SLAUGHTER BY PRODUCT

WINNING THE PRODUCTS LIABILITY CASE

EDWARD M. SWARTZ
Member of the Massachusetts Bar

KLUWER PRODUCTS LIABILITY LIBRARY

Kluwer Law Book Publishers, Inc.
New York, New York

Note: In this work, every effort has been made to use gender neutral language. Where clarity requires, however, the masculine pronoun has been used. The reader should note that it refers to persons of either gender.

Printed in the United States of America

91 90 89 88 87 86 7 6 5 4 3 2 1

Library of Congress Cataloging in Publication Data

Swartz, Edward M., 1934–
Slaughter by product.

(Kluwer products liability library)
Bibliography: p.
Includes index.
1. Products liability—United States—Trial practice.
2. Trial practice—United States. I. Title. II. Series.
KF8925.P7S92 1986 346.7303'82'0269 86–3002
ISBN 0–930273–54–0

(Pub. 73540)

ABOUT THE AUTHOR

EDWARD M. SWARTZ is one of this nation's most respected trial lawyers, authors, and consumer advocates. As a lawyer's lawyer, he has served as chief trial counsel in scores of million dollar record-setting landmark cases. He has represented injured consumers and, in many instances, their survivors, for injuries sustained as a result of defective products in their homes, their workplaces, and even in their schools.

Edward M. Swartz has sought to teach an entire generation of lawyers his successful strategies in order for them to obtain verdicts for their clients. He has made a career out of teaching his colleagues in the legal profession new techniques and methods of advocacy and accident prevention through speeches, lectures, and such publications as *Hazardous Products Litigation* and *Swartz Proof of Product Defect*.

Mr. Swartz's concerns and his crusade for safety cut across the entire spectrum of the American marketplace as he daily reinforces his reputation as one of the nation's foremost consumer advocates and the prime mover in products liability law. His message has been heard by millions of Americans through his appearances on such national programs as: The Today Show; 60 Minutes; The Dinah Shore Show; The Dick Cavett Show; The Merv Griffin Show; Miller's Court; The Larry King Show; CNN News; and network news programs. In 1981, he was presented with the "Ammy Award" by the American Lawyer Magazine for his outstanding work in the personal injury field.

Mr. Swartz graduated magna cum laude from Boston University School of Law, where he was Editor-in-Chief of the Law Review. He also received a graduate degree from the University of Michigan Law School where he was a W.C. Cook Fellow. He is Past President of the Massachusetts Trial Lawyers Association and former Chairman of The Association of Trial Lawyers of America's Continuing Legal Education Committee. He is a member of the Massachusetts Bar and is a partner in the Boston, Massachusetts firm of Swartz & Swartz.

In memory of my loving father,
Jacob W. Swartz.

ACKNOWLEDGMENTS

I wish to acknowledge and thank:

My colleagues who have shared the awesome responsibility of attempting to make corporate America more responsive to the safety needs and concerns of consumers.

The countless attorneys, physicians, and academicians, from every part of the country, who have so generously assisted me in my attempt to obtain justice for the aggrieved and crippled victims of our industrialized society.

The valuable editorial and research assistance of my associates, attorney Ron Wainrib and Professor Charles Kindregan. Their dedication to this volume was instrumental to its successful completion.

Jerome Nates, Esq., Kluwer's Editor-in-Chief, whose patience and advice is deeply appreciated.

My diligent office associates and colleagues, whose contributions to successful Swartz and Swartz litigation are evident throughout this text.

I must also extend my thanks to my loving wife, Linda, my children James, Joan, and Sharron, and my brothers, attorneys Frederic and Joseph Swartz for permitting me to take time away from our law practice to complete this important work.

PREFACE

Product litigation, fueled by defectively designed products, will continue to grow as seasoned lawyers learn to recognize and litigate new fact patterns, as young lawyers recognize the opportunities for personal success and contributions to the public good available in this field, and as law students take advantage of creative new curricula and clinical training to launch themselves into their future practices with a more realistic perspective.

Slaughter By Product: Winning the Products Liability Case will provide the trial lawyer with vivid illustrations of the potential for developing a products liability practice drawing examples from my twenty plus years of practice in this field. I hope to teach lawyers how to recognize potentially lucrative products cases that they might otherwise reject. Extensive litigation source materials are provided to aid in the lawyer's evaluation and preparation of new and significant cases.

The case studies, testimony excerpts, and litigation source material presented in this volume are intended to provide important guidelines for the practicing attorney. They illustrate the kinds of approaches that counsel should pursue in order to litigate cases of slaughter by product successfully. Counsel must tailor these techniques to the applicable laws, jurisdictional requirements, and fact patterns presented in each particular case.

I would like to thank Kluwer Law Book Publishers for allowing me to bring to practitioners a collection of sources and materials never before made available in this form. Hopefully, trial attorneys will utilize this volume to aid them in their efforts to reduce the staggering human suffering resulting from the continuing slaughter by product. For the first time, to my knowledge, attorneys and students will have before them a law book solely concerned with the theme that litigation techniques can have a deterrent effect on product-related injuries and deaths while at the same time providing a full, fair, and reasonable measure of redress to victims of slaughter by product.

This work should help attorneys to alert as many persons as possible about the dangers associated with many products. These warnings must be made by attorneys on as broad a basis as possible and should not be limited solely to their immediate clients and cases. It is equally clear that the public must be made aware of how important the existing consumer protection laws are to their everyday well-being.

Preface

This volume will provide attorneys with the necessary overview about product hazards so that they will be in a better position to make a concerted effort to preserve and improve on laws designed to protect consumers. A strong and vigorously pursued consumer case is still America's first line of defense against the onslaught of defective products. If only one lawyer is alerted to the merits of only one important consumer products case, then the effort that has gone into this text will not have been in vain.

Slaughter By Product should assist attorneys to convince manufacturers that their best hope to avoid continuing products liability lawsuits is to design safer products. I attempt in this work to show that the cause of consumer protection is dramatically aided by attorneys who expose the shortcomings of defective products through the litigation process. Such lawsuits should provide manufacturers with the incentive to provide for speedy and effective recalls as well as safer designs.

With the aid of this work, attorneys should be able to decipher the morass of technical obstacles woven into the actual process of bringing a products liability suit against producers of goods that maim or kill. If the cause of accident prevention is to be adequately served, it is important that attorneys recognize the potential for major product liability litigation when confronted with a myriad of differing and sometimes complex fact patterns. *Slaughter By Product* will assist the lawyer in making this diagnosis. Far too many important consumer cases are lost, not in the courtroom, but because attorneys neglect to pursue causes vigorously that they fail to perceive as actionable.

Unlike *Hazardous Products Litigation* and *Swartz Proof of Product Defect*, this volume teaches both in-courtroom techniques as well as those that can be utilized outside the courtroom. *Slaughter By Product* analyzes and reports on media efforts, industry public relations campaigns, and legislative conduct as such activity bears on pursuing the products liability case and consumer cause from start to finish.

It is my fervent hope that *Slaughter By Product* will prove to be a valuable aid to the legal profession, as well as to other professionals interested in the cause of accident prevention.

Edward M. Swartz
Boston, Massachusetts
March 1986

TABLE OF CONTENTS

III. Case Study: The Case of the "Heavenly Sleep" Comforter

IV. Other Flammable Products

V. Preventing Fabric-Related Burn Injuries

VI. Litigation Sources: Bibliography

Chapter 5
Electrical Mayhem

I. Introduction

II. Checklists

III. Case Study: The Case of the Too Hot Hair Dryer

IV. Other Electrical Hazards

V. Preventing Electrical-Related Injuries

VI. Litigation Sources: Bibliography

Chapter 6
Crippled at Leisure: Recreational Product-Related Torts

I. Introduction

II. Checklists

III. Case Study: The Case of the Backyard Country Club

IV. Other Recreational Product Hazards

III. Case Study: The Case of the Not-So-Playful Toy Figurine

IV. Other Toy Hazards

V. Preventing Toy-Related Injuries

Chapter 11
Closing the Case of Slaughter by Product

Chapter 1

RECOGNIZING "WINNABLE" FACT PATTERNS

KLUWER LITIGATION LIBRARY REFERENCES

HARLEY & MAGEE, WHAT'S IT WORTH? A GUIDE TO CURRENT PERSONAL INJURY AWARDS AND SETTLEMENTS.

JEANS, LITIGATION: Chapter 2, *Mind Set of the Advocate.*

SMITH & MALANDRO, COURTROOM COMMUNICATION STRATEGIES: Chapter 1, *Impression Formation in the Courtroom*; Chapter 2, *Persuasive Strategies in the Courtroom*; Chapter 5, *Preparing for Effective Courtroom Communication*.

§ 1.01 Introduction

Products litigation can be a lucrative area of legal practice. Yet, despite cries by members of the legal establishment about the "mania" of litigation and descriptions of our system as an "advocacy morass," it is my opinion—based on twenty years of representing injured plaintiffs, lecturing, writing, and counseling other trial lawyers—that products litigation is plagued by a woeful underutilization of our system of common law.

Every year, lawyers across America are turning down potentially big cases because they fail to recognize "winnable" fact patterns. These are cases that, if litigated, would serve the public good as well as the individual client. They never see the light of day, however, because lawyers throughout the country are applying the wrong standard of analysis. As a result, many potentially big cases are never initiated. They are lost in the offices of plaintiffs' attorneys, not in the courtrooms of America.

In a sense, this book represents a narrative of my personal involvement in this field. I have achieved record-setting verdicts in cases involving flammable fabrics,[1] hazardous toys,[2] and dangerous pools[3] because I have been able to demonstrate the utter disregard of the manufacturers and marketers of these products for the safety and well-being of their consumers. I have obtained landmark decisions and opened new frontiers with cases involving defective housing,[4] negligent publishing,[5] and hazardous household products[6] by taking creative and innovative approaches with the confidence that the common law could be molded to protect consumers in fields where they did not have that protection before. Finally, I have obtained million-dollar recoveries for clients in cases involving defective medical devices,[7] chemical cleaners,[8] defective LP gas-hot water heaters,[9] household appliances,[10] flammable children's

---

[1] Hinckley v. Eastman Kodak Co., No. 69–1338–J (D. Mass. 1973), $1.15 million settlement for young girl was largest individual recovery in product-related case at that time.

[2] Cunningham v. Quaker Oats Co., Fisher-Price Div., No. 1973–343 (W.D.N.Y. 1973), $3.1 million verdict was largest recovery for toy-related case at that time. Case is currently under appeal.

[3] Koenig v. Muskin Pools and W.T. Grant Co., No. 701, A–1973 (Pa. Ct. C.P., Erie Cty. Nov. 2, 1982), $6.5 million verdict was record for pool-related case at that time. Case is currently under appeal.

[4] Burnham v. Mark IV Homes, 387 Mass. 575, 441 N.E.2d 1027 (1982).

[5] Carter v. Rand McNally and Co., No. 76–1864–F (D. Mass. Sept. 1980).

[6] Larue v. National Union Electric Corp., 571 F.2d 51 (1st Cir. 1978).

[7] [Plaintiff] v. Atomic Energy of Canada, No. 3138–G (D. Mass. Jan, 21, 1983), $1.1 million.

[8] Drayton v. Jiffee Chemical Corp., 395 F. Supp. 1081 (N.D. Ohio 1975), *aff'd*, 591 F.2d 352 (6th Cir. 1978), lower court award of $1.7 million reduced to $700,000.

[9] Laaperi v. Sears, Roebuck, Inc., No. CA 79–2497–T, *et seq.* (D. Mass. Oct. 23, 1984).

[10] Gauthier v. [Major Stove Manufacturers], No. 76–1236G (D. Mass. 1982), $1.025 million.

ponchos,[11] and industrial plant explosions[12] because I fervently believe that all injured plaintiffs are entitled to full, fair, and reasonable compensation for the injuries they suffer as a result of defective products. The only language many corporations understand in designing and marketing their products is the economic price they must pay for their negligent or careless conduct.

§ 1.02 Creative and imaginative case analysis

Why are so many lawyers missing opportunities for potentially lucrative litigation? One reason is the way lawyers think about fact patterns. Some blame for this problem must be attributed to the inadequacies of legal education. With due apologies to the academic legal community, we must look first to what may be called the law school syndrome. Using the so-called case method approach, law students are taught very early in their education to begin each case analysis with the law found in appellate decisions. These students search for published appellate decisions whose fact patterns and theories best relate to the issue under consideration. As most seasoned trial lawyers know, these reports can make the most complex case appear relatively straightforward. These "reported" cases are often a far cry from the complex and difficult fact patterns that may face an attorney in his day-to-day practice. As a result, students are often left with misconceptions of real fact patterns and a shallow understanding of the scope of product defects. They fail to engage in creative and imaginative case analysis. All too often they carry this oversimplified approach into their law practices.

Lawyers need to learn new and more creative approaches for analyzing fact patterns. Most of the cases in which I have obtained large settlements and verdicts began with fact patterns that may have initially appeared outrageous, unexpected, or unusual. In many cases, a common initial reaction might have been, "That person doesn't deserve a dime." If I had turned those cases down, I would have rejected some of the most lucrative opportunities and significant cases of my practice. Yet all too many lawyers do just that.

§ 1.03 —Thinking in terms of specifics of product

My success as a trial lawyer has been based on my ability to focus properly on the facts in each case. Instead of thinking in the abstract,

---

[11] Jette v. Arlan Dep't Stores, No. 74–2400, M.C. (D. Mass. 1979), $1.14 million.

[12] Martel v. Peterson Puritan, No. 78–037 (D.R.I. 1982), $4.15 million.

which many lawyers tend to do, I think in terms of the specifics of that product. How was it defective? What was the environment in which it was used? How could it have been designed differently (i.e., made safer) to avoid this tragedy? These types of questions enable me to assess the product's potential defects in a manner that I can later convey to members of a jury.

In flammable fabrics cases, for example, plaintiffs' lawyers often fall into the trap set by defense counsel to focus on the source of ignition. This issue is a red herring. What is important in these types of cases is how the fabric reacted to a heat source. It doesn't matter whether the source is a match, portable heater, cigarette lighter, or stove. In a case involving the severe burn injuries of two young children caused by a hazardous, flammable comforter that burned when exposed to heat,[13] the product in question was totally destroyed. The source of ignition was unknown. It was also irrelevant! Whether that comforter was negligently manufactured or marketed depended on how it reacted to a heat source, whatever that source may have been. The important thing was that it melted into a hot, lavalike mass when exposed to heat. This hot mass stuck to the arms and faces of the two toddlers, burning them down to their very bones. The children's parents certainly did not know of this hazardous quality when they bought the cozy comforter to keep their children warm. The product's contact with a heat source was foreseeable and predictable. This case resulted in the first million-dollar settlement in a product-related personal injury case.[14]

Or consider the case of the teenager who was rendered permanently quadriplegic when his spinal cord was damaged after he dove into a uniformly four-foot-deep aboveground backyard pool.[15] A common reaction to this fact pattern might be, "Why did he do such a foolish thing?" Others might ask, "Didn't he know better than to dive into such shallow water?" Defendants had argued successfully for years that the hazards of diving into four feet of water were "open and obvious" and, therefore, that they should not be liable for such catastrophic injuries. My analysis took a different perspective. Did this young man really want to kill himself when he took that dive? No! Did he know that he would be rendered permanently quadriplegic? Of course not. I argued that anyone could tell by looking at the pool that the water was shallow. Yet,

---

[13] *See infra* Chapter 4, *The Case of the "Heavenly Sleep" Comforter*.

[14] Hinckley v. Eastman Kodak Co., *supra* note 1.

[15] *See infra*, Chapter 6, *The Case of the Backyard Country Club*.

through probing cross-examinations of company executives, I was able to elicit testimony that even they did not know that diving into the pool could cause quadriplegia until the first victims began to sue them in court. If the defendant's own executives didn't know about this hazard, I asked members of this Erie, Pennsylvania jury, then how could this young man be expected to know? How could the defendants argue that the danger was "open and obvious" when the company's own executives didn't recognize the quadriplegia threat? This plaintiff obtained a verdict of $6.5 million, including $500,000 in punitive damages against the pool's manufacturer. This verdict was, at that time, a record for a pool-related case.[16]

§ 1.04 —Thinking in terms of consumer protection

Above all else, products liability cases are consumer protection cases. If I know the product and I have a sensitivity for consumer issues, I can convey the product's hazards in a manner that the jury can understand. I often draw the jurors' attention to the consumer protection aspect of my case. They understand this approach, and I am able to convey my convictions of the plaintiff's right to compensation in a persuasive manner.

§ 1.05 Keeping abreast of new liability theories

Another reason why lawyers frequently miss opportunities for the big case is that they fail to keep abreast of new theories that can turn lackluster fact patterns into million-dollar verdicts and settlements. One example is the evolving concept of "defect."

A product need not be defective in the traditional sense of a broken part or other obvious fault in order for its manufacturer and marketer to be held liable and accountable for the destruction it causes. For example, a product may have a defective design that may cause injury or death. In one case, I represented a young child who was rendered severely and permanently brain damaged after a small toy figurine became lodged in his throat, cutting off the supply of oxygen to his brain.[17] The toy was designed small enough to fit into the toddler's mouth, but large enough to become lodged in his throat. A small, hooklike barb that was part of the toy's design dug into the child's throat tissue, preventing his parents from removing the toy before he became gravely injured. In another

[16] Koenig v. Muskin Pools and W.T. Grant Co., *supra* note 3.

[17] *See infra* Chapter 7, *The Case of the Not-So-Playful Toy Figurine*.

case, an eleven-year-old boy was injured when his penis became engaged in a vacuum cleaner motor fan. In representing this client, I drew the jurors' attention to the fact that the cleaner was designed without safety guards to prevent a child's extremities from entering the machine's housing. Under cross-examination, I elicited admissions from the defendant's executives that the machine's design permitted such dangerous human contact. The company designed and marketed safer models for its overseas markets where safety guards were required by law. In this country, where they were not required, they were not offered.[18]

Another defect may be a product's marketing scheme. The hazardous toy in the case referred to earlier was marketed in a package that bore the reassuring words "safe" and "safety first." These words lulled the toddler's parents into a false sense of security that the toy was safe. Under cross-examination, company executives admitted that safety was "not necessarily" first in the toy's design and that repeated use of the word "safe" was merely a marketing tool to build consumer confidence. Similarly, in the pool-related quadriplegia case mentioned earlier, the pool's manufacturer marketed its product with alluring advertisements depicting people diving into the water. A young man was seduced into taking his fateful dive by a company that cared more about selling its pools than about the safety of its customers. Additionally, in the case involving a flammable, polyester fiberfill comforter described previously, the manufacturer had adopted a highly sophisticated marketing gimmick to build consumer confidence in its product. Its marketing label describing the product as "certified" led one company executive to comment, "Whom are we trying to kid?"

A product can also be defective as a result of a failure to warn or to use adequate warnings. In a case involving an LP gas explosion, I represented the family of a young father of three who perished in an explosion triggered by liquefied petroleum gas leaking from his home's water heater. I successfully argued to an Ohio jury that the gas supplier's failure to provide adequate odorization to alert consumers to the presence of leaking propane gas, and its failure to educate consumers regarding the nature of the gas's artificial odorant, were elements in the defendant's liability for wrongful death.[19] Similarly, in a landmark case in which a junior high school student was severely burned when an explosion ripped through her chemistry laboratory as she followed the experiment direc-

---

[18]*See infra* Chapter 10, *The Case of the Vacuum Cleaner with Teeth*.

[19]*See infra* Chapter 2, *The Case of the Basement Booby Trap*.

tions printed in her school textbook, I argued that the textbook publisher should be liable based in part on its failure to provide adequate warnings of the experiment's explosive potential.[20]

A product may also be defective if it fails to meet the test of safety under "real conditions" of the home environment. In the gas explosion case previously discussed, the gas company's executive was forced to admit, under intensive cross-examination, that the product was never tested in a home environment to determine whether its artificial odorants were sufficient to alert homeowners to its danger or whether competing odors in a home environment might mask its odorant's smell, and thus make it ineffective to alert consumers before tragedy could strike. In the vacuum cleaner case discussed previously, I argued that a household product such as a vacuum cleaner must be designed in such a manner as to take into account children's creative, unpredictable, and forceful behavior, and that a manufacturer should be liable for the reasonably foreseeable misuse that may occur even when a child acts in a manner that places him at risk.

§ 1.06 Defendants' public relations efforts

One unfortunate result of the recent expansion of the common law recognition of consumers' rights has been a concerted effort on the part of manufacturers, marketers, and insurance companies with vested interests who are forced to pay the price for their corporate malfeasance to launch new public relations efforts. They have attempted to discredit injured consumers and their lawyers by charging them with excessive litigation. They say we are clogging the courts with costly and unnecessary lawsuits. They blame the contingency fee system for fueling the new rise in products litigation, and they charge lawyers with seeking the "pot of gold" at the end of the litigation rainbow.

Fortunately, these critics have not gone unanswered. Recent studies by leaders of the legal and business community have cast doubts on this strong rhetoric. A leading scholar has observed that much of the increased litigation, blamed so easily on our "litigious society," stems instead from such factors as the increased risks of injuries from the products of our highly advanced industrial society, a citizenry that is better educated and more aware of the causes of those injuries, and increased government intervention in the marketplace to reduce the risks

[20] *See infra* Chapter 10, *The Case of Slaughter by Textbook*.

posed by those hazardous products.[21] Such findings prompted a member of the federal judiciary to comment, "[v]iewed in this light, Americans' use of the courts is actually conservative."[22]

§ 1.07 Future trends

I have little doubt that the public relations efforts by those with the most to lose, and whose short-term interests are most threatened by the growth of products litigation, will continue as long as the scales of justice continue to tip in the consumers' direction. Although we have made some progress in recognizing consumers' rights to equal justice under the law, we still have a long way to go before justice for consumers is fully attained and their suffering at the hands of noncaring producers and marketers of goods comes to an end. Until that time, we have only seen the tip of the iceberg in terms of litigation for product-related injury victims.

Products litigation will continue to grow as seasoned lawyers learn to recognize and litigate new fact patterns; as young lawyers recognize the opportunities for personal success available in this field, as well as the contributions they can make to the public good; and as law students take advantage of creative new curricula and clinical training to launch themselves into their future practices with a more realistic perspective.

---

[21] Trubeck, *The Costs of Ordinary Litigation*, 31 U.C.L.A. L. REV. 72 (1983).

[22] Wald, *Litigation in America*, 31 U.C.L.A. L. REV. 1 (1983).

Chapter 2

COMBUSTION CATASTROPHES

VI. Litigation Sources: Bibliography

KLUWER LITIGATION LIBRARY REFERENCES

HARLEY & MAGEE, WHAT'S IT WORTH? A GUIDE TO CURRENT PERSONAL INJURY AWARDS AND SETTLEMENTS.

JEANS, LITIGATION: Chapter 4, *Discovery*; Chapter 8, *Direct Examination*; Chapter 9, *Direct Examination of Expert Witnesses*; Chapter 13, *Cross-Examination*; Chapter 14, *Cross-Examination of Expert Witnesses*.

SMITH & MALANDRO, COURTROOM COMMUNICATION STRATEGIES: Chapter 1, *Impression Formation in the Courtroom*; Chapter 2, *Persuasive Strategies in the Courtroom*; Chapter 5, *Preparing for Effective Courtroom Communication*; Chapter 8, *Direct Examination: Presenting the Evidence with Impact*; Chapter 9, *Cross-Examination: Controlling the Case*.

I. Introduction

§ 2.01 In general

Of all the hazardous products that I have encountered in my twenty-five years of trial practice, liquefied-petroleum (LP) gas is probably the source of greatest destruction. An estimated 15 million Americans rely on this product to fuel their stoves, heat their water, and operate their appliances. Inasmuch as gas is highly flammable, exposure to or contact with heat can lead quickly to an explosion. The explosive power of this fuel makes it a continuing threat in households where almost any heat source—a lighted match, electric spark, or even the heat generated by an ordinary light bulb—can ignite the leaking gas and trigger a catastrophic explosion. Moreover, its odorless and colorless nature makes it even more insidious. Most consumers don't realize that because of its odorless state, gas is artificially odorized before it reaches our homes.

The safety of appliances in which this product is burned, and the effectiveness of its odorization, are both vital ingredients in preventing catastrophic explosions. All too often home dwellers are unaware, before tragedy strikes, that leaking gas has rendered their homes into virtual time bombs. Industry members have taken some so-called safety measures, including use of artificial odorants to alert consumers to the presence of gas in their homes, but the massive destruction that I have witnessed in case after case has demonstrated to me that the so-called preventive measures currently taken to reduce the slaughter by this product are inadequate. I have represented too many families whose lives have been devastated and their homes destroyed by this silent killer. Suppliers of LP gas and manufacturers of gas-burning appliances permit these tragedies to occur by marketing their products without taking the care to make sure that they are safe for use in the home environment.

COMMENT: Inadequate odorization, the failure to warn and educate consumers regarding the detection of the artificial odorant, the failure to test the gas for odorization adequately, and defective gas-burning appliances that permit the volatile product to escape silently into the home environment, have all contributed to the destruction that has transformed people's homes into potential booby traps.

II. Checklists

§ 2.02 Checklist: Investigation of an LP gas explosion-related injury case

The following checklist is intended to aid counsel in preparing the LP gas explosion-related case. This investigation checklist will also be a valuable tool for counsel in preparing any other combustion-related injury case.

____ (1) Locate and interview all witnesses:

____(a) Ask each witness for a detailed impression of their recollections as to the sequence of events

____(b) Ask if the witness detected the odor associated with gas before the fire or explosion

____(c) Determine who was in charge of the premises, or of the particular task being undertaken at the time of the explosion, and what safety precautions had been taken prior to the fire or explosion

____ (2) Obtain possession of, or inspect, the gas equipment involved in the fire or explosion

____ (3) Obtain the reports of:

____(a) Fire marshal

____(b) Police

____(c) Plant security

____(d) Local, state, or federal investigation

____(e) Weather bureau records for the relevant period (weather may affect the degree of odorization needed)

____ (4) Retain the services of a chemist or chemical engineer as early as possible to serve as your expert and consultant throughout your investigation

____ (5) If the issue relates to the proper functioning of gas equipment or system, retain the services of a mechanical engineer as your expert-consultant

____ (6) Determine as early as possible what was the source of the ignition that caused the gas fire or explosion (sometimes the source of ignition is easy to ascertain from eyewitnesses)

____ (7) Determine what safety precautions, if any, were taken prior to the explosion or fire; for example:

____(a) Was a check made to determine the presence of gas vapors?

____(b) Was a gas odor ignored?

____(c) Were bystanders removed from the scene prior to work on a gas system?

____(d) Had a pilot light been turned off?

____(e) Were standard operating procedures followed or ignored?

____ (8) Determine who manufactured or installed the equipment used

____ (9) Note all serial and model numbers on the equipment

____(10) Check patent records regarding this equipment

____(11) Determine if the equipment used was originally manufactured for LP gas or for some other product

____(12) Determine if there was an automatic shut-off and if it was operating

____(13) Determine if all gas pipes in the area were properly capped

____(14) Determine if the equipment or connections were rusting

____(15) Do the records show how much fuel was in the tanks at the time of the fire or explosion?

____(16) Was all electrical equipment in the area properly grounded?

____(17) Were all code requirements complied with?

____(18) When was the last safety inspection prior to the fire or explosion? (Obtain all prior inspection reports)

____(19) What steps, if any, had been taken to remove or prevent sources of ignition in the area?

____(20) Were buildings and tanks in the area properly ventilated?

____(21) Was firefighting equipment provided and was it easily available?

____(22) Obtain a copy of the safety manual, work rules, instructions, or warnings given to employees or posted in the area

____(23) Were warnings given as to:

____(a) Safe use of equipment?

____(b) Avoidance of known dangers?

____(c) What to do if a gas odor was detected?

____(24) Had there been prior complaints about gas leaks?

____(25) Was the gas odor clearly distinguishable from other odors in the area?

____(26) Research law reviews and treatises on gas-related injury cases

____(27) Contact the following to determine what information, if any, is available regarding the product:

____(a) U.S. Consumer Product Safety Commission

____(b) U.S. Department of Health and Human Services

____(c) National Safety Council

____(d) National Fire Protection Association

____(e) American National Standards Institute

____(f) American Society for Testing and Materials

____(g) U.S. Department of Energy

____(h) National LP Gas Association

____(i) Underwriters' Laboratories

____(j) American Gas Association

____(k) ATLA Exchange

____(l) ATLA Law Reporter

____(m) ATLA Product Liability Law Reporter

§ 2.03 Checklist: Resources for a combustion-related injury case

The following resource checklist should be a valuable tool for counsel in preparing a combustion-related personal injury case.[1]

____ (1) Selected technical sources

____(a) New Scientist

____(b) Science News

____(c) Plant Engineering

____(d) Journal of Applied Physics

____(e) Pipeline and Gas Journal

____(f) Specifying Engineer

[1] *See, infra* §§ 2.21–2.25, for reference to specific articles contained in these publications.

____(g) Materials Performance

____(h) Electrical Construction and Maintenance

____(i) Journal of Organic Chemistry

____(j) Journal of Hazardous Material

____ (2) Selected popular sources

____(a) Consumer Reports

____(b) Popular Science

____(c) Family Handyman

____(d) Changing Times

____(e) Trailer Life

____(f) Mechanix Illustrated

____(g) Consumer's Digest

____(h) Popular Electronics

____(i) Which? (Great Britain)

____ (3) Selected government sources

____(a) U.S. Consumer Product Safety Commission

____(b) U.S. Department of Energy

____(c) U.S. Department of Commerce, National Bureau of Standards

____(d) Interstate Commerce Commission

____ (4) Selected industry sources

____(a) American Gas Association

____(b) Gas Research Institute

____(c) Natural Gas Supply Association

____(d) American Society of Gas Engineers

____(e) Butane-Propane News, Inc.

____(f) Interstate Natural Gas Association of America

____(g) National LP-Gas Association

____(h) Valve Manufacturers' Association

____(i) Better Heating-Cooling Council

III. Case Study: The Case of the Basement Booby Trap[2]

§ 2.04 Facts

Consider the case of a twenty-six-year-old father of four young children who lost his life when a catastrophic LP gas explosion ripped through his Bryan, Ohio home.

The morning that tragedy struck, the deceased was up early—around 6:30 to be exact. He had gone downstairs to the bathroom to shave, but found no hot water. He asked his wife to check the pilot light on the kitchen stove. The light was on. He then went to check the hot water heater in the basement.

His wife didn't see him after he left the bathroom and before tragedy struck. She heard him walk downstairs, first opening a small alcove door and then a second door just below ground level. The next thing she heard was the explosion. What she saw next would be etched in her mind for the rest of her life—her husband running upstairs, burning flesh hanging from his horribly disfigured body. She helped him into a cold tub of water and called the police. There was no way for her to know that her husband's burns were not limited to his skin, but had engulfed his respiratory system. He was rushed to the hospital, where four unimaginably painful hours later he succumbed to his injuries and died.

COMMENT: When his wife related the tragic events of that day to me, I knew from the start that her case, like those of other gas explosion victims I had represented in my practice, would not be easy. It would require extensive amounts of time, work, and perseverance. As the facts began to unfold from her obviously emotional recollections of that tragic day, however, I also knew that this family was ready for the struggle that lay ahead in their quest for justice.

---

[2] Hageman v. Signal L.P. Gas Co., 486 F.2d 479 (6th Cir. [Ohio] 1973).

§ 2.05 Analysis of case

At the start of this case, two primary parties appeared the most likely defendants: the company that manufactured the hot water heater and the company that supplied the LP gas to the plaintiff's home. As discovery of these defendants' witnesses proceeded, the evidence of their negligence in the manufacture, distribution, and supply of these products began to accumulate. The heater's burner head was so badly rusted that most of its portholes were closed, permitting the explosive gas to escape silently. No communications of any kind were made to the members of this family about the escaping gas or the defective nature of the burner; or the tendency of the gas to stratify in layers on the basement floor; or that the artificial odorant, used ostensibly to alert consumers to the presence of leaking gas, smells remarkably like the type of odors common in a rural home's basement. These, in large part, were the various pieces of the puzzle that I, as chief counsel, along with the plaintiff's local attorney, put together to obtain justice for this family against the purveyors of these hazardous products.

§ 2.06 The case against the hot water heater manufacturer

An expert in chemical engineering provided crucial testimony in support of the plaintiff's case against the hot water heater manufacturer. Through direct examination of this expert witness, I was able to elicit important testimony regarding: (1) the hazards posed by this appliance; (2) the fact that safer rust-resistant materials were available and were, in fact, being used on other parts of this appliance, and if used for the burner head may have avoided this catastrophe altogether; and (3) why, in this expert's opinion, the deceased was walking into a deadly booby trap when he opened his basement door.[3]

Q. You say that you found the burner head was constructed of improper materials. What were your reasons for that conclusion?

A. This burner head was analyzed spectrographically, and the analysis showed that it was just common basic cast iron. The kind of iron that has little or no resistance to corrosion, especially high-temperature oxidation corrosion, which you would expect from a burner head. And so the corrosion of the ports would be expected. . . . The small air shuttering was made out of corrosion-resistant material and also the little shield. It was

[3] *Id.*, testimony of Mr. M, expert witness for plaintiff.

made out of stainless steel and that shows little or no corrosion, and yet that got the major amount of condensation underneath the flue.

Q. Now, looking at this burner assembly, I notice that there is this piece of metal here, and I notice the top has rust on it, and the bottom of it is almost rust free. Does that have any significance to you?

A. The significance is that this burner sat inside of the heater's combustion chamber. The bottom is just painted aluminum; it shows little or no corrosion.

COMMENT: The witness continued his testimony by describing the defective condition of the burner.[4]

Q. Plaintiff's Exhibit ____, would you please tell us what it shows?

A. This is the burner assembly. . . . It shows the pilot burning, it shows flame around most, just practically around the entire periphery or circumference of the ports. It also shows something that is not right and that shows lifting of the flame from the ports where you do not see the flame right at the port. That was also a malfunction because of the corrosion.

Q. Plaintiff's Exhibit ____, would you please tell us what it shows?

A. This is the same burner—just happens to be late ignition, . . . where perhaps maybe four or five of the ports out of the seventy-two were burning and the rest were just leaking gas in my laboratory. And, in my opinion, this is also the type of thing that happened, unfortunately, in the __________ basement.

Q. What did you find out about the size of the ports in this burner head?

A. They varied all over the lot . . . from a 74 drill to a 42 drill. The average drill size was something like 58. I couldn't get the drill through some of the holes. They were practically plugged; you could say 90–95%.

---

[4] *Id.*

COMMENT: The defendant's engineer and Manager of Product Quality conceded in pretrial depositions that rust could form on the heater's cast iron burner heads, which could produce an explosive situation, and that other parts of the heater were made of the safer rust-resistant material. Adding the safer material to the burner head would have cost just two cents per unit. The company simply chose not to do so.[5]

Q. It is at least important that the burner ports be free and open, is that correct, in accordance with the tests that you have just described?

A. Essentially, yes.

Q. Why is that important?

A. If you have total blockage, the gas will not come out through the ports.

Q. What if you have partial blockage, that is, if some of the ports are blocked and some are not?

A. There is some latitude in the port area.

Q. At some point that latitude is exceeded, is it not?

A. Yes.

Q. When this latitude is exceeded, this could create a dangerous explosive situation, is that correct?

A. In the confines of the water heater. . . .

Q. Isn't it important to keep the ports clear?

A. From the point of performance, the ports should be essentially cleared.

Q. From the point of view of preventing unburned gas from escaping?

---

[5] *Hageman, supra* note 2, testimony of Mr. D, Engineering Manager of defendant ____________ Manufacturing Company, offered by plaintiff.

A. Yes.

Q. When it does become important, it could set up a dangerous explosive situation, is that correct?

A. Relating to time?

Q. Oh, sure. Is that correct?

A. It is possible.

Q. This possibility that you described, your company worked on that in order to make the product as safe as possible, correct?

A. Correct.

* * *

Q. One way your company worked on that, as I understand it, was to deal with the problem of rusting, because rusting could cause occlusion and closure of the ports?

A. It is one form.

Q. Because it is one form of the problem you have described, isn't this why it was an important consideration for your company from the point of view of consumer protection, one consideration?

A. It is a consideration.

Q. From the point of view of the ultimate consumer's safety, is that not so?

A. Yes.

Q. Why is that so?

A. To insure proper operation, safe operation of the unit.

Q. Since you get condensation in a water heater, isn't it important to be concerned with the rusting of the raw material you are making the burner unit from?

A. Correct.

Q. That is why you want to use whatever is scientifically available to inhibit rust formation, correct?

A. There is no metal material that doesn't corrode or rust.

Q. But there are ways to treat the metallic material either to retard or put off rusting?

A. You can retard it.

Q. What did your company do to retard rusting?

A. We have never found it necessary to do anything to cast iron.

COMMENT: Was this executive seeing the world through rose-colored glasses? Did he know what consumers were really experiencing? Apparently not, as evidenced by the following testimony of a plant manager employed by the manufacturing company. This witness had personally serviced the burners in consumers' homes. He admitted that he had seen many cast iron burners, such as the one in this case, that had rusted ports.[6]

Q. In your years of servicing hot water heaters, have you ever had occasion to find rust on the main burner heads?

A. Many times.

Q. And has it ever been your experience that those burner heads have not functioned properly because of the rust that is on them?

A. They would not function efficiently.

COMMENT: Under probing cross-examination, the engineering manager was forced to admit that cast iron could corrode, that his company did nothing to prevent rust formation, that other rust-resistant materials, such as stainless steel, were available and in fact were used elsewhere on this heater, but not for the burner head.[7]

Q. Is it fair to say, in the years you have been with the company,

[6] *Hageman, supra* note 2, testimony for defendant.

[7] *Hageman, supra* note 2, testimony of Mr. D, Engineering Manager of defendant ____________ Manufacturing Company, offered by plaintiff.

that the company didn't do anything to retard the rust formation in the cast iron that went into making burner units that were used for hot water heaters?

A. That is essentially true.

* * *

Q. Isn't stainless steel less likely to rust out than other types of material that you traditionally use?

A. Under certain given conditions, yes.

Q. Under virtually all conditions, stainless steel is likely to rust, is it not?

A. It depends upon the temperature range you are in.

Q. Generally speaking, from the point of view of home usage, it is fair to say stainless steel is less likely to rust, is that not correct, as a general statement?

A. In laymen's terms, yes.

Q. That is as true today as it was twenty years ago, right?

A. Twenty years ago, I was not in this business, but from what I read, essentially it would be true.

* * *

Q. In constructing the water heater burner, such as the kind that is depicted in both exhibits, did you use any special resistant alloys? [*Ed. note*: Exhibit not reproduced.]

A. The shield that was employed over the top of the burner was an alloy.

Q. A rust-resistant alloy?

A. Essentially, yes.

COMMENT: Shortly after this damaging testimony was elicted, the heater manufacturer agreed to settle the plaintiff's claim against it.[8] Our case continued against the gas supplier. This was the first time a major case was success-

[8] Case settled against defendant ____________ Manufacturing Company for $350,000.

fully brought against a hot water heater manufacturer on the basis of negligence for a rusted burner head.

---

§ 2.07 The case against the gas supplier

Our case against the gas supplier focused on this defendant's: (1) failure to odorize the propane gas adequately; (2) failure to warn this family adequately of the gas's explosive nature and the nature of the odorant used to alert consumers to the presence of leaking gas; and (3) failure to instruct consumers on how to respond when gas leaks into their homes.

In order to be alerted by a malodorant, you have to know what it smells like. As the following excerpt of the critical cross-examination of the defendant's assistant laboratory manager reveals, even gas company executives found it difficult to identify the malodorant odor adequately.[9]

Q. Do you know what kind of malodorant is used generally with propane gas or LP gas?

A. No, I don't.

Q. If I called it ethyl mercaptan, would that refresh your recollection?

A. No.

* * *

Q. On behalf of your company, you are aware, are you not, and have always been aware that water heaters are used in some instances in the basement of homes?

A. Correct.

Q. You do know that by basement I am talking about the lowest level of the home?

A. Correct.

Q. Do you know that the malodorant used in propane gas has a specific gravity greater than the propane and greater than air?

A. I did not know that.

---

[9] *Hageman, supra* note 2, testimony of Mr. T, Assistant Manager of Laboratory, witness called on behalf of defendant ____________ Gas Company. *See also* E. Swartz, Hazardous Products Litigation (Lawyers Co-op. Publishing Co., 1973 & Supps.).

* * *

Q. If I told you that ethyl mercaptan or the malodorant used in propane has a greater specific gravity than air and greater than the gas itself, would that information be important to your work from the standpoint of the ultimate consumer's usage of the product?

A. It would be something that would be open for investigation to see what relationship it had to the matter.

Q. It would become an important consideration at that point, correct?

A. In general, yes. In particular, I am not certain.

Q. Do you know what it smells like, the malodorant?

A. Essentially, yes.

Q. You are not entirely sure?

A. I would say the malodorants are usually common and I could detect it. I would assume it would be gas if I smelled the odor.

Q. Since you are a person who works with it all the time, you have smelled that malodorant many times in the past, is that correct?

A. That is correct.

* * *

Q. The propane gas that you smell and are able to detect, how would you describe the odor?

A. That is rather subjective. I am afraid I can't describe it in any terms other than being able to recognize it.

Q. It is a difficult thing?

A. Yes.

Q. Recognizing it requires experience, right?

A. I wouldn't say it is an odor that is different from anything that is common.

Q. Is that so?

A. I feel it is, that the odorants used in most gaseous fuels are there to call your attention to it.

Q. The fact that there is an odor?

A. Yes.

Q. Have you ever smelled rotten eggs?

A. Yes.

Q. Is it something like that?

A. No. That is hydrogen sulfide.

Q. Would you say it is something like cooking cabbage?

A. No.

Q. How about rotten potatoes? I am trying to analogize it to common odors.

A. I can't ever recall smelling rotten potatoes. If you are talking about vegetable matter, I wouldn't associate it with rotting vegetable matter per se.

Q. What would you analogize it to?

A. The only thing I can say would be gaseous fuel.

Q. If you were giving a warning to a member of the consuming public as to what type of odor to look out for, how would you describe it to that person short of letting them smell it themselves?

A. I would have to think about that. I can't find words to describe it fully. The best way to do it would be to have them smell it.

Q. And the best way to do it would be to send out a brochure or something that actually contained the odor so they could actually smell it, right?

A. Some means of doing it.

Q. Are you aware that there are gas companies that send out such a card in order to educate the consumer as to what the actual smell is?

A. I have never run into a case of that nature.

COMMENT: If this executive had such difficulty identifying the odor, I argued that the gas supplier could not reasonably expect the plaintiff, or any other consumers, to be alerted by it.

In handling a gas case, counsel should focus on the

odorization issue. For example: Was the odor strong? Could it be distinguished from competing odors?

As this witness' testimony continued, I was able to elicit equally crucial admissions regarding the difficulty of identifying this odorant.[10]

Q. Does it smell like rotten cabbage?

A. I think that people have a different sense of smell. I mean, what smells sweet to you might smell very bad to me.

Q. So it has a broad spectrum of odor, is that correct?

A. I think it is fairly definable from rotten cabbage and even the odor of a skunk.

Q. Does it smell like a dead mouse?

A. No.

Q. Does it smell like rotten cabbage?

A. Yes, it could to some people.

Q. But you are sure it doesn't smell like a dead mouse?

A. You asked an opinion of me, do I think it smells like a dead mouse. I'd say no, I don't think it smells like a dead mouse.

Q. So it would be fair to say if someone smelled a dead mouse, she shouldn't call the gas supplier?

A. I think it is up to the person involved.

Q. It is a difficult problem?

A. No, I don't think so. We are talking about a distinctive odor and I would assume that any time that you smelled anything unusual that you would wonder what is causing the odor.

Q. Does it smell like rotten potatoes?

A. Not to me it doesn't.

Q. So that if you smelled rotten potatoes in the basement of your home, you wouldn't be too concerned about it if you had some potatoes there, would you?

[10] *Id.*

A. You are asking me?

Q. Yes, you.

A. You are asking me some conjecture. As far as I am concerned, probably not.

COMMENT: The defendant's assistant laboratory manager also admitted that his company failed to test the gas product for adequate odorization to ensure consumer safety, despite the fact that it "didn't want to lose any customers."[11]

Q. You indicated that you are watchdogs for quality. If we had to describe it, that is your primary overall operational job?

A. That is essentially correct.

Q. And "watchdogs for quality," I suppose, means in part that you are concerned with consumer safety, are you not?

A. Absolutely, we don't want to lose any customers.

COMMENT: Under probing cross-examination, this witness also admitted that the gas company failed to test this odorant in its end use environment—the consumer's home.[12]

Q. End use means using the propane product in the home environment, does it not?

A. In some instances, yes.

Q. You know it is used commercially and in trailers, as well as in summer cottages, is it not?

---

11 *Id.*

12 *Id.*

A. It is even used in automobiles as fuel.

Q. But certainly one of its major uses is in homes, is it not?

A. I would say that is essentially true, yes, sir.

Q. And have you instituted any programs to run tests to determine what the safety of propane gas is from the point of view of its end use in the home?

A. Well, I would say this, that the standards have been pretty well established.

Q. I am asking what tests have [you] run?

A. What tests to determine safety?

Q. Yes.

A. . . . We run no tests to determine safety.

Q. So, from the point of view of consumer safety, which you said you are concerned about, you have performed no tests in the end use of the product? On your own, have you done any?

A. Yes, we have checked the mercaptan level of our propane.

Q. But have you ever run any practical, pragmatic tests in the home environment on the way your product is being used, from the point of view of end use?

A. That is not my function and my responsibility; no, sir.

COMMENT: Another of the defendant's expert witnesses admitted he'd "rather test [the heater] in a laboratory than in a home."[13]

Q. And is it fair to say that based upon the work that you have done to date, at least you do not know what the effect on the odor threshold is as a result of the interaction of other odors in our environment?

A. We have done that.

[13] *Hageman, supra* note 2, testimony of Mr. L, expert witness for defendant.

Q. And have you ever conducted any test in the basements of rural homes where propane is used, for example?

A. No, I haven't looked at a rural home.

Q. Do you think that this kind of testing, if it was ordered by the industry, would be helpful?

A. Well, I'd much rather do it under more controlled conditions than I could find in a cellar.

Q. You would rather do it in the laboratory?

A. Well, I can control things, and part of the problem of odor work has been the difficulty to control things.

COMMENT: This expert also admitted that what he believed was the malodorant's primary odor, an "earthy" smell, could easily go undetected in the "earthy" environment in the basement of a typical rural home like the plaintiff's.[14]

Q. Now, when you talked about the detection threshold, is it fair to say that the detection threshold of mercaptan is not reliable from the point of view of the consumers' end use of the product in the home? For example, because it can be affected by the subtle changes in background odor and by its very nature might result in a poorly defined odor response; is that a fair statement?

A. If you use the term detection threshold, you are correct.

Q. And so background odors, the other odors that you have in a room, would be material and important to you as a scientist in making a determination as to whether anything is adequate or inadequate as an odorant, correct?

A. Right, the background is of importance.

Q. And, of course, you do understand that in a basement in a ru-

[14] *Id.*

ral family house there are lots of competing odors, are there not?

A. It would have to be what is actually in existence at that time. If you go to my house or your house, we may differ.

Q. If you go to the basement of the average rural home, you can expect some competing odors, is that a fair statement? For example, you might expect to find a dead mouse in a rural basement occasionally, correct?

A. You might occasionally, correct.

Q. And this would be one type of competing odor, would it not?

A. It could be a competing odor.

Q. Mr. __________, His Honor asked you what ethyl mercaptan smelled like based on your studies, and what was your answer?

A. It has what I call a gassy pungent odor of irritation, and is similar to what I call a rotten vegetable or sulfidy kind of an odor.

Q. Would you describe it as an earthy odor?

A. To some extent I could describe it as earthy.

Q. And by earthy, you mean similar to that found in basements, correct?

A. Well, there are a number of materials that profess the earthy odor.

Q. That is a kind of odor one would expect to find in the basement of rural homes, the earthy odor?

A. Earthy in the sense of—my primary description of ethyl mercaptan would not be earthy, would be primarily gassy pungency, and then the sulfidy.

COMMENT: I proceeded to show to the witness, and the jury, a copy of an article the witness had authored on the subject of threshold odors of chemicals. In this particular article, the witness had stated that this malodorant produced a primarily "earthy" smell. Following is his response to my examination on this point.[15]

Q. I am going to show you the article, you are one of the coauthors?

A. Right.

Q. Now, let's take a table, you find it for me because you know what I am referring to, and ethyl mercaptan is listed, is it not?

A. Yes, it is.

Q. And what do you have for ethyl mercaptan?

A. It is what is called earthy and sulfidy.

Q. And what is listed first?

A. Earthy.

* * *

Q. Did you pick the word "earthy" in that study?

A. No. There was a panel of four trained people and these are not necessarily the consensus of the panel. Those descriptors are . . . typical kinds of things that could be used to describe it as earthy. But generally at the low level the earthiness was noted.

§ 2.08 —Failure to educate consumers regarding detection of odor

Another major argument in our case against the gas supply company was its failure to educate this family, and other consumers, regarding the hazards associated with LP gas and the odorants that were allegedly added to alert consumers to the presence of leaking gas. The defendant's own witnesses admitted that they failed to supply these consumers with information regarding their product. For example, one of its experts testified regarding ways in which this information, and important warnings, could have been provided to the plaintiffs and the public in general.[16]

Q. Now, have you endeavored to give any written instructions, pamphlets, or memoranda to large gas distributors such as

---

[15] *Id.*

[16] *Hageman, supra* note 2, testimony of Mr. T, Assistant Laboratory Manager, witness called on behalf of defendant ____________ Gas Company.

________________ Gas Company which helps them in their attempt, if there is such an attempt, to educate the ultimate user of this product in the environment in which it is going to be used?

A. It's not my function, sir.

Q. Does your company have any such program?

A. I'm not familiar with it; I don't know.

Q. Would you say that this aspect of consumer safety would be the concern of your large distributors?

A. I think it might be helpful.

Q. You think it would be helpful for large distributors of propane gas to have such an educational program from the point of view of the ultimate consumer?

A. That would be mere conjecture. I would merely say it might be helpful.

Q. There is nothing conjectural about consumer safety, is there, sir?

A. Not at all, sir.

Q. And when we started this conversation you indicated that your company, and you personally, were interested in that, right?

A. Quality control, yes.

Q. And quality control, you said, includes consumer safety, does it not?

A. I would say I made the statement. I believe, sir, if you want to check the record, that the company is interested in not losing any customers.

* * *

Q. When you say not losing any customers, there are two meanings—you don't want to lose any paying customers or you don't want to lose any lives?

A. I think you could say that either way.

Q. So this is the internal standard that you have at [your company], correct?

A. You asked me if this is my policy or [our company's]?

Q. Is it [your company's] policy that they don't want to lose any customers?

A. I would say that's a fair statement.

Q. And they wouldn't want to lose customers who are users of propane gas, correct, users of propane gas?

A. Certainly.

Q. Now, what do you do to educate large gas distributors about information they should pass on to the ultimate consumer so that they can protect themselves from some of the well-known hazards of propane gas? Do you do anything?

A. I personally do not.

Q. Does your company?

A. As far as I'm concerned, that is beyond the policy or the realms of my responsibility. I do not know.

Q. What about your company's responsibilities?

A. I can't speak for that.

Q. Okay. Now, wouldn't you say that this is something that your large distributor would be in a better position to accomplish, this educational process, from the point of view of consumer safety?

A. I don't know.

Q. You can't help us with that, can you?

A. No, I couldn't say that.

COMMENT: After a brief discussion of the tendency of LP gas to stratify, and its explosive potential if it leaks from a gas-fired appliance, this executive was forced to admit that instructions would have been helpful to the consumer.[17]

---

* * *

[17] *Id.*

A. . . .If you are within the explosibility limits of propane, then you could have a decided hazard, yes sir.

Q. In the basement of a home, for example?

A. Yes, sir.

Q. And this is one of the reasons, I suspect, from the point of view of consumer safety as you indicated, that special instructions should be given to homeowners with respect to this particular hazard; and would you recommend that?

A. I think that would be a reasonable assumption. . . .

COMMENT: The man who delivered the gas testified that "the consumer was not given any instructions as to any test to conduct to make sure there is enough odorant in the tank." Furthermore, the person who initially installed the plaintiffs' heater, and who was under contract to shut the machine down if he suspected any hazards, admitted that he never provided them with any information either. Subsequently, a chemical engineer called by the plaintiffs explained to the jury how the plaintiffs could have been trained to recognize the hazard that existed in their heater before tragedy struck: "They could be shown what is called lifting ports. Normally this burner should be burning with a very nice blue color flame that perhaps is in the order of a half to maybe one inch long. And a fair amount of yellow or flames that are not attached to the ports—which would be the most obvious type of symptoms."[18] This expert also stated his opinion that the gas supply company's failure to provide this information was an "improper" practice.[19]

Q. Now, with respect to the characteristics of propane and the nature of the odorants, do you have an opinion as to whether large retailers, prior to June 20, ____, such as __________, could have

[18] *Hageman, supra* note 2, testimony of Mr. M, expert witness for plaintiff.

[19] *Id*.

given more meaningful information and warnings to consumers about the hazards of that product?

A. Yes, I do.

Q. What is your opinion?

A. My opinion is they could have.

Q. And do you have an opinion as to whether the failure to give such warnings or instructions would be an improper practice?

A. Yes, I do.

Q. And what is your opinion?

A. It would be an improper practice not to give an adequate warning concerning odorization.

Q. And this unreasonable or unsafe practice—is that a fair word, unsafe, would you describe it as such?

A. Yes, they both mean the same to me.

COMMENT: The witness then provided further advice regarding alternative methods the defendants could have used to inform, educate, and warn the homeowner/consumer. In preparing his case, counsel will always want to consider and explore alternative safety features that the defendant did not employ.[20]

Q. Are there mechanical devices that would detect explosive concentrations of propane?

A. Yes, there are.

Q. That would set off an alarm that could be heard?

A. Yes, sir.

Q. And have these devices been known to the industry for at least the past fifteen years?

A. Oh, yes. When I design a system, not in a home, but whenever I design a system employing gas, I utilize what is called an explo-

[20] *Id.*

> sive—it is an explosive type of meter that would, for instance, be set on a wall with sensing devices and, at approximately one-fifth of the LEL, it either sounds an alarm or cuts off the gas supply automatically. There are three or four large manufacturers. On the market now, you are getting small lighter devices that you can buy for five or ten dollars that are doing the same thing, that will give you an auditory warning that you are building up an explosive concentration.

COMMENT: Extensive cross-examination led the defendant's assistant laboratory manager to concede that educating consumers regarding the product's hazards would have been helpful in preventing such tragedies, but his company failed to do it.

---

§ 2.09 Conclusion

In any trial, the time between presentation of the case and the return of the verdict is one of enormous emotion and anxiety. Years of preparation and investigation, reams of paper—briefs, motions, interrogatories, and depositions—all come down to those few hours of waiting for the jury's verdict. For this family, the wait was worth it. The U.S. District Court for the Northern District of Ohio, Eastern Division, found the defendant gas supplier liable for the wrongful death of the deceased and awarded $532,832. Their total recovery, including their settlement with the heater manufacturer, came to $882,800.[21]

IV. Other Combustion Products

§ 2.10 Gas stoves

The combination of defective appliances and dangerous gas threatens consumers from gas-fired appliances throughout their homes. In the following section, you will see how the lives of two small children were drastically altered because the gas-fueled kitchen range in their home was

[21] *Hageman, supra* note 2, verdict upheld on appeal.

not equipped with appropriate safety controls.[22]

§ 2.11 —Illustrative case

Curiosity seems to be an inevitable part of childhood. In case after case, I have argued that a manufacturer is responsible for taking into account the natural, foreseeable, and even unpredictable and outrageous behavior of children when designing and marketing products for the home environment. In the instant case, two young boys were horribly burned and permanently disfigured after their natural curiosity led them to climb atop the kitchen range in their home early one morning.[23] The children were aged one and two at the time of this terrifying incident. The two toddlers gained access to a can of cooking grease from cabinets above the stove and turned the control knob (no one knows who did it, why, or how). Within moments, these beautiful youngsters were transformed into human torches.

My investigation revealed two startling facts that so clearly established the liability of the defendant that the case was settled for more than $1 million before trial.[24] The first fact was that the range was designed with easy-to-turn gas control knobs. The stove manufacturer's executives testified that safer, two-step control knobs were commercially available and could have been used on this stove. They could have prevented this tragedy. The second fact was that the company used these safety controls on this very stove to operate the stove's clock timer! They were not used for the gas controls because they were not considered sufficiently attractive to promote product sales.

COMMENT: I wish that this was an isolated tragedy, but like so many cases of slaughter by product it is not. All too

---

[22] *See, infra* § 2.11.

[23] Gauthier v. [Major Stove Manufacturers], No. CA 76–1263K (D. Mass. July 13, 1982). One minor plaintiff received severe burns over 65% of his body, including his face, chest, abdomen, legs, hands, lower back, and buttocks. His wounds required more than 500 days of hospital treatment, including six months of intensive and painful reconstructive surgery as well as 24 separate readmissions during his long struggle to survive. The second minor plaintiff suffered burns over 40% of his body, including his face, legs, left hand, chest, and abdomen. The case was settled for $1.025 million. [The parties agreed not to divulge the identity of the defendants.]

[24] *Id.*

often, such natural activities as the exploratory climbing of a young child, or an adult's casual leaning against a stove or reaching across a burner while cooking, can lead to catastrophic burn injuries. Like other cases of slaughter by product, it is all too easy to blame the victim—the housewife who should have known better, the youngster who should not have been playing on the stove. Yet for all the excuses and pointed fingers, it is the product's manufacturer who ultimately can prevent these injuries by designing the product with safety protections against such foreseeable household use.

Two years prior to the boys' tragedy, research conducted by the federal government had documented the grave safety threats posed by hazardous stove design. The United States Public Health Service reported:[25]

> The victim's motivation in climbing onto the stovetop, into a chair or stool near the stove, or onto a countertop adjacent to the stove, included the desire to gain access to overhead cabinets, the desire to examine or retrieve an attractant stored in the stovetop, or the desire to check on the progress of food under preparation. . . . It is felt . . . that when the in-depth study of stove-related accidents enables us to identify certain design features or operational characteristics which contribute to serious injury, these factors and recommendations deserve careful consideration by those with an interest or responsibility in the field of consumer protection.

Among the identified hazards was the one-step easy-to-turn control.

In the early 1970's, one-step controls could be found on all of the defendant's stoves, although the company had used the two-step models for years on its ovens. Their protection against accidental turn-on by children was known throughout the industry. The company could have obtained the safety control from its supplier at an additional cost of just fifty cents and incorporated them with no substantial modification of the range. It simply chose not to use them. Why not? The defendant's former Director of Engineering Services provided some revealing answers in his sworn testimony pertaining to the company's previous use of the dual

---

[25] U.S. Pub. Health Serv., U.S. Food and Drug Admin., Boston Injury Unit, Burn Injury Study (1971).

controls.[26]

Q. Now, this series was marketed by _______ in the early 1960's?

A. Yes.

Q. And what was the purpose of having that feature on the oven control that you would have to push and turn at the same time?

A. It was a requirement, a standard at the time.

Q. There was, during a number of those years, a standard that required a locking valve for the oven control?

A. Yes.

Q. And was the purpose of that locking valve to prevent accidental turn-on of the gas to the oven?

A. Obviously to prevent it from being turned on accidentally, I'd have to say yes.

Q. Was the [two-step] control a standard control that your supplier was marketing at that time?

A. It was a standard control.

COMMENT: I learned from this witness that the technology for safer control knobs was feasible and available to the defendant as far back as 1969.[27]

Q. Was it technologically feasible to make such a top burner control in 1969?

A. Yes.

Q. In fact, in terms of how the control would operate, the two-operations feature, would there be any substantial difference between the two-operation feature for the oven control and the two-operation or locking valve feature for the top burner control?

---

[26] *Gauthier, supra* note 23, testimony of Mr. S, former Manager of Engineering for defendant C. Company.

[27] *Id.*

A. No.

Q. This was true in 1969 when you left your position as Chief Engineer for ___________?

A. Yes.

COMMENT: The witness explained that he left the company in 1969 and returned three years later. When he returned, the company still had not incorporated the safety features.[28]

Q. Was there any other device on any of these stoves . . . that would prevent accidental turning on of either the top burners or the oven burners?

A. No.

Q. Was it technically feasible [in 1972] to use the two-operational control for the top burners on gas stoves?

A. Yes.

COMMENT: Despite the general knowledge in the industry of the unsafe stove design and of the propensity of children to climb atop them, this witness admitted that the defendant neither consulted with experts to determine whether children could turn their controls nor discussed the hazards the company's product posed to children.[29]

Q. To your knowledge, has [your company] ever spoken with child psychologists, psychiatrists, or other specialists in child development and behavior concerning the ability of children to turn on [its] stoves?

---

[28] *Id.*

[29] *Id.*

A. No.

Q. Before 1969 did you ever attend any meetings in which the subject of the accidental turn-on of gas stove burners by children was discussed?

A. No.

Q. After you came back to the company in 1972, did you ever attend any such meetings?

A. No.

Q. Were you aware that any took place?

A. No.

COMMENT: This startling testimony led me to investigate the practice of the stove's marketer. I learned that this company, also, was fully aware of the feasibility and use of two-step controls. Company employees had raised the issue of safety controls during staff meetings. Additionally, this company used the safety knobs on other product lines, including washers and dryers. Despite these discussions, they did not convey their concerns up the distribution chain to the stove manufacturer. Why not? To this company's Product Marketing Specialist, it was a simple matter of aesthetics, convenience, and what would sell best in the marketplace. The following excerpt from this witness' testimony reveals this corporate philosophy.[30]

Q. Did you, in the course of considering what external appearance changes would be made [on this model], consider any changes to the external knobs?

A. For the knobs that are on the shaft of the burner valves, we did look at various possibilities and decided that, for the money, the standard ____ knob gave us the best appearance and that another knob would not change that appearance very dramati-

[30] *Gauthier, supra* note 23, testimony of Mr. M, Product Marketing Specialist, on behalf of defendant G. Company.

> cally. . . . We looked at various alternatives and decided that we could not differentiate it enough to make any relative difference in it. More as a convenience, we left them exactly the same.

COMMENT: A government study conducted a year later confirmed that "climbing around the range" was a primary hazard for young children, and concluded that "certain design modifications to the ranges will reduce the ignition hazard considerably. . . ."[31] It recommended that stove designs be altered to prevent the type of horrible injuries that befell the toddlers in this case. Why must innocent children be sacrificed because of industry's desire to save a few pennies or market a more attractive product?

---

§ 2.12 —Conclusion

A new industry standard, including use of two-step controls, was adopted in 1975. It was a voluntary standard, with no force of law to make manufacturers produce a safer product. That year, the Consumer Product Safety Commission estimated that 20,000 Americans were burned annually in incidents involving kitchen ranges. By 1981, the casualty rate had reached 40,000. Kitchen ranges had become the leading source of all household fires.

§ 2.13 Inadequately vented gas combustion

When gas is burned to heat our homes and run our appliances, the combustion produces two by-products: water vapor and carbon dioxide. When the combustion process is not complete, which is usually the case, deadly carbon monoxide is produced.

Carbon monoxide is an odorless, colorless, tasteless, and highly poisonous gas. The thought of carbon monoxide poisoning usually conjures up images of asphyxiation in a closed-up automobile. Yet the same combustion process that drives our cars also drives those appliances that heat

---

[31] *Kitchen Ranges in Fabric Fires*, Nat'l Bureau of Standards, Tech. Note 817 (1974).

our homes. When the carbon monoxide produced by this combustion process is not adequately vented out of the indoor environment, the results can be deadly.

Carbon monoxide gas gradually overcomes its victims. Poisoning symptoms at first resemble the flu: dizziness, nausea, headache, blurred vision, irritability. Later, as exposure increases, shortness of breath and convulsions can result. If the victim is sleeping, he can be poisoned and never wake up.

The case of the __________ family provides a vivid illustration of the hazards posed by inadequately vented gas combustion.[32] This family lived in a mobile home, equipped with its own gas-powered electric generator and motor. On December 8, 1973, the father drove his children from their home in Swansea, Massachusetts, to Auburn, Massachusetts, to attend Christmas parties at the ____________ Coach Association. He parked the vehicle in a field of tall grass, nearby the building where the party was to take place. The children attended their party in the afternoon and then asked to go to bed because they felt tired. The father felt tired and nauseous himself. He left the children with a baby-sitter at about 7:30 p.m. to attend the adult party. When he returned at 10:00 p.m., all the children and the baby-sitter were unconscious. Two of the children were later revived, but his youngest son died. He describes the horror in his own words:

> After three hours [at the party] I returned to get [the baby-sitter]. We found her unconscious in the rear, [my older boy] with a white paste on his lips, and [my daughter] with a mixture of blood and vomit through her nose and mouth. We tried to get [the babysitter] out. I remember opening the windows and turning on the air conditioner and fans . . . I carried [my daughter] out. She was lifeless and limp. I tried to listen for a heartbeat, but got none. I thought she was dead.[33]

The [plaintiff's] home was manufactured by the ____ Company. Eight months after the plaintiff's tragedy, two of own employees became ill in their motor home. Their illnesses prompted additional testing and action by the company. It found that carbon monoxide accumulated in the space beneath the vehicle.

---

[32] Derosier v. AVCO Corp., No. CA 75–2364F (D. Mass. Jan. 23, 1984), testimony of plaintiff.

[33] *Id*.

The company acknowledged the hazard in a letter to other motor home owners:

> The ____ Corporation has determined that a defect which relates to motor vehicle safety exists in some ____ . . . units with the side-mounted gasoline motor driven generator exhaust that is directed downward/undercoach. . . . The generator exhaust is piped into its high velocity cooling air discharge which is directed downward through the generator compartment toward the ground under the right rear corner of the motorcoach body. Under very still air conditions, with the coach completely closed, hazardous levels of carbon monoxide intrude into the coach. Parking the vehicle in tall grass accentuates the problem. . . . Occupants may be exposed to a hazardous level of carbon monoxide while the generator is running, in the subject coaches. . . . We regret the inconvenience. . . ."[34]

In another case, a woman found her son unconscious in his bedroom, carbon monoxide produced by the space heater that was keeping him warm had rendered him nearly lifeless. She related her tragic experience in testimony before the National Commission on Product Safety:[35]

> My son . . . was poisoned by carbon monoxide from an unvented gas heater. It happened on ________, 19__. We were living in a rented house at ____________ in ______, Georgia. We had lived there about a year. [He] was working at night and taking a course in radio and television repair. He was nineteen years old, and he was in perfect health until that day.
>
> The house had an unvented gas heater in every room when we rented it. We paid $95 a month. Those heaters were the only heat in the house. It was pretty chilly that day—it got down to twenty-one degrees. [He] went into the bedroom about 7:30 in the morning.
>
> I found him unconscious at about 7:00 p.m. The room was real hot. A friend called the police and firemen right away. They gave him artificial respiration just as soon as they got there, and rushed him to the hospital in ______. They put him in the intensive care room. He stayed there for three months. He went from 140 to 88 pounds. Then he was transferred to a nursing home in ________, Georgia. They kept him for four months, and then released him to my care.

---

[34] Letter from defendant ____ Motor Homes to plaintiff (January 22, 1975).

[35] Statement of Mrs. M before Nat'l Comm. on Prod. Safety (March 3, 1970).

After [he] came home, we had to bathe him and feed him like a baby. After a while he finally learned to feed and wash himself, but that's about all. The doctors say that part of his brain was completely destroyed, and he is mentally about eight or nine years old. He walks on his toes, and I can only understand what he is saying part of the time.

Two times since he came home, he has completely lost control of himself and become violent. He is dangerous when he is like that, and he had to be taken to the State Hospital for treatment. [He] had a psychiatric evaluation again last month, and the doctors said there is no need for any more appointments because he doesn't have any ability to comprehend.

He is on medication now, for his nerves, and so he can sleep. Last March, he had to go back to the State Hospital and he got out in December. He stays with me most of the time, and he has to be watched like a little child. . . . The doctors say there is no hope for recovery, and he will have to be cared for the rest of his life.

Those heaters were the only thing to keep the house warm. [He] never did like cold weather, so I suppose he closed the window to keep out the draft. We never knew that those unvented gas heaters could cause a thing like that. *There was nothing on the heater to warn us*. [Emphasis added.]

§ 2.14 Charcoal briquets

The horrors wrought by lethal carbon monoxide fumes are bad enough. When a company actually encourages indoor use of a product that it knows produces toxic carbon monoxide gases, this is inexcusable. Such was the case when four members of the Tennessee family perished in their home, overcome by deadly fumes from burning charcoal briquets. The briquets were sold in a bag labeled, "For Indoor Use."

Counsel facing a case involving death as a result of indoor exposure to toxic fumes from charcoal briquets may be tempted to ask, "Why did the fool use the briquets indoors to begin with?" As I learned in this case, the family that perished in this tragic occurrence was seduced by an orchestrated industry marketing campaign to use the product as they did. It was part of a calculated sales promotion campaign to encourage indoor, year-round use of their product. One industry publication boasted, "Briquets for All Seasons."[36] The campaign was launched despite safety experts' warnings over the years regarding the lethal consequences of carbon monoxide poisoning from indoor charcoal briquet use. Apparently, increased sales were more important to industry members than the lethal risks of toxic poisoning.

§ 2.15 —Illustrative case

The results of this industry campaign were predictably catastrophic. Across the country entire families were perishing as deadly fumes transformed family dinners into scenes of tragedy. I represented the estate of four members of a Tennessee family who perished in their home when they were overcome by deadly fumes from burning charcoal briquets.[37]

The company that manufactured the plaintiff's charcoal was the second leading manufacturer in the country at the time. The company's promotional efforts practically invited the plaintiffs to use their product indoors. The bag bore a label stating, in part, "For Indoor Use." The company then had the gall to add "Caution—Cook Only in Properly Ventilated Area."[38]

The company's Vice President admitted under oath that a partly open window would not be safe, that "well ventilated" might mean different things to different people, and that he did not know how many windows would have to be open for a room to be sufficiently "well ventilated" to meet the safety needs of consumers according to his company's so-called warning label.[39] This witness also admitted that he himself would not use the product indoors without a protective fireplace-type apparatus.[40]

> Q. You wouldn't recommend using charcoal briquets indoors unless they were used in a fireplace-type apparatus, would you?
>
> A. No, sir.
>
> Q. Under any circumstances, would you?
>
> A. No.

---

[36] Johnson v. Husky Indus., No. CA–3008 (E.D. Tenn. June 27, 1975), promotional materials with ______________ charcoal briquets used as evidence.

[37] *Johnson, supra* note 36.

[38] *Id*.

[39] *Johnson, supra* note 36, testimony of Mr. E, Vice President for defendant ______________ Industries.

[40] *Id*.

Q. That has always been true as long as you have been with the company, has it not?

A. To the best of my knowledge.

COMMENT: Not only were the product's hazards and limitations not divulged to consumers, they were not even shared with the company's own sales staff. Consider the following testimony of a company sales manager taken during depositions.

Q. When you became sales manager, as part of your training, did you receive in-company training there?

A. Not as such, no.

Q. They gave you material to read, did they not?

A. Yes.

Q. They gave you material pertaining to the advantages of the product, right?

A. We had several discussions about the nature of the product, the nature of the business.

Q. And the advantages of the product, certainly, as sales manager?

A. Yes.

Q. Likewise, they told you about the disadvantages of the briquets and any problems they had with it, correct?

A. I don't recall that we discussed disadvantages of our product. I don't recall that . . . we didn't talk about the negative aspects of the product.

Q. Did you talk about the safety aspects of the product?

A. I don't recall that, either.

Q. Did they discuss with you the fact that at least some persons had been killed when using or attempting to use charcoal briquets in the home, for example?

A. No.

My trial preparation revealed that this company's public relations campaign was just the tip of the iceberg. The following were just a sample of this company's negligent manufacturing and marketing practices:

(1) It conducted no adequate tests to determine the lethal effects of its product's toxic gases, the ventilation required to remove those gases from the indoor air, or the time it would take for carbon monoxide to reach fatal levels in an average size room;

(2) It employed no engineer or chemist with responsibility to study the uses to which consumers were likely to put its product;

(3) It kept no records of deaths or injuries resulting from the use of its product;

(4) Its executives were not aware of literature that dealt with similar products, or of articles concerning the toxic quality of charcoal combustion, proper ventilation, or the rate at which burning charcoal displaces air with carbon monoxide.

These failures are even more alarming when we consider the national publicity that charcoal-related poisonings had generated before the industry chose to initiate this campaign tactic. For example, in a published report, the National Safety Council had disclosed eighteen deaths from briquet poisoning. In addition, the U.S. Food and Drug Administration had warned consumers to "use charcoal briquets only outdoors because of the danger of carbon monoxide poisoning." The agency's files were filled with cases of carbon monoxide poisoning from the indoor use of charcoal briquets.

I pointed out that the defendant could have more adequately warned consumers of the hazardous nature of its product. The company had placed a more complete warning on some of its charcoal briquet bags the year before the plaintiff made his purchase. It also sent stick-on labels containing fuller warnings to its wholesalers. Yet it sent no such warnings to retailers concerning ______________ briquets. The only materials it provided to its retailers were the labels already printed on the bag. This failure to warn, in light of its demonstrated ability to do so, was a clear act of negligence on the part of this major manufacturer.

Our client received a $425,000 judgment for the wrongful death of this family of four. In its verdict the trial court held that, "officers of the defendant were aware prior to the accident involved herein that claims had been made against their company for deaths allegedly resulting from the use of its product . . . for indoor heating purposes."[41] Half of the judgment was for punitive damages against the defendant. The court determined that because the manufacturer distributed a product that was dangerous to human life, it "was under a duty to apprise the purchasing public, by labels or otherwise, of the manner in which the product might be safely used."[42] This the defendant failed to do.

V. Preventing Combustion-Related Injuries

§ 2.16 In general

There can be little question that gas will remain an important and growing home heating source in the foreseeable future. It is important, therefore, that gas suppliers, distributors, and appliance manufacturers take appropriate steps to reduce the perilous hazards resulting from household gas and gas appliance use. The gas itself, whether in the form of natural gas or liquefied-petroleum (LP) gas, must be adequately odorized, and alternative means for consumers to detect leaking gas in their homes must be provided. This program must include programs to educate consumers regarding gas detection equipment and detection of artificial odorants. Gas appliance manufacturers and marketers must incorporate safety precautions in their design of these products, as well as make certain that their products are guarded against such foreseeable household uses that may involve children's curious and adventuresome propensities and adults' inevitable moments of carelessness.

§ 2.17 Gas odorization

Household gas is usually supplied by a chain of companies involved in gas distribution. Each party along the route must be responsible for making sure that the gas they handle is adequately odorized. The traditional "sniff test" may not be sufficient for these purposes. These companies must take the responsibility to be certain that their gas is detectable in the home environment—even the rural home's basement environment, where a variety of earthy odors can compete with the artificial odorant currently being used.

In a government-sponsored study,[43] thousands of volunteers were

---

[41] *Johnson, supra* note 36.

[42] *Id.*

[43] M.L. Whisman, J.W. Goetzinger, C.J. Thompson, F.O. Cotton, O.W. Brinkman, *A*

tested to determine their ability to detect the smell of mercaptan and other additives used to odorize gas, and their ability to identify that smell as gas once they detected it. These researchers found that artificial odorizers are only as effective as the sense of smell of those people who occupy the room in which the odor is present. An estimated one out of every 500 people, according to this study, "have suffered complete loss of smell and would not be warned by any level of any odorant system."[44]

They also found that "unfortunately, a given environment as well as anxieties or mental distractions can produce reduced awareness to odorants intended to warn individuals of the presence of LP gas."[45] Age, too, can be a factor. As with our senses of hearing and vision, our sense of smell can deteriorate with age. The government also warned, "odor detection alone may be useless if the source of the odors is misinterpreted. . . . It was evident through the thousands of participants interviewed in this survey that a substantial portion of the general public has had little or no contact with LP gas and therefore failed to make the proper identification of odors provided them."[46] While 87% of the participants detected the odor upon entering the testing laboratory, only 58% correctly identified it as a gas-related smell. The government concluded:

> "[C]lassical methods of evaluating odorant levels required to provide a warning to LP-gas consumers probably approximate the levels that can be detected more nearly than the level that WILL be detected. Classical testing methods similar to the directed tests of this study may not define the level of odorants required to warn persons of the presence of gas in unfamiliar surroundings. . . . It seems probable that better education of the nonconsumer to the odors identified with LP-gas would raise the positive [identification] rate of the odor."[47]

Gas industry members must invest their resources in finding and developing alternative methods for gas leak detection. There is simply no excuse for the continued use of a system designed to prevent combustion catastrophes that is not adequate to the task.

New Look at Odorization Levels for Propane Gas, Bartlesville Energy Research Center, Energy Research and Dev. Admin. (March 1977).

[44] *Id*. at 3.

[45] *Id*. at Abstract.

[46] *Id*. at 62.

[47] *Id*. at 79.

Although technological breakthroughs in gas sensor and gas detection technology can be valuable in this endeavor, in the meantime, consumers should be (1) warned that current gas detection methods may not provide the safety protection that many consumers expect when they choose to heat their homes with gas and (2) informed of alternative gas detection devices available for their household.

Gas industry members must also develop innovative means for educating consumers regarding the odorization and detection of the artificial odorants currently in use. This may include the distribution of odorized products that provide consumers with examples of those odors to detect when gas is leaking in their homes. Adequate detection is vital if the catastrophes of exploding gas are to be prevented.

Code-setting bodies, including the National Fire Protection Association (N.F.P.A.) and American Gas Association (A.G.A.) must develop safety guidelines, including gas odorization levels, which provide for more reliable detection of leaking gas.

Professionals with technical expertise, including engineers and chemists, must seek out new and innovative means of testing, odorizing, and detecting leaking gas, and this information must be adopted efficiently into product lines for maximum consumer protection.

§ 2.18 Safety technology for gas appliances

Gas appliance manufacturers and marketers must design their products with all available safety equipment to ensure that the appliances shut down when gas is escaping before tragedy strikes. Those companies that fail to design their products with the most advanced available technology to prevent combustion catastrophes must realize that they will be held accountable in our courts for this practice, including the potential for an award of punitive damages against them when the appropriate proof is provided.

Manufacturers of kitchen ranges and other cooking equipment must design their products with safety devices to prevent foreseeable turn-on by curious and adventurous children. Safety technology and design are available, they just need to be used. Companies that choose not to employ safety designs because they are not required to, must also realize that they will pay the price for this practice.

§ 2.19 Safety in design and regulation of other combustion products

As consumers continue to import new heating fuels into their homes, standards and codes governing these products must keep up with the growth in demand. Coal and wood burning stoves, kerosene heaters, and portable gas heaters are just a few examples.

Code-setting bodies like the Underwriters' Laboratories and the National Fire Protection Association must develop safety standards that meet the needs and hazards posed by current product technology. The drafters of fire, electric, safety, and other building codes must also be alert to changes in product lines, product performance, and product risks in this area.

Manufacturers of these and other "alternative heat source" combustion products must invest both time and money to improve their safety technology, while at the same time warning consumers of their products' risks.

§ 2.20 What can lawyers do?

There is no question that gas explosion and similar combustion cases can be extremely complex and difficult to litigate. Nevertheless, lawyers provided the opportunity to litigate such cases should accept this challenge. In support of this work, I have provided in § 2.02 *supra*, an investigation checklist for guidance in preparing a gas explosion-related injury case. It is my hope that this checklist will prove helpful to the attorney and will contribute to increased litigation in this important and challenging product field.

I also encourage my fellow members of the bar to keep abreast of technological advancements in gas odorization and detection, gas appliance design and safety device development, and the innovative means employed by individual companies in communicating the hazards of their products to end-use consumers. The Gas Institute and other industry groups are constantly conducting research and publishing reports regarding technological advances in their field that may not, as yet, have been incorporated into home appliances and home gas use, but which certainly will be if sufficient pressure is placed on the industry by our government and our judiciary.

Finally, counsel should keep abreast of government and private standard and code-setting bodies' developments in regulating combustion products. Changes in this field can have important an impact on injury prevention and your case development.

VI. Litigation Sources: Bibliography

§ 2.21 Selected technical sources

Bellers & Susey, *Research Related to Appliance Utilization* (Am. Gas Ass'n 1975).

Blout, et al., *Crystal & Molecular Structure of 1,1,1,3,3,3,–Hexaphenaylpropane*, 47 J. Organic Chemistry 4359–61 (Oct. 22, 1982).

Cassidy, *Water Heaters*, 48 Specifying Engineer, No. 3 (Sept. 1982).

Chang & Reid, *Spreading—Boiling Model for Instantaneous Spills of LP Gas on Water*, 7 J. Hazardous Material 19–35 (Nov. 1982).

Charman, et al., *Materials Selection for Modern Gas Appliances and Systems*, 12 Metallic Materials Tech. 33–39, No. 1 (Jan. 1980).

Chou, *Combustible Gas Detectors: Toward Broader Standards*, 29 Instrumental Tech. 133–34 (Sept. 1982).

Delbourg & Purkis, *Interchangeable Gases and Appliance Standardization*, 182 Gas World Gas J. 4705 (Aug. 1977) (Interchangeability of gases and standardization of appliances in several countries, including Great Britain).

Dyabu, et al., *Sensing Characteristics of Tin Oxide Thick Film Gas Sensor*, 53 J. Applied Physics 7125–30 (Nov. 1982).

Gas/Vapor Sniffers Prevent Accidents (q & a), 81 Electrical Construction & Maintenance 36 (Sept. 1982).

Garman, *LPG Testing: Up Against the Wall*, 117 Sci. News 120 (Feb. 23, 1980).

Herbert, *On Line Laser Detection of Gases*, 29 Electronics & Power 316 (Apr. 1983).

Higgins, *Advances in Leak Detection Systems*, 58 Pipe Line Indus. 29–30 (Mar.-Apr. 1983).

Hillier, et al., *National Defect Monitoring Within the Concept of Quality Assurance* (Brit. Gas Corp. 1975). (Investigation of gas appliances defects in England.)

Hogan, *C.O. Sniffer Gives Duel-Level Alert*, 38 Design News 168–69 (Sept. 13, 1982).

Lauer, et al., *Mobile-Phase Transport Properties of Liquefied Gases in Near-Critical Supercritical Fluid Chromatography*, 55 Analytical Chemistry 1370–75 (July 1983).

Mount, *Acoustic Leak Detector in Development at LG+ pr GRC*, 209 Pipeline & Gas J. 22, No. 1 (May 1982).

Unsold Goods Threaten to Go With a Bang, 92 New Scientist 601 (Nov. 26, 1981).

Oyabu, *Sensing Characteristics of SuO_2 Thin Film Gas Sensor*, 53 J. Applied Physics 2785–87 (Apr. 1982).

Parcher & Lin, *Cooperative and Competitive Adsorption of Propane and Butane on Graphitized Carbon Black*, 53 Analytical Chemistry 1889–94 (Oct. 1981).

Pujado, et al., *LPG, A Direct Source of C3–C5 Olefins*, 81 Oil & Gas J. 71–74 (Mar. 28, 1983).

Reed, *Preventing Explosions and Fuel-Fed Fires*, 37 Plant Eng'g 81–82 (May 12, 1983).

Sakhuja, et al., *Improved Gas Fuel Appliances* (Proceedings of 5th Energy Technology Conference, Washington, D.C. 1978).

Singh, *Sizing vents for gas explosions*, 86 Chemical Eng'g 103–109 (Sept. 24, 1979).

Sliger & Serdahl, *Digital Monitoring of Combustible Gas*, 21 Computer Design 79–82 (Aug. 1982).

Stefanides, *Silicone Foam Ring Protects Against Explosions*, 35 Design News 138–39 (Apr. 23, 1979).

Yamaguchi, et al., *Combustion of Propane-Air Mixtures Ignited by Electrical Exploding Wire*, Bull. C. Eng'g Hosei U. 35–41, No. 19 (Mar. 1983).

§ 2.22 Selected popular sources

Blandy & Clark, *Hot New Developments in Home-Heating Technology*, 79 Mechanix Illustrated No. 665 (Oct. 1983).

Caughlin, *Troubleshooting & LP-Gas Systems*, 44 Trailer Life 106–12, No. 2 (Feb. 1984).

Safety Tips for Burner-Type Furnaces, 29 Changing Times 12, No. 11 (Nov. 1975).

Use Supplemental Heat Sources With Care, 9 Consumer News 2, No. 4 (Feb. 15, 1977).

Water Heaters: Gas & Electric, 41 Consumer Rep. 165–67, No. 3 (Mar. 1976).

Delrod, *How to Start Your Furnace When It Quits*, 15 Consumer's Digest 29–30, No. 7 (Nov.-Dec. 1976).

Emergency Cut-Off Valves—Where Are Yours?, 24 Fam. Handyman 50–53, No. 8 (Oct. 1974).

La Barge, *Tankless Water Heaters, How Good Are They?*, 79 Mechanix Illustrated 82, 113–14, No. 65 (Feb. 1983).

Powell, *How to Keep Yourself in Hot Water*, 204 Popular Sci. 110, No. 1 (Jan. 1974).

Focus on Fire Safety, 161 Redbook 204, No. 6 (Oct. 1983).

Thompson, *How to Handle LP Gas Safely*, 38 Trailer Life 84–90, No. 4 (Apr. 1978).

REVCO Gas Sniffer, 43 Trailer Life 1067, No. 10 (Oct. 1983).

§ 2.23 Selected government sources

O. Beedgen, *Fan-Type Gas Burners for Small Heat-Release Rates* (Report, Dec. 1980).

H. Coanda & G. Muresan, *Burner for Gaseous Fuel*, (Report, British Gas Corp., London, England 1982).

Y. Deschamps, *Gas Interchangeability as Applied to the Existing Range of Appliances* (British Gas Corp., London, England 1982) (Proposal of new method of gas interchangeability on an existing range of appliances actually in service).

D. DeWerth & S. Connelly, *Venting Requirements for High Efficiency Gas-Fired Heating Equipment* (Final Report, American Gas Ass'n Sept. 1983).

H. Dienelt & A. Fontana, *Application of Statistical Method to the Quality Control of Gas Appliances and to Testing Reliability with Particular Regard to Gas Meters* (Report, World Gas Conference 1982).

H. Grunes, *Development of a High Capacity Two-Phase Thermosypon*

Gas-Fired Water Heater (Final Report, June 1981–Dec. 1983, Gas Research Institute, Chicago, Ill. Jan. 1984).

P. Harsha, R. Edelman, et al., *Performance Modeling of Advanced Gas Burner Systems* (Final Report, Gas Research Institute, Chicago, Ill. July 1983).

R. Kolodgy & J. Fuller, *Pulse Combustion Residential Water Heater* (Dec. 1982–Nov. 1983, American Gas Ass'n Labs, Cleveland, Ohio, Gas Research Institute, Dec. 1983).

Introducing Supplemental Combustion Air to Gas-Fired Home Appliances (Report National Center for Appropriate Technology, Butte, Mont., U.S. Department of Energy Dec. 1983).

R. Pam & J. Kesselring, *Burner Survey for a High Efficiency Gas-Fired Heating Unit* (Report, Alzeta Corp., Mountain View, Cal. Jan. 31, 1984).

A. Vasilakis, G. Celorier & J. Gerstmann, *Integrated Gas-Fired Space Heating/Water Heating System with Electric Air Conditioning* (Annual Report, Advanced Mechanical Technology, Inc., Newton, Mass. Jan. 1984).

§ 2.24 Selected legal sources

Explosions and Explosives, 31 Am. Jur. 2d §§ 57 *et seq*. (1967).

Point of Origin of Fire: Improperly Installed or Maintained Heating Appliances, 27 Am. Jur. *P.O.F. 2d* 1 (1981).

Proof Regarding Negligence as Factor in Gas Explosions, 23 Am. Jur. *P.O.F.* 447 Gas Explosions (1976).

Liquefied Petroleum (LP) Gas Fires and Explosions, 14 Am. Jur. *Trials* 343 (1968).

Defective Heating Equipment, 1 A.L.R. 4th 748 (1980).

Products Liability: Liability for Injury or Death Allegedly Caused by Defect in Mobile Home or Trailer, 81 A.L.R. 3d 421 (1977).

Liability for One Selling or Distributing Liquid or Bottled Fuel Gas For Personal Injury, Death, or Property Damage, 41 A.L.R. 3d 782 (1972).

Liability of Manufacturer or Seller for Injury Caused by Explosions and Flammables, 80 A.L.R. 2d 488 (1961).

R. Hursch & H. Bailey, *American Law of Products Liability* (Lawyers Co-op., 2d ed. 1976).

§ 2.25 Selected newsletters

Gas

Butane/Propane:

International Butane/Propane Newsletter
Butane-Propane News, Inc.
P.O. Box 1408
Arcadia, Cal. 91006

Natural Gas News
Natural Gas Supply Association
1025 Conn Ave
Washington, D.C. 20036

NG News
Natural Gas Supply Association
1025 Connecticut Ave.
Washington, D.C. 20036

Tech Digest
American Society of Gas Engineers
P.O. Box 696
Ashland, N.H. 03217

Washington Letter
American Gas Association
1515 Wilson Blvd
Arlington, Va. 22209

GRID
Gas Research Institute
8600 West Bryn Mawr
Chicago, Ill. 60631

Heating and Ventilation:

Builder's Choice
Better Heating-Cooling Council
35 Russo Place
Berkeley Heights, N.J. 07922

HVAC Data File 1981
same as above

Pipe Lines:

INGAA Washington Report
Interstate Natural Gas Ass'n of America
1660 L St., N.W., Suite 601
Washington, D.C. 20036

Propane:

NLPGA Management News
National LP-Gas Assoc
1301 West 22d St
Oak Brook, Ill. 60521

Weekly Propane Newsletter
Butane-Propane News, Inc.
PO Box 1408
Arcadia, Cal. 91006

Valve Industry:

VMA Currents
Valve Manufacturers' Association
1050 17th St. N.W., Suite 701
Washington, D.C. 20036.

§ 2.26 Selected laws, regulations, and standards

Statutes

(1) Consumer Product Safety Act (CPSA), 15 U.S.C. §§ 2051–2083 (1985).

(2) Federal Hazardous Substances Act (FHSA), 15 U.S.C. §§ 1261–1276 (1985).

Regulations

(1) Labeling Requirements for Kerosene, 16 C.F.R. § 1500.14(a)(3) (1985)

(2) Labeling Requirements for Charcoal Briquettes, 16 C.F.R § 1500.14(b)(6) (1985)

(3) Method to Test for Flashpoint of Volatile Flammable Materials, 16 C.F.R. § 1500.32 (1985)

(4) Substances Requiring Special Packaging, 16 C.F.R. § 1700.14 (1985)

Industry Codes and Standards

(1) National Fire Protection Association (NFPA)
Battery March Park
Quincy, Mass. 02269

 (a) NFPA 501D: Fire Safety Criteria for Recreational Parks and Campgrounds

 (b) NFPA 58: Storage and Handling of LP Gas

 (c) NFPA 54: National Fuel Gas Code (also ANSI Z 223.1)

(2) American National Standards Institute (ANSI)
1430 Broadway
New York, N.Y. 10018

 (a) ANSI A 21.64: Direct Vent Central Furnaces

 (b) ANSI Z 21.54: Gas-Burning Appliances

 (c) ANSI Z 21.47: Gas-Fired Central Furnaces

 (d) ANSI Z 21.45: Connectors of other than all-metal construction for gas appliances

 (e) ANSI Z 21.44: Gas-Fired Gravity and Fan Type Direct Vent Wall Furnaces

 (f) ANSI Z 21.24: Connectors for Metal Gas Appliances

 (g) ANSI Z 21.18: Gas Appliances Pressure Regulators

 (h) ANSI Z 21.10.1: Hot Water Heaters, Automatic Storage Type

(3) American Society for Testing and Materials (ASTM)
1916 Race Street
Philadelphia, Pa. 19103

 (a) ASTM D1230–61

(4) Underwriters' Laboratories (UL)
333 Pfingsten Road
Northbrook, Ill. 60062

 (a) UL 307B: Gas Burning Heating Appliances for Mobile Homes and Recreational Vehicles

(b) UL 174: Household Electric, Storage-Tank Water Heaters

(c) UL 144: Valves for LP-Gas Pressure Regulating

(d) UL 132: Safety Relief Valves for Anhydrous Ammonia and LP Gas

§ 2.27 Selected cases

Hohlenkamp v. Rheem Mfg. Co., 134 Ariz. 208, 655 P.2d 32 (Ct. App. 1982), **gas-fired water heater;** fire loss; design defect.

Dennis v. Honeywell, No. 75–M–968 (D. Colo. Nov. 6, 1979), 23 ATLA L. Rep. 184 (May 1980), **water heater;** explosion; severe burns; defective control thermostat.

Van Hoose v. Blueflame Gas, Inc., 642 P.2d 36 (Colo. Ct. App. 1981), *aff'd*, 679 P.2d 579 (Colo. 1984), **hot water heater;** explosion; severe burns; failure to warn; defendant's burden to prove lack of defect on transfer of control.

Giglio v. Connecticut Light & Power Co., 180 Conn. 230, 429 A.2d 486 (1980), **home furnace;** duty to warn.

Travelers Ins. Co. v. Magic Chef, Inc. 483 A.2d 1115 (Del. 1984), **furnace;** furnace and blower manufacturers' concurrent negligence.

Douglas v. Smith, 578 F.2d 1169 (5th Cir. [Ga.] 1978), **LP gas;** explosion; personal injuries; supplier's liability for sale to unlicensed and uninsured dealer.

Kern v. Uregas Service of West Frankfort, Inc., 90 Ill. App. 3d 182, 45 Ill. Dec. 455, 412 N.E.2d 1037 (1980), **propane gas;** explosion; personal injuries and property damage; negligence in filling tank.

Gideon Service Div. v. Durham-Bush, Inc., 80 Ill. App. 3d 633, 35 Ill. Dec. 952, 400 N.E.2d 89 (1980), **furnace;** seller's untimely waiver of implied warranty.

Denniston v. Skelly Oil Co., 47 Ill. App. 3d 1054, 6 Ill. Dec. 77, 362 N.W.2d 712 (1977), **propane gas cylinders;** wrongful death; negligence of LP gas seller; failure to warn and to test gas lines.

Bainter v. Lamoine LP Gas Co., 24 Ill. App. 3d 913, 321 N.E.2d 744, (1974), **gas tank;** destruction of property; defective emergency pressure relief valve.

Hiltabrand v. Honeywell, Inc., No. 80 L 10837 (Ill. Cir. Ct. 1984), 27

ATLA L. Rep. 279 (Aug. 1984), **LP gas water heater;** explosion; wrongful death; settlement of $1.345 million.

Hughes v. Magic Chef, Inc., 288 N.W.2d 542 (Iowa 1980), **gas stove;** erroneous jury instructions.

Johnk v. Robertshaw Controls Co., No. 51078 (Iowa Dist. Ct. Aug. 16, 1982), **LP gas water heater;** defective safety control.

Brooks v. Dietz, No. 47,850 (Kan. Jan. 24, 1976), **furnace;** explosion.

Jones v. Hittle Service, Inc., 219 Kan. 627, 549 P.2d 1303 (1976), **propane gas;** distributor's warnings.

Briscoe v. Sears, Roebuck & Co., No. 78–C–116 (Kan. Dist. Ct. 1982), 24 ATLA L. Rep. 423 (Nov. 1981), **gas control;** gas leakage and explosion; burns over 47% of body; structured settlement of $270,000.

Harris v. Atlanta Stove Works, Inc., 428 So. 2d 1040 (La. Ct. App.), *cert. denied*, 434 So. 2d 1106 (La. 1983), **gas space heater;** carbon monoxide poisoning; wrongful death; latent defect.

O'Brien v. Delta Gas, Inc., 426 So. 2d 262 (La. Ct. App.), *cert. denied*, 433 So. 2d 163 (La. 1983), **home gas;** explosion; negligent failure to odorize gas adequately.

Kalmn, Inc. v. Empiregas Corp., 406 So. 2d 276 (La. Ct. App. 1981), **furnace;** insufficient malorant in gas causes explosion; destruction of farmhouse.

Allen v. Riley Mobile Home Sales, Inc., 307 So. 2d 773 (La. Ct. App. 1975), **butane for use in mobile homes;** seller's duty to inspect appliances for compatibility upon installation.

Pease v. Honeywell, Inc. (Me. Super. Ct. Aug. 19, 1980), 23 ATLA L. Rep. 422 (Nov. 1980), **LP gas;** burns; defective controls.

Butcher v. Robertshaw Controls Co., 550 F. Supp. 692 (D. Md. 1981), **gas run hot water heater;** severe burns; defective valve; no warnings; *settled*, No. 81–72 (D. Md. Jan. 14, 1983), for lifetime payout of $25 million.

Gauthier v. [Major Stove Manufacturers], No. CA 76–1263K (D. Mass. July 13, 1982), **gas stoves;** severe burns; settlement of $1.025 million.

Derosier v. AVCO Corp., No. CA 75–2364F, *et seq*. (D. Mass. June 13, 1975), **mobile home gas powered electric generator and motor;** carbon monoxide poisoning; wrongful death.

Stratton v. A.O. Smith Co., No. G 79–72 (W.D. Mich. 1981), 24 ATLA L. Rep. 328 (Sept. 1981), **water heater controls;** LP gas explosion; wrongful death; defective controls recalled; structured settlement of $604,000.

Woods v. Airstream, Inc. (Mich. Cir. Ct. 1981), 25 ATLA L. Rep. 227 (June 1982), **trailer furnace;** carbon monoxide poisoning from propane furnace; wrongful death; settlement of $1 million.

Jeadro v. Honeywell (Minn. Dist. Ct. 1984), 27 ATLA L. Rep. 371 (Oct. 1984), **gas furnace;** gas control valve; burns on explosion; settlement of $3.3 million.

Maertens v. White Rodgers Div. of Emerson Elec. Mfg. Co., No. 86215 (Minn. Dist. Ct. July 3, 1980), 23 ATLA L. Rep. 422 (Nov. 1980), **hot water heater;** explosion; burns; defective gas cock knob on control valve; structured settlement of $1.1 million.

Davolt v. Getty Refining and Marketing Co. (W.D. Mo. 1980), 23 ATLA L. Rep. 422 (Nov. 1980), **forced air gas furnace;** explosion; wrongful death; valve defects; settlement of $500,000.

Webster v. Empiregas, Inc. of Camdenton, 648 S.W.2d 198 (Mo. Ct. App. 1983), **space heater;** fire; defective and unreasonably dangerous product; damages to residence.

LaPlante v. Sears, Roebuck & Co., No. C–78–273–L (D.N.H. July 16, 1982), 26 ATLA L. Rep. 228 (June 1983), **hot water heater;** explosion; burns; settlement of $1.025 million.

Dempsey v. Magic Chef, No. 81–CV–780 (N.D.N.Y. 1983), 27 ATLA L. Rep. 133 (Apr. 1984), **gas stove;** gas control knobs ignited; severe burns; settlement with stove manufacturer for $1,100/month for life from age eighteen, increasing 5% annually plus future lump sum payments totaling $2.99 million; mobile home manufacturer contributed $250,000 to the settlement.

Lancaster Silo and Block Co. v. Northern Propane Gas Co., 75 A.D.2d 55, 427 N.Y.S.2d 1009 (1980), **propane gas cylinder;** gas leak; explosion; business property damage; action against propane supplier and manufacturers of tank component valve and regulator.

Bailey v. Baker's Air Force Gas Corp., 50 A.D.2d 129, 376 N.Y.S.2d 212 (1975), **liquid propane gas power unit on truck;** fire; property damage; seller's negligence for failure to shut primary valves, drain, and vent hoses.

Young v. Robertshaw Controls, 123 Misc. 2d 580, 474 N.Y.S.2d 886 (Sup. Ct. 1983), **water heater;** defective control valve; private fraud action proper for failure to disclose product information to the CPSC.

Flageman v. Signal L.P. Gas Co., 486 F.2d 479 (6th Cir. [Ohio] 1973), **LP gas hot water heater;** explosion; wrongful death.

Payne v. A.O. Smith, 99 F.R.D. 534 (S.D. Ohio 1983), **gas water heater;** explosion; introduction of evidence of prior, similar accidents.

Litowitz v. Buckeye Fire Equip. Co., No. 41145 (Cuyahoga, Ohio Cty. Ct. July 30, 1984), 27 ATLA L. Rep. 419 (Nov. 1984), **fire extinguisher;** jammed pin; wrongful death; improper testing and certification; structured settlement of $840,000.

Walsh v. Pennsylvania Gas and Water Co., 303 Pa. Super. 52, 449 A.2d 573 (1982), **gas range;** explosion; breach of implied warranty of merchantability.

Monchon's v. Erikson's Inc., 448 A.2d 776 (R.I. 1982), **electric range;** excessive verdict based on sympathy; new trial ordered.

Avery v. General Denko, No. 82–821–14 (D.S.C. 1983), 26 ATLA L. Rep. 181 (May 1983), **kerosene heater;** gasoline vapor ignites fire; wrongful death.

Johnson v. Husky Indus., No. CA–3008 (E.D. Tenn. June 27, 1975), **charcoal briquets;** carbon monoxide poisoning; wrongful death.

Rodriguez v. 7-11 Corp., No. 2362–81–E (Tex. Jud. Dist. Ct., Hidalgo Cty. 1982), 26 ATLA L. Rep. 412 (Nov. 1983), **gasoline container;** explosion; settlement of $15 million.

Dover Corp. v. Perez, 587 S.W.2d 761 (Tex. Civ. App. 1979), **wall heater;** wrongful death; design defect and inadequate warnings.

Cogswell v. Robertshaw Controls Co., No. 76–233 (Wis. Jan. 30, 1979), **water heater;** gas explosion; valve defect.

Chapter 3

HOUSEHOLD CHEMICAL THREATS

KLUWER LITIGATION LIBRARY REFERENCES

HARLEY & MAGEE, What's It Worth? A Guide to Current Personal Injury Awards and Settlements.

JEANS, LITIGATION: Chapter 4, *Discovery*; Chapter 8, *Direct Examination*; Chapter 9, *Direct Examination of Expert Witnesses*; Chapter 13, *Cross-Examination*; Chapter 14, *Cross-Examination of Expert Witnesses*.

SMITH & MALANDRO, COURTROOM COMMUNICATION STRATEGIES: Chapter 1, *Impression Formation in the Courtroom*; Chapter 2, *Persuasive Strategies in the Courtroom*; Chapter 5, *Preparing for Effective Courtroom Communication*; Chapter 8, *Direct Examination: Presenting the Evidence with Impact*; Chapter 9, *Cross-Examination*: *Controlling the Case*.

I. Introduction

§ 3.01 In general

Chemicals have become an important part of our lives. Their incorporation in a variety of household products makes our lives more enjoyable and our chores easier to accomplish. In our eagerness to obtain ever-faster and more effective panaceas, we have turned our homes into veritable warehouses of chemical ingredients. Over the years, however, we have become increasingly aware that many of these items can also cause grave harm both to ourselves and our children.

Household cleaners are but one example of those products that pose hazards of severe injury. The modern kitchen cabinet holds an array of cleaning agents for use on our stoves, ovens, drains, furniture, dishes, toilet bowls, and floors. These products are marketed with slick, expensive advertising campaigns designed to create a consumer demand for a product that is frequently more dangerous than is necessary for a particular task. Words like "powerful" and "muscleman" have come to symbolize the house cleaning industry in America.

This extra "power" all too often is provided by chemical ingredients that can produce tragic injuries if they come into contact with human skin or internal organs: caustic burns when alkali lye or sodium hydroxide spills on human skin or is ingested by a curious youngster, vision impairment or blindness when ingredients explode in a consumer's face, or poisoning when toxic vapor is inhaled.

For example, consider caustic household drain cleaners. As plumbers' rates have increased beyond the reach of many family budgets, the "quick fix" chemical drain cleaner has been marketed as a knight in shining armor riding to the rescue. In the world of drain cleaners, "strong" means using chemicals like sodium hydroxide—also known as lye. *Consumer Reports* magazine has described caustic cleaners as "among the most dangerous products on the consumer market."[1] And little wonder. While this chemical is strong enough to burn through the most heavily clogged drain, it is also strong enough to burn through human tissue almost instantly. If such a product is swallowed, the damage it can perpetrate on a person's internal organs is horrifying. In 1982, an estimated 13,000 consumers were poisoned when they ingested lye and other caus-

---

[1] 48 Consumer Rep. 146, No. 13 (Mar. 1983).

tic household cleaning agents.[2]

The hazardous effects of chemicals may be broadly classified into four categories: poisoning, burns, skin irritations, and explosions. Poisons can accidentally enter the system either by breathing vapors or by ingestion. Many organic compounds and some inorganic ones are rapidly absorbed through the skin. Strong acids and alkalies burn human tissue and will destroy it if they are not washed off immediately.[3]

Despite the staggering statistics and traumatic nature of chemical injuries, many manufacturers have marketed products for home use that disregard their foreseeable uses, childhood curiosity, accidental spillage, and resulting grave injuries.

This chapter on household chemical threats is not limited solely to chemical cleaners. It also includes discussions of other areas in our homes where our health and safety are vulnerable to the chemical threat. Of particular interest is the toxic threat posed by formaldehyde in many consumer products. The poisoned air that results when formaldehyde gas leaks from urea-formaldehyde foam insulation has received extensive publicity, but research has shown that other formaldehyde-based products, including plywood and particle board, can also emit toxic formaldehyde fumes. Consumer exposure to this threat can be most severe in mobile homes, where concentrations of ambient formaldehyde can unexpectedly poison and shatter families' lives.

§ 3.02 Focus on product itself

In my practice, I have witnessed the horrible and often life-threatening consequences of these hazardous chemical products firsthand, in circumstances that may at first glance seem unexpected, but after further study were clearly predictable in a household environment—the youngster whose face was burned beyond recognition and permanently disfigured after the contents of a container of liquid drain cleaner spilled over her head,[4] or the young child who was horribly burned when a can of cleaner toppled into her crib.[5]

Counsel, faced with a case involving injuries resulting from a hazard-

---

[2]U.S. Consumer Product Safety Commission, Annual Report at 37 (1982).

[3]Swartz, *Litigating Household Caustics Injuries*, CASE & COM. 3 (Mar.-Apr. 1983).

[4]Drayton v. Jiffee Chemical Corp., 395 F. Supp. 1081 (N.D. Ohio 1975), *aff'd*, 591 F.2d 352 (6th Cir. 1978).

[5]McGlaughlin v. Drackett Co., No. 71–925LC (D. Mass. Oct. 10, 1975).

ous household chemical product, should approach the case from the perspective of the product itself: its ingredients; ingredient concentrations; marketing strategies; warnings, if any, provided to consumers; the design of the product packaging; use of or failure to use available safety devices; testing procedures—was the product adequately tested for its hazardous nature before being placed on the market?; and safety practices used in the company's own laboratories when testing the product—are they more stringent than those recommended for consumers' use of the product in their homes?

COMMENT: In case after case, I have found that chemical product manufacturers never bothered to conduct appropriate tests to learn of their product's hazards in a home environment. To sell their products, they devise ingenious marketing schemes designed to invade consumers' homes with persuasive messages of the products' "strength" and "effectiveness," but provide no warnings of their hazards and threats to consumer safety. In my opinion, as I have stated in courtrooms across America, these practices represent a gross disregard for threats to consumer safety that may result from innocent user error or foreseeable childhood curiosity. I can only conclude from my experience that these manufacturers are, as a general rule, more concerned about the costs of providing safer products and adequate warnings than about preventing product-related tragedy.

I do not mean to suggest that a "vocabulary" of safety isn't part of the industry's lexicon. A brief review of technical and popular literature reveals extensive research materials devoted to the toxic and caustic effects of chemical ingredients, as well as safety precautions taken in laboratories to protect these companies' own employees from the chemicals' hazards.[6] These sources can often provide valuable information in support of the plaintiff's contention that the product contained an unreasonably dangerous concentration of caustic ingredients or that the defendant failed to meet its duty to warn consumers of its product's hazards and

[6] *See infra* §§ 3.29–3.30.

instruct them to appreciate the gravity and nature of the hazard. Similarly, consumer-oriented publications such as *Consumer Reports* and *Consumers' Research* magazine often provide valuable research and surveys regarding the relative effectiveness, safety, and merits of various household cleaning products,[7] even though they are often less technical in nature.

The dramatic case study that follows, *infra* §§ 3.05–3.15, illustrates: (1) the type of injury that can result from caustic drain cleaner ingredients, (2) the horrible impact on a child's life that can result when a product is manufactured and marketed for the convenience and benefit of the manufacturer rather than the home consumer, and (3) the culpability of a defendant who marketed a product as "safe" that was too hazardous for household use.

COMMENT: When a client suffering from an injury caused by a drain cleaner or other toxic cleaning product arrives in my office, certain fact patterns usually present themselves. Often the injured person is a child. A bottle of liquid drain cleaner tips over spilling its caustic contents over the head and face of a one-year-old girl. Or a can of granular drain cleaner is grabbed instinctively by a young boy; before his parents can respond, he has dug his hands in, placed a handful in his mouth, and swallowed the cleaner, causing permanent damage to his internal organs.

Despite the cries for justice and compensation for the victims of caustic cleaners, it is sometimes all too easy for attorneys or the public to respond initially to such tragedies with questions like, "How did he get that can in the first place?" or "Why did her father let her get so close when he was cleaning the drain?" This type of response may be one reason why household caustic chemical injuries are litigated in such a small percentage of cases relative to their frequency of occurrence. With the proper approach and understanding of the complex issues involved, however, an

[7] *See infra* § 3.30.

attorney handling a household caustics case can obtain justice for his client and a victory for the public interest.

II. Checklists

§ 3.03 Checklist: Investigation in a household chemical product-related injury case

The following checklist is intended to aid counsel in preparing his household chemical product-related personal injury case.

____ (1) Obtain the product causing the injury. If it is no longer available, locate and purchase the same product

____ (2) Determine the contents of the product:

____(a) Ingredients listed on container

____(b) Ingredients listed on package

____(c) Chemical analysis

____ (3) Determine the age of the product causing the injury

____ (4) Determine how the product was being used when the injury occurred

____ (5) Determine whether any other product or additive was being used in conjunction with the product at the time of the injury

____ (6) In the course of discovery determine:

____(a) Who was the manufacturer of the product's component parts

____(b) If the product was recalled or subject to other government action

____(c) Supplier of the container

____(d) Whether any warnings were ever issued concerning the product

____(e) If testing was ever done on the product

____(f) If there were any in-plant precautions taken during the manufacture of the product ____(g) If there were any records of quality control

____(h) If there were any records of inspection

____(i) What precautions were taken in product storage and transport

____(j) If there were any consumer complaints and instances of product-related injuries reported to the manufacturer or the U.S. Consumer Product Safety Commission

____ (7) Collect all advertising and promotional materials in connection with the product

____ (8) Examine the labeling of the product to determine:

____(a) Instructions for use

____(b) Warnings

____(c) Suggested household use

____(d) Restrictions on use

____(e) Storage recommendations

____ (9) Examine caps or closures to determine:

____(a) If child-resistant closures were used

____(b) If the product was easily spilled

____(c) If the product was subject to increased danger if exposed to heat or cold

____(10) Check the product's chemical composition to determine:

____(a) Toxicity

____(b) Flammability

____(c) Compatibility with other common household products

____(d) Chemical flashpoint

____(e) Effect of prolonged storage

____(f) Vapor density and pressure

____(g) Interaction of contents with packaging

____(11) Research law reviews and treatises on household caustic cases

____(12) Contact and check the following to determine what information, if any, is available regarding the product:

____(a) Consumer Product Safety Commission

____(b) U.S. Department of Health and Human Services

____(c) Underwriters' Laboratories

____(d) Occupational Safety and Health Administration

____(e) National Institute of Occupational Safety and Health

____(f) ATLA Exchange

____(g) ATLA Law Reporter

____(h) ATLA Product Liability Law Reporter

§ 3.04 Checklist: Resources for a household chemical product-related injury case

The following list can be a valuable source of information for counsel when preparing a household chemical product-related personal injury case.[8]

____(1) Selected technical sources

____(a) Clinical Toxicology

____(b) The New England Journal of Medicine

____(c) Science Digest

____(d) Alternative Methods Toxicology

____(e) American Journal of Ophthalmology

____(f) Annals of Emergency Medicine

____(g) Journal of Environmental Pathology and Toxicology

____(h) Chemical Age India

____(i) Pediatrics

____(j) American Industrial Hygiene Association Journal

____(k) Pediatric Clinics of North America

---

[8] *See infra* §§ 3.29–3.31, 3.33, for reference to specific articles contained in these publications.

____(2) Selected popular sources (periodicals)

____(a) Consumer Reports

____(b) Consumers' Research

____(c) Changing Times

____(d) Consumer's Digest

____(e) Family Health

____(f) Science Magazine

____(g) Parent Magazine

____(3) Selected government sources

____(a) U.S. Consumer Product Safety Commission

____(b) National Institute of Occupational Safety and Health

____(c) Occupational Safety and Health Administration

____(d) National Science Foundation

____(e) U.S. Food and Drug Administration

____(f) National Research Council

____(g) U.S. Environmental Protection Agency

____(h) U.S. Department of Energy

____(4) Selected industry sources

____(a) Association of Consulting Chemists and Chemical Engineers, Inc.

____(b) The American Institute of Chemists

____(c) The Formaldehyde Institute

____(d) Soap and Detergent Association

____(e) Center for Occupational Hazards

____(f) International Sanitary Suppliers Association

____(g) Drug, Chemical, and Allied Trades Association, Inc.

III. Case Study: The Case of the Silent Kitchen Assassin[9]

§ 3.05 Facts

The product involved in this case is sodium hydroxide, or lye. It is a caustic soda. How hazardous is it? As soon as human skin comes in contact with it, a process commences that transforms human skin into soap. It is irreversible. There is no known antidote. This is why many experts agree that this product should never be marketed for home use.[10]

In this case, a one-year-old girl was the innocent victim of a product described by its own manufacturer as "extremely dangerous," yet marketed as "safe"; a product so hazardous that the manufacturer's own employees were warned to take safety precautions when handling it—precautions never transmitted to American homeowners; a product that arrived in her home under false pretenses created by an expensive and sophisticated advertising campaign, and used by her father with no expectation of the tragedy it could cause; a product that did not have to be dangerous to get the job done—according to its manufacturer, it could have been more effective with a less hazardous formulation.

One afternoon, on a day that this minor plaintiff and her family would prefer to forget but simply cannot, her father, after arriving home, headed upstairs to clean the bathroom sink. On his way up, he picked up a can of liquid drain cleaner. When he got to the bathroom, he poured about half the contents of the can into the sink (following directions for its use on the bottle) and placed the bottle on the sink ledge. The next thing he knew, his daughter was tugging at his pants leg. He looked down to a sight he will probably never forget—his toddler screaming as the caustic contents of the tipped cleaner can rolled down her head and face, burning her to unrecognizable proportions. He grabbed her in his arms, placed a towel over her head, and ran downstairs. The plaintiff's mother rushed her to the hospital, where she had to undergo extensive and painful treatment.

---

[9] *See Drayton*, *supra* note 4. In this case a $1.1 million judgment for the minor plaintiff was returned by the jury.

[10] *See*, *e.g.*, *Drayton supra* note 4, testimony of Mr. B for the plaintiff.

COMMENT: Of course, my words and thoughts can hardly express the shock and fright that must have gone through the minds of this young child and her parents that day. Perhaps the most difficult part of counsel's job is to convey these human emotions in a court of law. To do this, counsel must ask family members and friends to recall the deeply emotional and painful memories associated with a loved one's tragedy. It's always difficult to talk about such horrible experiences. God knows, we don't want to raise these kinds of memories. In this case, the child's mother demonstrated the strength and courage to recall what she saw as plaintiff's father ran down the stairs with the plaintiff in his arms that god-awful afternoon.[11]

> To me, all I could see was like death. She looked like she was just parched or something. . . . Her face was all fused as if it were melted into one mound. . . . It was almost impossible to distinguish her nose, mouth, and her eyes. . . . She looked like a big blob of nothing. . . . One side of her face was her ear . . . there was like a gaping hole there that was parched black. . . . The top of her head near the forehead area was totally burned. . . . It was impossible to see her eyes because her eyelids were fused tight into big melted mounds. . . . The skin on her face was slimy, it looked like it had been turned into soap.

She recalled her frantic efforts to reach the hospital:

> During the whole trip, we couldn't tell whether she was crying or not because her eyes were fused; she was making gurgling sounds, as if she was trying to breathe or gasp for air. . . . She was moaning and groaning. . . . After a while at the hospital, we learned from the doctors that her entire nose cartilage was melted and fused and that she had no openings through her nose to breathe. . . . She was obviously in tremendous pain. . . . I had to hold her for long periods of time in order to get her to even fall asleep. . . . I still do . . . when she sleeps, her eyes appear to remain open, if you walked into her room when she was sleeping, it would look like she was awake be-

[11] *Drayton*, *supra* note 4, testimony of Mrs. D, the plaintiff's mother, witness for the plaintiff.

> cause they would be staring at you . . . even when she sleeps she wakes up screaming in the middle of the night . . . she says she has bad dreams.

The emotional strain on a witness who is so close to the victim can become truly overwhelming. When a friend of the family, who knew the plaintiff intimately before the tragedy and witnessed the changes in her personality since she returned home from the hospital the first time, agreed to testify, I asked her to write down her observations on a piece of paper before testifying. I also asked her if she'd like a glass of water. I hoped that these notes and some refreshment would make this task a little bit easier for her. Her testimony provided compelling evidence of the dramatic effect this injury had had on this little girl's life—socially, emotionally, and physically.[12]

> [She] was a very cheerful, joyful, bright child before the accident. She was a very pretty child. She was very outgoing. She was not afraid of anybody.
>
> * * *
>
> After the accident, she started to become withdrawn. She was very insecure. She always wanted somebody around that she knew. As she got older and grew, it was very hard for her to even face people. She would hide her face. She didn't want to be with other children. She constantly asked if she was pretty. She thought she was ugly. After the accident, [her] total mannerism changed. Her whole emotional stability collapsed. Her emotional life and her happiness had been ruined. She became clingy, insecure. She started to get shy and withdrawn, and as she got older, she started to ask questions about why kids didn't want to play with her, why people stared at her. Kids would cry when they saw her. . . . Whenever we took her places, kids called her ugly and said she looked like a monster. She got to be very remorseful and sad. She would want to know why. She would say things like "I'm ugly. They are afraid of me." And she got more and more withdrawn. . . . She would go sit in the corner. She just didn't want to be with other kids.
>
> * * *

---

[12] *Drayton, supra* note 4, testimony of Ms. S, the plaintiff's landlady, witness for the plaintiff.

> She thinks she is ugly. She believes nobody likes her, and she doesn't feel very good about herself.

By the age of seven, this child had been hospitalized eight different times, had undergone eleven operations, and had compiled a hospital record 190 pages long.

§ 3.06 Analysis of case

As horrifying as the little girl's injuries were, the facts that I discovered regarding the corporate decision making that produced this hazardous product in the first place, and resulted in a strategic national campaign to market this insidious product as "safe," were even more so. For example: (1) the company president admitted that no testing for safety was performed and that no specialists were hired to advise the company of the product's hazards and (2) the cleaner had a 26% concentration of caustic lye. As if this were not bad enough, this company provided no adequate warnings of its hazards and threats to human life; no adequate instructions for its use; what the company's own expert described during the trial as "confusing" directions for emergency aid if the product was ingested or touched; inadequate caps to prevent young children from gaining access to its hazardous contents; and hazardous containers designed for shipping convenience rather than consumer safety.

§ 3.07 Cross-examination of company president regarding product hazards

My examination of the defendant's president in a related case revealed that this company, which had become the largest drain cleaner distributor in the country, had been formed by three former truck drivers who knew nothing about chemistry. They found a gold mine—the American public's search for quick and easy solutions to their household cleaning problems—and a solution—a cleaning product that America wanted, or at least Americans were persuaded that they wanted after the company's shrewd and sophisticated advertising campaigns. By this company president's own admissions, his company did no testing for safety and hired no specialists to advise them of the product's hazards or risks in the home environment.[13]

Q. Did you organize the ____________ Chemical Company?

[13] *McLaughlin*, *supra* note 5, testimony of Mr. M, president of the defendant company, excerpt of deposition. For further discussion of this cross-examination, *see* Swartz, *Litigating Household Caustics Injuries*, 3 CASE & COM. (Mar.-Apr. 1983).

A. With the help of others.

Q. Were you one of the original incorporators?

A. That is right.

Q. And when was that?

A. 1951.

Q. Did you start marketing the product after you organized ____________, i.e., selling it on the market?

A. Well, that was the idea. It took several years to get much of it sold.

Q. Now, before you put it on the market, did you have it tested?

A. No.

Q. Were you familiar with the chemical properties of the product?

A. No.

* * *

Q. Were there any members in the original organization of the company who were chemists or familiar with the chemical properties of the ingredients?

A. No, only about the same knowledge that I had.

* * *

Q. Do you know what a caustic is?

A. No.

Q. Do you know what a caustic does? Do you know what the properties of a caustic are that make it work?

A. I don't know.

* * *

Q. Did you ever have the product tested for damage, if any, to human skin?

A. Not to my knowledge.

Q. Did you ever have the product tested for damage to esophageal tissue, the esophagus being the gullet you swallow through?

A. Not to my knowledge.

Q. Did you ever have the product tested for lye?

A. No, sir.

Q. Well, the tests that you had run were for its effectiveness? Wasn't that the purpose of the test that you had run?

A. It was tested for the purpose that it was designed for.

Q. It was tested whether it could do damage to pipes?

A. Yes, it had been tested for that.

Q. And whether it damaged septic tanks?

A. Yes, it was tested for that.

Q. Whether it would do damage to property?

A. Yes.

* * *

Q. Did you know what effect ____________ had on the skin?

A. No.

Q. Did you know what its effect was on the eyes?

A. No.

Q. Did you know what its effect was on the esophageal tissue?

A. No, I did not.

* * *

Q. Was the product ever tested to determine whether there was an effective antidote for it?

A. Not to my knowledge.

* * *

Q. Did your company ever consult a psychologist or a psychiatrist, particularly those specializing in child psychology or child psychiatry, concerning the format of the contents on your label?

A. Not to my knowledge. Nobody ever did.

* * *

Q. You were at one time the biggest distributor of liquid drain cleaners in America, were you not?

A. That is right.

* * *

Q. But you did consider, in the distribution and sale of the product, that you had a responsibility to produce a product that wasn't dangerous, didn't you?

A. Yes, we knew it.

§ 3.08 Testimony of chemical engineer regarding hazardous nature of product

All too often, caustic drain cleaners contain very dangerous chemicals although they could have been made just as cheaply and effectively with safe chemicals. This company developed a product with a dangerous concentration of caustic lye. Plaintiff's expert, an associate professor of chemical engineering, explained that the product could dissolve human tissue in a fraction of a second. The damage to human tissue occurs so fast and is so difficult to neutralize that it "renders the victim virtually helpless."[14]

COMMENT: Armed with plaintiff's expert's opinion of the hazardous nature of the cleaning product, I then attempted to elicit damaging testimony from the defendant's executives with regard to the product's hazards.

---

§ 3.09 Cross-examination of manager of specialty products regarding product hazards

The Manager of Specialty Products for the defendant-company testified under my extensive cross-examination that the product that so horribly disfigured the minor plaintiff was not only "extremely dangerous," but should have been banned. He admitted that in previous testimony he had stated that this product caused "severe, irreversible damage" and that "first aid was of minimal value."[15]

---

[14] *Drayton*, *supra* note 4, testimony of Prof. B, plaintiff's expert.

[15] *Drayton*, *supra* note 4, testimony of Mr. S, Manager of Specialty Products for the defendant.

COMMENT: It is sometimes worth the time and effort for counsel to research the public statements and speeches of officials of the defendant-corporation. If you find damaging admissions, you can make effective use of them on cross-examination.

The dangerously high concentration of sodium hydroxide that destroyed the plaintiff's face and hands was simply not necessary. It was, as this witness conceded under oath, counterproductive for the tasks at hand.[16]

Q. Now, . . . you found the old formulation to be ineffectual and that is why you looked for a new formulation, correct?

A. Yes, ineffectual on the grease.

Q. For the general purposes sold, you found that for some of its major applications, it was ineffectual, is that correct?

A. Yes.

Q. In addition to finding that the old ________ formulation was ineffectual, you were concerned . . . with the problem of safety?

A. Yes.

Q. In other words, you wanted to find some way, if possible, to reduce the causticity of the product, if you could, while increasing its effectiveness, correct?

A. Yes.

Q. And you did this primarily by using a potassium hydroxide solution in water, is that correct?

A. Yes.

Q. Now, potassium hydroxide was a well-known chemical known to chemists for hundreds of years, correct?

A. Yes.

* * *

Q. You found . . . , interestingly enough, that lesser concentrations

---

[16] *Id.*

of a caustic for the general purposes for which ___________ was sold would do a better job, . . . a more effectual job, than the higher concentrations, correct?

A. On the grease mainly. . . .

Q. But, generally speaking, that is true, correct?

A. Yes.

Q. And not only would it do a better job from the point of view that you just described, it was a far safer product, was it not?

A. It was certainly going in the right direction.

* * *

Q. You were asked a question whether, based on your training, experience, and the work you did in research and development, you agree . . . that liquid drain cleaners, including the old ___________, should be banned as a hazardous substance under the "Federal Hazardous Substance Act," and at that time your answer was yes. Is that still your answer?

A. Yes.

COMMENT: Safer formulations had been available for years to provide even more effective cleaning without the dangers posed by highly caustic ingredients. Prior to the minor plaintiff's tragedy, for instance, there was a product available in the marketplace that was both noncaustic and sold widely for opening drains. A former chief chemist for another major drain cleaner company conceded under oath in a related case that this product would be more effective for certain home applications than the highly caustic product.[17]

---

[17] *McGlaughlin*, *supra* note 5, testimony of Dr. R, former chief chemist for ___________ Products.

§ 3.10 Cross-examination of sales manager regarding misleading advertisements

How did a product that was so dangerous it should never have been marketed for household use nevertheless find its way into millions of households across America? It did so through slick and sophisticated marketing strategies that included advertisements and promotions of the product as "safe" and "effective," but omitted warnings of its capacity to gravely injure. The plaintiff challenged this marketing strategy by arguing that the defendant was negligent in its marketing practices.

COMMENT: Plaintiff's counsel should develop a strategy to challenge the marketing practices of the manufacturer. Rarely do marketing practices give sufficient attention to safety factors.

The cleaner had been advertised on television as "safe." This advertising program was designed to induce people to buy the product, lulling them into a false sense of security as to the true nature of its properties. The company admitted that it advertised the product on television and in the written media in Cleveland, Ohio; that its advertisements did not indicate that the product either contained sodium hydroxide or caustic soda; the defendant did not indicate that the product caused severe burns on contact; or that contact with skin, eyes, mucous membranes, and clothing should be avoided. Even the company's own sales representatives were kept in the dark about the product's hazards. Consider the following exchange I had with a company marketing representative.[18]

Q. Are you an advertising man, essentially, or a marketing man?

A. Marketing, yes.

Q. And you received all your technical information about the characteristics of ____________, from the home office, from the technical people?

A. Largely, yes.

---

[18] *Drayton*, *supra* note 4, testimony of Mr. J, Sales Manager for the defendant.

Q. And you were informed by them, were you not, that ____________ was a safe product?

A. Yes.

§ 3.11 Cross-examination of president of independent testing laboratory

This company's attempts to invade American households with this insidious product did not stop with misleading advertisements. The product's packaging also represented a callous attempt to hide the product's dangers from the American consumer while selling it as a necessary part of every American household. The cleaner was marketed in a plastic bottle with a screw-on top, with inadequate warnings of its hazards, inadequate antidotes, confusing directions should spillage or ingestion occur, inadequate closure to reduce the liquid flow from the bottle, and inadequate design intended for convenience in shipping rather than consumer safety.

The bottle was designed with a center of gravity such that slight contact would make it tip over. A more proper design would have been a bell-shaped bottle with a lower center of gravity that was stable. Although it was the most unsafe design for this bottle, it was adopted because it was the cheapest design to ship and pack.

Cost was also a factor in this company's choice of bottle caps. Before this tragedy, several cap designs were available that would have totally prevented the minor plaintiff's injuries even if the bottle had tipped. This company chose the screw-on cap instead because it was the cheapest cap available, under one-half cent per unit as compared to the one and one-half to two cent cost for the safer caps. This was one more example of how this company was willing to sacrifice the safety of America's children on the altar of short-term cost expediency.

My cross-examination of the defendant's expert witness is revealing.[19]

§ 3.12 —Regarding cap design

Q. Because of the hazardous nature of this product, I think we can agree that it would be impossible to guard the consumer against accidental spillage, wouldn't it, as a general proposition?

---

[19] Testimony of ______________, President of ______________ Laboratories, the defendant's expert witness in instant case. *See* Swartz, *supra* note 3, for further discussion of this cross-examination.

A. Yes.

Q. Would it be important to minimize the risks of such accidental spillage?

A. This would be an obvious thing that you want to do if you can.

Q. And one of the ways you could guard the consumer against accidental spillage is to attempt to design a cap that would minimize the risks of this spillage, correct?

A. All right.

Q. Why would you want to minimize the risks of accidental spillage in a household context?

A. To remove a source of danger.

Q. And to prevent personal injury, correct?

A. All right.

Q. What damage a caustic causes is a function of several things. One is the percentage of concentration of the caustic, correct?

A. That is correct.

Q. And the second thing is the volume of exposure of the person to that concentration, is that correct?

A. That is right.

Q. So that if you got a drop of a caustic on the hand of an adult male, you are not really talking about the same thing as getting a half bottle of ____________ on the face of a one-year-old baby, isn't that a fair statement?

A. I think that's probably true.

* * *

Q. You have talked about the interior cap that was on this product as not being suitable because of the viscosity of the liquid that is in it, correct?

A. That is right. . . . Because of the inherent viscosity and because it would hang up in the cap, the next time you want to pour it you would have a hard time getting that liquid to come out again, because of the plug that would form, as incidentally happens also in maple syrup. It makes a very bad situation. . . . I can take this off with impunity if it were the maple syrup bottle. No problem. But if I want to take it off to open up a can of

___________, I could also get contact with the fluid because it would shoot out of the bottle. That is why it is a bad situation for a liquid caustic container. It may be fine for maple syrup, but you are not dealing with a hazardous product there.

Q. You are aware that this cap was used on, among other products, maple syrup?

A. Yes.

Q. And how does the viscosity of maple syrup once again compare with ___________ formulation?

A. It is greater in viscosity. But it is also not a dangerous product. If you have this kind of situation on a dangerous product, you are just making it more dangerous.

* * *

Q. I think we can agree that if you cut down on the size of the hole, you are going to cut down on the volume of the contents of that bottle that someone is going to be exposed to in an accidental spillage, correct?

A. Yes.

Q. And to the extent that you cut down on the volume that gushes out of that bottle in the event of accidental spillage, you are contributing in that respect to the safety of the product, are you not?

A. Yes.

Q. And what you are saying is that you are making the product less hazardous from the point of view of a person coming in contact with the contents of the product because of accidental spillage, correct?

A. Yes.

* * *

Q. You mentioned automatic closure devices. What do you mean by an automatic closure device?

A. There are certain safety cans on the market that hold inflammable liquids like gasoline, and those are automatic closing devices. They are usually spring-loaded.

Q. They are what?

A. They are usually spring-loaded in the closed position requiring force to open them.

Q. Clearly, they were around before 1968, correct?

A. Yes.

Q. They were known to the trade for years, were they not?

A. That is right.

§ 3.13 —Regarding inadequate warnings

Q. Now, are you aware of what recommendations standard chemistry manuals make to protect people, sophisticated people, against such accidental spilling? Are you aware of any recommendations with regard to wearing protective clothing of some kind?

A. Wear gloves.

Q. You know that they recommend, to guard you against that kind of occurrence when you are using sodium hydroxide, that you wear protective gloves, correct?

A. That is right.

Q. And you also know that some of these standard chemistry manuals suggest that you wear a face shield or goggles to protect your eyes, right?

A. That is correct.

COMMENT: Yet no such warnings were given to the general public!

---

§ 3.14 —Regarding confusing and misleading antidotes

The antidote recommended on the bottle was misleading because it suggested to anyone who read it if it spilled that they could wash off this cleaning liquid with little difficulty or harm. The manufacturer did not tell the consumer what the corporate officials knew about the extreme dangers of human contact with their product. They built a wall of silence around the product's capacity to destroy body tissue irreversibly and permanently, as well as to cause permanent disfigurement. Even the defendant's expert admitted confusion.[20]

Q. What does an antidote suggest to you as a sophisticated user? Does it suggest that if you do certain things, you can reverse damage, or eliminate damage, or stop damage?

A. Yes.

Q. It says "Eyes—Flush with water at least twenty minutes," then it says "get prompt medical attention." Now, assume I am at home and have an accidental spillage situation. Now, I'm alone with a baby, let's say, and there is someone else in the basement of the home. Based on that direction, what would you want me to do first: flush with water at least twenty minutes or get prompt medical attention?

A. I would flush with water first.

Q. That is what you would do because you have superior knowledge to the average homeowner, don't you?

A. You said it. You are right.

Q. So to be fair, it says, "Flush with water at least twenty minutes; get prompt medical attention." Is there anything in that direction that tells you what to do first or what is more important?

A. It says, "Flush with water at least twenty minutes," and that is first.

Q. Because it comes first, right?

A. It comes first.

Q. Then it says "get prompt medical attention." And you think that direction, "get prompt medical attention," means twenty minutes later?

A. No. Of course not.

Q. Well, if you were in a situation where you had to do one or the other, which would you do first if you were the homeowner?

A. I would apply the water and then I would get the medical attention. But I would apply the first aid first.

* * *

---

[20] *Id.*

Q. I'm going to ask you to assume that an ordinary lay person, my wife or someone else's wife or someone's husband, is at home. They have a direction. They think the child's eyes are involved. Let's assume that. They certainly know the face is involved. The testimony is that the child's eyes swelled up instantly. And assume they read this direction carefully. It says "Flush with water at least twenty minutes"; "get prompt medical attention." Do you think it is reasonable to assume that someone who read that might be confused as to what to do first? Is it foreseeable that someone might be confused?

A. It is foreseeable.

* * *

Q. Now, on the bottom of this container it says, in large red letters, "Call physician immediately." If you read that direction, that is an unambiguous phrase, correct?

A. Yes.

Q. If someone said, "immediately," it is quite clear what is meant, correct?

A. That is right.

Q. Now, what would you do? Would you flush the eyes for twenty minutes or would you run to the hospital?

A. Give me time to answer one question at a time, please.

Q. Yes. Go ahead.

A. Now, what was the first question?

Q. In fairness, sir, based upon all of these directions, can't we agree that it is foreseeable that an ordinary lay person in a home context, faced with an emergency, might be confused as to what to do because of contradictory directions?

A. Except for the word contradictory that you used, those instructions are not contradictory.

Q. What you are talking about is confusion as to what to do first?

A. There could be confusion, but those instructions are not contradictory.

Q. But there could be confusion as to what to do first, correct? Is that what you mean?

A. That is right.

§ 3.15 Conclusion

It was foreseeable that the contents of this bottle would come into contact with human skin by spillage and other means. Company officials knew the product could effectively melt skin into soap on contact, and that this process was irreversible. Similarly, they knew the horrible consequences of their insidious product in terms of human suffering—they had a body count. Yet they continued to market the product as safe, to provide inadequate warnings as well as confusing and misleading antidotes; they chose the most expedient yet most dangerous means of designing the product's packaging, and they conducted no tests or research to assess its hazards and the ways to prevent them, although safer alternative formulations were available. In light of all the evidence, we charged this defendant with negligence, breach of warranty, and strict liability for the disfiguring and debilitating injuries the plaintiff suffered that fateful day.

Although it will never adequately repair the damage that has been done to this minor plaintiff, a Cleveland, Ohio court found the defendant negligent and awarded $1,712,460 million in damages.[21]

IV. Other Chemical Hazards

§ 3.16 Household cleaners—poisonous vapors

Household cleaning products can also produce poisonous fumes, especially when used in dangerous combinations. *Consumers' Research* magazine warned its readers that "care should be taken to avoid the inhaling of any irritating or toxic fumes that may be given off. . . . Since no two cleaners are formulated exactly the same, tragic results can and do occur when people try to mix various cleaning products."[22] Specifically, "[i]f Liquid Plumr, which contains sodium hypochlorite, should be mixed with an acidic household cleaner, such as a toilet bowl cleaner, highly poisonous chlorine gas may be released. This gas can be dangerously irritating or even fatal, depending upon its concentration. If Liquid Plumr happened to be mixed with Liquid Drano, which contains ammonium hydroxide, chloramine gas may be given off. Although the degree

[21] *Drayton*, *supra* note 4, on appeal, lower court award was reduced to $700,000.

[22] 62 Consumers' Research 13, No. 5 (May 1979).

of toxicity of this gas is not fully established, it is classified as being moderately toxic, and according to a publication of the American Medical Association, it can produce such symptoms as watery eyes, nausea, vomiting, and difficulty in breathing due to irritation of the upper respiratory tract."[23]

When *Consumer Reports* magazine studied household cleaners, it warned its readers that "the ingredients of [household] cleaners are a combination of detergents, grease-cutting agents, and, sometimes, fragrance, color, solvents, or germicides. Such chemicals make a somewhat dangerous combination, especially if accidentally swallowed or splashed in the eyes."[24]

Some cleaning products can release poisonous fumes even when they are not mixed with other products, particularly if they are used on a surface that contains other potentially toxic chemicals. Take, for example, the case of the 56-year-old woman who purchased a can of ____________ toilet bowl cleaner from her local store. She was looking for an effective cleaner and, like millions of other consumers, was attracted by the product's advertising. Late one evening, she used the cleaner to clean the toilet in her apartment. She followed the directions on the can, sprinkling the product into the bowl and vigorously scrubbing the bowl's interior surface with a short-handled brush, leaning over about twelve inches from the toilet bowl as she worked.

Suddenly, she began to choke and cough. She couldn't catch her breath. She left the bathroom and went outside to her porch for some fresh air. Her son rushed from his upstairs bedroom to find her weak and choking. He drove her to the hospital, where she was placed on oxygen and treated with adrenalin. Her physician testified that she was breathing rapidly, with wheezing that could be heard several feet away. He diagnosed her as suffering from a combination of acute bronchitis and bronchial asthma. He testified that her condition was brought on by an irritant, not an infection. He associated a direct relationship between the onset of her condition and her use of the toilet bowl cleaner.

A chemistry professor at Central Michigan University analyzed the contents of the cleaner that poisoned this woman. He testified that both hydrogen chloride and chlorine gas could be released when the product was used. It was his opinion that the chemicals were irritants, and would

---

[23] *Id.*

[24] 47 CONSUMER REP. 534, No. 10 (Oct. 1982).

produce harmful effects if inhaled: "___________ contains sodium bisulfate and a chloride ion which would react together and with iron oxide (in the rust of the toilet bowl), since iron oxide is both an oxidizing agent and a catalyst."

This woman, who was hospitalized for 122 days for respiratory problems caused by the cleaning product, recovered damages of $100,000.[25]

§ 3.17 Household cleaners—explosions

As if poisoning, burning, and toxic fumes were not enough, many household cleaning products can also be explosive, particularly when mixed with water. In one case, a woman lost the sight in her eyes when a can of Drano exploded. She had purchased the can the day before at her local store.

In holding the manufacturer liable for negligence, the Illinois Supreme Court[26] found that "Drano is a substance which will generate explosive hydrogen . . . due to the harmful propensities of the product upon contact with moisture. It was therefore highly essential for a tight closure between the cap and the can in which the product was placed."

The court had received evidence that moisture collection was a problem in Drano cans shipped for sale for a "considerable period." The court quoted the defendant's own Chief of Quality Control, who stated that the loose caps were "probably due to a maladjustment of the capper," that "the need for caution was imperative," and that "serious consideration should be given to maintaining operator control on the line. . . ." But "these warnings and admonitions went unheeded."[27]

The court found that "Drackett negligently failed to undertake tests to determine the properties of the can it used to withstand pressure or keep out moisture. Instead, the product was placed in a can with a screw-top without knowing whether, in the event of pressure within the can, the cap would blow off and act as a safety valve, or, as occurred in the present case, remain in position while the can itself burst. Not until after the accident here was it determined that a greater pressure was needed to blow the cap off than to burst the seam of the can."[28] Mrs. Moore recov-

---

[25] Shirley v. Drackett Products Co., 182 N.W.2d 726 (Mich. Ct. App. 1975).

[26] Moore v. Jewel Tea Co., 46 Ill. 2d 288, 263 N.E.2d 103 (1970).

[27] *Id.*

[28] *Id.*

ered compensatory damages of $900,000 and an additional $10,000 in punitive damages.[29]

COMMENT: Keep in mind that former employees of a defendant often make good witnesses for the plaintiff. They frequently have reservations about company policy that they are now free to expose.

The manufacturer knew that the product was explosive. This knowledge was stunningly revealed in a related case by the company's former senior research chemist.[30] This witness testified under oath that he conducted "several experiments" mixing the chemical cleaner with water in attempting to reduce the product's explosiveness. He witnessed eruptions in the laboratory, yet never measured the amount of force in those eruptions to determine whether they were sufficient to cause injury.

Q. Did you work on the formulation of the cleaner to determine whether you could make it less likely to erupt when moisture was added?

A. We did several experiments.

Q. To reduce the risk of eruption?

A. Specifically, not that I can recall.

Q. Did [the manufacturer], while you were working for them, have a consumer protection program to determine what hazards might result from the use of the product in a home environment?

A. Not that I know of. The cleaner erupts due to the reaction of water, and its contents produce heat. It's produced very fast. Reaction starts almost immediately, depending upon the amount of water and the amount of [cleaner]. When water is added, ammonia gases are generated.

Q. Did you ever do any tests to determine what comes out of the can in the way of gases when there's an eruption?

A. No.

---

[29] *Id.*

[30] *McGlaughlin*, *supra* note 5, testimony of Dr. R.

Q. Did you know—did [the manufacturer] know—when there was an eruption, what would come out?

A. Product and water would come out.

Q. If that material came out of the can on eruption and hit an eye, could that cause personal injury?

A. It can cause burns. On the label it says it can cause burns.

Q. But you never did any testing to determine under what conditions it could cause burns?

A. Correct.

Q. You, and when I say you, I mean [the manufacturer], never did any test to determine the severity of burns that could be caused?

A. As far as I know, that is correct.

Q. You have indicated to us that you have witnessed upon occasion the cap being blown off by the eruption of water and the product resulting in ammonia gas?

A. The eruption of water and the product will blow the cap off occasionally, yes.

Q. You also indicated that [the manufacturer] never determined what the forces of the eruption were, what the level of eruption was?

A. As far as I know, that is correct.

Q. Is it likewise true that [the manufacturer] never determined whether indeed the cap was being blown off with sufficient force to cause an eye injury?

A. I don't know.

Q. Based upon your knowledge, at least while you were with [the company], are you aware of any such knowledge or tests?

A. No.

Q. So you, indeed [the manufacturer], didn't know one way or the other, correct—whether the cap itself could cause an eye injury when it is blown off?

A. I don't know if it could or not.

Q. In working for [the manufacturer], in deciding whether to continue marketing this product, you indicated that you took into account the usefulness of the product?

A. Yes, correct.

Q. You compared its usefulness or its utility against the magnitude of any risk that might be created in any household context?

A. I didn't, no.

Q. Did you assume when you were testing this product that persons would always use the product as recommended?

A. No, that's why we were testing, adding water to the can.

Q. So you knew it was foreseeable that people would add water to the can?

A. It was conceivable that they would.

COMMENT: Thus, the company continued to market the product even while it knew full well that consumers would continue to mix their product with water, with potentially explosive results.

---

§ 3.18 Dishwashing detergents

Some products, such as dishwashing detergents, may be particularly hazardous because they are manufactured with a candy or fruitlike scent to promote their purchase. Unfortunately, this may also provide a particularly dangerous attraction to young children.

The tragic consequences of detergent poisoning were revealed by a mother who testified before the National Commission on Product Safety regarding her frantic experience when her one-year-old son ate some dishwashing detergent:[31]

> At 6:00 p.m. on ___________, while I was unloading the dishwasher, my son ___________, then just one, crawled behind me, climbed onto the open dishwasher lid, dipped his finger into one of the detergent dispensing cups, extracted a fingerful of partially wet, undischarged dishwashing detergent, and ate it.

---

[31] Statement of Mrs. S, *Hearings of National Commission on Product Safety* (Mar. 5, 1969).

One hour later—with second degree burns covering his lips, the inside of his mouth and the back of his throat, ____________ was admitted to the intensive care unit at Children's Orthopedic Hospital, where he remained and was treated for two days.

I realized what had happened when I heard him scream. As I turned toward him, my eye caught sight of the opened dispensing cup and the residue of detergent, something which had never happened with that particular dishwasher before.

I then picked [him] up, turned on the faucet, held his mouth open and hand-ladled water onto his face and into his mouth, pausing only long enough for him to breathe. Next, I grabbed the box for further instructions. Should I administer ipecac or is this a burning agent containing lye or its equivalent? The box said to "call my physician."

I dialed our doctor's number as per the instruction on the box, but his line was busy. All this time [he] screamed with pain and clutched me for the relief and comfort I could not supply.

I then wrapped him in a coat, left instructions for calling [his] physician and the hospital to alert them of our arrival and left for the hospital. Fortunately, my husband was walking in the door as I walked out with ____________, and he accompanied us to the hospital.

Children's Orthopedic Hospital is located approximately one-half mile from our home. On the way there [my son's] mouth and tongue became so swollen, and he was in such agony, was so confused, and was crying so hard that he stopped breathing.

In the hospital emergency room, the physicians positioned his head and mouth so that he could breathe, and again flushed his lips, mouth, and throat with water now diluted with vinegar. They apologized because they could not administer any pain reliever. It could have endangered [his] condition if he had gone into shock.

I left the emergency room to check on our physician's arrival and when I returned at 6:25 p.m.—only 25 minutes after [he] first ate the detergent—I was aghast. [His] cheeks were red, swollen, and blistered. The inside of his mouth and his tongue were white. If I had not known he was my child I would not have recognized him. And there was nothing the physicians, the nurses, or I could do to relieve his agonizing pain.

At 9:30, my husband and I left the hospital. [My son] had been admitted to the intensive care unit, had been given a sedative and was being cared for by the doctors and nurses. He was still crying, but the doctors thought he might sleep more easily if my husband and I were not at his bedside. Moreover, we were needed at home to care for our other children.

On November 1, when ___________ was released from the hospital, the only visible signs of his ordeal were a slightly inflamed uvula, three small white ulcers on his tongue, reddened lips, and two burn scabs on his cheeks. He suffered no permanent injuries or scars. We were lucky.

Why were we so fortunate?

Dishwashing compound is a burning agent when in contact with skin. If an area of the body is burned, the first and most effective thing one can do, obviously, is to remove the burning agent. If a hot iron burns an arm, first remove the iron.

In [my son's] case, I knew how to remove the burning agent. Instead of offering him a glass of water or fruit juice as per instructions on the box [something I cannot imagine a child suffering as much pain as ___________ was, accepting], I held his head next to the faucet and literally poured water over his face and into his mouth.

In serious burn cases, time is crucial. In [my son's] case, I knew that I could not wait for his physician to answer his telephone in order to get instructions. I knew I had to get [him] to the nearest emergency receiving hospital as fast as I could. In our case it takes only three minutes.

That evening another adult happened to be visiting during the dinner hour, so I could depend upon a responsible person to telephone the physician and hospital and care for my other two children. I did not have to waste a probable ten precious minutes telephoning neighbors and corralling children and jackets.

In [my son's] case, his father was there to hold him while I drove to the hospital. I don't know how I would have been able to drive and hold [him] screaming and writhing as he was.

And yet, with everything in [my son's] favor, he still sustained serious internal and external injuries from approximately one-eighth teaspoon of diluted ___________.

COMMENT: It must be recognized that many dishwasher detergent manufacturers have, in fact, reduced the caustic strength of their product since this boy's experience more than a decade ago. Yet *Consumer Reports* magazine later warned its readers that "detergents have to be strong to get dishes clean. But that strength means that they can irritate the eyes, or be harmful if swallowed. . . . All products could also irritate the skin. . . . [I]f you should get a bit of powder on your skin, rinse it off thoroughly—especially if your skin is sensitive."[32]

---

§ 3.19 Furniture polish

Furniture polishes pose similar unnecessary "invitations" to young children to mistake their contents for juice or candy. These products often contain few and inadequate warnings of their sometimes fatal threats. As *Consumer Reports* magazine warned its readers recently after surveying forty-one furniture polishes, "Some of the polishes also have an enticing scent, a soda-pop color, or a label that could tempt children to drink them (On ____________, for example, the words ____________ are much more prominent than the words 'Furniture Polish,' so it could be mistaken for salad dressing)."[33]

COMMENT: It should be noted that only six of the forty-one products surveyed by the magazine contained child-resistant closures, and that nearly half of them contained one or another ingredient that could be harmful or fatal if swallowed. Yet only fifteen of the forty-one bore labels warning of this danger.

---

[32] 45 CONSUMER REP. 371–373, No. 6 (June 1980).

[33] *Id*. at 373.

§ 3.20 Formaldehyde

Of all the chemicals that we use in our households, few are as mysterious as formaldehyde. For many consumers who have brought urea-formaldehyde foam insulation and other formaldehyde-based products into their homes, this exotic-sounding chemical has transformed their dream castles into chambers of toxic fumes.

A list of products containing formaldehyde reads like an inventory of every American home. Insulation, shampoo, toothpaste, natural gas, plywood, formica, permanent-pressed clothes, draperies, leather, and carpets are just a few of the more than one hundred products that contain the chemical. Formaldehyde is mystical in the variety of ways it can poison its victims and turn their world into a chemical jungle. It can transform routine errands to the store or a neighbor's home into traumatic struggles against formaldehyde-laden cigarette smoke, fabric, carpeting, or drapes. Because many of its symptoms are similar to the wintertime flu (irritated eyes and nose, sore throat, coughing, stomach pains, breathing problems), many victims go for months or even years before their ailments are correctly diagnosed, spending countless hard-earned dollars on "quick-fix" medications to relieve their discomfort.

Perhaps the most sinister weapon in this product's destructive arsenal is its potential to cause cancer. Government scientists asserted several years ago that "formaldehyde should be presumed to pose a carcinogenic risk to humans."[34] Because the cancerous effects may not reveal themselves for twenty or twenty-five years after the exposure takes place, however, consumers exposed today may not know for many years whether they have written their own cancer warrant.

COMMENT: I am presently representing a family who has lived with this fear since they installed urea-formaldehyde foam insulation in the walls of their home.[35] Like hundreds of thousands of other Americans, they turned to this product as a convenient way to save money and conserve energy as heating costs spiraled. The wife, however, subsequently developed growths in her nose—growths similar to those

[34] 47 Fed. Reg. 14,366 (Apr. 2, 1982).

[35] Vincent v. Combine Insulation Co., No. 81–1563 (Mass. Super. Ct., Essex Cty.) (case currently pending; opened July 20, 1981).

found in the laboratory rats that led scientists to conclude that there is a causal connection between formaldehyde exposure and cancer. She fears that she or her infant son, who was also exposed to formaldehyde gas leaking from the walls in his enclosed room, may become cancer victims in the years ahead.

---

§ 3.21 —Illustrative case

Another client of mine experienced so much agony after being poisoned by formaldehyde that she collapsed on her couch, truly believing that she was dying. When she finally recovered, she could not move back into her poisoned home.[36] This plaintiff's story, as she recounts it, is a moving, tortuous story of her struggle against an enemy she could not identify, and her eventual success in identifying that source of anguish and winning her personal war against it.[37]

> For many weeks [after installation], I had a vague awareness that something was not right, and then symptoms began to come and go: headaches, swollen glands, scratchy throat, tiredness but not sleepiness, diminished appetite. I went to see [my physician]. I asked him if he could prescribe some iron—the tiredness was the prominent symptom that day. He said that he couldn't prescribe iron without testing some blood to make sure I didn't have anemia. So the lab took a blood sample. The next evening [my husband] drove me back to [my physician] as my abdomen was hurting and I felt sure something could be detected by a doctor and I could finally get some relief from the bad feelings.
>
> The doctor examined me and could not explain what was wrong. I asked him if he had any experience dealing with the effect of formaldehyde insulation in the home [she had viewed a television program regarding its health effects the night before]. He said he had none. He ordered a urinalysis and another blood test.
>
> The following Monday, I visited a different doctor. He gave me some pills for energy. The next night, I experienced some really

---

[36] McGlew v. Countryside Insulators, No. 81–209 (Mass. Super. Ct., Essex Cty.) (case currently pending; opened Jan. 30, 1981).

[37] *Id*., testimony of plaintiff.

severe pain in my abdomen and knew that I had to get to the hospital—it seemed to me that it could be appendicitis. . . . The emergency room physician gave me a careful examination, took blood and urine to have tested and when the tests revealed nothing, said he thought my problem might be gynecologic, so the next day I made an appointment to see my gynecologist. He examined me and found no problems, but said if the abdominal discomfort persisted, he would do a laparoscopy.

The next day, I was feeling the absolute worst. I could just barely walk and got [my daughter] off to school and then laid down on the couch. All my strength was gone.

In these last weeks, additional symptoms had made appearances—vertigo, I fell coming downstairs, I lost my balance frequently, I was able to think but it was awfully hard to put my thoughts into words and to say what I meant—I could just barely drive as my arms felt so heavy. I had to cling to the bottom edge of the wheel and hold on because my arms felt as though they would fall down. It was a weariness that is just not possible to describe—as though instead of blood, I was made of lead.

As I lay on the couch, I became aware that I would never get up on my own strength, as it was gone. I knew that death was near. I knew that [my husband] was taking a shower and I called to him when he opened the door. When he sat down beside me, I told him that I knew I was dying and told him "goodbye" and that I loved him and asked him to tell the children that I loved them.

They took me to the hospital. The next thing I remember was the bustle of the men with a stretcher. I was extremely cold and a nurse wrapped my feet in lambswool. Then I began to experience abdominal pain in a severe way and it increased with time.

All tests proved negative, and I asked my doctor about contacting an allergist. He contacted a Dr. ____________ whom I had heard speak at a seminar once. They talked on the phone and Dr. ____________ said that it sounded to him as though I'd experienced an adverse reaction as a result of formaldehyde insulation.

I was released from the hospital a week after admission and Dr. ____________ saw me in his office. He urged me to come in for allergy tests and to go on a chemical-free diet until it could be determined what other things bothered me now that my body had reached a saturation point.

We could not live in our house any longer. . . . We had no idea what was going to happen as far as the insulation problem was concerned—or how soon—but we were hopeful that responsibility would be assumed [by the company], the problem would be solved, and we could go back home.

When September came and [my daughter] had to begin school, I had to drive her to __________ each morning and pick her up every afternoon. We began to look for an apartment in __________, but every place that had a vacancy wanted us to sign a year's lease and we couldn't do that—not knowing how long we'd need it.

Then the National Association of Foam Insulators put an air scrubber in our house and worked with the installer, drilling holes in the wooden shingles on the outside walls of our home, and installed a vent over the kitchen area and injected ammonia into the insulation to neutralize it.

We were optimistic about moving back but as a precaution [my husband] made the porch winter-ready. We had a phone extension put out there and decided that's where we'd sleep, eat, and generally spend our time—going into the house only when necessary. On nice days, I opened windows in the kitchen and put a fan on a window sill to bring in fresh air and began the big job of cleaning.

The evenings were cool enough for the furnace to work, and one cold and cloudy day I began to experience the symptoms again. We had realized two things: (1) that the efforts of the Association had not been successful and (2) that the air from all over the house was being heated in the furnace and forced out into the porch where we thought we'd be safe.

COMMENT: In February of 1982, the U.S. Consumer Product Safety Commission banned the manufacture, sale, and distribution of urea-formaldehyde foam insulation, calling it "an unreasonable risk to consumers [due to] the acute and chronic toxicity of the formaldehyde gas it releases."[38]

[38] *See supra* note 34.

However, the Commission's ban was overturned by a federal Court of Appeals.[39] On the other hand, several states have issued their own regulations regarding urea-formaldehyde foam insulation, including Massachusetts.[40] Massachusetts' ban has successfully withstood legal challenges by the formaldehyde industry.[41]

V. Preventing Household Chemical-Related Injuries

§ 3.22 In general

Household chemical cleaners are, in some instances, safer today than they were ten years ago. Caustic ingredient concentrations are decreasing, although they are still too high. Manufacturers are recognizing that the message they provide to consumers through product labels can be as important as the product's ingredients in determining their accountability to the public in a court of law. As stated in a recent article discussing product labeling, manufacturers can avoid the "expenses and embarrassment associated with personal injury suits"[42] by adopting product labels that meet suggested standards. Some manufacturers have taken this advice and provided more effective messages warning of their products' hazards and the dangerous consequences of ingestion or skin contact. Unfortunately, there is still a long way to go.

The most effective means of preventing chemical cleaner injuries would be to ban these products from household use. I'm sorry to say that four years after the U.S. Consumer Product Safety Commission was petitioned to ban sulphuric acid drain cleaners intended for use in or around the household,[43] the government agency rejected the petition.[44]

---

[39] Gulf South Insulation v. United States Consumer Product Safety Commission, No. 82–4218 *et seq.* (5th Cir. Apr. 7, 1983) (modified June 23, 1983).

[40] MASS. ADMIN. CODE §§ 650.000–650.990 (1979), *amended* §§ 650.220(2)–650.222 (1980).

[41] Borden, Inc. v. Commissioner of Public Health, No. S–2849 (Mass. Apr. 12, 1983).

[42] *See supra* note 1.

[43] Petition to Consumer Product Safety Commission (CPSC) from Hercules Chemical Company (HP 78–1).

[44] CPSC rejection of petition to ban sulphuric acid cleaners, 46 Fed. Reg. 51,427 (Oct. 20, 1981).

As long as caustic and toxic household cleaners remain on the market, there are several steps that can be taken by industry members to reduce the risks of injury posed by their products. These steps include the reduction of concentrations of highly caustic and dangerous ingredients, as well as providing for safer alternatives to the caustic product that can accomplish the same purpose; providing for adequate product labeling including warnings and clear advisories regarding safety equipment needed while using the product; effective and consistent remedial antidotes should be clearly printed on the label to prevent a bad situation from turning into a tragedy; children's access to dangerous products should be reduced through effective use of child-resistant enclosures.

§ 3.23 Reducing concentrations of caustic ingredients

In 1973, the Consumer Product Safety Commission, in an attempt to reduce household chemical threats, banned liquid lye products with high caustic concentrations.[45] However, the Commission exempted the most dangerous products of all—those containing solid or crystal lye. As a result, hazardous products with high caustic concentrations are still marketed for household use.

COMMENT: It should be noted that certain product formulas have not been changed since they were first introduced on the market over fifty years ago. This is so, even though there have been great advances made to reduce the threats posed by household chemical agents.

---

§ 3.24 Safer alternatives to caustic products

Advances are continuously being made in the science of noncaustic drain cleaning and other household cleaning chores.[46]

Scientists have discovered that genetic engineering may provide new sources of effective cleaning agents. One company announced that it has developed an enzyme-based drain cleaner that does not contain strong

[45] 15 C.F.R. 1500.17(a)(4)(1985).

[46] *See infra* § 3.29, *Selected technical sources*.

acids, caustics, or solvents and does not generate intense heat.[47]

COMMENT: I urge any lawyer who is preparing a drain cleaner or other household cleaner-related injury case to review these materials, as they represent the leading edge of technology to reduce the threats posed by traditional chemical cleaning agents.

More conventional alternatives to the traditional highly caustic chemical cleaners are also available. As previously noted, the same companies that produce these hazardous cleaners also may produce safer, noncaustic alternatives, but fail to promote them adequately. The use of mechanical means, the so-called "snake" method, remains the safest means for cleaning a clogged drain. Additionally, *Consumer Reports* magazine recently described four different drain openers designed to open clogged drains with blasts of gas or water.[48]

§ 3.25 Product labeling

The consumer who purchases and uses household cleaning products must be warned of the power and danger posed by the chemicals, of the necessity to use protective clothing and, as always, to keep the container away from children. Strong, effective warnings must be provided on the product's container (1) making the consumer aware, both as purchaser and user, that this product poses potentially serious health and safety threats and (2) providing needed information regarding effective antidotes in case an accident does occur.

Product surveys conducted by consumer magazines have found a consistent failure to provide consumers with adequate warnings on all forms of household cleaning products. For instance, a survey of glass and window cleaners conducted by *Consumers' Research* magazine found all cleaners except two to be excessively flammable, with flashpoints (the temperature at which the product may spontaneously ignite) well below the safe limit suggested by the National Fire Protection Association

[47] Genex Corp. announced new enzyme-based drain cleaner, Washington Post, Aug. 7, 1984, at El, col. 1.

[48] 8 CONSUMER REP. 148, No. 3. (Mar. 1983).

(NFPA), and below the limit established by the government. Despite these hazards, only two cleaners surveyed had a warning or cautionary statement on the label notifying the potential user of its flammable nature and one of those was, according to this publication, "somewhat lost in the wording pertaining to contents being under pressure. . . ."[49]

Consumer Reports magazine reported the same inadequate warnings when it tested all-purpose cleaners. The researchers found that "most of these cleaners could, conceivably, cause eye irritation, but only if you were unable to flush away the cleaner immediately after an accidental splash. Regrettably, some products—including four of those that we judged could be seriously irritating to the eye, carry no warnings or first-aid instructions on their label."[50] The magazine noted that one product with the potential for causing serious eye irritation had been ordered by the Consumer Product Safety Commission to incorporate a warning label on the can, but the researcher's samples had no warning.[51] The researchers expressed special concern about hazards posed by ammoniated liquids, particularly when mixed with chlorine bleach, hazards that they noted were not spelled out on product labels they surveyed:

> [S]uch cleaners should not be mixed with chlorine-type bleach because the acrid fumes that might result can bring on nausea, watery eyes, irritation to the nose and throat, or worse. Labels on three of the ammoniated liquids say nothing about this problem. One of the silent three contained more ammonia than any of the other ammoniated liquids.[52]

As noted earlier, recent research has also found inconsistencies and inadequacies in labeling of antidotes to deal with poisoning once it does occur.

COMMENT: The U.S. Consumer Product Safety Commission should follow the lead of the New York City Board of Health as well as Poison Control Centers across the nation in revising recommended antidotes. We must have stan-

[49] 61 CONSUMERS' RESEARCH 13, No. 7 (July 1978).

[50] 44 CONSUMER REP. 78, No. 2 (Feb. 1979).

[51] *Id.*

[52] *Id.*

dardized, consistent, effective antidote labeling before more children suffer unnecessarily.

---

§ 3.26 —Antidotes

I'm sorry to say that inadequate and misleading antidote labeling still remains a major problem. Of primary concern are the continued advisories to use citrus juices, vinegar, and/or oil as antidotes for ingestion of ammonia or lye-based products when milk or water is the preferred, and some say safer, antidote.

In a recent investigation, the New York City Poison Control Center stated:[53]

> Our experience has been that many consumer products lack complete ingredient information, thereby inhibiting a rational plan of action in the event of a poisoning. In addition, we suspected that first aid information on some products was outdated and would be dangerous if followed. . . .
>
> This study was performed to determine whether household product labels adequately assist the consumer in the event of a poisoning. The data supports our concerns that the qualitative and quantitative label information available for household items neither supplies the consumer with adequate ingredient data nor adequate advice in the event of a poisoning.

COMMENT: This agency surveyed 1,019 household product labels at retail markets in the New York City metropolitan area to determine whether those labels adequately defined what a consumer should do in the event of a poisoning, the quality of the poisoning warnings, the inadequacy of the first aid instructions, and the extent to which product ingredients were listed. Researchers found that 85% of the labels surveyed had inadequate first aid information; 53% demonstrated insufficient labeling; 6% had incor-

[53] Alderman, et al., Consumer Product Labels? An Investigation (New York City Poison Control Center, Dep't of Health, City of New York Sept. 3, 1981).

rect, potentially harmful instructions; 26% lacked instructions entirely; and 31% had no ingredients listed.

---

* * *

Advances in research and medical science have created a situation today where legal statutes, health codes, and product manufacturers may lag far behind the "state of the art" in medicine. This, however, does not release the manufacturer from liability. By not changing labels in light of current medical knowledge, the manufacturer is placing himself, his insurer, and the health of those persons using his product at an increased risk.

* * *

The results of our study clearly show a deficiency in adequate consumer product labeling. This is a serious problem. Incorrect or omitted labeling can have unfortunate consequences for the victim of an accidental ingestion, where time is a critical factor. . . .

When *Consumer Reports* magazine surveyed drain cleaners recently, its researchers found that more than one-third of the cleaners surveyed bore labels suggesting vinegar or citrus juice as ingestion antidotes, and noted that "the vinegar or citrus juice that they recommend as antidotes are no longer favored by some public health authorities."[54]

In another investigation, the New York State Consumer Protection Board found that, "Consumers are at risk if they follow instructions on some product labels."[55]

Testifying before the Consumer Product Safety Commission in April, 1983, this state agency's representative warned:

> Consumers should not follow first aid instructions provided on product labels. . . . Consumers who are continually warned to read and follow label instructions carefully are, according to experts in the health field, at risk if they follow instructions on some product labels. Water and milk, two readily available substances in almost every American home, are considered to be acceptable antidotes by

---

[54] *See supra* note 1.

[55] Testimony of Ms. L, N.Y. St. Consumer Protection Board, before U.S. Consumer Product Safety Commission (July 10, 1984).

every health official on a local, state, and federal level the Board contacted. However, due to the current CPSC labelling guide, the unacceptable citrus juice, vinegar and oil antidotes continue to appear, rather than milk and water. . . .

The New York State Consumer Protection Board has taken the position that in view of this controversy and the availability of alternative treatment, the CPSC should advise manufacturers to delete references to citrus juices, vinegar and oil on their labels, at least until all of the scientific evidence is in. As long as there is doubt, give consumers the benefit of that doubt. . . .[56]

COMMENT: The New York State Consumer Protection Board found alarming inconsistencies in antidote labeling. "There is substantial latitude in labelling guidelines for hazardous products, and instructions can vary considerably for products which seem to be identical. For instance, for spillage on the skin, one will advise, 'Flood the surface with water using soap freely, then cover with moist magnesia or baking soda. Call Physician Immediately.' While another says 'Immediately flood with water for 15 minutes. If irritation persists seek medical care.' While it may be true that neither set of instructions is wrong or harmful, one or a combination of the two may be most effective. The [Consumer Protection Board] position is that instructions should be standardized to a greater degree."

As the agency's former director warned, "I don't want the final study to occur in a child whose mother has read a label, and who has followed that label with perhaps disastrous results."[57]

§ 3.27 Reducing children's access

Another alternative to reducing the dangers of chemical cleaners is to make them less accessible to children. In 1970, Congress took a step in

[56] Testimony of Ms. B before Consumer Product Safety Commission Toxicological Advisory Board Meeting (Apr. 26–27, 1983).

[57] *Id.*

this direction when it adopted the Poison Prevention Packaging Act.[58] The Consumer Product Safety Commission has used its authority under the statute to promulgate regulations requiring child-resistant enclosures on many toxic household products and medications.[59]

COMMENT: The Consumer Product Safety Commission has indicated that the law has succeeded in reducing the plague of childhood poisonings by chemical products—the overall death rate has declined from 500 to 200 annually. However, that's still 200 too many!

It is imperative that manufacturers comply with these standards. It is also important for industry members, safety authorities, and members of the legal, medical, and pharmaceutical communities to warn consumers of the potentially tragic consequences of failing to use these safety devices after they bring these products into their homes.

§ 3.28 What can lawyers do?

Of course, the road to injury prevention is wide open. I urge my colleagues with interest and expertise in this area to become involved in injury prevention activities. Join or initiate poison prevention programs in your community. Pressure the Consumer Product Safety Commission to require more stringent, uniform, and effective antidote labeling on household chemical products. Educate the public regarding the importance of using child-resistant closures on all household chemical products. Promote the use and marketing of alternatives to traditional caustic drain cleaners for household use. Pressure government safety authorities for stringent and effective standards to reduce the toxic threats of formaldehyde in insulation, plywood, particle board, and other consumer products.

I also urge my colleagues to keep abreast of the latest technological developments in this field. With safer, noncaustic cleaners available, the issue of liability on the part of those companies that fail to pursue such

[58] Poison Prevention Packaging Act, Pub. L. No. 91–601, 84 Stat. 1670 (Dec. 30, 1970).

[59] 16 C.F.R. 1700 *et seq.* (1985).

safer designs may be a subject of important future litigation. The Association of Chemical Producers, Inc. (A.C.P.) has developed new "voluntary" industry standards regarding sulphuric acid drain cleaners that govern labeling and warning of hazards, safety packaging requirements, formulation, and testing.[60] I encourage you to become familiar with these standards, remembering that "voluntary" standards are not legally enforceable and that nearly one-third of this industry's members do not belong to this trade association. Our courts will determine whether these "minimal standards" are sufficient to protect consumers from sulphuric acid cleaner-related injuries.

COMMENT: I believe that chemical cleaner-related injury cases are not litigated in proportion to the number of poisonings and other product-related injuries that occur each year. This may be one reason why manufacturers have been so recalcitrant in developing safer alternatives and providing sufficient warnings on their products. It is my hope that increased litigation in this area will provide manufacturers with the incentive they need to provide safer and better protected household products in order to reduce the slaughter by product pervading America's homes today.

VI. Litigation Sources: Bibliography

§ 3.29 Selected technical sources

Abelson, *Laboratory Safety*, 211 Science 755 (May 1980).

Adhia, *Recent Developments in Chlor-Alkali Industry*, 31 Chemical Age India 411–18, No. 5 (1980).

Aleshaev & Nepomiashchaia, *Hydrodynamic Disorders in Alkaline Burns of the Eyeball*, 38 Ofthalmol-ZH 303–06, No. 5 (1983).

Exposures of Personnel to Laboratory Hazards, Am. Industrial Hygiene Ass'n J. (Aug. 1972).

---

[60] Minimum Standards for Sulphuric Acid Drain Cleaners (Ass'n Chem. Producers Oct. 15, 1983).

Balakrishnan & Saranthan, *Triple Effect Caustic Soda Evaporation System*, 31 Chemical Age India 553–55, No. 5 (1980).

Breault, *Five Years with Five Million Child-Resistant Containers*, 7 Clinical Toxicol. 91–95, No. 1 (1974).

Bucher, et al. *The Topically Irritant Substance: Essentials—Biotests—Predictions*, 11 Agents Actions 515–19, No. 5 (1981).

Burns & Hikes, *Irrigation of the Anterior Chamber for the Treatment of Alkali Burns*, 88 Am. J. Opthalmol. 119–20, No. 1 (1979).

Clinical Toxicology of Commercial Products, § 3, *Acute Poisoning* 206–12, *Lye* (4th ed. 1975).

Clinical Toxicology of Commercial Products, § 3, *Acute Poisoning* 2–6, *Acid* (4th ed. 1975).

Donaldson & Garnson, *Reporting Impurities in Commercial Products*, 51 Analytic Chemistry 441A-442 (Apr. 1979).

Douglas & Spillman, *In Vitro Ocular Irritancy Testing*, 1 Alternative Methods Toxicol. 205–230 (1983).

Faigel, *Hazards to Health—Mixtures of Household Cleaning Agents*, 271 New Eng. J. Med. (Sept. 17, 1964).

Goldman & Weigert, *Corrosive Substance Ingestion: A Review*, 79 Am. J. Gastroenterol, 285–88, No. 2 (Feb. 1984).

Hedbergs & Jensen, *Spill Control in the Laboratory*, 57 J. Chemical Educ. A16306 (May 1980).

Chemistry of Cleaning, 56 J. Chemical Educ. 610–611 (Summer 1979).

Michelotti, *Hazardous Chemical Safety in the Laboratory*, 51 Analytic Chemistry 441A–442 (Apr. 1979).

Moon & Robertson, *Retrospective Study of Alkali Burns of the Eye*, Austl. J. Ophthalmol. 282–86 (Nov. 11, 1983).

Motani, *The Tokuyama Soda Membrane Caustic-Chlorine Process*, 31 Chemical Age India 457–62, No. 5 (1980).

What Price Chemical Safety?—High Says ICI, 78 New Scientist 920 (June 29, 1978).

UK Detergents Come Clean, 82 New Scientist 894 (June 14, 1979).

O'Brien & Bennis, *Studies on the Interaction Between Eschericlua Coli Pyruvate Oxidase and a Detergent Activator by Utilization of the Flu-*

orescence Probe Bis 18-p-Toluidino-1-Naphthale Nesulfonate, 18 Biochemistry 804–09 (Mar. 6, 1979).

Renard, et al. *Corneal Changes Due to Alkali Burns*, 98(3) Trans-Ophthalmool-Soc-UK 379–82 (Sept. 1978).

Sahn & Good, *The Effect of Common Sclerosing Agents on the Rabbit Fleural Space*, 31 Am. Rev. Respiratory Disease 379–92, No. 5 (July 1981).

Salisbury, *Improvers of Caustic Soda*, 120 Brauwelt 358–62, No. 11 (1980).

Smith, *Laboratory Chemicals May Come Under Costly OSHA Restrictions*, 202 Science 496–499 (Nov. 3, 1978).

Starage, *Detergent Enzymes: Past, Present, and Future*, 60 J. Am. Oil and Chemical Soc'y 1025–27 (May 1983).

Labeling Chemicals—What's in a Name?, 86 Tech. Rev. 76–77 (Aug. 8, 1983).

Vancura, Clinton, Ruiz & Krenzelok, *Toxicity of Alkaline Solutions*, Annals Emergency Med. 118–122, No. 3 (Mar. 1980).

Zwicker, Allen & Stevens, *Toxicity of Aerosols of Sodium Reaction Products*, 2 J. Environmental Pathol. & Toxicol., No. 4 (Mar.-Apr. 1979).

§ 3.30 Selected popular sources

Test: Liquid Dish Detergents, 8 Canadian Consumer 21–23, No. 4 (Aug. 1978).

The Stuff That Unclogs Drains, 29 Changing Times 35–36, No. 3 (Mar. 1975).

Drain Cleaners, 48 Consumer Rep. 146, No. 3 (Mar. 1983).

All Purpose Cleaners, 47 Consumer Rep. 519–21, 534, No. 10 (Oct. 1982).

Oven Cleaners, 45 Consumer Rep. 598–99, No. 10 (Oct. 1980).

Glass Cleaners, 45 Consumer Rep. 570–71, No. 9, (Sept. 1980).

Toilet Bowl Cleaners, 45 Consumer Rep. 336–37, No. 5 (May 1980).

All-Purpose Cleaners, 44 Consumer Rep. 78–81, No. 2 (Feb. 1979).

Drain Cleaners, 41 Consumer Rep. 592–93, No. 10 (Oct. 1976).

Oven Cleaners, 41 Consumer Rep. 400–01, No. 7 (July 1976).

Toilet Bowl Cleaners, 40 Consumer Rep. 156–58, No. 3 (Mar. 1975).

Why Should a Child Swallow Drain Cleaner?, 36 Consumer Rep. 528–31, No. 9 (Sept. 1971).

Best Way to Unclog Drains, 16 Consumer's Digest 9, No. 6 (Nov.-Dec. 1975) (steps to unclog drains without using chemical product. Reasons for avoiding chemicals.)

Drain Cleaners, 62 Consumers' Research 12–15, No. 5 (May 1979).

General Purpose Household Cleaners, 60 Consumers' Research 1145, No. 5 (May 1977).

Day, *How to Handle Plugged Drains*, 28 Fam. Handyman, No. 5 (May-June 1978) (use of chemicals, plunger, plumber's snake, sewer tape, and so on.)

Guide to Laundry Aids, 84 Good Housekeeping 216, 218, 220, No. 5 (May 1977).

Jones, *Unstopping Clogged Drains*, 77 Mechanix Illustrated 24, 26, No. 643 (Dec. 1981).

§ 3.31 Selected government sources

First-Aid Labeling of Hazardous Household Product (Staff Briefing Package, Consumer Product Safety Comm'n Sept. 1984).

Voluntary Standard for Sulphuric Acid Drain Cleaners (Staff Briefing Package, Consumer Product Safety Comm'n Sept. 1984).

Technological Response to Environmental Protection Regulations and Energy/Supply Structure: A Case Study of Chlorine/Caustic Soda Manufacturing (Nat'l Sci. Found. Nov. 1981).

Pocket Guide to Chemical Hazards (Nat'l Inst. Occupational Safety & Health, DHEW pub. no. 78–710 Sept. 1978).

Poison Control Inquiry Data Base (Cumulates from June 1970, U.S. Food and Drug Admin., Division of Poison Control 1977).

Principles and Procedures for Evaluating the Toxicity of Household Substances (Nat'l Research Council, Washington, D.C. 1977).

Product Profile: Household Chemicals (Consumer Product Safety Comm'n Oct. 1976).

Drain Cleaners (Consumer Product Safety Comm'n, Fact Sheet No. 72, 1975).

Poisonous Household Products (Consumer Product Safety Comm'n, Fact Sheet No. 21, 1975).

Poison Prevention Packaging (Consumer Product Safety Comm'n, Fact Sheet No. 46, 1974).

§ 3.32 Selected legal sources

Products Liability: Drain Cleaners, 85 A.L.R. 3d 727 (1978).

Household Caustics Injury Actions, 28 Am. Jur. *Trials* 427 (1981).

5 R. Hursh & H. Bailey, *American Law and Products Liability*, § 30:7, *Drain Cleaners and Similar Caustics* (Lawyers Co-op., 2d ed. 1976).

Lambert, *Products Liability: A Trilogy of Duty-to-Warn Cases*, 36 ATLA L.J. 1 (1976), pt. II, *The Exploding Drano Case*, at 13–17.

E. Swartz, *Proof of Product Defect*, ch. 13, *Drain Cleaners* (Lawyers Co-op. 1985).

Swartz, *Litigating Household Caustic Cases*, 88 Case & Comment 3 (Mar.-Apr. 1983).

E. Swartz, *Hazardous Products Litigation* (Lawyers Co-op. 1973 & Supp.).

§ 3.33 Selected industry newsletters

Chemical Industry Updates
Predicasts, Inc.
11001 Cedar Ave.
Cleveland, Ohio 44106

Chemical Spotlight
P.O. Box 802
Ridgewood, N.J. 07451

Digest of Current Activities and Trends
Drug, Chemical, and Allied Trades Ass'n, Inc.
42–40 Bell Blvd., Suite 204
Bayside, N.Y. 11361

Index of Gov't Regulations
The Bureau of National Affairs, Inc.
1231 25th St., N.W.
Washington, D.C. 20037

Your Consultant
Ass'n of Consulting Chemists and Chemical Engineers, Inc.
50 East 41st St.
New York, N.Y. 10017

The Chemist
The American Institute of Chemists
7315 Wisconsin Ave.
Washington, D.C. 20014

ISSA Today
International Sanitary Supplier Ass'n
5330 North Elston Ave.
Chicago, Ill. 60630

SDA Newsletter
Soap and Detergent Ass'n
475 Park Ave. So.
New York, N.Y. 10016

Art Hazards News
Center for Occupational Hazards
5 Beekman St.
New York, N.Y. 10038

SDA Newsletter
Soap and Detergent Ass'n
475 Park Ave. So.
New York, N.Y. 10016

HBA Buyer
Dell Publishing Co, Inc.
245 East 47th St.
New York, N.Y. 10017

§ 3.34 Selected laws, regulations, and standards

Statutes

(1) Consumer Product Safety Act (CPSA), Pub. L. No. 92–573, 86 Stat. 1207, 15 U.S.C. §§ 2051–2083 (Oct. 27, 1982).

(2) Poison Prevention Packaging Act of 1970 (PPPA), Pub. L. No. 91–601, 84 Stat. 1670, 15 U.S.C. §§ 1471–1476 (Dec. 30, 1970).

(3) Federal Hazardous Substances Act (FHSA), Pub. L. No. 86–613, 74 Stat. 372, 15 U.S.C. §§ 1261–1276 (July 12, 1960).

Regulations

(1) CPSA Regulations, 16 C.F.R. § 1105 (1985).

(2) FHSA Regulations, 16 C.F.R. § 1500 (1985).

(3) PPPA Regulations, 16 C.F.R. § 1700 (1985).

§ 3.35 Selected cases

Heritage v. Pioneer Brokerage & Sales, Inc., 604 P.2d 1059 (Alaska 1979), **mobile home**; formaldehyde fumes; jury instruction on design defect.

Brown v. Clorox Co., No. 447–576–1 (Cal. July 7, 1978), 22 ATLA L. Rep. 34 (Feb. 1979), **drain cleaner**; ingestion by child; esophagus destroyed; settlement of $500,000.

Capers v. Drackett Prods. Co., 1 Civ. 33591 (Cal. App. Dep't Super. Ct. Aug. 28, 1975), 18 ATLA L. Rep. 423 (1975), **drain cleaner**; explosion; blinded boy; design defect in flip-top cap.

Cloroben Chemical Co. v. Comegys, 464 A.2d 887 (Del. 1983), **sulfuric acid drain cleaner**; plumber and distributor were joint tortfeasors.

Moore v. Jewel Tea Co., 46 Ill. 2d 288, 263 N.E.2d 103 (1970), **drain cleaner**; can exploded; woman blinded.

Clements v. Jiffee Chemical Corp., No. 74–153–C2 (D. Kan. June 19, 1980), 23 ATLA L. Rep. 472 (Dec. 1980), **drain cleaner**; ingestion by child; settlement of $850,000.

Shatswell v. Pennwalt, No. 74–35–C (D. Kan. Jan. 4, 1979), 22 ATLA L. Rep. 130 (Apr. 1979), **drain cleaner**; ingestion by child; settlement of $1.05 million.

Myers v. Jiffee Chemical Corp. (D. Kan. 1973), 16 ATLA L. Rep. 466 (1973), **drain cleaner**; ingestion by six children; contained 26% sodium hydroxide; settlement of $1.8 million.

Brummet v. Skyline Corp. (W.D. Ky. 1984), 27 ATLA L. Rep. 315 (Sept. 1984), **mobile homes**; formaldehyde fumes; economic injury; design defect; class action certification.

Guidry v. Kean Mfg. Co., 693 F.2d 426 (5th Cir. [La.] 1982), **drain cleaners**; liquid and granular cleaners mixed together; explosion partially blinded user; improper warning by one of the manufacturers.

Dongo v. Banks, 448 A.2d 885 (Me. 1982), **sulfuric acid drain cleaner**; splattered on children; settlement with some parties.

McGlaughlin v. Drackett Co., No. 71–925LC (D. Mass. 1975), **liquid drain cleaner with lye**; disfigurement.

Borden, Inc. v. Commissioner of Public Health, No. S–2849 (Mass. Apr. 12, 1983), **formaldehyde insulation**.

McGlew v. Countyside Insulators, No. 81–209 (Mass. Super. Ct., Essex Cty.)(case currently pending; opened Jan. 30, 1981), **formaldehyde insulation**.

Vincent v. Combine Insulation Co., No. 81–1563 (Mass. Super. Ct., Essex Cty.)(case currently pending; opened July 20, 1981), **urea-formaldehyde foam insulation**; link with cancer.

Carr v. Clorox Corp., No. 79–918–354 (Mich. Cir. Ct. Oct. 4, 1982), 26 ATLA L. Rep. 36 (Feb. 1983), **liquid drain cleaner**; ingestion by child; lack of child-proof cap; settlement of $1.5 million.

Eisert v. Greenberg Roofing and Sheet Metal Co., 314 N.W.2d 226 (Minn. 1982), **urethane spray foam insulation and intumescent paint**; toxic smoke fueled fire; wrongful death.

Laney v. Coleman, No. 82–0153–C(3) (E.D. Mo. July 19, 1983), 26 ATLA L. Rep. 374 (Oct. 1983), **camping fuel**; failure to have flash-back arrester.

Bersch v. Gold Seal, No. 79 Civ. 1671(EN) (E.D.N.Y. Mar. 14, 1983), 26 ATLA L. Rep. 181 (May 1983), **charcoal lighter**; explosion.

Hamlin v. Clorox, Inc., No. 71 Civ. 1522 (E.D.N.Y. Nov. 8, 1977), 21 ATLA L. Rep. 180 (May 1978), **drain cleaner**; ingestion by child; esophagus destroyed; settlement of $500,000.

Tucci v. Bossert, 53 A.D.2d 291, 385 N.Y.S.2d 328 (1976), **drain cleaner**; inadequate warnings on can; foreseeable misuse by infant.

Haran v. Union Carbide Corp., No. 13541/75 (N.Y. Sup. Ct. May 3, 1984), 28 ATLA L. Rep. 84 (Mar. 1985), **insect repellent**; spray ignited; severe burns.

Davis v. Siloo, Inc., 47 N.C. App. 237, 267 S.E.2d 354 (1980), **chemical solvent**; decedent sprayed with solvent; manufacturer's failure to warn of dangerous properties.

Davis v. Drackett Prods. Co., 536 F. Supp. 694 (S.D. Ohio 1982), **drain cleaning fluid**.

Drayton v. Jiffee Chemical Corp., 395 F. Supp. 1081 (N.D. Ohio 1975), *aff'd*, 591 F.2d 352 (6th Cir. 1978), **liquid drain cleaner with lye**; disfigurement.

Rogers v. Rapco Foam, Inc., No. 46791 (Ohio C.P. July 14, 1983), 26 ATLA L. Rep. 327 (Sept. 1983), **formaldehyde foam insulation**; respiratory problems; property damage; $300,000 total settlement for six families.

Vana v. Champion Int'l Corp., No. 27380 (Ohio C.P. Apr. 29, 1983), 26 ATLA L. Rep. 279 (Aug. 1983), **formaldehyde**; particle board flooring; psychological and respiratory injuries; settlement of $68,000.

Lancaster v. W.A. Hartzell & Assoc., 54 Or. App. 886, 637 P.2d 150 (1981), **wood stain**; ignited; defective labeling.

Ellis v. K-Lan Co., 695 F.2d 157 (5th Cir. [Tex.] 1983), **acid-based drain declogger**; chemical burns to child; expert's lack of knowledge of packaging legislation.

Boelens v. Redman Homes, Inc. (N.D. Tex. 1982), 26 ATLA L. Rep. 129 (Apr. 1983), **mobile home**; explosion of formaldehyde fumes from particle board.

Kindred v. Con/Chem, Inc., 650 S.W.2d 61 (Tex. 1983), **paint primer**; fire; personal injuries sustained by workers; design defect and failure to warn.

Tiderman v. Fleetwood Homes, 102 Wash. 2d 334, 684 P.2d 1302 (1984), **mobile homes**; formaldehyde emitted from particle board; jury instructions on warranty of merchantability and duty to warn.

Little v. PPG Indus., Inc. 92 Wash. 2d 118, 594 P.2d 911 (1979), **cleaning solvent**; duty to warn.

Chapter 4

FABRIC-RELATED BURN INJURIES—THE TORCH CASES

KLUWER LITIGATION LIBRARY REFERENCES

HARLEY & MAGEE, WHAT'S IT WORTH? A GUIDE TO CURRENT PERSONAL INJURY AWARDS AND SETTLEMENTS.

JEANS, LITIGATION: Chapter 4, *Discovery*; Chapter 8, *Direct Examination*; Chapter 9, *Direct Examination of Expert Witnesses*; Chapter 13, *Cross-Examination*; Chapter 14, *Cross-Examination of Expert Witnesses*.

SMITH & MALANDRO, COURTROOM COMMUNICATION STRATEGIES: Chapter 1, *Impression Formation in the Courtroom*; Chapter 2, *Persuasive Strategies in the Courtroom*; Chapter 5, *Preparing for Effective Courtroom Communication*; Chapter 8, *Direct Examination: Presenting the Evidence with Impact*; Chapter 9, *Cross-Examination: Controlling the Case*.

I. Introduction

§ 4.01 In general

Of all the product-related injuries I have dealt with in my trial practice, burn injuries resulting from flammable fabrics are the most traumatic. The severe burn traumatizes every part of the human person—physically, emotionally, and psychologically. Whether the product is an article of clothing, a cozy comforter, or any other fabric material, the evidence developed by experts in government, industry, and academia has demonstrated that fabric ignition heightens the effects of exposure to those heat sources that surround our lives. These experts also know that flame-retardancy technology has been available for years to reduce the threats to consumers from flammable fabric products. Yet, rather than exploring and developing new technologies, fabric industry members spent years hiding behind federal laws that provided the most minimal and inadequate flammability standards. In the end, it has been the American consumer who has paid the price in terms of the horrible pain and suffering produced by burn injuries. Yet consumers have fought back, and the flammable fabrics case has become a major area of product-related personal injury litigation.

COMMENT: In this chapter, we shall see how members of the fabric industry—manufacturers of clothing, upholstered furniture, and household carpeting—have provided the American consumer with products that may lead to disastrous fire if exposed to a household heat source, yet have steadfastly worked to hide this information from the American public.

---

§ 4.02 Focus on fabric itself

The first reaction to fabric-related burn injury cases is often "What was the source of ignition?" Or, when children are the burn victims, "Why weren't their parents watching them more closely?" or "Why were they playing with matches?" It has been my experience in handling fabric-related cases that focusing on the source of the ignition or the child's behavior is a misplaced attention. Rather, the important focus must be on the fabric itself: Why did it respond to the source of heat as it did? Why was it not designed with flame-retardant material or treatment to promote flame extinguishment when the source of heat was removed? Why was it not designed to permit easy removal from the child's body? Why was it designed with dangerously flammable fabric when safer, flame-retardant materials were readily available?[1]

COMMENT: My approach—focusing on the design of the fabric—has enabled me to obtain successful results and record judgments for consumers, particularly children, who have suffered the agonizing consequences of severe burn injuries and the often permanent physical and psychological scars that stay with them for the remainder of their lives.

The case study that follows in Part III, *infra*, illustrates the tragic consequences that can result when a manufacturer takes advantage of its national reputation for quality products by marketing a children's comforter that it knows is hazardous with marketing gimmicks so outrageous that they prompt one of the company's own executives to ask, "Whom are we trying to kid?"

II. Checklists

§ 4.03 Checklist: Investigation of a fabric-related burn injury case

The following checklist is provided as a guide for those colleagues wishing to prepare their flammable fabric-related case more adequately.

____ (1) Collect as much information as possible on the ignition that started the fire:

____(a) The source of ignition

____(b) The exact place on the fabric where the ignition

---

[1] *See infra* §§ 4.03 and 4.04, for further guidelines on the preparation of a fabric-related burn injury case.

first took place (e.g., cuff, hem, seam, trim, or middle of fabric)

____(c) How the fire spread after ignition

____(d) The distance between the fabric and the heat source when the ignition took place

____(e) Whether the fabric first smoldered before the flame appeared

____(f) The time between ignition and the extinguishment of the fire

____(g) Rate of flame spread and ignition

____ (2) Obtain possession of the fabric. If not available, locate another sample of the same type

____ (3) Collect all labels that were on, or had been on, the fabric, including the FTC registration number

____ (4) Ascertain the following information about the fabric:

____(a) When and where purchased

____(b) Any alterations made after it left the manufacturer and after it came into the client's possession

____(c) Length of time the fabric had been in use

____(d) Chemical treatment of fabric by owner, tailor, cleaner, or others

____(e) Normal use made of fabric

____(f) Fabric use at time of fire

____(g) Instructions for use and cleaning of fabric

____(h) Involvement of any other flammable household materials in the fire

____(i) Packaging of the fabric

____(j) Instructions or warnings with regard to the fabric

____ (5) Examine client and witnesses as to:

____(a) When and how the fire was discovered

____(b) Victim's immediate reaction

____(c) Reactions of others

____(d) How the fire was extinguished

____(e) Injuries to those attempting to extinguish the fire

____(f) How the ignited fabric was removed from the victim

____ (6) Obtain all reports from:

____(a) Fire marshal

____(b) Police

____(c) Other authorities

____ (7) Research law reviews and treatises on flammable fabrics cases

____ (8) Contact the following to determine what information, if any, is available regarding the product:

____(a) U.S. Consumer Product Safety Commission

____(b) U.S. Department of Commerce, National Bureau of Standards

____(c) U.S. Department of Health and Human Services

____(d) ATLA Exchange

____(e) ATLA Law Reporter

____(f) ATLA Product Liability Law Reporter

§ 4.04 Checklist: Resources for a fabric-related burn injury case

The following resource checklist should be a valuable tool for counsel in preparing a fabric-related burn injury case.[2]

____ (1) Selected technical sources

____(a) American Dyestuff Reporter

____(b) Chemical Engineering News

____(c) Textile Research Journal

____(d) Journal of Fire Retardant Chemistry

____(e) Journal of Consumer Product Flammability

____(f) Textile Industries

____(g) Science

[2] *See infra* §§ 4.27–4.31, for reference to specific articles contained in these publications.

____(h) Textile Chemist and Colorist

____ (2) Selected popular sources

____(a) Good Housekeeping Magazine

____(b) Consumer News

____(c) Consumers' Research

____(d) Ladies' Home Journal

____(e) Consumer Reports

____(f) Vogue

____(g) Which? (Great Britain)

____(h) Family Circle

____(i) Consumer's Digest

____ (3) Selected government sources

____(a) U.S. Consumer Product Safety Commission

____(b) U.S. Department of Commerce, National Bureau of Standards

____(c) U.S. Department of Health and Human Services

____(d) U.S. Food and Drug Administration

____ (4) Selected industry sources

____(a) American Association of Textile Chemists and Colorists

____(b) National Association of Textile and Apparel Distributors

____(c) Textile Research Institute

____(d) Textile Information Sources

____(e) National Association of Hosiery Manufacturers

____(f) National Association of Decorative Fabric Distributors

III. Case Study: The Case of the "Heavenly Sleep" Comforter[3]

§ 4.05 Facts

Two minor plaintiffs, ages 18 months and 28 months, were severely burned and permanently disfigured when a polyester fiberfill comforter on which they lay melted into a hot, lavalike mass when exposed to heat. The children's faces and hands were burned to their very bones.

The minor plaintiffs' tragic suffering began on a cold January morning when their parents were getting ready for a weekend trip to Cape Cod. As they loaded the family station wagon, they placed their two young children in the back of the wagon. They wrapped the kids in a cozy fiberfill comforter as added protection against the biting winter chill, and returned to the house to pick up some last minute supplies.

Suddenly, their mother looked out to see the car engulfed in a thick, black cloud of smoke. She and her husband dashed outside and began groping frantically for the two children. Mrs. H reached her daughter and was able to pull her to safety. Mr. H groped desperately for his son until he, too, was able to pull him out of the thick smoke. Both children were rushed to the hospital. The third and fourth degree burns they suffered rendered them almost unrecognizable, as melted and burned flesh clung from their faces and hands.

The children's battle for life continued in the hospital emergency room. Only around-the-clock care by a team of skilled doctors and nurses kept them alive. The director of the emergency surgical team said of their condition when they arrived:

> I think [the girl] was the sickest one at the time. . . . She was in severe respiratory distress, having a good deal of difficulty catching her breath. Our initial efforts were designed to resuscitate her and bring her back to a stable, vital-sign situation. . . . [The girl's] face was covered with a black type hard material . . . it was in a patchy distribution. . . . I couldn't identify it. . . . Just something very unusual we had not seen before. . . .[4]

For this plaintiff, the full dimensions of the accident took their toll psychologically as well. She drifted into a psychological state of with-

---

[3] Hinckley v. Eastman Kodak Co., No. 69–1338–J (D. Mass. June 6, 1973).

[4] *Id*., testimony of Dr. E., ____________ Children's Hospital.

drawal, communicating with nobody. A local newspaper described her status in this way:

> Little _______________, 18 months old, lies silently in a hospital crib in Boston. She has not spoken to anyone since being critically burned in a flash fire January 20.
>
> The bright-eyed youngster suffered such a traumatic experience while trapped in the blazing car that she has not said a word to anyone, including her parents. . . . Lisa remains in "good" condition but responds to any verbal communication by crying . . . the parents visit her daily but the scarred girl will not speak to anyone.[5]

COMMENT: Eventually, slowly, she began to speak again. But the depression, the withdrawal, the agony she must have been going through are simply impossible to imagine. The scars of this inner suffering must be just as deep and permanent as those she will always bear on her hands and face. As the advocate for such a victim, the plaintiff's lawyer must find a way to communicate such suffering to the court and jury.

---

§ 4.06 Analysis of case

What went wrong? How could this "heavenly" comforter produce such devastating tragedy that would permanently scar the lives of these two young children both physically and psychologically? The answer lies in the willingness of a nationally trusted company to misrepresent the true hazardous nature of its product behind an advertising facade designed to promote a false consumer confidence that its product was safe while perpetrating what can only be described as a cruel hoax on the consuming public.

The family purchased their comforter because, according to Mr. H, it "looked so very comfortable."[6] It was marketed with advertising and labeling intended to seduce the consumer into believing it was a safe,

[5] Woonsocket Call, Woonsocket, R.I., March 12, 1968.

[6] *Hinckley*, *supra* note 3, testimony of the plaintiff's father.

comfortable, and reliable product. They did not know that this "heavenly" comforter would produce a living hell when exposed to heat, that the comforter's polyester filler had the capacity to melt into a hot lavalike mass when exposed to the heat produced by the comforter's ignited rayon acetate shell, and burn the children's faces like napalm.

The plaintiffs could not have known the risk they were taking, but the defendant certainly did. This company knew that the fiberfill would melt when exposed to heat, that its flammability depended on the flammability of the comforter's outer shell, and that its own laboratory employees were trained and equipped with protective gear to avoid the risks of burn injuries.

§ 4.07 Cross-examination of defendant-company executives regarding hazardous nature of product

The following testimony from a supervisor at the defendant's __________ Testing Laboratories under probing cross-examination revealed this product's hazardous nature.

Q. If I asked you to comment on the burning characteristics of [this] polyester fiberfill when used in comforters, what would you inform me of if I were a buyer, say, for a manufacturer?

A. I would tell you that the __________ fiber per se is slow to ignite, that if sufficient energy is applied it might continue to burn, subject to the conditions of the testing at the time. That any cover fabrics that might be on the item would be a more critical thing for the manufacturer to concern himself with.

* * *

Q. What would you tell me about the covering material? Why would that be critical?

A. Conceivably, it could be some cover fabric that might flush and burn.

Q. Would that be hazardous?

A. Might be considered hazardous.

Q. Why is that?

A. Because it could propagate a flame.

Q. Why would that be hazardous?

A. It would spread to other things.

Q. Like the fiberfill?

A. Not necessarily. It might burn off the top.

Q. If it did spread to the fiberfill, would that pose any particular hazard?

A. Not that I would look at it as a hazard.

* * *

Q. What if the external fabric ignited, would the entire unit then support combustion?

A. It's very possible it would.

Q. Wouldn't that be the more relevant consideration from the point of view of the end use of the consumer, when you are talking about comforters?

A. It's a component of the finished product, yes.

Q. The burning characteristic of the end product, that would be the relevant consideration from the ultimate point of view of the consumer?

A. Yes.

* * *

Q. Melted __________ polyester fiberfill in your view doesn't present a hazard?

A. It is a condition. I don't classify it as a hazard.

Q. Does the melted polyester fiberfill adhere to human skin?

A. I would imagine if it—

Q. Could that cause burns?

A. In a localized area.

Q. Whatever area of the skin it came in contact with, is that what you are saying?

A. Yes.

Q. Could it cause deep burns?

A. It would be relative.

Q. And would you consider that to be a hazard?

A. Only if large quantities were involved.

Q. Such as a comforter?

A. If it were completely burning.

Q. Then that would be a hazard, correct?

A. Possibly.

Q. So it is fair to say, can we not agree, that the melting of a __________ fiberfill is hazardous?

A. Under certain circumstances it might be classified as hazardous. It would depend on the particular orientation of the fabric and the construction and many other things.

Q. But could it ignite?

A. Like all textiles' fibers, this product will burn under certain conditions.

Q. And unlike some other textile fibers, __________ will melt readily under certain conditions, will it not?

A. It will go through a melt phase before it burns, like many other fibers do.

* * *

Q. Whether a __________ polyester fiberfill has hazards associated with its use depends in part, does it not, on what kind of external covering is used, either for pillows or comforters, is that a fair statement?

A. Reasonably so.

Q. And in part, this end use depends upon what kind of product the fiberfill is used in conjunction with, correct?

A. Correct.

Q. So that it would be relevant in determining the end use safety of __________ polyester fiberfill to make a determination as to what
kind of external covering is used, either for pillows or comforters, correct?

A. It would be relatable.

Q. What do you mean by that?

A. Some cover fabrics might ignite more rapidly than others, and have a more rapid burning rate than others.

Q. It would be preferable when such a covering is used in conjunction with a polyester fiberfill such as your ________ polyester fiberfill, that the safest covering is used?

A. It might be desirable if the manufacturer wished it to be.

Q. Why would that be desirable?

A. Because the finished product manufacturer would be the one to decide what level of flammability resistance he might want to have built into his products.

* * *

COMMENT: The plaintiff's attorney should always investigate whether any safety procedures were adopted by the manufacturer to provide a safe workplace for his employee in the manufacturing process. Such procedures will often reveal the very dangers in the product from which the plaintiff was *not* protected. The following testimony from the Director of Plant Protection at the defendant's manufacturing facility conceded the safety threats posed by the material to employees during the manufacturing process.

Q. The ingredients that go into making your synthetic fibers, can any of those ingredients cause burns?

A. Oh, I am sure we use acids and caustics in the process somewhere along the line in making these chemicals.

Q. Will you describe how it is done?

A. It is an extrusion process, a material is forced through a small opening.

Q. In what form is the material forced through that small opening? Is it liquid?

A. Liquid, semisolid.

Q. Is the liquid hot?

A. Yes.

Q. Have you had burn injuries in the plant from people coming in contact with this hot liquid?

A. Yes.

* * *

Q. Can this hot liquid cause *serious* burn injuries if someone comes in contact with it?

A. Well, we haven't had such because [the seriousness] is related to the area covered, naturally, as with any other burn.

Q. What area would be covered in this instance that you are describing?

A. Oh, maybe a spot on a person's hand, most likely.

Q. Is that a common burn injury in the plant?

A. No, we don't have many of them.

Q. Is this one of the hazards you have warned your people about?

A. Yes.

Q. How have you warned your employees about this hazard?

A. There is on the job training.

COMMENT: The family's comforter bore the message: "This comforter is certified to contain 100% virgin ____________ polyester fiberfill, count on ____________, member of the ____________ family. This manufactured product is certified to meet ____________ polyester fiberfill weight specifications."[7] The name ____________ appeared on the upturned corner, a gimmick that a previous witness (Supervisor at ____________ Testing Laboratory) admitted under oath was intentionally designed to promote product sales.

Counsel should examine the product and its advertising with a view toward finding the defendant's subtle and not-so-subtle methods of convincing the public that the product is safe. If the defendant sold his product as safe and reli-

[7] *Hinckley*, *supra* note 3, promotional materials accompanying plaintiff's fiberfill comforter.

able, then he must be willing to face the consequences when it turns out not to be so.

Q. I notice at the bottom of the page it says, "Count on ________, member of the ____________ family."

A. Yes.

Q. You know that slogan has been used widely in newspaper advertisements, in magazine advertisements, and throughout the country on a mass media basis, is that correct?

A. Yes.

Q. And the expression, "Member of the ________ family," has been widely disseminated in the public media, newspaper advertisements, etc., correct?

A. Yes.

Q. And that logo, "Count on ________, Member of the ____________ family," was used prior to ____________ was it not?

A. Yes.

Q. And extensively throughout the country, was it not?

A. Yes.

Q. When an American consumer, as a marketing expert, reads the expression, "Count on ________, Member of the ____________ family," what do you hope to impart when you say "Count on ________"?

A. We would like her to associate the selling points that have been made for our fiber as they would relate to the finished product that she has purchased or is considering buying.

Q. Now, to the extent that in order to get fiber, she has to buy the finished product, obviously you are inducing the purchaser of the finished product also with this advertising campaign, are you not?

A. Indirectly.

Q. That has always been true, has it not?

A. It has been the marketing objective.

Q. Since you have been with the company?

A. Yes.

Q. What else did your specification certification program consist of?

A. It required the manufacturer to make use of 100% ____________ fiber . . . to verify that he used our fiber and that it was virgin materials.

Q. Aside from insuring that they were going to use your product to sell in turn to the consumer, did the certification program amount to anything else, in truth?

A. That if the specifications were followed, Mrs. Consumer would attain the selling points that the manufacturer wished to put on his particular promotional piece.

COMMENT: Crucial evidence of this company's real intentions came in the form of an internal company memorandum discussing changes in the marketing program, including a change in language from "Certified Fabrics Program" to a "Fabrics Registration Program." One executive's handwritten note read, "According to Webster, registered—legally certified or authenticated. Whom are we trying to kid?" Consider the following revealing testimony in which this executive explained his comments.[8]

Q. You once wrote a memorandum entitled "Whom are we trying to kid?" and in fairness to you I want to show this to you. Is this your handwriting?

A. Yes.

Q. Will you please read your handwriting, the handwritten portions?

A. This is in response to the question from someone who signed his name Jim, directed to me, June 16, "[Mr. . . .], any comments?" I then started off,

[8] *Hinckley*, *supra* note 3, testimony of Mr. T, supervisor at defendant's testing laboratories.

"I will try. Our objective was to update our program to be consistent with limited testing we are able to do with our limited facilities and with expanding fiber sales. Our old program started with ____________ lending its turned-up corner to certify that the quality of the fabrics was [up to its standards] and, for a long time, it truly was. But then we had to sell more fiber so we all know the rest. Now we use the term registered to indicate that a converter has submitted fabric to us and we know its case history. . . . So the difference in the use of these terms is that we told the consumer in our tags that the fabric was certified quality, whereas now we use the term registered internally to indicate the status of fabric for ____________ marketing programs. It is solely between ____________ and its converters."

Q. How would an ____________ name help market textile fabrics?

A. It created an association with the . . . organization.

* * *

Q. So that in essence your Education Division designed a labeling program that would induce consumer confidence in ____________ products, correct?

A. That would acquaint consumers with an awareness of our fibers as an ____________ product.

Q. And to build up their confidence in ____________ products, correct?

A. To build up confidence.

Q. The ____________ name means something, correct?

A. Yes.

Q. It means something or showed meaning to the American consumer from the point of view of safety, among other things, correct?

A. Not necessarily, but it could be.

Q. You don't think an American consumer is entitled to rely on the ____________ name from the point of view of safety?

A. To a degree, yes.

Q. That has always been true, has it not?

A. Fairly so.

* * *

Q. The label that appears on the package of some of these products, as you indicated, is there to induce consumer confidence in the product as a whole, correct?

A. To create an awareness that the product contains our fiber.

Q. And to induce the ultimate consumer to buy that product, correct?

A. As an aid in helping them make a decision.

Q. That has always been true, I suppose, has it not been?

A. Yes.

Q. The product as a whole at least has the _____________ family, if you want to use that expression, has the confidence of the _____________ family, correct?

A. It has an association with the _____________ name.

COMMENT: To make matters worse, if that was possible, the defendant's executives admitted under oath their failure to test this product adequately for flammability. This was so even though the company had testing facilities and adequate resources available, and had tested its products to make sure that they contained the amount of fiberfill per weight as required in their contracts. Ironically, they did have programs for testing flammability of other products, including mattress pads, mattresses, quilted robes, padded bras, rugs, and blankets. Again, the testimony of the testing laboratory supervisor is revealing.[9]

Q. Neither you nor _____________ ever developed an acceptable test method for comforters, did you?

A. No.

---

[9] *Id.*

Q. There is no question that you did some testing with respect to National Fire Protection Association Standard 701, did you not?

A. That is right.

Q. And you did that prior to ______________. That is clear, is it not?

A. Yes.

Q. That is sort of an end-use test, is it not, a practical test?

A. Yes.

Q. You never used FPA Standard 701 with respect to comforters, did you, at any time?

A. No.

* * *

Q. Prior to ______________, your company conducted flammability tests on the exterior covers of mattresses, did they not?

A. Yes.

Q. Were you aware that your company did testing on the exterior fabric of pillows filled with the polyester fiberfill?

A. In a vague way, I recall that.

Q. Were you aware that your company did flammability testing on bedspreads filled with __________ fiberfill, polyester fiberfill, are you aware of that?

A. They might have simulated—

Q. A test on a bedspread?

A. Yes.

Q. But they never actually did tests on a bedspread filled with ____ fiberfill, did they?

A. Not that I am aware of.

* * *

Q. Did you ever test the comforters or bedspreads from the point of view of the National Fire Protection Association's Standards, which is concerned with consumer end use?

A. I have tested the cover fabrics as you have asked in accordance with NFPA 702 and they would pass the test.

Q. The ones you tested?

A. Yes.

Q. And NFPA 701 also?

A. They would fail 701.

* * *

Q. Which is the more stringent standard from the point of view of benefiting the consumer?

A. In my opinion, 701 is a very strict test method. [*Note*: This test was to become the government's stringent flame-retardancy test for children's sleepwear].

COMMENT: The company had done flammability testing on some products made with ____________ fiber: carpets and rugs, for instance. Those tests demonstrated that ____________ fiber, exposed to flame, tends to melt. They did not examine the proportions of the melt, or of the residue, or the precise temperature at which the product melts.

As if to justify his company's failure to test its comforters, this executive attempted to hide behind the rationale that no government regulations required it to test the comforters for flammability. I was able to discredit this argument, however, by eliciting his admission that the company did test other products, including doll hair, even though no standard or government regulations required such testing, but failed to do the same for its comforters, although flammability testing for child safety was, he agreed, a good idea.

Failure to test the safety of a product adequately makes a good case for negligence—yet many lawyers fail to consider or pursue this issue.

Q. Were you aware that your company tested dolls' acetate hair for flammability?

A. Yes.

Q. Why was it important to do that?

A. It was of interest to us to see how our fiber would compare with competitive fibers.

Q. So to that extent, you were interested in the safety of children with respect to dolls' hair?

A. Yes.

Q. And you are aware, of course, that your company has tested dolls' clothing, for example, from the point of view of flammability?

A. Yes.

Q. Are you aware that your company has tested articles of children's clothing?

A. All apparel has to pass C.S. 191–53 [government flammability standard—16 C.F.R. 1610].

Q. And the dolls' acetate hair did not have to pass that test, did it? There was no standard with respect to dolls' acetate hair, no government standard, was there?

A. No.

Q. But you still endeavored to test dolls' acetate hair from the point of view of trying to contribute to the ultimate safety of the child consumer, did you not?

A. We tested.

* * *

Q. You indicated a moment ago that when your company tested acetate dolls' hair there were no federal standards with respect to that, correct?

A. Yes.

Q. You also indicated it was important to do this testing from the point of view of attempting to protect, in some way, the ultimate child consumer, did you not?

A. We were doing our testing in order to compare our product with competitive products.

* * *

Q. To the extent that you conducted these tests and obtained some knowledge with respect to acetate dolls' hair, you were interested in protecting the ultimate child consumer, were you not?

A. It had its ultimate effect.

Q. So that you would be interested in protecting the ultimate child consumer with respect to at least the acetate product involved in dolls' hair, would you not be?

A. It's always been an area of interest to try to improve products, yes.

Q. That's a salutary approach, is it not?

A. That is correct.

COMMENT: This company's selectivity also applied to the information it was willing to divulge to its customers and to the consuming public. They did not tell the public that their comforters failed to pass stringent flammability tests. They would not tell their customers this fact until they were asked. Under my cross-examination, this same witness conceded that the underlying marketing rationale for the company's failure to disclose such information was the risk of losing sales![10]

Q. Did you ever tell the manufacturers of your products that used the ____________ name on it that the cover would fail the NFPA 701 test?

A. If they asked, we would have told them.

Q. If they didn't ask, you certainly wouldn't tell them, correct?

A. That is correct.

* * *

Q. You sent out a lot of material about fiberfill to customers that included not only customers' names, but educators, retailers, and manufacturers, in order to attempt to promote your product, did you not?

[10] *Id.*

A. Yes.

Q. And they didn't request that information all the time, did they?

A. No.

Q. When you placed advertisements in papers talking about the properties and values of ______________ polyester fiberfill, that was done as part of your marketing program to sell your product, to assist your customers?

A. Yes.

Q. No one necessarily had to request that information about the properties of this fiberfill, did they?

A. No.

* * *

Q. [T]o the extent that you don't talk about the negative aspects of your products in advertisements, in the media, and in communications to the public, generally, that is to induce sales, correct?

A. Yes.

Q. And to increase profits, right, as a result of increasing sales, correct?

A. It goes together.

COMMENT: This company was also silent when it came to safer, flame-retardant alternative fabrics for its comforters. Although flame-retardant fabrics were available and could have been used for this product, this defendant did not use them. Although other items in its product line were designed with flame-retardant materials and promoted for their safety, no mention of safety risks were made in this company's marketing of its comforters.

Another executive admitted on cross-examination that promotional material for the company's other flame-retardant products made frequent reference to their low flammability and high safety.[11] Sales pitches for this product, on the

[11] *Hinckley*, *supra* note 3, testimony of Mr. L, Assistant Superintendent of Fiber Development, Division of ______________ Company.

other hand, were silent on flammability. Is it any wonder the plaintiffs were never warned or informed of the risks posed to their children when they purchased their "heavenly sleep" comforter? Consider the following testimony of this witness.[12]

Q. It is not slow burning when used in combination with other fabrics, is it?

A. Well, the fiber, itself, is basically a slow-burning fiber.

Q. But when the fiber is exposed to the flame by something that is not slow burning, does that affect the burning characteristics of the ______________, itself?

A. Well, if you build a fire under it with some other source, it would certainly affect the way it burns.

Q. If it is surrounded by a rayon acetate covering, for example, would that affect the way it burns?

A. It would depend on the particular orientation of the fabric and the construction and many other things whether it would actually ignite.

Q. But could it ignite?

A. Like all textile fibers, it will burn under certain conditions.

Q. And, unlike some other textile fibers, ______________ will melt readily under certain conditions, will it not?

A. It will go through a melt phase before it burns, like many other fibers do.

Q. You say it goes through a melt phase before it burns, is that correct?

A. Yes.

Q. And that is true for both kinds of ______________?

A. Yes.

Q. Is there anything in that brochure that you distributed to the

---

[12] *Id.*

trade that talks about its melting characteristics in the way we have just described it?

A. I will have to look at this. Yes, under the Thermal Properties, we comment that polyester fibers burn slowly, but melt and drop off when hanging free.

Q. What you mean by melt and drop off when hanging free?

A. Well, as ______________ fiber ignites, it will melt prior to beginning to burn. This is assuming you have enough of a flame source to get it to ignite. That melt that is formed would tend to burn slowly, and when you were holding this material up, it would tend to fall in usually small droplets onto—whatever is below.

Q. That is if it is held in a vertical position?

A. Yes.

Q. Of course, comforters aren't ordinarily held in that position, isn't that true?

A. Yes.

Q. Is there anything in that brochure that talks about the melting characteristics of ______________ when it is held in positions other than vertical?

A. The reference is obvious to a vertical test when you say melting and drop off.

Q. There is nothing in there that talks about the melting characteristics of ______________ when it is held in positions other than vertical, is there?

A. Such as horizontal?

Q. Yes.

A. No.

Q. And there is nothing in there that talks about the melt itself, as to its characteristics, is there?

A. No.

Q. And there is nothing in there that talks about the risk to anyone that comes in contact with the melt, is there?

A. There is nothing in that book that deals with that kind of subject.

Q. Was there anything put out by ______________ at any time that deals with that kind of subject?

A. Not to my knowledge.

§ 4.08 Conclusion

These two minor plaintiffs were victims of a system in which an unsafe fabric was manufactured by one company, made into an unsafe product by another, sold by a third, and purchased by an unwary consumer (their mother). They were victims of a system that was totally lacking in accountability, permitting each party along the chain to hide behind a shield of irresponsibility with no effective standards to ensure the product's safety.

The parents of these tragically injured children had been conned into purchasing a product whose manufacturer did not test for flammability and purchased its materials from other companies that did not check for flammability. The company that sold it naively relied on the reputation of its suppliers and their products to provide a safe product.

The plaintiffs received a settlement of $1,415,000, which at the time was a national record for a flammable fabrics personal injury case.[13]

IV. Other Flammable Products

§ 4.09 Clothing, generally

The horror and deformity of burned skin is made many times worse by our use of flammable materials in our clothing. While our homes are filled with flammable products—bedding, upholstery, draperies, carpets, and rugs—clothing seems to be most damaging in its ability to transform a small spot burn as a result of contact with a lighted match or other flame source into a catastrophic torch of flame. I've seen children at the Shriner's Burn Institute with burns over 50% to 85% of their bodies. These same children, had they been clothed in flame retardant material, would have had burns that were, at most, the size of a quarter.

For years, government research has drawn the same conclusion: flam-

[13] The little girl received $1,015,000, which was, at that time, the largest single result for money damages for a single personal injury or death resulting from injuries inflicted by a flammable fabric or garment, and the largest single amount ever received for personal injuries or death in any category in New England. The boy received $310,000 and the parents received $90,000 for the children's medical expenses.

mable clothing means more serious burns. One study found that clothing fire victims were four times more likely to die from their burns than those whose clothing did not ignite.[14] The following contrasting scenarios provided by the U.S. Department of Health, Education and Welfare illustrate the devastating impact of clothing fire burns:

> A young mother awoke to find her house on fire. She ran to get her two-year-old daughter out of bed. To get the child, she had to step through surging flames. The bottoms of her feet and her nylon nightgown ignited. Although the flames were at her feet, the nightgown fire resulted in severe burns affecting the upper part of her torso and arms. She suffered burns over 37% of her body. Her hospital costs ran to $14,582.95. She has scars that will never disappear.[15]
>
> A young father awoke in a similar house fire. Unclothed, he rushed downstairs to rescue his baby son. On his return, he had to step down the burning staircase, badly burning the bottoms of his feet. He also burned his left leg, left hand, and face. Yet, since clothing was not ignited, his injuries were only 10% of his body. His medical bills totalled only $1,217.15.[16]

This is not a new and previously unknown horror. More than 120 years ago, *Scientific American* magazine described the firsthand account of one of our nation's most famous historical figures:[17]

> The public has been painfully startled by the death of Henry Wadsworth Longfellow's wife which occurred in Cambridge on the tenth instant. Mrs. Longfellow was seated in her library and was in the act of making seals with sealing wax. A bit of paper caught fire and before the blaze could be controlled, she was painfully burned. . . . Although we have urged the preparation of ladies' dresses with non-flammable materials, we trust that the subject of

---

[14] U.S. Dep't of Health, Education and Welfare, Third Annual Report to the President and Congress on the Studies of Deaths, Injuries, and Economic Losses Resulting From Accidental Burning of Products, Fabrics, or Related Materials, D.H.E.W. Publication # 72–7013 at 36 (1971).

[15] *Id*. at 9.

[16] *Id*.

[17] *Scientific American*, July 1861, cited in remarks presented by William V. White, Preventing Burns from Clothing Fires: The Public Health Approach (National Fire Protection Association, 70th Annual Meeting, Chicago, Ill., May 16–20, 1966).

safety clothing will receive more attention from ladies. Their own sense demands it.

Although no data is available on the number of our forefathers who met fates similar to Mrs. Longfellow's, candlelight fire and flammable clothing was certainly a daily threat.

Our more advanced communications systems have provided us more information on just how widespread the danger of clothing ignition really is. Statistics first collected in the 1950's showed 250,000 Americans falling victim to clothing-related fires every year. This evidence prompted Congress to pass the first legislation to deal with the problem on a national scale, the Flammable Fabrics Act of 1953.[18] Despite the public's hopes and expectations that that law would help to eradicate the national plague of clothing fires, the law passed by Congress chose simply to adopt the existing textile industry standard that applied to extremely flammable garments,[19] but none other. It left the overwhelming majority of clothing, and consumers, unprotected from a fire's scourge. Instead of curing the nation's clothing fire plague, the Act has simply prolonged the human misery of fabric burns.

The textile industry has been aware of this problem for decades. The industry's own leaders have admitted under oath that they have known the dangers caused by the flammability of the clothing they produce.[20] Despite this knowledge, they have consistently failed to use existing technology or invest adequately in research and development for new technology to provide flame-retardant products. The textile industry's failure to act is shocking. Of course, manufacturers are in business to make a profit, and they will produce only those products that they expect will sell. But economics will not justify such a wanton disregard for human safety as has been demonstrated by the textile industry. When industry fails to act, government must intervene to enforce the consumer's right to safety. Federal officials have this authority under existing law.[21] They

---

[18] 15 U.S.C. § 1191 *et seq*. (1972).

[19] Commercial Standard (C.S.) 191–53, originally developed by the American Association of Textile Chemists and Colorists (A.A.T.C.C.). The standard for the flammability of clothing textiles is now found in 16 C.F.R. 1610 (1985).

[20] Welkovsky v. Crown Tex. Corp., No. CA 69–1339G (D. Mass.), testimony of Mr. L, ______________ Fabric Co., Welkovsky v. Zayre of Roxbury, Inc., No. CA 71–912G (D. Mass.). Cases remanded to Mass. Super. Ct., Middlesex Cty., Dec. 20, 1971, No. CA 308906 (1975).

[21] Consumer Product Safety Act of 1972, 15 U.S.C. § 2051 *et seq.* (1972).

also know the human misery produced by flammable clothing and other flammable products.

> **COMMENT:** I believe that the failure of public officials to use their authority to require industry action is a breach of the public trust. These are strong words, I know. But after more than a decade of seeing, knowing, and representing burn victims, and knowing full well that their overwhelming anguish and suffering simply did not have to be, I believe these words are well justified.

---

§ 4.10 Children's sleepwear

The following two fact patterns, and the discussions that follow, are illustrative of the types of cases that may be encountered by the attorney handling a fabric-related burn injury case involving children's sleepwear. Plaintiff's counsel must remember that in preparing and trying this type of case, he should not be drawn by defense counsel into focusing on the precise source of ignition or the plaintiff's reaction after his clothing ignited. These are traps set to divert his attention from his crucial focus on the fabric itself.

A five-year-old girl was wearing only her cotton flannelette nightgown when she decided to make some hot chocolate one fateful Sunday morning. She climbed atop her kitchen stove to reach for the chocolate in the cabinets above, and inadvertently turned on the gas. Her nightgown quickly ignited, turning her into a ball of fire. Her mother rushed to her aid as she screamed, "Mommy, I am on fire." Her mother remembers:

> All I could see was [my daughter] in flames, [she was] running around the house. I was trying to put it out with my hands. . . . The flames came up above her head. . . . It was very hot. . . . It just went up so fast. . . . I tried to catch her to put it out. . . . I couldn't catch her . . . she was screaming . . . [the clothing] was still smoldering on the way to the hospital. It was stuck to her skin. . . .[22]

[22] Teixiera v. Her Majesties Industries, Inc., CA No. 73-567-C (D. Mass. February 23, 1979), testimony of the plaintiff's mother.

This minor plaintiff had received second and third degree burns over 60% of her body. Her mother recalls: "[She] and I were both screaming. She was screaming, 'Mommy, help me,' and I couldn't help her. The more she screamed, I said, 'I will help you. Wait. . . .' She looked like a little mummy."[23] She was transferred to ______________ Burn Institute for extensive treatment. She stayed there for over a year. Her initial treatment was followed by eighteen readmissions over the next five years. By the time plaintiff was eleven years old, she was still returning weekly for corrective treatment.

Similarly, consider the case of another young girl who was playing with a trick candle her parents had purchased and used for her father's birthday party when tragedy struck. The plaintiff recalls:

> I was upstairs and got two candles, one for [my friend] and one for me and I lit one and [he] lit the other, and we went downstairs. We were watching T.V., so I blew out the candle and put it on my lap and after awhile there was smoke and stuff and I ran upstairs. . . . I ran into the bathroom. . . . My mother came and she told me to roll on the floor. I said no. . . . I turned the water on in the bathtub . . . and I jumped in the bathtub.[24]

This plaintiff received severe burns over 85% of her body, including her neck, chest, both thighs, abdomen, right calf, both arms, and buttocks. She incurred permanent damage and destruction of her muscle, skin, and underlying soft tissue; permanent and grotesque scarring; permanent functional disability; and severely disabling psychological reactions. She was admitted ten separate times for extensive treatment at ______________ Burn Institute over a three-year period, during which time she was treated by thirty different doctors. In addition, she was seen by hospital physicians during thirteen different admissions at the Institute's outpatient clinic. She underwent at least sixty different operations during this time.

The girl's father described her battle for survival:

> [She] was moved to a hospital, I came up to the hospital, a surgeon cousin of mine came out of New York, plastic surgeons came out of New York. The only thing I was interested in at that time was [her] living. She was given up for dead in New York. The doc-

[23] *Id.*

[24] Rosenberg v. Pioneer Products, Inc., CA No. 77–3936–G (D. Mass. Feb. 13, 1984), testimony of plaintiff.

> tor told me she would not make it through the next day. . . . My cousin told me, "She cannot remain here. She has to be moved out." The hospital in New York said she should remain; it was too dangerous to move her. Dr. _____________ said she would die, and be prepared that she was dying. I, like a fool, asked him, "What's her percentages of living?" And he told me, "If you want to be a fool, it's a 5% chance she would live."[25]

He also described the impact the accident had on his daughter's life:

> [S]he is a child that is burned, is hurt, is maimed, and she will have certain problems as far as a woman is concerned. She will have no breasts, natural breasts, anyway. . . . [She] does what she wants to do in school. She's got a 149 I.Q., and is basically not interested in school. She just saw too much. The doctors say that she lived with death too long, and she has missed so much of her youth, adolescence, child years, baby years, that she wants to play. . . .[26]

COMMENT: When tragedies like this happen to little children, the entire family goes through a severe trauma. All too often, parents compound the horrible effects of the accident by blaming themselves. They yearn to turn back the clock, torturing themselves with thoughts of what they might or might not have done to prevent it.

---

§ 4.11 —Development of flame-retardant technology

The nightgowns that ignited and so wronged these children were the product of a complex industry and a long chain of events. Fabric manufacturers, garment manufacturers, distributors, marketers, and retailers each contribute to the end result: a product manufactured for consumers, in this case, children, to wear in their homes. Ironically, experts within the textile industry had known for years that children were suffering horrible and painful burn injuries from sleepwear ignition, and that flame retardant technology was available to reduce children's risks of

[25] *Id*., testimony of plaintiff's father.

[26] *Id*.

harm. They also have known for years that the federal flammability standard's tests are inadequate and that the true test of flame-resistance is not how many seconds it takes a piece of clothing to ignite, but rather whether or not the fabric is self-extinguishing.[27] One respected industry member admitted in sworn testimony that the whole game of playing with seconds—how many seconds does it take a five-inch strip of fabric to burn—is nonsense. The real test, he said, is that the garment should self-extinguish when the source of ignition is removed.[28]

Mr. L was Director of Research and Development at one of the nation's largest fabric houses, during the early years of development of flame-retardant technology. He admitted on the witness stand that sleepers were indeed being manufactured with flame-retardant finishes in the early 1960's.[29]

Q. Fire-retardant sleepwear fabrics made from modacrylics such as ______________ were available, were they not, in the mid-1960's?

A. I do not know of any woven ______________ available in the mid-60's. I seem to remember some knitted sleepers.

Q. By a sleeper, you mean the kind of thing that looks like a blanket with a zipper, which the child gets into, and can be used like pajamas?

A. The thing that looks like a blanket with legs and feet on them that you zip the child up into.

Q. That is what you mean by a sleeper?

A. Yes.

Q. So, it was available in the mid-60's from the point of view of that kind of product?

A. I believe it was.

COMMENT: Mr. L conceded under examination that the fabrics that they were supplying to children's sleepwear

[27] Testimony of Mr. L, ______________ Fabric Co., Welkovsky v. Crown Tex Corp., *supra* note 20.

[28] *Id*.

[29] *Id*.

manufacturers in 1966 were flammable and posed an inherent threat to the safety of children. Published statistics showed that thousands of young children were burned every year when their sleepwear ignited. Children who had been injured, as well as the families of children who had been killed as a result of clothing ignition, had begun to file suit. In 1966, Mr. L tested fabrics and witnessed them igniting.[30]

Q. Those samples that you tested and these tests you observed back in 1966 in the laboratory, do you recall earlier testifying about those? . . . Do you recall testifying about your witnessing some tests that were done, . . . , are vertical tests done in the laboratory?

A. Yes.

Q. What did you observe about the flannelette when it was exposed to an ignition source on this occasion?

A. It burned.

Q. Rapidly?

A. At about the same rate as any other fabric of its weight.

Q. How would you describe the burning rate?

A. By and large, fabrics burn in the reverse relationship to their weight. This is a well-known, fairly constant rate of mass burning. And all cotton fabrics burn according to this general scheme and the flannel burns at the rate you would expect from its weight.

Q. What is that?

A. I don't know how to say this. Faster than a pair of pants; slower than a voile scarf.

Q. It wasn't self-extinguishing, was it?

A. No.

---

[30] *Id.*

COMMENT: Mr. L had earlier testified that for consumer safety, the important factor was not how long it took for the fabric to ignite, as measured in the federal flammability standards, but whether the product was self-extinguishing. He also admitted that a fabric must be self-extinguishing in order to be considered flame-retardant.[31]

Q. In 1965, did [the company] recognize or did you, for [the company], recognize the inherent dangers that flammable fabrics could mean to children?

A. If the emphasis is on the company, I have to say the answer is yes. . . .

* * *

Q. In order to be effective from the point of view of consumer protection, you were interested in developing a program, were you not, that produced a safer fabric . . . from the point of view of its ultimate end uses in a home environment or other applications, is this correct?

A. We were looking at improving safety with particular attention to apparel.

Q. So that in attempting to develop this consumer protection program, you were concerned with the end use application of the fabrics that you were testing, correct?

A. We did not see any sense in looking and aiming at anything other than self-extinguishing properties. During this early work, we believed that the rate of burning had little to do with the incidents of injury.

Q. That it was from the point of view of consumer protection, as you indicated, to have a self-extinguishing fabric?

A. Correct.

Q. Why is that so? Explain it to us.

---

[31] *Id*.

A. If a garment becomes ignited, if a fabric becomes ignited with a small child, the time required to remove that garment from the child is long enough so that any difference in the rate of the burning is meaningless. The only way you can offer any protection is by arranging the fabric—the flame on the fabric goes out when the flame is removed.

* * *

Q. Virtually all fabrics in the marketplace back in 1966, as far as flannelettes, passed the then existing federal standard, did they not?

A. Yes.

Q. Almost without exception, I think we can agree, can we not?

A. I would think so.

COMMENT: Children wearing these garments would be exposed to heat sources in the home that would ignite the material: kitchen stoves, matches, candles, and the like. Such contact was foreseeable, yet this company made no adequate effort to warn consumers of those hazards. No adequate instructions or warnings were placed on the product. The failure of the defendant-manufacturer to communicate known dangers to the public is common because of the adverse impact such warnings would have on sales. Such conduct cannot be justified, however, either legally or morally. Plaintiffs' lawyers must vigorously pursue this issue in investigation, discovery, pleading, and at trial.

Mr. L also admitted under oath the company's lack of any program to communicate safety information to the consumer.[32]

Q. Let me ask you, back in 1965 and 1966, you certainly knew how to get the warning or instructions out to the trades and consum-

[32] *Id*.

ers, generally, about flammability problems, if you were so inclined, is that not true?

A. Yes.

Q. If there was a practical way to develop a program or to do something that would protect children, [the company] would do that as soon as a method was available, would they not?

A. Yes.

Q. That has always been true for as long as you have been with [the company]?

A. Yes.

Q. That would be true whether we are talking about warnings or instructions or a flame retardancy program?

A. Flame retardancy programs, yes. The philosophy—

Q. Not philosophy. We are not talking about philosophy. Would that be correct with respect to warnings and instructions?

A. No.

Q. Why?

A. The fabrics did not suddenly become dangerous. The fabrics are the same fabrics that had been in commerce for two hundred or three hundred years. The odds are that—I say the odds are that the exposure to flame has been reduced rather than increased over the years because of sophistication in central heating and what have you. As a commercial matter, it is not possible for one company, one isolated company, to insist that people who buy its fabrics put a label on saying, "Dangerous, keep away from fire". . . . This does not make economic sense at all. . . .

COMMENT: After learning of this failure to warn consumers of the product's hazards, it came as little surprise to learn that the company had not invested adequate money and or developed adequate programs for communicating safety information to consumers.

Q. You did have some program, as you indicated, in 1966 dealing with the language of communications, as far as testing methods to get information across to your customers, your trade, and to consumers, generally, did you not? Some portion of your budget was spent for that in 1966, was it not?

A. Some portion of our budget must obviously have been spent in studying test methods, flammability test methods.

Q. What about studying labeling techniques from the point of view of communicating safety information to trade accounts and buyers, etc.?

A. I don't believe we spent any money on that.

Q. There was no program then, is that fair to say, that teaches your executives, your advertising executives, and other people who have to deal with the public, that teaches them how to communicate safety information to members of the public generally and your trade accounts, is that accurate?

A. No. For 1966, there was no such program to communicate safety information to customers.

Q. Neither trade nor consumers?

A. Neither trade nor consumers.

Q. That was true for 1967?

A. That was true for 1967.

Q. That was true for 1965?

A. That was true for 1965.

COMMENT: It was subsequently brought out that the company waited until it began marketing its own flame-retardant fabric, to acknowledge publicly those hazards it had known about for years, and to warn the public about the flammability of its product. When it finally acknowledged the dangers, its incentive was profit: to sell its own new flame-retardant product.

---

§ 4.12 —Marketing of flame-retardant sleepwear

For consumers, safe apparel depended on the marketing whims of textile retailers as well as the research and development whims of textile manufacturers. Even when national retailers began marketing flame-resistant sleepwear their self-protective attitude immediately created a self-fulfilling prophecy of failure.

Consider the case of a well-known national company. It launched an advertising campaign, telling consumers that their flame-retardant nightwear was comfortable and durable, and that it cost more than the nonflame-retardant traditional model (It priced the flame-retardant garment at $3.95, compared to the flammable model price of $2.95). Following its national campaign, this company announced that its trial marketing venture was a disappointment, and blamed the failure on a lack of consumer interest in flame-retardant sleepwear for children.[33] Yet, even Mr. L of the ______________ Fabric Company conceded that the advertisements did not fully inform consumers of the importance of the flame-retardant alternative and of the fire dangers associated with cotton flannelette and other hazardous children's sleepwear.[34] None of the advertisements disclosed how quickly the nonflame-retardant sleepwear would ignite. They did not show or describe the consequences to children burned by nonflame-retardant sleepwear. The primary reason that the flame-retardant sleepwear did not sell was because the average consumer—the average mother, father, or grandparent—did not understand or appreciate the magnitude of the dangers involved. Consumers remained uninformed, and they naturally tended to purchase the lower priced garment available.

COMMENT: The textile industry understood the public's ignorance of the importance of flame-retardant sleepwear very well. A recognized leader and spokesperson for the textile industry told the New York Chapter of the American Association for Textile Technology that public ignorance was the real culprit in the industry's apparent inability to

[33] Statement of Mr. Q, ______________ Co., Hearing on Proposed Standard for Flammability of Children's Sleepwear, D.O.C. P.F.F. 3–70 (U.S. Dep't of Commerce, January 14, 1971).

[34] *Welkovsky*, *supra* note 20.

> market the flame-retardant product. He told his audience that, "possibly most significantly, the consumer fails to appreciate the protection advantages of flame-retardant textiles."[35]

§ 4.13 —Government involvement forces industry action

By the early 1970's, the federal government was working to amend the flammability standard, as it concerned children's sleepwear, to require that all children's sleepwear marketed to America's children be flame retardant. The industry's own publications reflected its concerns about being forced to manufacture a safe garment. In its December 1971 issue, for example, *Earnshaw's Review*, an industry periodical, carried the story headline, "Feds Make It Hot."[36] The story communicated the message from industry leaders decrying the pending standards as the death knell for their industry. The President of the William Carter Company warned that: "It is my opinion that sleepwear will not be made in this country after next year unless there is some change in the standard or the way it is enforced."[37]

By 1972, with the federal sleepwear standards rapidly approaching, firms switched from wholesale denial of their ability to meet the standards to an intense competition to develop flame-retardant products. By January 1973, *Textile Industries* magazine could report that:

> [W]ith less than a year remaining before the children's sleepwear standard goes into full effect, there is a noticeable escalation of activity among chemical makers and fiber producers . . . to meet the July 29, 1973 deadline. . . . [B]eginning in the Spring of 1972, one development followed another in rapid succession. . . . Monsanto announced a self-extinguishing fiber in April. . . . [T]he MRC's fiber division disclosed a joint development with Guilford Mills. . . . Lowenstein announced all-polyester wovens and knits to add to the Fire Gard line of all cotton flame-retardants developed in 1968 . . .

[35] Address by Richard A. Feis, Member of Executive Committee, American Association for Textile Technology (A.A.T.T.), remarks before New York Chapter of American Association for Textile Technology, MODERN TEXTILES MAGAZINE, at 54 (July 1968).

[36] Van Olinda, *Feds Make It Hot*, EARNSHAW'S REVIEW (Dec. 1971), at 26.

[37] Leo J. Feuer, President, The William Carter Company, EARNSHAW'S REVIEW (Dec. 1971), at 31.

> and early in the Fall, the giant of the sleepwear business, the William Carter Company, began marketing an all-polyester garment, following an extensive field testing and "excellent response". . . . This was not all![38]

The field was wide open. In effect, cotton-based manufacturers, after protesting for years that they could not provide a flame-retardant garment for children's sleepwear, were suddenly challenged by the synthetic fiber industry: rayon, polyester, and other synthetics. One textile firm scientist observed: "[T]he cotton people are worried. If there is no progress in treating tubular cotton knits, other fibers could move in."[39] *Textile Industries* magazine further reported: " [T]hus the cotton growers have at last come to realize that thousands of bales of cotton may be lost to man-made fibers in the children's sleepwear markets alone—60,000 to be exact."[40]

By mid-October, 1972, Cotton, Inc., the cotton industry trade association, made its move. "[S]pokesmen from [Cotton, Inc. and United Merchants and Manufacturers, Inc.] reported that the process, known as Fire-Stop cotton, will surpass the recently imposed federal flame-retardant standard for children's sleepwear, and United's Ameritex Division will begin marketing fabrics immediately."[41] Cotton, Inc., had invested a reported $41 million annually in research to obtain a flame-retardant fabric.

Competitive language, too, was starting to appear in industry press releases. For example, Robert Benheim, Chairman and Chief Executive of Lowenstein Fabric Company, boasted: "This new fire-retardant capability means that Lowenstein has the most diversified selection of fire-retardant fabrics for apparel in the market today. We can now offer a complete line of year-round fire-retardant wovens and knits in the latest fashion, colors, and prints."[42]

Under the hammer of mandatory government standards, textile manufacturers were competing for the consumer dollar once again, this time for safety. Since the sleepwear standard became mandatory almost a decade ago, the number of children burned by sleepwear fires has de-

---

[38] Sucheski, *On the Flammability Front: Polyester Moves In and Cotton Fights Back*, TEXTILE INDUSTRIES, at 67 (Jan. 1973).

[39] *Id*. at 72.

[40] *Id*.

[41] *Id*. at 67.

[42] *Id*. at 68.

clined dramatically.[43]

§ 4.14 Children's nonsleepwear apparel

Parents shopping for safe children's sleepwear today clearly have more variety to choose from than their counterparts of a decade ago. Most of the sleepwear products on our stores' shelves are flame-retardant, and are so labeled. Unfortunately, however, the same does not hold for other children's garments. The sad fact is that the government has not extended its requirements for flame-retardancy to cover other children's clothing, and manufacturers certainly have not been beating down their doors to do so on their own. The child climbing on the kitchen stove, blowing out candles, or otherwise coming into contact with flame, remains a time bomb for catastrophe. Such a catastrophe could be avoided, however, if industry and government only had the will to do what should be done.

COMMENT: The attorney representing a child who has sustained severe burn injuries, therefore, may very well be dealing with a garment that has caught fire after a brief exposure to a heat source, yet has passed whatever government flammability standard exists. In this circumstance, the attorney should approach the liability issue based on the inadequacy of the product's design. He must also consider any private regulatory standards, as well as determine the ease of ignition, flame intensity, heat generation, heat transfer, flame-spread time independent of ignition time, and the fabric's self-extinguishing capability when the source of heat is removed. These factors will all come into play in determining whether the article of clothing was negligently designed.

Consider the case of an eight-year-old boy, who was severely burned when a terry cloth novelty bib he had received in a Christmas package ignited as he was lighting the family's Christmas wreath on the dining room table. The bib extended the length of his chest, from his neck to his

[43] U.S. Consumer Prod. Safety Comm'n, Annual Report, at 237 (1981).

waist. The area and extent of his burn matched exactly the dimensions of the bib.[44]

His mother described the accident:

> [He] leaned toward the candles and the bottom of the bib caught fire and burned very, very fast. [my other son] said that [his brother] was lighting the candle, he leaned, the bib went into the fire and it caught fire, and that is when he came to get me. [The injured plaintiff] said, "I didn't forget to stand still, I didn't run."[45]

The manufacturer of this minor plaintiff's bib also manufactured dishcloths, aprons, and towels, primarily terry cloth products. The children's bibs were manufactured and marketed specifically for the Christmas-time market. The company's Secretary of Production conceded under questioning that his company did not take the safety of the consumer (young children) into account in manufacturing their product. Consider this excerpt from his testimony.[46]

Q. Are there any safety factors that your company takes into account when it decides whether or not to market a new item?

A. No.

Q. Did ____________ (supplier of the fabric used in the bibs) ever supply to you, in the course of supplying towel blanks, any statements concerning flammability of the product?

A. No.

Q. Did your company conduct any tests on flammability of those Christmas bibs?

A. No.

Q. Did your company retain any outside independent laboratory to test the flammability of the bibs?

A. Not of the bibs.

Q. Did you retain any such independent testing laboratory for material used in the bibs?

---

[44] Belanger, PPA v. Barth and Dreyfuss, Inc. and Cannon Mills Co., CA No. 73–747–C (D. Mass. May 6, 1976), case settled for $390,000.

[45] *Id*., testimony of plaintiff's mother.

[46] *Id*., testimony of Mr. B, Secretary of Production for defendant; these questions pertained to actions taken by the company before the date of the accident, December 15, 1970.

A. Not the material, no.

Q. Did you have any flammability standards or criteria that you expected these bibs to meet?

A. No.

Q. Were you aware that terry cloth could catch fire?

A. No.

Q. Were you aware of any of the combustion characteristics of terry cloth?

A. No.

Q. Was there anyone involved in the manufacture or marketing of the Christmas bibs who would have greater expertise or better knowledge of these subjects than yourself?

A. No.

Q. It would be fair to say then that you were marketing these bibs without any knowledge as to their flammability characteristics?

A. It would be fair to say that.

Q. Catalogues refer to the various bib styles as children's bibs, is that correct?

A. That is correct.

Q. Does that refresh your memory as to the particular age category for which the product was marketed?

A. No, in fact that is the first time I really read it to see that it said children's bibs.

Q. In view of the fact that these bibs were marketed as children's bibs, did your company take any specific safety precautions with regard to the flammability of the bib?

A. No.

Or consider the case of a five-year-old girl who was severely burned when the poncho she was wearing caught fire. It was a new, plaid poncho, made from a synthetic material, with a decorative cotton fringe along the edges. The fringe caught fire, and the entire poncho soon became engulfed in flames. The little girl sustained massive and disfiguring burn injuries.[47] A company executive admitted under direct examination

[47] Jette v. Arlan's Dep't Stores and Gort Industries, No. 74–2400 (D. Mass. 1979).

that the company did conduct some limited flammability testing: "[O]n a couple of occasions I remember applying a match to a piece of fabric to see if it would smoulder or curl or ball up . . . [to measure] the degree of flammability in the eye judgment test."[48]

Q. When you did this match test back in the mid-1960's, would you put a match to the edge of the garment?

A. Not the garment, a swatch of fabric.

Q. You would take a piece of this material and you would put a match to the end of it to see how fast it burned?

A. That's right.

Q. And if it burned too fast, you rejected it?

A. I would mention to [the] New York [office] the results of the test.

Q. You were trying to find out if it was hazardous?

A. Right.

Q. And if, based on the eye judgment test, it burned too fast, you would reject it?

A. Well, I wouldn't have the power to reject it.

Q. You would recommend rejection?

A. Right.

Q. And who would you make those recommendations to?

A. To the principals.

* * *

Q. Now, of course, if you tested fabric that came in contact with a match, do you ever recall testing the fringe?

A. No, I never tested the fringe.

Q. Why would that be?

A. Well, our concern at that time was with fabric. We didn't think in terms of flammability or inflammability of trims.

Q. Occasionally, from 1965 to 1970, when you notified the principals about a problem with a fabric that you tested, the adminis-

---

[48] *Id.*, testimony of Mr. B, witness called by plaintiffs.

trative decision would be made to go ahead and use the fabric despite your objections, is that correct?

A. To use the fabric, yes.

Q. And even when you recommended a product not be marketed because it failed the test in your mind, occasionally [they] would tell you to make it, is that correct?

A. Right.

COMMENT: In this examination, we see how a company can place into the stream of commerce, clothing products for little children that they know full well are dangerously flammable! To make matters even worse, this executive admitted that the company had no program for informing consumers of this product hazard.[49]

Q. Did your company ever, aside from what the government required, send out a newsletter or put out a label that talked about flammability hazards?

A. No.

* * *

Q. Did they ever put anything on the labels, precautionary warnings of any kind?

A. Not that I remember.

Q. Did your company ever institute a recall of any of its products?

A. Not that I was aware of.

COMMENT: Yet the company was, in this official's own words, fully aware of the risks to little children caused by

[49] *Id.*

their hazardously flammable products.[50]

Q. To be fair, say from about 1965 on, you were quite aware of the problem of the hazards associated with flammability?

A. I'd say that would be a fair estimate.

Q. And a lot of statistics were being published as to how many children were being injured?

A. These things would come up at convention meetings that we had in the industry. In September our industry met and it was a big topic of discussion at that time.

Q. [So that] you are aware of the magnitude of the risk when you make a product for a child, are you not? As a father, you know that to be true?

A. Yes, I imagine so.

Q. And you knew [when you were conducting those tests], and that is why you tested, that children have fertile imaginations?

A. Yes.

Q. And they are exposed to flame sources more than the general population?

A. That's true.

Q. Therefore they are entitled to a larger measure of protection than you or I would be?

A. It sounds logical.

Q. And it is because they are entitled to this larger measure of protection that you instituted this child protection program?

A. That is correct.

Q. So when you talked about your testing program, your motivation for it, one of the considerations was to protect the child, is that correct?

A. Yes.

Q. And the reason you protect the child is for the sake of humanity in general, is that correct?

---

[50] *Id.*

A. Yes.

Q. And, by doing that, you also help yourself by avoiding the expense of lawsuits, is that correct?

A. Yes.

Q. That is just plain common sense, isn't it?

A. Yes.

§ 4.15 Adult apparel

Although the destruction of children by unsafe, flammable clothing is a horror, adults are also victims of products that they expect to be safe. They rely on their clothing to provide warmth, comfort, and attractiveness. Yet, just as the more stringent flammability standards for children's sleepwear have not been extended to other children's clothing, adult apparel likewise remains dangerously flammable.[51]

COMMENT: The physical limitations of the elderly and disabled may make them more vulnerable to accidents and injuries involving home heat sources. For those with arthritis or other impairments, lighting matches, heaters, or ovens may be a cumbersome and hazardous task. Moreover, with restricted mobility, their ability to escape from or extinguish a fire once it begins may be reduced.

Of course, adult clothing is not always worn by adults. When children fit into adult sizes, they literally fall between the cracks in the "protection system."

---

§ 4.16 —Women's robes and nightgowns

Women's robes and nightgowns are particularly hazardous. Their loose-fitting sleeves, flowing trellises, and frilly hems are prone to contact with in-home heat sources. I have seen, in my practice, the horrible results of several flash fires that resulted when people inadvertently

[51] *See infra* § 4.18, discussing judicial intervention to impose liability on manufacturer's of adult clothing regardless of flammability standards.

dropped a cigarette ash, match, or lighter on their lap, and were transformed into human torches in a matter of moments.

In one case, for example, a woman wearing a cotton chenille bathrobe was lighting a cigarette when she suddenly felt a sensation around her legs. She looked down and, to her horror, saw a rush of flames climbing toward her face. She collapsed on the stairway landing.[52] During the investigation of the case, it was discovered that the government's Consumer Product Safety Commission had issued an administrative complaint against this company after finding its garments to be in violation of federal flammability standards. The safety agency's records indicated at least four other consumer complaints, including one death, as a result of ignition of the company's robes.[53]

COMMENT: The following excerpts from testimony of the company's president reveal this defendant's callous and indifferent attitude toward consumer safety in producing and marketing this product:[54]

Q. At some time did you have a problem with the flammability characteristics of the ______________ garment?

A. I did not have a problem with it.

Q. Were you advised by any government agency that the ______________ garment was excessively flammable?

A. Yes.

Q. When were you so advised?

A. In the summer of 1979.

Q. And who notified you?

A. The Consumer Product Safety Commission.

Q. And what did they say to you?

---

52 Sabean v. Edgewood Chenille, Inc., No. 82–2047T (D. Mass. Oct. 23, 1984).

53 47 Fed. Reg. 33,733 (1982), Consumer Product Safety Guide (CCH) ¶ 45,943 (August 4, 1982).

54 *Sabean*, *supra* note 52, testimony of Mrs. G, President, ______________, witness called by plaintiff.

A. They said that they had a customer complaint and that they had tested some garments and that they had failed.

Q. They had failed the C.S. 191–53 test? [now 16 C.F.R. 1610]

A. Yes.

* * *

COMMENT: Apparently, the company was aware of flame-retardant technology. This executive admitted that in prior years the company had contracted with other firms to use flame-retardant chenille fabric.[55]

Q. At any time in the seventies, either prior to the manufacture of the ______________ garment or subsequent to the manufacture of the ______________ garment, did you have the chenille treated for flame retardancy?

A. At one time we did.

Q. When was that time?

A. Prior to 1975. It must have been 1974.

* * *

Q. And why was it that you flame retarded the chenille fabric prior to 1975 and did not subsequently thereto?

A. Prior to 1975 we were doing this on contract for another firm and they were the ones who had it treated. Flame retarded.

* * *

COMMENT: Despite the garment's failure to pass federal flammability tests, the defendant guaranteed the garments' flame retardancy as required under the federal flammability

---

[55] *Id.*

act.[56] (Guarantees of flammability standard compliance were preprinted on all company invoices, as required under the Federal Flammable Fabrics Act.) To this plaintiff and consumers across America, these garments were safe. Plaintiff never had any reason to believe otherwise.

---

§ 4.17 Inaction by government and industry

Despite the availability of flame-retardant techniques and flame-resistant fibers for nearly twenty years, little has been done to give the public an effective choice between safe and unsafe products. Consumers have been kept in the dark by industry about the true nature and extent of the risks involved. Industry spokesmen have repeatedly asserted that the consumer would not pay the increased price for safety and that flame-retardant fabrics or treatments would be stiff or otherwise unacceptable to the consumer.[57] Thus, although government and industry officials have been aware of the horrors associated with burn injuries, many consumers remain uninformed and unaware that their clothing may be a fire hazard.

§ 4.18 Judicial intervention

Where industry and government have failed to act, the legal system has stepped in to ensure that justice is done. In a court of law, the source of ignition of a flammable garment may be irrelevant. The standard by which manufacturers are going to be judged is how this product acts when exposed to any source of ignition—e.g., ignition rate, burning rate, and flame temperature or intensity. Courts throughout the country have found that industry compliance with the Flammable Fabrics Act is not a defense to a products liability action, since industry knows full well the standard's inadequacies.[58] An item of clothing or other fabric-related article that meets these standards can still be considered negligently

---

[56] Federal Flammable Fabrics Act, Pub. L. No. 83–629, 68 Stat. 770 (1954).

[57] George F. Buck, Jr. (Research Director for the Nat'l Cotton Council), Final Report of the Joint Special Committee to Make an Investigation and Study Relative to the Manufacture, Sale, and Use of Flammable Clothing, at 37 (Commonwealth of Massachusetts, Nov. 1972).

[58] *See infra* § 4.32.

designed and manufactured or an unreasonably dangerous product.[59] Young children have recently won major victories when the courts found the manufacturers of flammable sleepwear negligent even though the garments were manufactured before the more stringent federal sleepwear standards went into effect. In the landmark decision of *Gryc v. Dayton Hudson Corp.*,[60] the Minnesota Supreme Court affirmed a $1 million punitive damage award against a children's sleepwear manufacturer, ruling that the company's conduct in manufacturing and marketing such a highly flammable garment created a substantial danger to the public. In *Gryc*, a five-year-old girl wearing a cotton flannelette nightgown was severely burned when she climbed on a hot kitchen oven to turn off a clock timer. The manufacturer raised as its defense its compliance with the federal flammability standard (the girl's garment was manufactured before the children's sleepwear standard required it to be flame-retardant), and that flame-retardant fabrics were not available at the time. The court found that flame-retardant technology had been available for years before the girl's garment was manufactured. The fact that the law did not require its use was no defense to the company's negligence.

V. Preventing Fabric-Related Burn Injuries

§ 4.19 Working for injury prevention

The agony of burn injuries resulting from ignition of clothing and other flammable household fabrics is not new, but we have today, as we have had for more than twenty years, the technology for ridding our marketplace of this menace. Just as the development and marketing of flame-retardant children's sleepwear produced important results in the reduction of children's burn injuries, similar aggressive research and manufacturing procedures must be initiated to spread this protection to other articles of clothing and other household products, such as upholstered furniture, carpets, and rugs.

Similarly, the federal government must formally recognize the failures of its so-called flammability standards and strive toward providing stringent, effective, mandatory standards for protecting all Americans from

---

[59] *See* Restatement (Second) of Torts § 402A (1965), pursuant to which strict liability may be imposed upon the company.

[60] 297 N.W.2d 727 (Minn.), *cert. denied*, 449 U.S. 921, 101 S. Ct. 320, 66 L. Ed. 2d 149 (1980).

the scourge of fabric-related burn injuries from synthetic as well as natural textile fabrics.

In the meantime, communications with consumers in the form of adequate warnings and education regarding fabric flammability are essential. Given that our households are surrounded by heat sources, including fireplaces, stoves, matches, cigarette lighters, and barbecue grills, it is absolutely imperative that consumers be educated regarding the hazards posed by flammable fabric combustion.

§ 4.20 Flame retardancy: protecting all Americans from flammable fabrics

Effective flame retardancy is that which causes a fabric to self-extinguish after a source of heat is removed. Technology to accomplish this purpose has been available for many years, but has been resisted by an industry more concerned about salability than safety.

More than ten years ago, strong and repeated consumer advocacy led the federal government to establish stringent mandatory standards requiring manufacture of flame-retardant sleepwear for children. At that time, industry members voiced opposition to this government initiative with claims that such standards would mean the death knell for their industry. Similar advocacy is needed today to provide these protections for all wearing apparel and other fabric products. It simply makes no sense that we should protect our children while they sleep, but not devote the resources to protect them while they are actively climbing atop kitchen ranges, playing near heaters, and otherwise making inevitable and foreseeable contacts with home heat sources. Nor does it make any sense not to extend this protection to all other Americans, particularly senior citizens whose physical aging may restrict their mobility and ability to escape once a fire ignites. If the technology is available for making our apparel and other household items flame retardant, which it is, then what are we waiting for other than the garment and textile industry's fear that flame-retardant products won't sell? Once it is forced to act, this industry will respond with a safer and marketable product. There is simply no need for the continued manufacture and marketing of flammable fabric products.

§ 4.21 Revising and strengthening flammability standards

It has been widely recognized for years that the federal government's so-called flammability safety standards are inadequate to protect consumers from fabric-related burn injuries.[61] Most of the tests mandated by the federal government have little relation to actual full-scale fire environments. With the exception of standards for children's sleepwear, current federal requirements take no account of major advances in the development of flame-retardant processes. Testing procedures are inadequate and do not effectively simulate normal use conditions or common accident patterns. Under these standards, the average, fully clothed adult or child, when exposed to a source of ignition, will become a human torch in a matter of moments.

Of immediate concern is the standard's failure to test for the meltdown reaction of many synthetic textiles. As demonstrated in *Hinckley*,[62] this deficiency permits the continued marketing of synthetic fabric-based products that, when exposed to heat, can melt into a sticky, lavalike mass that clings to human skin and causes serious burn injuries. Yet current standards are silent on this melting characteristic of the fabric residue. It is imperative that standard-setting authorities in government and the private sector take these hazards into account when formulating new and more stringent fabric flammability standards.

Flammability standards must also be revised to establish quantitative measures for ease of ignition, flame intensity, heat generation, and heat transfer; for flame-spread time independent of ignition time; and for the fabric's self-extinguishing capability when the source of heat is removed.

§ 4.22 Enforcing existing standards

Despite their obvious deficiencies, some manufacturers continue to manufacture and market products that fail even existing flammability standards. The federal government's Consumer Product Safety Commission recently brought an administrative action against one company whose garments failed to pass these standards.[63] Several consumers were horribly burned and some died when these products ignited. This agency, and applicable state agencies, must continue to monitor the marketplace aggressively to identify and seize dangerous fabric products before tragic burn injuries can strike.

---

[61] *See supra* note 19. *See also* E. SWARTZ, PROOF OF PRODUCT DEFECTS, ch. 7, *Flammable Fabrics* (Lawyers Co-op. 1985).

[62] *Hinckley*, supra note 3.

[63] *See supra* note 53.

§ 4.23 Reducing hazards from unsafe fabric design

In case after case involving flammable clothing, I have witnessed the hazardous nature of flammable fabric exacerbated by the product's unsafe design. One example is the design of children's garments with buttons down the back. Should the garment ignite, this design makes removal before serious injury occurs all but impossible. Another example is the flowing sleeves on women's bathrobes and gowns, an open invitation to disaster from such an everyday act as leaning over a kitchen stove to heat a pot of coffee.

§ 4.24 Sounding the alarm for safer products

Manufacturers like to tell us that fabric-related burn injuries are our own fault, not theirs, and that they should not be held responsible for our "carelessness." We can all be careless at times. Yet it is not sufficient to say that it is a damned foolish thing to put a flammable garment in a situation where there are matches, cigarettes, kitchen stoves, or other ignition sources. It is not sufficient because we know that we are going to lean over our stoves, smoke our cigarettes, and light our matches, and that some accidents will, indeed, happen. We also know that flames can start when flammable garments are exposed to these ignition sources. To make matters worse, the manufacturers know this. However, they have consistently failed to warn consumers that their products are flammable and that tragedy can strike at the drop of a match!

Why the silence? One overriding reason accounts for it—fear of reduced sales. Despite the availability for more than two decades of flame-retardant techniques and inherently flame-retardant fibers, little effort has been made either to give the public an effective choice between safe and unsafe products or to give effective warnings that the products they buy may be time bombs ready to ignite. Industry officials have repeatedly stated their position that consumers would not pay the additional price required for flame-retardant fabrics or that flame-retardant fabrics would be stiff or otherwise unacceptable to consumers. These excuses merely disguise an appalling and pervasive lack of concern for safety in the marketing of fabrics.

When will this silence end? When will industry members adopt new technologies to protect Americans from the flammable fabrics? And when will our public safety officials take firm action to force renewed research, development, and application of flame-retardant technologies to prevent further torch-case tragedies?

§ 4.25 A joint effort for injury prevention

Members of the medical, scientific, government, and legal communities can and must work together to eradicate the plague of burn injuries produced by combustion of flammable fabrics. Members of these professions can be the consumer's most effective spokesmen in forcing industries to rework their products in consideration of safety. Attorneys and members of the medical profession deal daily with the victims of this assault on the human person. Our access and credibility enables us to influence members of industry and government officials toward greater recognition of safety in the products they produce and, hopefully, the elimination of flammability hazards from textiles and other fabric products. We must work together to make injury prevention a priority in our professions and share our knowledge of flammable fabrics with the public at large.

We must also work hand in hand with members of the scientific community, whose expertise and research advances have led to the development of technologies for preventing burn injuries. These technologies must be incorporated in fabric product development as well as those standards and regulations that govern this process. Only then will we ensure the protection of American consumers from the scourge of fabric-related burn injuries.

§ 4.26 What can lawyers do?

Lawyers have an important and vital role to play in the prevention of burn injuries from flammable fabrics. Our skills and training make us particularly well-suited to lead the fight for safer clothing and other fabric-related articles. We understand the workings of state and federal governments; we are skilled in the ways of legislative and regulatory drafting; and we have the resources to challenge the purveyors of flammable fabrics in the courts, to make them pay the price for continued marketing of flammable products.

Can lawyers make an impact on industry members who are hesitant to produce safe products for economic reasons? Consider the following excerpt from an industry publication:

> A $1,415,000 judgment this past June resulted from a lawsuit against a manufacturer and distributor of a blanket which caught fire and burned two children. This was the largest single money judgment ever given in the nation for personal injury inflicted by

> flammable fabrics, according to the court. What is obvious from this case is shocking enough. Multiply the number of units you produced last year by $1.4 million, and add reported legal fees of more than half a million dollars for each such case, and it becomes even more shocking. Lurking "beneath the water" is the fact that the plaintiff's lawyer in this case revealed that he was handling more than 22 flammable fabrics cases at that time. *How many can you afford before you lost product liability coverage*? [emphasis added][64]

While the deterrent impact of large money judgments is certainly encouraging, we must still wonder when industry will learn that it is more economical to prevent burn injuries before they occur than to pay the cost of compensating burned victims for injuries that can only be described as among the worst known to man.

VI. Litigation Sources: Bibliography

§ 4.27 Selected technical sources

1982 Flame Retardant Buyers' Guide, 71 Am. Dyestuff Rep. 17–20 (Jan. 1982).

Study sees Europeans increasing fire retardant chemicals consumption, 10 Am. Dyestuff Rep. 51 (June 1981).

Flame Retardants Buyers' Guide, 70 Am. Dyestuff Rep. 15–20 (Jan. 1981).

Baltinger & Haynes, *Furniture Flammability: fabric opportunities*, 50 Textile Research J. 201–4 (Mar. 1980).

Bandyopadhyay, Mehta & D'Souza, *Evaluation of Flame-Retardant Textiles in Retrospect*, *Flame-Retardant Finishing of Textiles*, The State of the Art in India 229–264 (May 1982).

Beninate, et al., *Durable flame-retardant treatments for blends of cotton, wool, and polyester*, 51 Textile Research J. 217–24 (Apr. 1981).

Benisek & Craven, *Machine Washable, Flame-Retardant, Water, Oil, Petrol, and Acid Repellent Wool*, 54 Textile Research J. 350–352, No. 5 (May 1984).

Crangle & Hanvey, *Flame Retardant Polypropylene Textiles, Poly-*

[64] Swartz, *Techniques of Direct Examination: Illustrative Testimony in a Flammable Fabrics Case*, in PERSONAL INJURY ANNUAL (Matthew Bender & Co. 1974).

propylene Fibres and Textiles (Third Int'l Conference Oct. 4–6, 1983).

Crown & Brown, *Flame retardance as a criterion in textile product evaluation: a conjoint analysis approach*, 8 J. Consumer Product Flammability 221–34 (Dec. 1981).

Daigle & Frank, *Chemistry of Hydroxymethyl Phosphorous Compounds, part 4: Ammonia, Amines, and THPOH: A Chemical Approach to Flame Retardancy*, 52 Textile Research J. 738–750, No. 12 (Dec. 1982).

Damant, et al., *Cigarette Ignition Behavior of Commercial Upholstery Cover Fabrics*, 9 J. Consumer Product Flammability 31–46 (Mar. 1982).

Dardis & Stremel, *Economic Analysis of a Flammability Standard for Adult Clothing*, 8 J. Consumer Product Flammability 16–26 (Mar. 1981).

Day, et al., *Systematic study of the effects of individual constructional components on the flammability characteristics of a carpet*, 49 Textile Research J. 88–93 (Feb. 1979).

Dufresne, *Status of Flammability Standards*, 70 Am. Dyestuff Rep. 27 (Jan. 1981).

Gadalla, et al., *Kinetics of Pyrolysis of Some Fire Retardants and Treated Fabrics*, 30 Am. Inst. Chemical Engineers' J. 50–55 (Jan. 1984).

Gerber & Sallay, *New Flame Retardant Compositions*, 62 Chemical Engineering News 4–5, No. 15 (Apr. 9, 1984).

Gonzalez & Kullman, *Flame Retardant Durable Press Finishing of Lightweight Cotton/Polyester Fabrics*, 7 J. Consumer Product Flammability 218–28 (Dec. 1980).

Holme & Patel, *Effects of N-Methylol Finishing Treatments on the Flammability of Polyester Cotton Fabrics, in Blended Textiles* 354–372 (38th All India Textile Conference Papers Nov. 18–20, 1981).

Hsieh & Hardin, *Effects of Selected Inorganic Salts on Cotton Flammability: Untreated Cotton in the Vertical Test and Oxygen Index Text*, 54 Textile Research J. 171–9 (Mar. 1984).

Textile Flammability: An Industry Update, 61 Industrial Fabric Products Rev. 52, No. 1 (May 1984).

Where Do We Stand On Flammability?, 169 Int'l Dyer, Textile Printer, and Bleacher, and Finisher 30, No. 1 (Jan. 1984).

Le Blanc, *Textile Flammability Update*, 144 Textile Indus. 82–83 (Feb. 1980).

LeBlanc, *What's Available for FR Textiles*, 143 Textile Indus., 78–80 (Feb. 1979).

Mehta, *Fire Retardant/Durable Press Finishing of Lightweight Cotton/Polyester Fabric*, 70 Am. Dyestuff Rep. 27–33 (Aug. 1981).

Miles, et al., *Extinguishability of Flammable Textiles*, 5 J. Consumer Product Flammability, 135–162 (Sept. 1980).

Miller, et al., *Fabric Ignition by Flame Impingement*, 50 Textile Research J. 256–60 (Aug. 1980).

Mock, *An Update in Flame Retardants*, 28 Plastic Engineering 17–19 (Feb. 1982).

Needles, *Care of Flame Retardant Treated Fabrics*, 8 J. Consumer Product Flammability 27–34 (Mar. 1981).

Neumeyer, *Comparison of Smolder Resistance Standards for Boric Acid Treated Cotton Batting*, 9 J. Consumer Product Flammability 3–10 (Mar. 1982).

Niemann, *Flame Retardant Bedding with Help of Trevira CS*, 35 Reiniger-Waescher 28 (Dec. 1982).

Pintauro & Buchanan, *Ignition Process in Single and Multicomponent Polyester/Cotton Textile Structures*, 49 Textile Research J. 326–34 (June 1979).

Reeves, *Comparing some flame tests on slow-burning fabrics*, 71 Am. Dyestuff Rep. 12–13 (Jan. 1982).

Reeves & Hammons, *Horizontal burning rates of fabrics with low add-ons of fire retardant*, 50 Textile Research J. 245–49 (Apr. 1980).

Robenstine & Blouin, *Effects of education and other factors on consumers' priorities for flame retardant protection in apparel fabrics*, 8 J. Consumer Product Flammability 144–57 (Sept. 1981).

Roschke, *Development of Textile Flammability Standards in Australia*, 7 J. Consumer Product Flammability 133–46 (Sept. 1980).

Rowland & Hobart, *Flame temperatures and burning rates of cotton and two flame retardant cotton fabrics*, 9 J. Fire Retardant Chemistry 135–52 (May 1982).

Rucker, *Consumer Concerns About Furniture Flammability*, 7 J. Consumer Product Flammability 235–49 (Dec. 1980).

Rucker, et al., *Evaluation of Three Types of Flame Retardant Children's Sleepwear Before and After Home Use*, 8 J. Consumer Product Flammability 169–82 (S 1981).

Seidel, *Flame-Safe SEF Modacrylic*, 145 Textile Indus. 54 (Dec. 1981).

Spivak, et al., *Impact of two potential flammability standards on adult sleepwear and dresses*, 9 J. Consumer Product Flammability 66–76 (June 1982).

Summers, et al., *Durable fire resistant durable press finish for cotton and polyester cotton fabrics*, 70 Am. Dyestuff Rep. 24–26 (Jan. 1981).

Tesoro, *Fire Safety of Upholstered Furniture: An Evaluation of the State-of-the Art and Potential Improvements*, 8 J. Consumer Product Flammability 132–43 (June 1981).

A Review of New Products, 15 Textile Chemist & Colorist 37–50 (Jan. 1983).

Toner, *Ignition of Foam/Fabric Composites in Residential Upholstered Furniture*, 9 J. Consumer Product Flammability 85–95 (June 1982).

Trask, et al., *Flammability Rates of Flame Retardant Cotton Blends After Surface and Edge Ignition*, 9 J. Fire Retardant Chemistry 53–69 (May 1982).

Trent, et al., *Design and construction of a thermally-instrumented mannequin for measuring the burn injury potential of wearing apparel*, 49 Textile Research J. 639–47 (Nov. 1979).

Vail, Daigle & Frank, *Chemistry of Hydroxymethyl Phosphorous Compounds, Part 1: Introduction*, 52 Textile Research J. 671–77 (Nov. 1982).

Weil, Fearing & Jaffe, *Oligomeric Phosphorous Esters with Flame Retardant Utility*, 9 J. Fire Retardant Chemistry 39–49 (Feb. 1982).

§ 4.28 Selected popular sources

Alter, *Family Circle's Guide to Easy-Care Fabrics*, 95 Fam. Circle 109, No. 3 (Feb. 23, 1982).

More Cotton on Men's Durable Press Shirts, 60 Consumers' Research 24–25, No. 3 (1977).

Thermal Underwear: Which is Warmest?, 193 Good Housekeeping 232, No. 4 (Oct. 1981).

S-T-R-E-T-C-H Fabrics, 192 Good Housekeeping 236, No. 5 (May 1981).

Men's Shirts: Our Textiles Experts Answer Your Biggest Questions, 182 Good Housekeeping 183, No. 6 (June 1976).

Ralph Nader Reports, 93 Ladies Home J. 58, No. 3 (1976).

Nader, *4,000 Fatal Fabric Fires: The Burned Children*, 165 New Republic 19–21 (July 3, 1971).

Richards, *The Complex Problem of Flammability Legislation*, 55 Consumer Bull. 20–22 (Sept. 1972).

Russell, *Sounding the Alarm for Better Burns Treatment*, 54 Today's Health 40–43 (Mar. 1976).

Satterfield, *Warming Up With Down*, 22 Consumers Digest 37–39, No. 6 (Sept.-Oct. 1983).

Trunzo, *Super Sweaters*, 10 Money 133–134, No. 10 (Oct. 1981).

§ 4.29 Selected government sources

Guide to Fabric Flammability (Consumer Product Safety Comm'n June 1976).

Children's Sleepwear 1975: Consumer Deputy Program (Final Report, Consumer Product Safety Comm'n 1975).

Fire Safety Research (N.B.S. Special Publication 411, U.S. Dep't of Commerce 1974).

Fire Incidents Involving Sleepwear Worn by Children Ages 6–12 (N.B.S. Tech. Note No. 810, U.S. Dep't of Commerce 1973).

Mathers & Klam, *When Clothing Ignites* (FDA Consumer, U.S. Dep't of Health, Education & Welfare Oct. 1972).

Matches and Lighters in Flammable Fabric Incidents: The Magnitude of the Problem (N.B.S. Tech. Note No. 750, 1972).

Young, *Burn-Resistant Fabrics: There's Hope Ahead* (FDA Papers July-Aug. 1971).

FDA Papers (FDA Annual Report 1971).

Fibers and Fabrics (N.B.S., U.S. Dep't of Commerce 1970).

A Community Action Approach for Prevention of Burn Injuries (U.S. Dep't of Health, Education & Welfare 1969).

The Silent Epidemic (Medical Communications Dep't Shriner's Burn Institute, Galveston Unit).

Flammable Fabrics and the Elderly (Consumer Product Safety Comm'n).

Fire Incidents Involving the Ignition of Sleepwear Worn by Children Under the Age of Three (N.B.S. Tech. Note No. 815, U.S. Dep't of Commerce Feb. 1974).

§ 4.30 Selected legal sources

Flammability of Fabrics, 14 Am. Jur. *P.O.F.* (1964).

Textile Identification and Clothing Hazards, 13 Am. Jur. *P.O.F.* 649 (1963).

The Use of Discovery in Product-Related Burn Injury Cases, 22 Am. Jur. *Trials* 199 (1975).

Products Liability: Protective Clothing and Equipment, 27 A.L.R. 4th 815 (1984).

Products Liability: Flammable Clothing, 1 A.L.R. 4th 251 (1980).

Expert and Opinion Evidence as to Cause or Origin of Fire, 88 A.L.R. 2d 230 (1963).

Armstrong, *The Human Torch—An Exegesis About the Clothes We Wear*, 23 S.C.L. Rev. 787-803 (1971).

15 ATLA Newsletter 105 (Apr. 1972) (the plaintiff's experts demonstrate that ordinary toilet paper can pass the federal flammability standard).

Campbell & Vargo, *The Flammable Fabrics Act and Strict Liability in Tort*, 9 Ind. L. Rev. 395 (1976).

Church, *Scientific Aspects of Clothing Fires*, 1 J. Prod. Liability No. 1 (1977).

Comment, *Dressed to Kill—The Flammable Fabrics Act of 1953—Twenty Years in Retrospect*, 4 Cum.-Sam. L. Rev. 358 (1973).

Hoffman & Hoffman, *Use of Standards in Products Liability Litigation*, 30 Drake L. Rev. 283 (1980-81).

R. Hursch & H. Bailey, *American Law of Products Liability*, ch. 31, *Lia-*

bility for Injury Caused by Clothing or Wearing Apparel, Combs, and Like Products, (Lawyers Co-op, 2d ed. 1976).

Note, *The Flammable Fabrics Act Protection: Fire Resistants vs. Industry Resistants*, 39 Geo. Wash. L. Rev. 608 (1971).

E. Swartz, *Proof of Product Defect*, ch. 7, *Flammable Fabrics* (Lawyers Co-op. 1984).

Swartz, *Will It Happen Again?*, 104 Archives of Surgery 19 (1972).

Swartz, *The Torch Cases*, 67 Case & Comment, No. 1 (Jan.-Feb. 1971).

Swartz, *Preventing Burn Injuries*, 8 J. of Nursing Ad. 9, No. 1 (Jan.-Feb. 1973).

E. Swartz, *Hazardous Products Litigation* (Lawyers Co-op. 1973 & Supps.).

§ 4.31 Selected newsletters

APBIC News
Action for Prevention of Burn Injuries to Children
P.O. Box 347
Burlington, Mass. 01803

Am. Burn Ass'n Newsletter
c/o C.F. Hartford, M.D.
Crozer-Chester Medical Center
15th and Upland
Chester, Pa. 19013

The Icarus File
The Phoenix Society, Inc.
11 Rust Hill Rd.
Levittown, Pa. 19056

International Soc'y for Burn Injuries Newsletter
4200 East 9th Ave.
Box C–309
Denver, Colo. 80262

Fabrics: Retail

Swatches
National Ass'n of Decorative Fabric Distributors
180 North Michigan Ave., Suite 1710
Chicago, Ill. 60601

SFM
California State Fire Marshall's Office
7171 Bowling Drive
Suite 800
Sacramento, Cal. 95823

Fire News
National Fire Protection Ass'n
Battery Park March
Quincy, Mass. 02269

Firewatch
National Ass'n of Fire Equipment Distributors
111 East Wacker Drive
Chicago, Ill. 60601

Sparky News
National Fire Protection Ass'n
Battery Park March
Quincy, Mass. 02269

Upholstered Furniture Manufacturers' Ass'n
Bulletin
276 5th Ave.
New York, N.Y. 10001

Hosiery Newsletter
National Ass'n of Hosiery Mfrs.
516 Charlottetown Mall
Charlotte, N.C. 28204

NATAD Newsletter
National Ass'n of Textile and Apparel Distributors
New York Statler Hotel, Rm. 104
401 7th Ave.
New York, N.Y. 10001

TRI News and Research Briefs
Textile Research Institute
P.O. Box 625
Princeton, N.J. 08540

Textile Info Sources and Resources
Textile Information Sources
1587 3rd Ave.
New York, N.Y. 10028

Textile News and Notes
Schumann Intergroup, Inc.
18 Monterey Drive
Manhasset Hills, N.Y. 11040

The Textile Booklist
Textile Information Sources
1587 3rd Ave.
New York, N.Y. 10028

§ 4.32 Selected laws and standards

Statutes

(1) Consumer Product Safety Act of 1972, 15 U.S.C. §§ 2051–2086 (1972).

(2) Federal Flammable Fabrics Act, 15 U.S.C. §§ 1191–1204 (1972).

Federal Flammability Standards

(1) Standard for the flammability of clothing textiles, 16 C.F.R.§ 1610 (1985).

(2) Standard for the flammability of children's sleepwear sizes 0–6x, 16 C.F.R. § 1615 (1985).

(3) Standard for the flammability of children's sleepwear sizes 7–14, 16 C.F.R. § 1616 (1985).

(4) Standard for the surface flammability of carpets and rugs, 16 C.F.R. § 1630 (1985).

(5) Standard for the surface flammability of small carpets and rugs, 16 C.F.R. § 1631 (1985).

(6) Standard for the flammability of mattress (and mattress pads), 16 C.F.R. § 1632 (1985).

Voluntary Standards

(1) American Society for Testing Materials (ASTM):

- (a) D 461: Felt.
- (b) D 1230: Clothing Textiles.
- (c) D 4108: Thermal Clothing.

(d) D 4151: Blankets.

(2) National Fire Protection Association (NFPA):

(a) NFPA FC–260A–83: Cigarette Ignition Resistance in Components of Upholstered Furniture.

(b) NFPA FC–701–77: Flame Resistant Textiles and Films.

(c) NFPA FC–702–80: Flammability of Wearing Apparel.

§ 4.33 Selected cases

Montano v. Lees Mfg. Co., No. 173577 (Cal. Super. Ct. Mar. 15, 1979), 22 ATLA L. Rep. 232 (June 1979), **polyester-filled quilted robe**.

Sears, Roebuck & Co. v. Reliance Ins. Co., 654 F.2d 494 (7th Cir. [Ill.] 1981), **girl's slacks**; wrongful death.

Ervin v. Sears, Roebuck & Co., 36 Ill. App. 3d 64, 343 N.E.2d 220, *aff'd*, 65 Ill. 2d 140, 357 N.E.2d 500 (1976), **thermal underwear**.

Dyson v. Sears, Roebuck & Co., No. 73–L–10391 (Ill. Cir. Ct. May 30, 1979), **cotton nightgown**; settlement of $1 million.

Nichols v. Union Underwear Co., 602 S.W.2d 429 (Ky. 1980), **child's t-shirt**; design defect.

Howard v. McCreary Corp., 601 F.2d 133 (4th Cir. [Md.] 1979), **bathrobe**; child's death; relevancy of federal standards.

Sabean v. Edgewood Chenille, Inc., No. 82–2047T (D. Mass. Oct. 23, 1984), **cotton chenille bathrobe**; federal flammability standards.

Koslowski v. Sears, Roebuck & Co., No. 75–1370–J (D. Mass. Apr. 1981), 24 ATLA L. Rep. 202 (June 1981), **child's flannelette pajamas**; settled during trial for $250,000.

Jette v. Arlan's Dep't Stores and Gort Industries, No. 74–2400 (D. Mass. 1979), **synthetic poncho**; severe burns.

Teixeira v. Her Majesties Industries, No. CA–73–567–C (D. Mass. Feb. 23, 1979), **cotton flannelette nightgown**; severe burns.

Billings v. W.T. Grant, Inc. (D. Mass. 1979), 23 ATLA L. Rep. 60 (Mar. 1980), **flannelette nightgown homemade with cotton and rayon fibers**; settlement of $1.5 million.

Hinckley v. Eastman Kodak Co., No. 69–1338–J (D. Mass. June 6, 1973), **polyester fiberfill comforter**; burns cause disfigurement.

Belanger, PPA v. Barth, No. CA–73–747–C (D. Mass.), **terry cloth novelty bib**; severe burns; settlement of $390,000.

Gryc v. Dayton Hudson Corp., 297 N.W.2d 727 (Minn.), *cert. denied*, 449 U.S. 921, 101 S. Ct. 320, 66 L. Ed. 2d 149 (1980), **flannelette children's pajamas**; compliance with federal standards does not bar punitive damages award.

Bigham v. J.C. Penney Co., 268 N.W.2d 892 (Minn. 1978), **polyester cotton work shirt**; "melt and cling" effect; failure to warn.

Raymond v. Riegel Textile Corp., 484 F.2d 1025 (1st Cir. [N.H.] 1973), **flannelette nightgown**; state recovery despite compliance with federal standards.

Paculius v. Guilford Mills, No. L–45057–74 (N.J. Super. Ct. Sept. 20, 1977), 21 ATLA L. Rep. 180 (May 1978), **triacetate robe**; settlement of $50,000.

Stephens v. Alexander's Inc. (N.Y. Sup. Ct. 1983), 27 ATLA L. Rep. 182 (May 1984), **polyester leisure suit**; 100% retailer liability; $1.1 million settlement in lieu of appeal.

Shanks v. K-Mart Dep't Store, No. D–90609 (N.Y. Sup. Ct. Oct. 3, 1979), 23 ATLA L. Rep. 406 (Feb. 1980), **polyester t-shirt**; settlement of $160,000.

Genesco Inc. v. Cone Mills Corp., 604 F.2d 281 (4th Cir. [N.C.] 1979), **nightgown**.

Ross v. Spiegel, 53 Ohio App. 2d 297, 7 Ohio Op. 3d 385, 373 N.W.2d 1288 (1977), **pajamas**; wrongful death.

Ethredge v. Amway Corp. (N.D. Okla. 1982), 26 ATLA L. Rep. 36 (Feb. 1983), **cotton chenille lounger**; settlement of $1 million.

Spenser v. Nelson Sales Co., 620 P.2d 477 (Okla. Ct. App. 1980), **long quilted, insulated underwear**; design defect; improper jury instruction.

Smith v. J.C. Penney Co., 269 Or. 643, 525 P.2d 1299 (1974), **synthetic "fake fur" coat**.

Weems v. CBS Imports Corp., 46 Or. App. 539, 612 P.2d 323 (1980), **cotton flannel pajamas**; failure to treat with flame retardant; design defect; improper jury instruction.

Carter v. Joseph Bancroft & Sons, Co., 360 F. Supp. 1103 (E.D. Pa. 1973), **"Ban-Lon" dress**; liability of trademark licensor.

Walason v. Ann & Hope Factory Outlet, Inc., No. 74–3510 (R.I. Super. Ct. Feb. 28, 1979), 22 ATLA L. Rep. 232 (June 1979), **cotton flannel pajamas**; inadequate treatment with flame retardant; settlement of $50,000.

Nelson By Carson v. Park Indus., Inc., 717 F.2d 1120 (7th Cir. [Wis.] 1983), **flannel shirt**.

Stick v. K-Mart Apparel of Wis., No. 450–569 (Wis. Cty. Cir. Ct. Nov. 27, 1979), 23 ATLA L. Rep. 60 (Mar. 1980), **100% interwoven cotton flannel pajamas**; failure to pass federal flammability standards for children's sleepwear; settlement of $4.7 million.

Schwenn v. Pamida, 392 F. Supp. 69 (D. Wyo. 1975), **nylon jacket**.

Chapter 5

ELECTRICAL MAYHEM

KLUWER LITIGATION LIBRARY REFERENCES

HARLEY & MAGEE, WHAT'S IT WORTH? A GUIDE TO CURRENT PERSONAL INJURY AWARDS AND SETTLEMENTS.

JEANS, LITIGATION: Chapter 4, *Discovery*; Chapter 8, *Direct Examination*; Chapter 9, *Direct Examination of Expert Witnesses*; Chapter 13, *Cross-Examination*; Chapter 14, *Cross-Examination of Expert Witnesses*.

SMITH & MALANDRO, COURTROOM COMMUNICATION STRATEGIES: Chapter 1, *Impression Formation in the Courtroom*; Chapter 2, *Persuasive Strategies in the Courtroom*; Chapter 5, *Preparing for Effective Courtroom Communication*; Chapter 8, *Direct Examination: Presenting the Evidence with Impact*; Chapter 9, *Cross-Examination: Controlling the Case*.

I. Introduction

§ 5.01 In general

American households are filled with electrically operated devices and gadgets that provide us with worlds of pleasure and convenience when they are designed for safety and function properly. When they are defective, however, the damage they cause can be devastating. For a consumer using a defective hair dryer, electric blanket, smoke detector, or automobile battery, or whose home is not correctly wired or is wired with a product that is not designed for safety, slaughter by product can mean catastrophic fire or explosion.

§ 5.02 Focus on product itself

In my practice, I have continually represented consumers who have fallen victim to these defective products: the girl who was brutally burned when her portable hair dryer overheated because it was designed without safety thermostats or adequate warnings for safe use because such warnings would not be "aesthetically pleasing";[1] the father whose three children perished in a blaze that consumed their household when the smoke detector he had purchased to protect his family from such a disaster failed to sound its alarm the night that fire broke out;[2] or the young man who lost sight in one of his eyes when his automobile battery exploded without warning.[3]

Like other cases of slaughter by product, it's easy, at first glance, to question the fact pattern and ask whether it presents a viable case for liability. In the case study that follows,[4] a seven-year-old girl was horribly burned and permanently disfigured when her hair dryer overheated in her bed, igniting nearby bedding and transforming her room into a mass of flame. The minor plaintiff was using the product in her bed to warm her feet. Should she have known better? Was she at fault for using this product for this purpose? Were the companies that manufactured and distributed this product responsible for protecting young children from what they alleged was misuse of their product? By asking the right questions, I was able to learn how the companies responsible for manufacturing and marketing the culpable product chose to design it without available safety technology and to keep consumers in the dark regarding its dangers. This case illustrates how an effective approach can reveal the callous, corporate attitude and negligent manufacturing and marketing practices that resulted in a living hell for an unsuspecting child.

---

[1] Toman v. Superior Elec. Prod., No. 73–4091–S (D. Mass. May 11, 1978).

[2] Laaperi v. Sears, Roebuck & Co., No. 79–2497–T, *et seq*. (D. Mass. Oct. 23, 1984).

[3] Boyd v. General Motors, No. 61472 (Mass. Super. Ct. Feb. 23, 1979).

[4] *See infra* §§ 5.05 *et seq*.

II. Checklists

§ 5.03 Checklist: Investigation of an electrical appliance-related injury case

The following checklist is intended to assist counsel in the preparation of an electrical appliance injury claim:

____(1) Take immediate steps to gain possession and secure the appliance

____(2) From the victim or from witnesses, reconstruct exactly what happened at the time of injury

____(3) Obtain the following information:

____(a) Manufacturer of appliance

____(b) Retailer of appliance

____(c) Serial and model number

____(d) Date of manufacture

____(e) Public records relating to patents on appliance

____(4) Obtain either the original or a duplicate of the packaging of the appliance

____(5) Collect all advertisements and promotional materials for the appliance

____(6) Collect any inserts, warnings, warranties, instructions, safety tags, or other relevant materials packaged with the product

____(7) Develop potential theories of liability and consider all potential defendants against whom such theories might be asserted:

____(a) Design defect

____(b) Manufacturing defect

____(c) Failure to warn

____(d) Breach of warranty

____(e) Strict liability

____(f) Unreasonably dangerous

____(g) Negligence

____(h) Other

____(8) Determine if the appliance has ever been recalled

____(9) Determine if any modifications were made to the appliance by:

____(a) Vendor

____(b) Customer

____(c) Repairman

____(d) User

____(10) Determine what safety testing, if any, had been done on this appliance

____(11) Determine if safety features of appliances were available on competing models but not on the model that caused the injury

____(12) Examine the medical literature to determine if there are reports of other injuries from this product

____(13) Research law reviews and treatises on electrical appliance cases

____(14) Contact the following to determine what information, if any, is available regarding the product:

____(a) U.S. Consumer Product Safety Commission

____(b) American Society of Mechanical Engineers

____(c) Underwriters Laboratories

____(d) U.S. Department of Commerce, National Bureau of Standards

____(e) ATLA Exchange

____(f) ATLA Law Reporter

____(g) ATLA Product Liability Law Reporter

§ 5.04 Checklist: Resources for an electrical product-related injury case

The following list can be a valuable source of information for counsel when preparing his electrical product-related personal injury case.

____(1) Selected technical sources

____(a) Electrical Engineering

____(b) Electrotech

____(c) Journal of Scientific Instruments

____(d) Electronics Journal

____(e) General Electronics Review

____(f) Product Engineering

____(g) Journal of Applied Physics

____(h) Machine Design

____(i) Electrical Manufacturing

____(j) Journal of the American Society of Safety Engineers

____(k) Electron Power

____(2) Selected popular sources

____(a) Consumer Reports

____(b) Popular Science

____(c) Mechanix Illustrated

____(d) Consumers' Research

____(e) Canadian Consumer

____(f) Which? (Great Britain)

____(g) Popular Electronics

____(3) Selected government sources

____(a) U.S. Consumer Product Safety Commission

____(b) U.S. Department of Commerce, National Bureau of Standards

____(c) U.S. Army Research and Development Command

____(4) Selected industry sources

____(a) Association of Home Appliance Manufacturers

____(b) National Electrical Manufacturers Association

____(c) The Electrical Women's Round Table, Inc.

____(d) International Association of Electrical Leagues

____(e) International Association of Electrical Inspectors

____(f) American Society of Safety Engineers

____(g) Electric Technicians' Association

III. Case Study: The Case of the Too Hot Hair Dryer[5]

§ 5.05 Facts

I like to tell my fellow members of the bar that there are three things a good plaintiff's lawyer needs to be successful: compassion, a sense of timing, and a killer instinct. I had the opportunity to use all three in a case involving an item found in almost any household across America—a portable electric hair dryer. All hair dryers produce heat. Most are designed with safety features to prevent them from overheating. Unfortunately, not this one.

The victim of this hazardous product was a seven-year-old girl. The night tragedy struck, this minor plaintiff apparently had carried the dryer into the bedroom and placed it next to her feet. In the middle of the night, she awoke to find her bed and her pajamas on fire. Her mother recalled what happened next:[6]

> I woke up. . . . She was screaming. I came to her room I found her ablaze, standing like a torch in the doorway. I dragged her. . . . I just dragged her to the bathroom to douse her with water to extinguish the flames. . . . I put her under the shower . . . and she kept screaming. . . . My husband came to the shower, and he turned off the water, and she jumped out of the shower, trembling and shaking. . . . The next thing I remember was somebody [handing] me a blanket and my extinguishing her with it. Then running to the bedroom. . . . I think she was naked. After she was extinguished, I called up the Fire Department. . . . Then I kept her in the bedroom, trying not to hurt. She was jumping with fright, she just—must have been in terrible pain, she just kept jumping and screaming, and I was crying and waiting for the ambulance to come and take her to the hospital.

COMMENT: On direct examination the injured client should give a vivid and detailed explanation of what happened. The horror of reliving those events will be difficult, but the jury must be brought to stand in the shoes of the

[5] *See supra* note 1.

[6] *Toman, supra* note 1, testimony of the plaintiff's mother, witness for the plaintiff.

victim and experience the horror. The witness must be properly prepared for this moment, for it is a critical stage of the plaintiff's case.

---

§ 5.06 Analysis of case

When an item is designed for marketability, such as this one was, with no adequate warnings to consumers of its capacity to overheat and ignite into flames, somebody must pay the price of this uncaring practice. Should it be the child who is horribly burned and permanently disfigured over 50% of her body after the dryer ignites her bedding in the middle of the night as she lies asleep in her bed? I don't think so. Responsibility must lie with the company that: (1) continues to manufacture and market this product without a safety device that would prevent a tragedy by shutting off the appliance before overheating could produce catastrophe; (2) has notice of ignitions and consumer complaints of fires igniting when their dryers overheated, yet fails to warn consumers adequately of this safety risk; and (3) knows consumers use the product for other uses besides drying hair. Additionally, responsibility must lie with the company that marketed the product even though its president testified under oath that warnings of safe use and the product's propensity to overheat if its vents are covered were not provided because such a warning would not be "aesthetically pleasing."[7]

§ 5.07 Foreseeable use of product

An important step in any product liability lawsuit is establishing that the use of the product by the injured consumer was foreseeable to the manufacturer. In this case, the president of the manufacturing company conceded in trial depositions that the dryer was being used in an ordinary and foreseeable manner at the time of the accident.[8]

Q. Could you warm your hands with it?

A. I suppose you could.

Q. Could you warm your face with it, if you were chilly?

---

[7] *Toman, supra* note 1, testimony of Mr. S, president, ______________, witness for the defendant.

[8] *Toman, supra* note 1, testimony of Mr. B, president, ______________, witness for the defendant.

A. If you wished, yes.

Q. You could dry your hair with it, right?

A. That's right.

Q. So it could be used to provide heat for either drying hair or warming your person?

A. It could be.

The defendant's answers to requests for admissions revealed its knowledge of this foreseeable use of its product, and that such use could result in a tragic fire.[9]

> 193. [A] hair dryer, such as the hair dryer involved in this lawsuit, could possibly be used by a person sitting in bed. Admitted.
>
> * * *
>
> 206. [I]t is foreseeable that a hair dryer, such as the hair dryer involved in this lawsuit, may be used to warm a user's face and hands. Admitted.
>
> * * *
>
> 210. There is a danger in using a hair dryer, such as the hair dryer involved in this lawsuit, in bed, that a fire will result from the hair dryer getting covered up and the heating element getting heated. Admitted.

§ 5.08 Marketing of product without safety thermostat

This minor plaintiff received second and third degree burns over her chest, arms, neck, and legs. No one knows for sure how the product got onto her bed. It may have fallen there, or she may have gotten up and placed it there. That wasn't important. The important question was why did this appliance overheat while the plaintiff slept, igniting her bedding and awakening her to a frightening world of fire and pain?

Less than one month after this tragedy occurred, a partial answer was provided by investigators at the Massachusetts Department of Public Safety. They had conducted tests that demonstrated that the hair dryer lacked a safety thermostat, which would prevent it from attaining sufficient heat to ignite surrounding fabrics. With its intake airflow restricted

---

[9] *Toman, supra* note 1, defendant ____________ responses to plaintiff's requests to admit facts.

by a cloth towel, the dryer's temperature rapidly rose to a dangerous 520°F, hot enough to incinerate the towel. Responding to these test results, a consulting engineer described the dryer as "unreasonably dangerous and improperly designed"[10] because of its lack of a high temperature shutoff control.

Similarly, the president of the dryer distributor described the thermostat's safety function on the witness stand at trial.[11]

Q. How does [this device] work?

A. If the dryer is placed on its back and the airflow cut off, when the heating wires reach a certain temperature, it should shut off.

Q. What is the purpose of having that sort of device?

A. Safety.

Q. Okay, to protect the consumer from getting burned in any way?

A. To protect the consumer from his stupidity.

Q. That would include placing the unit in such a way that the air intake was blocked?

A. Yes.

§ 5.09 —Testimony of distributor's consulting engineer

A consulting engineer, hired as an expert by the dryer distributor admitted under my cross-examination that designing this product without a safety thermostat would be hazardous.[12]

Q. With respect to portable hair dryers such as plaintiff's exhibit in this case, would it be important from the point of view of consumer safety, considering the end use of these products, that they have some kind of temperature control or shutoff device, such as bimetallic stripping, so that the device shuts down when it reaches certain temperatures? Generally, would that be important?

---

[10] *Toman, supra* note 1, letter from Mr. R. B., consulting engineer, Report of Inspection and Test of ____________ Portable Hair Dryer (June 13, 1973).

[11] *Toman, supra* note 1, testimony of Mr. S, president of ____________, witness for the defendant.

[12] *Toman, supra* note 1, testimony of Mr. L, consulting engineer for ____________, witness for the defendant.

A. In my opinion, under situations of possible abnormal use I, as an engineer, would design a control into such a device.

Q. When you talk about abnormal use or misuse, what you are talking about are things that could happen, foreseeable uses that could happen in the marketplace, correct?

A. Oh, yes. . . . Something created by the consumer in a manner for which the device was originally not intended, yes.

* * *

Q. If you have a hand hair dryer made for consumer use that, when covered by let's say a bedsheet or a Turkish towel, ignited the fabric in under ten minutes, would you consider that product, in all fairness now, to be unsuitable from the point of view of consumer use?

A. According to my standards or requirements, I would say yes.

Q. And that's your opinion as a professional engineer?

A. Yes.

COMMENT: Careful examination of the defendant's experts can produce damaging admissions. Most experts are honest men and women with professional reputations to protect. Counsel should construct a strategy for bringing them into confrontation with the truth.

This witness also admitted that the length of time it would take an overheated dryer to ignite surrounding fabric was not important—the fact that it could attain sufficient heat to trigger dangerous ignition was important.[13]

Q. A while ago I asked you a question, if [this dryer] ignited the fabric or reached temperatures, to use your phraseology, that could ignite fabric in ten minutes or under, I suppose it wouldn't make any difference in what time it reached those temperatures.

---

[13] *Id.*

It just shouldn't reach those temperatures. Is that the way I understand your answer?

A. Yes.

Q. So whether it's ten minutes, an hour, or two-and-a-half hours, it wouldn't make any difference? It shouldn't reach temperatures hot enough to ignite fabrics, correct?

A. The [thermostat] should function in such a way that it should not result in a fire hazard.

This witness also admitted that if a thermostat had been incorporated in this machine, and in other hair dryers marketed by this company, it could not have attained the dangerous temperatures that caused this tragedy.[14]

Q. Referring to Plaintiff's Exhibit 2, sir, that's an example of a marketed hair dryer that you are familiar with, I take it? [*Ed. note*: Exhibit not supplied]

A. Yes.

Q. And could you tell us what kind of heat shutoff device this would have?

A. A bimetallic strip . . . located where the heating element is located so that if there is any restriction in airflow, either air in or air out, the radiant energy which would not be dissipated because of normal airflow would cause the thermostat to shut off, making the whole device inoperative.

Q. And you'd set it so that it would shut off at temperatures obviously that were at safe limits, that would not ignite, let's say, adjoining fabrics or things of that kind, correct?

A. Yes, and including keeping temperatures of the device itself. . .

Q. And so in designing a hair dryer you'd want to have not only the bimetallic type of stripping that you talked about, but you'd want to have the kind of housing that was compatible to the guts of the machine?

A. Yes.

Q. And that would be most safe from the point of view of not conducting heat at high temperatures, is that not correct?

---

[14] *Id*.

A. Not conducting excessive heat, yes.

* * *

Q. And that's a very critical factor from the point of view of end use and consumer safety?

A. Yes.

Q. In an attempt to avoid ignition of fabrics and clothing, among other things?

A. Yes.

Q. In other words, to prevent fires?

A. Yes.

Q. And that's always been an important consideration for you as long as you've been an engineer, correct?

A. Yes.

COMMENT: Plaintiff's counsel should make every effort to pin down the defendant's officers, experts, and engineers on how their product could be made safer and their reasons for not incorporating specific safety features. Such admissions can vividly demonstrate to the jury the carelessness and utter disregard of safety these corporate officials exhibited.

The dryer could have been designed with a safety thermostat. The president of the manufacturing company admitted under oath that commercial thermostats were available prior to the time the dryer was manufactured. His company had been incorporating them into its appliances for years. How much would they have cost? Mere pennies, according to the defendant's own engineering consultant as his testimony continued.[15]

Q. [Showing witness similar hair dryer of same manufacturer equipped with thermostat.] Approximately what would be the per unit cost of the bimetallic stripping?

---

[15] *Id*.

A. It would vary anywhere from ten cents to sixteen cents. . . . [In previous years] they would have been more expensive. . . .

Q. When you say more expensive, you are talking in terms of pennies?

A. Strictly pennies, right.

Q. On a per unit cost basis?

A. Yes.

COMMENT: Establishing the small cost of adding a safety feature is an effective way to show the extent of the defendant's wrongdoing in failing to protect the consumer.

---

§ 5.10 —Testimony of distributor's president

The dryer distributor's president knew that consumers had experienced fires and burn injuries when their dryers overheated. He knew that blockage of air intake vents was a major cause of product failure. He also had known for years how consumers could avoid forseeable injuries. As is shown in the following excerpt, this executive acknowledged the company's notice of its product's hazardous nature.[16]

Q. All right. Prior to April of this year, how many complaints or communications had your company received with respect to overheating of the portable dryer that your company had marketed?

A. What period of time are you talking about?

Q. Say from the 1950's all the way up. Give me a rough approximation.

A. A rough estimate would be fifty.

Q. Have you received complaints regarding overheating of the unit?

A. Yes.

Q. Did your company respond to those complaints?

---

[16] *Toman, supra* note 1, testimony of Mr. S.

A. We did.

Q. Did you investigate what caused the unit to overheat?

A. Yes.

Q. And in these cases, did you determine that the overheating was, in many instances, caused by blockage or obstruction of the air intake?

A. I would say, based on my knowledge at the moment, I'd say 98% were caused by someone using the dryer while the telephone was ringing and not switching it off and putting it down on the table in the most convenient way and going to answer the phone.

Q. Would it be fair to say that any design of the dryer which would enable you to lay it with the air intake flat down on the table, or down on any flat table surface, would have been a factor of this incidence of complaint caused by the blockage of the air intake?

A. I'd say the only factor.

§ 5.11 Failure to warn: testimony of distributor's president

Despite this knowledge of the consequences to consumer safety, the distributor did not warn consumers to avoid this hazard. The distributor's president admitted that consumers might not know of the hazards of overheating and that warnings might prevent tragedies like that which befell the young plaintiff.[17]

Q. You didn't know much more about the temperatures which this product could reach, both with the air intake blocked or unblocked, than the ordinary consumer who bought it in the drugstore would know?

A. That is right.

Q. And certainly you wouldn't expect a consumer who did not receive the warning that we talked about, about not blocking the air intake, to have any greater knowledge of that than yourself, your company itself did?

A. [No response.]

Q. If the consumer didn't receive a warning or instruction about not blocking the air intake, would you expect a consumer without

---

[17] *Id.*

that knowledge to know that blocking the air intake would result in increasing the temperature of the unit?

A. Average judgment, yes.

Q. Would you expect that there would be a great many consumers who might not know this?

A. Based on a number of complaints and the number of those that were sold, the assumption is everybody understood what they were supposed to do with it and the usage.

Q. Of course, you don't know of every problem of overheating of this unit.

A. They would have returned it because there would always be an over-the-counter guarantee on our product.

Q. If the air intake of the unit was blocked and the unit overheated in such a way as not to result in a breakdown of the unit, there wouldn't be any return, would there?

A. Normally, no.

Q. So it is possible to have a customer who might block the air intake and not cause enough damage to the unit to have it come to your attention in any way?

A. That is right.

Q. You were aware that the customer might not know about keeping the intake free?

A. If they were normal human beings, I would expect they would.

Q. But there were some people who did not know that?

A. That, I can't answer. I can't answer as to some people. I can only answer to what I know.

Q. From the complaints that you received, were you aware that there were people who did not know about the dangers of blocking the air intake?

A. I would say one or two, yes.

Q. This was a class of people, and no matter how small or how large, you don't know who might not have had this knowledge, is that right?

A. Misused it, yes.

Q. In respect to this Model ____________, did you ever place on it any warnings or instructions stating that the product was not supposed to be used by children?

A. No.

Q. And were you not aware when you marketed this product that one of the foreseeable uses was that children might get hold of it?

A. I couldn't answer that. A child could get a hold of an automobile, too, and have it go down a hill and the manufacturer isn't going to put this in his guarantee.

Q. Why would it be important, if at all, to keep this product out of the reach of a child?

A. Because it is not meant for them. It is an adult product.

Q. In terms of providing warnings and instructions to the consumer, you wanted to prevent this type of misuse, didn't you?

A. Yes.

* * *

Q. You wouldn't expect a child to have the same sophistication and knowledge about this product as an adult, would you?

A. That is right. It is not meant for a child.

Q. Now, in your experience with the product and the complaints about the product, were you aware of any occasion on which a child came in contact with this product?

A. No.

Q. Did you place any warnings or instructions on this product saying keep out of the reach of children?

A. No, it is not a toy.

Q. That is clear. Did you ever say that on your product?

A. No.

Q. What danger would exist if a child used this product?

A. Misuse.

Q. What type of misuse?

A. To lay it down somewhere where it could be snuffed, prohibiting air from going into it to keep it cool, because it must have an airflow.

Q. What might result from that type of misuse by a child?

A. It could burn something.

Q. No further questions.

COMMENT: From a businessman's point of view, an aesthetic consideration that relates to sales is an important self-justifying feature. From the viewpoint of trial counsel and the jury, placing aesthetics over safety is a disaster. This must be brought out effectively. The testimony of the distributor's president continues:[18]

---

* * *

Q. Was there any label or words on the product itself instructing the user not to block the air intake?

A. No, not on that.

Q. Was there any instruction or warning on the product telling the consumer what the effect of blocking the air intake would be in raising the temperature of the heating element or of the unit or of the air coming out of the nozzle?

A. None.

Q. But you know people wouldn't know enough to keep the air intake clear?

A. I can't assume that.

Q. From your own experience with people who sent back hair dryers that you knew about?

A. There might have been a couple, yes, that were in that condition and the assumption was that this is what happened.

Q. Now, did your company at any time in the fifties market together with the hair dryers any instructions as to their use?

A. There were guarantees against manufacturing defects enclosed

---

[18] *Id.*

with them. I think it did have something on it stating something to the effect that the air intake should not be blocked.

Q. And did your company, with each model hair dryer in the fifties, also market such an instruction?

A. Yes, on the guarantee. Yes, there was something like it.

Q. Was there any instruction on the unit itself?

A. None.

Q. Did your company ever attempt to determine what increased cost, if any, there would be to put a sticker or label to that effect on the unit itself?

A. Nothing was ever put on it because aesthetically it wouldn't look good.

Q. It wasn't cost?

A. Cost was not important.

Q. It was just an aesthetic consideration?

A. Yes.

COMMENT: When the distributor finally did request the use of a warning, it was because the company learned that blockage of the air intake could damage the hair dryer, not because it could cause injury. Again, testimony by this company's president is revealing.[19]

Q. And were you familiar with incidents of blocking the airflow into the air intake with the [other model] hair dryers that you marketed in the fifties?

A. Yes.

Q. The same phenomenon occurred only if it was placed down on the table in different ways, put down on the bed in a different way?

A. Right.

---

[19] *Id.*

Q. And was it based in part on your experience with those hair dryers that you first requested the introduction of the warnings and instructions?

A. No. It was a test I gave it at that time, while I was playing with it and running it in this factory. . . . When I asked the question of why the motor was starting to bind, [I was given an] answer about blocking of the air intake, at which time we came up with a warning notice.

Q. That's when you realized that blocking of the air intake could cause overheating?

A. Could damage the dryer.

Q. Could damage the hair dryer?

A. That is right.

§ 5.12 —Testimony of manufacturer's consulting engineer

The testimony by the defendant's consulting engineer as to the importance of warnings provided on the appliance itself was important to plaintiff's case on this issue.[20]

Q. I think we can agree that if there's a risk that in terms of potential for injury is a great risk and it was something that, as a professional engineer, you wanted to make recommendations as to an adequate warning and instruction, can we agree that the most visible and lasting place to put such an instruction would be on the product itself?

A. Not necessarily.

Q. Where would you put it?

A. I would generally put either a warning or a reference to the warning on the product . . . then coupled perhaps with a circular, a use and care booklet, and an indication on the packaging if it were necessary to do this.

* * *

Q. As an engineer you are quite aware that products generally—if things are as they are in my home and, I suspect, even your

[20] *Toman, supra* note 1, testimony of Mr. L, consulting engineer for ____________, witness for defendant.

home—are removed from packages and used by people who don't see the original package, is that true?

A. I agree.

Q. Because of that, certainly as a professional engineer, and one that's interested in consumer safety, I think we can agree that considering, for example, a risk of fire, you'd want to have that kind of warning or instruction put in a conspicuous place where it would be seen by all potential users, correct?

A. Or reference to something that would so state it, yes.

Q. Then is it your best professional judgment that this warning, instruction, or reference, as you call it, would best be put on the product itself?

A. In conjunction with some other place. There should be something perhaps that appears on the product.

Q. And there is no question about that in your professional judgment, correct?

A. I would say no at this point

IV. Other Electrical Hazards

§ 5.13 Electric blankets

Another preventable threat is the continuing fire risk from electric blankets. According to the U.S. Consumer Product Safety Commission, nearly 7,000 fires involving electric blankets occurred in 1979, including 16 deaths and 875 injuries.[21] The most commonly identified failures involved the cord or cord/blanket junction, the thermostat, and heat entrapment.

COMMENT: Because electric blankets are used while the person is asleep, they constitute a major threat to the user. In preparing the case, plaintiff's counsel should put great

[21] Consumer Prod. Safety Comm'n, *Briefing Papers on Electric Blankets* (Nov. 5, 1982).

stress on the increased risk of fire during the time when the consumer is most vulnerable.

Consider the plaintiff who was awakened early one morning by flames rising from her electric blanket. She and her husband immediately tried to squelch the flames, but to no avail. The fire spread through their home, injuring the plaintiffs and destroying their dwelling.[22] At first glance, the case may not have appeared viable. The plaintiffs had spent a considerable amount of valuable time in their home attempting to put out the blaze. Worse, most of the potential evidence was destroyed, including the electrical receptacle and the plug connecting the cord for the controls to the blanket's inner network of wires. Despite this lack of evidence, the plaintiff's expert asserted that the blanket had been ignited by heat from a short circuit arc, or a spark, near the connector at the foot of the blanket. Based on circumstantial evidence, the plaintiff successfully argued that the blanket was responsible for the fire that erupted in plaintiffs' home and the plaintiffs obtained a jury verdict against the manufacturer of the blanket.[23]

For years, consumer advocates warned that these cozy oases of packaged heat did not contain sufficient numbers of heat-restricting thermostats to prevent ignition from overheating. Blanket manufacturers and testing agencies contended that the existing thermostat load was sufficient. This comment by W.A. Farquhar, Vice President of Underwriters' Laboratories, before the National Commission on Product Safety, is illustrative:

> The safety thermostats are sufficient in number and so placed that the possibility of localized heating not affecting at least one thermostat and thus shutting off power has been demonstrated to be extremely unlikely.[24]

Despite these reassuring words, the blankets were marketed with long lists of "don'ts" to prevent overheating: "don't bundle, don't fold, don't bunch, and don't lie atop" to name a few. The reason for all these "don'ts" is basic to the blanket's design. Between two layers of blanket lies a network of wires that are heated by electric current. Spaced peri-

---

[22] Gediman v. Sears, Roebuck & Co., 484 F. Supp. 1244 (D. Mass. 1980).

[23] *Id.*

[24] Nat'l Comm'n on Prod. Safety, VI–273 (June 19, 1969).

odically throughout this network are a series of thermostats. As with hair dryers and other appliances, these thermostats are often the only things that stand between pleasurable warmth and devastating fire. Around each thermostat is an insulating plastic sheath. If moisture should enter this sheath, the thermostat can fail. If too much wire is bunched together in one spot, it can generate excessive heat.

COMMENT: All too often, consumers don't discover the long list of "don'ts" that accompany the product until after they've brought it home: don't bundle, don't fold, don't cover, don't even lie on the blanket or let your child or pet lie on it, don't dry clean it (cleaning solvent can harm insulation around the wiring). In short, don't do all those things that we do so naturally and automatically when we curl up in bed or get out of bed.

In 1982, the Underwriters' Laboratories revised its electric blanket standards to require more thermostats in all size blankets and more stringent testing requirements.[25]

§ 5.14 Smoke detectors

Of all the false assurances of safety, few compare with those provided by defective smoke detectors. No product is purchased with as much expectation and reliance for proper functioning and performance. When a smoke detector fails to perform as expected, human lives can, and usually do, hang in the balance. For this reason, it is all the more important that adequate warnings be provided by detector manufacturers when they know that their product will not function adequately in a foreseeable situation. When detector manufacturers fail to provide safe products or fail to warn of deficiencies that can cost consumers their lives, our courts must and have played the role of marketplace monitor.

[25] UL 964: Standard for Electric-Heated Bedding.

§ 5.15 —Illustrative case

Three teenage children in the plaintiff's family perished when a fire consumed their Massachusetts home.[26] Ironically, the father had purchased and installed a smoke detector to protect his family against just such a disaster. The night that fire erupted, the detector never sounded its alarm. Three of the family's children died from smoke inhalation in the fire. A fourth child suffered severe burns, but survived.

COMMENT: In smoke detector cases, the failure of the product to respond in emergencies is critical. The lawyer for the plaintiff should ask himself if the manufacturer took reasonable steps in manufacturing and promoting its product to be sure that it would function in an emergency.

The smoke detector purchased by the father ran on electrical power. He installed the product in a doorway between two upstairs bedrooms. On the night of the fire, the detector was plugged in and power was feeding the receptacle. It never sounded. Fire investigators later determined why—the fire had originated in a defective extension cord, which had shorted the wires and blew the circuit fuse into which the detector was plugged. The detector was rendered useless.

This tragedy occurred because the company that manufactured this detector did not include a battery-powered component as a backup for those situations where the home's electrical system is shut off or disabled and did not warn the family that their detector would fail to function in the event of household current interruption. In sworn testimony, company executives admitted that the detector was promoted to provide early warning of a residential fire and thus to save lives.[27] The consumer was advised when purchasing the product that he was buying a lifesaving device and that the product was designed to detect fire and provide a warning long before the products of combustion became life threatening.[28]

---

[26] *Laaperi, supra* note 2.

[27] *Laaperi, supra* note 2, testimony of Mr. S, design engineer for the defendant.

[28] *Id*.

One year prior to this tragedy, the manufacturer conceived the design of a safer model detector, an electrically powered detector with a battery backup. This model would remain operational in the event of an electrical outage. The company promoted the battery backup feature of this model as an additional safety feature. The company's president admitted that this model provided an extra layer of protection in the event of a loss of household power.[29] Similarly, the company's chairman of the board testified that in the event that electrical power went off, the new model would provide an extra degree of safety because the smoke detector would operate by battery.[30]

Despite the fact that the company's own standard in marketing its smoke detectors was that one injury or death would be one too many if it could be avoided,[31] the defendant's actions evinced a shocking disregard for the safety of consumers who purchased and used its products. Nowhere in the packaging or the owner's manual was there any mention of the advantages of a combination smoke detector operated by both battery and electric current. It was never recommended to the consumer that he buy two units, one powered by electrical current and one powered by battery. As a matter of fact, the defendant's design engineer admitted that such a recommendation was not made because no regulations required it.[32] He also admitted that the defendant never gave consideration to selling one AC-powered unit and one DC-powered unit in the same package.[33]

Prior to the plaintiff's tragedy, the defendant's executives admitted they were aware that, in the event of a loss of power, the plaintiff's detector would not function,[34] but they did not advise consumers of this risk.[35] These same executives also admitted: (1) that if power outages during fires were even an occasional occurrence, this would be significant information to pass on to the consumer to use a backup battery-powered source,[36] and (2) that "lots of fires" develop from electrical failure and

---

[29] *Laaperi, supra* note 2, testimony of Mr. C, president for the defendant.

[30] *Laaperi, supra* note 2, testimony of Mr. H, chairman of the board for the defendant.

[31] *Laaperi, supra* note 2, testimony of Mr. S.

[32] *Id.*

[33] *Id.*

[34] *Laaperi, supra* note 2, testimony of Mr. C.

[35] *Laaperi, supra* note 2, testimony of Mr. H.

[36] *Id.*

wipe out the electrical current.[37]

In effect, the defendant left the plaintiff (and all consumers) in the dark regarding its product's defects and the need for additional protection to obtain the security the plaintiff thought he was purchasing when he bought the culpable product. As the defendant's president was forced to concede, if the unit in the plaintiff's home on the night of the fire had contained a battery backup, it would have been operational.[38] Had the alarm sounded, in all probability the entire family would have heard it and been able to escape. If the family's detector had not been negligently marketed, three of the plaintiff's children may not have lost their lives.

§ 5.16 Exploding automobile batteries

I have often stated that a major cause of slaughter by product is the "body count" approach to consumer safety taken by many manufacturers and industries when it comes to injury prevention. All too often, the testing grounds for hazardous products is the American marketplace. As reports of consumer injuries are received, and as their count mounts high enough that the excuse of "freak accident" is embarrassing even to the product manufacturer, a company or industry will finally decide that significant design changes or clear warnings on the product are as important for their own legal protection as for the protection of the consumer. That is when action will come.

A classic case of "body count" consumerism, and the effectiveness of legal action in forcing a change to safer product design, can be seen in the manufacture of another electrical product, automobile batteries. Manufacturers and their engineering staffs have known for more than thirty years that the batteries they built and distributed could explode, and that unsuspecting people were becoming the victims of these hazardous products. Yet they made no effort to change the battery design, or provide warnings on the batteries of the hazards they posed, until lawsuits by injured consumers pressed them into action.

COMMENT: In an exploding battery case, counsel should emphasize that safety devices have existed for decades,

[37] *Laaperi, supra* note 2, testimony of Mr. C.

[38] *Id*.

and that failure to incorporate them cannot be justified by cost or other factors.

---

§ 5.17 —Illustrative case

A Whitman, Massachusetts man was working at a local service station when a customer brought in a car with an old battery that he wished to exchange for a new one. As he attempted to recharge the battery on his station's charging machine, the battery blew up in his face. He had just pulled the caps off the battery, preparing to recharge it. He recalls what happened next: "I went to hook the battery charger up and that was it . . . bing! . . . that thing came up and hit me in the face."[39]

A registered engineer explained the hazardous nature of this battery and other batteries manufactured for our automobiles:

> The normal, anticipated, expected, foreseeable use of an automotive battery the way they have been designed and the way they're used is that it's just to be expected. You're generating hydrogen in the normal course of usage, and sparking and arcing is characteristic at the terminals. . . . There are literally hundreds upon hundreds of battery explosions throughout the country every year.[40]

The plaintiff's expert then provided an important and detailed explanation of how and why a battery explodes:

> [If] you generate hydrogen on the order of 4% by volume in the presence of a spark and air, you'll sustain an explosion. What you do is sustain ignition and burning of the hydrogen. The burning flame front travels back to the source of the greater concentration, and that's through the cell caps or through the cell openings, inside the battery. The battery casing itself is a very weak structural element. It cannot sustain a rapid expansion of gases, and so it gives and explodes with the fragmentation of the battery case, just as happened in the [instant] case."[41]

He examined the battery in detail, describing it as a "potential bomb." He identified at least three different defects that justified this description:

---

[39] *Boyd, supra* note 3, testimony of the plaintiff.

[40] *Boyd, supra* note 3, testimony of Mr. M.

[41] *Id.*

the location of its terminals, its lack of a flame arrestor, and the lack of warnings to users of its explosiveness. The terminals' location at the top of the battery placed them in easy reach of the battery's explosive gases. It didn't have to be designed that way. According to this engineer, other manufacturers were designing safer batteries, with terminals on the side rather than the top, when the plaintiff's battery was produced. This design alternative, he explained, "reduces sufficiently and substantially the chance of explosion."[42]

COMMENT: It was brought out by several other company officials that this safer design was available as far back as the 1960's, and required no major new technical innovations to produce.

The company's former assistant chief engineer for batteries conceded that the company had the technology for side-terminal devices in the 1960's.[43]

Q. Company X had the technology and the know-how, and indeed the experience, in side-terminal batteries back at least as far as 1960, did they not?

A. Well, the technology, the know-how, and the experience. . .

Flame arrestors also might have prevented the explosion if they had been incorporated on the battery. These had been available, according to this expert, for fifteen years before the plaintiff's battery exploded. Automobile battery manufacturers simply refused to allocate their resources for their development to protect customers. It was a clear case of "body count" consumerism.

The defendant's own officials admitted during depositions that they had known of their product's explosiveness since 1957, yet waited fifteen years before they developed the flame arrestor as a safety program. This same executive admitted his knowledge of the batteries' hazards:[44]

---

[42] *Id.*

[43] *Boyd, supra* note 3, testimony of Mr. W, witness for the defendant.

[44] *Id.*

Q. Since 1957, you have been aware that batteries can explode under some circumstances?

A. Yes.

Q. And from time to time you have heard of battery explosions?

A. Yes.

Q. When did you start hearing about them with frequency or regularity?

Q. Sometime in the 1960's, late 1960's, perhaps.

The defendant's manager of reliability was responsible for ensureing the reliability of the company's products. He conceded the company's "body count" approach to consumer safety:[45]

Q. Has something happened since 1969 that now makes this something that you might be able to do?

A. No, I don't believe so. It's a matter of development rather than breakthrough of any kind.

Q. It's now a matter of spending your energies on this as opposed to something else?

A. Yes.

Q. It's a matter of allocation of priorities within [your] company that prevented you from doing it earlier?

A. There is some indication here that there were more complaints from the field, more claims that caused us to consider what [we could] do to minimize the hazards, you know, particularly in the case of the uninformed person handling a battery.

Q. The complaints were becoming more frequent?

A. Yes.

Q. To the point where it now became a matter of corporate concern that you should undertake to do something to prevent, diminish, or reduce that risk or hazard?

A. To explore if there was some way.

COMMENT: Injured consumers were not only winning,

[45] *Boyd, supra* note 3, testimony of Mr. K, witness for the defendant.

> they were also helping millions of other consumers by forcing the industry to act. Under the pressure of litigation, batteries suddenly appeared with labels warning of their explosiveness. The industry's own newsletter reveals its concern about its legal liability, and the influence that courts have had in shaping industry practice to meet consumer needs:
>
> "Hazardous explosion warnings are not defined by the [government] at this time, but it is likely that they will be defined in the future. However, they are interpreted in the general language of the law and are desirable from a liability standpoint. . . . These instructions are not required by the Government at this time. However, legal opinions state, 'such labels should be sufficiently explicit that the product can be safely handled.' . . .Recent court rulings state that 'plastering warnings about Poison on labels and advising antidotes is not enough. You have to tell how to use it.' "[46]

It was also conceded by the defendant that the warnings could easily have been placed on the batteries many years earlier:[47]

Q. What was involved, other than the formation of the language itself and finally settling on the language, what is involved in putting the label on?

A. Mechanically?

Q. Yes.

A. There are certain technical considerations of adherence, acid resistance, and assembly considerations.

Q. This wasn't any insurmountable or particularly difficult thing?

A. No.

Q. There wasn't anything that was unknown in the state of the art, say, in the early 1960's, was there?

A. No.

---

[46] Newsletter, Battery Council Int'l (Mar. 24, 1974).

[47] *Boyd, supra* note 43, testimony of Mr. W.

Q. And would the cost be more, in terms of a cent or a few cents per battery, as opposed to a dollar a battery?

A. I don't know what the cost of the label is, but it does not approach a dollar a battery. I know that.

COMMENT: Thus, injured consumers and their lawyers had acted through the courts to force an industry to act where Congress and the federal bureaucracy had failed.

V. Preventing Electrical-Related Injuries

§ 5.18 In general

Manufacturers, code writers, engineers, public officials, product testers, and lawyers all have important roles to play in reducing casualties produced by household electrical products. Manufacturers must invest resources to develop products of safer design and provide adequate warnings to consumers when household use of the product, by adults or by children, can result in avoidable death or injury. Engineers and other technical experts must apply their expertise to promoting advances in electrical product technology with the goal of reducing recognized risks. Product testers must recognize the need for improved communication to the public regarding product hazards, and the need for improved product design to reduce safety threats. Public officials must recognize the need to establish stringent safety standards for electrically operated products, and take firm action against manufacturers that continue to market products without sufficient regard to their end use safety.

Special concern and attention must be paid to those responsible for writing codes regulating household electrical safety, including the National Electric Code. This model code, prepared under the auspices of the National Fire Protection Association (NFPA), is used as the basis for state and local electric and safety codes nationwide.[48]

[48] NFPA 70–1984.

§ 5.19 Adopting safety technology to reduce shock risks

Two areas that call for immediate action on this front are protections against appliance-related electrocutions by using Ground Fault Circuit Interruptors (GFCI's) in household wiring systems,[49] and protections against smoke alarm malfunctions by requiring battery backups for electrically operated household smoke detectors.

Household electrocutions can be prevented if technological advances are incorporated into electrical appliances and household wiring systems. GFCI's represent one technological advance that can contribute to injury prevention. It is imperative that appliance manufacturers, code drafters, and other professionals concerned with injury prevention address this and other potentially lifesaving engineering advances.

§ 5.20 —Providing adequate warnings

Consumers continue to be needlessly electrocuted in their own homes. It is imperative that household appliances bear adequate warnings of the fatal risks associated with using electrical appliances, particularly in bathrooms and other locations where water and electricity can combine to create deadly results. All household electrical appliances should bear clear, conspicuous, and adequate warnings of this lethal threat.

§ 5.21 Adopting safety technology to reduce fire risks

Technology is available to protect homedwellers against fire by detecting gas and smoke before tragedy strikes. Advances in smoke and gas detector technology must be shared with the American public to enable consumers to protect themselves by purchasing the maximum fire protection. Electrically operated detectors must be equipped with battery backups or marketed with accompanying battery-operated devices.

Consumers must be warned that smoke detectors are often not designed to detect toxic gases emitted before fire breaks out. Household plastic products, including wiring, piping, wallpaper, and other items, can be the source of deadly hydrogen chloride gas well before detectable combustion products trigger the home's smoke alarm system.

Electrical, fire, and related residential safety codes must be revised to incorporate requirements for adequate safety technology and warnings to

---

[49] *See also* E. SWARTZ, PROOF OF PRODUCT DEFECTS, ch. 16, dealing with small household appliances (Lawyers' Co-op. Publishing Co. 1985).

consumers. This must be changed. Gas detection technology must be required as well as smoke detection technology to provide consumers with adequate fire protection.

§ 5.22 Adequate testing for electrical appliance safety

Many organizations test electrical appliances for compliance with product standards. Foremost in the electrical field is Underwriters Laboratories (UL). UL "lists" products that pass its tests in compliance with existing standards. Who writes these standards? Industry members, of course. Many consumers mistake the UL emblem on a product as an indication of safety. They do not understand that the standards against which these products are tested are developed by industry members to meet their own interests. They also do not understand that UL works under contract with product manufacturers and, as such, has a vested interest in pleasing their contractor with positive test results. Public education in this field can promote injury prevention by increasing consumers' awareness that products marketed with UL labels are not necessarily "safe."

§ 5.23 What can lawyers do?

Lawyers can play a special role in this area. Lawyers are highly skilled professionals who understand the relationship between consumer safety and the regulatory responsibilities of code setting organizations, and who see the tragic results of inadequate safety precautions firsthand. We are particularly suited to work with code setting bodies to establish standards and regulations that meet consumers' needs before inadequate codes result in tragic deaths and injuries. We are also in a prime position to share information with code drafters and product safety authorities regarding the need for injury prevention through appropriate rules and regulations.

Of course, the most obvious role we lawyers can play in this field is through increased litigation. A clear example of how litigation can impact on injury prevention by forcing manufacturers to take consumer interests into account in their product design and marketing was provided in the case of the exploding automobile battery.[50] It is my hope that increased litigation regarding smoke detectors, for example, will (1) heighten the public's awareness of the defects in these devices that we rely on so heavily for lifesaving fire protection, (2) heighten the aware-

[50] *See supra* §§ 5.16, 5.17.

ness by public safety officials and code drafters of the need for new directions in electrical system and fire detection safety, and (3) provide the necessary motivation for smoke detector manufacturers to invest in and promote new technologies to protect against foreseeable tragedies.

VI. Litigation Sources: Bibliography

§ 5.24 Selected technical sources

How to Achieve Electrical Safety, 27 Actual Specifying Engineer, No. 5 (May 1972).

C. Alban, *Thermostatic Bimetals*, in *Handbook of Engineering Materials* (John Wiley & Sons, Inc., 1st ed. 1955).

Allen, *Thermal Switch Gives 30 Second Range Heating*, Electrical Manufacturing (Mar. 1955).

Allison, *Ground Fault Circuit Interrupters*, J. Am. Soc'y Safety Engineers (Nov. 1975).

A. Ansley, *Temperature Control* (University College of the South West of England, Exeter, Chapman & Hall, Ltd., London 1942).

Applications of Thermometals (H. Wiggin & Co. 1949).

G. Brady, *Materials Handbook* (An Encyclopedia for Purchasing Agents, Engineers, Executives, and Foremen) (McGraw-Hill Book Co. 1956, 1963).

Black, *A Sensitive Thermo-Regulator*, 5 J. Sci. Instruments (1928).

Carissimi, *Automatic Cooking Control*, Electrical Manufacturing (Aug. 1956).

Dahlen, *Design Factors in Thermostatic Selection*, Electrical Manufacturing (Nov. 1958).

Dalziel, *Effects of Electric Current on Man*, Am. Soc'y Safety Engineers (June 1973).

Dalziel, *Effect of Electric Current on Man*, Electrical Engineering (Feb. 1974).

Dalziel, *The Ground Fault Circuit Interrupter in 1974*, I.A.E.I. News (Nov./Dec. 1974).

P. Dike, *Thermoelectric Thermometry* (Leads & Northrup Co. Sept. 1954).

Dufton, *The Eupatheoscope*, 6 J. Sci. Instruments (1929).

N. Ebihara, T. Handa, S. Yoshizawwa, et al., *Flame Retardant Paper Base Phenol Laminate for Household Electric Appliance*, in Proc. Int'l Conf. on Electr & Electron Mater., Millbrae, Cal., Jan. 8–9, 1980, at 19–59 (Product Safety Corp., Sunnyvale, Cal. 1980).

Electric Motor Operated Appliances for Domestic and Similar Purposes (CEE 10, Am. Nat'l Standards Inst. 1953).

For Control of Heat or Cold, 22 Electrical Manufacturing No. 5 (1938).

Maintaining Electrical Machines: The Need for Systematic Planning, 19 Electron Power No. 8 (May 3, 1973).

Ein Leistungsfaehiges Buegeleret fuer Haushalt und Gewerbe, 71 Elektrotech. Z. (Apr. 20, 1950).

Testing and Accuracy of Thermal Circuit Breakers—Motor Protecting Cut-Offs, 56 Elektrotech. Z. (1935).

Temperature Regulation in Electric Irons, 55 Elektrotech. Z. (1934).

Advances in the Technology of Domestic Electric Heating, 47 Elektrotech. Z. (1926).

A New Motor Switch with a Heat Protecting Relay, 47 Elektrotech Z. (1926).

The Operation of an Electric Iron and the Need of Temperature Regulation, 26 Elektizitat (1927).

Farrell, *Motor Overload Protection for Domestic Appliances*, Electrical Engineering (Aug. 1953).

Four Monographs on Electrical Safety (Instrument Soc'y of America 1969, 1972).

Greve, *Which Thermostat*, Machine Design (Aug. 1942).

Haviland, *Thermostatic Controls*, Machine Design (Apr. 3, 1958).

Heumann, *Overload Relays and Circuit Breakers for Protecting Motorized Appliances and Their Branch Circuits*, Electrical Engineering (Dec. 1953).

Hirsch, *Electrical Uses of Thermostat Metals*, 12 Electrical Manufacturing No. 3 (1933).

IEC Recommendations 175 AC Electric Table Type Fans and Regulators (Am. Nat'l Standards Inst., 1st ed. 1965).

Ireton, *Making Electrical and Electronic Products Safe*, Am. Soc'y Safety Engineers (Sept. 1971).

Jones & Heck, *A Study of Fires Involving Alternative Heating Equipment*, 77 Fire J. No. 5 (Sept. 1983).

Temperature-Measuring Equipment, 2 J. Applied Physics No. 6 (June 1940).

P.A. Kinzie, *Thermocouple Temperature Measurement* (John Wiley & Sons, Inc. 1973).

Kostylev, Drapitskaya & Volkova, *New Trends in Electrical-Heating Devices for Food Preparation*, 50 Soviet Electrical Engineering 59–62, No. 8 (1979) (New technical and economic trends in the development of designs for traditional food preparation appliances are discussed).

Larson, *Motors that Protect Themselves*, 32 Electronics J. (1935).

Leonard, *The Clampdown on Electrical Hazards*, J. Am. Soc'y Safety Engineers (Sept. 1975).

Maeda, et al., *4-Bit One-Chip Microcomputer-Based Controllers for Home Appliances*, 26 Nat'l Tech. Rep. Matsushita Electr. Indus. 718–727, No. 4 (Aug. 1980).

A.H. McKinney & H.G. Conner, *Electrical Safety Abstracts* (Instrument Soc'y of America, 4th ed. 1972).

M.L. Miller, *Automation in Electrical Testing* (Am. Soc'y of Safety Engineers Oct. 1962).

Moorhead, *Applying BiMetal Thermostats*, Product Engineering (Nov. 1947).

Morath, *Designing and Manufacturing of Electrical Cooking Appliances Using PBIP*, 73 Kunstst Ger Plast 6–8, No. 2 (Feb. 1983) (Development of engineering plastics had led to material that now meets relevant requirements for electrical cooking appliances. One of these materials is the thermoplastic polyester polybutylene tereghthalate. This report deals with various problem solutions).

R.L. Nailen, *Is That Motor Really Overloaded?* (Louis Allis Co.).

Fundamentals of Electrical Hazards, Nat'l Safety News (June 1967).

Guidelines for application and use of interlock safety devices, Nat'l Tech. Information Services Order No. PB 83–120162.

Nohara, *Appliance Power Switch Trends and Safety Standards*, 19 J. Electron Engineering 52–55, No. 188 (Aug. 1982).

M. Pickett, M. Arnold & L. Ketterer, *Household Equipment in Residential Design* (John Wiley & Sons, Inc. 9th ed. 1986).

Ground Systems for Better Protection, 117 Power No. 2 (Feb. 1973).

Thermostat Mechanisms, 6 Product Engineering (1935).

The Protection of Alternating Current Motors by Circuit Breakers, 32 Rev. Gen. Elect. (1927).

Riley, *Where and How Thermostat Metals Are Used*, Materials & Methods (Apr. 1954).

Robbins, *Protecting the Electricity User*, Electronics & Power (June 1971).

Schad, *Improvements in the Construction of Thermostats for Heating Pads*, 39 Helios Fachteil (1933).

The Snapping-Bug Thermostat, 132 Sci. Am. (1925).

H. Scott, *Thermostatic Metal—or Bimetal Nature and Utility*, in *Metal Progress* (Am. Soc'y for Steel Treating Nov. 1932).

Plastics in Appliances, in Regional Tech. Conf. of the Soc'y of Plastic Engineers, Inc. (Soc'y of Plastic Engineers, Kentuckiana sect. 1980).

Stevens, *Bimetal Thermostats for Products of Tomorrow*, Electrical Manufacturing (Feb. 1945).

Stevens, *Thermal Controls: Their Location, Range, and Frequency of Operation Have Important Effects on Performance*, Machine Design (Apr. 1947).

Birka Regulators and Their Use in Domestic Electric Heating Work, 55 Tek. Tidsk. (Feb. 2, 1924).

The Ways Things Work (Simon & Schuster 1967).

Thorper, *Establishing Design Defect as Proximate Cause of Injury in a Portable Household Blender Accident*, ASME Paper 81–WA/DE–5 (Analysis of alleged design defect in a product liability case involving hand injuries allegedly caused by a portable household blender. Risk-utility analysis of design choices made by defendant blender manufacturer).

Thermostats for Electrical Appliances, Westinghouse Engineering (July 1949).

§ 5.25 Selected popular sources

Balakier, *A Major Boom in Minor Appliances*, 74 Mechanix Illustrated 84, No. 602 (July 1978).

Blow Dryers, 49 Consumer Rep. 132, 136, No. 6 (June 1984).

Electric Blankets, 43 Consumer Rep. 562, No. 10 (Oct. 1978).

Electric Drip Coffeemakers, 61 Consumers' Research 7–11, No. 11 (Nov. 1978).

Irons, 61 Consumers' Research 13–16, No. 5 (May 1978).

Automatic Electric Clothes Dryers, 61 Consumers' Research 24–29, No. 6 (June 1978).

Powell, *Small Appliance Repair*, 212 Popular Sci. 46, No. 6 (June 1978).

International

Test: Coffee Makers, 8 Can. Consumer No. 2 (Aug. 1978).

Test: Dishwashers, 8 Can. Consumer 9–14, No. 1 (Feb. 1978).

§ 5.26 Selected government sources

Morrissey, et al., Army Research and Development Command, *Measurement of Carbon Fiber Exposure to Failure and Possible Shock Hazard for Household Equipment* (Final Report Mar. 1980).

Consumer Product Safety Comm'n, *Electric Baseboard Heaters*, Fact Sheet No. 54 (Rev. May 1978).

Consumer Product Safety Comm'n, *The Home Electrical System*, Fact Sheet No. 18 (July 1979).

Consumer Product Safety Comm'n, *Smoke Detectors*, Fact Sheet No. 57 (Rev. May 1978).

Consumer Product Safety Comm'n, *Extension Cords and Wall Outlets*, Fact Sheet No. 16 (Rev. May 1978).

Consumer Product Safety Comm'n, *Antenna Electrocutions*, Fact Sheet No. 88 (Jan. 1976).

Consumer Product Safety Comm'n, *Electrical Products*, Fact Sheet No. 61 (Sept. 1975).

Consumer Product Safety Comm'n, *Hair Dryers and Stylers*, Fact Sheet No. 35 (Sept. 1975).

Consumer Product Safety Comm'n, *Electric Blenders, Mixers, Choppers/ Slicers, and Grinders*, Fact Sheet No. 50 (May 1975).

Consumer Product Safety Comm'n, *Kitchen Ranges*, Fact Sheet No. 9 (May 1975).

Consumer Product Safety Comm'n, Bureau of Epidemiology, *Hazard Analysis on Aluminum Wiring* (Apr. 1975).

Consumer Product Safety Comm'n, Bureau of Epidemiology, *Hazard Analysis of Appliance Cords, Extension Cords, and Replacement Wire* (Nov. 1974).

Consumer Product Safety Comm'n, Bureau of Epidemiology, *Hazard Analysis on Television Sets* (Oct. 1974).

Consumer Product Safety Comm'n, *Fondue Pots*, Fact Sheet No. 45 (Aug. 1974).

Vickers, Nat'l Bureau of Standards, *Kitchen Ranges in Fabric Fires*, Technical Report Note 817 (Apr. 1974).

General Services Admin., *Washers and Dryers*, Consumer Information Series No. 8, Stock No. 2200–0079 (Sept. 1972).

Denver Injury Study Unit, *Injuries from the Upset Electric Countertop Cooking and Heating Appliances from Cord Tension* (Jan. 1971).

§ 5.27 Selected legal sources

Products Liability: Clothes Dryers, 6 A.L.R. 4th 1262 (1981).

Products Liability: Defective Heating Equipment, 1 A.L.R. 4th 748 (1980).

Products Liability: Modern Cases Determining Whether Product is Defectively Designed, 96 A.L.R. 3d 22 (1979).

Products Liability: Duty of Manufacturer to Equip Product with Safety Device to Protect Against Patent or Obvious Danger, 95 A.L.R. 3d 1066 (1979).

Products Liability: Stoves, 93 A.L.R. 3d 99 (1979).

Liability of Manufacturer or Seller for Personal Injury or Property Damage Caused by Television Set, 89 A.L.R. 3d 210 (1979).

Liability of Owner or Operator of Self-Service Laundry for Personal Injury or Damage to Patron or Frequenter of Premises from Defect in Premises or Appliances, 23 A.L.R. 3d 1246 (1969).

Liability of Manufacturer or Seller for Injury Caused by Household or Domestic Machinery, Appliance, Furnishing, or Equipment, 80 A.L.R. 2d 401 (1961).

Liability for Injury or Damage from Escaping Refrigerant, 74 A.L.R. 2d 894 (1960).

§ 5.28 Selected industry newsletters

AHAM Appliances Letter
Ass'n of Home Appliances Manufacturers
20 North Wacker Drive
Chicago, Ill. 60606

NEMA News Bulletin
Nat'l Electrical Manufacturers Ass'n
2101 L Street, N.W.
Washington, D.C. 20037

EWRT National Newsletter
The Electrical Women's Round Table, Inc.
6130 Sunbury Road, Suite C
Westerville, Ohio 43081

Electrical Industry Hotline
Int'l Ass'n of Electrical Leagues
2101 L Street, N.W.
Washington, D.C. 20037

Biomedical Electronics
Girard Associates
P.O. Box 455
Mt. Arlington, N.J. 07856

Electric Industries Ass'n—Executive Report
2001 Eye Street, N.W.
Washington, D.C. 20006

Electronics Technicians Ass'n
Association News
Route 3, Box 564
Greencastle, Ind. 46135

IAEI News
Int'l Ass'n of Electrical Inspectors

802 Busse Highway
Park Ridge, Ill. 60068

Engineers:

Hawkeye Safety News
American Soc'y of Safety Engineers
Hawkeye Chapter
Safety Education Building
Iowa State University
Ames, Iowa 50010

§ 5.29 Selected laws, regulations, and standards

Statutes

(1) Consumer Product Safety Act (CPSA), 15 U.S.C. §§ 2051–2083 *et seq*. (1985).

(2) Refrigerator Safety Act, 15 U.S.C. § § 1211 *et seq*. (1956).

Regulations

(1) Antennas (CB Base Station and TV), 16 C.F.R. 1402 (1985).

(2) Refrigerator Safety Act Regulations, 16 C.F.R. 1750 (1985).

Industry Codes and Standards

(1) National Fire Protection Association (NFPA)
  (a) NFPA 70: National Electric Code

(2) Underwriters' Laboratories (UL)
  (a) UL 1556: Coin-Operated Clothes Drying Equipment
  (b) UL 1555: Electric, Coin-Operated Clothes Washing Equipment
  (c) UL 1438: Household Drip-Type Electric Coffeemakers
  (d) UL 1413: High Voltage Components for Television Appliances
  (e) UL 1410: Television Receivers and High Voltage Video Products
  (f) UL 1240: Electric, Commercial Clothes Drying Equipment

(g) UL 1206: Electric, Commercial Clothes Washing Equipment

(h) UL 1086: Household Trash Compactors

(i) UL 1083: Household Electric Skillets and Frying-Type Appliances

(j) UL 1075: Gas-Fired Cooking Appliances for Recreational Vehicles

(k) UL 1028: Electric Hair-Clipping and Shaving Appliances

(l) UL 1026: Household Electric Cooking and Food-Serving Appliances

(m) UL 1025: Electric Air Heaters

(n) UL 1017: Electric Vacuum Cleaning Machines and Blower Cleaners

(o) UL 982: Household Motor-Operated Food Preparing Machines

(p) UL 923: Microwave Cooking Appliances

(q) UL 921: Commercial Electric Dishwashers

(r) UL 859: Electric Personal Grooming Appliances

(s) UL 749: Household Electric Dishwashers

(t) UL 621: Ice Cream Makers

(u) UL 507: Electric Fans

(v) UL 499: Electric Heating Appliances

(w) UL 484: Room Air Conditioners

(x) UL 482: Portable Sun/Heat Lamps

(y) UL 474: Dehumidifiers

(z) UL 430: Electric Waste Disposers

(aa) UL 298: Portable Electric Hand Lamps

(bb) UL 250: Household Refrigerators and Freezers

(cc) UL 197: Commercial Electric Cooking Appliances

(dd) UL 153: Portable Electric Lamps

(ee) UL 136: Pressure Cookers

(ff) UL 130: Electric Heating Pads

(gg) UL 73: Electric Motor-Operated Appliances

(3) Other Voluntary Appliance Standards[51]

(a) ANSI/AHAM FWD–1–1983: Method for Measuring Performance of Household Food Waste Disposers

(b) ANSI/AHAM DW–1–1982: Household Dishwashers

(c) ANSI/AHAM RAC–1–1982: Room Air Conditioners

(d) ANSI/AHAM CI–1–1981: Method for Measuring Performance of Household Electric Curling Irons

(e) ANSI/AHAM MA–1–PS–1980: Pre-Shipment Test Standard for Packaged Major Appliances

(f) ANSI/AHAM HLW–1–1980: Performance Evaluation Procedure for Clothes Washers

(g) ANSI/AHAM FM–1–1980: Method for Measuring Performance of Household Electric Food Mixers

(h) ANSI/AHAM DH–1–1980: Dehumidifier Standard

(i) ANSI/AHAM HD–1–1980: Method for Measuring Performance of Household Electric Hair Dryers

(j) ANSI/AHAM HU–1–1980: Methods of Measuring Performance of Appliance Humidifiers

(k) ANSI/AHAM HRF–1–1979: Method for Measuring Performance of Household Refrigerators, Combination Refrigerator–Freezers, and Household Freezers

(l) ANSI/AHAM FB–1–1978: Method for Measuring Performance of Household Electric Food Blenders

(m) ANSI/AHAM CO–1–1978: Method for Measuring Performance of Household Electric Can Openers

(n) ANSI/AHAM HLD–1–1975: Performance Evaluation Procedure for Household Tumble Type Clothes Dryers

(o) ANSI/AHAM CO–1–1978: Method for Measuring Performance of Household Electric Coffeemakers

---

[51] ASTM: American Society for Testing and Materials; ANSI: American National Standards Institute; AHAM: Association of Home Appliance Manufacturers; UL: Underwriters' Laboratories.

(p) ANSI/AHAM FB–1–1978: Method for Measuring Performance of Household Electric Frypans

(q) ANSI/AHAM I–1–1978: Method for Measuring Performance of Household Electric Irons

(r) ANSI/AHAM T–1–1977: Method for Measuring Performance of Household Electric Toasters

(s) ANSI/AHAM TC–1–1976: Performance Evaluation Procedure for Household Trash Compactors

(t) ANSI/AHAM WBSG–1–1984: Method for Measuring Performance of Household Electric Waffle Bakers/ Sandwich Grills

(u) ANSI/ASTM F430–75: Testing Paper Used for Vacuum Cleaner Filter Bags

(v) ANSI/ASTM F655–80: Test Carpets and Pads for Vacuum Cleaner Testing

(w) ANSI/ASTM F630–80: Specifications for Safety Considerations for Household Vacuum Cleaners

(x) ANSI/ASTM F431: Air Performance Measurement Plenum Chamber for Vacuum Cleaners

(y) ANSI C101.1–1973: Leakage Current for Appliances

§ 5.30 Selected cases

Pierce v. Pacific Gas & Elec. Co., 166 Cal. App. 3d 68, 212 Cal. Rptr. 283 (1985), **defective transformer;** electricity furnished by utility is a "product."

Wehman v. Broaster Co., No. 279865 (Cal. App. Dep't Super. Ct. July 21, 1980), 23 ATLA L. Rep. 473 (Dec. 1980), **commercial pressure cooker;** burns suffered while cleaning; $260,000 settlement.

Cassisi v. Maytag Co., 396 So. 2d 1140 (Fla. Ct. App. 1980), **clothes dryer**.

Smith v. Godfrey, 155 Ga. App. 113, 270 S.E.2d 322 (1980), **heating and air conditioning system;** fire loss; alleged defective heat pump compressor; industry standards.

Boudreau v. General Elec. Co., No. 6094 (Hawaii Ct. App. Mar. 10, 1981), **washer/dryer;** explosion; improper jury instructions.

Lindroth v. Walgreen Co., 407 Ill. 121, 94 N.E.2d 847 (1950), **electric vaporizer;** fire; design defect.

Spesco, Inc. v. General Elec. Co., 719 F.2d 233 (7th Cir. [Ind.] 1983), **fluorescent light fixture;** ballast contained no thermal protector; loft fire.

SCM v. Letterer, 448 N.E.2d 686 (Ind. Ct. App. 1983), **toaster oven;** property damage.

Granger v. Montgomery Ward & Co., 408 So. 2d 320 (La. Ct. App. 1981), *cert. denied*, 412 So. 2d 1097 (La. 1982), **batteries.**

American Guaranty & Liability Ins. Co. v. Little, 328 So. 2d 706 (La. Ct. App. 1976), **stereo receiver-amplifier;** failure to warn.

Goodman v. Magnavox Co., 443 A.2d 945 (Me. 1982), **television;** damage to home; negligence claim accrued on date of fire.

Gediman v. Sears, Roebuck & Co., 484 F. Supp. 1244 (D. Mass. 1980), **electric blanket;** destruction of home.

Hayes v. Hobart Corp., 7 Mass. App. 889, 387 N.E.2d 176 (1979), **food chopper;** design defect.

Conkright v. Ballantyne of Omaha, Inc., 496 F. Supp. 147 (W.D. Mich. 1980), **deep fat fryer.**

Piper v. Tensor Corp., 71 Mich. App. 658, 248 N.W.2d 659 (1976), **high intensity lamp;** inference of defect.

Ryan v. McDonough Power Equipment, Inc., No. 6–81–373 (D. Minn. June 15, 1982); 25 ATLA L. Rep. 423 (Nov. 1982), **lawn mower;** foot amputation.

McCormack v. Hankscraft Co., 278 Minn. 322, 154 N.W.2d 488 (1967), **electric steam vaporizer;** burns from spillage; design defect.

Price v. Admiral Corp., 527 F.2d 412 (5th Cir. [Miss.] 1976), **refrigerator;** destruction of home; product defect.

Lovelace v. Astra Trading Corp., 439 F. Supp. 753 (D. Miss. 1977), **imported mini hair dryer;** heart damage, allegedly caused by fire, could be recoverable as personal injury if causal relationship was established.

Fain v. GTE Sylvania, Inc., 652 S.W.2d 163 (Mo. Ct. App. 1983) **television;** property damage to retailer's place of business; defective product.

Winters v. Sears, Roebuck & Co., 554 S.W.2d 565 (Mo. Ct. App. 1977), **television;** defective heating coil in picture tube.

Sapp v. Carrier Corp., No. 83750 (Mo. Cir. Ct. July 11, 1983), 26 ATLA L. Rep. 423 (Nov. 1983), **air conditioner;** electrocution of repairman; design change; failure to recall.

Butler v. Pittway Corp., 770 F.2d 7 (2d Cir. [N.Y.] 1985), **smoke detectors;** admission of evidence that failure to sound resulted in exposure to unreasonably dangerous condition.

Voss v. Black & Decker Mfg. Co., 59 N.Y.2d 102, 450 N.E.2d 204, 463 N.Y.S.2d 398 (1983), **circular power saw;** use in mobile home; inadequate guard.

Bartlett v. General Elec. Co., 90 A.D.2d 183, 457 N.Y.S.2d 628 (1982), **extension cord;** injuries resulting from bite by child; admissible evidence of subsequent cord design changes.

Mead v. Warren Pruyn Div., Finch Pruyn Sales, Inc., 57 A.D.2d 340, 394 N.Y.S.2d 483 (1977), **refrigerator;** wrongful death; retailer liable for latent manufacturing defects.

Fischer v. General Elec. Hotpoint, 108 Misc. 2d 683, 438 N.Y.S.2d 690 (Suffolk Cty. Dist. Ct. 1981), **refrigerator;** recovery for loss of spoiled food; breach of warranty.

Maccaro v. Twin Grand Central Drugs, Inc., No. 16060 (N.Y. Sup. Ct. Feb. 2, 1978), 21 ATLA L. Rep. 323 (Sept. 1978), **hair dryer;** fell into the bathtub; electrocution; wrongful death; settlement $25,000.

Fowler v. General Elec. Co., 40 N.C. App. 301, 252 S.E.2d 862 (1979), **refrigerator;** house burned; negligent design of thermostat.

Gillham v. Admiral Corp., 523 F.2d 102 (6th Cir. [Ohio] 1975), *cert. denied*, 424 U.S. 913, 96 S. Ct. 1113, 476 L. Ed. 2d 318 (1976), **television set;** design defect; failure to warn.

McDonough v. Teledyne, Inc., No. 77–968026 (Ohio Ct. C.P., Cuyahoga Cty. Feb. 1980), 24 ATLA L. Rep. 88 (Mar. 1981), **television;** house fire; wrongful death; settlement.

Cheney v. RCA, No. 78–980041 (Ohio Ct. C.P., Cuyahoga Cty. Apr. 1980), 24 ATLA L. Rep. 88 (Mar. 1981), **portable color television set;** house fire; wrongful deaths; settlement.

Lawrimore v. Bosman Indus., Inc., No. IV–82–516–T (W.D. Okla. Feb. 14, 1983), **pressure "Cajun" cooker;** severe burns on foot when pan of hot grease fell; $135,000 settlement.

Baird v. Electro Mart Factory Direct, Inc., 47 Or. App. 565, 615 P.2d 335 (1980), **television;** time limitations.

Breidor v. Sears, Roebuck & Co., 722 F.2d 1134 (3rd Cir. [Pa.] 1983), **refrigerator;** destruction of home; expert testimony on malfunction.

Pearsall v. Sanhart Indus., 599 F. Supp. 207 (E.D. Pa. 1984), **smoke detector;** wrongful death; failure to warn.

Freeman v. Avco Corp., No. 76–472 (D.S.C. Mar. 9, 1978), **refrigerator;** wrongful death due to suffocation in refrigerator equipped with latch-lock door; $30,000 settlement.

A.L. Crandell v. Larkin & Jones Appliance Co., 334 N.W.2d 31 (S.D. 1983), **reconditioned clothes dryer;** fire from overheating in drum; implied warranty of merchantability.

Miller v. Bock Laundry Machine Co., No. B–6857 (Tex. Dec. 30, 1977), **clothes dryer;** loss of boy's arm; safety device preventing lid from opening during spin cycle failed.

Bosanko v. Carol Cable Co., No. 84–2128C (Tex. Jud. Dist. Ct. Feb. 15, 1985), **extension cord;** wrongful death; settlement $650,000.

Alvarado v. Rodriguez, No. 81C1 13528 (Tex. Jud. Dist. Ct. Oct. 8, 1982), 26 ATLA L. Rep. 126 (Apr. 1983), **electric fan;** hand injury; settlement $110,500.

Hopkins v. Yaskawa Elec. Mfg Co., No. C81–7933 (Utah Dist. Ct. Salt Lake Cty. Oct. 28, 1983), 26 ATLA L. Rep. 467 (Dec. 1983), **automatic garage door;** descending door; child brain damaged; $1 million settlement.

Clay v. Carrier Corp., No. 77–349–A (E.D. Va. Dec. 16, 1977), 21 ATLA L. Rep. 230 (June 1978), **air conditioner;** compressor exploded; $235,000 settlement.

Bica v. General Elec. Co., 27 Wash. App. 25, 614 P.2d 1323 (1980), **transformer;** design defect.

Pearson Construction Corp. v. Intertherm, Inc., 18 Wash. App. 17, 566 P.2d 575 (1977), **electric heater;** fire damage resulting from arc in attached cord.

Chapter 6

CRIPPLED AT LEISURE: RECREATIONAL PRODUCT-RELATED TORTS

KLUWER LITIGATION LIBRARY REFERENCES

HARLEY & MAGEE, WHAT'S IT WORTH? A GUIDE TO CURRENT PERSONAL INJURY AWARDS AND SETTLEMENTS.

JEANS, LITIGATION: Chapter 4, *Discovery*; Chapter 8, *Direct Examination*; Chapter 9, *Direct Examination of Expert Witnesses*; Chapter 13, *Cross-Examination*; Chapter 14, *Cross-Examination of Expert Witnesses*.

SMITH & MALANDRO, COURTROOM COMMUNICATION STRATEGIES: Chapter 1, *Impression Formation in the Courtroom*; Chapter 2, *Persuasive Strategies in the Courtroom*; Chapter 5, *Preparing for Effective Courtroom Communication*; Chapter 8, *Direct Examination: Presenting the Evidence With Impact*; Chapter 9, *Cross-Examination: Controlling the Case*.

I. Introduction

§ 6.01 In general

The most dramatic thing that comes to my mind when I think about recreational product-related cases is the devastating and crippling nature of spinal cord injuries that are often caused by defective recreational products. Despite the traumatic nature of these injuries, many lawyers fail to pursue these cases. They become trapped, at least at first, in the industry's ploy of blaming the injured party. Once they understand the total fact pattern and the nature of the industry that has designed, manufactured, and marketed the product, these lawyers will understand (1) that the product's dangerous design is all too often a result of conscious choice rather than happenstance, and (2) that consumers are often kept in the dark about crippling injury risks so that companies can maintain product sales. Then they will understand why recreational product cases are such an important part of the trial lawyer's consumer protection arsenal.

Recreational injuries often occur when we least expect them. Plaintiff's guard may be down as he enjoys the pleasures of swimming, boating, bicycling, skiing, snowmobiling, or some other recreational activity. But what about those products used to enjoy this leisure time? While American enterprise has been more than willing to meet our thirst for fun with scores of leisure time products, they have been less than diligent in designing these products for safety or in warning us adequately of hazards that could lead to devastating and crippling injuries. I believe that these products present insidious threats. It is so easy to get caught up in the excitement of play that we lower our guard and, as a result, fall easy prey to products not manufactured with safety in mind.

Perhaps my feelings about these products stem from my experience in representing the tragic victims of these products—young, healthy people struck down in the prime of their lives (most spinal cord injury victims are between the ages of eighteen and twenty-five[1]) because the products they relied on for fun and recreation were not manufactured for safety.

All too often, consumers just don't know the magnitude of the risks they face. They know nothing about these dangers because no one ever told them. Consider the case of a thirteen-year-old girl who was playing with her sister and a friend in a neighbor's new backyard pool.[2] The girl's parents were very concerned about her safety. They were especially wary of the dangers of drowning and had set strict rules for her pool conduct. Conspicuously absent was any rule regarding diving into a shallow backyard pool.

The girls had spent the summer afternoon playing in the pool when tragedy struck. Taking their last dive of the afternoon, the girl's two playmates sat in shock as she failed to come up after them. They looked into the pool to see the horrifying spectacle of her body floating apparently lifeless, bubbles coming out of her mouth. Plaintiff was rushed to the hospital. Her life was saved. But the spinal cord injury she had suffered during that fateful dive rendered her permanently quadriplegic.

Reflecting on his daughter's tragedy, plaintiff's father echoed the response so indicative of this industry's failures: "I was not aware, actually, of such an accident ever happening. It was never in my mind."[3]

---

[1] J. YOUNG, ET AL., SPINAL CORD INJURY STATISTICS, EXPERIENCE OF THE REGINAL SPINAL CORD INJURY SYSTEMS, (Good Samaritan Medical Center, Phoenix, Ariz. 1982).

[2] Berube v. Muskin Corp., No. 77–2230M (D. Mass. Nov. 13, 1981).

[3] *Id*.

These are just a few examples that come to mind. Law books are filled with cases in which snowmobiles,[4] skis,[5] bicycles,[6] boats,[7] pools,[8] recreational vehicles,[9] motorcycles,[10] and many other recreational products have been the source of crippling injury and death.

COMMENT: With the right approach and the right strategy, recreational product cases can be an important part of a product liability trial practice, while at the same time contributing to a national reduction in recreational product-related injuries.

---

§ 6.02 Focus on foreseeable use of product

Why does this slaughter by leisure time products continue? Is it because, as some industry spokespersons and others would have us believe, the people who suffer these injuries are simply fooling around, are not following directions, or should have known better? Are they right when they claim that the risk of quadriplegia from diving into four feet of water is "open and obvious" and, therefore, the injured party assumed the risk or was contributorily negligent by diving in? I don't think so. I have been able to establish, in case after case, that the fault for these

[4] Butaud v. Suburban Marine & Sporting Goods, 543 P.2d 209 (Alaska 1975), *modified*, 555 P.2d 42 (Alaska 1975); Smith v. Ariens Co., 375 Mass. 633, 378 N.E.2d 954 (1978); Bjorkland v. Hantz, 296 Minn. 298, 208 N.W.2d 722 (1973).

[5] Anderson v. Heron Engineering Co., 198 Colo. 391, 604 P.2d 674 (1979).

[6] Walden v. Sears, Roebuck & Co., 654 F.2d 443 (5th Cir. 1981); Caporale v. Raleigh Indus. of America, 382 So. 2d 849 (D. Fla. 1980); Hunt v. City of Los Angeles, C–167–528 (Cal. Super. Ct. 1981); Ries v. MTD Products, No. 1099 (Pa. Super. Ct.).

[7] Lykes Bros. S.S. Co. v. Waukesha Bearing Co., 502 F. Supp. 1163 (E.D. La. 1980); Falcon Tankers, Inc. v. Litton Sys., 380 A.2d 569 (Del. Super. Ct. 1977); Harris v. Bardwell, 373 So. 2d 777 (La. 1979).

[8] Anthony Pools v. Sheehan, 295 Md. 285, 455 A.2d 434 (Ct. App. 1983); O'Brien v. Muskin Corp., 94 N.J. 169, 463 A.2d 298 (1983); Koenig v. Muskin Corp. & W.T. Grant Co., No. 701, A–1973 (Pa. Ct. C.P. Nov. 8, 1982).

[9] Nolan v. Reynolds Trailer Sales, No. 74–183 (D.N.H. 1974); Harrington v. Holiday Rambler Corp., 176 Mont. 37, 575 P.2d 578 (1978).

[10] Winkler v. American Safety Equipment Corp., 43 Colo. App. 241, 604 P.2d 693 (1979); Koons v. Walker, 76 Mich. App. 726, 257 N.W.2d 229 (1977).

injuries does not lie with the injured party, but with the industry and manufacturer of the product who knew full well that a crippling injury could result from the foreseeable use of the product. For reasons of expediency, short-term profits, or just plain greed, the manufacturer often chooses to continue marketing the product despite mounting body counts of catastrophic injury and death, with no significant design changes to reduce the injury risks or adequate warnings to refrain from foreseeably hazardous end use.

COMMENT: No group of products illustrates this failure more graphically than the uniformly four-foot-deep aboveground backyard pool. The very design of these cylinders that hold water invites users to take a fateful dive. Counsel should focus on design issues in preparing the case and ask: "how could the pool have been designed with safety in mind?"

At least 500 diving-related spinal cord injuries occur every year.[11] Many are associated with these products marketed as "backyard country clubs."[12] In 1981, the Council for National Cooperation in Aquatics (CNCA) published what is considered the definitive book on diving-related accidents. Researchers studied 132 diving-related spinal cord injury cases and discovered that all the injured people had sustained their injuries by striking the bottom of the pool (or other water area). They concluded: "A dominant consideration of the study is that the diver is not aware of the actual risk encountered in the head-first entry into water."[13]

These experts place a considerable amount of responsibility on the manufacturer to build and market a product that is free from design features proven to produce such human catastrophe.

---

[11] *See supra* note 1.

[12] *Koenig, supra* note 8, defendant's own promotional literature.

[13] Diving Injuries—Prevention of the Most Catastrophic of All Sports-Related Injuries (A Critical Insight & Recommendations) (M.A. Gabrielson, ed., Nova Univ. Ft. Lauderdale, Fla. 1981) (In cooperation with Aquatic Program of Indiana University of Pennsylvania).

> The intended use of a swimming pool and its attendant equipment should be anticipated and established by the manufacturer and/or builder of the pool and ultimately must be reflected in the pool's design and operating instructions issued to potential users and owners of the pools. . . . *To assume that people of all ages and varying ability are knowledgeable about safe practices in and around the pool is extremely risky*." [Emphasis added.] . . .
>
> Sixty-one of the quadriplegias were the result of people diving into the shallow portions of the pool. . . . Only three of the accident locations had any warning signs calling attention to any potential hazard or restricting people from diving in the area where the accident occurred.[14]

Pool manufacturers know full well that their product can cripple its users if they dive into it. It is up to the plaintiff's attorney to demonstrate this knowledge in establishing the manufacturer's liability and to raise the important questions of why the product was designed and marketed as it was, and why the injured party acted as he did. In many cases, I have discovered that the severely injured person was seduced into acting as he did by a conscious and sophisticated marketing strategy on the part of the product manufacturer that was designed to sell the product regardless of the risks involved. Because recreational products are marketed for fun and enjoyment, lowering our guard of caution and our inhibitions may be an intended and foreseeable use of the product. A good consumer advocate lawyer will not let the defendant's attorneys cajole him into thinking anything less.

COMMENT: Pool cases also provide an opportunity for plaintiffs' lawyers to clarify the distinctions between adequate warnings and instructions, to stress accurate product classification, and to question the validity of end use testing that does not include testing in the ultimate end use environment. Can the product be classified as a sporting good, or is it really a toy? How was the product marketed? Was it accompanied by seductive marketing techniques showing the very act that led to tragedy? Was it tested before being marketed? Was it tested in its end use environment or the

[14] *Id*.

restricted confines of a laboratory? Are adequate warnings provided, or merely instructions for use that the manufacturer tries to pass off as adequate warnings? These are the kinds of questions that I raised in a case tried on behalf of a young man who was rendered permanently quadriplegic in a diving-related case.[15]

II. Checklists

§ 6.03 Checklist: Investigation of a recreational product-related injury case

The following checklist is intended to aid counsel in preparing the recreational product-related injury case. While devoted specifically to the swimming pool case, this checklist is an illustration of the kinds of specific concerns that should draw the attention of the plaintiff's lawyer. The wide variety of applications of leisure time products—ranging from those that are used thousands of feet above the ground to thousands of feet below sea level, and from totally solo activities to activities involving thousands of people—precludes the development of a single checklist suitable for all leisure time products. Nevertheless, as in the pool case, emphasis should be placed on marketing practices that induce the consumer to enter into a relaxing, unconcerned activity while at the same time exposing him to highly dangerous risks. In this sense, the preparation of a case involving an aboveground pool is a good prototype for other types of claims based on leisure time product-related injuries.

____ (1) Consider the following questions in relation to the particular pool:

____(a) Was its depth suitable for swimming?

____(b) Was its depth suitable for diving?

____(c) Did it have a suitable means for entering and leaving the pool?

____(d) Did it have a deck or platform that made it attractive for diving?

---

[15] *Koenig, supra* note 8.

____(e) Were additional safety features sold as "extras" and available at extra cost?

____(f) Did the pool have cushioning to protect against spinal cord or head injuries?

____(g) Were the materials and liners used the safest available?

____ (2) Were specific warnings provided in advertisements, manuals, instructions, directions, or on the pool itself regarding:

____(a) The danger of diving?

____(b) The risks of serious injury or quadriplegia?

____(c) The danger of adding extensions to the pool such as platforms or decks?

____(d) The danger of not erecting the pool according to precise instructions?

____ (3) Did the pool come equipped with warnings, danger signs, or other external notices posted in prominent places to warn users of known dangers?

____ (4) Did the manufacturer or distributor recommend fencing the pool?

____ (5) Locate all print advertisements, promotional literature, and television ads showing use of the pool. Does such material depict people diving into the pool?

____ (6) Was the pool an "attractive nuisance" under applicable law and, if so, did the manufacturer or distributor provide suggestions to minimize the danger?

____ (7) In the course of discovery determine the following:

____(a) Who designed the pool?

____(b) Was the pool subject to a recall or warnings from safety authorities?

____(c) Were additional safety features added after the pool was manufactured?

____(d) Has the manufacturer attempted to warn consumers of postmanufacture hazards?

____(e) Has the manufacturer received notices or complaints about injuries caused by the pool?

____(f) Have added safety features ever been recommended to the pool manufacturer?

____ (8) Contact the following to determine what information they may have on pool-related injuries:

____(a) Spinal Cord Injury Foundation

____(b) Council for National Cooperation in Aquatics

____(c) U.S. Consumer Product Safety Commission

____(d) ATLA Exchange

____(e) ATLA Law Reporter

____(f) ATLA Product Liability Law Reporter

____(g) National Swimming Pool Institute

____ (9) Research law reviews and treatises on recreational product-related cases

§ 6.04 Checklist: Resources in a recreational product-related injury case

The following resources checklist is provided to assist counsel in preparation of a recreational product-related injury case.

____ (1) Selected technical sources

____(a) Society of Automotive Engineers

____(b) Council for National Cooperation in Aquatics

____(c) Swimming Pool Age

____(d) Journal of Biomechanics

____(e) Journal of Safety Research

____(f) American Bicyclist and Motorcyclist

____(g) The Physician and Sports Medicine

____(h) Journal of Trauma

____(i) Machine Design

____(j) Journal of Engineering

____(k) Human Factors

____(l) ASSE Journal

____ (2) Selected popular sources

____(a) Skiing Magazine

____(b) Ski Area Management

____(c) Mechanical Engineering

____(d) American Journal of Public Health

____(e) Engineering

____(f) Mechanix Illustrated

____(g) Consumer Reports

____(h) Physics Teacher

____(i) New Scientist

____(j) Environment

____ (3) Selected government sources

____(a) U.S. Consumer Product Safety Commission

____(b) National Highway Traffic Safety Administration

____(c) National Technical Information Service

____(d) U.S. Coast Guard

____(e) U.S. Parks Service

____(f) U.S. Department of Interior

____ (4) Selected industry sources

____(a) American Alliance for Health, Physical Education and Recreation

____(b) National Pool and Spa Institute

____(c) National Bicycle Dealers' Association

____(d) National Association of Engine and Boat Manufacturers

____(e) Intergovernmental Association of Amusement Parks and Attractions

____(f) National Marine Manufacturers' Association

____(g) RV Industry Association

____(h) U.S. Ski Association

____(i) U.S. Ski Coaches Association

III. Case Study: The Case of the Backyard Country Club[16]

§ 6.05 Facts

On June 26, 1971, the fifteen-year-old plaintiff was cooling off in his neighbor's four-foot-deep, aboveground, backyard pool. He had launched a racing-type dive from a platform adjacent to the pool when he spotted his friend swimming below. He shortened his dive to avoid hitting his friend when disaster struck. The plaintiff's head hit the pool bottom. His spinal cord was fractured. He was rendered permanently quadriplegic, paralyzed from the neck down.

This case is one of several in my files with similar tragic fact patterns: the unsuspecting young man or woman enjoying the cool waters of a backyard pool on a hot, summer day, having fun, diving into the pool water. No one told them that their "fun" could result in a lifetime of paralysis. On the contrary, industry-sponsored advertisements in their local media had depicted the fun of diving into these "backyard country clubs."[17]

§ 6.06 Analysis of case

Many attorneys faced with this fact pattern might initially ask: "Why did he dive into four feet of water, anyway?" They don't recognize the true dimension of the product's defects and the potential liability of all parties along the chain of distribution for the catastrophic spinal cord injuries that result when an unsuspecting consumer dives into shallow pool waters. They don't understand that, as I argued in a recent case, this person was likely doing precisely what that pool's manufacturer and marketers expected him to do—take a dive.

When I first became involved with this plaintiff's case, I was all too familiar with the horrible consequences of spinal cord injuries, including quadriplegia and paraplegia. The excruciating rehabilitation, around-the-clock care, accompanying medical complications, and enormous ex-

---

[16] *Koenig, supra* note 8; in this litigation, the jury returned a record verdict at that time for a pool-related quadriplegia case, and the highest verdict at that time for any product liability case in the history of Pennsylvania—$6.5 million including $500,000 in punitive damages against the pool manufacturer. At the time of publication, this case was on appeal.

[17] *Koenig, supra* note 8.

penses involved in attempting to gain a sense of independence despite these crippling injuries are certainly an overwhelming struggle.

I also knew something else—that the courts were not supportive of plaintiffs' positions in aboveground pool cases. The leading case, also a Pennsylvania case,[18] upheld the defense's argument that the hazards posed by aboveground pools were "open and obvious." Defense attorneys had been using this argument ever since. In effect, they argued that the pool's depth was open and obvious to the injured party and, therefore, that person assumed the risk of diving in. Defense attorneys were baiting the trap and plaintiffs' lawyers were falling right in. Too many plaintiffs' cases have been hurt by using self-defeating arguments such as "even though the pool is sitting aboveground, when you look down, its depth is deceptive." The truth is, these pools are defective in many significant ways. The water depth is only a condition that makes all these defects potentially deadly.

I knew when I entered this case that history would have to be changed. This is what the common law is all about. It is founded on change and creativity. As a noted common law expert instructs: "The law of liability is not what the court said the last time but what it will say in your case. . . . The law is never settled until it is right and it is never right until it is just and serves society to the maximum."[19]

The direction of prevailing case law would have to be altered if I hoped to succeed for my client. Justice required that this plaintiff be duly compensated for his injuries by those ultimately responsible for causing them. Justice also required that the pool's manufacturer be charged punitive damages for its wanton and callous marketing of this hazardous product. The challenge was set.

Like other recreational injury cases, the first questions raised by defendants in pool-related quadriplegia cases are often directed at the conduct of the injured party. Why wasn't he more careful? Why did he dive into four feet of water? As stated previously, this question is usually couched by the defense in language like "open and obvious"—surely he knew that diving into such shallow water could be dangerous?

My approach to these questions is twofold. First, look at the big picture. Why did this young man dive into that pool? Did he want to kill

---

[18] Colosimo v. May Dep't Store Co., 466 F.2d 1234 (3d Cir. 1972).

[19] H. Philo, Lawyers' Desk Reference, at xiii (Lawyers Co-op. Publishing Co., 6th ed. 1979).

himself? Did he know that he could be paralyzed for life as a result of his actions? Ask your client these questions, as I did mine, and you'll get the answer, a resounding "no!"

Why, then? The answer is simple. Like other leisure products, swimming pools bring out the relaxed, uninhibited part of our human nature. We let our guard down, maybe fool around a little, enjoying the pleasure that the product is designed to provide. In my experience, recreational tragedy often strikes under these circumstances. We might be swimming or boating, motorcycling or skiing. We let our guard down and become vulnerable to product hazards.

This may explain our behavior, but isn't it the plaintiff's fault if he was fooling around? Maybe if he was more careful, tragedy could have been avoided? This line of thinking raises the second argument, and a major part of my case against the defendant in the instant case: this young man was doing exactly what the pool's manufacturer and marketers wanted him to do when he took that dive! That fateful dive was only the culmination of a sophisticated marketing strategy that had been developed in a corporate boardroom years earlier—create a new product market for pools that are larger than traditional backyard wading pools but smaller than conventional all-purpose in-ground pools. Market them as "backyard country clubs," all-purpose pools that can turn the backyards of America into instant summer resorts at the cost of a week's vacation, and sell-sell-sell.

That was the scheme and it worked, until lawyers began to challenge it in court. The media carried advertisements depicting the fun and excitement of these "cylinders that hold water." Pictures of happy people diving into the pools were shown in newspapers to increase sales. And it worked. In a few years, more than five million pools were dotting the American landscape! For the pool industry, it was a marketing bonanza. For the consumer, it was a seduction to disaster. For the consumer's attorney, it formed the basis of a claim for negligent marketing.

§ 6.07 Improper use of advertisements showing diving

Some of the most incriminating testimony of this case was provided by the defendant's own expert on the subject of this pool's marketing. Under cross-examination, this expert admitted that using pictures of people diving into the pool's shallow water could be "improper."[20]

---

[20] *Koenig, supra* note 8, testimony of Mr. W, expert witness for the defense in a related case, Berube v. Muskin Pools, Inc., No. 77–2230M (D. Mass. Nov. 13, 1981).

Q. Would it be improper for the manufacturer and/or retailer to advertise these pools showing people diving into them and encouraging that kind of use?

A. No, if the manufacturer had drawings or films that show people literally diving into a pool—not children, now, but adults diving into a pool, I would say that would be improper.

The plaintiff's own expert used stronger language in his testimony regarding these advertisements. He called them "outrageous." "They have photographs with their pools showing people diving through a tube," this expert explained, "and I think there's one with a kid diving from the side. It's outrageous to put advertising like that into the public's hands."[21]

One former company executive admitted that a product line—"Add A Deck"—was actually developed and marketed to encourage diving into the company's pools.[22] Company literature actually referred to this decking as a diving platform.

Q. Can you identify the document?

A. It says "____________ [Name of Store] sun decks and safety fence."

Q. Can you tell us what year or years those decks were manufactured and sold?

A. I can't give you the exact year. It would have been 1970 or 1971.

Q. Can you tell us whether or not this was the type of document that was prepared by the [advertising] Agency that was initially sent to [the defendant] and, in turn, sent to [the retailer] for dissemination?

A. The diagrams in this catalog appear to be the same as what I've seen with [the defendant] diagrams from the [advertising] Agency, but I don't know how it came about to be in [the store's] advertising.

---

[21] *Koenig, supra* note 8, testimony of Mr. P, Professor of Mechanical Engineering, witness for plaintiff.

[22] *Koenig, supra* note 8, testimony of Mr. S, former customer services director, witness for the defense.

§ 6.08 Defendant's knowledge of product's risks created by hazardous design

Such advertising would have been bad enough if the company had not known of the product's risks. And, ironically, this defendant initially argued just that: People were diving into their pools all the time, and this was all right! Sworn testimony from the company's senior executives revealed an alarming attitude that diving was an acceptable and foreseeable use of the pool. They claimed that they had no knowledge when the pool was being designed that diving into its shallow waters could result in quadriplegia. This claim of ignorance was made despite studies and warnings from experts that diving into 3½ or four feet of water was a hazardous practice and should never be allowed.[23] But they also wanted to argue that the risk to this young man was "open and obvious." If it was not obvious to them, I argued, how could it have been obvious to this young man?

Testimony by the defendant's expert was again revealing, as he admitted the risks created by this pool's hazardous design.[24]

> A. [In] most of the cases when you dive into 3½ feet of water, you can keep yourself safe. There are circumstances where you can't, where you may lose control of yourself. Under those circumstances, obviously, whether you dive into 3½ feet of water in an aboveground pool or an in-ground pool, you are going to get yourself into trouble. . . . In general, my feeling is that you shouldn't dive into 3½ feet of water in an aboveground pool, and I don't think my opinion is any different than the manufacturer's.
>
> * * *
>
> Q. Have you ever seen anyone jump [into these pools] feet first?
>
> A. I haven't seen it—I take it back. I have seen several people, adults, jump in feet first.
>
> Q. And probably you have seen, from time to time, people dive into these things?
>
> A. No, I haven't seen people dive into them—but I am aware people have dived into them.

---

[23] *See supra* note 21.

[24] *Koenig, supra* note 8, testimony of Mr. W.

Q. You are aware that it's foreseeable that people would dive into them?

A. Foreseeable that people would dive into a pool.

* * *

Q. Should anyone be permitted to dive into a four-foot pool?

A. No, I don't think diving should be allowed in any aboveground pool.

Q. Period?

A. Period, right.

Q. [I]t would be improper to suggest or recommend to anyone that they do so?

A. Correct.

§ 6.09 Pools sold without ready means of ingress or egress

The manufacturer's executives knew the pool's hazards. They knew that people were diving into their pools, an activity that could have tragic consequences. They knew that these "large, water-filled cylinders" were being sold without ready means of ingress or egress. They knew that ladders, decks, and other ingress and egress means were being sold as expensive optional equipment, and that those ladders that were sold separately were designed in ways that invited diving. They knew that many consumers were rejecting the offered optional equipment for their own homemade makeshift platforms or decks. Others were using any available means as a way of entering the pools: rooftops of their homes and garages, or even trees. I have argued repeatedly that selling a pool without a ready means of ingress and egress is like selling a car without brakes. It is a prescription for disaster.

COMMENT: These pools should not be marketed in the first place, but if they are, they should be equipped with ready means of ingress and egress as a standard item.

---

§ 6.10 —Testimony of pool's designer

Testimony from the pool's designer revealed to the jury his knowledge that diving into the pool's shallow waters could be dangerous, and that consumers would take that dive. He knew that consumers would purchase the pool from one manufacturer and the equipment from another, or build their own means of egress or ingress, and that it would be unsafe to dive from those devices into the pools.[25]

> Q. You were aware [when you were affiliated with the defendant] that, on occasion, many homeowners purchased your pool without any ladder at all?
>
> A. I would say it was possible that they would do that from a dealer.
>
> Q. Or perhaps build their own ladder?
>
> A. I would say it was assumed that the dealer would sell them a ladder or platform for use with the pool.
>
> Q. Or that the homeowner would make one if they were handy?
>
> A. I would say that's a possibility.
>
> Q. It would be important, at least while you were with [the defendant], for the homeowner to pick out an appropriate design ladder for the pool he purchased?
>
> A. I wouldn't say the homeowner necessarily picked it out. I would say the dealer or the outlet would recommend one or have a ladder for the homeowner to purchase.
>
> Q. When you were with [the defendant], did you give the homeowner or the user of the pool any instructions as to what height ladder to use or what height platform to use with their pools?
>
> A. I don't recall specifically. I know ladders of specific heights were provided with pools of certain heights.
>
> Q. Was it unsafe to dive into one of those pool . . . from the ladder that you helped design while you were with [the defendant]?
>
> A. I would say it was not unsafe to perform a shallow dive. Professional diving, yes, a deep dive.

---

[25] *Koenig, supra* note 8, testimony of Mr. B, pool designer, witness for the defense.

§ 6.11 —Testimony of former company director of customer services

Another company executive who handled the company's product liability claims admitted the widespread use of homemade decks.[26]

Q. Back in 1969 and 1970, had you ever seen [the defendant's] pools with a homemade deck constructed at or near it?

A. Yes.

Q. Where had you seen them?

A. Quite a few places, all over. I've traveled extensively for [the defendant] throughout the United States, looking at consumers' pools and dealers' pools; likewise, I've seen a few homemade pool decks.

Q. And to your knowledge, did [the defendant] give the consumer of the pool who did not buy a deck any directions or instructions as to how to construct the deck?

A. No.

COMMENT: This former executive conceded that only three to five percent of this manufacturer's pools were sold with decks. He also knew full well that consumers were building their own decks around this company's pools, and diving into their pools from those decks and from the rungs and platforms of the ladders.[27]

Q. You indicated previously that children or teenagers had used your deck or the rim of your pool [Mr. S.'s own backyard pool] for the purposes of diving into the pool?

A. Yes.

Q. What was your understanding of the general frequency of that practice being followed by other people who owned ____________ pools?

---

[26] *Koenig, supra* note 8, testimony of Mr. S.

[27] *Id.*

A. There's a lot of diving done—quite a bit.

Q. That's generally been your findings, all the way from 1968 or 1969 to the present time?

A. Oh, yes, even if they don't have a deck, they'll dive from a ladder.

Q. That would be the ladder you're talking about? [Pointing to exhibit.]

A. The in and out ladder.

Q. And customarily where do they stand when they start their dive into the pool?

A. On the rung of the ladder, or maybe the top rung or second top rung of the ladder.

§ 6.12 —Testimony of store employee

A buyer for the store that sold the pool involved in this case conceded under oath that this type of equipment was not provided to the purchasing consumer.[28]

Q. Did any of your aboveground pools, during the period of time that you had a responsibility for buying them for [the store], come with any egress-ingress equipment as part of the pool, or was it always an extra?

A. I think it was an extra, as far as the consumer was concerned.

Q. In selling the pools and considering the safety aspect, as you said you did, one of the things that you would want to consider is the reliability of the method of egress and ingress to the pool, is that correct?

A. Yes.

Q. What warnings or instructions did you give a customer who purchased an aboveground pool, but did not purchase a method of egress or ingress?

A. I don't remember. Those instructions would have been issued with whatever instructions would have gone with that product and would have been shipped with the product by the manufacturer.

---

[28] *Koenig, supra* note 8, testimony of Mr. H, buyer for pool retailer.

Q. We can agree, I suppose, that those instructions themselves would be most important to give. Certainly, you would want the customer to receive them as a responsible buyer, wouldn't you?

A. That's correct.

COMMENT: This witness also agreed that platforms would provide a foreseeable base for diving into the pool, an activity that he admitted would be unsafe.[29]

Q. Can you dive and jump when you get to the top platform [of a ladder]? Would that be all right?

A. To the top ladder rung?

Q. I call it a platform.

A. It is permissible. It might be. Would I recommend it? No.

Q. So that while it is permissible during the period of time you were charged with the responsibility for buying aboveground pools, it is not something that you personally would have recommended during that period of time, correct?

A. I never would have recommended it during that time.

COMMENT: He also knew that consumers used this equipment for diving into the pools, and agreed that warnings of the danger of that activity should have been incorporated, for safety reasons, into the pool owner's manual.[30]

---

[29] *Id*.

[30] *Id. See also infra* §§ 6.14–6.17.

§ 6.13 Defendant's failure to investigate cause of prior quadriplegia cases

By the time of this plaintiff's injury, the company already had a record of four quadriplegia cases. By the time our case reached trial, this horrible toll had climbed to thirty-six. Despite this toll, the company made no effort before marketing the pool either to investigate the cause of these injuries or to determine whether they could be prevented in the future. The testimony of one of the company's officials is once again revealing.[31]

Q. And prior to ______ knowledge of the happening in the *Colosimo* case,[32] do you recall any concern or considerations regarding the potential for spinal cord injuries from diving into those aboveground pools?

A. No.

Q. And apparently you have acknowledged the *Colosimo* case as of 1968?

A. Yes.

Q. And after the occurrences in the *Colosimo* case became known, can you tell us whether or not, to your knowledge, the [manufacturer] tried to understand or anticipate how many future diving accidents involving spinal cord injuries could occur?

A. I don't think we had a program to investigate or anticipate how many people would dive into the pool and become injured.

Q. Was there any study in either 1968, 1969, or 1970 to try to identify either the magnitude of these types of injuries or the number of injuries that had occurred?

A. No.

Q. Was that ever done, at any time between 1968 and the present time, by ____________?

A. No.

Q. From your knowledge in dealing with the __________ people, was it your understanding or anticipation that, over the next decade, approximately thirty or thirty-five spinal cord-type injuries might occur?

---

[31] *Koenig, supra* note 8, testimony of Mr. S.

[32] *Colosimo, supra* note 18.

A. I didn't anticipate, and I don't think ________ anticipated that there would be that amount of spinal cord injuries.

Q. Was there any number that you had any idea of what you could reasonably anticipate?

A. No . . . in 1968 I don't believe we anticipated any.

§ 6.14 Inadequate warnings

An important element in the plaintiff's case was a failure to warn plaintiff of the pool's quadriplegia risks. Defendant argued that the message "Do Not Dive" in the owner's manual provided an adequate warning. Plaintiff countered that this was not an adequate warning at all, but an instruction for the pool's use.

§ 6.15 —Distinction between "instruction" and "warning"

Testimony elicited from defendant's expert in a related case[33] assisted plaintiff in communicating this important point to the jury in the instant case. This witness conceded that the "Do Not Dive" message is an instruction for the use of the pool, not a warning. He agreed that for warnings to be adequate, they must tell the user why there is a danger and how he can save himself. This is particularly vital when the risk of injury is of the magnitude of quadriplegia.

COMMENT: The distinction between warnings and instructions can be critical to plaintiff's case, and should be clearly explained and set out for the jury by counsel. For example, if a doctor tells me to "take two aspirins for your cold," that is an instruction. If he tells me, "take two aspirins. If you take more than two, it will make you ill," that is a warning. For consumers of four-feet deep aboveground pools, the risks of quadriplegia that result from diving into the pool's shallow waters require both an instruction *and* an adequate warning.

---

[33] *Koenig*, *supra* note 8, testimony of Mr. W, taken in case of Berube v. Muskin, Inc., No. 77–2230M (D. Mass. Nov. 13, 1981).

§ 6.16 Effectiveness of warning

Q. We have agreed, have we not, that in cases where the risk of injury or the degree of injury is great or serious, that both warnings and instructions should be given, correct?

A. I would say so, yes.

COMMENT: Appropriate warnings, according to this expert, must contain the word "caution" or "danger," be of an acceptable color and size, and be located in a visible position on the pool.[34] To promote consumer safety, these warnings should contain, for example, pictures of a person diving with a red slash through it. All children learn that warning in school. This witness admitted that "it would have been better if the manufacturer had employed such a warning" on the plaintiff's pool.[35]

Q. You would pay some attention, as you indicated earlier, to the magnitude of the risk? In other words, someone is more likely to heed a warning or an instruction if they know that to violate the warning and instruction could result in death or quadriplegia?

A. I would imagine if you put the word "Caution" or "Danger," it's a high-level word, and the word "Danger" you would certainly know in this type of accident, if I was going to write a warning, would be appropriate.

Q. What type of picture would you design in this type of case to inform the consumer or the user of the seriousness of this problem?

A. I think all that's necessary is essentially to put a logo on there with a person in a diving position and the line through it.

Q. You'd put a red slash through it?

A. Yes, because even kids understand that. They see it in their

---

[34] *Id.*

[35] *Id.*

daily life in school and so forth, and it's something that they would respond to.

Q. And as a safety expert, you know that's the new wave of giving a warning instruction, to use a universal sign language?

A. That's right.

Q. So when you see a "No Smoking" sign, what you have is a cigarette with a red slash through the circle?

A. Right.

Q. So that's the kind of thing you are talking about? Right?

A. Yes.

Q. Did you determine in this instance whether the "Do Not Dive" label, if indeed this pool carried such an admonishment, if you can call it that, had the word "Caution" on it?

A. It did not.

§ 6.17 —Warning should have been more explicit

In the opinion of our expert,[36] warnings regarding the hazards of diving into these pools should be even more explicit.

* * *

A. There should have been very distinct danger warning signs located both on the exterior of the pool in each section . . . and on the inside on the liner of the pool around the edge.

Q. Are there any practical problems involved in putting warnings on liners?

A. I'm not sure what you mean by a practical problem. They put nice designs into liners. There is no technical or practical problem in putting warnings into vinyl.

Q. What are some of the ways that could be done?

A. Essentially, including the warning in the color texture of the vinyl floor.

Q. In the manufacturing process of the vinyl, you mean?

A. Sure.

---

[36] *Koenig, supra* note 8, testimony of Mr. P.

§ 6.18 Trade-off of safety for sales

In devastating testimony, one of the defendant's experts conceded that this company's motivation for not providing warnings regarding the risks of quadriplegia from diving into its product was an economic one: the fear of lost sales.[37] In short, consumers were the victims of an industry trade-off of safety for sales.[38]

* * *

A. I think you know as well as I do that there's a constant battle between the reality of the marketplace and safety.

Q. So you are saying that the reason that those kinds of warnings and instructions usually aren't given, in your experience, is a fear? Is that a marketing idea?

A. Well, it's a fear.

Q. A fear that it might deter sales?

A. That's right.

COMMENT: Counsel should always try and focus on the economic factors involved in a manufacturer's decision not to post warnings. Has he put money over safety in his decision-making process? The jury should be made to understand the impact that economic and marketing decisions have on safety considerations.

---

§ 6.19 Closing argument to jury

In my closing argument to the jury, I focused on the defendant's own witness' admission that this pool should never have been marketed.[39] The following is an excerpt from my closing.

You know this case really comes down to one question and an-

[37] *Koenig, supra* note 8, testimony of Mr. W.

[38] *Id*.

[39] *See generally infra*, Chapter 11, *Closing the Case of Slaughter By Product*.

swer. Consider this portion of the defendant witness' deposition taken under oath.

> Q. You indicated that with regard to the conclusion relating to diving that it was potentially very dangerous and actually discouraged. I would like to ask you about that. Do you agree with that, as it applies to aboveground swimming pools?
>
> A. What kind of aboveground swimming pool?
>
> Q. Four-foot aboveground swimming pools of the type we have in this particular case.
>
> A. I concur at this point in time that a four-foot aboveground swimming pool that is sold for residential use with no control over the level of supervision provided or the level of training provided to people that might potentially dive should be prohibited.

If there was not another single piece of evidence in the case, it would seem that this statement made under oath by one of their witnesses should be dispositive of whether this type of pool was safe for diving and whether it should be permitted on the market.

A product must be judged by the way it is sold, by whom it is to be used, and where it is to be used. It is in the backyards and it is a circle, with no deep and no shallow end, and they sold it for all purposes. It is not right. It is for you to say, however.

The bottom line is, with respect to pool safety: Was that pool marketed in a responsible way or was it marketed in a defective way? His Honor will give you a series of questions that itemize some of the defects and I pray, with the right conclusion, this jury will work for the purpose of safety in the future. Thank you.

§ 6.20 —Balancing product's utility against its risk

One test used by courts around the country to determine whether a product is defective is to balance that product's utility against its risk.[40] It is important for the jury to consider this balancing test, and the related question of who should bear the responsibility of the enormous costs of those risks: the product manufacturer and marketer or the injured party?

---

[40] *See, e.g.*, Barker v. Lull Eng. Co., 20 Cal. 3d 413, 573 P.2d 443, 143 Cal. Rptr. 225 (1978).

In order to bring this to the jury's attention during closing argument, it is vitally important to ask the right questions. Consider the following simplified, illustrative approach:[41]

> As between the individual marketer of the product who, for economic reasons—admittedly so—chose to market a product without adequate warnings or instructions, or without other kinds of safety improvements that could have been made, in a manner that exposed users to unnecessary risks, in order to make more money—because they didn't want to affect sales—who should bear the burden of the cost of the injury? The person who is making an extra buck because he didn't do what the law, I respectfully submit, requires him to do or the young man who is now part of the body count, a statistic?

§ 6.21 —Isolating specific product defects

It is important that you isolate various specific product defects for the jury before they leave for their deliberations. A checklist of potential defects may prove helpful. This might include items such as "the pool was defective and of an inadequate depth for recreational family swimming and diving"; "the pool was defective in that it was sold and promoted for uses other than wading or swimming"; or "the pool was defective in that it was sold without means of entering and exiting." Notice the communications to the jury in laymen's terms, rather than the more technical "ingress and egress" language used in examinations of expert witnesses. In those jurisdictions where a defective warning or instruction is also considered a product defect, that type of defect should also be emphasized and listed separately for members of the jury.

§ 6.22 Conclusion

This itemization of possible product defects makes the jurors' job easier and less confusing. When the Erie, Pennsylvania jury returned with its verdict in the instant case, it had responded to special interrogatories and found the pool in question defective on four, separate grounds.[42]

(1) not suitable for any type of diving;

(2) unsafe because it lacked adequate safety devices such as a cushioned bottom, safety ladder, and suitable assembly for entering and exiting;

---

[41] *See supra* note 39.

[42] *Koenig, supra* note 8.

(3) sold without adequate warnings; and

(4) sold without adequate instructions.

This plaintiff was awarded $6.5 million in damages, a record for a pool-related case, of which $500,000 was for punitive damages against the manufacturer only.[43]

We had uncovered overwhelming evidence that this defendant had deliberately marketed a defective product with full knowledge of a mounting body count of quadriplegia victims. Because it wanted to maintain product sales, this defendant deliberately failed to educate or notify potential pool users of the risks of quadriplegia or death associated with diving into the pools. The product was marketed in such a way as to increase the risk of injury by seducing people like my client into diving into the pool. We argued that this willful and wanton behavior entitled the plaintiff to collect punitive damages from the pool manufacturer, and the jury agreed.

IV. Other Recreational Product Hazards

§ 6.23 Bicycles

No single group of consumer products is associated with more injuries each year than the bicycle. According to the Consumer Product Safety Commission, an estimated 500,000 Americans suffer bicycle-related deaths and injuries each year.[44] The victims of this national plague come in all ages: young children whose low profile, often brakeless, "Big Wheels" plastic tricycles are not seen by a driver before tragedy strikes when their acceleration carries these innocent children into the street; youngsters riding the popular "high-rise" bikes, designed for aesthetic appeal and brinkmanship rather than safety; adults on racing bikes designed and marketed as "innovative" with "guarantees" of safety, yet designed with frames known to fail.[45] Like other recreational products cases, victims of bicycle-related injuries often are seduced by a combination of sophisticated marketing techniques and callous manufacturing practices that lead to predictable and avoidable tragedy.

---

[43] *Id.*

[44] U.S. Consumer Product Safety Comm'n, Annual Reports (1981, 1982).

[45] Willette v. Yamaha Int'l Corp., No. 80–1403–T (D. Mass. Mar. 11, 1985).

§ 6.24 Racing bicycles: illustrative case

Consider the case of a husband and wife who had purchased their new racing bicycles—bicycles that were advertised and promoted as new, innovative, lugless frames, "guaranteed" not to fail.

This "innovative" design became the source of tragedy as this couple took their new bikes on a cross-country tour. Riding down a long, winding, mountain road, the young man suddenly felt his bike begin to wobble. His handlebars began to shake. He sensed the bicycle give way underneath him. Before he knew what had happened, he was thrown twenty-five feet through the air, landing in a ditch, unable to move from his neck down. His spinal cord had been damaged. He would be a paraplegic for the remainder of his life.

§ 6.25 —Analysis of case

Like many other product-related injuries, this plaintiff's fate was the tragic culmination of a story that really began in a corporate boardroom several years earlier and many miles away. There the officials of this international bicycle distributor made their decisions to distribute a cheap, lightweight product with no frame lugs, to substitute slick salesmanship for quality parts, and to market as "new" and "innovative" a product that was destined to fail. During the preparation of this case, I reviewed the evidence of this company's marketing practices from its own files. I uncovered what I can only describe as a corporate-inspired quota for disaster—a company that knew and expected a certain percentage of its bicycles to fail, just as the plaintiff's bicycle had failed, but simply counted that human toll in its corporate ledgers when determining whether this product would be profitable to the company.

§ 6.26 —Company's Quality Assurance Plan

The remarkable evidence of this policy came in the form of a Quality Assurance Plan developed for this distributor by a private consultant and obtained by my staff. What more compelling evidence of corporate callousness and cold-blooded acceptance of human tragedy as the price for corporate profit do we need than the words of its own "Plan," an excerpt of which follows.[46]

> An average commuter will ride a bicycle about 42,000 miles in 10 years. . . . Based upon vibration data obtained at Viking Laborato-

[46] *Id*. Quality Assurance Plan (prepared by defendant's consultant Mr. B) at 2.

ries . . . and tubing and brazed-joint strength data . . . the probability calculations indicate that only 5 ____________ "double-brazed" frames out of 100,000 may fail in 42,000 miles of rough road usage. Of the five that may fail, one will last at least 2 years, the second will last at least 4 years, and so on. . . . In general, the numbers mean that no ____________ frame, no matter what its use, will fail in one year. In general, there are 3 chances in 100,000 that a ____________ frame may fail in five years of riding, no matter what its use. If the company guarantees the frame for five years and offers to replace the entire damaged bicycle free of charge, then the cost would not exceed about .08% loss in gross profit per year assuming that replacement costs are three times the original cost of the first bicycle, and 100,000 bicycles are sold per year. If the company guarantees the frame for a lifetime (about 10 years) then the cost would not exceed .15% loss in gross profit, assuming that replacement costs are five times the original cost of the first bicycle and 100,000 bicycles are sold per year.

§ 6.27 —Failure to investigate product's failure

It wasn't long before cracked frames began to pile up in the company's offices, the ugly remains of an uglier corporate policy. Along with the frames came letters—complaints from consumers writing of their personal experiences with these racing bikes, and calling on the company to replace their defective products in their so-called "warranty" program. Apparently, in this corporate mind, the piles of returned frames and outraged consumers' letters were but the price to be paid for marketing a product that would sell. No tests were conducted on the returned frames to learn the source of failure. Their paid consultant took them home to use them as scrap metal. As for the letters, the company's response was similar: no tests, no questions asked, and no communications to other consumers or the company's dealers of this mounting evidence of product failure.

The responses of defendant's product service manager to the plaintiff's questions during cross-examination was revealing of this alarming company nonresponse.[47]

> Q. Over the course of the three years that you were the service manager in charge of this department, did you have frequent claims alleging problems with the top tube and down tube?

[47] *Willette, supra* note 45, testimony of Mr. S, witness for the defense.

A. You have in front of you obvious claims that were made in that regard. . . . We had claims—

Q. Do you know how many?

A. No.

Q. And when the bikes came in for the inspection of the frame, for example, who would do the actual inspection?

A. I would do some of them . . .

Q. And in your inspections, do you recall instances of frames being mailed back to you showing separation of the top tube and down tube from the head tube?

A. I had seen where there had been some cracks.

Q. Have you seen total separation?

A. Yes, I have.

Q. Do you recall whether there was any consistency when there were cracks in the down tube and top tube, or were they all different?

A. They were all in a similar area.

Q. Which was?

A. Just aft of the head tube.

Q. Now, if something is recurring over and over again, or some defect frequently occurred enough times, would you notify anybody within the company that you were getting a series of complaints involving the same particular area?

A. If we had a problem, if we've got something that's recurring, I don't remember the exact procedure, but we communicated with people not only within the company but with the supplier that they were having problems.

Q. All right. Then how many times would it have to occur to be—

A. I can't remember.

Q. Was there an amount?

A. No, no rule of thumb.

Q. To your knowledge, had you ever or did you ever notify any of the dealers who were selling this bicycle, the ____________ bicycle, that you had occasion to see a number of bikes that were either fractured at the top tube or down tube or both?

A. Did I notify the dealers that I had seen bicycles that had frames that had cracked down tubes? No. In a general mailing or general notification-type process? Is that the question?

Q. Yes, sure.

A. No.

Q. Now, if you became aware of a problem associated with the bicycles, who in the company, or maybe it was yourself, would have been responsible to communicate that to the dealers?

A. Well, the sales department would have, but it would not have been their normal function.

Q. Would it have been the service department?

A. Sure.

Q. All right. And at any time during the three years that you were selling the bikes, or subsequently, did you or anyone on your behalf every notify the dealers about any problems with the bicycle at all? Did it ever happen, in other words?

A. Not until we came to this recall.

Q. So the very first time, at least to your knowledge, that you notified dealers was the recall following the front fork assembly failure?

A. That was the first time we notified dealers.

Q. And as we previously established, at no time was any dealer ever notified of any problem associated with either the top tube, down tube, or head tube?

A. Correct.

* * *

Q. Have you ever known, or did you ever know, if anyone ever alleged that they were injured as a result of the head tube—or down tube or the top tube coming apart from the head tube without any—

A. Injured without litigation?

Q. Yes, were you ever notified of any personal injury?

A. I recall there were a couple of cases.

Q. And those couple of cases involved the down tube and top tube?

A. I can't state categorically that it was— you know—

Q. What's your recollection?

A. My recollection is that the person crashed on the bicycle and— but I don't remember the particulars.

* * *

Q. To your knowledge, has your company or anyone in your company instituted any tests of any type to determine why the up tube and down tube of these bicycles were caused to crack or come apart?

A. Did we institute any tests as to why?

Q. Yes.

A. I don't know that we—to my knowledge, we did not have any specific analysis of these.

This failure to investigate was also confirmed by the testimony of a company vice president.[48]

Q. Has anybody to your knowledge, whether it be a governmental agency or private agency, done any investigation about the structural integrity of any other part of the bike other than the fork assembly?

A. Not to my knowledge.

Q. As far as you know, there has been no testing nor any work done to determine whether or not there are any problems with the low tube/top tube, where it meets the head tube?

A. None to my knowledge.

Q. Now, after this fatigue problem took place that caused the collapse, did you contract with anybody to test the remaining portions of the bicycle further to be sure that there were no fatigue problems in any other sections of the bike? Did you ever take any steps to determine whether this fatigue problem occurred in any other portion of this particular bicycle?

A. Not to my knowledge.

---

[48] *Willette, supra* note 45, testimony of Mr. O, witness for the defense.

Q. Did you ever ask anybody, after you found out about this particular litigation, to test the head tube not in preparation for litigation, but for the integrity of the bike?

A. No.

Q. Had anybody, whether it was yourself or somebody else, been concerned that there might be a structural integrity problem with the bike?

A. Not to my knowledge.

Q. Is there anybody in the company that would know, to your knowledge?

A. I don't think there would be anybody who could answer as to why it is. None of us are engineers or metallurgists. We know that a fatigue crack develops, but I don't think there is anybody capable to say why it is developing.

Q. But despite the fact that you knew there was a fatigue problem with the fork assembly, to your knowledge, there has never been any testing by the company for fatigue stress of other areas of the bike other than the front fork assembly? And this is so even after you found out about the cracking?

A. Not to my knowledge, no.

COMMENT: Plaintiff's counsel should work to develop evidence regarding the callous attitude of the manufacturer toward injured consumers. This can become an important part of the plaintiff's case.

As this witness conceded under oath, this was yet another classic case of body count consumerism: don't correct the product until sufficient numbers of consumers have been injured to justify the corrective action.[49]

Q. The only time you would recall a product or make a correction on a product—you would replace a front fork assembly, for instance—was such time when you found out through instances

[49] *Id.*

occurring that there was something wrong with the bike; isn't that so?

A. Logically, the only time you would replace something is when there is a problem.

Q. For example, in the situation with the front fork assembly, it became knowledgeable to you through feedback from consumers that bought the bike, and maybe perhaps the Consumer Product Safety Commission, that the front assembly was fatigue cracking and when you found out there were enough instances of this happening, you set out to find the problem and correct it?

A. Yes.

Q. And we would agree, would we not, that based upon that procedure, if you ever did learn that there was a problem with the bike, with the upper tube and lower tube coming apart from the frame, you might or might not take the same action, based upon the information that you received?

A. We would have to see what the information is.

* * *

Q. Someone in the warranties [consumer complaints] department wrote you and said there has been a separation of one of the tubes from the head tube?

A. Yes.

Q. So, then, we can say now that you know about two of them, two separations of the tube, whatever the reasons may be, right?

A. Yes.

Q. How many instances or allegations of the separation of the tube would or would not alert you to do something about it? What's the rule of thumb . . . if there is any?

A. There is no rule of thumb.

Q. Is there any standard that your company has pertaining to whether or not there is—

A. No.

Q. All right. That's just a decision you would make or wouldn't make?

A. Yes.

Q. So, what happened with that case, with the tube that separated when it hit the curb?

A. I don't know. I would have to read the whole file.

Q. There is a file?

A. Yes.

§ 6.28 —Conclusion

Eventually these bicycles were recalled by this company under pressure from the Consumer Product Safety Commission. In 1981, 30,000 _____________ bicycles were recalled because of their hazardous lugless design.[50] Company executives admitted that recall letters had been sent to only 12,000 to 15,000 people, and only "8,000 dangerous forks were replaced."[51] That leaves 22,000 Americans riding bicycles that could cripple them for life.

This company's orchestrated quota for disaster produced a bicycle that was bound to fail. And fail it did. But consumers fought back. As one company vice president was forced to admit, at least fifteen lawsuits had been filed against this company by consumers injured as a result of fork failure (as of 1982).[52] Eventually, this company will be forced by our legal system to pay the price for its marketing practices. It is unfortunate, however, that this plaintiff and so many other Americans have to suffer such tragedy in the meantime.

§ 6.29 High-rise bicycles

The consequences of unsafe products are often most tragic when children are involved, and bicycles are no exception. Yet most bicycle-related injuries occur to children aged five to fourteen.[53] To the growing child, a bicycle is an adventure, a new freedom, and they make the most of it.

Consider the high-rise bicycle with the large banana seat. When this product arrived on the market several years ago, it literally invited young children to engage in the unsafe practice of riding double on the seat.

---

[50] Consumer Product Safety Comm'n (Press Release, July 10, 1981).

[51] *Willette, supra* note 45, testimony of Mr. O.

[52] *Id.*

[53] Data provided by Nat'l Injury Information Clearinghouse, Consumer Product Safety Comm'n (1983).

Why not? The large seat provided ample room. It also invited that other youthful game, the "wheelie." The seat's design, slightly raised at the rear, was perfectly suited to the young rider shifting his weight to the back, and pulling up on the handlebars. The design of the handlebars encouraged these and other hazardous riding practices, while providing no protection whatsoever upon impact.

§ 6.30 —Parent's testimony before National Commission on Product Safety

Those parents whose children are thrown headfirst over these handlebars know firsthand the pain and suffering they must endure. One mother of a young girl who was injured in this manner testified about her daughter's devastating experience before the National Commission on Product Safety. Because her testimony was so vital and poignant, I have set forth for you its major parts:[54]

> My name is _______. I live in Cincinnati, and I am the mother of three children, two girls, and one boy. I am a housewife, and I also work for four suburban newspapers.
>
> The Thursday before Labor Day this last fall, I received a call from a woman to tell me that my nine-year-old daughter had had a bike accident in front of her house and that she might need or require some stitches. I immediately went a few blocks away to where she was and found that she did, indeed, require a few stitches . . . in her lip, her chin, and where the doctors also removed a teaspoon of fragments that had chipped off when she landed on her chin. There were also stitches needed in her hand, and around the skin graft that was necessary on one of her fingers, plus the ones around . . . her arm. After the stitches, she had her broken arm set and they took many, many X-rays to determine whether or not her jaw was broken. It was, and required setting, and the placement of arch-bars in her mouth, which kept her jaws clamped together. She was on a liquid diet for eight weeks.
>
> This all happened in about three seconds to a bright, pretty, little girl with straight bones, straight teeth, and, fortunately, an irrepressible spirit, having never known one day of serious illness.
>
> * * *

[54] Statement of Mrs. M, Nat'l Comm'n on Product Safety (Mar. 4, 1970).

One of the doctors at Children's Hospital told me that all of his broken jaw cases that summer had been children who were riding on this type of bicycle. He said that riding up in the air, as they must on these high seats, and with their arms spread out to grip the handlebars, there is no protection whatsoever in the event of any impact, such as hitting a curb, and that the riders are actually propelled forward, usually landing on their chins. He also told us that some of these cases had resulted in complete reconstruction of the face, because these children had not been lucky enough to just land on their chins, instead they had just landed facedown with rather catastrophic results. In his opinion, and mine too now, the joy of a child having such a super-bike is not worth the anguish and extra danger of having a wreck on one.

Unfortunately, the same thing that happened to our daughter could happen to any child whose loving parents have purchased for them what seems to be their heart's desire—a bicycle with the little wheels, high banana seats—which are conducive to riding double—and handlebars that are widely spread apart at the grips. These bikes are the rage with the young bike-riding set, and you have probably seen them going up and down the streets. But what we did not know then, but have since learned through our bitter experience, is that their design makes them perhaps the unsafest means of transportation yet devised.

§ 6.31 —Manufacturer's testimony before National Commission on Product Safety

Manufacturers not only knew that children would follow their natural instincts for play and adventure on these bicycles, they actually encouraged it. Their advertising campaigns were built around themes of adventure and danger. They were designed to encourage daredevil activity. Mr. S was President of ____________ Bicycles when he represented the Bicycle Manufacturers Association of America in testimony before the National Commission on Product Safety. He boasted under questioning from the Commission Chairman that the high-rise bicycles were toys, and that children were expected to "have fun" on them.[55]

Q. A witness earlier this morning referred to the influence of advertising on product misuse by a consumer. The staff has collected a number of advertisements for bicycles which certainly suggest

[55] Statement of Mr. S, Nat'l Comm'n on Product Safety (Mar. 4, 1970).

a misuse on the part of youngsters. For example, the first one . . . shows a lad with all of his weight on the back wheel, and the front wheel up in the air. A youngster, seeing that, would desire to influence his parents to buy that bicycle and would want to get hold of it to try that stunt. The names used to advertise the bicycle seem to suggest that the advertiser desires youngsters to use it for acrobatics. . . . The names are "Barracuda," "Beast," "Screamer." . . . Are you familiar with these advertisements? You must be.

A. Yes, I am familiar with them. I am also familiar with the names . . . today the list is crowded with automobile names. . . . Well, it is a fun product; there is no question about it. The children use it in that sense. It is not primarily a product for transportation, this one; it is for fun.

Mr. S later admitted that the product was marketed before the scientific facts to support its marketing were even known. In effect, the industry saw a potential market, knew children's yearnings for it would be irresistible, and pushed forward. Consider this dialogue.[56]

Q. [Y]ou think it is safe, but apparently you have not made any in-depth study to determine whether it is or not. . . . It bothers us that you think these bicycles are as safe as the standard or traditional form of bicycle. I rather feel that you should not be expressing that kind of opinion based on your contingencies or theories without some scientific facts to back it up.

A. We intend to develop some scientific facts—

Q. Well, you intend to. This means you have not done it. I do not think you are in a good position to think they are safe, when there is some scientific evidence to the effect that they are not as safe. That is what bothers me.

A. I think we are perhaps differing on what evidence is available.

Q. Well, at our very first hearing a year ago November, the Chairman of the Pediatrics Committee of the American Medical Association testified that they were getting a great incidence of chin bone injuries, quite severe ones, due to the high handlebars. That statement has been available for well over a year now. In your own examination of data, have you attempted to determine

---

[56] *Id.*

any degree of severity? Has there been an increase in more severe accidents?

A. Well, we are in the process of doing that, to find out if they are more severe. That evidence is not all in. I was asked by the Commission . . . whether we crash-tested vehicles as a means of checking severity of accidents. The answer to that is, "No, we have not done that." It is not part of our normal practice to crash-test to find out what happens in the event there is an accident.

Q. But as an individual manufacturer, what engineering studies have you made?

A. Well, we did not crash-test the bicycle, we have never crash-tested bicycles of any configuration, but we did consumer-test this product in the hands of children to find out if it was less safe than a conventional design, and we concluded it was not, in the hands of the user.

COMMENT: An important aspect of a products liability case can be the defendant's failure to test the product for safety before marketing it. Especially if the product is developed in response to market demand, the safety tests may be less than adequate because they detract from the time needed to get the product onto the market. This is a prime issue for plaintiff's discovery.

---

§ 6.32 Plastic tricycles

For younger children, the counterpart to the high-riser is the three-wheeled plastic tricycle. These plastic tricycles have seemingly replaced the traditional metal product in meeting the bicycling needs for our youngest children. As I can attest from my own practice, the low height of these cycles, combined with the lack of breaking mechanism in many models, can prove deadly to a small child.

The combination of young children, the thrill of increased speed, the lack of brakes, and the cycle's low profile create an inevitable prescription for disaster.

Consider the five-year-old girl who was crossing the street on her plastic tricycle one afternoon as her mother sat waiting for her.[57] Suddenly, a car turned the corner and slammed into the plaintiff. The girl suffered severe and permanent injuries. Sworn testimony from company executives revealed that they had not tested the tricycle adequately for its visibility to oncoming automobiles. They rejected advice from their staff to add a "safety flag" to increase the tricycle's visibility.[58]

Similarly, the manufacturer's negligence in designing a similar cycle was demonstrated dramatically in a New Jersey case in which a seven-year-old boy was struck as he was riding his brother's "Big Wheels."[59] A safety engineer testified that the cycle was unsafe because it lacked a mechanical braking system. Had it been equipped with brakes, the injury could have been reduced or avoided altogether.

Adequate braking systems were known, were available to the manufacturer, and were technologically feasible when the plaintiff's "Big Wheels" was built. The manufacturer claimed that it was not economically feasible to add a brake mechanism to that bike. Yet, he admitted that models built before the accident did include such a braking mechanism, as well as models built after the accident. The court concluded that "the later model manufactured by defendant incorporated a hand-operated lever brake, a fact which would appear to question [the defendant's witness'] opinion that such a brake would not be economically feasible."[60]

Clearly, manufacturers can design a safer product. They can incorporate braking mechanisms and a projection device to increase the low cycle's visibility to motorists. As our children's demand for plastic tricycles continues to grow, their safety hangs in the balance.

§ 6.33 Winter sports

Like swimming and bicycling, winter sports-related cases may lead counsel to question at first glance the behavior of the injured party. The

---

[57] Vincent v. Louis Marx Co., No. CA 80–738–MC (D. Mass.). Case currently pending. Opened April 18, 1980).

[58] *Id.*

[59] Lavin v. Fauci, 170 N.J. Super. 403, 406 A.2d 978 (1979).

[60] *Id.*

plaintiff who is rendered quadriplegic in a snowmobiling accident, for example. Was he traveling too fast when the snowmobile jumped unexpectedly? Was he hotdogging it on a frozen lake?

§ 6.34 —Snowmobiles

Every year, thousands of people are injured, some severely, in snowmobile accidents.[61] One common cause of severe injury is the snowmobile's "jump" when it encounters a raised object, hill, or other surface irregularity in its path. When it "jumps," the occupant's body, particularly the spine, bears the brunt of the force.

I represented one woman who suffered a fractured spine when she was riding her snowmobile while vacationing in Maine.[62] She was driving her machine on a frozen lake covered with snow when the accident occurred.

> I was on the other side of the lake. It was a wide span of snow and quite flat. . . . I was trying to see how it was running. . . . I was going quite fast, then I saw up ahead of me, it looked like an irregularity, some snow, so I throttled down and started braking, and I realized I couldn't stop, and I went over a little bump, and then I hit the ice. . . . When I came back up again, there was a higher bump. . . . I went over the top of that, I came down, and hurt my back.[63]

Her snowmobile had a braking device, but it was not designed to stop her immediately, as in an automobile.

> I couldn't stop, I realized that . . . it had a hand brake, and you just press on it . . . it stops the tread, but it doesn't stop it immediately. To brake down, it takes a while . . . it doesn't lock.
>
> When I landed, I really hit it. It was a hard impact. I felt it right up my spine. The first thing I felt was tremendous pain up my spine . . . then the feeling of hurting on the side toward the back . . . the machine just came to a stop. . . . I just sat there . . . I saw some people off in the distance, and I was trying to get their attention . . . then the emergency patrol arrived. . . . I couldn't seem to hold myself, my body up. . . . I was in pain, it was more like numbness . . . it

---

[61] In 1980, the Consumer Product Safety Commission estimated that 18,000 people suffered snowmobile-related injuries.

[62] Sabo v. Bombardier, Ltd., No. 73–22T (D. Mass. Oct. 9, 1975).

[63] *Id.*, testimony of the plaintiff.

> was my lower back and the back of my hip, my sacroiliac.[64]

The plaintiff was rushed to the hospital with a compression fracture of her lower spine. She spent six weeks hospitalized in a prone position, then underwent physical therapy to regain her strength and mobility.[65]

Is such a plaintiff to blame for her permanent crippling injuries? I don't think so. Not if we consider that members of the snowmobile industry have known for years that their products have jumping problems, and that jumping the vehicles is the most prevalent cause of broken backs. They also know that spinal cord injury victims often engage in their risky behavior in response to the industry's promotional literature.

§ 6.35 —Skiing

Skiing is another national winter pasttime that involves millions of Americans in the pursuit of leisure. The thrill, challenge, and excitement of pitting one's own skills against the environment force the skier to rely heavily on safe and effective equipment. It is all too easy to accept skiing injuries as inevitable and unfortunate consequences of the ski experience. Undoubtedly, many such injuries are the result of improper behavior or inadequate training. All too often, however, a cursory examination will lead counsel to overlook the design of the skis or ski bindings as a cause of the plaintiff's injuries.

Releasable ski bindings are designed to free the boot from the ski before the forces created by falling cause injury. If they fail to perform adequately, the result can be injury for the unsuspecting skier.

A client of mine was skiing at Vail, Colorado, when his binding failed to release.[66] He had set out with his brother and some friends for a day on the slopes. He recalled,

> We headed up to Flapjack on line number six. I liked Flapjack, having skied it at least ten times before. . . . It was an intermediate run, and offered no real challenge. . . . I skied down about two hundred yards. . . . I remember attempting a right turn on a slope and catching the tip of my left ski. This caused me to fall forward and tumble down the slope in a slow twisting turn to the right. . . . My skis did not release. . . . I felt a sharp pain in my right ankle. . . .

---

[64] *Id*.

[65] *See supra* note 62.

[66] Hodge v. Tennis & Squash Shop, No. 76–2374T (D. Mass. July 17, 1980).

> I slid another six feet before coming to a rest. I realized right there that my leg was broken and that I needed help.
>
> I managed to release my right boot, which was still firmly bound to the ski. My brother was immediately on the scene. He helped me out of both skis and I got in the most comfortable position I could to wait for the Ski Patrol. . . . The pain in my leg became sharp whenever I moved. . . . The Ski Patrol arrived, splinted my leg, and took me to the Vail Clinic. On the way down the mountain, my thoughts were how stupid it was to break one's leg when no special risks were being taken, and why hadn't my bindings released.[67]

Our discovery in this case revealed that the defendant's director of engineering was advised by his own consultant of the boot binding's potentially unsafe design. His decision to ignore these warnings, revealed in his responses to my examination, provided important evidence in plaintiff's case.[68]

* * *

A. ____________ said that when the binding is released, the upper part of the boot can come in contact with one of the wings of the binding.

Q. With what effect?

A. It would affect the release of the binding.

Q. In what way?

A. It could increase the setting or the effective release force.

Q. The force necessary before the boot will release from the binding will be a greater force under the circumstances just described than would be the force necessary, or the force, rather, at which the release mechanism of the binding was set. Is that clear to you?

A. Yes.

Q. Do you know whether Mr. L found that it would be greater?

A. Yes, I think he found that it would increase.

Even after he learned of the potential design defects, this company executive made no effort to spread the information within the corpora-

---

[67] *Id.*

[68] *Hodge, supra* note 66, testimony of Mr. C.

tion, within the industry, or to an unsuspecting public.[69]

Q. When did you first learn of Mr. L's findings with respect to the binding and boot?

A. Oh, I'd say we discussed it probably in 1974 or 1975.

Q. And did you discuss it at that time with anyone else in the ____________ Corporation?

A. No.

Q. Did you make any memorandum of that conversation?

A. No.

Q. And did Mr. L, to your knowledge, discuss it with anyone else in the ____________ Corporation?

A. Not that I know of.

Q. To your knowledge, after the findings were reported to you by Mr. L, did [the corporation] make any communications to retailers or consumers of the equipment—

A. No.

Hazards of ski bindings are not new to skiing enthusiasts. As one industry expert recalled:[70]

> In the early days of Alpine skiing, retention was the only thing that mattered in evaluating bindings. By the [1950's], when bindings began to provide releasable features, safety became an issue for the first time. By the 1960's, the emphasis had shifted back to retention because of the unpredictable performance of many early release bindings. In the 1970's, the manufacturers again turned their attention to the development of safer designs.

Also in the 1970's, the U.S. Consumer Product Safety Commission warned consumers:

> [W]hen a skier loses control, the binding must release him from the skis before he suffers a serious injury. At the same time, the binding should not release too easily, exposing the skier to injury from an unnecessary fall. . . . For the beginner skier, a good general rule in selecting bindings is that the more ways a binding releases, the

[69] *Id*.

[70] Ettinger, *Bindings '83*, 35 SKIING MAG. 162 (Sept. 1982).

better.[71]

In the 1980's, incompatible equipment remains a threat to consumer safety. One expert warned of this threat in *Skiing Magazine*, "In the current decade, there has been a recognition of problems of compatibility between boot and binding, first addressed by the early plate designs. . . ."[72]

The federal government estimates that 50,000 Americans received hospital care for ski-related injuries in 1980.[73] Yet, the agency with the authority to act, the Consumer Product Safety Commission, has set no standards for ski safety. It has developed no controls to reduce the unnecessary injuries in what is a major American leisure time activity.

V. Preventing Recreational Product-Related Injuries

§ 6.36 In general

I have been stating publicly for years that the uniformly four-foot-deep aboveground pool is too hazardous to be marketed and should be banned by the government. Experts agree that these pools present invitations to dive, and that diving can produce catastrophic, crippling, spinal cord injuries.

As long as these pools continue to be marketed, manufacturers and sellers must take some fundamental steps to prevent quadriplegic injuries. These include: selling these products with prescribed, required, and safe methods of ingress and egress that are an integral part of the pool; providing explicit and conspicuous warnings of spinal cord injury risks both on the pools themselves and in accompanying literature; providing clear and explicit warnings against using homemade platforms, decks, and other means that can inadvertently be transformed into agents of destruction when unsuspecting friends or neighbors proceed to take a dive; ceasing to market these pools with means of ingress and egress including stairways, platforms, and decks, as extras, which present convenient and inviting places to launch a dive and usually cost as much as the pool itself; ceasing to market these pools with advertising that depicts people diving into the pools' inviting waters; providing ladders of safe design that do not encourage diving; not providing the six- or eight-inch

[71] Consumer Product Safety Comm'n, *Ski Equipment* (Fact Sheet Apr. 1975).

[72] Ettinger, *supra* note 70.

[73] Consumer Product Safety Comm'n (Annual Report 1980).

rims that go around pools that are cosmetic embellishments, providing no additional structural support, but posing unnecessary hazards when children use them to jump or dive; and designing these pools with liners designed to provide friction when a diver's hands make contact with the pool's bottom.

In addition, federal, state, and local safety authorities, as well as pool industry members, should develop uniform safety requirements governing the design of these pools. Apparently, this safety threat has slipped between the cracks of public safety officials' regulatory agendas, and has been all but ignored by members of the swimming pool industry.

§ 6.37 Prescribed, safe methods of ingress and egress

There is no excuse for this industry's continued failure to meet the public's safety needs. Consumers who purchase these pools without such prescribed means will find their own improvised means including makeshift platforms, decks, and other homemade entryways, with no guidance or warning of their grave risks.

Moreover, selling these items as expensive "extras" only encourages consumers to reject them in favor of their own alternate means. Often, surrounding rooftops, tree limbs, and other convenient structures become the natural substitute for expensive but safer ingress and egress means.

§ 6.38 Explicit and conspicuous warnings

The apparent industry philosophy that adequate warnings will deter pool sales has contributed to this product's hazardous nature. These pools must be marketed with clear, conspicuous warnings that diving is a dangerous act with catastrophic consequences—quadriplegia, paraplegia, and death. This industry's use of "DO NOT DIVE" decals and descriptions of them as adequate warnings of their products' risks is one more example of their callous indifference to human safety. Their own experts have admitted under oath that these messages are instructions, not warnings, and that warnings are required in light of the level of risk posed by these products.[74]

These so-called "swimming pools" should be accompanied by permanently affixed warnings at several locations on the pool itself—in addition to the accompanying literature, owner's manual, promotional materials,

[74] *Koenig*, *supra* note 8, testimony of Mr. W.

and advertising—that diving into this product has and can result in crippling spinal cord injuries, including quadriplegia, paraplegia, and death. Diagrams should be provided to illustrate graphically how this crippling injury occurs. Depictions of people diving with red slashes through the illustration, as in other safety literature, will clarify the warning and the risks.

§ 6.39 Warnings against use of makeshift means of ingress and egress

All pool users must be provided adequate and clear warnings that use of makeshift platforms, decks, and other means of entry for diving or jumping including nearby roofs, tree limbs, and other structures can lead to catastrophic injury or death, and are therefore not worth the risk. This warning, in promotional literature and owners' manuals, as well as on the pool itself, must be provided in the hope of preventing further tragedy before it can strike.

§ 6.40 Ceasing alluring advertising depicting diving

We don't have to look far to find advertising of aboveground four-foot-deep pools that contain alluring and seductive pictures or illustrations of people taking a dive. The use of seductive advertising, which encourages this dangerous activity, must be recognized publicly as an outrageous and negligent act. There is no excuse for this continued marketing practice.

§ 6.41 Ladders, rims, and other unnecessary invitations to dive

Pool industry members will do almost anything to make their product more attractive to increase sales, including using such aesthetically pleasing embellishments as six- and eight-inch rims that go around these pools. These rims provide no additional structural support, yet pose unnecessary hazards when children use them as platforms for diving and jumping. Other invitations to dive include A-frame ladders with top steps above the rim. These ladders can be designed so that they are below the rim on interior and exterior sides of the pool, where they do not encourage diving or other hazardous pool uses.

§ 6.42 Alternative pool liners

Other design improvements that can reduce the diver's risk of catastrophic injury include less slippery pool liners. All too often, slippery vinyl liners make a hazardous situation even worse when a diver's outstretched hands slip upon contact with the pool bottom, leaving his head and spinal cord to bear the full brunt of impact pressure. Safer pool liners have been available for years and have been espoused by pool safety advocates. What excuse is there to not take such steps, which may reduce the risks of quadriplegic injury?

§ 6.43 Stringent government action

The Consumer Product Safety Commission has known for years that aboveground uniformly four-foot-deep pools pose grave risks of spinal cord injury. As previously noted, this agency's investigative reports have revealed this threat since the late 1970's.[75] Yet this agency has failed to take significant action to reduce this product's safety risks. With no safety standards for these products at either the federal or state levels, consumers remain at the mercy of an industry whose callous attitude to consumer safety is a matter of record. There is no excuse for this continued failure of our safety authorities to take firm and swift action to remove this dangerous product from the streams of commerce.

§ 6.44 What can lawyers do?

Litigation has already had an impact in this field, but we have a long way to go. Pool industry executives admit that their development of "DO NOT DIVE" decals for their products was initiated in response to litigation. Unfortunately, these manufacturers then tried to hide behind these so-called "warnings" as a shield against liability in subsequent suits. As I demonstrated in *Koenig*, this industry tactic is no longer acceptable, and courts have recognized that this decal is not a sufficient warning in light of the catastrophic injury risks these products impose on the American consumer.[76] Because plaintiffs' attorneys have been successful in litigation brought against pool manufacturers and distributors, including *Koenig*, the industry is finally beginning to come around and recognize its responsibility to warn the American public regarding their products' threats. A recent industry brochure bears this message on page one.

But this is not enough. How many consumers and pool users will re-

---

[75] Medical Analysis of Swimming Pool Injuries (Study conducted for U.S. Consumer Product Safety Commission by Department of Orthopedics and Rehabilitation and Department of Neurosurgery of Univ. of Miami School of Law and Nova Univ. Dec. 1977).

[76] *See supra* note 36.

ceive this message? How many manufacturers will tell consumers the truth on the pool itself, that "DIVING INTO THIS POOL CAN CAUSE CRIPPLING SPINAL CORD INJURY"?

The pressure brought upon the industry must be increased until this industry recognizes that because of their continued marketing of this hazardous product, they will (1) pay on that valued bottom line of their quarterly profit ledger, and (2) tarnish their cherished public image.

Lawyers can also press for stringent, effective government action to ban from the marketplace these "cylinders that hold water." The Consumer Product Safety Commission has known for years that these products pose grave safety risks, but has failed to take effective action to remove this risk from the marketplace. I have shared revealing evidence from my practice with agency attorneys in the hope of encouraging their prompt action. I also encourage my colleagues to share their pertinent information with this agency, and to press the agency for firm action to ban these hazardous products before further tragedy strikes.

VI. Litigation Sources: Bibliography

§ 6.45 Selected technical sources

Pools

American National Red Cross, *Swimming and Water Safety* (Doubleday & Co. Inc. 1968).

American National Red Cross, *Basic Rescue and Water Safety* (1974).

Conference for National Cooperation in Aquatics, *The Outdoor Swimming Pool: A Study Report* (Temple University 1956).

Conference for National Cooperation in Aquatics, *Lifeguard Training Manual* (Association Press 1964).

Council for National Cooperation in Aquatics, *Swimming Pools, A Guide to Their Planning, Design and Operation* (Washington, D.C., 3d ed. 1975).

Council for National Cooperation in Aquatics, *Diving Injuries: Prevention of the Most Catastrophic Sport Related Injuries* (M.A. Gabrielson, ed., Indiana University of Pennsylvania 1981).

C. Batterman, *The Techniques of Springboard Diving* (MIT Press 1968).

G. Butler, *Outdoor Swimming Pools* (Nat'l Recreation Ass'n 1955).

Fabian & Dietrich, *Modern Swimming Pools of the World* (Nat'l Pool Equip. Co. 1958).

M.A. Gabrielson, et al., *Sports and Recreational Facilities—For School and Community* (Prentice-Hall 1958).

Gabrielson, Spears & Gabrielson, *Aquatics Handbook* (Prentice-Hall, 2d ed. 1966).

Guide for Planning Facilities for Athletics, Recreation, and Health Education (Athletic Ins., Inc. 1965).

P. Jones, *Swimming Pools* (Doubleday & Co., Inc. 1982).

J. McElhaney, R. Snyder, J. States & M. Gabrielson, *Biomechanical Analysis of Swimming Pool Neck Injuries* (Soc'y of Automotive Engineers, Inc. 1979).

Modern Swimming Pool Data and Design. A Guide for Consulting Engineers on the Design and Operation of Swimming Pools and Swimming Pool Equipment (Refinite Corp. 1953).

L. Murphy, *Planning the Outdoor Swimming Pool* (Iowa State College 1931).

C. Nicholls, *Municipal Swimming Pools*, Parks & Recreation (Mar. 1948).

D. Neilson & J. Nixon, *Swimming Pools for Schools* (Stanford University Press 1954).

P.H. Perkins, *Swimming Pools* (Elsevier Publishing Co., Ltd. 1971).

R.N. Perkins, *Swimming Pool Operator's Manual* (Perkins Laboratories 1950).

R.M. Scharff, *Swimming Pool Book* (Barrows & Co. 1958).

Swimming Pools—A Guide to Their Planning, Design and Operation (M. Gabrielson, ed., Hoffman Publications 1973).

University of Miami School of Medicine & Nova University, *Medical Analysis of Swimming Pool Injuries* (Consumer Product Safety Comm'n 1977) (A report of case studies of 72 swimming pool injuries).

J. Young, et al., *Spinal Cord Injury Statistics, Experience of the Reginal Spinal Cord Injury Systems* (Good Samaritan Medical Center 1982).

Bicycles

Bicycle Accident: An Exhaustive Study, 92 Am. Bicyclist & Motorcyclist No. 12 (Dec. 1971).

Bohlmann, *Injuries in Competitive Cycling*, 9 Physician & Sportsmedicine No. 5 (May 1981).

Daniels, Zajkowski & Drury, *Bicycle Riding Performance* (6th Congress of the Int'l Ergonomics Ass'n July 11, 1976).

Davis & Hull, *Measurement of Pedal Loading in Bicycling, Analysis and Results*, 14 J. Biomechanics 857–72, No. 12 (1981).

Drury & Daniels, *Predicting Bicycle Riding Performance Under Controlled Conditions*, 13 J. Safety Research No. 2 (Summer 1980).

Kobas & Drury, *Bicyclist's Exposure to Risk* (6th Congress of the Int'l Ergonomics Ass'n July 11, 1976).

Lakshmikanthan & Sensupta, *Control of Runner Defects in Cycle Rim Manufacture* 4 Q.R.J. No. 3 (Sept. 1977).

Miller & Ross, *Design of Variable Ratio Chain Drives for Bicycles and Ergometers—Application to a Maximum Power Bicycle Drive* (Int'l Conf. on Medical Devices & Sports Equip., Century 2—Emerging Tech. Conf., San Francisco, Cal. Aug. 1980, ASME 1980).

Soden & Adeyefa, *Forces Applied to a Bicycle During Normal Cycling*, 12 J. Biomechanics 517–541, No. 7 (1979).

Zhao, et al., *Research of Welding Front Bicycle Fork with Mag Welding*, Tiajin Daxue Xuebuo No. 2 (1983).

Skiing

Bahniuk, *The Biomechanics of Ski Boots*, J. Safety Research (Mar. 1974).

Erskine, *Recent Change in the Pattern of Ski Injuries*, J. Trauma (Jan. 1974).

Gaylor & Rombold, *Handbook for Ski Slope Development* (Am. Inst. of Park Executive, Inc. 1964).

O'Malley, *Trends in Skiing Injuries*, Physician & Sportsmedicine (Dec. 1978).

Outwater, *The Engineering Problems of Ski Safety*.

Shealy, *ASTM Standards for Ski Binding Performance: Environmental Testing of Releasable Ski Bindings* (Congress of the Int'l Ergonometrics Ass'n, 6th & Tech. Program of the Annual Meeting of the Human Factors Soc'y, 20th July 11–16,1976).

Von Allmen, *Beat; Safety of Ski Sloper* (Part of Masters Thesis in M.E., University of Vermont 1971).

Zimmerman, *New Technology Protects Skiers from Themselves*, 51 Machine Design 20–22, No. 1 (Jan. 11, 1979).

Football

Torg & Quedenfeld, *Effect of Shoe Type and Cleat Length on Incidence and Severity of Knee Injuries Among High School Football Players*, Research Q. (Temple University 1971).

Boating

The Application of the Federal Boat Safety Act to Boat and Associated Equipment Manufacturers (Soc'y of Automotive Engineers, Tech. Paper No. 2, 1978).

Motorcycles

Muller, *Evaluation of Costs and Benefits of Motorcycle Helmet Law*, 70 Am. J. Pub. Health 586–92 (June 1980).

Muller, *Evaluation of Effectiveness of Motorcycle Daytime Headlight Laws*, 72 Am. J. Pub. Health 11 (Oct. 6, 1982).

How Crash Helmets Can Cause Accidents, 93 New Scientist 777 (Mar. 25, 1982).

Watson, et al., *Repeal of Helmet Use Laws and Increased Motorcyclist Mortality in U.S. (1975-76)*, 70 Am. J. Pub. Health 579–85 (June 1980).

§ 6.46 Selected popular sources

Auran, *Ski Gear 81: New Boots*, 33 Skiing 88–94, No. 1 (Sept. 1980).

Berto, *The New Stuff for 1984*, 25 Bicycling 150–52, No. 4 (May 1984).

Brown & Allen, *Five New Folding Bicycles*, 25 Bicycling 103–09, No. 4 (May 1984).

The Center for Auto Safety, *Snowmobiles and Snowmobs: A Critical Look at a New Industry* (1972).

Elder, *'85 Snowmobiles: New Stars on the Great White Way*, 161 Popular Mechanics 98–99, No. 11 (Nov. 1984).

Ettinger, *Ski Gear '81: The New Bindings*, 33 Skiing 98–104, No. 1 (Sept. 1980).

Ettinger, *The 21st Century Bindings*, 32 Skiing 100, No. 7 (Spring 1980).

Masia, *First Glance*, 48 Ski 18, No. 8 (Apr. 1984).

§ 6.47 Selected government sources

Bicycle Safety and Transportation (1964–June 1983, NTIS government publications data base citations July 1983).

Watts, *Pedal Cycle Spacers—A Study Involving School Children, Transport and Road Research Law* (Report, Crowthorne, England 1983).

Blomberg, et al., *Identification and Development of Countermeasures for Bicyclist/Motor Vehicle Problem Types*, 3 Model Regulations (Report, Dep't of Transp. Aug. 1982).

Hurnall, *Bike Plan Australia '81—Conference Proceedings* (Summary, Geelong Bike Plan Committee, Australia 1981).

Chang, *Bicycle-Safe Grate Inlets Design Manual (Implementation Package* (Water & Resources Service, Denver, Colo. Dec. 1980).

Consumer Products Safety Comm'n, *NEISS NEWS* (1976).

Consumer Products Safety Comm'n, *Swimming Pools*, Fact Sheet No. 8 (1976).

Swimming Pools—Safety and Disease Control Through Proper Design and Operation (U.S. Dep't of Health, Education & Welfare, Public Health Center for Disease Control, Atlanta, Ga. 1976).

Home Safety (U.S. Dep't of Housing & Urban Development 1972).

§ 6.48 Selected legal sources

Pools

Swimming Pool Accidents, 15 Am. Jur. *P.O.F.* 411 (1964).

Defectively Designed or Constructed Swimming Pool, 12 Am. Jur. *P.O.F.* 2d 545 (1977).

Swimming Pool Accidents, 7 Am. Jur. *Trials* 643 (1964).

Products Liability: Swimming Pools and Accessories, 6 A.L.R. 4th 492 (1981).

Liability of Swimming Facility Operator for Injury or Death Inflicted by Third Person, 90 A.L.R. 3d 533 (1979).

Liability of Swimming Facility Operator for Injury to or Death of Trespassing Child, 88 A.L.R. 3d 1197 (1978).

Liability of Operator of Nonresidential Swimming Facility for Injury or Death Allegedly Resulting from Failure to Provide or Exercise Proper Supervision, 87 A.L.R. 3d 1032 (1978).

Liability of Swimming Facility Operator for Injury or Death Allegedly Caused by Failure to Adequately Fence Facility, 87 A.L.R. 3d 886 (1978).

Liability of Swimming Facility Operator for Injury to or Death of Swimmer Allegedly Resulting from Hazardous Condition in Water, 86 A.L.R. 3d 1021 (1978).

Liability of Swimming Facility Operator for Injury or Death Allegedly Resulting from Condition of Deck, Bathhouse, or Other Area in Vicinity of Water, 86 A.L.R. 3d 388 (1978).

Liability of Swimming Facility Operator for Injury or Death Allegedly Resulting from Defects of Diving Board, Slide, or Other Swimming Pool Equipment, 85 A.L.R. 3d 849 (1978).

Liability of Swimming Facility Operator for Injury to or Death of Diver Allegedly Resulting from Hazardous Condition in Water, 85 A.L.R. 3d 750 (1978).

Liability of Owner of Private Residential Swimming Pool for Injury or Death Occasioned Thereby, 20 A.L.R. 3d 1395 (1968).

Statutes, Ordinances, or Regulations, Relating to Private Residential Swimming Pools, 92 A.L.R. 2d 1283 (1963).

Municipal Operation of Bathing Beach of Swimming Pool as Governmental or Proprietary Function, for Purposes of Tort Liability, 55 A.L.R. 2d 1434 (1957).

Liability of Private Owner or Operator of Bathing Resort or Swimming Pool for Injury or Death of Patron, 48 A.L.R. 2d 104, § 4, *Presumption of Negligence; Res Ipsa Loquitur* (1956).

Liability of Municipality in Respect of Municipal Bathhouses, Bathing

Beaches, and Swimming Pools, 51 A.L.R. 370 (1927), 57 A.L.R. 406 (1928).

Begam & Begam, *A Day in the Life of a Quadriplegic*, 14 Trial 24 (Mar. 1978).

Gabrielson & Rennolenn, *Swimming Pool Litigation: Educating for Safety*, Trial (Feb. 1982).

J. Hendry, *Handbook of Swimming Pool Liability, Annotated* (1976).

Kewalramani & Taylor, *Injuries to the Cervical Spine from Diving Accidents*, 15 J. Trauma 130 (Feb. 1975).

H. Philo, *Lawyers Desk Reference* §§ 24:1–24:18, *Swimming Pools* (Lawyers Co-op. Publishing Co., 6th ed. 1979 & Supps.).

Football

Football Injuries, 22 Am. Jur. *P.O.F*. 287 (1969).

The "Booby Trap": Does the Violent Nature of Professional Football Vitiate the Doctrine of Due Care in Participant Tort Litigation?, 10 Conn. L. Rev. 365 (Winter 1978).

Collision with Spring-Loaded Football Tackling and Blocking Dummies, 236 J. A.M.A. 1270, No. 11 (Sept. 13, 1970).

Albright, et al., *Nonfatal Cervical Spine Injuries in Interscholastic Football*, 236 J. A.M.A. 1246, No. 11 (Sept. 13, 1970).

Matthews, *Footballer's Migraine*, 2 Brit. Med. J. 326 (May 6, 1972).

Phill & Steine, *The Liability Path to Safer Helmets*, 13 Trial 33, No. 1 (Jan. 1977).

Bicycles

Defective Bicycle Design, 16 Am. Jur. *P.O.F. 2d* 447 (1978).

Skis

Liability for Skiing Accident, 20 Am. Jur. *P.O.F. 2d* 1 (1979).

Gaines, *Skiing Accident Litigation*, 15 Am. Jur. *Trials* 147 (1968).

Liability for Injury or Death from Ski Lift, Ski Tow, or Similar Device, 95 A.L.R. 3d 203 (1979).

Private Owner's Liability to Trespassing Children for Injury Sustained by Sledding, Tobogganing, Skiing, Skating, or Otherwise Sliding on His Land, 19 A.L.R. 3d 184 (1968).

Trine, *Ski Litigation: Elements of the Successful Case*, 18 Trial 32 (1982).

Motorcycles and Snowmobiles

Snowmobile Accidents, 29 Am. Jur. *P.O.F*. 641 (1972).

Motorcycle Accidents, 25 Am. Jur. *P.O.F*. 1 (1970).

Products Liability: Liability for Injury or Death Allegedly Caused by Defect in Snowmobile or Other Recreational-Purpose Vehicle, 81 A.L.R. 3d 394 (1977).

Accidents Involving Negligence in Operation of Snowmobile, Skimobile, or Similar Vehicle, 42 A.L.R. 3d 1422 (1972).

Boats and Water Skiing

Construction and Effect of Provision of Homeowner's, Premises, or Personal Liability Insurance Policy Covering or Excluding Watercraft, 26 A.L.R. 4th 967 (1983).

Products Liability: Liability of Manufacturer or Seller for Injury or Death Caused by Defect in Boat or Its Parts, Supplies, or Equipment, 1 A.L.R. 4th 411 (1980).

Liability of Owner or Operator of Powered Pleasure Boat for Injuries to Swimmer or Bather Struck by Boat, 98 A.L.R. 3d 1127 (1980).

Liability of Owner or Powerboat for Injury or Death Allegedly Caused by One Permitted to Operate Boat by Owner, 71 A.L.R. 3d 1018 (1976).

Liability for Injury or Death of Nonparticipant Caused by Water Skiing, 67 A.L.R. 3d 1218 (1975).

Liability for Injuries to or Death of Water Skiers, 8 A.L.R. 3d 675 (1966).

Action for Death Caused by Maritime Tort Within a State's Territorial Waters, 71 A.L.R. 2d 1296 (1960).

Liability of Owner or Operator of Motorboat for Injury or Damage, 63 A.L.R. 2d 343, § 3, *Standard of Care and Duty* (1959).

Bernhart, *The Weekend Seaman—Small Boat Liability for Personal Injuries*, 19 Practical Lawyer 43, No. 1 (Jan. 1973).

Comment, *Unseaworthiness and Evidence of Subsequent Repairs*, 19 Cal. Western L. Rev. 450 (Spring 1983).

Haskell, *A Look at the Law and Pleasure Boating*, 32 Ins. Counsel J. 66, No. 1 (1965).

Recreational Boating Law in Wisconsin, Whipple, 61 Marquette L. Rev. 425 (Spring 1978).

Norris, *The Law of Maritime Personal Injuries* (Lawyers Co-op. Publishing Co. 3d ed. 1975).

Prince, *Liability of the Owner of Pleasurecraft for Injury or Property Damage to Persons Aboard Other Watercraft*, 47 Ins. Counsel J. 317 (July 1980).

Rich, *Torts on Boats and Yachts*, 19 Cleveland St. Law Rev. 509, No. 3 (Sept. 1970).

Tiffany, *Limitations of Liability and Pleasure Boats: 65 Years of Judicial Misinterpretation of the Intent of Congress*, 12 Transportation L.J. 249, No. 2 (1982).

§ 6.49 Selected newsletters

Amusement Parks

Actionews
Int'l Ass'n of Amusement Parks & Attractions
7222 West Cermak Road, Suite 303
North Riverside, Ill. 60546

Nat'l Amusement Park Historical News
Nat'l Amusement Park Historical Ass'n
P.O. Box 83
Mt. Prospect, Ill. 60056

Aqua Notes
American Alliance for Health, Physical Education,
and Recreation
Indiana University of Pennsylvania
Indiana, Pa. 15705

Bicycle Industry—Retail Trade

Professional Bicycle Dealer Newsletter
Nat'l Bicycle Dealers Ass'n, Inc.
29023 Euclid Avenue
Wickliffe, Ohio 44092

Boats/Boating Industry

ABYC News
American Boat and Yacht Council, Inc.
15 East 26th Street
New York, N.Y. 10010

American Boat Builders & Repairers Ass'n Bulletin
2488 Grand Concourse
Bronx, N.Y. 10458

Affiliate File
Nat'l Ass'n of Engine & Boat Manufacturers
P.O. Box 5555
Grand Central Station
New York, N.Y. 10017

Boating News
Nat'l Ass'n of Engine & Boat Manufacturers
P.O. Box 5555
Grand Central Station
New York, N.Y. 10017

Monday Morning Report
Int'l Marine Expositions, Inc. (MAREX)
401 North Michigan Avenue
Chicago, Ill. 60660

At Your Service
Boat Owners Ass'n of the United States
880 South Picket Street
Alexandria, Va. 22304

Boating News
Nat'l Marine Manufacturers' Ass'n
401 North Michigan Avenue
Chicago, Ill. 60660

Interom
Nat'l Ass'n of Engine & Boat Manufacturers
P.O. Box 5555
Grand Central Station
New York, N.Y. 10017

The Lookout
Nat'l Boating Federation
P.O. Box 296
Bryn Athyn, Pa. 19009

The Telltale Compass
18418 South Old River Drive
Lake Oswego, Or. 97034

Safe Boating
Office of Boating Safety
U.S. Coast Guard
Washington, D.C. 20593

The Leisure Industry Digest
Property Invsetments, Inc.
350 Fifth Avenue
New York, N.Y. 10118

Motorcycle Industry

Motorcycle Business Newsletter
Parkhurst Publishing Co.
1812 Alaska Avenue
Costa Mesa, Cal. 92626

Off-Road RV's

The ORV Monitor
Sierra Club
P.O. Box 7959
Rincon Annex
San Francisco, Cal. 94120

Paralysis

Progress in Research
Research Division
American Paralysis Ass'n
7655 Old Spring House Road
McLean, Va. 22102

Recreational Vehicles

RV Financial Facts
RV Industry Ass'n
P.O. Box 204
Chantilly, Va. 22021

Tech Talk Newsletter
Bernie and Ruth Fuller
P.O. Box 2870
MCCA 8378
Estes Park, Colo. 80517

United's Voice
United Four-Wheel Drive Ass'ns
6793 CTH C
De Forest, Wis. 53532

Swimming Pools

Swimming Pleasure
Nat'l Ass'n of Pool Owners
570 Hillside Avenue
Needham, Mass. 02194

Skiing

The Ski Industry Letter
Washington Business Information, Inc.
235 National Press Building
Washington, D.C. 20045

Skier
U.S. Ski Ass'n, Eastern Division
22 High Street
Brattleboro, Vt. 05301

U.S. Ski Coaches Bulletin
U.S. Ski Coaches Ass'n
P.O. Box 1747
Park City, Utah 84060

Recreational

Recreation Newsletter
National Safety Council
444 North Michigan Avenue
Chicago, Ill. 60611

§ 6.50 Selected laws, regulations, and standards

Statutes

(1) Consumer Product Safety Act (CPSA), 15 U.S.C. §§ 2051 to 2083 (1972).

Regulations

(1) Mandatory Safety Standards for Bicycles, 16 C.F.R. 1512 (1985).

(2) Mandatory Safety Standards for Swimming Pool Slides, 16 C.F.R. 1207 (1985).

Voluntary Standards

Swimming Pools

(1) National Spa & Pool Institute

- (a) Suggested Minimum Standards for Residential Swimming Pools (1961, 1969, 1972, 1974).
- (b) Suggested Minimum Standards for Public Swimming Pools (1958, 1962, 1969, 1977).
- (c) Standards for Residential Aboveground, Portable Swimming Pools, Ladders, and Filters (1980).

(2) American Public Health Association

- (a) Suggested Ordinance and Regulations Covering Private Residential Swimming Pools (1970).
- (b) Suggested Ordinance and Regulations Covering Public Swimming Pools (1964).

Skis and Snowmobiles

(1) ASTM F504-77: Measuring Release Movements of Adult Alpine Ski Bindings.

(2) ASTM F498-77: Test for Center Spring Constant and Spring Constant Balance of Alpine Skis.

(3) ASTM F475: Specifications for Test Screws Used in Screw-Retention Test of Binding Mounting Area on Alpine Skis.

(4) ASTM F472: Geometric Terms and Definitions for Alpine Skis.

(5) Safety Code for Aerial Passenger Tramways B77.1 (1973).

§ 6.51 Selected cases

Butaud v. Suburban Marine & Sporting Goods, Inc., 543 P.2d 209, *modified*, 555 P.2d 42 (Alaska 1975), **snow machine**.

Byrns v. Riddell, Inc., 113 Ariz. 264, 550 P.2d 1065 (1976), **football helmet;** head injury.

Cota v. Harley-Davidson, Division of AMF, Inc., 141 Ariz. 7, 684 P.2d 888 (Ct. App. 1984), **motorcycle;** design defect.

Hauter v. Zogarts, 14 Cal. 3d 104, 120 Cal. Rptr. 681, 534 P.2d 377 (1975), **golf training device;** design defect.

Kavanaugh v. Geye, No. C287 196 (Cal. Super. Ct. May 17, 1984), 27 ATLA L. Rep. 327 (Sept. 1984), **ski bindings;** sudden release.

Columbo v. Trans World Int'l, Cal., No. C223796 (Cal. Super. Ct. Sept. 23, 1982), 26 ATLA L. Rep. 37 (Feb. 1983), **weight support apparatus**.

Lombardi v. AMF, Inc., No. 149–840 (Cal. Super. Ct. Apr. 14, 1982), 25 ATLA L. Rep. 467 (Dec. 1982), **motorcycle;** system defect; structured settlement $1.6 million.

Hunt v. City of Los Angeles, No. C 167 528 (Cal. Super. Ct. Aug. 10, 1981), 25 ATLA L. Rep. 124 (Apr. 1982), **bicycle;** brake failure; brain damage.

Anderson v. Heron Engineering Co., 198 Colo. 391, 604 P.2d 674 (1979), **ski chair lift**.

Whitlock v. Gym Master, No. 78CV7008 (Colo. Dist. Ct. May 28, 1982), 26 ATLA L. Rep. 32 (Feb. 1983), **trampoline;** inadequate maintenance.

Schenck v. Pelkey, 176 Conn. 245, 405 A.2d 665 (1978), **swimming pool slide;** implied warranty of merchantability.

Spoto v. Hayward Mfg. Co., 2 Conn. App. 663, 482 A.2d 91 (1984), **swimming pool;** quadriplegia after dive; expert testimony on indentation at pool's bottom.

Taylor v. American Honda Motor Corp., No. 81–62–Civ–Oc (M.D. Fla. Nov. 1, 1982), 555 F. Supp. 59 (1982), **motorcycle**.

Votour v. American Honda Motor Co., No. 79–4686 CA (L)01 B (Fla. Cir. Ct., Palm Beach Cty. Nov. 3, 1983), 27 ATLA L. Rep. 83 (Mar. 1984), **motorcycle;** absence of lower leg protection; settlement $1.05 million.

McCann v. Murray Chris-Craft Cruisers, Inc., No. 82–12168 (Fla. Cir. Ct. Mar. 29, 1983), 26 ATLA L. Rep. 373 (Oct. 1983), **boat cleat;** quadriplegia; structured settlement $6.6 million.

Berry v. Dudley Sports Co., No. 78–3820 (Fla. Cir. Ct. Jan. 26, 1982), 25 ATLA L. Rep. 226 (June 1982), **baseball pitching machine;** settlement $1.108 million.

Yowler v. Brunswick Corp., No. 80–741 (Fla. Cir. Ct. Mar. 20, 1981), 25 ATLA L. Rep. 374 (Oct. 1982), **outboard motor;** design defect.

Caporale v. Raleigh Industries of America, Inc., 382 So. 2d 849 (Fla. Dist. Ct. App. 1980), **bicycle;** improper assembly.

Aquino v. Pepsico Inc., No. 79–0019 (D. Hawaii Aug. 15, 1983), 26 ATLA L. Rep. 425 (Nov. 1983), **football helmet;** brain stem injury; structured settlement.

Galindo v. Riddell, 107 Ill. App. 3d 139, 62 Ill. Dec. 849, 437 N.E.2d 376 (1982), **football helmet;** quadriplegia.

Sipari v. Villa Oliva Country Club, 63 Ill. App. 3d 985, 20 Ill. Dec. 610, 380 N.E.2d 819 (1978), **golf cart**.

Pell v. School District 230, No. 81 L8639 (Ill. Cir. Ct. Aug. 10, 1982), 25 ATLA L. Rep. 467 (Dec. 1982), **trampoline;** failure to warn; quadriplegia.

Nissen Trampoline Co. v. Terre Haute First Nat'l Bank, 265 Ind. 457, 358 N.E.2d 974 (1976), **aqua diver;** failure to warn; unreasonably dangerous product.

Woods v. International Harvester Co., 697 F.2d 635 (5th Cir. [La.] 1983), **four-wheel drive Scout II;** carbon monoxide poisoning; unreasonably dangerous for normal use.

Pawlak v. Brown, 430 So. 2d 1346 (La. Ct. App), *cert. denied*, 439 So. 2d 1072 (La. 1983), **motorcycle;** failure to warn; design defect.

Harper v. Liggett Group, Inc., No. 246,652 (La. Dist. Ct. Mar. 10, 1983),

26 ATLA L. Rep. 327 (Sept. 1983), **racquetball racquet;** defective "safety thong."

Harris v. Bardwell, 373 So. 2d 777 (La. Ct. App. 1979), **fiberglass boat;** pedestal mounted seat; defective installation.

Anthony Pools v. Sheehan, 295 Md. 285, 455 A.2d 434 (Ct. App. 1983), **swimming pool;** implied warranty of merchantability.

Carrier v. Becton, Dickinson & Co., No. 80–2565–2 (D. Mass. Feb. 29, 1984), 24 ATLA L. Rep. 326 (Sept. 1984), **football helmet;** quadriplegia; failure to warn; failure to absorb on impact; structured settlement.

Everett v. Bucky Warren, Inc., 376 Mass. 280, 380 N.E.2d 653 (1978), **hockey helmet;** head injury.

Smith v. Ariens Co., 375 Mass. 620, 377 N.E.2d 954 (1978), **snowmobile;** design defect.

Panosso v. Huffy Corp., No. 76–10119 (E.D. Mich. Jan. 23, 1979), 22 ATLA L. Rep. 129 (Apr. 1979), **bicycle**.

Durkee v. Cooper of Canada, Ltd., 99 Mich. App. 693, 298 N.W.2d 620 (1980), **hockey helmet;** test for negligent design.

Koons v. Walker, 76 Mich. App. 726, 257 N.W.2d 229 (1977), **motorcycle helmet**.

Soutee v. Pro-Tec, Inc., No. 81–1638–C(2) (E.D. Mo. June 4, 1982), 25 ATLA L. Rep. 375 (Oct. 1982), **sports goggle;** settlement $150,000.

Blevins v. Cushman Motors, 551 S.W.2d 602 (Mo. 1977), **golf cart;** design defect.

Harrington v. Holiday Rambler Corp., 176 Mont. 37, 575 P.2d 578 (1987), **travel trailer**.

Tassie v. Tram Diamond Corp., No. C–80–189–L (D.N.H. June 21, 1982), 26 ATLA L. Rep. 180 (May 1983), **CB radio;** electrocution; improper grounding instructions and warnings; structured settlement $3.3 million.

Wentworth v. Kawasaki, Inc. Snojet, Inc., 508 F. Supp. 1114 (D.N.H. 1981), **snowmobile**.

O'Brien v. Muskin Co., 94 N.J. 169, 463 A.2d 298 (1983), **aboveground swimming pool;** design defect; state-of-the-art evidence.

Gentile v. MacGregor Mfg., 201 N.J. Super. 612, 493 A.2d 647 (1985),

(*Text continued following illustrations.*)

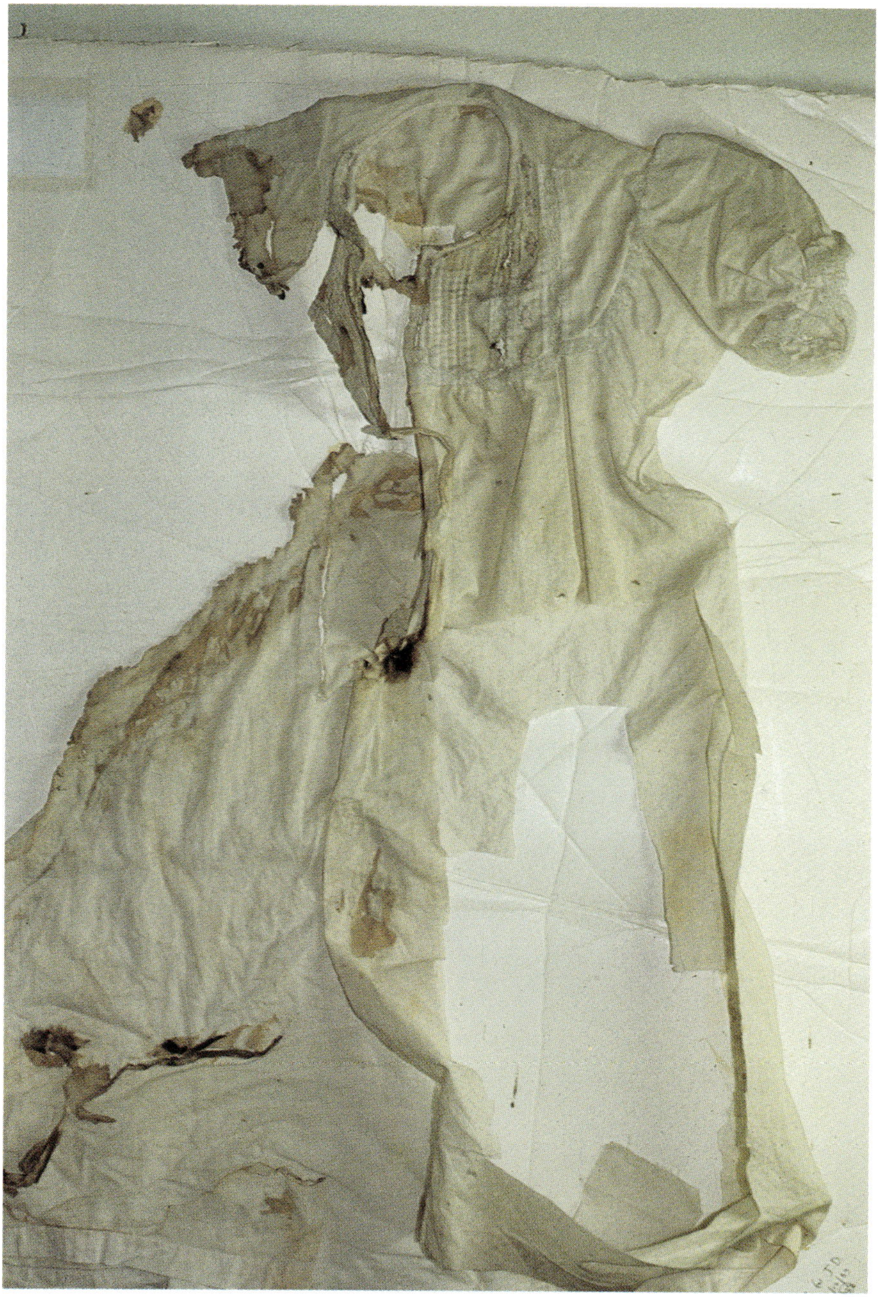

Figure 1
Flammable Nightgown

This flammable nightgown ignited when exposed to heat, resulting in severe and disfiguring burn injuries. The nightgown was designed without available flame-retardant material that could have prevented the tragedy. (*See* Chapter 4, *Fabric-Related Burn Injuries—The Torch Cases*.)

I N T E R O F F I C E   M E M O : . . . . . .   *File*

TO: DATE: October 29, 1970

FROM:

SUBJECT: "DO NOT DIVE" LABELS

This is to confirm our discussion on placing "Do Not Dive" labels on all our pools. Effective immediately, change all the bills of material on walls to show the "Do Not Dive" label.

In addition, we will put in each steel ladder carton one label which the consumer should attach to the ladder. Please make sure that our instruction sheets state that diving should not be permitted.

DO NOT DIVE

Figure 2
Do Not Dive Decals

Pool manufacturers responded to litigation with inadequate "Do Not Dive" decals similar to the one contained in the above memorandum. (*See* Chapter 6, *Crippled at Leisure: Recreational Product-Related Torts*, §§ 6.05–6.22.)

Figure 3
Person Diving Into Four-Foot-Deep Pool

A pool manufacturer used an advertisement such as this one encouraging consumers to dive into its pools' shallow waters to market its four-foot-deep aboveground pools. This manufacturer already had reports of diving-related quadriplegia and paraplegia. (*See* Chapter 6, *Crippled at Leisure: Recreational Product-Related Torts*, §§ 6.05–6.22.)

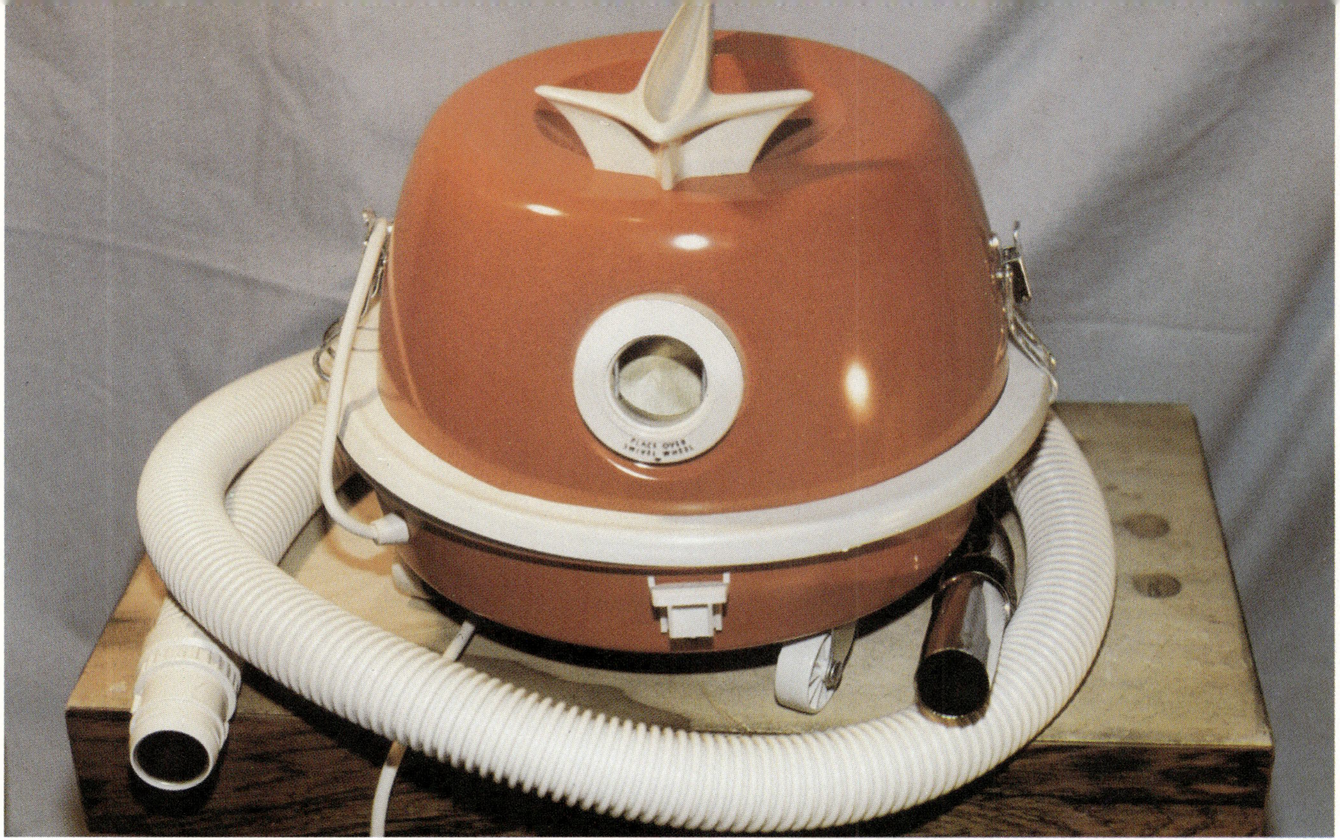

Figure 4
Vacuum Cleaner

Vacuum cleaner model, like the one above, was designed without an effective motor housing guard, causing the laceration of a young boy's penis. (*See* Chapter 10, *Opening New Doors: Landmark Litigation*, §§ 10.02–10.09.)

Figure 5
Plastic Tricycle

Plastic tricycles, such as this one, have caused many deaths and severe injuries due to their low design resulting in a lack of visibility to oncoming cars. (*See* Chapter 6, *Crippled at Leisure: Recreational Product-Related Torts*, §§ 6.29–6.32.)

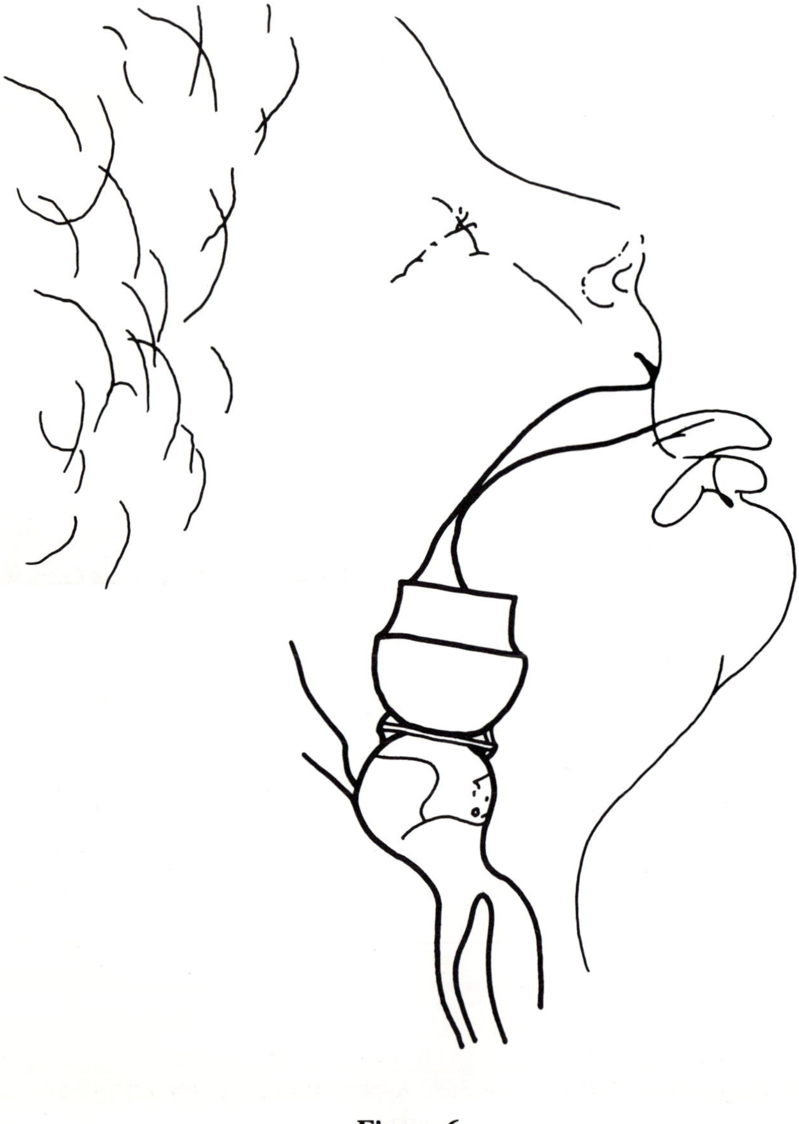

Figure 6
Toy Ingestion

Graphic depiction of a small toy figurine that lodged in the throat of a fourteen-month-old boy resulting in severe and irreversible brain damage. (*See* Chapter 7, *In The Nursery: Toys That Injure and Maim*, §§ 7.05–7.24.)

Figure 7
Kitchen Stove

Two young children were severely burned and permanently disfigured after they climbed atop a kitchen stove, similar to the one above, and turned on its gas burners. The burner was designed with easy-to-turn knobs, resulting in tragic injuries. (*See* Chapter 2, *Combustion Catastrophes*, §§ 2.10–2.12.)

Figure 8
Stove Safety Tag

A safety tag similar to this one illustrates how hazardous stoves could have been designed and marketed for safety, rather than sales, to prevent devastating burn injuries. (*See* Chapter 2, *Combustion Catastrophes*, §§ 2.10–2.12.)

football helmet; reconditioner strictly liable for defects created by original manufacturer.

Skolka v. Kratz, No. L–65667–80 (N.J. Super. Ct., Middlesex Cty. Jan. 23, 1984), 27 ATLA L. Rep. 183 (May 1984), **aboveground pool;** quadriplegia; settlement $1.025 million.

Scerbak v. Segarra & AMF Harley-Davidson Motor Co., No. L–62366–78 (N.J. Super. Ct., Morris Cty. Oct. 1, 1981), 25 ATLA L. Rep. 86 (Mar. 1982), **motorcycle half-helmet;** failure to recall.

Lavin v. Fauci, 170 N.J. Super. 403, 406 A.2d 978 (1979), **toy "Big Wheel" vehicle;** evidence of subsequent changes in product.

Ashwal v. Friedman, No. 179/77 (N.Y. Sup. Ct., Richmond Cty. Nov. 20, 1984), 28 ATLA L. Rep. 131 (Apr. 1985), **lawn swing;** thigh fracture; design defect.

Somella v. Union Carbide Corp., No. 1068/80 (N.Y. Sup. Ct., Queens Cty. Oct. 12, 1983), **in-ground pool;** quadriplegia; structured settlement $1,325,000.

Rusa v. Sears, Roebuck & Co., (N.Y. Sup. Ct. 1981), 25 ATLA L. Rep. 227 (June 1982), **tent;** flammability; wrongful death.

Maybank v. S.S. Kresge Co., 46 N.C. App. 687, 266 S.E.2d 409 (1980), **flashcube;** exploded in face; implied warranty of merchantability.

Randall v. Warnaco Inc., 677 F.2d 1266 (8th Cir. [N.D.] 1982), **tent fire;** admissibility of videotaped experiment.

Beauregard v. Rick Case Motors, Inc., No. 31441 (Ohio Ct. C.P., Cayuga Cty. Dec. 8, 1983), 27 ATLA L. Rep. 134 (Apr. 1984), **motorcycle;** rendered paraplegic when kickstand struck ground during turn.

Kearney v. Montgomery Ward & Co., 55 Or. App. 64, 639 P.2d 682 (1982), **bicycle;** time limitations.

Dyches v. Benjamin Franklin Federal Savings & Loan, No. A7607–09750 (Or. Cir. Ct., Multnomah Cty. Jan. 24, 1979), 22 ATLA L. Rep. 129 (Apr. 1979), **ten-speed bicycle;** wrongful death; defective mechanical linkage in brake system; settlement during trial $280,000.

Matsko v. Harley-Davidson Motor Co., 325 Pa. Super. 452, 473 A.2d 155 (1984), **motorcycle;** evidence of subsequent repairs.

Ries v. MTD Products, Inc., 310 Pa. Super. 118, 456 A.2d 211 (1981), **bicycle;** sale in partially assembled condition.

McKinley v. Honda Motor Co., No. 81–CV102674 (Pa. Ct. C.P. May 25,

1984), 27 ATLA L. Rep. 327 (Sept. 1984), **three-wheel recreational vehicle;** quadriplegia.

Fiske v. MacGregor, Division of Brunswick, 464 A.2d 719 (R.I. 1983), **football helmet;** defectively designed for game conditions.

Romano v. Ann & Hope Factory Outlet, Inc., 417 A.2d 1375 (R.I. 1980), **bicycle;** defective design.

Evridge v. American Honda Motor Co., 685 S.W.2d 632 (Tenn. 1985), **motorbike;** adequacy of warning; negligent design.

Walden v. Sears, Roebuck & Co., 654 F.2d 443 (5th Cir. [Tex.] 1981), **bicycle;** admission of deposition testimony of minor.

Reese v. Mercury Marine, No. B–83–1195 (E.D. Tex. Mar. 29, 1985), **outboard motor;** wrongful death; inadequate warnings.

Howard v. Chris-Craft Corp., No. TY–80–407–CA (E.D. Tex. Aug. 19, 1982), 26 ATLA L. Rep. 82 (Mar. 1983), **19' trihull stern-drive outboard motor boat;** $1.3 million settlement.

Rawlings Sporting Goods, Inc. v. Daniels, 619 S.W.2d 435 (Tex. Ct. Civ. App. 1981), **football helmet;** duty to warn; defectively manufactured.

Shugar v. Pat Walker Figure Perfection Salons Int'l, 541 S.W.2d 511 (Tex. Ct. Civ. App. 1976), **vibrating/reducing machine;** failure to warn.

Todd v. Hill-McDonald Boats & Motors, Inc., No. 1,157,910 (Tex. Jud. Dist. Ct., Harris Cty. Mar. 3, 1983), 26 ATLA L. Rep. 180 (May 1983), **bass boat;** wrongful death; $615,000 settlement.

Beaton v. Everlast Sporting Goods Mfg. Co., No. 79–0013–C (W.D. Va. June 5, 1981), 25 ATLA L. Rep. 133 (Apr. 1982), **minitrampoline;** quadriplegia; structured settlement $875,000.

Noto v. Pico Peak Corp., 469 F.2d 358 (2d Cir. [Vt.] 1972), **ski lift;** defective seal and inadequate lubrication on bull wheel.

Fischer v. Weatherking Products, Inc., No. S14–80CnC (Vt. Super. Ct., Chittenden Cty. Dec. 8, 1983), 27 ATLA L. Rep. 182 (May 1984), **in-ground swimming pool;** two-tone bottom; dangerous to dive; quadriplegia; structured settlement $1.6 million.

Myette v. Fort Wayne Pool Equip., Inc., No. S122–79CnC (Vt. Super. Ct., Chittenden Cty. Oct. 1, 1982), 26 ATLA L. Rep. 37 (Feb. 1983), **in-ground pool;** quadriplegia; $1.1 million settlement.

Clark v. Leisure Vehicles, Inc., 96 Wis. 2d 607, 292 N.W.2d 630 (1980), **snowmobile**.

Ekern v. Nissen Corp., No. 79CV99 (Wis. Cir. Ct. Jan. 26, 1983), 26 ATLA L. Rep. 132 (Apr. 1983), **trampoline;** quadriplegia.

McGinnis v. Harley-Davidson Motor Co., No. 579–634 (Wis. Cir. Ct., Milwaukee Cty. Dec. 23, 1983), 27 ATLA L. Rep. 83 (Mar. 1984), **motorcycle;** paraplegia.

Chapter 7

IN THE NURSERY: TOYS THAT INJURE AND MAIM

IV. Other Toy Hazards

V. Preventing Toy-Related Injuries

VI. Litigation Sources: Bibliography

KLUWER LITIGATION LIBRARY REFERENCES

HARLEY & MAGEE, WHAT'S IT WORTH? A GUIDE TO CURRENT PERSONAL INJURY AWARDS AND SETTLEMENTS.

JEANS, LITIGATION: Chapter 4, *Discovery*; Chapter 8, *Direct Examination*; Chapter 9, *Direct Examination of Expert Witnesses*; Chapter 13, *Cross-Examination*; Chapter 14, *Cross-Examination of Expert Witnesses*.

SMITH & MALANDRO, COURTROOM COMMUNICATION STRATEGIES: Chapter 1, *Impression Formation in the Courtroom*; Chapter 2, *Persuasive Strategies in the Courtroom*; Chapter 5, *Preparing for Effective Courtroom Communication*; Chapter 8, *Direct Examination: Presenting the Evidence With Impact*; Chapter 9, *Cross-Examination: Controlling the Case*.

I. Introduction

§ 7.01 In general

Every year, toys kill or injure more than 500,000 American children.[1] The toll is considerably higher if we include playground equipment, children's furnishings, and bicycles. With this staggering toll, we might expect that our courts would be filled with cases involving toy-related deaths and injuries. But they are not.

§ 7.02 Focus on product itself

One reason is the failure by many parents to recognize that they may have a case. Years of effective public relations by the toy industry and government authorities have indoctrinated parents to blame themselves or their children when tragedy strikes, rather than the culpable toy. Plaintiffs' lawyers have also fallen into this industry's public relations

[1] According to the Federal Centers for Disease Control, 588,700 children received hospital treatment for toy-related injuries in 1984.

trap. They tend to focus blame and attention on the child's use or alleged misuse of the toy or the parents' alleged failure to supervise the child at play adequately instead of focusing on the product itself. For example, why the toy was designed the way it was with no protections against a child's foreseeable and creative, if unpredictable, behavior; whether the toy could have been designed more safely or whether the hazards, once identified, could have been designed out of the culpable product; why the toy was marketed despite its hazards, and what methods were used to market the toy by building consumer confidence and increasing toy sales?

In my practice, I have learned to see through this industry's public relations ploys and to recognize evidence of the industry's gimmickry and false representations in their own corporate files. I have also learned to recognize how toys can be defective and/or hazardous in their design, manufacture, and marketing practices.

"Do I have a case?" This is a question I am often asked by attorneys who are inexperienced in dealing with toy-related deaths and injuries and who are suspicious of the pleasant-sounding pronouncements they hear from government and industry spokespersons. As the case study in Part III illustrates, justice can be obtained for injured children and their families for the tragedies that are inflicted by hazardous toys. You may have a potentially important case if you know what questions to ask, how to ask them, and where to look for the answers.

II. Checklists

§ 7.03 Checklist: Investigation of a toy-related injury case

The following checklist is intended to assist counsel in preparation of a toy-related personal injury case.

____(1) Collect as much information as possible on the injured child, including:

- ____(a) Age
- ____(b) Level of education
- ____(c) Motor development
- ____(d) Hobbies
- ____(e) Mental or physical handicaps
- ____(f) Prior experience with or use of the toy

____(2) Construct exactly, minute by minute, what happened when the injury occurred

____(3) Was an adult or mature minor present when the injury occurred?

  ____(a) Names

  ____(b) Was the parent present as a supervisor of the injured child?

  ____(c) Relationship to child?

____(4) Description of the injury?

____(5) Exact description of the toy

____(6) Manufacturer of the toy

____(7) Serial number, model number of the toy

____(8) Manufacturer[s] of component parts

____(9) Take possession of:

  ____(a) The toy itself

  ____(b) If toy was part of a set, complete set

  ____(c) Packaging in which the toy was sold

  ____(d) Instructions provided with toy

  ____(e) Advertisements for toy

  ____(f) Any warnings provided with toy

  ____(g) Sales slips or receipts

  ____(h) If toy causing injury is not available, then purchase same model, or one as similar as possible

____(10) Get detailed information on prior uses and experience with toy from parents, guardians, teachers, and so on

____(11) Carefully examine packaging, advertisements, and television videotapes, if available, to determine what representations were made about uses of toy

____(12) Determine what warranties were made in reference to the toy

____(13) Identify retail seller of toy

____(14) Were any modifications made to toy?

____(15) Consider the design of the toy—was it made "child-proof," in regard to the following:

____(a) Size of toy

____(b) Sharp edges

____(c) Hidden dangers

____(d) Paint used

____(e) Flammability

____(f) Potential psychological effect of usage

____(g) Easily ingestible parts

____(h) Easily adaptable to dangerous use

____(i) Unsafe packaging (including plastic wrap)

____(j) Contain projectiles

____(k) Easily shatterable

____(l) Use of hazardous household electricity

____(m) Contain toxic, nonsterile, or allergenic stuffing or other materials

____(16) List potential defendants:

____(a) Manufacturer of toy or parts

____(b) Assembler of toy

____(c) Toy designer

____(d) Testing laboratory

____(e) Toy wholesalers

____(f) Toy retailers

____(g) Toy packagers

____(h) Toy marketers

____(i) Toy advertisers

____(j) Toy owner (if not client)

____(17) Retain an expert

____(a) What is the nature of his expertise?

____(b) Does he have experience with this toy?

____(c) Prior testimony record

____(d) Determine potential problems with expert if he will be used as a witness

____(e) Provide toys, accessories, packaging, and advertisements to expert and work with him during testing

____(f) Use expert closely in preparation for settlement or trial

____(18) Has the toy ever been recalled?

____(19) Has government agency issued any warnings regarding toy hazards?

____(20) Has company notified government (Consumer Product Safety Commission) that toy presents substantial product hazard?

____(21) Has federal government or company received consumer complaints about the toy?

____(22) Have prior injuries been reported in medical literature regarding this toy?

____(23) Does consumer literature report safety risks for this toy?

____(24) Determine testing done on toy

____(25) Evaluate potential theories of liability

____(a) Negligence

____(b) Breach of Warranty

____(c) Strict Liability

____(26) Research applicable statutes:

____(a) Consumer Product Safety Act

____(b) Food, Drug and Cosmetic Act

____(c) Flammable Fabrics Act

____(d) Federal Hazardous Substances Act

____(e) Relevant state statutes

____(27) Ascertain special damages

____(a) Medical

____(b) Dental

____(c) Nursing care

____(d) Special care

____(e) Rehabilitation

____(f) Hospitalization

____(g) Education

____(h) Ambulance service

____(i) Drugs

____(j) Braces and medical devices

____(k) Lost earning capacity

____(28) Determine general damages. Details of pain and suffering should be carefully ascertained

____(29) Obtain expert opinions as to impact of toy-related injury on child:

____(a) Physical impact

____(b) Psychological impact

____(c) Impact on educational development

____(d) Impact on earning capacity

____(e) Impact on social development

____(30) Research law reviews and treatises on toy cases

____(31) Contact the following to determine what information, if any, is available regarding the product:

____(a) U.S. Consumer Product Safety Commission

____(b) United States Testing Co., Inc.

____(c) U.S. Department of Commerce, National Bureau of Standards

____(d) Underwriters' Laboratories

____(e) ATLA Law Reporter

____(f) ATLA Exchange

____(g) ATLA Product Liability Law Reporter

§ 7.04 Checklist: Resources in a toy-related injury case

The following checklist of resources should prove valuable for counsel preparing a toy-related personal injury case.

____(1) Selected technical sources

____(a) Pediatrics

____(b) Physics Teacher

____(c) New Scientist

____(d) Scientific American

____(e) American Journal of Physics

____(f) Psychology Today

____(2) Selected popular sources

____(a) Parent

____(b) Sunset

____(c) Consumer Reports

____(d) Consumers' Research

____(e) Which? (Great Britain)

____(f) Canadian Consumer

____(g) Changing Times

____(h) Good Housekeeping

____(3) Selected government sources

____(a) U.S. Consumer Product Safety Commission

____(b) U.S. Department of Commerce, National Bureau of Standards

____(4) Selected industry sources

____(a) Toy Manufacturers of America

____(b) Juvenile Products Manufacturers Association

III. Case Study: The Case of the Not-So-Playful Toy Figurine[2]

§ 7.05 Facts

One of the most appalling examples of callousness and negligent, corporate decision making that I have come across in my twenty-five years

[2] Cunningham v. Quaker Oats Co., Fisher Price Div., No. 1973–343 (W.D.N.Y. 1973). This case resulted in a verdict of $3.1 million. This case is currently under appeal.

of practice occurred in this case involving an innocent-looking, but lethal, children's toy figurine. Despite my years of involvement in representing the victims of slaughter by product, my blood still boils when I come across a case like this. A young child, barely more than one year old, was playing with his toy figurines on the living room floor of his home—the kinds of play figures that can be found in millions of homes across America. His mother was sitting close by. As his father walked by them into the kitchen, the plaintiff stood up to follow. Suddenly, he began to gag and his body stiffened. He had placed one of the figurines in his mouth, as all youngsters of that age are prone to do, and it had become lodged in his throat. The boy's mother recalls the traumatic moments that followed.[3]

> [H]e got up and toddled off into the kitchen . . . the next thing I saw he stopped dead in his tracks, like just stopped, and I saw him stiffen and I heard him gag as though he had some obstruction. . . . I immediately thought he swallowed something and I got up and ran to him. . . . I said to [my husband], "he's got something in his throat."
>
> [My husband] turned him upside down and I got underneath, I was kneeling. . . . And I put my hand up, I could get my fingers in until he was biting down on my hand. But . . . I couldn't get very far . . . it was painful on my fingers . . . I slapped him on the back, but nothing happened.
>
> [My boy] was making gagging noises. I told [my husband] "we better take him into emergency." [H]e went to the telephone and phoned for an ambulance and I said "we'll get there faster ourselves." . . . While he went to get the car I had [my boy] in my arms with his head down, below his feet. . . . There was blood coming out of his mouth.
>
> When we got into the car I turned him over on my lap . . . he was facing up with his head back . . . when his teeth became unclenched, I thought I'd have another try to see whether I could get the toy out. . . . I put my fingers in his mouth . . . I could barely feel the tip, just barely. . . . I felt something in the back of his mouth or throat area. . . . I could feel the hole, the little round hole. . . . I felt the end of something. . . . But I couldn't grasp anything. . . . He was obviously in difficulty.

---

[3] *Cunningham*, *supra* note 2, testimony of Mrs. C, the plaintiff's mother, on behalf of the plaintiff.

> When we had been in the car a little while, I don't know how long, his body just went limp. . . . He apparently had given up the struggle. . . . I told [my husband], "he's stopped breathing." I said, "I can't give him mouth-to-mouth resuscitation because there is something blocking it." . . . He said, "try mouth-to-nose resuscitation," which I did. And his chest did fill with air. I continued the mouth-to-nose resuscitation until we arrived at the hospital.

His father brought him into the emergency room, and the seemingly endless wait for news began. Later that day, the plaintiff's pediatrician brought them the news: Their son had suffered severe and irreversible brain damage. His father recalls, "We were told he was in a coma. . . . He was in an oxygen tent, lying very, very still. . . . The hospital neurologist told us that [our son's] life was very much in the balance, and to prepare for him not pulling through."[4]

A few days later, the family received the gift of their lives: the boy's eyes opened and he began to cry.

Their son's life had been spared, but his valiant struggle to regain the mobility and coordination that most of us take for granted had just begun. He was about to enter into a period of intensive, excruciating, and painstaking rehabilitation, the type of therapy that is typical for victims of catastrophic brain damage.

This family's inspiring story of courage and determination did not stop with their struggle for the boy's recovery. They also set out to wage their fight against those responsible for their son's devastating injury—the company that manufactured and marketed the toy that should never have been of a size that could fit into their son's mouth.

COMMENT: As their lawyer, I had the privilege of using the common law to obtain a fair and reasonable compensation for this injured child, as well as to expose this appalling case of negligent corporate decision making. As a concerned professional, I consider it my obligation to share the horrifying facts uncovered in this case with my fellow members of the legal profession and the public, in the hopes that

[4] *Cunningham*, *supra* note 2, testimony of Mr. C., the plaintiff's father, on behalf of the plaintiff.

armed with this knowledge, similar tragedies can be averted in the future.

---

§ 7.06 Analysis of case

As I prepared the family's case, my research took me into the company president's office, into his files, and into his corporate philosophy. I uncovered startling evidence of this company's toy design, manufacturing, and marketing practices, which demonstrated to me and to the jury the company's total indifference to this child's safety. Testimony offered by the company's executives revealed the company's negligent failure to test the toy for safety, its negligent use of marketing practices that falsely assured consumers that this toy was safe, its negligent use of inadequate age grading, its failure to warn consumers of the toy's hazards, and its failure to respond to repeated warnings that the toy's hazardous design could result in the particular tragic incident that occurred in this case. One executive actually misrepresented the facts in order, apparently, to save the company's name.

COMMENT: In a products case, it is vital for counsel to leave no stone unturned during the discovery process. Information useful to the plaintiff's case may rest unnoticed in many places. Modern discovery techniques give the lawyer the tools he needs to uncover this information.

Testimony provided by doctors and other medical experts enlightened the jury concerning the catastrophic impact that this injury had on this child's life. Testimony of an economist also assisted this jury in making its determination of damages—an award of $3.1 million, which was, at that time, a national record in a toy-related personal injury case.

§ 7.07 Negligent design

I said that this child's injury was the beginning of this story. Let me correct myself. This boy's injury was just the culmination of a tragic sequence of events that began in a corporate boardroom seven years earlier, when the company that manufactured this toy made a marketing decision. For several years, this company had been designing, manufacturing, and marketing toys accompanied by so-called play figures—figures that can be found today in toy chests all across America. In fact, the company invented the concept. A bus was one of these toys. It had been marketed since 1959. In 1964, the company's management decided to change the toy's design. They wanted to make the school bus more aesthetically appealing, so they needed a design that was something in between the two existing sizes. As the toy's designer candidly admitted, "It was a design option to make a more attractive, more appealing toy."[5] They thought that a scaled down, smaller bus would be more salable. Smaller figurines would be needed to fit the smaller bus' holes. A smaller figurine would also allow the company to fit seven small figures into a bus instead of five.

At the bottom line, the figures had to be designed in such a way that they would fit into the bus, shoe, and other products that the company was marketing at the time. The orders from senior management were clear: "Design a toy to fit into existing toy holes."[6] Its overall size could be anywhere between that of the larger figure and the smaller one, but its base had to be cylindrical to fit into the existing holes.

§ 7.08 Manufacturer's prior knowledge of risks

An important part of the plaintiff's case was evidence demonstrating that the defendant had been put on notice by a safety expert and concerned consumers regarding its product's propensity to cause grave harm. Apparently, the company chose to ignore these warnings and, instead, decided to maintain its existing product line.

§ 7.09 —Put on notice by safety expert

Poring through this company's files, I found important evidence that the company had been put on notice because of this newly designed toy's deadly potential. In 1965, the company's manager of research and development asked a safety organization for guidance on a safe size for the company's figures. He recognized the potential hazards of children choking on small toys, and sought advice on designing a toy to avoid

---

[5] *Cunningham*, *supra* note 2, testimony of Mr. O, toy designer.

[6] *Id*.

such risks.[7] The organization forwarded this letter to a member of its advisory council, who also served as the medical assistant to the Department of Public Health in the State of Illinois. In an important response, this individual wrote back that the company could avoid the choking and suffocation risk presented by this toy by designing it large enough so as not to fit into a child's mouth. Following is an excerpt from that letter:

> I am not sure of the economic and technical aspects of manufacturing objects of various sizes, but it occurred to me that in order to avoid this it would simply be necessary to make the toys of sufficient size so that they could not be completely inserted into the mouth of an infant. This would mean that at least one diameter of the toy would have to be four or five inches long. The exact length you get either from an anatomy book or calling the pathologist in Buffalo, New York, who does autopsies on infants and children of this size regularly.[8]

This executive considered this advice, but rejected it. Why? Because it would mean replacing an entire toy line! In his words, to follow it would "not be practical . . . [it] would have eliminated all these products."[9] In order words, the entire line of toys would need to be redesigned. In this company's philosophy, this was apparently too high a price to pay to secure the safety and well-being of our children.

§ 7.10 —Put on notice by consumers

As if this were not evidence enough of this company's philosophy regarding safety, the company's files also revealed a series of warnings in the form of letters from consumers whose children had suffered the consequences of this toy's hazardous design, and had been spared only by their parents' ability to remove the toys from their throats. A mother wrote of her son's frightening near-miss incident when a figurine became lodged in his throat. She alerted the company that the toy was a "death trap."[10] Similarly, the wife of a pediatric intern wrote of her husband's medical experience with children who were suffocated when similar, small toys became lodged in their throats. She warned that the company

---

[7] Letter from Mr. H, manager of product development of the defendant to __________, Mar. 30, 1965.

[8] Letter from Dr. P to Mr. H, Apr. 21, 1965.

[9] *Cunningham*, *supra* note 2, testimony of Mr. H, on behalf of the defendant.

[10] Letter from Mrs. S to the defendant, Jan. 6, 1968.

should redesign this toy before tragedy could strike![11]

§ 7.11 —Manufacturer's response to warnings

These letters should have served as large, red flags of caution to this company that its product was hazardous and that steps should be taken to stop production and reevaluate the toy's design. Unfortunately, neither of these steps were taken. Behind corporate boardroom doors, the warnings were written off as freak accidents and ignored. The following excerpt from my cross-examination of this company's president, taken during pretrial depositions and read as evidence during the trial, reveals this corporation's philosophy and practice.[12]

Q. Did you ever receive any complaints prior to the date of the occurrence about a child either ingesting, swallowing, or having a problem with respect to one of the figurines coming in contact with his mouth or other portions of the human anatomy?

A. I can recall one case where we did receive a letter.

Q. Have you seen the letter recently?

A. Yes.

Q. How recently?

A. Oh, I reviewed it within the last week.

Q. Now, for the record, will you identify this letter?

A. Yes, yes. This is the letter written in January 1968.

Q. And received by [your company]?

A. Received by [us].

Q. Were you president of the company when this letter came in?

A. 1968, yes.

* * *

Q. Now we are both looking at Plaintiff's Exhibit 3, and you say this is a copy of a letter, the original of which is still in the [defendant's] files? [*Ed. Note*: Exhibit not supplied.]

A. Yes.

Q. Now, the age of the child is a sixteen-month-old child that re-

[11] Letter from Mrs. B to the defendant, Nov. 24, 1970.

[12] *Cunningham*, *supra*, note 2, testimony of Mr. C, president of the defendant.

ceived a present for Christmas? The next sentence says, "the day after Christmas I heard my son choking and upon investigation found he had one of the [figurines] in his mouth." Is that accurate?

A. Yes.

Q. "I reached into his mouth and to my surprise I was unable to pull the," and then she says, "the object out." Correct?

A. Right.

Q. "My husband was home and he then reached in our son's mouth and pulled it out."

A. "And pulled," period.

Q. Okay, "pulled," and what does it say there?

A. "All he got was blood."

Q. Can you read the next sentence?

A. "He then gave a very hard jerk and out came the death trap."

Q. And then after that sentence, "death trap," they describe what came out of his mouth, correct?

A. Yes.

Q. Do you agree that it was one of the [defendant's] figurines? Is that here now?

A. No.

Q. But it's one of the little figures, correct?

A. Right.

* * *

Q. Okay; so after the word "death trap," on that letter, January 1968, what's the next sentence?

A. "It was the ____________ with his baseball cap on sideways."

Q. Go ahead.

A. "[Its bill] had acted much like a barb on a fishhook and was preventing us from pulling the thing out of his throat."

Q. After you got notice of that in January of 1968, did you make any study to determine whether, in the event of such an occurrence such as described in this letter, it would have been easier for the parents to pull out a smooth-headed figurine as compared to one that had a hat or hair on it, such as the one that accompanied Plaintiff's Exhibit 1? [*Ed. Note*: Exhibit not supplied.]

A. I'm not familiar with any studies of that nature.

Q. Or test?

A. Or test, particularly of tests.

Q. Continue reading please.

A. "Upon looking at the other [figurines] we noticed the little girls are even worse. . .".

Q. Go ahead.

A. "Ours has a happy ending, thank God, as our son received nothing more than a small gash in his throat on the inside, and small children do heal fast. I am writing this letter, however, as a helpful hint. I hope, in order to prevent some other child from perhaps a far more serious accident, as once one of these barbs get locked in a child's throat, some other mother may not be able to pull it free."

* * *

Q. After receiving the January 1968 letter, did you, when I say "you" I mean [the company], based upon the warning that was contained in the January 1968 letter, did you amend or add to the instructions that accompanied toys similar to or the same as that?

A. No.

Q. Did you change your instructions in any way after the January letter with regard to toys the same as or similar to those talked about in that letter?

A. No.

Q. Did you change the design of the toy or toys in any way as a consequence of receiving that notice in January of 1968?

A. We constantly change our design and there have been design changes, but not with respect to the baseball cap on a figure.

Q. Well, you're limiting yourself to the baseball cap and I'm asking you, as a result of receiving this letter, did you make any safety changes in the design of the toy complained of or one similar to it?

A. Prior to the date of the occurrence?

Q. Yes, to the child [plaintiff].

A. I don't think so.

COMMENT: Instead of reevaluating its product, this executive responded by telling the mother that hers was an isolated case, a freak accident.[13]

Q. Did your company answer that letter?

A. Yes.

Q. Do you have your response?

A. Not with me, no.

Q. What did you tell her in response?

A. I can't recall it verbatim, but we expressed surprise in that, that this was a first, that that was the first occurrence we have heard of in over a million toys. I don't recall the complete response. I can get it for you.

COMMENT: What he actually told her was "Your letter of January 6 was a real shock to us. We are very upset to know that your baby was hurt while playing with a . . . toy, and are thankful that you and your husband were both on hand to deal so effectively with what can only be described as a 'freak' accident. The __________ has always been considered one of our safest toys, and there are over a million of them in homes all over the country . . .".[14]

---

[13] *Id.*

[14] *Id.*

The one person who could have made a real difference, had he known about these letters of warning, was the toy's designer. This official testified that he never was informed of the warning from the safety expert regarding the toy's hazardous design or of the complaint letters from consumers alerting the company to the toy's hazards! If he had that information, he testified, he likely would have acted to redesign the toy to avoid the tragedy that subsequently took place.[15]

§ 7.12 Lack of safety considerations

The startling lack of safety input into this toy's design process was revealed in testimony given by executives from the company president on down: no information, no research, no consultation, no testing. The company had received no reports of injuries from its earlier toy designs, and felt no reason to expect them from this new product. They knew the toy could fit in a child's mouth. But could it be ingested? Could it block a child's airways? No one knew, or even tried to find out. The toy would be designed to fit into the existing toy line. That was the company's concern, and the guiding force behind the toy's design, as revealed in the following excerpt of testimony by the toy's designer.[16]

Q. Who was in charge of the relative safety, from the point of view of the child, of the ____________ series of figurines?

A. I don't know that it would have been any one person, but rather the team developing any particular toy.

Q. Was it your responsibility?

A. Partly.

Q. Okay. You say as part of that team, a portion of that responsibility was yours. What did you do to carry out those responsibilities, and what did that responsibility consist of, if anything?

A. If there were concerns expressed by any member of the team, from Mr. ________ on down, and the team decided that certain changes or modifications to a design of a toy were necessary, and it was a toy that I was assigned to work on, then it was my responsibility to translate those concerns into physical changes.

Q. Did you recommend any changes related to safety, or have any

---

[15] *Cunningham*, *supra* note 2, testimony of Mr. O.

[16] *Id*.

suggestions at the time you were working on the development of the toys we're questioning?

A. No.

Q. Okay. Did you read any material—have any input about safety considerations regarding the toy during the period of time we're talking about—when you initially got involved in the development of the figurines?

A. No.

Q. Did you receive any safety input at that time from any other member of the team that you tried to incorporate into the design of the __________ series figurines?

A. Not in the figures themselves.

Q. So in essence, prior to the time that they were marketed, there was no safety input with respect to the __________ series of figurines? Correct me, if you will, sir, if I'm wrong in any way.

A. Not with the specific figure that we are referring to, which is the evolutionary figure, the one that I designed specifically. . . .

COMMENT: He knew that this toy could fit into a child's mouth and that children might put the toy into their mouths. Yet he checked no medical texts, and made no literature search to determine what the appropriate size should be to ensure a child's safety! His ignorance is revealed in the following cross-examination excerpt.[17]

Q. At the time you were designing this toy, it was pretty standard pediatric teaching that a toddler should not be permitted to walk with objects that could fit into his mouth; were you aware of that?

A. No, I didn't know that.

Q. Okay. As a designer of toys, do you feel there is any hazard at all associated with a child of one year or two years walking with

[17] *Id.*

an object such as Plaintiff's Exhibit 1, for example, that could fit completely in his mouth? [*Ed. Note*: Exhibit not supplied.]

A. Yes, there can be hazard associated with that.

Q. Would asphyxiation or choking be one of those hazards?

A. I don't know.

Q. To this moment you don't know?

A. It would depend on what happened when the child fell.

Q. At least you didn't consider when you were designing this toy, aside from a chipped tooth or a lacerated mouth, the possibility that if a toy fits into a toddler's mouth, it could cause an occlusion of the airway resulting in suffocation?

A. We felt that the size we were working with was safe.

Q. You didn't consider the possibility, did you, that a child might have his airway blocked with a toy that fitted into his mouth, a toddler?

A. We did consider that possibility.

Q. You did, and how did you consider it? Did you consult any medical books?

A. No, we did not.

Q. Did you hire any medical consultants?

A. No, I didn't.

Q. Did [the company]?

A. Not that I am aware of.

COMMENT: This executive's ignorance was not an isolated case. The company had no books, no library, no expertise to evaluate this toy's safety adequately and make sure that tragedies like this one could be avoided. As a postscript to this chain of events, this company still made no significant design changes even after this young boy's horrible injury. Two years later, another child fell victim to this hazardous toy. He lost his life when a smaller figurine became lodged in his throat. Since that time, two more children were reported to have lost their lives after similar incidents.

---

§ 7.13 Saving face: misrepresentations under oath

Not only did this company fail to heed the warning flags regarding this toy's killer potential, one company executive misrepresented the facts in an apparent attempt to save the company's reputation. In pretrial depositions taken in a related case,[18] this executive claimed to have consulted with a series of medical experts in Buffalo, New York, regarding the safety of the toy figurine's design in 1955. On the witness stand at trial, he changed his story, claiming now that these meetings took place in 1965. He admitted that one of these "consultants" was his father-in-law and another was his cousin-in-law. He steadfastly maintained, however, that he had met with these medical experts and that they had advised him that this toy was safe. He also testified that it was his belief that at least two of the physicians with whom he had consulted had since died.

When it was my turn to cross-examine this witness, I shocked the court, the jury, and the defendants by calling to the witness stand those two doctors who were allegedly deceased! Both physicians testified that they had never consulted with this man regarding this toy, and that they could not express a medical opinion that the toy was safe!

COMMENT: Never assume that any evidence you have been told is unavailable is actually not to be found. Keep digging—the so-called "dead" witness, or the missing page, may prove to be very much available.

---

§ 7.14 —Direct examination of company executive

The following excerpt from the direct examination of the company's manager of product development reveals this executive's attempt to con-

[18] *Cunningham*, *supra* note 2, direct examination of Mr. H by defense counsel.

ceal the truth from the jury.[19]

Q. All right. Mr. H, prior to the adjournment I was inquiring about what you did after the receipt of the letter from [the safety expert], and you had already described that you looked at some anatomy books and that you considered the matter carefully, and I think you then said that you went to see a Dr. D; is that right, sir?

A. Yes, sir.

Q. Now, first of all, tell the jury if Dr. D is alive.

A. No, he is not.

Q. Tell us who Dr. D was, and what his specialty and background was?

A. Dr. D was one of the senior members of the ________ Medical Community, to my knowledge. He was an anesthesiologist at the ____________ General Hospital, which I think I previously said, I had been led to believe dealt with emergency situations having to do with the throat area.

Q. All right, sir, and did you have a meeting with Dr. D, the anesthesiologist, in person?

A. Yes, I did.

Q. And did you take anything with you when you went to see him?

A. Yes, I took some ____________ figurines.

Q. Now, state what your reason was for going to see Dr. D following the receipt of the [safety expert's] letter?

A. Well, [the] letter did not speak specifically to the problem that I had outlined, and he had said simply to make all the toys greater than four or five inches, which did not seem to be an acceptable solution in view of what had gone on for fifty years, so the fundamental reason I went was to get more information.

Q. All right, sir, and then you had an actual consultation with Dr. D after that?

A. Yes, I did.

Q. And you took with you the various samples?

---

[19] Dorsett v. Quaker Oats Co., Fisher Price Div., No. CA 77–2061, Civ. T–H (M.D. Fla. Oct. 22, 1981).

A. Various figures.

Q. Examples of figures?

A. Yes.

Q. Do you recall how long you were with him?

A. On the first meeting, maybe an hour and a half, an hour.

Q. Did you show Dr. D the figures?

A. Yes.

Q. Following the meeting, did you make any change in the manufacturing techniques that were followed in making the ____________?

A. No.

Q. Did you change the design of the ____________ figures following your meeting with Dr. D?

A. No.

Q. Now, sir, following receipt of the [safety expert's] letter that you previously identified, did you see or consult with any other physicians?

A. Yes.

Q. Did you ask Dr. D whether [you] should make any changes, or whether he saw any problems in connection with the design of the figures and in connection with the manner in which they were being merchandised or sold? Did you ask Dr. D that in words or substance?

A. Yes, I simply asked him that question. I don't think I asked him if we should make any changes, in those words.

Q. Did you ask him if he saw any problems in the design?

A. Yes, very definitely.

Q. You specifically asked him in words or substance whether or not he saw any problem in the design?

A. Yes, I did.

Q. Did you ask Dr. B essentially the same question?

A. Yes, I did.

Q. And your testimony is that following each of those meetings, you made no change in either the design, manufacturing, or any other matter concerning which I asked you?

A. That's correct.

Q. Who else did you consult with?

A. Dr. B, who was with the __________ Hospital in __________.

Q. And who is Dr. B, where does he live, and what was his position at the time you went to see him?

A. He was a private practitioner in pediatrics associated with the __________ Children's Hospital. I believe he is also deceased.

Q. All right, sir. Did you go to see him following receipt of the letter?

A. Yes.

Q. What, if anything, did you take with you when you went to see him?

A. I took examples of the __________ figurines as well as some other products that the company produced.

* * *

Q. How much time did you spend with Dr. B?

A. In the order of a half an hour.

Q. Following that meeting, did you make any changes in the __________ figurines?

A. No, I did not.

Q. Did you change the design of the __________ figures in any respect?

A. No.

§ 7.15 —Cross-examination of company executive

In the following testimony, the witness affected his own credibility with his confusion over the dates of his alleged meetings [excerpt taken from the author's cross-examination of this witness].

Q. Referring to page 78 [of witness' deposition], do you see that down at line 22, the year 1955 or 1956? Does that refresh your recollection as to when you consulted with [these doctors]? Can you now tell us what year it was that you communicated with those mentioned as well as Dr. D?

A. Yes, I think it does refresh my memory.

Q. And what year was that?

A. I think it was 1965 or 1966.

Q. Does the deposition indicate your answer was at that time 1955 or 1956?

A. Yes, it does.

Q. And was your recollection on the date that this deposition was taken better than it is now with respect to those dates?

A. Yes, it is.

Q. So can we now agree it was 1955 or 1956?

A. Plus or minus, yes.

Q. Okay. Of course, in 1955 or 1956, Plaintiff's Exhibit 1 was not in existence, isn't that correct? [*Ed. Note*: Exhibit not supplied.]

A. Yes.

Q. So you didn't have any consultation with those doctors with respect to the adequacy or inadequacy of Plaintiff's Exhibit 1, is that correct?

A. That's correct.

§ 7.16 —Testimony of physicians

The following testimony reveals the real story [excerpt taken from the author's direct examination of these witnesses].

Examination of Dr. D[20]

Q. Did you ever consult with Mr. H or any other executive of [the defendant] in any way concerning Plaintiff's Exhibit Figure 1?

A. No.

Q. Or others like it?

A. No.

Q. Did you ever consult with him informally?

---

[20] *Cunningham*, *supra* note 2, direct examination by the author.

A. No.

* * *

Q. Did Mr. H ever come to your office with a series of figurines and spend an hour and a half with you consulting about these figurines?

A. He did not.

Q. Do you have an opinion, as an anesthesiologist, one way or the other about the safety or adequacy or inadequacy of [this toy] or others like it?

A. No.

Examination of Dr. B[21]

Q. Did you ever consult professionally with Mr. H or any other executive of [the defendant] concerning in any way Plaintiff's Exhibit 1 or other figurines like it?

A. I did not consult with Mr. H referable to the toy in issue, or any other member of the [defendant] Company.

Q. Did you ever consult with him informally?

A. No.

* * *

Q. With respect to Plaintiff's Exhibit 1, do you have an opinion one way or the other as to the safety of this particular toy for infants?

A. I have no opinion.

§ 7.17 Inadequate testing

Premarket testing for safety is not required for toys by any laws or regulations. Yet, one would think that a company that had enjoyed the kind of reputation for safety that this company had for so many years would endeavor to make sure that a toy it was designing and marketing was safe. For this particular toy, this was simply not the case. Company executives admitted that the company failed to test this product adequately before it was marketed to make sure that it was safe.

The company president, who was also at that time president of the toy industry's trade association, admitted that he knew that this toy could fit

[21] *Id.*

in a young child's mouth, but that he did not know whether, once a child placed this toy in his or her mouth, it could be swallowed or ingested, or block the child's airways with lethal consequences. Unfortunately, the company conducted no tests to find out. Consider these excerpts from his cross-examination.[22]

Q. Did [the defendant] do any test to determine whether the figurines that accompanied [this toy] could be mouthed?

A. It's obvious that the toy can be admitted into the oral cavity.

Q. Did [the defendant] do any tests to determine whether the play figurines that accompanied [this toy] could be swallowed?

A. No.

Q. How far beyond the mouth can they be admitted?

A. I'm afraid I'm not capable of answering that question.

Q. Who in [the defendant's company] is capable of answering that question?

A. I don't know if anyone in [the company] is capable of answering that question.

Q. Do you understand the term "blocking an airway?"

A. I understand the term "blockage," but I don't understand the intricacies of a child's body. I understand the term "blockage."

Q. Does blockage involve a suffocation hazard?

A. I don't know that.

Q. Did [the defendant] ever do any tests to determine that?

A. Not to my knowledge.

Q. Did [the defendant] do any test to determine whether, after a toy was admitted to the oral cavity, these figurines could block the airway or airways of preschool children of different ages?

A. You're saying "tests"?

Q. Yes.

A. No.

---

[22] *Cunningham*, *supra* note 2, testimony of Mr. C.

COMMENT: The company's so-called "tests" consisted of observing children at play, with the toys, before the company knew if the toys could be swallowed or fit in the child's throat, but while it knew they could fit in a child's mouth! Again, consider the testimony of the company president.[23]

Q. Did [you] do anything other than tests to determine that [a toy could be swallowed]?

A. Yes.

Q. What?

A. [We] observed children at play.

Q. You let children play with these things before you determined whether they were safe from the point of view of swallowability?

A. You're confusing [again] swallowability and admittance into the mouth.

Q. Well, mouthability. Did you let children play with these to determine whether [they were] safe from the point of view of mouthability?

A. You know that they can be admitted into the mouth.

§ 7.18 Alternative designs

Perhaps the cruelest part of this tragedy was the evidence elicited from the toy's designer that this toy could have been made in other, safer designs, that would have eliminated the hazard that caused this child's brain damage and the death of another. A different shape, a larger base, different materials, or even a hole drilled through the body of the toy to permit air to flow through it might have avoided the catastrophic consequences we witnessed in this case.

COMMENT: The plaintiff's witness, a child development

[23] *Id.*

expert, explained why drilling a hole would be so important to save a child's life. "[It] would . . . at least provide a temporary airway . . . it would sustain accessed air . . . not for long . . . [but] for the twenty, thirty minutes that you have got, at least it gives you a shot at it."[24]

According to the toy's designer, all of these design alternatives were feasible, but none were used because of the requirements for the figures to fit into the existing toy holes.[25]

Q. What alternative designs did you consider for the ____________ figurines that you are testifying about?

A. The only alternate aspects were the different hairstyles and the color and shape of the hats.

Q. Cosmetic things?

A. Cosmetic things.

Q. Thinking about the ____________ figurines at that time, did you consider any shape other than the cylindrical shape that it took?

A. Not at the base, because they had to fit in the holes of existing toys . . . to be compatible with other toys already on the market that had these holes.

Q. In other words, there was a line of vehicles and toys out at that time and these figurines were going to be redesigned, but they had to fit into that production, prior production as far as the size holes?

A. That was one of the requirements, that it be compatible with earlier products. . . .

Q. You didn't consider alternative materials?

A. No.

Several years later, the company still had not made any significant changes in the toy's design. A newspaper carried the following account of the same official's reaction when asked again whether the drilling of a hole was considered to avoid such a catastrophe in the future:

[24] *Cunningham*, *supra* note 2, testimony of Mr. K, M.C., Ph.D., Tufts New England Medical Center, on behalf of the plaintiff.

[25] *Cunningham*, *supra* note 2, testimony of Mr. O.

"Oh, boy, if you changed ____________, my God, all of our ____________ toys and all of the little recesses [the holes the toys fit into]—everything is designed proportionately." Such a change, he said, would cost the company millions of dollars.[26]

§ 7.19 Marketing strategy regarding safety

This toy company spent a lot of time and money cultivating a public image of being concerned about safety and manufacturing safe, high quality products. Its marketing strategy for this toy took full advantage of this image, from its repeated assurances that this toy was safe. The toy's package bore the word "safe" in at least three different places including, as part of its logo, "safety first." This image and reputation made its executives' testimony—that safety was not first, that indeed many factors came before safety, and that the very use of the word "safe" on the packaging was a promotional gimmick to build consumer confidence—most shocking. Consider the following excerpt from the testimony of the company's manager of research and development.[27]

Q. Now, the word "safe" is used several times [on the package], is it not?

A. This?

Q. On the box?

A. I am sure it is. I see at least two with a quick look.

Q. Yes, satisfy yourself?

A. Yes.

Q. A parent who is buying that toy, would they be entitled to rely on that word "safe" in all respects?

A. I am sure you would find and our research has shown quite a variance in the acceptance of packaging information, so I can't generalize. I would say probably less than half would.

Q. Less than half the people in a marketing area would rely on the word "safe"?

A. Yeah.

Q. But an appreciable number would?

A. Some would.

---

[26] Baltimore Sun, Nov. 22, 1978, at B1, col. 1.

[27] *Cunningham*, *supra* note 2, testimony of Mr. H.

Q. Is that one of the reasons it's put on the package, to assist sales?

A. Because we feel the product is safe, yes.

Q. And that would assist sales, wouldn't it?

A. Confidence, yes.

COMMENT: Despite this company's logo of "safety first," the toy designer's testimony shed the light of day on this cruel misrepresentation.[28]

Q. I notice that on the box marked as Plaintiff's Exhibit 10 for identification, on one of the panels, . . . there is some language and . . . that says "safety first," correct? [*Ed. Note*: Exhibit not supplied]

A. Correct.

Q. Well, when you were designing toys such as the ones that were contained in [this box], of all considerations you had to make, was safety your first consideration?

A. Not necessarily.

§ 7.20 Marketing strategy regarding age grading

Age grading was another element in this marketing gimmickry. Before they purchased this toy, the plaintiff's parents had seen a similar toy advertised in a company brochure with age recommendations for children aged one to five. They relied on these recommendations when they purchased the toy in the instant case, a toy that came with age recommendations for children two to five. The company used this age grading in its callous attempts to shift blame for this tragedy to the child's parents.

The president of the company responded to a letter from a friend of the aggrieved family writing of their tragedy by implying that the tragedy was brought on by the parents' purchasing toys for their fourteen-month-old son that bore age recommendations for "children 2–5." He stated

---

[28] *Cunningham*, *supra* note 2, testimony of Mr. O.

that:[29]

> [P]arents are inclined to ignore the studied recommendations of the manufacturer. We find that practically all difficulties with our toys are caused by giving the child a toy for which . . . is not ready.

Under cross-examination, this company president commented.[30]

> A. I think what I said in this letter is that we have age recommendations; we have many toys that were recommended for children one and two. These two particular toys that had been bought for this child were inappropriate and when the parents do this they have to supervise their children in their play.

This same official went on to testify that this toy would be safe for a one-year-old child, and that the same figurines were marketed with other toys marketed for one-year-old children. The toy's designer testified that the company expected age recommendations to be interpreted within a range of plus or minus one year. In other words, a toy recommended for children aged two to five was expected by the company to be purchased for children aged one to six:[31]

> The emotional or intellectual content of the toy was geared to a median age. I think the toys were always designed so they would accept a variant above and below that age. . . . I don't recall exactly where that toy was age graded. . . . I think if we check the catalog age gradings, then, I think that a range of a year below and above the recommended ranges are acceptable. . . . We knew that parents don't always purchase the toy precisely for the age range we put on the package, that's correct.

The toy's designer also admitted that age gradings, contrary to popular belief, have nothing to do with safety, but are based on the intellectual interest presented by the toy.[32]

COMMENT: This might come as a surprise to millions of parents, and our government's safety authorities who for

[29] Letter from Mr. H to Mr. C, Apr. 27, 1971. Second letter from Mr. H to Mr. C, June 15, 1971. *See also infra* § 7.21.

[30] *Cunningham*, *supra* note 2, testimony of Mr. C.

[31] *Cunningham*, *supra* note 2, testimony of Mr. O.

[32] *Id*.

years have urged parents to follow the toy's age recommendations to safeguard their children's safety.

It is well recognized by experts in child development that any child under the age of five is still going through the oral stage of development, placing any article, including toys, seemingly automatically into his or her mouth.[33] One must ask then why this toy that could fit in a young child's mouth was marketed for children aged one to six? The answer was apparently simple, though frightening: the age recommendation was a carryover from the toy's larger predecessor. Because company officials believed that age recommendations connoted "play value" rather than a toy's safety, they made no effort to change the age grading for the new, smaller model, nor even to consider the greater hazards that this in-between size toy would pose to young children. Excerpts from the designer's testimony under cross-examination are revealing.[34]

Q. When you received your assignment, you were asked to design a toy that would have been marketable for ages two to five?

A. I believe it was the same, whatever the age recommendation was on the original [toy], we would have been designing the revision with the same age group.

Q. Whatever the age recommendation was for the larger figurines on the larger [toy]?

A. The [toy] as a play item, that's correct.

Q. Okay, fine. You would carry over that recommendation to the new line?

A. That would be the general idea, right.

Subsequently, this same official admitted that it did not occur to anyone while designing the toy and deciding what was going to go on its package that the smaller, in-between size might be more hazardous than the size previously marketed: "We kept the same age grading because it was still the ____________ and the ____________ appeals to a child two to five years of age."[35]

---

[33] *Cunningham*, *supra* note 2, testimony of Dr. K.

[34] *Cunningham*, *supra* note 2, testimony of Mr. O.

[35] *Id*.

§ 7.21 Parental supervision

As members of the toy industry have attempted to shift the blame for toy-related injuries away from their products and onto parents and children, "parental supervision" has become a code word for "don't blame us." Throughout the preparation of this case, it became clear that this company was no exception.

This callousness was exemplified in the company's reply to the letter from the family friend that I have previously discussed. The president wrote, "All we can do is continue to stress to parents the importance of giving their children only those toys that are designed for their age level and depend upon those parents to supervise the play of their children during this vulnerable period . . .".[36] Yet, in sworn testimony, the company's president admitted that the company made no mention of or gave any warnings regarding parental supervision on this toy. In fact, the toy's box bore a picture of a young child playing with the toy—by himself!

Other company executives testified that the toy was intended and marketed as a creative play toy, and it was expected to be used without parental supervision. The toy's designer testified that he knew that the figures would be played with by unsupervised children, and that in his opinion the toy was safe to be used in this way. The company's manager of product development agreed.[37]

Q. It's perfectly all right for that child to use [this toy] unsupervised?

A. Yes.

Q. Indeed, that toy and others like it are marketed as an activity toy, are they not?

A. Yes, they are.

Q. And they are intended to be used by children within their own little world so they can create their own images and create their own play patterns?

A. That's right.

---

[36] Letter from Mr. C, company president, to Mr. H, June 23, 1971. *See supra* note 29.

[37] *See also* note 9, *supra*.

§ 7.22 Impact of injury on plaintiff's life

The plaintiff's expert in child development was helpful in conveying the impact of this boy's injury to the jury. The following is an excerpt from this witness's testimony.[38]

> [This child] is an eleven-and-a-half-year-old boy who has a severe physical handicap. He has difficulty walking. He moves about more easily on all fours around his home. His arms are limited in their movement. They are spastic. His hands are also spastic. He has a motor level of development of approximately a two-year-old. [A two-year-old child would be much more capable of moving easier through his environment than. . .].
>
> [He] has a mental handicap, in my opinion, based on the evaluations that I made and others have made, of about five or six years of age. His physical handicap and his mental handicap are permanent. They are not going to go away. He will continue for the rest of his life to be a severely physically and mentally handicapped human being, and there is no reason to suppose that his life is going to be shortened. He will require continuing medical treatment, physical therapy, speech therapy, and occupational therapy. He will undoubtedly require psychiatric treatment. He is going to have severe problems. . . .

COMMENT: Up to this time, the boy's parents had been caring for him and providing these treatments in his home environment with the help of scores of volunteers working around the clock for several years. This expert called the progress the child had made under this care a "miracle." But could it last?

> I think it is inconceivable to think that these two parents can continue all by themselves to take on this awesome task of caring for a child who will soon be an adult, who has the mind of a five year old, and is not going to get much further on. The older that [the boy]

[38] *Cunningham*, *supra* note 2, testimony of Dr. K.

gets, the greater the problem becomes. . . . [39]

Both doctors and economists play a vital role in any personal injury litigation. In this case, I was able to call on a series of medical specialists—pediatricians, a neurologist, child development and disability experts, and others who treated this young boy since his injury. Their opinions regarding the extent of this boy's injury, the likelihood of long-term consequences, the impact of that injury on his life, and the care and treatment required to allow him to lead as normal a life as possible, all were presented as part of the case, and all contributed to the jury's determination of a record damages award.

§ 7.23 —Testimony of pediatrician and neurologist

A pediatrician specializing in children's developmental disabilities and the care and management of handicapped children testified that when he first saw the plaintiff in 1977, he saw a young boy who was suffering from cerebral palsy, with "a general delay in development,"[40] who was "unable to coordinate and use his muscles in a normal fashion."[41] Although the plaintiff was 7½ years old at that time, he was functioning, in this doctor's opinion, at a motor level of a twelve- to fifteen-month-old child (his age at the time of injury), and at an intellectual level that this doctor described as mentally retarded. The plaintiff's difficulties, according to this doctor, included "difficulties with self-help skills: dressing, classroom exercises like using a pencil, and other daily activities requiring hand coordination."[42] As for the future, this doctor's prognosis was that drastic changes were unlikely.

A neurologist diagnosed the plaintiff's condition as "brain dysfunction from a lack of oxygen"[43] caused by "something in the throat causing respiratory arrest, cardiac arrest, and lack of oxygen to the brain."[44] He also described the boy's future outlook for normality as poor, explaining that "once the damage is done, it is permanent."[45]

---

[39] *Id.*

[40] *Cunningham*, *supra* note 2, testimony of Dr. D, on behalf of the plaintiff.

[41] *Id.*

[42] *Id.*

[43] *Cunningham*, *supra* note 2, testimony of Dr. G on behalf of the plaintiff.

[44] *Id.*

[45] *Id.*

§ 7.24 Conclusion

As I stated in my closing remarks to this jury, the plaintiff was seeking justice, not sympathy. Full justice to compensate him for his injury, his lost opportunities of life, and to compensate his family for their suffering and the care they had already provided and would have to provide for the remainder of his life.

In June 1981, this jury, in the defendant's own home territory, found this company negligent in its design, manufacture, and marketing of this toy, and awarded my client $3.1 million in damages.[46]

All the money in the world cannot, of course, undo or correct the damage done to this child. However, it can help meet the monumental expenses incurred by this family, provide some compensation for their pain and grief, and substitute, to some degree, for the income and earnings this young person would have attained had he been allowed to live his normal, expected life.

IV. Other Toy Hazards

§ 7.25 In general

Toys' threats come in many shapes and forms including: hazardous small parts, long strings or cords, sharp edges and sharp points, projectile weaponry, flammable fabrics, and electricity.[47] In the sections that follow, you will see just how dangerous these toys can be.

§ 7.26 Ingestion of small parts

Nothing is more natural in a young child's oral stage of development than placing almost anything he touches into his mouth. Child care experts agree that this "oral stage" of development is not only common to all children, but an integral part of their formative years.[48] It is bad enough that our homes are filled with small items, such as paper clips

---

[46] *See supra* note 2. This award included $800,000 for future medical expenses, $500,000 for pain and suffering along with lost amenities of life, and $500,000 for loss of future earning capacity. The plaintiff's parents received $1.3 million, including $300,000 for their son's medical care and $1 million for loss of their son's services and companionship.

[47] *See* E. Swartz, Toys That Don't Care, *How Toys are Unsafe* (Gambit, Inc. 1971).

[48] *Cunningham*, *supra* note 2, testimony of Dr. K.

and rubber bands, that we must continually remind ourselves to keep away from our children. It is little surprise, therefore, that hospital emergency rooms report thousands of children being rushed for treatment after ingesting small objects every year.[49]

Small parts present several hazards to young children, particularly those under the age of five: they can be placed in a child's mouth and swallowed, or become trapped in the child's throat and block his airways; they can enter a child's nose and become lodged in his breathing passages or be aspirated into his lungs; or they can block a child's breathing, causing suffocation, as in the case of a rattle or squeeze toy when its narrow end becomes caught in the child's throat.

Small toy threats also come in a variety of shapes and sizes. In some cases, the toy itself can pose ingestion threats: the small figurines that were the subject of the preceding case are one example.[50] Other threats come from larger toys with parts that can be easily removed by a child: small noses or other articles that are pulled off of stuffed dolls, or small wheels that can be pulled off of toy cars are just two examples.

In 1978, the Consumer Product Safety Commission issued its so-called "ban" on small toys and toys with small parts.[51] Any toy containing small parts had to be marketed for children over the age of three. A so-called small parts "test" accompanied this regulation. The test was inadequate from the start. It was developed to meet the needs of manufacturers whose interest was that then-existing toy lines did not have to be redesigned or taken off the market. For years, I have warned publicly that this so-called safety test was inadequate to prevent children's deaths and severe injuries from choking. At least thirty-seven children have died as a result of choking on so-called "safe" toys.[52] Recently, the CPSC's own studies have revealed these inadequacies.[53] Still, toys are manufactured that meet this standard and are marketed with the government's benediction that the toy is "safe." This same government study

---

[49] According to the Consumer Product Safety Commission (CPSC), in 1976, the last year for which such statistics are available, an estimated 46,500 children under the age of 10 were treated for small parts-related injuries.

[50] *See supra* §§ 7.05–7.24.

[51] 16 C.F.R. 1501 *et seq.* (1985).

[52] Consumer Product Safety Comm'n, *Choking Hazards Associated with Squeeze Toys and Similar Infant Products* (Briefing Package Nov. 1983). This number includes choking on toys that pass small parts, rattle, and pacifier choking tests.

[53] *Id*.

also found that all current standards are inadequate to protect America's children from the ingestion hazards posed by squeeze toys. The pliable nature of these infant toys makes them a continuing threat to lodge in children's throats.

§ 7.27 Strangulation

The threat of strangulation lurks behind every toy sold with an elastic or string of dangerous length. No danger illustrates my call for action against killer toys on the loose as well as the crib gym set that recently struck its second victim—a young child that died from strangulation when its clothing became entangled on a crib gym set. The toy's manufacturer and government safety agency had known of this toy's record of death since 1980, when the first child lost its life in a similar manner. Instead of recalling this killer toy, or ordering production stopped and seizing all toys in the company's inventory, this government agency permitted the toy to remain on the market, with no adequate warnings of its potential to kill. Only a caution was added, that "entanglement" could occur if the toy remained in the crib after a child could lift up on its hands or knees.[54]

Even more outrageous, if that is possible, is the response by this agency and manufacturer after the second death. Still no recall! Still no firm action to remove this killer from the marketplace! Still no adequate warnings! Only a so-called "safety alert" that the toy should be removed from the crib when a child attains the ability to pull himself up.[55] Other manufacturers, apparently ignoring this tragic record, continue to market their crib gym toys for children beyond the age when they attain this mobility. A 10½-month-old child died from strangulation on a gym that was marketed for children from the ages of birth to twenty-four months.

COMMENT: Crib gyms and other toys designed to be strung across cribs or playpens should be banned from the market entirely, since no parent can predict with certainty when their child will attain this mobility and place himself at risk. By the time parents learn that their child can pull him-

[54] The label on this toy read: "CAUTION: To Prevent Possible Entanglement Injury Remove Toy When Baby is 5 Months Old and Begins to Push Up On Hands and Knees."

[55] Consumer Product Safety Comm'n, *Safety Alert* (Press Release Oct. 10, 1984).

self up, it may be too late. Many other toys and children's products also pose lethal strangulation threats: toy telephones and other toys with long cords, lacing toys with long strings, pull toys, and mobiles are just a few that come to mind.

None of these toys are currently covered by mandatory government safety standards. Even government authorities criticize industry standards as being inadequate to protect children from strangulation threats.[56] Yet these toys are marketed as "safe" with no adequate warnings of their potential to kill.

§ 7.28 Sharp points and sharp edges

Cuts, abrasions, punctures, lacerations, bruises, and eye injuries are just some of the hazards posed by toys with sharp parts and sharp points. According to the federal government, in 1977, more than 43,000 children were injured from the sharp points or edges on their toys or other playthings.[57] Government regulations provide for so-called "tests," which toys with sharp points and edges must comply with, but only if they are marketed to children under the age of eight. Despite the regulations, toys with sharp points and edges continue to plague our children's nurseries. A recent government survey found that seventeen out of twenty-two toys tested failed to comply with the safety standards.[58]

Even those standards that exist contain a major loophole: toys with "functional" sharp points or edges are exempted.[59] This exemption was designed to cover such "obvious" and "part of the toy" hazards as the needle on a phonograph or sewing machine. Yet, ingenious manufacturers have used the loophole to create more deceptively hazardous products. For example, one manufacturer last year marketed a "pen" with a sharp, ballpoint tip, that was designed to look like a car, with wheels and

[56] Consumer Product Safety Comm'n, *Alternative Strategies to Address Accidental Ligature Strangulations of Children Less Than Five Years of Age* (Briefing Package May 1982).

[57] S. Brobeck & A. Averyt, The Product Safety Book (E.P. Dutton, Inc. 1983).

[58] Consumer Product Safety Comm'n, *Toys Hobbies and Crafts Magazine*, Toy Compliance Program Results 37, col. 2 (Nov. 1982).

[59] 16 C.F.R. 1500.18 (1985).

a sleak, plastic body. Because it was a "pen," it supposedly avoided compliance with the safety standards. How many children are running through their homes with this play vehicle, with its sharp point exposed, ready to penetrate someone's eye?

§ 7.29 Flammability

We saw in Chapter 4 how devastating burn injuries can be, particularly to children. Toys are often marketed with labels assuring consumers that they are "flame-retardant" or that they comply with "existing government requirements for flame retardancy." All too often, however, this assurance refers to the inadequate standards incorporated in the federal Flammable Fabrics Act, not the more stringent standards for flame-retardant children's sleepwear.[60]

The same polyester fiberfill that produced such horrible burns to the two youngsters in the *Hinckley* case (discussed in Chapter 4) can also be found in children's dolls and other items. No standards protect children from the devastating burn injuries these fabrics can produce.

COMMENT: Isn't it ironic that we can provide our children with flame-retardant sleepwear, but their dolls' clothing, or their tents, or comforters, can produce tragedy if they come into contact with heat sources around the home!

---

§ 7.30 Electrical hazards

We know that electricity can be dangerous, yet toys continue to be marketed that operate on dangerous, 120-volt, household current. Under government regulations, warnings must be provided on those toys where burns or shock can result.[61] Noticeably absent are any requirements that manufacturers equip these products with step-down transformers, as are required in Great Britain and other nations around the world, to reduce the threats of injury to our children.

In *Toys That Don't Care*, I complained about toys such as ovens and

[60] 16 C.F.R. 1615 *et seq.* (1985).

[61] 16 C.F.R. 1505 *et seq.* (1985).

irons that use real 120-volt, household current.[62] Admirably, many manufacturers ceased making such toys. However, a notable exception is ____________ Easy-Bake Oven. The box advertises that the oven has "built-in safety features" and that it is "simple-safe-fun." Despite these safety features, the warnings on the box reveal the manufacturer's acknowledgement of its hazards: "DANGER, TO PREVENT ELECTRIC SHOCK DO NOT IMMERSE IN WATER. WARNING: SHOCK HAZARD, DO NOT USE LIGHT BULB LARGER THAN 60 WATTS." Inside the box, other hazards are divulged: "HOT OVEN INTERIOR, OVEN TOP, OVEN BACK—DO NOT TOUCH. HOT PANS AND FOOD, HANDLE CAREFULLY. SHOCK HAZARD, PULL PLUG BEFORE CHANGING LIGHT BULBS."

Another manufacturer produces a microwave Style Electric Bake Oven. This "toy" uses 115-volt, household current and "cooks" with a 100-watt light bulb. This product contains many of the same warnings as its counterpart, but adds the following: "PARENT PLEASE NOTE! PERIODICALLY EXAMINE YOUR CHILD'S OVEN CORD AND LAMP SOCKET TO DETERMINE IF ANY DAMAGE HAS OCCURRED OR HAZARD EXISTS. ALL SUCH CONDITIONS MUST BE CORRECTED BEFORE USE."

COMMENT: Real electricity is not a toy and it is my belief that "electric" toys are never appropriate for small children. Because of government and industry safety standards, the manufacturer is required to sell this product to children ages eight and over. This caution appears on the toy box. Yet no child should be encouraged to treat cooking as a "play activity" when the potential for harm is so great.

---

§ 7.31 Projectile weapons

Projectile products come in a wide range of shapes and forms. All are dangerous. Many should not be sold as children's "toys" at all. Many others should be marketed only under strict safety requirements which,

[62] *See* E. Swartz, Toys That Don't Care 23–24, 109–110, 124 (Gambit, Inc. 1971).

as we shall see, have not been developed by the industry or by government authorities charged with protecting consumer safety.

Products like darts, BB's, pellets, arrows, and other projectile weapons can produce permanent injuries to the eyes of children and their playmates. Some of these products operate through a spring mechanism, building up sufficient energy to propel the product through the air. Others use air pumps or other energy-storage mechanisms. The latest craze of missile-firing "space toys" only adds to the jungle of eye-threatening products available for our children's use.

§ 7.32 Toy marketing

Any trip to the toy store will reveal the ingenious marketing schemes used to sell toys. It's hard to find a toy that doesn't bear the message "safe," "safety-tested," or "in compliance with safety standards" to lull consumers into a false sense of security that the product they are purchasing is safe. Recall, if you will, the admission by one toy company executive under oath that the word "safe" was used to "build consumer confidence,"[63] and another executive's sworn testimony that the "safety first" label on his company's toy was "not necessarily" accurate.[64]

Perhaps the most insidious of all toy marketing gimmicks are the so-called "age gradings" allegedly provided to help American consumers purchase toys that are "safe" for their children. Industry members concede in their own memoranda that age grades are used as a marketing gimmick by toy marketers to increase toy sales.[65] Government safety authorities acknowledge that age grades are inconsistent and inadequate,[66] yet they continue to urge consumers in so-called "toy safety" campaigns to follow toy age recommendations to prevent toy-related injuries.

These marketing gimmicks, combined with extremely sophisticated and expensive advertising blitzes on television and in the print media, leave American consumers with the false impression that the toys they buy are safe, fun, and educational, and that if hazards do exist, those in charge will act to remove them from the marketplace.

---

[63] *Cunningham*, *supra* note 2, testimony of Mr. H.

[64] *Cunningham*, *supra* note 2, testimony of Mr. O.

[65] Draft Memorandum of Toy Manufacturers of America, Mar. 24, 1982, at 1.

[66] Consumer Product Safety Comm'n, *Age Labeling of Toys* (Briefing Package Apr. 3, 1984).

COMMENT: I have publicly labeled this hoax perpetuated on the American public as a "conspiracy of silence."[67] Knowledge of toy dangers—of killer toys that remain lurking in children's nurseries and toy store shelves, of age gradings that are only marketing gimmicks, and of false assurances of safety that simply do not hold up under close scrutiny—are not being shared with the American public because the toy industry, and government safety agencies, would rather have it that way.

§ 7.33 Other children's product hazards

Other products designed, manufactured, and marketed for children pose fatal risks that can be prevented, but are not because manufacturers and marketers do not want to risk losing product sales. Cribs, playpens, toy chests, baby gates, baby corrals, and playground equipment all fall into this category.

§ 7.34 —Cribs

Ten years ago, the CPSC promulgated its first mandatory crib safety standards in response to reports that 200 children were dying from strangulation in hazardous cribs every year.[68] The agency mandated that cribs be designed to eliminate hazards of crib slats spaced so far apart that children's heads could fit and become lodged between them; mattresses fitting so poorly that children's heads became caught between mattresses and crib frames; loose-fitting locking mechanisms that permitted crib sides to fall without warning; and sharp metal surfaces that enabled children to suffer cuts, bruises, and lacerations in their own cribs.

Unfortunately, the agency's own files continue to document the tragic consequences of hazardous cribs: a nine-month-old girl died of asphyxiation when her neck became caught and was compressed between the fold-

---

[67] Swartz, Press Release on Dangerous Toys (Nov. 27, 1984).

[68] 16 C.F.R. 1508 *et seq.* (1985).

down slats in the crib side rail;[69] a six-month-old boy was found hanging by the head between the springs and side rail after he crawled between a foam mattress and side rail;[70] a four-month-old baby girl died of asphyxiation from chest compression when she became trapped between the crib rail and mattress edge.[71]

Other hazards persist that were not covered by these standards. Every year children are needlessly strangled to death when their clothing, toys, or other articles become caught on dangerous crib cornerposts.[72] In one recent year, the CPSC found that one-third of all crib-related injuries it investigated involved strangulation on finials.[73] Twenty-five children lost their lives to these decorative but utterly nonfunctional posts ranging from one inch to six inches in height.[74] In one case, a fifteen-month-old boy was strangled when his T-shirt caught on a crib finial. The young boy fell outside of his crib, his arm slipped out of its sleeve, and his weight caused the shirt to press on his throat.[75] In another case, an eleven-month-old child was fatally hanged on the inside of a crib when a string from a hat she was wearing became caught on the cornerpost.[76] According to government estimates, the majority of the twenty million cribs on the market today have potentially deadly cornerposts.[77] In 1981, Canada set limits on heights of crib finials sold in that country to one centimeter.[78] The American safety agency has studied the problem for years, but has not yet established stringent, mandatory, safety standards.

Recently, another crib hazard was brought to the public's attention: death from suffocation in mesh-sided cribs.[79] At least eleven children were reported to have died when the side of the crib was left down and the child crawled or rolled under the mesh covering and was suffocated when his head became trapped underneath. The safety agency responded

---

[69] Consumer Product Safety Comm'n, Injury Reports provided to the author by the National Injury Information Clearinghouse (1983).

[70] *Id.*

[71] *Id.*

[72] Consumer Product Safety Comm'n Briefing Package, *supra* note 57.

[73] *Id.*

[74] *Id.*

[75] *Id.*

[76] *Id.*

[77] *Id.*

[78] *Id.*

[79] Consumer Product Safety Comm'n Press Release (May 11, 1983).

to these tragedies by issuing so-called "safety alerts" for parents to make certain that they kept the crib sides in the "up" position.[80]

§ 7.35 —Toy chests

By government estimates, twenty-one children have lost their lives, while others have been rendered permanently brain damaged, paralyzed, or blind after swiftly falling toy chest lids came crashing down as they peered inside.[81] The dangers posed by these rapidly falling lids is not new. More than ten years ago, consumer advocates, including myself, were calling for prompt, stringent action to remove this lethal threat from our children's nurseries. Half of the 700,000 toy chests on the market have hinged lids.[82] The cost of redesigning these products to avoid tragedy would have been mere pennies.[83] In 1983, the safety agency was finally prepared to promulgate mandatory standards requiring use of safety hinges to prevent these tragedies. Its own experts warned that a mandatory standard was required to ensure compliance and provide adequate protections for America's children.[84]

The mandatory standards never went into effect. Instead, the agency voted to reject this approach in favor of so-called "voluntary" standards being developed by the toy industry. Trade association representatives assured the government that this time compliance would be full. Never mind that the agency's own staff acknowledged that the likelihood for compliance with voluntary standards was not good, or that many toy chest manufacturers were not members of the industry's trade association and, even if they were, the association had no legal means of enforcing the standard. The agency knew that only fourteen of thirty toy chest manufacturers were even members of industry trade associations and, only 46% of all toy chests were manufactured by association members.[85]

The comments of one agency commissioner following this vote summarized this agency's continuing preference to sacrifice the safety of America's children for industry's interests and pressure:

Considering the unfathomable recalcitrance of the industry over the

---

[80] *Id.*

[81] Consumer Product Safety Comm'n, *Toy Chests* (Briefing Package Aug. 8, 1983).

[82] *Id.*

[83] *Id.*

[84] *Id.*

[85] *Id.*

> past nine years to address this hazard, even as the deaths rose with grim precision, I am not persuaded that the presence on paper of a voluntary standard is likely to result in a substantial compliance. . . . The Commission, it appears, has given this industry the benefit of considerable doubt. I wish it had extended that same courtesy to the nation's children.[86]

Another commissioner termed the decision "dangerous" and commented, "We should be sure, not sorry. Great expectations are fine for a novel, but child safety should not have to run the risk of possible fiction."[87]

§ 7.36 —Baby gates and baby corrals

Ironically, both of these products are purchased and used for safety purposes. Corrals are designed to provide children with safe play areas outside, to permit parents to focus on other matters while children engage in carefree play. Their design also provides invitations to tragedy, with "V"-shaped peaks and diamond-shaped bottoms that can catch children's necks and heads, posing risks of serious injury and death. In one case, a thirteen-month-old girl wedged her head between the slats of a wooden corral.[88] In another, a twelve-month-old died of asphyxiation after her neck became entrapped in the "V" section of a wooden, expandable, accordian-type corral.[89]

Baby gates pose similar hazards. Like corrals, these products are marketed for use particularly when a child is to be left unattended. The gate's design has resulted in at least eight reported deaths and seventeen near-misses when children's necks or heads became trapped in the top "V" or bottom "diamond" shapes.[90] Recently, manufacturers of accordian-style gates have ceased marketing the product, but have refused to recall the estimated ten to fifteen million gates already in consumers'

---

[86] Consumer Product Safety Comm'n, Opinion and Ballot of Commissioner Edith Barksdale Sloan in the Matter of Toy Chests, at 2 (Aug. 17, 1983).

[87] Consumer Product Safety Comm'n, Dissenting Opinion of Commissioner Sam Zagoria in the Matter of Comm'n Vote on Toy Chests Draft Standard (Aug. 17, 1983).

[88] Information provided to the author by National Injury Information Clearinghouse, Consumer Product Safety Comm'n (1983).

[89] *Id*.

[90] Consumer Product Safety Comm'n, *Expandable Accordian-Style Baby Gates* (Information Package Dec. 6, 1984).

homes and retailers' inventories.[91]

§ 7.37 —Playpens

Playpens can prove fatal to children in several respects: choking threats from plastic or vinyl padding, strangulation from nylon thread that unravels from the playpen's padding, and strangulation when the child's clothing buttons or other articles become caught on the playpen's mesh covering.

For example, one parent found her one-year-old son choking and unable to breathe in his playpen. The toddler had chewed off a piece of vinyl plastic from the playpen and attempted to swallow it. Fortunately, this parent was able to remove the plastic piece from her youngster's throat before tragedy could strike.[92] Another parent found her one-year-old son "turning colors" after he ingested vinyl materials from his playpen. She forced him to regurgitate the material by placing her finger down his throat.[93] Similarly, a nineteen-month-old toddler nearly strangled when a string of padding filament, used to bind the playpen's mesh sides to its padded protections, became loose and wound around his neck.[94]

§ 7.38 —Playground equipment

Hazards of defective playground equipment are not new. In *Toys That Don't Care*, I described the hazards as follows:

> Watch out for such recurrent problems as toxic paints, splintering wooden parts, and generally unstable frames. We should ask whether the units (such as swings, for instance) are spaced far enough apart from each other, and built only for a back-and-forth and not a 360° movement. If they are not, then collisions with other units or with inattentive bystanders are very likely. . . . Be sure to examine every aspect of any gym set to make certain that there are no closely meshing metal parts into which children could put their hands or fingers. . . . [Some] ordinary back-and-forth swings are made with adjustable "S" hooks which can be used to suspend the

[91] Consumer Product Safety Comm'n News Release, Jan. 24, 1985. *See also* CONSUMER PROD. SAFETY REP. (CCH) 46,892.

[92] *See supra* note 89.

[93] *Id.*

[94] *Id.*

> swing set at varying distances from the ground in order to accomodate children of different ages and sizes. Children may stand up on the swings or climb up the chains. The danger of these practices is compounded on the adjustable models by the fact that the youngsters may shimmy on the chains, catching their clothes, fingers, or genitals on the S-shaped hooks.[95]

Ladders and slides have also been the source of injuries and death when children's bodies or their clothing became entangled on protrusions causing lacerations or lethal strangulation.

The Consumer Product Safety Commission estimates that 200,000 children suffer playground equipment-related injuries every year.[96] Despite this staggering toll, little adequate effort has been made by federal safety authorities to require safer playground design.

V. Preventing Toy-Related Injuries

§ 7.39 In general

Three factors affect the safety of any product: manufacturers' concerns about the product's safety, consumers' awareness of the hazards associated with the product, and the diligence of public authorities in forcing manufacturers to meet the public's need by producing and marketing safe products. In the case of the toy industry, all of these factors have been historically lacking. The prevention of injuries from toys and other children's products requires a new vigorous effort by all parties concerned.

§ 7.40 Industry action needed

Industry members must make certain that their products are designed for safety. As a first step, they must comply with their own often proclaimed standard that "one injury to one child is one too many." They must tell American consumers the whole story about toy safety, including the various hazards their products might pose, instead of blithely labeling their products as "safe" when they have not tested them for safety and they know the label is used only to increase product sales. If they use a system of age grading, this system must be uniform, consistent, and include explanations of the reasons for the particular age rec-

---

[95] *See* SWARTZ, *supra*, note 63 at 237–41.

[96] *See* Consumer Product Safety Comm'n Annual Reports, 1980, 1981, 1982.

ommendations on each toy. They must comply with existing laws, regulations, and safety standards. They must share information regarding toy hazards with American consumers instead of hiding them as part of the current "conspiracy of silence." Finally, the industry must cease shifting blame for toy-related deaths and injuries to the injured children or their parents, and admit that hazardous toys are also to blame. As producers of products designed and intended for children's use in the home environment, there is no excuse for a lack of diligence in designing products that are safe and providing adequate warnings for those products that may be safe for older children but pose dangers to their younger siblings.

The toy industry must recognize and publicly acknowledge the failure of its industry-wide voluntary toy safety standard[97] to protect children adequately from harm caused by their toys and other products. Recent proposed revisions by the American Society for Testing Materials (ASTM)[98] continue the deficiencies of the existing standards for all toy hazards, including small toy ingestion, strangulation, flammability, electrical toys, and projectiles. Many toys currently sold as "safe" because they conform to the industry's standards are simply too dangerous and should not be permitted on the market. It is imperative that the industry make an honest and diligent effort to reduce toy hazards by developing and revising its voluntary standards to accomplish this end.

Toy safety standards, bans, statutory requirements for reporting product defects, and recalls of hazardous products must be complied with, monitored, and pursued with diligence and commitment.

§ 7.41 Government action needed

Government safety authorities, particularly officials of the Consumer Product Safety Commission, have an important and immediate responsibility to fulfill in preventing children's toy-related injuries. For ten years, this federal agency has had the authority and responsibility to take firm action needed to protect children from hazardous toys.[99]

Recent congressional passage of the Toy Safety Act of 1984[100] has ex-

---

[97] P.S. 72–76.

[98] Revisions to P.S. 72–76 by American Society for Testing Materials (1985).

[99] Federal Hazardous Substances Act, 15 U.S.C. § 1261 *et seq.* (1978).

[100] Toy Safety Act of 1984, amendments to Federal Hazardous Substances Act, 15 U.S.C. § 1261 *et seq.* (1984).

panded the CPSC's authority to act swiftly and firmly against defective toys. Still needed is a requirement for uniform, across-the-board, premarket testing of all toys for safety.

Several measures must be forthcoming from the CPSC to prevent further toy-related injuries and deaths: recognizing the inadequacies and failures of current so-called toy "safety" standards and regulations; establishing revised or, if necessary, new standards or other regulatory measures to protect America's children adequately from hazardous toys; acting firmly to ban, recall, seize, warn consumers, and otherwise remove from the marketplace toys that have track records of death; ceasing espousal the toy industry's self-serving interests in the so-called annual "toy safety" campaign; telling American consumers the whole story about toy hazards instead of joining the toy industry in shifting blame for toy-related injuries to injured children and their families; mandating and stringently enforcing uniform, effective, and meaningful age grade labeling, including clear warnings and explanations of the reasons for particular age grades; stringently enforcing all toy safety standards, statutory defective product reporting requirements, and recalls of hazardous toys; and using its new authority under the Toy Safety Act of 1984[101] to recall defective toys quickly and efficiently.

Instead of effective action, we have seen only weak words from this agency. Instead of banning toy weaponry, we see a proliferation of these products, some marketed to children as young as three years of age. Instead of setting mandatory safety standards, we see coloring books, so-called advisories on product packages not to fire weaponry toward someone's face and to use it only with parental supervision. It is no secret that many of these products are toy industry staple items, and that toy industry pressure has prevented this safety agency from taking strong, effective action.

It's also time for the safety agency to acknowledge that the standards in the United States are in many instances far less stringent and less protective than those provided by other nations around the world to protect their children.[102]

---

[101] *Id.*

[102] Electrical toys, for example, must be accompanied by step-down transformers to reduce the operating voltage to safe levels in Great Britain and Australia. Projectile toys and toys with sharp points and edges are governed by stringent standards in Canada. Toys with flammable fabrics are under stringent flame-retardancy requirements in Great Britain, Canada, Australia, and the European Community.

COMMENT: The CPSC must stop playing games with children's lives. Firm action is needed immediately to establish stringent and effective standards and to ban products that are too dangerous to be marketed to children.

The reduction in the CPSC's budget and staff in recent years has been accompanied by a new industry attitude that they can get away with violating even the existing inadequate standards. The agency's own surveys have found consistently high rates of noncompliance with safety standards and with statutory requirements such as the reporting of identified product hazards.[103]

Recalls are also notoriously ineffective. Those toys that are recalled may linger in children's nurseries for years because the message never is adequately conveyed to the consumer. The agency must amplify its efforts to inform consumers of product recalls, including distribution of "WANTED" posters in retail outlets, doctors' offices, hospitals, and other appropriate locations across the country. It must also recognize the inherent deficiencies in recall procedures and push for mandatory across-the-board, premarket testing of toys for safety.

The safety agency has many options for firm action against toys that have a record of death. It can classify the product as an imminent hazard because it presents an "imminent and unreasonable risk of death, serious illness, or severe personal injury,"[104] and it can ask a court to order the product seized and production halted.[105] It can also order the toy immediately recalled.[106]

The CPSC should require that toy age recommendations appear on the toys themselves in addition to the box or package in which they are sold. Many toys are sold without packaging and bear no age recommendation. All toys are removed from their packaging after they are brought home,

---

[103] Consumer Product Safety Comm'n, *Evaluation of Toy Compliance* (1982), *supra* note 59.

[104] Federal Hazardous Substances Act, *supra* note 100.

[105] *Id.*

[106] Toy Safety Act of 1984, *supra* note 101.

if not before. Permanent age grades on the toy package, with adequate explanations and warnings of the risks of use by children not of the recommended age, will serve as a constant reminder of the dangers posed and the need for vigilence in preventing toy-related tragedies.

A favorite marketing gimmick of toy manufacturers are labels stating a toy is "safe," "safety-tested," or "complies with safety standards." The CPSC must require manufacturers to include explanations of what these so-called safety references mean. Whose standards do they comply with? Can a flammable toy burn or will it self-extinguish when a heat source is removed? Can a small toy fit in a child's mouth? Can it obstruct a child's airway? Can a toy that is safe for a six- or seven-year-old pose harm to a younger sibling? Manufacturers have a duty to end the conspiracy of silence surrounding toy hazards. If they won't, public officials must step in. The conspiracy of silence regarding toy-related hazards must end.

COMMENT: Each year, this safety agency joins hands with the toy industry in their so-called "toy safety" campaign. It's time this agency ceased spending taxpayer dollars to espouse and promote the industry's arguments that toys are safe, that blame for toy-related deaths and injuries lies with the injured child or his family rather than the hazardous toy, and that consumers wanting to protect their children should follow manufacturers' age grading.

It is ironic that this agency endorses the industry's line that toys are safe, while at the same time publishing the grim statistics of toy-related injuries and deaths. Instead of advising consumers to be careful of toys with small parts, sharp points, and the like, why not acknowledge publicly that hazardous toys continue to pollute the marketplace, and use its resources to identify and eliminate those toys?

---

§ 7.42 Consumer action

Until these steps are taken, consumers will have to take their own actions to prevent toy-related injuries. These include: shopping wisely; to the extent they can, testing toys in the store before purchasing them; reporting suspicious toy hazards to the appropriate government authorities; writing letters to manufacturers regarding suspect toy hazards; calling for prompt action to remove those hazards from the marketplace; generating publicity in the local media for toy safety and regarding toy hazards; joining or starting local toy safety organizations to keep a "watch" on the toy industry and prevent hazardous toys from entering the marketplace; and writing to members of Congress and CPSC Commissioners regarding the need for effective toy safety action and across-the-board, premarket testing of all toys for safety.

§ 7.43 The media

The mass media has a less widely recognized, but equally vital, role to play.

For too many years, time and space in electronic and print media has been monopolized by industry interests. Advertising is one reason why. Each year the toy industry spends hundreds of millions of dollars in toy advertising aimed at children and their parents.[107] Much of this budget is allocated to the pre-Christmas, toy-purchasing season. For many years, consumer advocates have protested the manner in which toys are advertised, particularly on children's television programming. They have warned that the sophisticated ads take undue advantage of children's inability to distinguish fantasy from reality. Why not ban television toy advertising on children's programming altogether?

Television news and talk shows present another problem. All too often, toy companies are prime sponsors for these programs. Is it any wonder that the information shared with the public reflects the industry's biases? When toy hazards are discussed, they are often placed in the content of the parents' or child's behavior rather than the toy's potential to kill because of its hazardous design. More complete coverage of this subject likely requires a broad education of the media members as to toy hazards and the culpability of the toy industry in polluting our marketplace with hazardous products.

COMMENT: The consumer's perspective on the preven-

[107] The top five toy industry members spent an estimated $100 million on television advertising in 1981, as reported in *Toys, Hobbies and Crafts Magazine* (Oct. 1982).

tion of toy injuries and toy safety has been historically lacking. This deficiency is beginning to give way to a broader approach by many members of the print and electronic media, particularly consumer-oriented reporters. This trend must continue and grow for consumers to get the whole story about toy safety.

---

§ 7.44 What can lawyers do?

Lawyers have a vital role to play in the prevention of toy-related injuries. I have demonstrated in the last fifteen years of my practice how one person can make a difference. I learned about toy industry practices and the tragic consequences of hazardous toys first-hand through my representation of injured children. I used my skills as a trial lawyer to represent injured children in the courts of our land, exposing the negligent and callous practices of toy industry leaders who prefer short-term profits to preventing toy-related injuries. I used my skills as a lawyer and advocate to share the hazards I found in the marketplace and the sorry state of toy injury prevention when I testified before the National Commission on Product Safety[108] and the Senate Committee on Commerce.[109] I used my skills as a researcher and writer to expose the toy industry's deadly game in *Toys That Don't Care*,[110] and to share my concerns about prevention of toy-related injuries in numerous articles for legal journals,[111] comments on pending legislative and regulatory decisions, drafting reform legislation, and pressing public safety authorities to take firm action to remove hazardous toys from the marketplace.

I have used my skills as an advocate by drawing the public's attention to toy hazards in my annual nominees of the "Ten Worst Toys" and in countless appearances on the media, including *60 Minutes*, *To Tell the*

---

[108] National Commission on Product Safety, testimony of Edward M. Swartz (Dec. 18, 1968).

[109] *Consumer Product Safety Act of 1971 in support of S. 983 of the Senate Comm. on Commerce*, testimony of Edward M. Swartz (July 28, 1971).

[110] Swartz, *supra* note 48.

[111] *Toys That Don't Care*, 76 CASE & COM. No. 6 (Nov.-Dec. 1976); *Inside Santa's Bag of Tricks*, ENVIRONMENTAL QUALITY (Dec. 1972); *Blindness in the Toy Box*, 43 SIGHT SAVING REV. No. 2 (1973); *Toys-R-Dangerous*, TRIAL (Feb. 1982); *Toys That Harm*, TRIAL (Dec. 1976).

Truth, *The Dick Cavett Show*, the *Dinah Shore Show*, and the *Larry King Show*. Moreover, I have used my skills as a public speaker and teacher to talk and lecture on the subject of toy safety and injury prevention before community organizations, consumer groups, legal audiences, medical associations, law students, libraries, industry groups, students, government officials, and others concerned about children's safety and the need to prevent toy-related deaths and injuries.

COMMENT: I have demonstrated what one person can do. But that is not enough. I believe that all members of the legal profession who know the horrors of toy-related injuries from their own work and have access to information that can prevent toy-related injuries have an obligation to share this information with the American public. Not only lawyers, but doctors, child development experts, engineers, government officials, and others have the obligation to work together to raise the public's consciousness regarding toy hazards and press industry and government officials into action for safer toys and other children's products.

I have devoted much of my lifetime to the cause of preventing children's injuries. I invite those readers who wish to become more actively involved in the prevention of toy-related injuries to take an active role for toy safety in your community. Write letters and articles regarding recognized toy hazards. Pressure the Consumer Product Safety Commission for firm and swift action to remove hazardous toys from the marketplace. Participate in drafting and revising toy safety standards to promote more stringent and effective standard criteria. Promote toy safety through your local media, raising the public's awareness of toy hazards. Finally, communicate your concerns to other members of the legal community, including lawyers, law professors, and law students, to promote their participation in this effort.

VI. Litigation Sources: Bibliography

§ 7.45 Selected technical sources

Aubrecht, *Mechanical Toy: The Gee-Haw Whammy-Diddle*, 20 Physics Teacher 614 (Dec. 1982).

Bevry, *Perpetual Motion Toys*, 20 Physics Teacher 319 (May 1982).

Blocker, et al., *Serious Air Rifle Injuries in Children*, 69 Pediatrics 751–54, No. 6 (June 1982).

Bryan, *Head Injuries in Children*, in *Developmental Medicine and Child Neurology* (1972), at 137–47.

Fox, *Figuratively Speaking*, 94 New Scientist 2–5 (Apr. 29, 1982).

Gardner, *Toys With a Mind of Their Own*, 13 Psychology Today 93–95 (Nov. 1979).

Greenslade, *Electrostatic Toys*, 20 Physics Teacher 552 (Nov. 6, 1982).

Hanna, *Spring-Wound Toy Cars: Experiments in Mechanics*, 21 Physics Teacher 177–81 (Mar. 1983).

Harris, et al., *BB and Pellet Guns—Toys or Deadly Weapons?*, 23 J. Trauma 566–69, No. 7 (July 1983).

Hope, *Toying with Legal Action*, 86 New Scientist 27 (Apr. 3, 1980).

Levenstein, *Physics of Toys*, 20 Physics Teacher 358–65 (Sept. 1982).

Mulder, *Children's Toys*, 18 Physics Teacher 134–35 (Feb. 1980).

Tilting Toy Train, 96 New Scientist 117 (Oct. 14, 1982).

Electronic Maths, 92 New Scientist 24 (Oct. 1, 1981).

Top Secret is Topped, 80 New Scientist 359 (Nov. 2, 1978).

Accidental Falls from Elevated Surfaces in Infants from Birth To One Year of Age, 44 Pediatrics 869–75, No. 5, Part. II (Nov. 1969).

Rice, *Manipulation: Ho, Ho, Children, Here Comes Guilta Claus*, 15 Psychology Today 32 (Apr. 1981).

Ridenour, *Variability in Flight Patterns of Projectiles from Toy Guns*, 59 Perceptual & Motor Skills 707–10 (1984).

Steganine, *Behavior of a Real Top*, 41 Am. J. Physics 346–50 (Apr. 1979).

Walker, *Physics of Spinning Tops, Including Some Far-Out Ones*, 244 Sci. Am. 182 (Mar. 1981).

Walker, *More Effects, The Kaleidoscope, and Other Victorian Diversions*, 239 Sci. Supp. 82–86 (Dec. 1978).

Werner, *Playground Injuries and Voluntary Product Standards for Home and Public Playgrounds* 69 Pediatrics No. 1 (Jan. 1982).

§ 7.46 Selected popular sources

Campbell, *How To: Playground Equipment: Making Your Backyard Safe*, 55 Parent No. 5 (May 1980).

Canadian Toy Testing Council, *Toy Buying Guide*, 6 Can. Consumer No. 5 (Oct. 1976).

Too Many Playgrounds Are Unsafe, 35 Changing Times 70–72, No. 5 (May 1981).

Crib Standards, 6 Consumer News No. 18 (Sept. 15, 1976).

Playpens, Consumer Rep. (Aug. 1981).

High Chairs' Safety, Comfort, Convenience, Consumer Rep. (Mar. 1975).

Sleds and Other Things To Ride Down a Snowy Hill, Consumer Rep. 776–778 (Nov. 1974).

Child Safety Gates, 38 Consumer Rep. 14–17, No. 1 (Jan. 1973).

Toy Construction Sets, 60 Consumers' Research No. 12 (Dec. 1977).

Hazards in Arts & Crafts, 60 Consumers' Research No. 7 (July 1977).

High Chairs 59 Consumers' Research No. 11 (Nov. 1976).

Denenberg, *Denenberg Says: Balloons Can Be Killers*, 11 Caveat Emptor 20, No. 3 (Mar. 1981).

Fireworks Incidents, 1974, Fire J. (Nov. 1974).

Your Baby's Crib May be Dangerous, 178 Good Housekeeping No. 5 (May 1974).

McAskin, *The Canadian Toy Testing Council; In Your Child's Best Interest*, 4 Can. Consumer No. 5 (Oct. 1974).

Paul, *What We Must Do To Prevent a Child From Being Injured by a Toy*, 57 Consumers' Research No. 12 (Dec. 1974).

Sage, *The ABC: Dick Sage, Reviews Fundamental Principles and Desira-*

ble Features of the Bow, Arrow, and Bowst, 47 Archery No. 2 (Feb. 1975).

Schultz, *How To: Safety on Wheels*, 56 Parent No. 7 (July 1981).

Impact: The Art of Falling, 2 Skateboarder 46–49, No. 2 (Fall 1975).

Blocks for Young Builders, 167 Sunset 136, No. 6 (Dec. 1981).

§ 7.47 Selected government sources

Choking Incidents in Children, Human Factors Analysis (Consumer Product Safety Comm'n 1983).

Projectile Toys (Briefing Package, Consumer Product Safety Comm'n 1981).

Toy Chests (Briefing Package, Consumer Product Safety Comm'n 1982).

Squeeze Toys and Other Small Toys (Briefing Package Consumer Product Safety Comm'n 1983).

Strangulation Hazards from Toys (Briefing Package, Consumer Products Safety Comm'n 1981).

Structural and Hardware Failure of Cribs (Briefing Package, Consumer Product Safety Comm'n 1984).

Toy Boxes and Toy Chests (Fact Sheet No. 74, Consumer Product Safety Comm'n Apr. 1979).

Toys (Fact Sheet No. 47, Consumer Product Safety Comm'n June 1979).

Skateboards (Fact Sheet No. 93, Consumer Product Safety Comm'n Aug. 1978).

Electrically Operated Toys and Childrens Articles (Fact Sheet No. 61, Consumer Product Safety Comm'n Apr. 1979).

Fireworks (Fact Sheet No. 12, Consumer Product Safety Comm'n Apr. 1977).

Baby Walkers, Jumpers (Fact Sheet No. 66, Consumer Product Safety Comm'n Aug. 1980).

Tricycles (Fact Sheet No. 15, Consumer Prod. Safety Comm'n).

Sleds, Toboggans, and Snow Disks (Fact Sheet No. 49, Consumer Product Safety Comm'n 1976).

Baby Rattles (Fact Sheet No. 86, Consumer Product Safety Comm'n May 1978).

High Chairs (Fact Sheet No. 70, Consumer Product Safety Comm'n).

Roller Skates and Ice Skates (Fact Sheet No. 84, Consumer Product Safety Comm'n 1979).

A Handbook for Public Playground Safety (Consumer Product Safety Comm'n 1981).

Toy Chests: Related Injuries (Consumer Product Safety Comm'n Hazard Analysis 1983).

§ 7.48 Selected legal sources

Cain, *Toys Causing Injury and Disease*, 23 Am. Jur. *P.O.F.* 393; 23 Supp. ch. 9, § 4 (1969).

Robbins, *Special Handling of Children's Cases*, 12 Am. Jur. *Trials* 184–92 (1966).

Rothenberg, *Attractive Nuisance Cases*, 16 Am. Jur. *Trials* 6–7 (1969).

Soehnel, *Products Liability: Toys and Games*, 95 A.L.R. 3d 386 (1979).

Soehnel, *Products Liability: Air Guns and BB Guns*, 94 A.L.R. 3d 291 (1979).

Swartz, *Household Caustics Injury Actions*, 28 Am. Jur. *Trials* (1981).

Swartz, *Litigating Household Caustics Injuries*, 88 Case & Com. No. 1 (1971).

Swartz, *Product Liability: The Torch Cases*, 76 Case & Com. No. 1 (1971).

Swartz, *Inside Santa's Bag of Tricks*, Environmental Quality (Dec. 1972).

E. Swartz, *Hazardous Products Litigation* (Lawyers Co-op. Publishing Co. 1973 & Supps.).

Swartz, *Legal Approaches to Injury Prevention*, Pediatric Clinics of North America (Feb. 1985).

Swartz, *Blindness in the Toy Box*, 43 Sight Saving Rev. No. 2 (1973).

E. Swartz, *Toys That Don't Care* (Gambit, Inc. 1971).

Swartz, *Toys-R-Dangerous*, Trial (Feb. 1982).

Swartz, *You Can't Judge a Book by Its Cover*, Trial (Nov. 1981).

Swartz, *Toys That Harm*, Trial (Dec. 1976).

§ 7.49 Selected newsletters

Darts

American Dart Association News
128 North Main Street
Ashley, Pa. 18706

Model Rockets

Model Rocket News
Estes Industries
P.O. Box 227
Penrose, Colo. 81240

§ 7.50 Selected laws, regulations, and standards

Laws Affecting Safety of Toys and Other Children's Products

(1) Consumer Product Safety Act, 15 U.S.C. §§ 2051 to 2083 (1972).

(2) Federal Hazardous Substances Act, 15 U.S.C. §§ 1261 to 1276 (1978).

(3) Toy Safety Act of 1984, *amending* Federal Hazardous Substances Act, 15 U.S.C. § 1261 *et seq.*

(4) Federal Flammable Fabrics Act, 15 U.S.C. §§ 1191 to 1204 (1972).

(5) Federal Poison Prevention Packaging Act of 1970, 15 U.S.C. §§ 1471 to 1476.

Regulations

(1) Method for identifying toys and other articles intended for use by children under three years of age which present choking, aspiration, or ingestion hazards because of small parts, 16 C.F.R. 1501 (1985).

(2) Requirements for electrically operated toys or other electrically operated articles intended for use by children, 16 C.F.R. 1505 (1985).

(3) Fireworks Devices, 16 C.F.R. 1507 (1985).

(4) Requirements for Non-Full-Size Baby Cribs, 16 C.F.R. 1509 (1985).

(5) Requirements for Rattles, 16 C.F.R. 1510 (1985).

(6) Requirements for Pacifiers, 16 C.F.R. 1511 (1985).

Voluntary Standards

(1) P.S. 72–76: Voluntary Standard for Toys

International Standards

COMMENT: Recently, I conducted a study of toy regulation and safety standards around the world to compare them with the standards offered to protect children in the United States. In almost every country that I studied, I found standards in many cases more stringent than those in the United States governing particular toy hazards.

Following are examples of other nations' standards that are more stringent than those in the United States.

---

(1) Toys that use electricity must be designed to operate on a maximum 24 volts, using a step-down transformer if they connect with household, electric current (Great Britain, Australia).

In the United States, toy standards permit the sale of toys that operate on dangerous, household current.

(2) Projectile toys are governed by mandatory government safety regulations (Canada).

In the United States, no mandatory government safety standards govern projectile toys.

(3) Toy weapons are banned or strictly regulated and licensed (Japan, West Germany, Great Britain).

In the United States, toy weapons are not governed by mandatory government safety standards. Many of these products are expressly excluded from American toy industry standards.

(4) Projectile toys and weapons must be accompanied by warnings of injury risks (Great Britain, Australia).

In the United States, no warnings are required of injury risks, including blindness and other eye injury.

(5) Toys with small parts are governed by stringent requirements with no exemptions (Canada, Australia, Great Britain, European Community).

In the United States, the toy safety standards for small toys and toy parts include a long list of exempted products, including balloons.

(6) Toys with sharp points and sharp edges are governed by stringent mandatory requirements, with no exceptions or age limitations (Canada).

In the United States, only toys intended for children under age eight are governed by safety standards, and all toys with "functional" sharp points and sharp edges are exempted.

(7) Playgrounds are stringently regulated to reduce risks of injury (Great Britain).

In the United States, no government safety standards govern playground equipment.

(8) Crib cornerposts are limited to one inch maximum to avoid strangulation risks (Canada).

In the United States, no requirements for cornerposts, despite body counts of deaths by strangulation.

(9) Toys with flammable fabrics are under stringent flame-retardancy requirements (Great Britain, Canada, Australia, European Community).

In the United States, discredited and weak federal flammability standards govern toys and other fabric products. Stringent flame-retardancy requirements for children's sleepwear have not been extended to other children's toy products.

§ 7.51 Selected cases

Bailey v. Montgomery Ward & Co., 6 Ariz. App. 213, 431 P.2d 108 (1967), **pogo stick**; eye injuries; supplier's responsibility for public safety.

Schleininger v. Questor Corp., 153 Cal. App. 3d 762, 200 Cal. Rptr. 634 (1984), **infant auto seat**; state-of-the-art evidence.

Flores v. Carolina Enterprises, Inc., No. EAC 25312 (Cal. Super. Ct. Sept. 20, 1982), 26 ATLA L. Rep. 228 (June 1983), **plastic tricycle**; absence of brakes or warning flag.

Gobin v. Avenue Food Mart, 345 P.2d 89 (Cal. Ct. App. 1959), **plastic toy dart gun**; res ipsa loquitur.

Roberts v. Amsco Indus., No. 75970 (Cal. Super. Ct., Santa Barbara Cty. Feb. 29, 1968), **"Hooper-Dooper" toy**; child struck in eye by toy's rubber band; risks inherent in using rubber bands in action toys.

McBurnette v. Playground Equipment Corp., 137 So. 2d 563 (Fla.), *on remand*, 138 So. 2d 372 (Fla. Dist. Ct. App. 1962), **swing**; vertical bar; loss of part of finger.

Pudlo v. Dubiel, 273 Mass. 172, 173 N.E. 536 (1930), **air rifle**; BB shot; retailer liable for sale to minor.

Rosenberg v. Placo Products Co., No. 131703 (Mass. Super. Ct. Aug. 12, 1983), 27 ATLA L. Rep. 321 (Sept. 1984), **dart gun**; eye injury; settlement $104,000.

Moning v. Alfono, 400 Mich. 425, 254 N.W.2d 759 (Mich. 1977), **sling shot**; loss of sight by pellet.

Estes v. Collier Keyworth, No. 81 131 631 NI (Mich. Cir. Ct. Mar. 19, 1985), 28 ATLA L. Rep. 331 (Sept. 1985), **infant car seat**; inadequate padding; cerebral palsy.

Mitchell v. R&R Toy Co., No. 71 14553-4NP (Mich. Cir. Ct., Saginaw Cty. Jan. 20, 1977), 20 ATLA L. Rep. 228 (June 1977), **stuffed "Snoopy Dog"**; suffocation; infant death.

Savoia v. F.W. Woolworth Co., 88 N.J. Super. 153, 211 A.2d 214 (1965), **mechanically operated hobby horse**.

Gearghty v. Collier Keyworth Co., No. 84 Civ. 0563 (TCP) (E.D.N.Y. Jan. 3, 1985), 28 ATLA L. Rep. 84 (Mar. 1985), **infant high chair**; tray-locking device; head injuries; settlement $500,000.

Gittelson v. Gotham Pressed Steel Corp., 266 A.D. 866, 42 N.Y.S.2d 341 (1943), **toy top**; tack flew out and struck eye.

Crist v. Art Metal Works, 230 A.D. 114, 243 N.Y.S. 496, *aff'd*, 255 N.Y. 624, 175 N.E. 341 (1930), **toy revolver**; advertised as "absolutely harmless"; ignited costume.

Tirino v. Kenner Prod. Co., 72 Misc. 2d 1094, 341 N.Y.S.2d 61 (N.Y. Civ. Ct. 1973), **"Lightning Bug Glo-Juice"**; "non-toxic" label; express warranty.

Henningsen v. Markowitz, 132 Misc. 547, 230 N.Y.S. 313 (N.Y. Sup. Ct. 1928), **air rifle**; sale to minor.

Continental Insurance Co. v. Louis Marx and Co., 64 Ohio St. 2d 399, 18 Ohio Ops. 3d 539, 415 N.E.2d 315 (Ohio 1980), **"Wild Rider" six-wheeled toy**.

Poe v. Canton-Mansfield Dry Goods Co., 36 Ohio App. 395, 173 N.E. 318 (1929), **air gun**; sale to minor.

Guiher v. Lujan's Kent Burger Boy, Inc., No. 77 2 0495 (Ohio Ct. C.P., Summit Cty. Feb. 17, 1978), 21 ATLA L. Rep. 274 (Aug. 1978), **toy rocket**; eye injury from rubber band on toy; free promotional item by restaurant; $150,000 jury verdict.

Fenton v. McCrory Corp., 47 F.R.D. 260 (W.D. Pa. 1969), **toy bow and arrow**; eye injuries; defective arrow suction cups.

Kelly v. Hanscom Brothers, 231 Pa. Super. 357, 331 A.2d 737 (1974), **squeeze toy**; infant choked to death.

Pizzo v. Wiemann, 149 Wis. 235, 134 N.W. 899 (1912), **toy pistols**; wholesaler's liability.

Chapter 8

MEDICAL PRODUCTS THAT DO NOT HEAL

V. Litigation Sources: Bibliography

KLUWER LITIGATION LIBRARY REFERENCES

HARLEY & MAGEE, WHAT'S IT WORTH? A GUIDE TO CURRENT PERSONAL INJURY AWARDS AND SETTLEMENTS.

JEANS, LITIGATION: Chapter 4, *Discovery*; Chapter 8, *Direct Examination*; Chapter 9, *Direct Examination of Expert Witnesses*; Chapter 13, *Cross-Examination*; Chapter 14, *Cross-Examination of Expert Witnesses*.

SMITH & MALANDRO, COURTROOM COMMUNICATION STRATEGIES: Chapter 1, *Impression Formation in the Courtroom*; Chapter 2, *Persuasive Strategies in the Courtroom*; Chapter 5, *Preparing for Effective Courtroom Communication*; Chapter 8, *Direct Examination: Presenting the Evidence with Impact*; Chapter 9, *Cross-Examination: Controlling the Case*.

I. Introduction

§ 8.01 In general

Everyone recognizes that medical devices provide tremendous benefits to society. Rather than merely looking to physicians or hospitals for compensation, however, counsel should always consider whether a defective medical instrument was the source of the client's injury.[1]

[1] *See* Swartz, *Malpractice From the Viewpoint of the Trial Attorney*, in THE UNFAVORABLE RESULT IN PLASTIC SURGERY (Little, Brown & Co. 1984); Swartz, *Defective Medi-*

§ 8.02 Focus on product itself

As with other types of products discussed throughout this book, counsel should focus on the product itself rather than totally on the actions of the individual plaintiffs or defendants. By this, I mean that counsel should always think in terms of the manufacturer, designer, and marketer of the product.

II. Checklists

§ 8.03 Checklist: Investigation of a medical device-related injury case

The following checklist is intended to aid counsel in the preparation of a claim based on an injury caused by a medical device. Obviously, many of the factors found in the checklists in other chapters in this book will also have relevance to such a claim, but there are some matters that are particularly relevant to injuries caused by medical devices.

____ (1) Investigate the circumstances surrounding the injury as soon as possible. In many cases involving injuries caused by medical devices, there are witnesses, and they should be located and questioned as early as possible:

____(a) Physicians, nurses, and other health care professionals

____(b) Technicians

____(c) Hospital or clinic support staff

____(d) Other patients

____(e) Maintenance people called to the scene when the machine or device malfunctioned

____ (2) Visit the site of the injury as soon as possible and observe the scene

____ (3) Research the device, learning as much as you can about it from:

____(a) Medical journals

____(b) Engineering journals

---

cal Devices, in PROOF OF PRODUCT DEFECT ch. 18 (Lawyers Co-op. Publishing Co. 1985).

____(c) Advertisements

____(d) Discussions with health professionals

____(e) Reported cases involving the same device

____(f) Low level or former employees of the manufacturer

____ (4) Retain an expert as early as possible, and involve him in the investigation and preparation of the case

____ (5) If available, examine the device that caused the injury or a duplicate of it. Take your expert with you

____ (6) Determine if the device has ever been the subject of a recall

____ (7) Determine if the device has been superseded by the latest state-of-the-art medical technology

____ (8) Determine if safety guards or improvements have become available since the device was manufactured, or were available as options, but were not added

____ (9) Determine what warnings or instructions were given:

____(a) In manuals

____(b) In inserts

____(c) In posted work rules

____(d) In oral communications

____(e) In staff meetings

____(f) On signs or symbols on the device

____(g) On packaging

____(10) Determine how the device is classified under the May 28, 1976 amendments to the U.S. Food, Drug and Cosmetics Act (21 U.S.C. § 321 *et seq*.)

____(a) Class I under 21 U.S.C. § 360c(a)(1)(A), devices for which specific performance standards or premarket approval is not required

____(b) Class II under 21 U.S.C. § 360c(a)(1)(B), devices for which general controls are not sufficient, but for which performance standards can be enunciated to adequately assure that the goals of safety and effectiveness will be met

____(c) Class III under 21 U.S.C. § 360c(a)(1)(C), devices that require premarket approval because they are intended for use in life-supporting or life-sustaining situations, or because they present a potential unreasonable risk of illness or injury

____(11) Determine if the device or drug causing the injury has met all FDA standards, including:

____(a) Animal testing

____(b) Human testing

____(c) Review of package insert or labeling

____(12) Review all available medical literature and relevant government reports to determine if the device has been the subject of prior action or reports of injury

____(13) Consult *Physician's Desk Reference*

____(14) Check with the Bureau of Medical Devices of the FDA to determine if there are prior complaints about the device

____(15) Check patent records on the device

____(16) Draw up a preliminary list of potential defendants and possible theories of recovery

____(17) Research law reviews and treatises on medical device cases to understand possible legal and factual theories underlying your claim better

____(18) Contact the following to determine what information, if any, is available regarding the device:

____(a) U.S. Food and Drug Administration

____(b) U.S. Consumer Product Safety Commission

____(c) U.S. Department of Commerce

____(d) American National Standards Institute

____(e) ATLA Law Reporter

____(f) ATLA Products Liability Reporter

____(g) ATLA Exchange

§ 8.04 Checklist: Resources for a medical device-related injury case

The following list should prove helpful to counsel preparing for a medical device-related personal injury case.

____ (1) Selected technical sources

____(a) Hospital Engineer

____(b) Contemporary Anesthesia Practice

____(c) International Anesthesiology Clinics

____(d) Anesthesiology

____(e) Medical Electronics

____(f) Canadian Anesthesiology Society Journal

____(g) Medical Instruments

____(h) Journal of Clinical Engineering

____(i) Health and Social Services Journal

____(j) Journal of Medical Engineering Technology

____(k) Journal of Thoracic Cardiovascular Surgery

____(l) Critical Care Monitor

____ (2) Selected popular sources

____(a) American Journal of Nursing

____(b) Hospital Risk Management

____(c) Professional Safety

____(d) AORN Journal

____(e) Hospital Purchasing Management

____(f) American Journal of Cardiology

____(g) Hospital Pharmacy

____(h) Modern Health Care

____(i) Canadian Nurse

____(j) Critical Care Nurse

____ (3) Selected government sources

____(a) U.S. Food and Drug Administration

____(b) U.S. Consumer Product Safety Commission

____(c) U.S. Department of Commerce

____(d) National Center for Disease Control

____(e) National Institute for Health

____(f) National Center for Devices and Radiological Health

____(g) U.S. Department of Energy

____(h) National Research Council

____(i) National Academy of Sciences

____ (4) Selected industry sources

____(a) Association for Advancement of Medical Instrumentation

____(b) Emergency Care Research Institute

____(c) International Biomedical Information Services, Inc.

____(d) American Hospital Association

____(e) Drug Research Reports, Inc.

____(f) International Techniquest

III. Case Study: The Case of the "Unstoppable" X-Ray Machine[2]

§ 8.05 Facts

A sixty-five-year-old woman was lying on the table of a therapy machine receiving radiation therapy for her cancer when the machine malfunctioned. As she was being raised for treatment and her body approached the breast cone on the collimator, something went wrong. The stretcher would not stop. It moved inexorably closer to the machine's head, as a technician tried to stop its movement. Those efforts proved fruitless. As the stretcher continued to rise, the collimator and breast cone crushed into her chest. After what must have been unimaginably painful moments, this woman died from asphyxiation.

The culprit was a Theratron 80—a cobalt teletherapy machine designed for the treatment of cancer by gamma radiation, with main

[2] [Plaintiff] v. General Electric, et al., C.A. No. 76–3138–G (D. Mass. Jan. 21, 1983), case settled for $1.375 million.

frame and base, a device known as a collimator through which the beams are targeted to the patient's body, and a motorized stretcher unit attached at the base. A steel breast plate called a breast cone or beam splitter had been attached to the collimator for purposes of this treatment. The on-off switches to this machine, as well as other operating controls, were placed outside the therapy room. A hand control at the machine itself contained controls to elevate and otherwise direct the stretcher. This hand control also included a switch to activate the stretcher's elevation drive motor relay. The operator could raise the stretcher by pressing the up button and stop it by releasing that button. If the hand control became inoperable, as happened in this case, there are no other means within the operator's immediate reach for stopping the stretcher's upward movement. The effective and safe operation of this complex machine is dependent upon the relay contact as well as the other components working properly.

The procedure used by the technician in this case was to position the rotary switch on the hand control to "vertical," depress the push button designed for up/clockwise motion, hold the button down until the patient's chest came to within a finger's width distance of the breast cone and then release it, stopping the stretcher's upward movement. Normally, releasing the button would de-energize the relay supplying power to the stretcher's vertical drive motor, thus stopping the stretcher. Apparently, the machine's vertical drive relay had remained stuck in a closed position, thus not stopping the flow of electricity and providing for the stretcher's upward movement. The technician released the button, but it did not stop. She then pressed the emergency stop button on the hand control, but the stretcher continued to rise.

§ 8.06 Analysis of case

This case illustrates two important elements of medical device litigation. First, the catastrophic consequences that can occur when the sophisticated, modern equipment we rely on for advanced medical treatment fails to function properly. Second, the importance of including the manufacturer, designer, and marketers of medical devices in your preparation of a medical treatment case.

Through the discovery process, we learned that this highly complex machine was designed with components that were not adequate to ensure its safe performance. Specifically, as one company representative admitted under cross-examination, the machine's contact relay and hand controls were not designed for maximum safety. Perhaps most tragic of all, this company engineer also admitted under oath that a safety device that could have prevented this injury by stopping the stretcher before it could make contact with the collimator was not provided as standard equipment with the machine, but were unavailable as an optional extra.

§ 8.07 Testimony of defendant's design engineer

The testimony of the defendant's design engineer provided valuable evidence of this company's failure to provide a machine designed for safety, and its responsibility, in part, for this plaintiff's death.

§ 8.08 —Regarding emergency button

Consider the following illustrative and revealing testimony in which this witness admitted that: "If the stretcher assembly was not responding correctly, the emergency button which is located on the hand control and also on the control console would be the primary safety device."[3]

Q. Let's start with the hand control that malfunctioned. Now where is the other emergency button located?

A. On the control console.

Q. Which is where?

A. Which is located just outside the room normally in front of the window.

Q. So the operator would have to leave the room if somebody was in the other room and push the button?

A. They could push that button or they could use the main circuit breaker that would be located in the room . . . on the wall beside the unit. . . . [Although] the wall one is not really considered an emergency shut-off. It is considered as a safety device to ensure that there is no electric current going into the machine during servicing and this type of thing. It isn't primarily the emergency shut-off.

Q. Did your company, when they were marketing this machine, recommend or suggest to people who were purchasing the machine that they have another means or emergency button to stop the rise of the stretcher other than the hand unit that we know about?

[3] *Id*., testimony of Mr. S.

A. No, sir.

* * *

Q. When you installed these machines, did your company ever insist or recommend that there be a switch within reach of the operator that would have shut off all the current going to that machine?

A. We recommended a circuit breaker in the room, but not as you describe. We recommended certain, you know, a breaker to shut off the current in the machine.

Q. But not for the reason I described?

A. It could have been implied, but it wasn't explicit.

COMMENT: Ironically, this witness admitted that the console emergency shutoff was designed as a backup system in case of machine failure—a foreseeable event in the use of this machine.[4]

Q. Now why is it that you had a shut-off switch on the console as well as on the hand control?

A. In case of malfunction during treatment, and the safety device didn't work, you still had that emergency console shut-off device in case there was a mechanical or an electrical malfunction, for whatever reason, however unlikely it was.

Q. In other words, it was a backup system to the hand control in the event of a malfunction?

A. It was a backup system to the total unit, not specifically to the hand control.

§ 8.09 —Regarding safety device

A separate collision device was provided for instances when the stretcher was being rotated, to stop the stretcher when there was the possibility of a collision between the arm head assembly and the stretcher.

[4] *Id.*

This collision device was not designed and was not intended, as this witness admitted, to stop the stretcher in the elevation mode. It was designed to halt the arm rotation only when the moving arm contacts the stretcher top. It had no effect whatsoever on the stretcher's upward movement. Thus, the stretcher continues to move until stopped manually. This so-called safety device provided no safety protection for this plaintiff or for anyone else whose fate lay with the sound performance of the stretcher controls.

§ 8.10 —Regarding safety clearance

The defendant's design engineer then explained that a gap of approximately twelve inches between the collimator and the stretcher at its maximum height would prevent such tragedy from occurring even upon a relay malfunction.[5]

Q. So, in other words, the machine was designed so that there was clearance between the head and the stretcher no matter how high or how much the stretcher would rise?

A. That is right.

Q. What was the clearance, roughly?

A. It would be in excess of twelve inches.

What this company, by its spokesman's own admissions, failed to take into account was the hospital's use of an additional device on the machine to direct the gamma radiation in the treatment therapy. Known as a beam splitter or breast cone, this device could direct the beams directly to the patient's needs. As this witness was forced to admit, this device was at least the size of the gap that he testified was designed to prevent contact between the collimator and the rising stretcher. In other words, anyone using this breast cone would be eliminating this so-called safety design feature and placing the patient's life in jeopardy. The defendant knew that this hospital used this device, in fact it provided these devices itself for use with its machines, but failed to warn either administering doctors or their patients of its potentially deadly consequences. Again, the witness' testimony provided important information for the plaintiff's case against the therapy machine manufacturer:[6]

Q. Did you ever contemplate, when you designed this machine, that

---

[5] *Id.*

[6] *Id.*

if an operator could not stop the stretcher from rising with the hand unit that there would be a time gap from the time the operator put the hand unit down until he went into the other room and pressed the other stop button?

A. Basically the design parameters were such that that wasn't really a consideration, because when the couch was going in the vertical position, even with a patient, there was ample clearance between the collimator and the stretcher top.

Q. Now, in this particular instance, there was a device that was added to the machine. Wasn't there a beam splitter of some sort?

A. Yes. Breast cone as they call them.

Q. What is that?

A. That is basically used for the treatment of chest cavities; say, after a radical mastectomy or for a tumor in the breast, depending on the procedure or protocol and the prescription that the doctor elected. It is used to prevent excessive radiation getting to the chest cavity. . . .

Q. And how long have those devices been in use?

A. Approximately since 1958, at the ____________ Hospital.

Q. You were aware, were you not, that these devices were being used with the Theratron 80?

A. Yes, sir.

Q. How many inches would the [beam splitter] extend down from the head, roughly?

A. Eighty centimeters . . . a foot.

Q. So that if somebody was using a beam splitter with the Theratron 80, we would lose some of that twelve-inch clearance you told me about, wouldn't we?

A. Yes.

Q. As a matter of fact, we would lose it all, wouldn't we?

A. Yes, sir.

COMMENT: Despite the fact that this device eliminated the machine's so-called built-in safety factor, the company did not change its emergency shut-off device to take this added feature into account.

---

§ 8.11 —Regarding ring-type collision device

Perhaps the most important testimony from this witness concerned a safety device that was not provided on this machine. This is a ring-type collision device, which by this witness' admissions would have prevented this tragedy had it been provided as standard equipment rather than an optional "extra."[7]

Q. Now was there any optional safety equipment that came along with the machinery and similar machines you sold?

A. Yes.

Q. What were they?

A. Specifically, there was what we call the ring-type collision device that was mounted on the head. And it was mounted on the post that could be moved up and down and locked into place by the operator, so it would indicate or sense collision of something, be it patient or the machine coming up toward the unit.

Q. Would it generally be just above the patient's body?

A. Somewhere between the patient and the machine.

Q. That safety ring would have been marketed prior to the time this machine was sold?

A. Yes, sir.

Q. And had that ring safety device been on this machine, would it have prevented the stretcher assembly from coming into approximate contact with the head assembly?

A. If the operator located it properly, yes, it would have.

* * *

Q. Had this safety ring been on the Theratron 80 that was involved in the accident here today, could this accident have occurred?

---

[7] *Id.*

A. If it was properly in place, the accident probably would not have occurred.

* * *

Q. One of the reasons the mechanical/electrical safety ring was designed and developed by your company was to afford additional protection to the patient who was on the stretcher, isn't that so?

A. Yes, sir.

COMMENT: Subsequent testimony by the company's electrical engineer affirmed this argument for the plaintiff.[8] The electrical engineer admitted that had this machine been equipped with a safety ring, it wouldn't have mattered if the relay failed, the fail-safe button failed, or there was a misuse of the hand control by the hospital personnel; the accident would not have happened if they had had the safety ring in its proper place.

The price of this optional safety device, according to the design engineer, would have been less than $790, a small price to pay for preventing a patient's death, considering this witness' estimate of the price of the machine itself at up to $100,000!

Why weren't these devices included as standard equipment? "Convenience" is the answer in short. It seems that many customers didn't like them and, in some cases, were removing them. A manufacturer faced with this situation has two choices: either affix the device permanently to ensure a safer machine because it cannot be removed, or remove it altogether and avoid complaints from customers. This company apparently thought it could gain a competitive edge in the marketplace by providing the machines without them.

This witness also admitted that safety was not a selling point for this product—that the safety benefits of purchasing the safety ring were not

[8] *See supra* note 2, testimony of Mr. U, defendant's Electrical Engineer.

even mentioned in the product's promotional literature.[9]

Q. What promotional literature do you recall being associated with the safety ring?

A. There was a sales specification sheet that had been distributed and in that literature that particular safety ring was described.

Q. Did you ever encourage a customer to purchase it for safety reasons?

A. It would have been the practice of the salesmen to encourage the purchase of those rings, yes.

Q. The answer to my question is that there was no literature that encouraged it, correct?

A. You mean a sales promotion?

Q. Yes.

A. Encouraging salesmen to do this?

Q. Yes.

A. No, that would have been done verbally with the salesmen.

* * *

Q. Keeping in mind that the safety ring was an option and was offered to customers who chose to purchase it, at any time subsequent to the accident involved in this litigation, did your company ever send out any literature to anybody who was using the Theratron 80 machine that they should consider, or ought to consider, putting on this safety ring?

A. I am not aware of any personally.

Q. Did you send out any literature to any of your customers advising them or telling them that they should not use the beam splitter or breast cone in a straight down position with the use of your machines?

A. I am not aware of any literature.

We also learned from the witness' testimony that this company had received numerous complaints regarding this equipment shortly after it was installed, with respect to the machine's automatic controls. "There were a number of misunderstandings and also a number of things that

---

[9] *See supra* note 2, testimony of Mr. S.

were not properly installed,"[10] including the cable and hand control mechanisms. One of those parts was the contact relay, an electromechanical device that works from an electrical signal, and performs the mechanical function to close contacts in order to allow electricity to flow from one point to another. If that relay failed to function, it would allow the stretcher to continue its inexorable and deadly rise after the operator released the hand control switch. After the tragedy, it was shown that the accident was caused by the vertical relay being in a sticking position (closed) allowing the current to continue through.

§ 8.12 Testimony of defendant's electrical engineer regarding cause of accident

Part of the defendant's electrical engineer's testimony consisted of his reading from a report of the investigation's findings.[11]

* * *

A. The investigating team determined that one of the relays was in a condition where the contacts were being in an energized position, that would be—

Q. What do you mean by that?

A. That would be in the same position if the power had been applied to the relay source.

Q. So what would that mean in terms of the function of the machine, if anything?

A. It would mean that this relay would be stuck in the up position.

Q. And if that relay is stuck in the up position, would that mean, in essence, that if the machine was operating, the couch would continue to rise?

A. That is correct.

This witness then presented his opinions as to the cause of the machine's failure.[12]

Q. Now you said the main points were: one, the relay contacts sticking, correct?

---

[10] *Id*.

[11] *See supra* note 2, testimony of Mr. U.

[12] *Id*.

A. Yes.

Q. And the miswiring of the hand control emergency buttons?

A. Yes.

Q. And did you mean by that, it was your opinion at that point in time that those were two of the main points involved in causing this particular accident?

A. Yes.

This witness subsequently admitted in his testimony that changes to correct these design defects could have been incorporated into the original manufacture of the machine.

COMMENT: We also learned that the U.S. Food and Drug Administration had identified this product's hazardous design and had prepared a report documenting those defects, in which the emergency switch circuitry was singled out: "The emergency switch circuit design could be improved. Failure of the master key switch to return from the start position to the on position would render both hand switch and console emergency switch ineffective. . . . The hand control switch has a history of broken wiring. . . . *The elevation motor relay has a history of sticking contacts with extended use*. . . . Relays of this nature are not expected to have a long extended life and require maintenance or cleaning often. The relay K310 [in this machine] that was found stuck in the closed position had pitted and burnt contacts."[13] [Emphasis added.] The FDA asked the company to recall the product because of its defective circuitry.

Under FDA pressure, the company made changes in its product's design. These changes, the company's electrical engineer conceded, would have prevented this tragedy had they been made earlier.[14]

---

[13] U.S. Food and Drug Administration, Memorandum from Thomas L. Hooker to Earl V. Burton, Director, Investigations Branch, Re: Theratron 80 Radiation Therapy Unit, at 15 (Apr. 2, 1974).

[14] *See supra* note 2, testimony of Mr. U.

Q. It is your opinion that if the machine had been wired at the time of the accident in accordance with the way it has been wired since the FDA requested your company to rewire the machine, that the accident would have been avoided, unless there was a certain type of short circuit?

A. Assuming the conditions, then the power would have been off the unit, stopping the motion of the vertical [relay].

IV. Preventing Medical Device-Related Injuries

§ 8.13 In general

The prevention of medical device-related injuries must become a priority for members of the medical device industry, health care service professions, the scientific community, and the legal profession. It is particularly important that physicians and other members of the medical profession recognize the value of safety in the design and marketing of those products they depend on in their work. Product manufacturers must provide adequate warnings regarding potential product-related hazards. Product manufacturers and health care providers must initiate and participate in patient education programs so that health care consumers are given adequate information and warnings regarding the device's use, potential risks, and benefits. This is particularly important in light of the new medical technology that is rapidly developing.

The federal government must also play an active role. New reporting requirements for hazardous medical devices can play an important part in the national injury prevention effort.[15]

§ 8.14 Injury prevention as a joint effort

Members of all healing professions have a stake in reducing the toll produced by defective medical and surgical devices. Surgeons, physicians, nurses, hospital staff, and health care technicians can all contribute in this effort by learning how their equipment works and identifying defects in operation that may lead to harmful consequences for the patient or technician. Effective communication between health service providers and medical device manufacturers and marketers is vital in this regard. Product manufacturers and marketers must provide adequate informa-

---

[15] 49 Fed. Reg. 36,326 (Sept. 14, 1984) corrected at 49 Fed. Reg. 36,644 (Sept. 19, 1984).

tion and warnings regarding product operation, performance, and design. The health service provider must be alerted to any and all safety devices and other available means for stopping the machinery in case of an emergency. This information and adequate warnings must be conveyed in written and oral form, through product promotional literature, operations manuals, trade advertisements, and personal communications between product manufacturers, suppliers, and health care service providers. These health care providers must also be able and willing to convey any suspicious or questionable product performance to manufacturers and suppliers to reduce the risks of avoidable death or injury.

§ 8.15 Recognizing role of defective medical products in health care deaths and injuries

It is important for members of the medical profession to recognize the hazards posed by defective medical devices and the importance of selecting and using safe devices to prevent health care-related deaths and injuries. Physicians and other medical specialists must recognize that those tools on which they rely to care for their patients can be just as defective as the products offered in the consumer marketplace. These products are often designed, manufactured, and marketed by companies with the same bottom-line concern for profit as those marketing consumer goods. In the health care field, the need for adequate safety protections, adequate warnings of potential product hazards, and adequate directions for use are no less vital than in the consumer goods field.

§ 8.16 Patient education for safety

The basic rights of the medical patient include the right to informed consent. With the advent of new technologies and complex medical procedures, the need for coordinated patient education regarding the risks and benefits of surgical procedures and the products used in those procedures is more important than ever. This education must be shared by all members of the health service profession, as well as manufacturers and suppliers of medical and health care equipment. Thus, doctors, nurses, medical specialists, technicians, hospital staff, product suppliers, and product manufacturers must all share in developing and communicating information in written, oral, electronic, and other forms. Skilled professionals must be hired, if necessary, to communicate this information in formats and media that the patient can understand.

§ 8.17 Incorporating safety-related technological advances in medical products

Technological advances have reduced the risks posed by many health care devices, but they can also be the basis for the liability of a manufacturer or health care provider who is not employing the up-to-date devices or techniques. For example, numerous procedures are available today to locate and remove lost catheters, including radiopaque techniques. As a result, a non-radiopaque catheter could be found to be defective if the lack of radiopaqueness impeded prompt catheter location and removal. Catheter manufacturers should mark the catheter tip distinctively to promote efficient location. The failure to do so may also serve as a basis for liability.

§ 8.18 Firm action by FDA to enforce new reporting requirements

Recently, the U.S. Food and Drug Administration issued new regulations requiring manufacturers and importers of medical devices to report to the FDA whenever the manufacturer or importer became aware of information that reasonably suggested that one of its marketed devices may have caused or contributed to a death or injury, or had malfunctioned and that the device or any other device marketed by the manufacturer or importer would be likely to cause or contribute to a death or serious injury if the malfunction were to occur.[16] The purpose of the new rule is to assure that the FDA is informed promptly of all serious or potentially serious problems associated with marketed devices.[17]

The FDA must vigorously and firmly enforce this new rule. It is important that this information be conveyed to those concerned with injury prevention, including consumers, health care providers, government authorities, and others so that preventive measures can be taken before tragedy strikes.

§ 8.19 What can lawyers do?

Lawyers must work closely with members of the medical profession to identify product-related hazards, to educate the public regarding these hazards, to keep abreast of new technological advances that can increase medical device safety, and to keep the pressure on manufacturers for

[16] *Id.*

[17] *Id.*

safer product designs and effective communications with patients and medical care professionals regarding their products' hazards.

As I have stated previously, the common law has historically been marked by a paucity of litigation in the medical device field. Perhaps this is because many attorneys have traditionally focused on health care providers, particularly physicians, in legal actions resulting from medical-related injuries. Perhaps it is because injured patients have not been sufficiently educated regarding their rights to challenge the manufacturers and suppliers of medical supplies and equipment when they have suffered medical care-related injuries. Or perhaps it is because many members of the medical profession are not sufficiently aware of the role of defective instruments and the potential liability of defective instrument manufacturers and suppliers in traditional medical malpractice litigation. Regardless of the reason, it is important that lawyers recognize the failures of traditional approaches in medical negligence cases and focus on the product manufacturers as potential parties in litigation. As medical product litigation increases, those who manufacture and market their products will come to know, as those in the consumer product market already know, that they will pay a price in the courts of our land for purveying products that can kill instead of heal.

V. Litigation Sources: Bibliography

§ 8.20 Selected technical sources

Azar, *Anesthetic Gas Spillage and Scavenging*, 19 Int'l Anesthesiol. Clinics 1–37, No. 4 (Winter 1981).

Bilitch, Hauser, Goldman, Furman & Parsonnet, *Performance of Cardiac Pacemaker Pulse Generators*, 4 PACE 730–35, No. 6 (Nov. 1981).

Carter & Shaw, *Telfer AB Tourniquets for Surgery: Safety Aspects*, 7 J. Med. Eng'g Tech. 136–39, No. 3 (May–June 1983).

Cooper, et al., *An Analysis of Major Errors and Equipment Failures in Anesthesia Management: Considerations for Prevention and Detection*, 60 Anesthesiol. 34–42, No. 1 (Jan. 1984).

Cooper & Newbower, *The Boston Anesthesia System*, 8 Contemp. Anesthesia Prac. 207–19 (1984).

Duberman & Bendixen, *Concepts of Failsafe in Anesthetic Practice*, 22 Int'l Anesthesiol. Clinics 149–65, No. 2 (Summer 1984).

Duberman & Wald, *An Integrated Quality Control Program for Anesthesia Equipment*, 9 Quality Rev. Bull. 328–36, No. 11 (Nov. 1983).

Eschelbach, *'ASAP': A Microcomputer-Based Automated Safety and Performance Testing System*, 9 J. Clinical Eng'g 21–27, No. 1 (Jan.–Mar. 1984).

Fialla, *Installation and Use of Clinical Anesthetics: Safety Precautions*, 35 Hosp. Engineer 10–14, No. 5 (June 1981).

Gallo, et al., *Five-to Eight-Year Follow-Up of Patients with the Hancock Cardiac Bioprosthesis*, 86 J. Thoracic Cardiovascular Surgery 897–902, No. 6 (Dec. 1983).

Hargest, *Recommendations for Designing Device Improvements*, 17 Med. Instruments 431–32, No. 6 (Nov.–Dec. 1983).

Syringe Pumps, 92 Health Social Services J. No. 4821 (Nov. 4, 1982).

Heath, *Accidents Associated with Equipment*, 39 Anaesthesia 57–60, No. 1 (Jan. 1984).

Humphrey, *A New Anaesthetic Breathing System Combining Mapleson A, D and E Principals. A Simple Apparatus for Low Flow Universal Use Without Carbon Dioxide Absorption*, 38 Anaesthesia 361–72, No. 4 (Apr. 1983).

Hyman, *Evaluation of Alarm System for Medical Equipment*, 7 J. Clinical Eng'g 223–27, No. 3 (July–Sept. 1982).

Hyman & Orinker, *Design of Medical Device Alarm Systems*, 19 Med. Instruments 103–106, No. 2 (Mar.–Apr. 1983).

Karmann & Roth, *Prevention of Accidents Associated with Air-Oxygen Mixers*, 37 Anaesthesia 860–62, No. 6 (June 1982).

Marsh, *ECG Lead Checker*, 38 Hosp. Engineer 7, No. 1 (Feb. 1984).

Morse, *Hospital and Incubator Manufacturer Sued by Parents of Premature Baby with Central Nervous Disorder*, 13 Med. Electronics No. 6 (Dec. 1982).

Morse, *Is Hospital or Supplier of X-Ray Machine Liable for Accident Injury?*, 13 Med. Electronics 26, No. 5 (Oct. 1982).

Neufeld, Johnson, & deVeth, *Safety of Anesthesia Breathing Circuit Connectors*, 36 Can. Anasthesiol. Soc'y J. 646–52, No. 6 (Nov. 1983).

Neuman, Flammer & O'Connor, *Safety Devices for Neonatal Intensive Care*, 7 J. Clinical Eng'g 51–62, No. 1 (Jan.–Mar. 1982).

O'Connor, *A Pacemaker Monitoring System*, 7 J. Clinical Eng'g 305–307, No. 4 (Oct.–Dec. 1982).

Oviatt, *Biosafety for Hospital Engineers*, 37 Hosp. Eng'g 20–22, No. 10 (Dec. 1983).

Phillips & Jorkasky, *Hazards Associated with Returned and Field Serviced Medical Devices and Equipment*, 2 J. Hosp. Supply Process Distribution 69–71, No. 2 (Mar.–Apr. 1984).

Rendell-Baker, *Standards for Anaesthesia: The Issues*, 8 Contemp. Anesthesia Practice 59–88 (1984).

Saunders, *What Do We Do Until the Future Gets Here?*, 8 Contemp. Anesthesia Practice 237–44 (1984).

Spooner & Kirby, *Equipment-Related Anesthetic Incidents*, 22 Int'l Anesthesiol. Clinics 133–47, No. 2 (Summer 1984).

Whelpton, *Will Good Manufacturing Practice Produce Acceptable Equipment*, 8 J. Medical Eng'g Tech. No. 1 (Jan.–Feb. 1984).

§ 8.21 Selected popular sources

Austin, Preis, Crampton, et al., *Analysis of Pacemaker Malfunction and Complications of Temporary Pacing in the Coronary Care Unit*, 49 Am. J. Cardiol. 301–306, No. 2 (Feb. 1, 1982).

Carnevale, *Maintaining Intravascular Catheter Patency Safely in Children*, 4 Critical Care Nurse No. 2 (Apr. 1984).

Curran & Delaney, *Oxygen Analyzers Create Liability If Not Used Consistently [Interview]*, 4 Hosp. Risk Management 152–55, No. 11 (Nov. 1982).

Decker, *Who Is Liable for Equipment Failure?*, 6 Hosp. Purchasing Management 16, No. 10 (Oct. 1981).

Fielden, *Surgical Implants, Consumer Aspects*, 37 AORN J. 1315–16, No. 7 (June 1983).

Horty, *Manufacturer, Not Hospital or M.D., Responsible in Product Liability Case*, 12 Mod. Health Care 115–118, No. 12 (Dec. 1982).

CAT Scanners Pose Radiation Risk to Patients, 5 Hosp. Risk Management 81–82, No. 6 (June 1983).

Holzer, *Share Hospital Liability with Products' Manufacturers, Sellers [Interview]*, 4 Hosp. Risk Management 41–44, No. 4 (Apr. 1982).

Janowski, *Accidental Disconnections from Breathing Systems, What FDA Found—and What You Can Do About It*, 84 Am. J. Nursing No. 2 (Feb. 1984).

Jennings, Schad & Kaurich, *Recycled Unused Pissyback Admixtures Through the Use of Tamper-Proof Safety Caps*, 17 Hosp. Pharmacy 643–45, No. 12 (Dec. 1982).

Hazards in Health Care: DHSS Hazard Notification System, 18 NATNEWS 24, No. 9 (Sept. 1981).

Osman, *Apnea Monitors: False Security?*, 80 Can. Nurse 42–43, No. 5 (May 1984).

Pilot, *Product Recalls*, 1 J. Hosp. Supply Process Distribution 45–47, No. 3 (Nov.–Dec. 1983).

Riley & Cochran, *Deacy JE Warning Label Design*, 26 Professional Safety 44–46, No. 10 (Oct. 1981).

Smith, *Microbiological Safety Index*, 36 AORN J. 311–16, No. 2 (Aug. 1982).

§ 8.22 Selected government sources

Department of Energy, *Instrument Is Developed for Ramp Injection of Radiotracers for Blood Flow Measurement by Emission Tomography* (July 1984).

Department of Health and Social Security, *Health Equipment Information Number 120* (London, England, Apr. 1984).

NASA, *Development of a New, Completely Implantable Intraventricular Pressure Meter and Preliminary Report of Its Clinical Experience* (July 1982).

National Center for Devices and Radiological Health, *Administration of the Radiation Control for Health Safety Act of 1968, Public Law 90–602* (Annual Report 1983).

National Center for Devices and Radiological Health, *Study of the Common Characteristics, Hazards, and Performance Problems of Endoscopes and Endoscopic Accessories* (Apr. 1981).

National Center for Toxicological Research, *Chronic Indwelling Catheters in Fetal Rhesus Monkeys* (Aug. 1981).

National Research Council, Final Report, *Guidelines for the Prevention of Disease Transmission in the Use of CPR Manikins* (Jan. 1984).

§ 8.23 Selected legal sources

Excessive Radiation, 17 Am. Jur. *P.O.F.2d* 575 (1978).

Anesthesia, 12 Am. Jur. *P.O.F.* 453–522 (1962).

Shots, Injections and Other Needling Procedures, 10 Am. Jur. *P.O.F.* 479–516 (1961).

Products Liability in Connection with Prosthesis or Other Product Designed to be Surgically Implanted in Patient's Body, 1 A.L.R. 4th 921 (1980).

Application of Rule of Strict Liability in Tort to Person or Entity Rendering Medical Services, 100 A.L.R. 3d 1205 (1980).

Malpractice: Liability of Anesthetist for Injuries from Spinal Anesthetics, 90 A.L.R. 3d 775 (1979).

When Statute of Limitations Commences to Run Against Malpractice Action Based on Leaving Foreign Substance in Patient's Body, 70 A.L.R. 3d 7 (1976).

Physicians; Hospitals—Strict Liability, 54 A.L.R. 3d 258 (1973).

Medical Malpractice: Liability for Injury Allegedly Resulting from Negligence in Making Hypodermic Injections, 45 A.L.R. 3d 731 (1972).

Hospital's Liability for Injury or Death to Patient Resulting from or Connected with Administration of Anesthetic, 31 A.L.R. 3d 1114 (1970).

Malpractice: Liability in Connection with Insertion of Prosthetic or Other Corrective Devices in Patient's Body, 14 A.L.R. 3d 967 (1967).

Malpractice: Liability of Physician, Surgeon, Anesthetist, or Dentist for Injury Resulting from Foreign Object Left in Patient, 10 A.L.R. 3d 9 (1966).

Gingerich, *Medical Product Liability* (F&S Press 1981).

Philo, *Lawyer's Desk Reference* ch. 2 (Lawyers' Co-op. Publishing Co., 6th ed. 1979 & Supps.).

§ 8.24 Selected newsletters

AAMI News
Ass'n for Advancement of Medical Instrumentation
1901 North Fort Myers Drive
Suite 602
Arlington, Va. 22209

Bio-Medical Insight
Int'l Bio-Medical Information Services, Inc.
P.O. Box 752
Miami, Fla. 33156

Changing Medical Markets
Theta Technology Corp.
462 Ridge Road
Wethersfield, Conn. 06109

Health Devices Alerts
Emergency Care Research Institute
5200 Butler Pike
Plymouth Meeting, Pa. 19462

Hospital Technology Alerts
American Hospital Ass'n
840 North Lake Shore Drive
Chicago, Ill. 60611

Hospital Technology Series
American Hospital Ass'n
840 North Lake Shore Drive
Chicago, Ill. 60611

Medical Devices, Diagnostics, and Instrumentation

"The Gray Sheet"
Drug Research Reports, Inc.
National Press Building
Washington, D.C. 20045

Tech Scanner
Int'l Techniquest
P.O. Box 10006
Minneapolis, Minn. 55440

Washington Drug and Device Letter
Capitol Publications, Inc.
2430 Pennsylvania Ave, N.W.
Suite 612
Washington, D.C. 20037

Devices and Diagnostics Letter
Washington Business Information, Inc.
235 National Press Bldg.
Washington, D.C. 20045

§ 8.25 Selected laws, regulations, and standards

Federal Laws

(1) U.S. Food and Drug Administration, U.S. Department of Health and Human Services

(a) Federal Food, Drug, and Cosmetic Act, 21 U.S.C. 301. *See also* implementing regulations of FDA.

(b) Public Health Service Act, Radiation Control for Health and Safety, 21 U.S.C. § 263. *See also* implementing regulations of FDA.

(c) Fair Packaging and Labeling Act 21 U.S.C. § 451. *See also* implementing regulations of FDA.

(d) The Medical Devices Act of 1976, 21 U.S.C. § 21. *See also* implementing regulations of FDA.

Voluntary Standards

(1) UL (Underwriters' Laboratories)

(a) UL 1067: Electrically Conductive Equipment and Materials for Use in Flammable Anesthesizing Locations.

(b) UL 913: Intrinsically Safe Apparatus and Associated Apparatus for use in Class I, II, and II, Division I Hazardous Locations.

(c) UL 674: Electric Motors and Generators for Use in Hazardous Locations, Class I, Groups C and D, Class II, Groups E, F, and G.

(d) UL 544: Electric Medical and Dental Equipment

(e) UL 416: Refrigerated Medical Equipment

(f) UL 187: X-Ray Equipment

(2) ANSI (American National Standards Institute)

Anesthetic Equipment

(a) ANSI Z79.16

(b) ANSI Z79.8

(c) ANSI Z79.4

(d) ANSI Z79.7

(e) ANSI Z79.6

(f) ANSI Z79.9

(g) ANSI Z79.3

(h) ANSI Z79.10

(i) ANSI Z79.13

(j) ANSI Z79.11

(k) ANSI Z79.14

(l) ANSI Z79.2

Health Care Facilities

(a) ANSI/NFPA 76C

(b) ANSI/NFPA 56D

§ 8.26 Selected cases

Simmons First National Bank v. Abbot, No. Civ. 80–440 (Ark. Cir. Ct., Saline Cty. Sept. 16, 1981), 25 ATLA L. Rep. 181 (May. 1982), **oxygen and anesthetic gas hoses;** misconnection to Airco ventilator; permanent brain damage.

Mattie v. Picker Corp., No. 444 398 (Cal. Super. Ct. Jan. 25, 1984), 27 ATLA L. Rep. 421 (Nov. 1984), **X-ray machine;** radiation exposure.

Vossler v. Richards Mfg. Co., 143 Cal. App. 3d 952, 192 Cal. Rptr. 219 (1983), **prosthetic knee device;** defect concealed.

Putensen v. Clay Adams, Inc., 12 Cal. App. 3d 1062, 91 Cal. Rptr. 319 (1970), **polyethylene tubing;** manufacturer's failure to inspect for defects.

Inouye v. Black, 238 Cal. App. 2d 31, 47 Cal. Rptr. 313 (1965), **wire;** holding vertebrae in place broke.

C.R. Bard v. Mason, 247 So. 2d 471 (Fla. Dist. Ct. App.), *cert. denied*, 251 So. 2d 878 (Fla. 1971), **catheter**.

Kincl v. Hycel, Inc., 56 Ill. App. 3d 772, 14 Ill. Dec. 374, 372 N.E.2d 385 (1977), **PMS blood test;** brain damage; failure to warn.

McKasson v. Zimmer Manufacturing Co., 12 Ill. App. 3d 429, 299 N.E.2d 38 (1973), **intramedullary rod;** defective manufacture and imperfections in metal.

Bowles v. Zimmer Mfg. Co., 277 F.2d 868 (7th Cir. [Ind.] 1960), **intramedullary pin.**

Terre Haute First Nat'l Bank v. Air Shields, Inc., No. C–75–240 (Ind. Cir. Ct. June 24, 1983), 26 ATLA L. Rep. 425 (Nov. 1983), **incubator;** oxygen explosion blinds infant; $733,333 settlement.

Richard v. Southwest Louisiana Hospital Ass'n, 383 So. 2d 83 (La. Ct. App.), *cert. denied*, 385 So. 2d 274 (La. 1980), **Foley catheter;** surgical difficulties; hospital found negligent for use of defective catheter.

Plaintiff v. New England Medical Center, No. 76–3138 G (D. Mass. Jan. 1983), 26 ATLA L. Rep. 343 (Oct. 1983), **therapeutic radiation machine;** crushed to death between stretcher assembly; pretrial cash settlement $1.375 million.

Hoffman v. Howmedica, Inc., 373 Mass. 32, 364 N.E.2d 1215 (1977), **hip prothesis;** cracked; manufacturer's breach of warranty.

Zeller v. American Safety Razor Corp., 15 Mass. App. 919, 443 N.E.2d 1349, *app. denied*, 388 Mass. 1104, 447 N.E.2d 670 (1983), **surgical blade;** broke off in patient's disc space; possible danger on movement; "knife blade phobia."

Keefer v. C.R. Bard, Inc., 110 Mich. App. 563, 313 N.W.2d 151 (1981), **catheter needle;** in-court demonstration.

Whitney v. Gallagher, 64 Mich. App. 46, 235 N.W.2d 57 (1975), **catheter;** broke during arteriogram; time runs from discovery of injury.

Ferren v. Richards Mfg. Co., No. CV 81–4131–CV (W.D. Mo. Apr. 22, 1983), **hip prosthesis;** cracked.

Bhagvandross v. Cockrell, No. 23JUN80 40 4672 (Mo. Cir. Ct. Aug. 8, 1984), **surgical bandage;** contamination.

Monaco v. G.D. Searle Co., No. 79–1513 (D.N.J. July 16, 1982), 26 ATLA L. Rep. 227 (June 1983), **aldactone;** abnormal breast development in man; information withheld from FDA.

Anderson v. Somberg, 67 N.J. 291, 338 A.2d 1, *cert. denied*, 423 U.S. 929, 96 S. Ct. 279, 46 L. Ed. 2d 258 (1975), **forceps (angulated pituitary rongeur);** burden of proof.

Sinatra v. National X-Ray Prod. Corp., 26 N.J. 546, 141 A.2d 28 (1958), **X-ray machine;** defective cable; manufacturer's duty to inspect for defects.

Goffe v. Pharmaceutical Laboratories, Inc., 90 N.M. 753, 568 P.2d 589 (1977), **K-2R Kaslow intestional tube**.

Michael v. Warner/Chilcott, 91 N.M. 651, 579 P.2d 183 (Ct. App. 1978), **sinus congestion tablets**; adequacy of warnings.

Klein v. Dow Corning Corp., 661 F.2d 998 (2d Cir. [N.Y.] 1981), **silicone breast prosthesis;** time limitation.

Liberatore v. National Cylinder Gas Co., 193 F.2d 429 (2d Cir. [N.Y.] 1952), **oxygen cylinder;** negligent manufacture.

Martin v. Edwards Laboratories, 60 N.Y.2d 417, 457 N.E.2d 1150, 469 N.Y.S.2d 923 (1983), **artificial heart valve;** time limitation runs from malfunction.

Fogal v. Genesee Hospital, 41 A.D.2d 468, 344 N.Y.S.2d 552 (1973), **hypothermia machine;** defective electronic temperature control unit.

Murphy v. St. Charles Hospital, 35 A.D.2d 64, 312 N.Y.S.2d 978 (1970), **hip prosthesis;** cracked; statute of limitations runs from breakage.

Peluso v. Gambro, No. 5170/76 (N.Y. Sup. Ct. June 15, 1984), 28 ATLA L. Rep. 179 (May 1985), **dialyzer;** failure to warn; hearing loss.

Patel v. Albany Medical Center Hospital, 101 Misc. 2d 457, 421 N.Y.S.2d 182 (Sup. Ct. 1979), **anesthesia machine;** wrongful death.

James v. Keefe & Keefe, Inc., 85 Misc. 2d 301, 379 N.Y.S.2d 576 (Sup. Ct.), *rev'd*, 50 A.D.2d 741, 377 N.Y.S.2d 991 (1st Dept. 1975), **glass jar humidifier attached to oxygen tank;** explosion sufficient evidence of defect to allow jury to infer negligence.

Danilla v. Botti, No. 30338 (Ohio Ct. C.P. Feb. 4, 1983), 26 ATLA L. Rep. 327 (Sept. 1983), **pacemaker;** malfunction; wrongful death.

Neese v. Shawnee Medical Center Hospital, Inc., 626 P.2d 1327 (Okla. 1981), **forceps (pituitary rongeur);** broke off in spinal column during laminectomy.

Oksenholt v. Lederle Laboratories, 294 Or. 213, 656 P.2d 293 (1982), **nyambutol;** manufacturer's failure to warn.

Thomas v. American Cystoscope Makers, Inc., 414 F. Supp. 255 (E.D. Pa. 1976), **resectoscope;** electrical burn to physician's cornea.

Ayers v. Morgan, 397 Pa. 282, 154 A.2d 788 (1959), **sponge;** remained in abdomen; action accrues on discovery.

Grubb v. Albert Einstein Medical Center, 255 Pa. Super. 381, 387 A.2d 480 (1978), **Stryker 4 plug (bone) cutter**.

Vergott v. Deseret Pharmaceutical Co., 463 F.2d 12 (5th Cir. [Tex.] 1972), **Bardic-Deseret intracath catheter;** unfit for intended use.

Olsen v. Royal Metals Corp., 392 F.2d 116 (5th Cir. [Tex.] 1968), **hospital bed;** breach of implied warranty.

Oswald v. United States, No. SA–82–CA–211 (W.D. Tex. June 9, 1983), 27 ATLA L. Rep. 85 (Mar. 1984), **blood warming device;** newborn is brain damaged; $1.37 million settlement.

Travenol Laboratories, Inc. v. Bandy Laboratories, Inc., 608 S.W.2d 308 (Tex. Civ. App. 1980), **sterile latex surgeon's gloves;** contaminated by rabies vaccine due to alleged pinholes in gloves.

Air Shields v. Spears, 590 S.W.2d 574 (Tex. Civ. App. 1979), **incubator;** failure to warn of oxygen use in incubator; blindness.

E.R. Squibb & Sons v. Heflin, 579 S.W.2d 19 (Tex. Civ. App. 1979), **Renografin-60 X-ray diagnostic fluid;** failure to warn.

V. Hueller & Co. v. Corley, 570 S.W.2d 140 (Tex. Civ. App. 1978), **breast implant prosthesis;** break in envelope required removal.

Ethicon v. Parten, 520 S.W.2d 527 (Tex. Civ. App. 1975), **surgical needle;** evidence that manufacturing process had resulted in cracked needles.

Thomas v. Pugh, 6 S.W.2d 202 (Tex. Civ. App. 1928), **X-ray machine;** release of manufacturer did not release retailer.

Conlee v. McGhan Medical Corp., No. 81–4062–F (Tex. Jud. Dist. Ct. Dec. 13, 1983), 27 ATLA L. Rep. 134 (Apr. 1984), **saline breast implant;** deflation; fraud; identical to implant removed from market earlier.

Kennedy v. Bird Corp., No. C–79–1148 (Utah Dist. Ct. June 23, 1983), 26 ATLA L. Rep. 326 (Sept. 1983), **infant respirator;** brain damage; settlement $1.2 million.

Orthopedic Equipment Co. v. Eustler, 276 F.2d 455 (4th Cir. [Va.] 1960), **intramedullary nail;** incurable bone infection; negligence per se.

Ohler v. Tacoma General Hospital, 92 Wash. 2d 507, 598 P.2d 1358 (1979), **incubator;** blindness.

Chapter 9

INDUSTRIAL ACCIDENTS: DEATH AT THE WORKPLACE

KLUWER LITIGATION LIBRARY REFERENCES

HARLEY & MAGEE, WHAT'S IT WORTH? A GUIDE TO CURRENT PERSONAL INJURY AWARDS AND SETTLEMENTS.

JEANS, LITIGATION: Chapter 4, *Discovery*; Chapter 8, *Direct Examination*; Chapter 13, *Cross-Examination*; Chapter 14, *Cross-Examination of Expert Witnesses*.

SMITH & MALANDRO, COURTROOM COMMUNICATION STRATEGIES: Chapter 1, *Impression Formation in the Courtroom*; Chapter 2, *Persuasive Strategies in the Courtroom*; Chapter 5, *Preparing for Effective Courtroom Communication*; Chapter 9, *Cross-Examination: Controlling the Case*.

I. Introduction

§ 9.01 In general

"His poverty, not his will, consented to incur the danger."[1] This principle of economic compulsion proclaimed in English common law nearly

[1] Thrussell v. Handyside, 20 Q.B.D. 359 (Eng. 1888), this was a ruling in favor of a workman who was struck on the head by an iron bolt falling from construction work

a century ago still holds true today. Consumers have the freedom to choose among products they bring into their homes, but the worker has no such choice. He stays on the job because he needs to support himself and his family. The worker accepts the products provided by his employer to accomplish his given tasks. He is paid to produce, regardless of the job's safety.

More than a century ago, the common law served notice that workers' rights to safety at the workplace would be protected, and that economic compulsion could not deprive them of their right to justice.

American courts have also concerned themselves with the rights of workers. In *Independent Nail & Packing Co. v. Mitchell*,[2] my client was injured while constructing a chicken roost in a pole barn in Newton, Illinois. He was striking a series of nails with a hammer when one of the nails fractured at the tip. The broken piece flew off and struck him in the right eye, blinding him in that eye. Ruling for my client, the United States Court of Appeals for the First Circuit stated: "[T]he manufacturer should have anticipated that the employee might, through economic compulsion, as here, be reasonable in running the risk that it had created." In this chapter, I will focus on some of the risks and dangers that confront working men and women in the United States, and the response of our legal system when these risks and dangers result in injury or death.

II. Checklists

§ 9.02 Checklist: Investigation of an industrial product-related injury case

The following checklist is intended to aid counsel in the preparation of a claim involving an injury caused by a product in an employment context.

____ (1) How did the injury occur? Investigate by interviewing as many witnesses as possible, as soon as possible. Since the injury took place in the workplace, it is likely that there are a number of witnesses who are still working for the

---

taking place above him. The English court stated, "If the plaintiff could have gone away from the dangerous place without incurring the risk of losing his means of livelihood, the case might have been different; but he was obliged to be there; his poverty, not his will, consented to incur the danger."

[2] 343 F.2d 819 (1st Cir. 1965).

same employer. Locating one such witness through information provided by your client or his family will likely lead you to other such witnesses (*see* (2) below).

____ (2) Locate witnesses to the incident, including:

____(a) Co-workers

____(b) Former workers

____(c) Union officials

____(d) Visitors to the workplace at the time of the injury

____(e) First aid station staff, ambulance drivers, emergency room employees, and others who may have treated victims immediately after the injury

____(f) Media employees who may have gone to the scene immediately after the incident to report it

____ (3) Where did the injury occur? If possible, visit the site and observe the surrounding circumstances. Many employment-related injuries take place in public places to which you will have free access.

____ (4) From the witnesses and your client develop a detailed statement of the machine, vehicle, or other product that caused the injury.

____ (5) Attempt to locate the actual machine, vehicle, or product that caused the injury and inspect it as early as possible. Take your consultant-expert with you.

____ (6) Question the client and/or fellow workers about prior experiences with the machine, vehicle, or product.

____ (7) Determine the following about the machine, product, or vehicle that caused the work-related injury:

____(a) Manufactured by

____(b) Manufactured at

____(c) Date of manufacture

____(d) Patent number[s]

____(e) Model number[s]

____(f) Serial number[s]

____(g) Brand name

____(h) Modifications to product

____ (8) Locate copies of all investigations of the incidents including:

____(a) Police reports

____(b) Fire reports

____(c) Union reports

____(d) Coroner's reports

____(e) Reports prepared by state or federal safety and/or health inspectors

____ (9) Was there a prior malfunction or report of injury in connection with this machine or a similar machine?

____(10) Locate reports or witnesses to prior malfunctions or injuries

____(11) Make every effort to determine what warnings, if any, were given about the dangers associated with using the machine, vehicle, or product, including:

____(a) Signs

____(b) Symbols

____(c) Labels

____(d) Available manuals

____(e) Posted work rules

____(f) Memoranda

____(g) Oral warnings

____(h) Safety meetings

(If any such warnings were apparently given, investigate how, and in what context, they were given to workers.)

____(12) Make a preliminary list of the potential defendants:

____(a) Employer

____(b) Manufacturer

____(c) Assembler

____(d) Successor corporation

____(e) Repairer

____(f) Person or agency responsible for maintenance

____(g) Designer of machine

____(h) Tester

____(i) Inspector

____(j) Vendor of product

____(k) Other

____(13) Investigate possible legal theories that might be used against each defendant:

____(a) Design defect

____(b) Manufacturing defect

____(c) Failure to warn of danger

____(d) Strict liability

____(e) Breach of implied warranty

____(f) Negligence

____(g) Failure to inspect

____(h) Failure to improve safety features

____(i) Unreasonably dangerous

____(j) Violation of code

____(k) Violation of statute

____(l) Other

____(14) As early as possible, assist your client in locating alternative sources of income while he is out of work. This will help him to get through a difficult period and reduce the danger that he will otherwise be tempted to settle a good claim for much less than he is entitled to because of his decreased economic circumstances. Investigate:

____(a) Private disability insurance

____(b) Government or employer sponsored disability insurance

____(c) Health and accident insurance

____(d) Workmen's compensation (be careful not to do or agree to anything that will waive the right to file a tort claim)

____(e) Sick leave

____(f) Social Security

____(g) Private sources

____(15) Research law reviews and treatises on work related injury cases

____(16) Contact the following to determine what information, if any, is available regarding the machine, product, or vehicle:

____(a) National Institute for Occupational Safety and Health

____(b) Occupational Safety and Health Administration

____(c) ATLA Exchange

____(d) ATLA Law Reporter

____(e) ATLA Products Liability Law Reporter

§ 9.03 Checklist: Resources for an industrial product-related injury case

The following checklist of litigation sources should be of valuable assistance to counsel when preparing for an industrial product-related case.

____(1) Selected technical sources

____(a) Professional Safety

____(b) American Machinist

____(c) National Safety Council

____(d) Industrial Medicine

____(e) Journal of Trauma

____(f) Annals of Occupational Hygiene

____(g) Accidents

____(h) Journal of Occupational Medicine

____(2) Selected government sources

____(a) Occupational Safety and Health Administration

____(b) National Institute of Occupational Safety and Health

____(c) National Aeronautic and Space Administration

____(d) U.S. Department of Defense

____ (3) Industry sources

____(a) Society for Occupational Safety and Health

____(b) National Tool, Dye, and Precision Machinery Association

____(c) National Safety Council

____(d) U.S. Chamber of Commerce

____(e) National Association of Manufacturers

____(f) American Public Works Association

____(g) Associated Equipment Distributors

III. Case Study: The Case of the Exploding Plant[3]

§ 9.04 Facts

An aerosol packaging plant in Cumberland, Rhode Island, was the site of a tragic explosion on January 16, 1976. The plant used gas to package a variety of consumer aerosol products: perfumes, hair spray, and shaving cream among them. Because so many different products required different types of propellant gas, a "changeover" procedure accompanied each change in production to meet the requirements of the next order. Gases used for one production job would be removed from the system, while those required for the next job would be supplied. Elaborate systems of switches, valves, and gauges had to be performed properly for smooth and safe changeover operations.

The morning of the explosion, plant employees were just completing this changeover. They were preparing for a large production that would require a colorless, odorless, highly flammable propellant known as isobutane. Despite the dangerously flammable and explosive nature of this and other gases, plant employees did not receive the most rudimentary safety protection: a functioning gas detection system to alert them to leaking gas.

The plaintiff was one of several employees who became the victims of several defendants' negligent practices when leaking propellant gas exploded at the plant on January 16, 1976. He was lucky. At least five of

[3] Martel v. Peterson Puritan, No. 78–037 (D.R.I. Dec. 15, 1982).

his fellow workers lost their lives in the blast. He recalled that fateful day, "I was in my office when it occurred. . . . [I heard] a very loud boom and next thing I know I was surrounded with flames burning up. I tried to get out the door and my hand stuck to the brass doorknob. I went to the floor, the sprinklers came on, and I remember walking out the door and getting in a vehicle to go to the hospital."[4]

The plaintiff was rushed to the hospital where he slipped into a coma. Even when he regained consciousness, his recovery was slow and painful. He was readmitted at least eight times for skin grafts aimed at healing his severely burned body. Five years later, he still felt the tragedy's effects:

> "My legs give way on me without any notice, I fall downstairs, fall [on the ground just] walking, just croak and go down . . . . I have very little strength in my hands. I don't want to stay as an invalid at home all day the rest of my life. My kids have been deprived of fathership for the last six years. . . . I have boys that needed me playing ball and everything else, which I always did, which I'm not able to do now."[5]

§ 9.05 Analysis of case

Soon after my investigation into this tragedy began, I recognized that this would be an extremely complex and difficult case. At one point, twenty-four different parties were joined in the action. The chalkboard in my office listing these parties and their role in our state and federal court actions became an object of interest to my staff and friends alike. Guests and clients touring my offices often asked about that "chart with all the names on it." Before those names were erased, the sworn testimony of dozens of witnesses provided the ammunition I needed to win a major legal victory, and thus uphold the common law tradition of protecting the rights of workers to safe working conditions.[6]

Who had responsibility for this tragedy? Who made the decisions to use this dangerous product? Did the gas suppliers provide adequate warnings and instructions for safe use? Armed with these and similar questions, I set out to find the answers. I learned that two companies supplied the gases for this aerosol operation, ____________ Company and ____________ Company. In sworn testimony, executives of both

---

[4] *Id.*, testimony of the plaintiff.

[5] *Id.*

[6] *See infra* § 9.11.

companies admitted that they knew that isobutane was extremely flammable and explosive and would pose safety hazards if used in any plant that lacked gas leak detection systems. They were aware of detection systems that could be installed to reduce the safety risks of leaking gas explosions. Yet they failed to inform the plant of those alternative detection systems, and continued to sell the gases to this company nevertheless.

§ 9.06 Cross-examination of vice president of operations for gas supplier regarding safety matters

Mr. C, vice president of operations for ____________ Chemicals, was responsible for supplying propellant products to the defendant-aerosol plant. He admitted under oath that he permitted the sale of this odorless, volatile gas to the plant despite the fact that he did not know that this customer lacked a functioning gas detection system. He knew the gas was hazardous and that safety detection systems were available. His company had safety information available, but provided this potentially lifesaving information to its customers only when they asked for it. Plant officials never asked for the information, and the information was never volunteered. Consider these excerpts from my cross-examination of this high ranking company official.[7]

Q. Did you know that when you were supplying [the plant] with propellants, that they did not have a gas detection system?

A. I was not aware of that situation.

Q. Did you ever become aware of that situation, that they did not have a gas detection system?

A. I was not aware of—if they did or did not have, either one, no, sir. [*Ed. Note*: Mr. C visited the plant after the explosion.]

Q. Well, did you become aware at that time when you visited the site that there was no operating gas detection system in the gas house at the ____________ plant?

A. No, sir.

Q. Well, would you supply your propellants to a purchaser whom you knew, or your company knew, not to have a gas detection system?

A. Yes, sir.

---

[7] Testimony of Mr. C, vice president of operations, ____________ Chemical Company.

Q. And the propellants that you sell and the ones used by the consumer, or the purchaser, they're odorless, are they not?

A. Yes, sir.

Q. Invisible?

A. Yes, sir.

Q. And explosive or flammable?

A. Yes, sir.

Q. Did your company have any safety programs that they would urge purchasers to follow, any organized safety program?

A. Safety programs were available upon request.

Q. What were they?

A. Safety programs are available; they would consist of an instruction program, incorporating the handling of aerosol propellants.

Q. And how would that be done; would the people advise the suppliers, or the purchasers, is that what they would do, your people?

A. Yes, sir.

Q. And did you ever distribute any literature to your customers about the use or the installation of gas detection systems?

A. No, sir.

Q. Did you ever encourage your purchasers by any means to employ the use of a gas detection system?

A. When consulted, yes.

Q. When you say "when consulted," do you mean, in other words, if a purchaser came up to you and said, can you give me some information on a gas detection system, is that what you mean, something like that?

A. Yes, sir.

Q. You never volunteered, or at least it wasn't the policy of your company, to volunteer this information?

A. No, sir.

Q. When your engineer goes on the site of a plant, for whatever reason, is he ever given any instruction to determine whether or not there is a gas detection system?

A. No, sir.

Q. Is he ever given any instruction to encourage the purchaser to use one?

A. If consulted, yes.

Q. If asked, once again?

A. Yes, sir.

COMMENT: Despite his company's lack of initiative in providing safety information to the customer, this witness conceded that detection systems were the only means of alerting workers to the leaking hazardous gas. He stated that he had been aware of such systems for fifteen years. Although he claimed he was "concerned,"[8] he admitted that information on these systems came only on request from the customer. This company never volunteered such information, even though it was selling a highly flammable and dangerous product.

Admissions by senior company executives as to what they failed to do to promote safety in the workplace can help to establish the defendant's liability. Many jurors are workers who have a suspicion about corporate executives' concern for their safety.

I asked the witness if customers had to meet any requirements before his company would sell them this explosive product. He responded that the customer had to be "competent."[9] When asked what this meant, he replied: "There is no specific program. The evaluation is predicated upon contracts established with a customer."[10] When I asked if it concerned him as a manufacturer and a supplier of an invisible, odorless, flammable mixture that the mixture was being supplied to a customer who had no detection equipment, he replied, "No."[11] "And why not?", I

[8] *Id.*

[9] *Id.*

[10] *Id.*

[11] *Id.*

asked. Because, he said, such safety systems were not required by government regulations! Consider this exchange:[12]

> Q. So what you're saying, in essence, is that even if the purchaser didn't have a gas detection—any gas detection equipment, you'd still supply it to them, as long as they met whatever the regulations were at the time?
>
> A. Yes, sir.

Yet, the official admitted that in this case, the company did not even determine the customer's compliance with state and federal requirements before it supplied the product.[13]

§ 9.07 Cross-examination of marketing manager for gas supplier regarding lack of safety equipment

The other company, ___________ Petroleum, sold aerosol propellants to the plant and did not inspect the customer's plant to see how the propellants were being used, either. This company's marketing manager admitted under extensive cross-examination that he did not know whether the defendant had gas detection equipment or not. However, he conceded that the customer's lack of safety equipment would not prevent the sale of the explosive gas. Again, consider the following excerpt from this official's sworn testimony.[14]

> Q. When you sold these propellants, did you ever make plant inspections as to how they're using the product, storing it, or disbursing it in any way? Prior to the accident?
>
> A. No.
>
> Q. Sir, as a salesman of propellants, they are flammable, aren't they?
>
> A. That's correct.
>
> Q. Well, actually, they can reach explosive levels?
>
> A. They can.
>
> Q. Was it the practice of your company, in 1976 or before, to sup-

---

[12] *Id.*

[13] *Id.*

[14] *Martel, supra* note 3, testimony of Mr. C, marketing manager for defendant-___________ Petroleum.

ply propellants to a purchaser if you knew they did not have detection equipment?

A. I don't think I know the answer to that question.

Q. Well, you as a salesperson would visit a plant, correct?

A. That's right.

Q. And you'd sell propellants in certain quantities?

A. Anything from a one pound cylinder to a 30,000 gallon tank car.

Q. Now, assuming you were supplying a 30,000 gallon tank car to a supplier, if you, as a sales manager or person who was making a sale to a manufacturer, knew that the plant did not have detection equipment, would that prevent you from making a sale?

A. No.

Q. Did you at any time prior to supplying the [aerosol plant] with your propellants, ever have knowledge of whether or not they had a gas detection system?

A. No.

Q. Did you ever inquire?

A. I don't recall inquiring.

COMMENT: This company was also well aware of the importance of safety devices in the proper use of its product. One company executive had written and published articles on the subject of aerosol safety. Yet, like its competitor, this company only offered the information when it was requested. It failed to volunteer the information needed to promote the safe use of its product.

---

§ 9.08 Inspection of plant facilities by parent company

The lack of diligence on the part of propellant suppliers was compounded by a lack of diligence on the part of the parent company. This defendant hired a private safety engineering firm to conduct safety inspections of its plants. This firm's president inspected the aerosol plant just eight months before the explosion, but he admitted that he had very limited knowledge of the plant's operations before undertaking the assignment.[15] He did not know that the plant used odorless, colorless gas. He did not even attempt to determine what chemicals were being used. He knew for certain that the plant was using gases that were flammable only "when I heard about the explosion!"[16] His ignorance may have contributed to his failure to learn whether the plant had a gas detection system, since he never asked about such a safety system during his inspection.

§ 9.09 Inspection of plant facilities by insurance carrier

The parent company's insurance carrier also conducted inspections of the plant. Although the company's "risk control" manager personally visited the plant one year before the explosion, his lack of knowledge regarding the company's explosive gases also made his inspection largely ineffective, as illustrated in the following excerpt from his sworn testimony.[17]

> Q. Sir, it is my understanding that when you inspect these plants, you do so in order to make sure sure that it's a safe environment, relatively safe environment for the working man, right?
>
> A. Yes.
>
> Q. And in determining whether or not there is a safe environment for the working man, you have to familiarize yourself somewhat with the type of machinery or product that the working man is exposed to, correct?
>
> A. Yes.
>
> Q. Did you familiarize yourself with the type of gases or chemicals that the plant utilized in the production of its product?
>
> A. No.
>
> Q. I assume that your inspection was concerned with the efforts of the company to protect the working man in the area effectively, was it not?
>
> A. To provide a safe environment for the worker.

---

[15] *Martel*, *supra* note 3, testimony of Mr. G, president of ___________.

[16] *Id*.

[17] *Martel, supra* note 3, testimony of Mr. A, risk control manager for ___________ Ins. Co.

Q. Were you aware, at the time that you performed this safety inspection, that the plant utilized explosive gases in the area of the working environment?

A. No.

Q. You didn't realize at that time that they produced aerosol?

A. Yes, I was aware that it was an aerosol packaging plant.

Q. But you didn't know at that time that some of the material that went into those cans was a gas, explosive gas mixture, is that correct?

A. No, it didn't occur to me at that time.

Q. But you knew, didn't you, that they were in the business of filling aerosol spray cans, did you not?

A. Yes.

Q. And you knew, did you not, that some sort of a gas was injected into those cans?

A. Yes.

Q. And, as a matter of fact, not knowing, sir, that the gases were potentially explosive gases in the plant at the time that you inspected it, then I assume that you made no inspection pertaining to any explosive gases, correct?

A. Yes.

Q. Did you know what the chemical isobutane was before you went out and made the inspection?

A. No.

Q. If you had known or had reason to know that flammable or explosive gases were being used in conjunction with the product being manufactured in that plant, would you have asked any questions pertaining to explosive materials?

A. Possibly.

Q. You were the supervisor of risk control, were you not?

A. Yes.

Q. And in the capacity of that particular job, isn't it part of your job or your responsibility to know whether or not a man who is working in a factory is being exposed to an explosive, colorless, and odorless gas?

A. Yes.

Q. When you inspected this plant, did you check to see if there were gas detection or alarm systems?

A. No.

Q. Were you ever made aware or did you ever know that the gases that were being used in conjunction with the product manufactured at the plant were odorless and colorless?

A. No.

Q. Had you been aware of that, sir, prior to your inspection in January of 1975, would you have done anything differently when you visited the plant that day?

A. I am not sure.

§ 9.10 Cross-examination of vice president of parent company regarding safety at plant

When the plant was finally renovated for safety, after the explosion, the parent company's vice president reluctantly admitted that the plant had not been as safe as it could have been, that after the explosion he had "begun to pay a lot more attention to what was being done in the area of safety. . . ."[18] Consider the following excerpted testimony.[19]

Q. Did [the parent company] institute any policies after this explosion to be incorporated at the ____________ plant?

A. We were very much concerned, as was [the defendant-plant], that when the plant was rebuilt, that it was made as absolutely safe as we thought—no reason to believe it was not—but in the course of the reconstruction, using new techniques and new things, we authorized the expenditure of several more millions of dollars, which required merely to replace the plant and kind of to augment as much as possible all the safety procedures and bring it right up to date. . . .

Q. Did you find out about any deficiencies subsequent to the explosion?

A. Deficiency, I think is the wrong word. We found things where

---

[18] *Martel, supra* note 3, testimony of Mr. L, vice president, ____________.

[19] *Id*.

improvements could be made, but I think that's different from saying that there were deficiences. . . .

Q. Did anyone from [the parent-company] inquire whether there was ever a gas detection system installed?

A. Not to my knowledge.

Q. Is it your testimony today that up to this point in time, as we sit here today, you do not know whether or not [the plant] has a gas detection system installed in its plant?

A. I do know that in all of our plants there are gas detection systems, at least that's my belief.

Q. Well, how do you know that all your plants have gas detection systems?

A. Because, as I said, after this event occurred, and we began making a major project to upgrade and do the most we could to prevent any recurrence, any possible recurrences, and we looked—and *I paid a lot more attention then to what was being done in the area of safety*. [Emphasis added.]

Q. In other words, after this explosion, you made it a point to try to determine that in any of the plants that you either owned or ran, that they had proper detection equipment, is that right?

A. Right.

§ 9.11 Conclusion

The plant's employees were the victims of a chain of corporate decision making that permitted unsafe working conditions to continue behind the mask of "all's clear" inspection reports, and of gas suppliers who knew about the lack of safety equipment, yet felt it was not their place to volunteer the information that could have prevented the explosion from ever taking place.

Not surprisingly, when officials of the Occupational Safety and Health Administration (OSHA) investigated the plant after the explosion, they found numerous safety violations that they linked directly to the explosion. The Agency's regional director termed four of the seven alleged violations "serious."

My client and the other plaintiffs received damages totaling over $4 million from the many companies whose negligence contributed to this catastrophic, and unnecessary, tragedy.[20]

IV. Other Workplace Hazards

§ 9.12 Lethal utility plant

A twenty-five-year-old employee of an independent contractor hired by an electric utility company to clean the preheater in its Sandwich, Massachusetts, power plant was killed when he slipped on the wet, sloping floor and his body became caught in the machine's turning rotor.[21] The six-story preheater provided the necessary heat exchange for the utility's operations. The heat exchange took place through a revolving rotor. This rotor was periodically cleaned in order to maintain maximum performance.

The plaintiff supervised the cleaning team assigned to clean the preheater. The night that tragedy struck, the plaintiff's work crew had just completed their cleaning assignment. The cleaning process was performed with the rotor turning. Water was pumped or jetted through the rotor area at high force. When the cleaning was complete, an inspection was performed to determine whether the rotor was sufficiently clean. The inspection involved one employee shining a flashlight on the rotor blades from one side of the preheater while the other employee stood on the other side to observe the light through the rotor blades. On previous occasions, the utility company would assign its own employee to supervise the cleaning and inspection procedure. On this occasion, its executive had left the premises with no one assigned to this task.

When plaintiff's co-worker joined him to inspect the job, he suddenly heard a moan. He called out the plaintiff's name, but there was no reply. He moved over to the plaintiff's side and found the plaintiff's hard hat lying on the manway. Apparently he had been caught by the turning rotor. His body was crushed between the rotor and the sector plate that housed it and dropped into the air intake level below. A watch engineer found the plaintiff first. His right leg was severed. His chest was crushed. His excruciating pain lasted for approximately one-half hour. Rescue personnel arrived and rushed him to the hospital, but it was too late. The plaintiff succumbed to death during the ambulance ride to a

---

[20] *See Martel, supra* note 3.

[21] Conner, Admx. v. Canal Electric Co., et al., CA No. 78–2398–S (D. Mass. Nov. 8, 1984).

Cape Cod hospital.[22]

COMMENT: To try and establish his case, the plaintiff should call on the help of experts whose testimony can reveal the defendant's negligent practices to the members of the jury.

The plaintiff's expert testified that the utility company was negligent both in failing to warn the plaintiff's employer of the extreme hazards associated with the preheater and in failing to provide a liaison safety officer to supervise plaintiff's work.[23] The utility company failed to take any safety precautions whatsoever to reduce the hazards to the contractor's personnel. It also failed to install guardrails, nonskid surfaces, warning signs, interlocks, or safety cables, despite its knowledge that the work area was extremely hazardous while the rotor was turning due to its darkness and slippery, sloping floor. Furthermore, this expert testified that the utility company negligently allowed the cleaning to occur on the sixth level of the preheater rather than the fourth level, despite knowing that conditions on the fourth level were inherently safer.[24] This expert also testified as to the negligence of the product's manufacturer—for manufacturing a product that was defective in that it had no safety devices that would have ameliorated the hazard posed to employees working in the preheater chamber. The product was also defective in that it totally lacked guardrails, interlocks, and warnings of the hazards associated with entering the access space with the rotor turning. On the contrary, this company suggested in its service manual describing cleaning procedures that the cleaning and inspection be performed with the rotor turning![25] This manual provided no warnings of any kind regarding the hazards of entering the preheater chamber with the rotor turning.[26]

[22] *Id.*

[23] *Id.*, testimony of Mr. M on behalf of the plaintiff.

[24] *Id.*

[25] *Id.*

[26] *Conner, supra* note 21, service manual accompanying preheater, Plaintiff's Exhibit 163.

COMMENT: In addition to helpful evidence provided by the plaintiff's experts, it is always valuable to obtain vital evidence of the defendant's negligence from its own employees. In this case, the utility company's production supervisor provided revealing testimony of his company's gross negligence and reckless and wanton conduct with respect to their practices of operating the subject preheater.[27] The evidence indicated that this company was acutely aware of the hazards of entering the preheater chamber from the cold end side of level six with the rotor turning, yet negligently and recklessly failed to take any action to convey the existence of these hazards to its employees.

The defendant's production supervisor acknowledged under oath that he knew about the dark nature of level six of the preheater chamber, that the entrance area on level six tended to accumulate water and become slippery, and that the floor at the entranceway to the chamber was sloped downward with a pitch pointed directly toward the area where the rotor was located.[28] He also acknowledged that it was hazardous to enter the preheater chamber with the rotor turning. Yet, he had previously inspected the rotor inside the preheater chamber with the plaintiff while the rotor was turning, from the same sloped and slippery side that the plaintiff had entered the chamber the night that tragedy struck.[29] Despite knowledge of these hazards, the defendant permitted cleaning operations on level six instead of the flatter level four. (The flat surface of level four would have prevented the hazard of being drawn into the rotor and pulled between the rotor seal and sector plate.)

This executive also testified that he had, on previous occasions, assigned members of his staff to supervise the contractor's employees during cleaning operations.[30] He had the authority to assign such personnel

---

[27] *Conner, supra* note 21, testimony of Mr. R, production supervisor, __________ Elec. Co.

[28] *Id.*

[29] *Id.*

[30] *Id.*

on the date tragedy struck, but failed to do so. He did instruct a watch engineer already on duty to make occasional checks to make sure that everything was safe with respect to the cleaning operation. This engineer was the individual who first found the plaintiff when the incident occurred.

The client's day cleaning crew had had a preliminary meeting with this company executive, who requested that they call him forty-five minutes before the job was done so that he could inspect the work. He did not warn them against entering the preheater chamber with the rotor turning.[31] He did not show the workers where the shut-off switch was located or how to operate it (control of this switch remained exclusively in the hands of defendant's employees). A member of that crew testified that this executive did not assign any member of his staff to assist the plaintiff and his co-workers during the cleaning operations, although he had provided such assistance on previous assignments.[32]

One of plaintiff's co-workers testified that when the plaintiff's crew arrived for their work that evening, no one instructed them against entering the preheater chamber with the motor turning.[33] Another co-worker testified that there was no control available for them to use to turn the rotor on or off.[34]

COMMENT: Former executives can also provide valuable testimony to help establish corporate liability for the manufacture of defective products. Such was the case here, where testimony by the former manager of the direction service department for the company that manufactured the product revealed this company's grossly negligent and seriously deficient practices in connection with the design and marketing of the preheater.[35]

---

[31] *Id.*

[32] *Id.*

[33] *Conner, supra* note 21, testimony of Mr. O.

[34] *Conner, supra* note 21, testimony of Mr. D.

[35] *Conner, supra* note 21, testimony of Mr. C, former manager of direction service department.

According to testimony by the manufacturer's former manager of direction service, this company was aware, prior to the time that the preheater was designed, that during its lifetime of use there would be occasions when people would be working inside the preheater chamber.[36] He also acknowledged that persons entering the chamber would step on a slanted plate, and that he knew before the preheater was built that persons might enter the preheater chamber without knowing in advance of the sloping pitch of the floor.[37] Despite this knowledge, this witness conceded, the company did not provide any signs, warnings, or labels to warn workers that the slanting pitch of the floor led directly toward the rotor blades although he admitted it would have been feasible to provide such warnings.[38]

The company that manufactured the product recommended no safety devices or procedures to protect a person entering the chamber with the rotor turning. Why not? Because, according to its answers to the plaintiff's interrogatories, entry should not be made with the rotor turning. Despite this statement, this former executive testified that he and other employees of the defendant entered the preheater chambers to make inspections while the rotor was turning.[39]

COMMENT: Counsel seeking evidence of the defendant's corporate policies should not overlook an examination of the defendant's product service manuals.

Valuable evidence for the plaintiff in this case was provided by the service manual that actually encouraged workers to enter the preheater chamber with the rotor turning.[40] In this manual, distributed by the manufacturer prior to marketing the product in question, the defendant described out-of-service washing procedures as follows.

Out-Of-Service preheater washing is accomplished when the boiler

[36] *Id.*

[37] *Id.*

[38] *Id.*

[39] *Conner, supra* note 21, defendant's answer to plaintiff's Interrogatory No. 14.

[40] *Conner, supra* note 21, Water Washing Procedures Manual, Plaintiff's Exhibit 163.

> is shut down for a normal pre-scheduled inspection or for repair work. *Out-Of-Service washing affords the best possible opportunity for close control of the washing operation and for making a thorough inspection of the heating surface to determine its degree of cleanliness, both during and after completion of the wash.* The air preheater may be washed at any time after the boiler has been shut down. *The preheater rotor can be allowed to turn at normal speed during the operation*; but, if it is necessary to restrict the discharge of the wash water as much as possible to one side of the preheater, some type of auxiliary drive may be employed to reduce the rotor speed. After the drainage system has been checked to see that no obstructions exist, water should be admitted to both the hot and cold end devices. *The heating surface should be visually inspected periodically throughout the washing cycle to determine its degree of cleanliness*. When it is observed that the heating surface has been thoroughly cleaned, the unit should be allowed to completely dry before being put back into service.[41] [Emphasis added.]

This kind of evidence coupled with the damaging statements from its employees and the plaintiff's experts, contributed to a jury verdict of $2.6 million for the plaintiff.[42]

§ 9.13 Crane calamities

"It's funny, when you depend on the equipment you think you're safe. You think you're sitting in your living room and then, all of a sudden, whack, you're out."[43]

The man who uttered these words had just witnessed his twenty-four-year-old co-worker fall to his death when a defective construction crane collapsed. His words reflect the feelings of frustration of those workers who must live with the continuing knowledge that their lives are dependent on the safe design of equipment they use every day. Although the company that manufactured this crane knew for years that the crane was unsafe, the plaintiff never knew. The message did not reach his employer until ten days after the plaintiff died.

Another co-worker recalled the accident scene:

---

[41] *Id*. at 13. Case against preheater manufacturer, company that developed manual, was settled during trial.

[42] *Conner, supra* note 21.

[43] Estate of Gulla v. Walter Kiddie & Co., No. 77–97F (Feb. 22, 1982), testimony of the plaintiff's co-worker.

> "[After he completed his work] I saw plaintiff lean over the basket and he gave me the signal to come down. . . . I moved the manual controls to bring them in. . . . As soon as I moved the controls, I heard a crash and bang. The section flew in at the same time the basket dipped forward. It happened so quick. . . . The basket tipped. . . . I couldn't tell but it looked like plaintiff was hanging on. . . . I saw him fall. . . . There wasn't enough time for me to do anything. There was no warning. . . . I saw [him] moving so I went to him. There was too much blood. . . . [He] was moaning . . . his eyes were open. He didn't say anything. I took my jacket off and covered him. . . . The police came . . . the ambulance took him away."[44]

The plaintiff was rushed to the Massachusetts General Hospital where he underwent emergency surgery. He died a few hours later.

COMMENT: Counsel should always check previous communications between the plaintiff's employer and product suppliers. These communications, often in the form of company service bulletins, can provide evidence that the product supplier or manufacturer had knowledge of the product's hazards before tragedy struck.

The company that manufactured the crane knew the extreme dangers that faced anyone using its product. Four years before the accident, this defendant had communicated the crane's hazard potential to its customers in the form of a service bulletin.[45] Six months later, the company recognized that its cranes had not been modified and again warned its distributors of a potentially dangerous situation: ". . .The previous method of using set screws to secure this shaft is satisfactory. *However, if they should become loose, an unsafe condition could be created which would be unknown to the user*." [Emphasis added.] Distributors were told to notify their customers of the problem and conduct immediate safety inspections: "[I]f there is any evidence or indication of lateral shaft movement, the shaft must be properly aligned and we recommend

[44] *Id*.

[45] ____________ Service Bulletin (Aug. 1972) *supra* note 43.

that this improvement be incorporated. Regardless, when disassembly is required for any other reason, the improvement should be incorporated at that time."[46]

Eighteen months later, defective cranes were still in service, as the company acknowledged in its third warning: "[W]e again stress that all units must immediately be inspected for lateral shaft movement. . . . If any lateral movement is found, an unsafe condition exists which can properly be remedied by installation of an anchor shaft as detailed in Service Bulletin #73–141. For your convenience, we have again attached instructions for accomplishing this. . . . *Owners of cranes who fail to make these inspections and installations of anchor shafts when necessary, assume all risks which may be attendant to continued operation in an unsafe condition*."[47] [Emphasis added.]

The company's director of product safety and reliability admitted in depositions that his company knew three years before the accident that the cranes could be unsafe. The company expected its distributors to provide the information regarding its hazards to their customers. It distributed its latest advisory because its distributors did not respond adequately to its earlier ones, although this official admitted that he had no employees assigned to enforce compliance with the company warnings. Consider this excerpt from the company's director of product safety and reliability:[48]

Q. At the time of the issuance of this memo of January 12, 1973, you people were aware that if the set screws became loose, an unsafe condition would result, that is correct, isn't it?

A. Yes.

Q. The reason for this modification was that the experience of [your company] had indicated that the set screws were sometimes not being placed in the recesses in the shaft that were designed to accommodate them, that is right, isn't it?

A. Yes.

Q. And this you were learning as a result of your reports from the field, reports from distributors, and so on?

---

[46] __________ Service Bulletin (Jan. 12, 1973) *supra* note 43.

[47] __________ Service Bulletin (Aug. 1974) *supra* note 43.

[48] *Burke, supra* note 43, testimony of Mr. R, Director of Product Safety and Reliability.

A. I believe this is how they came upon it, yes, sir.

Q. And this came to your personal attention, didn't it, sir?

A. Yes, sir, I was aware of it, sir.

Q. And, in fact, you participated or people under your supervision participated in drafting the notice to the distributors dated August 9, 1972, is that so?

A. Yes, sir.

Q. Did you expect that your distributors would advise all their customers who had this type of crane of this modification requirement?

A. Yes.

Q. Does anyone in [your company] have responsibility to insure that these service bulletins were complied with?

A. No.

He also admitted that the modifications, as proposed in the service bulletin, would have prevented the accident that took this young man's life. I asked him, "Is it fair to say that if the modification that you recommend in your directives had been made on this particular machine, the telescoping boom, the breaking off of the bushing from the portion of the machine to which it was welded, would not have occurred?" He replied "yes."[49]

Unfortunately, the distributors themselves were not always diligent in responding to these service warnings. In the instant case, the distributor's service manager admitted that the company had received the defendant manufacturer's "Service Bulletins" warning of the product hazards, yet chose to ignore them because he "didn't see anything to get excited about."[50] He simply "filed them away" in his desk. Consider this revealing exchange between myself and this company official.[51]

Q. All right, Mr. R, I hand you an original document which has on the top of it ___________ Service Bulletin Number DLD–1063 and a date 9 August 1972, and I ask you, sir, if that is a ___________ service bulletin?

---

[49] *Id.*

[50] *Burke, supra* note 43, testimony of Mr. R, service manager, ___________ Equipment Co.

[51] *Id.*

A. Yes.

Q. Have you seen that 1972 bulletin before, sir?

A. Yes.

Q. The 1972 Service Bulletin also has a red border across the top and bottom on the first page, does it not?

A. Yes.

Q. Do you recall, sir, receiving that service bulletin from Mr. P or any other source?

A. I believe so, yes.

Q. What, if anything, sir, did you do with the service bulletin, Exhibit 4, when you received it? [*Ed. Note*: Exhibit not included.]

A. Read it, put it in the file, didn't see anything to get excited about.

Q. Did you bring the contents of the Exhibit 4 service bulletin to anyone else's attention, sir, at any time after you received it and prior to October 9, 1975 [date of the accident]?

A. I can't remember, but I must have. It's the usual practice.

Q. Well, your usual practice would have been to bring it to whose attention, sir?

A. The mechanic's.

Q. Assuming that the accident occurred on the 9th of October, 1975, did you have a mechanic working for you at that point?

A. I believe so.

Q. Did you bring the contents of Exhibit 4, the 1972 service bulletin, to [the mechanic's] attention, sir?

A. No.

Q. Sir, did you ever perform, prior to October 9, 1975, the modification that is outlined in Exhibit 4 on any ____________ Crane?

A. Before when?

Q. Before the accident that is the subject of this lawsuit, sir, which was October 9, 1975.

A. To the best of my knowledge, I don't believe so.

When this company finally decided that there might be a problem, it wrote to its customers as recommended by the manufacturer. It never sent a notice to the plaintiff's employer.

The master mechanic responsible for repairing all of the equipment used by the plaintiff's employer stated in sworn testimony that he never received any information or notification regarding the hazards associated with the crane: not from the manufacturer, distributor, or any other source.[52]

The plaintiff's employer's failure to modify the crane may have been excusable in light of its failure to receive the warnings from the other parties. However, the employer compounded the problem by attaching a basket to its crane that was not designed for use with the crane. The employer failed to contact the manufacturer, as instructed, before attaching the basket. The manufacturing company's director of product safety and reliability admitted that the company required all of its customers to get its approval before attaching baskets not approved by the company for its cranes, and that use of the company's cranes with baskets that did not receive its approval would be hazardous.[53] According to this official, the company never received a request from the deceased's employer, nor any notice that the company was using a nonconforming basket.[54] In his opinion, the bucket used by this company would not have been approved by the manufacturer, appeared to fail government safety standards, and did not even meet industry-wide product standards.[55]

This young man was just doing his job. His safety depended on the diligence of his employer, and those who provided his equipment. He paid for this dependence with his life.

§ 9.14 Plastic poison

I represented a woman who worked as a grocery store meat wrapper.[56] She had been wrapping meat for nearly twenty years when the store shifted from clear, cellophane meat wrap to plastic, polyvinyl chloride wrap. Shortly after this change, her health began to deteriorate rapidly. She developed dry throat, hacking coughs, wheezing, bad chest pains, and a variety of other respiratory problems. After three years, her health was so endangered that she was forced to quit her job to stay alive. She later learned that she was the victim of a condition sometimes called

---

[52] *Burke, supra* note 43, testimony of Mr. M, master mechanic, ____________ Co.

[53] *Burke, supra* note 43, testimony of Mr. R, director of product safety and reliability.

[54] *Id.*

[55] *Id.*

[56] Schofield v. Borden, Inc., CA 75–2934MC (D. Mass. Mar. 5, 1984).

"meat packer's asthma," a reaction to the toxic hydrogen chloride fumes given off by the plastic wrap.

This woman initially thought her illness was just a common cold: "My throat would get constantly dry and then my nose would get dry. . . . I was having trouble breathing. I was getting what I thought were colds." As things got worse, she went to see her doctor. "First, he figured it was a cold. Then he said it was a flu. Then bronchitis. It was everything."[57]

Her health was clearly tied to her work. When she stayed home, her symptoms disappeared. Feeling better, she returned to work, and the entire problem began again.

> "I'd be home for two days, and I was just wonderful. I'd call my doctor and say 'I feel great. Can I go back to work?' I'd go back to work. After two or three days, being in the same place, the same thing happened to me. I got another cold again. It would just continue and continue and continue. . . . I would come home, I would be coughing all night long. . . . I used to sit on the edge of the bed until three o'clock in the morning, coughing. I couldn't catch my breath. I would finally fall asleep, then, lo and behold, I was up at six o'clock to be at work at seven. It was getting so I would get home and I was a basket case. . . . My doctor couldn't figure out what was doing it."[58]

COMMENT: As in so many cases involving defective products, the victim often blames himself for the pain and suffering he experiences. Because plaintiff's very job may be on the line, he will endure great suffering before believing that the blame may lie with his employer or its products. This is one of the greatest barriers counsel must overcome in preparing his case.

She finally told her doctor about the smoke and fumes at work. He told her she had to quit her job. The toxic fumes, he warned, were mak-

[57] *Id*., testimony of the plaintiff.

[58] *Id*.

ing her sick. She could not accept his advice. Her fear of losing her job was simply too strong. She preferred to blame everything else, including herself. "I had been on this job for 24 years. I was a young woman, and I wasn't about to quit. I said, 'No, I won't quit.' "[59] Every time she called her doctor, he told her it was suicide if she didn't quit. "But I didn't want to admit to myself that it was the paper that was causing it. I didn't want to blame it on the machine because I didn't want to quit working. I was hoping it wasn't, but I was only kidding myself."[60]

A year later, her chest pains got worse. "I used to get these pains in my chest in the middle of the night, well, my husband thought I was going to die. I couldn't breathe. I just couldn't catch my breath."[61]

Six years after the plastic wrap was brought into the store, she was finally forced to quit. She remembers that her last day of work was devastating:

> "It was the week before Christmas. I went to work. I wasn't feeling good, but I did want to go in. [My boss] was short of help and I didn't want to leave him in the lurch. I went into work and I don't think I was there more than an hour when I started getting short of breath. I did go upstairs on my coffee break. We had a couch up there and I laid down. When I came down, I just couldn't breathe. I worked for a half hour and had to call a cab and get to the doctor's. That was it."[62]

COMMENT: Counsel should focus attention on when the product manufacturer first learned of the product's hazards. This notice helps establish defendant's knowledge of its product's defects.

Officials of the company that manufactured the plastic wrapping material admitted under oath that they first learned of workers' adverse reactions to the product in 1969. Unfortunately, the company made no effort

---

[59] *Id*.

[60] *Id*.

[61] *Id*.

[62] *Id*.

to inform its customers of this hazard until four years later, as revealed in the following excerpt of testimony by the company's quality control manager.[63]

Q. To your knowledge, was 1969 the first year any complaints were received pertaining to the use of the product as an irritant?

A. To my knowledge, it was the first I heard of any.

Q. As part of your responsibility in your department, the department which you took over in 1969, was it your function to make recommendations as to what kind of information you were to pass on to consumers pertaining to your product, namely this resin material?

A. Yes.

Q. Did you, between the years 1969 and 1973, ever suggest to the company that they send out notices to customers regarding the complaints which you had been receiving pertaining to lung irritations and complications?

A. No.

Q. At any time from 1969 to 1973, did you personally ever send a questionnaire or any communication to users of your product to be on the lookout for possible lung irritation problems?

A. No, sir. I did not.

Q. Did you, at any time from 1969 to 1973, suggest that anybody do so?

A. No, sir, not to my knowledge.

This witness conceded that people were complaining of respiratory problems. He explained that the company advised its customers to keep their wire below 300°F because, "there had been some questions raised about the cutting of PVC [polyvinyl chloride] film. We know that HCL comes off as a degradation product and HCL is an irritant, and anything we could do to minimize any of the questions would be in the best interests of everyone."[64]

Four years after it first learned of PVC-related illnesses, the company developed a safer device known as a "cool rod" for cutting its plastic

---

[63] *Schoefield, supra* note 56, testimony of Dr. J, quality control manager, ___________ Chemical Co., the defendant's witness.

[64] *Id.*

wrap. A company official who participated in the company's "cool rod" development admitted to me that "the cutting of the cool rod does totally eliminate any possibility for the development of fumes."[65] Despite this acknowledgment, this official conceded that the company made no effort to recall the hot wires already in use. And despite its acknowledgment of consumer complaints, he admitted that the company did not conduct any tests of its own to determine an association between its product and the complaints of respiratory problems.

Although my client's employer did change to the safer "cool rod" shortly after the plaintiff left her job, the manufacturer made little effort to warn other customers either of its product's hazards or the safer cutting device. The company could have alerted its customers of the hazards of the hot wire method, and the safer alternatives available, by placing warnings on the product itself, or at least on the carton in which the product was packaged. It failed to take either of these remedial actions.

COMMENT: Until such companies realize that an ounce of prevention is worth a pound of cure, people whose lives have been ruined will continue to challenge them through the legal system. It is apparent that only if such companies are held legally accountable will they ever begin to weigh human safety as a factor when they estimate their costs of doing business.

V. Preventing Industrial Product-Related Injuries

§ 9.15 In general

All too often, workplace injuries result from defective industrial products that are not manufactured with proper consideration of the worker's safety. In many cases, product manufacturers and suppliers know the product's hazards, but they fail or refuse to convey this information or to provide adequate warnings to those who need them.

[65] *Id.*

Injury prevention in the workplace requires a concerted effort on the part of all parties involved—product manufacturers, distributors, and suppliers; plant managers and owners; insurance company representatives and inspectors; government officials who establish safety standards and inspect workplace environments to make certain that those standards are adequate and are complied with; and the workers themselves—to make certain that the products are designed with necessary safeguards, that they are marketed with adequate warnings and instructions regarding their hazards and their safe use, that they are used in a manner that maintains their safety, that the overall plant design is conducive to safe operations, and that the workers themselves are informed of the risks posed by the products and environment on which they depend for their livelihood.

§ 9.16 Adequate design

As with consumer products, those products used in the workplace environment must be designed with all available safety features and devices. For example, machines must be permanently guarded; explosive gases must be adequately odorized; and construction equipment must be adequately designed to prevent foreseeable tragedies. There is simply no excuse for marketing industrial products without the safest designs. All parties in the product distribution chain must take the responsibility for making certain that this is done, and that any changes, modifications, or alterations in product design that limit its safety are corrected immediately. Injuries resulting from defectively designed industrial products are foreseeable. All parties have a duty to provide safe machine design to prevent such injuries from occurring.

§ 9.17 Adequate warnings

It is essential that information, instructions, and warnings regarding product hazards be expressly communicated to all parties affected by those products. This can take the form of warnings permanently placed on machinery; warnings placed in training manuals; warnings placed on posters or other visible means of internal plant communication, oral communication through seminars, discussions, training programs; and or other means. There is simply no excuse for failing to convey safe use of industrial equipment, as well as warnings of the consequences of failing to use the equipment in the prescribed manner.

§ 9.18 Adequate plant maintenance

Often the equipment or products brought into a workplace require particular environmental maintenance to ensure their safe use and operation. Explosive gases, for instance, require adequate gas detection systems to stop the flow of gas and sound an alarm before volatile gas can result in catastrophe. It is vital that those parties responsible for supplying such products make certain that the workplace environment is sufficiently protected. It is also vital that those responsible for plant management make the safety of plant employees a paramount consideration when allocating resources. Plant safety must become a priority before tragedy strikes, not after.

§ 9.19 Adequate plant inspection

Many parties are responsible for inspecting industrial sites to promote worker safety. Government officials, insurance company representatives, plant executives, and equipment suppliers must all make adequate and effective inspections to be certain that the working conditions are safe. Those who conduct on-site inspections must be sufficiently trained and alerted to the potential hazards they might find, and the technology involved in plant equipment and supplies. Management must cooperate with inspection representatives to be certain that all aspects of the plant environment are covered. Inspection reports must be comprehensive, detailed, and provide adequate warnings of potentially hazardous conditions to those with authority to act. These inspections must be conducted regularly and frequently. When conditions require remedial action, this action must be taken. Policy-making officials must be held accountable for their failure to respond to warnings of danger.

§ 9.20 Informing workers of their rights

Workers are captive consumers at their workplaces. They must know their rights and be informed of hazards. They must have the power to request action before tragedy strikes, and to seek redress through our legal system against those responsible for defective equipment. Protection must also be provided through legislation. "Right-to-know" laws that clearly describe the hazards posed by workplace chemicals must be adopted. Workers must also be informed about the safety requirements of federal regulations promulgated by the Occupational Safety and Health Administration (OSHA). Although these are only minimal standards, failure to comply with them may be a signal of other practices on the part of plant management or product marketers that threaten workers' safety.

§ 9.21 What can lawyers do?

Injury prevention in the workplace depends on a vigorous and committed pursuit of justice through effective enforcement of stringent safety rules and standards, and the willingness to challenge the system through legal action. Lawyers must recognize this and work to educate workers with regard to their legal rights when they sustain workplace injuries. They must also work to strengthen and press for enforcement of stringent safety standards governing industrial products and workplace environments.

Increased litigation in this field will provide additional pressure on product manufacturers, suppliers, and distributors, as well as plant owners, to take those steps necessary to prevent workplace-related injuries. They must see that the costs of subjecting workers to inferior or defective equipment in workplace environments is simply too high a price to pay.

VI. Litigation Sources: Bibliography

§ 9.22 Selected technical sources

Safeguarding of Mechanical Power Presses, Accidents 5–15, No. 81 (1969).

Improved Safety Devices Curtail Machine Shop Accidents in England, Am. Machinist 130–36 (May 10, 1945).

E. Browning, *Aromatic Hydrocarbons, Toxicity and Metabolism of Industrial Solvents* 1–65 (Elsevier Publishing Co. 1965).

Browning, *Industrial Solvents: The Aromatic and Cyclic Hydrocarbons*, 7 Brit. Med. Bull. 19–22, No. 1–2 (1950).

Firth, *Accidents in the Printing Industry*, 16 Annals of Occupational Hygiene 151–62, No. 2 (Aug. 1973).

Faulkner, *Don't Overlook Operator Safety in Press-Tool Design*, Am. Machinist 121–34 (Sept. 1, 1952).

Garde, *The Effects of Mode of Operation on Press Safety*, Professional Safety 33 (Mar. 1975).

Graves, et al., *Respiratory Effects of Two Types of Solder Flux Used in the Electronics Industry*, 26 J. Occupational Med. 81–85, No. 2 (1984).

Griffin, *Safety for Industrial Robotic Applications*, Professional Safety 22–26 (1983).

Howard, *The History of Occupational Injuries in the United States*, 27 J. Trauma 411–18, No. 6 (1977).

Joint Standing Committee on Safety in the Use of Power Presses, *Seventh Report: Safety in the Use of Press Brakes* (Her Majesty's Stationery Office 1969).

The Roll-Bar Hand, Rollover Injuries of the Upper Extremity, 18 J. Trauma 601–607, No. 8 (Aug. 1978).

MacCollum, *Critical Hazard Analysis of Crane Design* (4th Int'l System Safety Conference Proceedings July 1979).

Meldrum, *The Elimination of Safety Hazards in Press Operations*, General Motors Eng'g J. 15–21 (Nov.-Dec. 1953).

Montgomery, *Machine Guarding*, 74 ASSE J. 57–60, No. 5 (Nov. 1956).

National Safety Council Data Sheet 506, *Masonry Saws (Stationary Single-Blade Type)* (Revision A 1971).

National Safety Council Safe Practices, *Power Presses*, (Pamphlet No. 18 Dec. 1918, revised May 1929, Sept. 1942).

Fork-Lift Accident Checklist, Nat'l Safety News 77 (Apr. 1969).

Ofjalik, *Research Finds Aromatic Amines Exposure Cause of Increased Number of Tumors*, 44 Int'l J. Occupational Health & Safety 46–47, No. 5 (Sept.–Oct. 1975).

The Construction Machine and Power Line Hazard, Professional Safety 15–20 (Sept. 1979).

Quadland, *Reports of Occupational Injuries Attributed to Volatile Solvents*, 12 Industrial Med. 734–37, No. 11 (Nov. 1943).

Vollmer, *Punch Presses Can Be Safe*, Am. Machinist 99–103 (July 3, 1947).

§ 9.23 Selected government sources

Cloe & Breslin, *Occupational Fatalities Related to Scaffolds as Found in Reports of OSHA Fatality/Catastrophy Investigations* (Occupational Safety and Health Administration May 1979).

DHEW, *Criteria for a Recommended Standard. . .Occupational Exposure to Tungsten and Cemented Tungsten Carbide* (Publication No. 77–117 Sept. 1977).

Fattal, Mullen & Hunt, *Analysis of Scaffolding Accident Records and Related Employee Casualties* (National Institute of Occupational Safety and Health, NBSIR 79–19–5555 Jan. 1980).

Kusnetz & Hutchison, eds., *A Guide to Work-Relatedness of Disease* (National Institute of Occupational Safety and Health, Publication 79–116 Jan. 1979).

NASA, *Final Report: Osha Medical and Workplace Surveillance Requirements and Niosh Recommendations (For Employees Exposed to Toxic Substances and Other Work Hazards* (Aug. 1983).

NASA, *Handbook for Industrial Noise Control* (1981).

NASA (Sponsor), *Final Report: Safety and Technical Optimization of Belt Transfer Points with Special Consideration for the Suppression of Noxious and Explosive Dusts* (In German, with English summary, Dec. 1980).

NASA (Sponsor), *Standard Specification for Industrial Safety-Belt Assemblies* (South African Bureau of Standards Nov. 1980).

National Board of Occupational Safety and Health, *Directions Concerning the Construction, Care, and Use of Eccentric Power Presses Including Mechanical Press Brakes* (Directions No. 35 Dec. 1972).

National Institute for Occupational Safety and Health (NIOSH) Certified Equipment List (Sept. 1983).

National Institute for Occupational Health and Safety, *Evaluation of Environmental Instrumentation (Black Globe Thermometer) Project* (1982).

National Institute for Occupational Safety and Health (NIOSH), *Arsine (Arsenic Hydride) Poisoning in the Workplace* (Bulletin 32 Aug. 3, 1979).

National Institute for Occupational Safety and Health, *Criteria for a Recommended Standard . . . Occupational Exposure to Carbon Black* (Publication No. 78–204 Sept. 1978).

Occupational Safety and Health Symposia, National Institute of Occupational Safety and Health, *Occupational Lung Diseases—General Principles and Selected Topics* 103–107 (June 1979).

Science Applications, *Analytical Models for Industrial Gas Burner Design, Part 1, Modeling Methods* (Jan. 1983).

Vira, *Occupational Fatalities Related to Ladders as Found in Reports of OSHA Fatality/Catastrophe Investigations* (Occupational Safety and Health Administration Nov. 1979).

§ 9.24 Selected legal sources

Dangerous Scaffolding, 11 Am. Jur. *P.O.F.2d* 579 (1976).

Failure to Provide Safe Place to Work, 2 Am. Jur. *P.O.F.2d* 517 (1974).

Inherently Dangerous Nature of Work Performed by Independent Contractor, 34 Am. Jur. *P.O.F.2d* 483 (1983).

What Constitutes "Willful" Violation for Purposes of Sections 17(a) and (e) of Occupational Safety and Health Act of 1970, 31 A.L.R. Fed. 551 (1977).

Validity, Construction, and Application of Personal Protective Equipment Subpart of OSHA General Industry Standards, 29 C.F.R. § 1910.132–1910.140, 39 A.L.R. Fed. 141 (1978).

Industrial Accidents Involving Conveyor Belts or Systems, 2 A.L.R. 4th 262 (1980).

When Statute of Limitations Begins to Run As to Cause of Action for Development of Latent Industrial or Occupational Disease, 1 A.L.R. 4th 117 (1980).

Violation of OSHA Regulation as Affecting Tort Liability, 79 A.L.R. 3d 962 (1977).

Industrial or Occupational Disease or Poisoning Under FELA, 30 A.L.R. 3d 735 (1970).

Liability of Manufacturer or Seller for Injury Caused by Industrial or Business Tools, Equipment, or Materials, 78 A.L.R. 3d 594 (1961).

Brown, *Occupational Safety and Health*, 38 Law & Contemp. Probs. 174 (1974).

Mitchell, *Products Liability, Worker's Compensation, and the Industrial Accident*, 14 Duquesne L. Rev. 349 (1976).

Mansfield, *Asbestos: The Insurance Problem*, 15 Forum 860 (1980).

Pomerantz, *Products Liability Insurance in the New Industrial Revolution*, 1980 Ins. L.J. 129 (1980).

Henderson, *Products Liability Disease Litigation: Blueprint for Occupational Safety and Health*, 16 Trial 25 (1980).

Davis, *Interaction of Worker's Compensation and Products Liability*, 15 Trial 31 (1979).

Note, *Use of OSHA in Products Liability Suits Against the Manufacturers of Industrial Machinery*, 11 Val. U.L. Rev. 37 (1976).

§ 9.25 Selected newsletters

Construction Equipment

Distributor Executive Contact
Associated Equipment Distributors
615 W. 22st
Oak Brook, Ill. 60521

Equipment Maintenance
Institute for Equipment Services Newsletter
American Public Works Ass'n
1313 East 60th Street
Chicago, Ill. 60637

Job Safety and Health
The Bureau of National Affairs, Inc.
1231 25th Street, N.W.
Washington, D.C. 20037

Job Safety and Health Report
Business Publishers, Inc.
818 Roeder Road
Suite 711
Silver Spring, Md. 20710

Labor Occupational Health Program—Monitor
Institute of Industrial Relations
University of California
2521 Channing Way
Berkeley, Cal. 94720

Labor Safety Newsletter
National Safety Council
444 North Michigan Ave.
Chicago, Ill. 60611

Occupational Safety and Health Reporter
The Bureau of National Affairs, Inc.
1231 25th Street, N.W.
Washington, D.C. 20037

Safety and Health Report
The Bureau of National Affairs, Inc.
1231 25th Street, N.W.
Washington, D.C. 20037

Society for Occupational and Environmental Health—Letter
806 15th Street, N.W.
Suite 450
Washington, D.C. 20005

Trades and Services Newsletter
National Safety Council
444 North Michigan Ave.
Chicago, Ill. 60601

Machine Tools

NTDPMA Newsletter
National Tool, Die, and Precision Machinery Ass'n
9300 Livingston Road
Washington, D.C. 20022

§ 9.26 Selected laws, regulations, and standards

Statutes

Federal

(1) Occupational Safety and Health Act of 1970, Pub. L. No. 91–596.

(2) Contract Work Hours and Safety Standards Act (Construction Safety Act), Pub. L. No. 87–581 (amended Aug. 13, 1962, Aug. 9, 1969).

States

(1) OSHA approves state plans that may be more stringent than OSHA requirements. Approximately twenty states have developed their own plans.

Regulations

Federal

(1) Occupational Safety and Health Standards, 29 C.F.R. 1910 *et. seq*. (1985).

Selected Federal Standards

(1) Safety Requirements for Scaffolding, 29 C.F.R. 1910.28 (1985).

(2) Powered Platforms, Manlifts, and Vehicle-Mounted Working Platforms, 29 C.F.R. 1910.66 (1985).

(3) Ionizing and Nonionizing Radiation, 29 C.F.R. 1910.96–1910.97 (1985).

(4) Compressed Gases, 29 C.F.R. 1910.101 (1985).

(5) Flammable and Combustible Liquids, 29 C.F.R. 1910.106 (1985).

(6) Explosives and Blasting Agents, LP Gas Storage and Handling, Anhydrous Ammonia Storage and Handling, 29 C.F.R. 1910.109–1910.116 (1985).

(7) Personal Protective Equipment, Storage and Handling, 29 C.F.R. 1910.132 (1985).

(8) Accident Prevention Signs and Tags, 29 C.F.R. 1910.144–1910.149 (1985).

§ 9.27 Selected cases

River v. Stihl, Inc., 434 So. 2d 766 (Ala. 1983), **chain saw**.

Harned v. Dura Corp., 665 P.2d 5 (Alaska 1983), *later app*., 703 P.2d 396 (Alaska 1985), **portable compressed air tank;** jury instruction on industry standards.

Hopkins v. Chip-In-Saw, Inc., 630 F.2d 616 (8th Cir. [Ark.] 1980), **lumber machine;** death of operator; duty to affix warning onto machine itself.

Cipres v. Bonus Bilt, Inc., No. C291776 (Los Angeles, Cal. Cty. Ct. Apr. 20, 1984), 28 ATLA 131 (Apr. 1985), **foldable mail cart;** design defect.

Martinez v. C&C Corp., No. SEC 34153 (Los Angeles, Cal. Cty. Ct. Mar. 15, 1984), 27 ATLA L. Rep. 470 (Dec. 1984), **buffing machine;** defectively designed guards.

Reno v. Champ Corp., No. NWC–76796 (Cal. Super. Ct. Jan. 10, 1983), 26 ATLA L. Rep. 227 (June 1983), **forklift;** collapse; settlement $1.5 million.

Albanese v. Emerson Elec. Co., 552 F. Supp. 694 (D. Del. 1982), **chain saw.**

Ford v. Highlands Ins. Co., 369 So. 2d 77 (Fla. Dist. Ct. App.), *cert. denied*, 378 So. 2d 345 (Fla. 1979), **truck crane;** "obvious danger" doctrine not complete bar to recovery; failure to equip with warning device.

Jarriel v. Skil Corp., No. C–31361 (Ga. Oct. 26, 1984), 28 ATLA L. Rep. 179 (May 1985), **commercial drill;** electrocution; lack of insulation.

Dintelman v. Alliance Machine Co., 117 Ill. App. 3d 344, 72 Ill. Dec. 823, 453 N.E.2d 128 (1983), **crane and trolley;** time limitations; design defect.

Soto v. E.W. Bliss Div. of Gulf & Western Mfg. Co., 116 Ill. App. 3d 880, 72 Ill. Dec. 319, 452 N.E.2d 572 (1983), **punch press;** unreasonably dangerous; lack of warning.

Kozlowski v. General Elec. Co., No. 77 L 12075 (Ill. Cir. Ct. June 13, 1983), 26 ATLA L. Rep. 279 (Aug. 1983), **electrical switch;** wrongful death; settlement $1.25 million.

Newton v. G.F. Goodman & Son, 519 F. Supp. 1301 (N.D. Ind. 1981), **automatic rubber cutting machine;** design defect.

Hoffman v. E.W. Bliss Co., 448 N.E.2d 277 (Ind. 1983), **punch press;** adequacy of instructions for use; duty to warn of latent defect.

Rexrode v. American Laundry Press Co., 674 F.2d 826 (10th Cir. [Kan.]), *cert. denied*, 459 U.S. 862, 103 S. Ct. 137, 74 L. Ed. 2d 117 (1982), **laundry press;** relevancy to other accidents.

Jenkins v. E.I. Du Pont de Nemours, No. 81–52 (E.D. La. Apr. 23, 1982), 26 ATLA L. Rep. 71 (Mar. 1983), **chlorine gas;** gas released from phlange bolts that had not been purged for twenty-eight hours.

Perkins v. Emerson Electric Co., 482 F. Supp. 1347 (W.D. La. 1980), **chain saw;** failure to install known safety devices.

Uloth v. City Tank Corp., 376 Mass. 874, 384 N.E.2d 1188 (1978), **garbage truck;** design defect.

Burnett v. Mackworth G. Rees, Inc., 109 Mich. App. 547, 311 N.W.2d 417 (1981), **punch press;** design defect.

Hall v. Hydraulic Pumps, Inc., No. 81–12–164 (Miss. Cir. Ct. Oct. 7, 1982), 26 ATLA L. Rep. 118 (Apr. 1983), **vacuum tank;** explosion.

Kayser v. Rockwell Graphics Systems, 666 F.2d 1233 (8th Cir. [Mo.] 1982), **high-speed letter press;** design defect.

Soler v. Castmater, Division of H.P.M. Corp., 98 N.J. 137, 484 A.2d 1225 (1984), **die-casting machine;** design defect.

Bexiga v. Havir Mfg. Corp., 60 N.J. 402, 290 A.2d 281 (1972), **ten-ton power punch press;** hand crushed; inadequate safety devices.

Queiros v. Miller Electric Co., No. L51272–81 (N.J. Super. Ct. Apr. 3, 1984), 27 ATLA L. Rep. 371 (Oct. 1984), **utility light**.

Gross v. Tracy Val Co., No. 81 CIV 6121 (S.D.N.Y. Nov. 8, 1984), 28 ATLA L. Rep. 179 (May 1985), **record press;** hand crushed.

Micallef v. Miehle Co., 39 N.Y.2d 376, 348 N.E.2d 571, 384 N.Y.S.2d 115 (1976), **high-powered photo-offset printing machine;** contributory fault is no defense if encounter with known risk is usual job practice.

Victorson v. Bock Laundry Machine Co., 37 N.Y.2d 395, 335 N.E.2d 275, 373 N.Y.S.2d 39 (1975), **laundry centrifuge extractor;** remote users; strict time limitations; runs from injury.

Kritz v. Mister Machine Co., 69 Ohio St. 2d 460, 23 Ohio Ops. 3d 403, 432 N.E.2d 814, *cert. denied*, 459 U.S. 857, 103 S. Ct. 127, 74 L. Ed. 2d 110 (1982), **punch press;** design defect.

Walker v. Armco, 446 U.S. 740, 100 S. Ct. 1978, 64 L. Ed. 2d 659, *affirming* 592 F.2d 1133 (10th Cir. [Okla.] 1980), **nail;** shattered; eye injury.

Stewart v. Scott-Kitz Miller Co., 626 P.2d 329 (Okla. Ct. App. 1981), **forklift;** design defect in bolts.

Christner v. E.W. Bliss Co., 524 F. Supp. 1122 (M.D. Pa. 1981), **punch press;** custom in trade and safety standards admissible.

Dunne v. Philadelphia Gas Works, No. 79–10–2488 (Pa. Ct. C.P. Apr. 22, 1983), 26 ATLA L. Rep. 118 (Apr. 1983), **sewage treatment facility;** gas explosion.

Kerby v. Xomox, No. H 80–2002 (S.D. Tex. 1983), 26 ATLA L. Rep. 83 (Mar. 1983), **flow control valve**.

Wood v. Stihl, Inc., 705 F.2d 1101 (9th Cir. [Wash.] 1983), **chain saw**.

Santee v. Eastern Association Coal Corp., No. 80–1403 (W. Va. Cir. Ct. June 25, 1982), 26 ATLA L. Rep. 21 (Jan. 1983), **hydraulic jack;** collapse in coal mine.

Chapter 10

OPENING NEW DOORS: LANDMARK LITIGATION

KLUWER LITIGATION LIBRARY REFERENCES

HARLEY & MAGEE, WHAT'S IT WORTH? A GUIDE TO CURRENT PERSONAL INJURY AWARDS AND SETTLEMENTS.

JEANS, LITIGATION: Chapter 4, *Discovery*; Chapter 8, *Direct Examination*; Chapter 9, *Direct Examination of Expert Witnesses*; Chapter 13, *Cross-Examination*; Chapter 14, *Cross-Examination of Expert Witnesses*.

SMITH & MALANDRO, COURTROOM COMMUNICATION STRATEGIES: Chapter 1, *Impression Formation in the Courtroom*; Chapter 2, *Persuasive Strategies in the Courtroom*; Chapter 5, *Preparing for Effective Courtroom Communication*; Chapter 8, *Direct Examination: Presenting the Evidence with Impact*; Chapter 9, *Cross-Examination: Controlling the Case*.

§ 10.01 Introduction

The common law is most vibrant and alive when it is molded to fit new fact patterns and to bring justice to those injured in what might otherwise seem to be unusual ways. I have been privileged to represent clients whose cases against purveyors of defective products resulted in landmark litigation, securing justice for my clients and establishing new law to protect consumers in the future.

The three cases presented in this chapter reflect a most challenging and exciting aspect of my products liability practice. In the first case, the United States District Court in Boston (affirmed by the First Circuit U.S. Court of Appeals[1]) took a major step in protecting children against hazardous products intended for use in the home environment by holding that a child's natural, and sometimes bizarre, but foreseeable behavior must be taken into account by a product manufacturer as a necessary element of the product's home use environment when designing the

[1] Larue v. National Union Electric Co., 571 F.2d 51 (1st Cir. 1978), jury award of $125,000 reduced to $93,750 because of the plaintiff's contributory negligence.

product. The court recognized that children's behavior foreseeably includes the tendency to follow impulses to play. Thus, where children are involved or are likely to be involved, the manufacturer who owes the duty of ordinary care must take this tendency into account.

In the second case, the Massachusetts Supreme Judicial Court established the right of consumers to bring suit against purveyors of defective homes and recognized their right to a trial by a jury of their peers under the state's stringent Consumer Protection Laws, based on their claim of fraud and misrepresentation in the sale of their homes.[2]

The third case established that a textbook publisher can be held accountable for the negligent publishing of a junior high school science textbook that led to devastating burn injuries of a student in her science classroom when one of the book's experiments created a violent explosion.[3] It was the first time that a textbook publisher had been held liable for negligent publishing that resulted in a dramatic personal injury.

§ 10.02 Case study: The case of the vacuum cleaner with teeth[4]

Children are blessed with active imaginations and a high degree of inventiveness. All too often, these basic qualities of childhood lead youngsters to have contact with household products in ways we might at first glance consider bizarre or unusual. Such was the case when the mother of a young boy came to my office and described her son's traumatic experience with her household vacuum cleaner. She told me how her eleven-year-old son had lacerated his penis while he was playing on her vacuum cleaner. She had changed the cleaner's filter the night before leaving its top open with the machine plugged in overnight. Her two children had been alone at home when the incident occurred. Her son had been in his pajamas, sitting on the machine playing "horsey" when the machine suddenly turned on. Somehow his penis made contact with the machine's whirling fan. The two children ran to a neighbor's house for help, leaving a bloody trail along their path. When the boy's father got home, he saw the blood—everywhere. When he examined the machine he found the penis head and flesh in the motor housing.

Many attorneys hearing this mother's story may have thought, at least

---

[2] Burnham v. Mark IV Homes, Inc., 287 Mass. 575, 441 N.E.2d 1027 (1982).

[3] Carter v. Rand McNally & Co., No 76-1864F (D. Mass. Sept. 1980).

[4] *See Larue*, *supra* note 1.

initially, "Come on, now. Not all injuries are compensable." They may have stopped right there and not taken the case. My colleagues who knew me expected something more—and they were right.

§ 10.03 —Analysis of case

My experience with the common law led me to approach this case not from the perspective of "what was that kid doing playing with the cleaner like that?" or "why did his mother leave the vacuum plugged in?", but rather as a case of failure to guard. There is a common law duty of care to protect persons from moving machinery. Does it matter whether the human part being protected is a finger, toe, hair, or other extremity, including a penis? No! If there is moving machinery that exposes a human being to a hazard, the common law does not demand that the plaintiff meet the burden of predicting the exact nature of the injury that occurred. On the contrary, it is clear that under the common law, it is not essential that the precise manner in which injuries might have occurred or were sustained be foreseeable or foreseen.

COMMENT: Defendants will frequently argue that the injury was unforeseeable. The plaintiff should show that the exposure to the risk was perfectly foreseeable. A product is used in a context, the home environment, by real people, including children. It is not used in a vacuum. The manufacturer should foresee this context, and its dangers.

The more I thought about it, the more I realized that this case was not impossible. It might be a challenge, but isn't that what the practice of law is all about—challenging the purveyors of products that could be designed for safety to avoid these kinds of injuries around the house? Despite the initial raised eyebrows from my colleagues and staff, I accepted the case. Little did I know that the information I would uncover would reveal as clear a case of negligence on the part of this appliance's manufacturer as I have found in any other case in my files, and that the case would result in a landmark decision protecting the rights of America's children to a safe home environment!

§ 10.04 —Evidence regarding availability of safer model

Some of the most important evidence came from the defendant's own executives. Under my cross-examination, one senior executive admitted that human contact with the appliance's engine parts was possible, and that the company could have provided a safety screen to shield the motor fan from user contact. Perhaps the most damaging testimony of all came when this executive admitted that safer models, equipped with guards to prevent foreseeable human contact, were manufactured for the company's overseas markets where it was required by law. With no such requirements in the United States, the safer machines were not even offered to American consumers. The following testimony reveals this company's culpable practices.[5]

Q. Certainly you would have to tell me that it was foreseeable in some way or the another that somewhere along the line a part of the human anatomy, whether it be a finger or what, might come in contact with that fan?

A. Possibly, but unlikely.

Q. How would you guard against that possibility; how could you make it safer to guard against a part of the human anatomy, like a finger or a penis, coming in contact with the machine?

A. It's possible to redesign it, yes.

Q. How would that be accomplished?

A. [T]here are many approaches . . . it could be moved away from the fan a little bit, some of the apertures made somewhat smaller, the amount smaller would be dictated by air performance.

Q. Are you aware of your company making a canister-type vacuum cleaner for industrial or commercial use that has the housing completely encased?

A. I have seen them, not completely encased. It can't be completely.

Q. What have you seen that fits that particular description?

A. I have seen a cover over the unit with holes in it.

Q. What model was that?

---

[5] *Larue*, *supra* note 1, testimony of Mr. B, Chief Engineer for the defendant.

A. The 4001 is one.

Q. Do you still make it?

A. No.

Q. In what period of time was that made?

A. During this same period, I wouldn't have a time sequence on it.

Q. Was that for home use, also?

A. Yes.

Q. Was that a canister?

A. Yes.

Q. How was the thing filtered in that connection?

A. The filter was on top of a metal can that fit over the motor . . . that had small perforations.

Q. Even if you took off the top, it would have a filter holder?

A. No.

Q. So the filter was fixed right on top of that?

A. Right.

Q. This housing that was used in the 4001 for the motor, which you placed the filter on top of, was it a metal housing with small holes?

A. No.

Q. You couldn't fit a finger through it?

A. No.

Q. No part of the human anatomy could come in contact with the fan unit?

A. Unless you took it off.

Q. How was it fastened?

A. With screws.

Q. It was permanently affixed. . . ?

A. Right.

Q. And it wasn't necessary to remove it to change the filter, or whatever?

A. No, just the same as the 842A [plaintiff's model], it wasn't necessary.

Q. Except for the difference that with the 842A you could fit a finger through the apparatus, correct?

A. You could.

Q. Was the 4001 unit safer from the point of view of not being able to put a finger in it?

A. Yes.

* * *

Q. Was [the 4001] competitive with other series?

A. It was used for export.

Q. Where did you export it?

A. France . . . and Sweden.

Q. Why was the design—

* * *

A. The regulatory agency required different construction, not only that, but other items.

Q. Which country's regulatory agency required [the motor housing] be encased that way?

A. I believe it's ___________ of Sweden.

Q. What does that stand for?

A. It's a regulatory group.

Q. Were any of these manufactured in this country?

A. Not to my knowledge.

Q. Were they available for sale through your dealers?

A. Not to my knowledge.

Q. Was a choice given the American purchaser, so that they could have purchased the 4001 had they been aware of it?

A. Not to my knowledge.

§ 10.05 —Evidence regarding safety shut-off device

Many accidents, such as this one, could also have been avoided if the manufacturer had incorporated a simple safety shut-off device, or interlock, on the machine. This device was available and had been used regularly on electrical appliances for twenty-five years. This device would automatically shut the machine off as soon as the lid was lifted. A company vice-president admitted that this company simply did not consider safety interlocks for the plaintiff's machine, that the company had never used such a device and never considered using it and, to his knowledge, had never even conducted any cost analyses to determine whether it would be beneficial for the company to adopt that safety device into the design of its machines.[6] Another company official admitted that the addition of an interlock device to the appliance would have added to the machine's safety, yet the company simply did not consider it a required part.[7]

According to the plaintiff's expert engineer, the additional cost of incorporating an interlock on the plaintiff's cleaner model would have been twenty-five to thirty cents.[8]

COMMENT: This company compounded its injustice to consumers by providing no warnings on the machine concerning its hazardous nature and its ability to lacerate any human extremity that came near it. The advertising promotions that accompanied the machine were silent regarding its dangers. The question of safety was simply never mentioned. The only labels provided were stick-on instructions about machine upkeep and the use of correct vacuum bags. In short, there were instructions to protect the machine, but none to protect the safety of its users. The plaintiff's lawyer must emphasize such gross failure to provide for safety.

---

[6] *Larue*, *supra* note 1, testimony of Mr. D, vice president.

[7] *Larue*, *supra* note 1, testimony of Mr. B.

[8] *Larue*, *supra* note 1, testimony of Mr. P.

§ 10.06 —Cross-examination of consulting engineer

As in so many products liability cases, important testimony supporting the plaintiff's case was provided during the cross-examination of the defendant's own expert witness. In this case, a consulting engineer was called to the stand by the defense to state that in his opinion the plaintiff's injury could not have been caused by the motor fan. Responding to defense counsel's direct examination, this witness stated:

> The cutting edge of the fan motor is recessed an inch and an eighth below the surface of this filter support. Under the circumstances . . . the contact with the penis under these conditions, I do not see how it could have occurred.[9]

When it was my turn to cross-examine this witness, I was able to transform his apparently damaging testimony into supportive testimony for the plaintiff's case. Under probing questions, he was forced to admit that a human extremity could be injured in this machine, that it was foreseeable that children would play with it in a home environment, that warnings of its hazardous nature would have been beneficial, and that the plaintiff's injury would not have occurred if the machine was designed with a protective guard. Following are excerpts from this important testimony.[10]

Q. And is that fan housing dangerous?

A. In normal use, it is not dangerous. In this use, with this filter support, it is not dangerous.

Q. Would you say it presents a hazard to someone's fingers?

A. I would say so, yes, sir.

Q. So in that context, it is dangerous, is it not?

A. In that context, yes, sir.

Q. And, of course, the vacuum cleaner is used in the context of a home environment, isn't it?

A. A vacuum cleaner is used in a home environment, yes, sir.

Q. It is foreseeable that a vacuum cleaner will come in contact with children in play, correct?

A. Yes, children will come in contact with a vacuum cleaner.

---

[9] *Larue*, *supra* note 1, testimony of Mr. P, expert witness for the defendant.

[10] *Id.*

Q. And in your experience in ordinary household products, based upon your qualifications, preventive engineering means that we try to guard against accidents or injuries that could occur to children in a household, correct?

A. That's an industrial standard, but perfection is never 100%.

Q. I'm not talking about industrial standards. I'm talking about a household.

A. Even a household. Look at the accidents that happen around the house.

Q. That's correct. We try to eliminate accidents if we can with good sound engineering practices, right?

A. Yes, not keeping a vacuum cleaner plugged in.

Q. That would be something to communicate to the housewife?

A. Not keeping an appliance plugged in.

Q. Does that cause an electrical hazard?

A. I think its common sense, whether it's an iron, a vacuum cleaner, or anything else, that people shouldn't keep appliances plugged in when they are not used.

Q. Do you think common sense would indicate to anyone, an average child or an average housewife, that under that filter there is a piece of machinery which would cause an amputating injury?

A. I don't think a housewife or a child would be [able to discern] what is under a piece of machinery, no.

Q. So we agree they couldn't have that knowledge?

A. No, I wouldn't expect them to have that knowledge.

Q. Therefore, if there was a hazard under that filter holder, would it be good, sound practice to at least warn them about the hazard?

A. Well, warnings are always beneficial; but the hazard only becomes operational if the appliance is plugged in. I perceive that no warning should be on a product in this part of the twentieth century telling people to unplug an appliance.

Q. And yet you know, don't you, that in the ordinary course of a busy household day that occasionally people might be changing filter pads while the appliance is plugged in. Isn't that foreseeable?

A. You could change the filter pad with an appliance operating because there is a bottom filter pad underneath it. This is a two-part pad.

* * *

Q. You wouldn't want anyone to put a hand in this area while it is moving, right?

A. Of course not.

Q. Because it could cause an amputating injury, correct?

A. That is part of the reason.

Q. In view of the very severe risk, there is a warning. It says "warning" on that cover, right?

A. That warning, as I read it, only relates to damage to the equipment if the filters were dirty, and that could be a consequence of causing an electrical fire.

Q. If you were going to warn against damage to the equipment, do you think at the same time, under these circumstances, it would have been prudent to warn about the possibility of an amputating injury to the person?

A. Sir, every day at the hospital I see children who have been poisoned and warnings are all over the bottle. You can't warn against every possible contingency. Certainly warnings are beneficial.

Q. They would have been beneficial here, right?

A. Sure.

Q. But the best method to protect against amputating injury, I would suspect, would be to put a guard on it such as the Swedish version of this vacuum cleaner, which is Plaintiff's Exhibit 6. [*Ed. Note*: Exhibit not reproduced.] With respect to the ____________ cleaner, there is a guard on that, right?

A. Yes.

Q. If that guard were in place, there is no question that the injury to this young boy could not have occurred, correct?

A. That is a fact.

§ 10.07 —Cross-examination of medical witness

The most significant moment of the case came when I had the opportunity to cross-examine the defendant's expert medical witness. By attacking this expert's conclusions with probing questions, I was able to expose his lack of knowledge concerning how the product worked and the fact that he failed to consider that blood was found on the product's motor unit.[11]

Q. Dr. ____________, you stated as one of the reasons for your opinion about the hose that you had a prior case involving a vacuum, is that right?

A. That's correct.

Q. And that was the only reason you gave, is that right?

A. That was the only one I stated.

Q. If you had not had that prior case, I would suspect you wouldn't have known that that plastic hose was capable of permanent injury, is that a fair statement?

A. Yes.

Q. So you, as a professional person, wouldn't be able to tell if a vacuum cleaner was on and if a child, for whatever purpose, inserted ____________ into the end of the vacuum cleaner, you wouldn't know, without any prior experience, that that would cause injury, correct?

A. Correct.

Q. And you learned that from your experience as a physician?

A. Correct.

Q. As a physician, one of your responsibilities is—and I know this is true—that you are interested in the prevention of injury or accidents, correct?

A. Yes.

Q. Did you do any tests with the end of that hose to determine if your thesis was right?

A. No.

[11] *Larue*, *supra* note 1, testimony of Dr. R, urologist, expert witness for the defendant.

Q. Was the other vacuum cleaner a similar make, was it a ______________?

A. I have no idea.

Q. Do you know what design it was?

A. No.

Q. Do you know what the motor capacity was?

A. No.

Q. Do you know what the suction capacity was?

A. No.

Q. So you don't know then, as a matter of fact, whether this particular vacuum cleaner is capable of producing that kind of harm without that information, correct?

A. Correct.

Q. And you weren't provided that information, correct?

A. Correct.

* * *

Q. Did you see any tests to determine what the hazards of the motor housing itself were?

A. No.

Q. Showing you Plaintiff's Exhibit 1, there is a yellow filter holder on top of it, correct?

A. Yes.

Q. Did you see that in operation?

A. No.

Q. When it was plugged in?

A. No.

Q. Not at any time?

A. Well, I saw a similar vacuum to this plugged in with the motor running.

Q. Do you know what the capacity of the motor housing is to cut?

A. No.

Q. Were you given any information in that regard?

A. No.

Q. Do you specifically know where on this unit, Plaintiff's Exhibit 1, the boy was sitting?

A. No, just that he was sitting on the top.

Q. He could have been sitting over the center back line, correct?

A. Yes.

Q. And if he was, of course, that would change your opinion because the position of his penis would be changed?

A. Yes.

Q. To what extent would it have changed your opinion?

A. If he were not in a squatting position?

Q. Yes.

A. And were more prone, so that his abdomen was facing down on the machine with his penis hanging down, then it would change the position.

Q. Oh, if he fell forward?

A. Well, he would be in the prone position at that time.

* * *

Q. Did you examine this hose prior to testifying to see whether it was a cutting edge?

A. This particular hose right here that you are holding?

Q. Yes.

A. No.

Q. Did you see any reference in any of the material that you were given or any of the records to indicate that there was any blood or other material found at the end of that hose?

A. No.

Q. If I told you the only testimony was that there was no blood in the area of the filter holder on Plaintiff's Exhibit 1 and that his penis, as counsel pointed out, was found in the area of the motor housing, but that there was no evidence of blood found on the end of the hose, would that make a difference to you?

A. Yes.

Q. And why would that make a difference?

A. Because if the injury would have occurred at the end of the house, naturally, there would have been some bleeding at the point of injury.

* * *

Q. You told us previously that you didn't know what the capacity of that vacuum cleaner was in terms of horsepower, its suction, and its various other physical characteristics, and you say this information was not given to you, is that correct?

A. That's correct.

Q. You don't know whether it was as powerful as the prior vacuum cleaner that you were involved with, is that correct?

A. That's correct.

Q. And you also said that it would affect your opinion if indeed the evidence was such that there was no blood or no evidence of blood on the end of the hose, did you not?

A. I did.

Q. You indicated earlier that you didn't have information with respect to the vacuum cleaner's capacity, its horsepower, its drawing power, its suction power, the type of motor, the type of voltage used—information about whether the lid was up or down and what its suction capacity is when it is up compared to when it is down. You indicated that you based your opinion, at least in major part, on your experience, which you related to us, with a prior vacuum cleaner. You told us you didn't remember the vacuum cleaner; you don't know what kind of vacuum cleaner it was, what the power was, or what the capacity was compared to this domestic vacuum cleaner. You indicated that you would want to know those things in order to render a definitive opinion in this case, is that a fair statement?

A. No, I don't think so.

Q. You don't need to know any of those things?

A. I don't think I indicated that.

Q. Do you need to know any of those things to render an opinion in this case?

A. About the actual mechanics of the vacuum cleaner?

Q. Sure.

A. I think they would be helpful, yes.

Q. Why would that be helpful?

A. I don't claim to be an engineer. But it has been my experience and my opinion that a domestic vacuum cleaner, as you so stated, is capable of causing the injuries so described.

* * *

Q. Is it fair to say that in order to give the opinion asked of you, you would at least want to know those things?

A. I would be more interested in knowing whether or not there was blood, as you so stated, on the end of the tube.

Q. Well, if I told you that there was no evidence of blood at the end of the hose, would that affect your opinion?

A. Yes.

Q. Why?

A. It would be more evidence that that part of the machine was directly involved in the injury.

Q. And without that evidence, you wouldn't be willing to state the opinion you did?

A. Not necessarily. . . . It is possible for it to have happened, but it would be helpful to know whether or not there was blood there.

Q. Possible for it to have happened, but certainly, it wouldn't be probable to have happened without that evidence, correct?

A. It wouldn't be probable for it to happen without that.

Q. Without the evidence of blood?

A. True.

This witness' responses were so revealing and so destructive to his credibility that the court upheld the plaintiff's motion to strike the witness' entire testimony because his conclusions were based on possibilities without adequate supporting evidence, rather than on probabilities and reasonable medical certainty.

§ 10.08 —Experiment demonstrating hazardous nature of vacuum

In representing the victims of hazardous products, real evidence is always the most effective, when it is available, in demonstrating the product's defects to members of a jury. To get the point across, trial lawyers must sometimes engage in novel strategies.

I had no films, no slides, no ready means of demonstrating this appliance's treacherous and hazardous threats to human body parts. What did I do? I devised an experiment. The vacuum cleaner and a pocketful of hot dogs became my apparatus. I said to the judge something along these lines: "Your Honor, I'm going to do a demonstration. I don't have any films. I don't have any pictures. I can't show how this hazard works. I don't know any way to demonstrate it. The fans go around so fast you can't see them. I know it's a little gross but we'll condition the jury for it. I think this is the only way I've got of showing the cutting capacity of these blades."

His Honor asked the defense counsel for any objections. To my surprise, he had none. He perhaps thought, "Now Swartz has gone too far," or "He's getting desperate, now. He's overtrying his case. Let him make a fool of himself." Thus, armed with a breastpocket full of different sized hot dogs and a working vacuum cleaner, I walked to the center of the courtroom, in full view of an extremely curious jury. I turned the machine on and, one by one, fed the hot dogs into its rapidly whirling blades. Confetti-sized bits of meat soon filled this federal courtroom.

The impact was dramatic. The jurors witnessed the cutting power of this appliance firsthand. They saw that the hazard was so severe and so treacherous that from the point of view of a defect, it really makes little difference whether the "appendage" involved is one's toe, finger, or penis.

§ 10.09 —Conclusion

When the jury returned its verdict, it found the defendant negligent for manufacturing a hazardous machine. On appeal, the U.S. Court of Appeals for the First Circuit stated the doctrine of a manufacturer's duty to design a product intended for use in a home environment in which the play of children may include reasonably foreseeable misuse of the product:

> In determining what kind of reasonable foreseeable misuse might arise from the play of children [we recognize that] children as old as

> thirteen years of age are likely to act dangerously to themselves even though, upon reflection, they know better. . . . It should be emphasized that it is unessential that the *precise* manner in which injuries might have occurred, or were sustained, be foreseeable, or foreseen. It is sufficient that there is a reasonable generalized gamut of greater than ordinary dangers of injury and that the sustaining of injury was within this range. . . .
>
> It was undisputed that [defendant] realized its ____________ vacuum cleaner would be used in households where children would be present and appreciated the risks of children playing with the insides of the machine. Based on all the evidence presented at trial, there was a sufficient basis for holding that the vacuum cleaner presented an unreasonable risk of harm to children who might reasonably be foreseen to explore and fiddle with the device. The inadvertent intrusion of [the plaintiff's] penis into the fan, perhaps the product of the machine's suction, fell within this class of dangers, even though the precise circumstances of the accident might have been improbable.[12]

§ 10.10 Case study: The case of the homes that leaked[13]

Few cases in my practice have provided the opportunities to forge new law and expand the rights of consumers for safe products than the recent case in which nine families brought suit against a manufacturer of defective mobile homes. The field of housing transactions has traditionally been one of the last areas of resistance to the growth in products litigation. Realty transactions were marked by the wide gulf between the dashed expectations of the purchasing public and the prevailing principle of "let the buyer beware." While evolving case law had recognized the rights of injured consumers to seek redress against the manufacturer and seller of defective housing, the facts in this case and the trial court's holdings presented the prime opportunity to steer the law on a further course away from the traditional barriers and to take advantage of the state's stringent consumer protection laws to seek justice for these plaintiffs.

Several Massachusetts families purchased mobile homes in a new housing development. The homes were known as "double-wides" because of their construction, which involved attaching two separate pieces together into one unit with resulting extra space inside. They were man-

[12] *See Larue*, *supra* note 1, at 56–57.

[13] *Burnham*, *supra* note 2.

ufactured at the defendant's plant, shipped to dealers' lots, and then shipped to purchasers' housing sites; they came with a ninety day manufacturer's warranty. These consumers didn't know when they purchased their homes that their roofs would spring leaks after the first rainy or snowy day, or would get so bad that they would produce almost unlivable conditions.

§ 10.11 —Analysis of case

After months and, in some cases, years of asking for, and then demanding, adequate roof repairs by the manufacturer, these homeowners sought justice through the courts. Some wanted their roofs replaced; some had already replaced the defective roofs themselves and now wanted to be compensated for their expenses. All wanted to be compensated for the damage to their property—the doors that wouldn't close, floors warped by persistent puddles, frozen pipes and windows, and walls so saturated with water that electrical circuitry was perilously exposed. All charged the defendant with negligence in the design, distribution, and marketing of their homes, as well as with a breach of implied warranty of habitability. What made this case unique was the plaintiffs' additional charge that the defendant violated the state's consumer protection laws, and their demand of a trial by jury to determine whether the defendant had violated that law. While other courts had broken the traditional barriers of privity and caveat emptor in real estate and housing transactions by holding strict liability, negligence, and breach of warranty applicable in cases of defective housing, this case represented something new for the consumer.

Massachusetts' consumer protection law provides consumers with redress against misrepresentation and nondisclosure in product transactions, as well as attorneys fees and double (or treble) damages as penalties against those parties knowingly violating the law.[14]

The trial court granted the defendant's motion to dismiss that count of the complaint charging a violation of the consumer protection statute. After reviewing the facts and the trial transcripts, my instincts and experience told me that if Massachusetts' highest court could be convinced that these plaintiffs had a right to a jury determination of the defendant's statutory violations, that new law could be forged for these consumers and a new era of consumer protection opened in the state.

[14] MASS. GEN. LAWS ANN. ch. 93A (West 1984).

My instincts were right. When you read those portions of the revealing trial transcript that follow, you will understand the conditions under which the plaintiffs were forced to live and the practices of this defendant in marketing these products knowing full well their defective condition.[15]

> **COMMENT:** For the trial lawyer, the opportunity to create new law is one that provides an enormous challenge, and it is an enormously gratifying part of one's products liability practice. Given the historical intransigence of the law to protect consumers in the field of housing transactions, this challenge became a crusade for lawyers in search of justice.

---

§ 10.12 —Testimony of plaintiff-homeowner regarding unlivable conditions

Mrs. H was one of the first of the plaintiffs to purchase the defendant's home. Portions of her testimony vividly illustrate the conditions that she and the other plaintiffs had to live under, and demonstrate why she chose to bring suit against the defendants in this case.[16]

> About a week and a half after we moved in, we noticed a large sagging in our dining room ceiling. My husband took down a little piece of the panel and water just gushed out onto the floor. I called [the installer]. He sent a man down who drained the water. Then he patched the room. It was fine for about a week, then it started all over again, springing leaks everywhere around my front window, all the seams would leak down through the middle of the living room. It just didn't stop.
>
> I called [the company's representative] who sent down two more men. They put coating on the roof again. This time it lasted two or

---

[15] The dramatic examinations and cross-examinations in this case study were conducted by two fellow Massachusetts trial lawyers, Jan Schlictmann, Esq., and Marguerite Dolan, Esq.

[16] *Larue*, *supra* note 1, testimony of Mrs. H, plaintiff. Several other injured consumers were co-plaintiffs in this litigation.

> three months before it started leaking again. It was leaking all over the place—coming down through the side walls and onto the floors. My living room was just a mess! My rug was saturated all the time. I called him again, he sent men who patched the roof again, and it just kept leaking. After that I couldn't reach the company again. Mr. ____________ was not available and no one would come out to my home.

Mrs. H then described her first winter in her new home.[17]

> Ice would build up on the roof and sides of the home and it just stayed there. The windows were sealed with ice. My back door sometimes froze so solid I had to chop it to get in and out. It would seal the whole door. The door warped real bad and I had a space through the middle of it. It was just terrible. None of my windows would close. They were all warped by the ice. Ice got in between the sealing parts of the windows and they just wouldn't lock up tight. Water was coming down the side walls; my floors started rotting out. I tried to reach the company, but Mr. ____________ was never available. He left messages that he'd get back to me, but he never did. I wrote a letter to the company, but it was never answered.

Then she described the extent of damage to her home's interior.[18]

> All my ceilings were damaged, my paneling in my kitchen became completely warped out of shape. The back door was a total mess, we couldn't close it properly—at one point we had to tie it to keep it shut. My front door paneling is stained. The floor is rotted so bad it is beginning to give way. It keeps peeling and the holes keep getting larger. I have a lot of damage on the floors and the walls. Every winter, my pipes freeze. They break under the home and are always leaking in the kitchen. My kitchen faucet rotted, and fell through the kitchen counter.

Frustrated at her failure to get help, she eventually took matters into her own hands.[19]

> I repaired a lot of the problems myself—my husband and I coated the roof four times ourselves; my husband installed a new water heater; I have patched floors and put on numerous moldings around

---

[17] *Id.*

[18] *Id.*

[19] *Id.*

> the windows and doorways; we put the back door on; we've put combination doors on; we've chopped windows; we've had to paint numerous ceilings; we put boards up to hold the living room ceilings up; we patched pipes, put heat tape on them, and put plastic around them; I've had to replace my living room rug; this year I replaced all the windows except for those in my living room and dining room; I've had to replace the floor registers for my furnaces as they kept rusting out and the inner flaps would fall out from them; I've had to reseal my toilet three times; and we've had to replace the kitchen counter tops and the kitchen faucet.

This plaintiff estimated that she and her husband spent more than 1,500 hours doing repairs to survive in their own home. Even then, the conditions became unbearable at times. She recalls, "my roof was so bad it was unlivable. I had buckets on the floor to catch the water."[20]

§ 10.13 —Expert testimony regarding roof defects

Testimony by a general contractor-roofer regarding the defects of plaintiffs' roofs drew a graphic picture for the jury of the causal connection between the product and the plaintiffs' plight.[21]

> Q. Mr. H, do you have an opinion as to what caused the roof leaks and the ice formations that you testified to previously?
>
> A. In my opinion, it is the general construction of the modular home roof. Start with the roof supports. They are inadequate with 2 x 2, sixteen inches on center to take the live load and dead load of ice and snow, and the weight of the roof itself. . .
>
> Q. What is the basis of your opinion?
>
> A. It would be the lack of an overhang on the edge of the modular home, which created the ice down the side of the windows and the doors.
>
> The size of the gutter, which was installed on the eave edge—as a matter of fact, all edges of the modular home had the same size gutter. The pitch of the room which is an inch and a half to twelve to the bottom of that beam cap, it's based two inches to the top of the beam cap, which is a very low pitch for the New England area, the tremendous heat loss from the ceiling to the galvanized decking

---

[20] *Id.*

[21] *Burnham*, *supra* note 2, testimony of Mr. H, expert witness called by the plaintiffs.

created very large ice build-up on the edge of the room which would create a dam on the edge of the room.

So, when the water melted from above and flowed toward the ice on the edge of the roof, it creates a dam on the edge.

So, if you have a two to twelve inch pitch, if you add eight inches of ice and eight inches of water backed up behind that ice, then the water would be four feet up the edge of the roof right here.

This would create a tremendous load on the roof decking which spans sixteen inches, the roof decking which is two feet wide, and truss sixteen inches, would create sags with your expansion and contraction of galvanized decking running both vertically and horizontally. It wouldn't take much to open the seam of this and if the seam was under water as it opened up, the water would flow right into the modular home. The roof vents sometimes are located within four or five feet of the edges of the modular home; the water got built up so high, it would get in those vents, would cause water problems right there. This is part of the flashing problem.

If the ice builds up further up the roof right at the beam cap which joins the two modular sections together, as the beam cap flashing comes down over the decking, in my opinion the way the roofers would do it in the New England area it should come down further onto the roof right there so it would allow water to come up underneath and leak through the beam cap where the two sections come together.

§ 10.14 —Testimony regarding company's failure to train its dealers

Mr. W was an executive in charge of design and engineering for the defendant during the time that these homes were manufactured. He testified that, to his knowledge, the defendant did not provide any programs to train its dealers in the proper assembly of its homes, or provide instructions to the homeowner regarding proper assembly. Yet he admitted that it would be helpful for the homeowner to have had that information.[22]

Similarly, a company vice president admitted the company's failure to

[22] *Burnham*, *supra* note 2, testimony of Mr. W, witness called by the plaintiff.

train its dealers:[23]

Q. There was no formal program?

A. No formal program.

Q. You didn't train dealers in the installation of the home?

A. At their request we would train them.

Q. They had to request you to train them?

A. Yes.

Q. You didn't go out and train them?

A. No.

Q. In fact, you sold the homes to dealers who you didn't train in the installation of the homes, is that correct?

A. That's correct.

A sales manager for the defendant also conceded this company's failure to train its sales personnel.[24]

Q. Do you know if the company in 1973, or at any time prior to that, had any program for its dealers to train them in the proper assembly of the home?

A. Not to my knowledge.

Q. Were the salesmen, in your opinion, qualified to answer questions that might be directed at them by dealers pertaining to the assembly of the ____________ homes?

A. I do not know that.

Q. Well, you didn't train them in assembly, other than giving them the assembly instructions, correct?

A. Yes.

Q. So, I'm asking you whether the training program that you set up for your salesmen was directed toward sales or toward the technical aspects of the homes.

A. At that time, it was directed toward sales.

Q. Back in 1972 and 1973, do you have any knowledge of any in-

---

[23] *Burnham*, *supra* note 2, testimony for Mr. B, witness called by the defendant, examined by the plaintiff.

[24] *Burnham*, *supra* note 2, testimony of Mr. S, sales manager for the defendant.

structions or directions being given to dealers on the application of roof coating on the double-wide ___________ homes?

A. We did not provide any written instructions on the application.

Q. What about oral instructions?

A. Not really. The roof coating was not a necessary item.

Q. And, in fact, you didn't put it on at the factory.

A. We didn't.

Q. Right?

A. That's correct.

* * *

Q. As far as you know, then, you don't know of any recommendations that a roof coating be put on the roof on the double-wide homes after assembly on the site?

A. No recommendations that I know of.

* * *

Q. Back in 1973, do you feel it would have been helpful to the homeowner to have instructions or directions for use with his home? At least helpful?

A. Yes.

Q. And not every person who purchases a metal home knows, for example, that a roof coating should be applied.

A. I always thought it was up to the dealer to try to inform them.

* * *

Q. I'm talking about the general consumer, someone who ultimately purchased a home; and whether you provided written instructions that went to every consumer, not just someone who came into the plant with a question?

A. We didn't do it. We didn't supply what you are asking for. No one else ever supplied any of these types of information.

Q. But in 1973 and 1974, what you are telling me is that ___________ Homes didn't perceive a need to disseminate that type of information to the consumer or purchaser of the home. Correct?

A. Right.

§ 10.15 —Testimony regarding company's failure to coat roofs

A company spokesman admitted that the homes' roofs should be coated to prevent leaking, but that the company did not coat the roofs before placing them on the market.[25]

Q. Do you recommend to your assemblers that a roof coating or some other additional protection device be placed on top of that galvanized steel roof?

A. It's been a standard practice—I don't know if you will find that in the instructions for putting it together, but it's been a standard practice with the industry that, in order to protect the galvanized roof, people would coat their roof after they purchased the house, and it acts as a sealer and it prevents the roof from rusting and from deteriorating.

Q. But your company . . . did not provide this additional roof coating?

A. No, we did not.

Q. Did you ever consider supplying or recommending the use of a roof coating to dealers?

A. If the topic ever came up, yes, I did personally discuss it with particular dealers that would come to the factory.

Q. At your staff meetings, was this a suggestion that you brought up to other employees and officers . . . , that the company should recommend to their dealers that the homes be sealed or that a sealer be supplied with the home when it was sent out for shipment?

A. No.

Q. That is despite the fact that . . . you knew that if the roof wasn't sealed that it would deteriorate and possibly leak within a rather short period of time?

A. Yes.

Q. Well, there are goals that the construction industry is supposed to meet. You are supposed to have a home that's safe, healthful, and comfortable. Right?

---

[25] *Burnham*, *supra* note 2, testimony of Mr. W.

A. Yes.

Q. It's supposed to provide structural strength and rigidity sufficient for design loads.

A. Yes.

Q. And by design loads, we are also talking about loads that could be applied to the roof by virtue of the weight of snow?

A. Yes.

Q. And that the homes are supposed to provide reasonable protection against rain and snow?

A. Yes.

COMMENT: Despite the hazardous nature of this company's product, its corporate officials admitted under oath that the company had no real safety program and did not adequately test its product for safety before placing it on the market.

---

§ 10.16 —Testimony regarding company's inadequate quality control

Another company spokesman admitted that despite the company's so-called "quality control" program, these homes were never tested for their watertightness before leaving the company's premises.[26]

Q. You told the jury about some of the things that ____________ Homes did about quality control, do you remember that?

A. Yes.

Q. As a matter of fact, you testified that they had a man who was in charge of quality control there at the plant, isn't that correct?

A. Yes.

Q. And every morning, I think you said, this man would check out each of the products as they came off the line, is that correct?

[26] *Burnham*, *supra* note 2, testimony of Mr. B.

This man monitored the construction of the home as it was being manufactured?

A. Yes.

Q. And he was in charge of making sure that the home was built as it was designed, is that correct?

A. Yes.

Q. And he made sure that the walls were built the way they were designed, is that correct?

A. Yes.

Q. And he made sure that all the other connections and facilities into the home were all built to the design requirements, is that correct?

A. Yes.

Q. Including the electrical system, is that correct?

A. Yes.

Q. And the heating system?

A. Yes.

Q. And the plumbing system?

A. Yes.

Q. He would go everywhere to make sure that the building was built as designed?

A. Yes.

Q. At the end he would sign off the building and say this is all correct as designed, is that correct?

A. He would sign the paper saying it was complete as far as the quality, yes.

Q. You take the building and ship it to the dealer for installation for the consumer?

A. Not quite that fast. It would go into the yard, which was a storage area, until such time as it was shipped, yes.

Q. When it went into the yard, the building was never actually installed, was it?

A. No.

Q. So it was never put together until it was actually installed for the consumer, is that correct?

A. Completely, no.

Q. Is that correct?

A. Yes.

Q. In other words, you never made any tests on the building as it was to be installed at the site to determine whether it was watertight or weatherproof, is that correct?

A. That's correct.

Q. No tests at all, is that correct?

A. As far as watertight or waterproof, that's correct.

A defense-hired consulting engineer affirmed this lack of adequate quality control.[27]

Q. These homes, after they were manufactured, you said they were checked, is that correct?

A. Yes.

Q. All right. And when they were checked, did they pour water on the building?

A. No, they allowed it to rain.

Q. Did they set the building up, install it the way they are supposed to be on the field, and wait for a rainstorm?

A. They put them outside in the field.

Q. After they came out of the factory, they installed them?

A. If by installed you mean did they connect them together, no.

Q. They didn't install them after they came off the factory line, isn't that correct?

A. They didn't connect them together, they did not assemble them, no.

---

[27] *Burnham*, *supra* note 2, testimony of Mr. C, witness called by the defendant, examined by the plaintiff.

§ 10.17 —Testimony regarding product's failure to meet industry safety standards

This consulting engineer also provided valuable testimony under cross-examination regarding this product's failure to meet the industry's own safety standards.[28]

Q. If a mobile home let in the rain or the snow, would it meet the ANSI standards?

A. No.

Q. Isn't it true that the ANSI standards require that a mobile home provide safe, healthful, and comfortable living facilities with adequate storage space and economy of maintenance?

A. Yes.

Q. So that a home, a mobile home that did not provide a safe, healthful, or comfortable living facility would not meet the standards under ANSI, would it?

A. No.

Q. Would you consider a mobile home that let in the rain and the snow to be safe, healthful, or comfortable?

A. No.

* * *

Q. Isn't it a fact that just mere temperature differences will open up roof joints because of the extremes of hot and cold allowing the leak to come in, isn't that true?

A. If the thermal changes are great enough, it could happen.

Q. Aside from the extremes of hot and cold, these panels also react to wind vibration, is that correct?

A. Yes.

Q. In conjunction with wind vibration and rippling effect and extremes of hot and cold, that could also open up these joints, is that correct?

A. If the winds are great enough, yes.

Q. And isn't it a fact that regular preventive maintenance is neces-

---

[28] *Id.*

sary to avoid possible damage and discomfort from leaks that may develop due to heat expansion and wind vibration?

A. [S]ome maintenance would be required if these homes were subject to extreme changes in temperatures or extreme winds.

Q. And, in your opinion, how regular should that be?

A. Well, at least with every change in season.

Q. Every change in season, there should be something done to that roof?

A. When you go from warm to cold and cold to warm, it would be advisable.

Q. So, twice a year?

A. To do some preventive maintenance.

Q. To prevent leaks from normal heat and cold expansion and wind vibration?

A. To prevent possible leaks.

Previous expert witnesses had testified that these homes could have been designed with increased safety if overhangs were provided on the roofs. Ironically, this witness admitted, these homes could have been produced with roof overhangs. Other models from this manufacturer had this safer design. The defendant simply chose not to incorporate them in this model, but rather to provide them as expensive "extras."[29]

Overhangs weren't the only safety feature sold as an expensive "extra." The defendant's expert testified that consumers could also purchase pitched roofs, shingles, and other features to increase the roof's safety, all as "extras."[30]

Q. If the people wanted an overhang, greater pitch, or shingles, that would be an extra, is that correct?

A. They could have ordered a mobile home with a shingled pitched roof.

Q. All right. And that would have been an extra?

A. Yes, it would have cost more.

Q. Is a roof that doesn't leak an extra?

---

[29] *Id.*

[30] *Id.*

A. I don't know how to answer that.

COMMENT: The fact is, consumers were not informed of the homes' hazards. In part because, as we've seen, the dealers themselves were not trained and in part because the information simply was not conveyed to the consumer. Not that the company didn't have the information. Several years later, when the federal government instituted regulations requiring that owners' manuals be supplied for these homes, suddenly this type of information was provided. Unfortunately, this was several years too late for the plaintiffs who relied on the product's manufacturer to provide complete disclosure of information regarding safety of the home without being forced to by government mandates.

---

§ 10.18 —Testimony regarding prior nature of defective condition

An important part of the plaintiff's case under the Consumer Protection Laws of Massachusetts was establishing that this defendant continued to market its product despite notice of its defective condition. Important evidence establishing this notice was provided by a witness who had purchased mobile homes from this defendant for sale in Pennsylvania, and who testified about his purchase and complaints of leaky roofs prior to the time that the homes were sold to the plaintiffs. He recalled first notifying the defendant after receiving complaints from his customers: "I talked to ____________, I told them, 'We have a problem with this, what do you suggest?' They said they didn't have anybody available."[31] As the leaks continued, he called again: "I asked [them], 'please go and look at it to see if there couldn't be a permanent fixing job on it to stop future leaks.' Their response was, 'We're extremely busy.' "[32] Consider the following excerpts from this witness's testimony.[33]

[31] *Burnham*, *supra* note 2, testimony of Mr. B, called by the plaintiffs.

[32] *Id.*

[33] *Id.*

Q. We're interested in the phone calls when you told Mr. G about the roof leak problems. You said you developed leaks two months after you sold the home?

A. Yes.

Q. When, within that two month period, do you remember making the first call to Mr. G specifically complaining about roof leaks?

A. Approximately the middle of April we started making phone calls to [Mr. G] involving roof leaks in the first mobile home.

Q. This phone call, what did you say to Mr. G and what did he say to you?

A. I said to him, "We have roof leaks with the double-wide, what are we going to do? Can you get somebody up here and see if they can't take a look at it and solve the problem?"

Q. What did he say?

A. He says, "I will have to check my schedule and get back to you."

Q. Okay.

A. When he got back to me he said, "We're extremely busy, the only thing I can say is you'll have to try to roof coat it or solve the problem the best way you can."

Q. Did you then call him again about the roof?

A. When we received the second complaint, approximately a month later, I contacted Mr. G; he said, "The service people are extremely busy, I can't get to you."

Several weeks later, another home purchaser complained, and he called again.[34]

Q. That's when you called Mr. G again?

A. I called Mr. G.

Q. What exactly did you say to him?

A. "We have a serious problem with roof leaks on this unit, we have to get something done to it."

Q. What did he say?

A. He says, "I don't have control of the service people, I'm going to have to get back to you." He got back to me and said, "We're

[34] *Id.*

going to be two weeks out." And meantime, I said, "I can't wait." He says, "Well, you're going to have to do what you have to do." I kept calling. At that point we're calling approximately every two or three days asking for some kind of help.

Q. Did you actually talk to Mr. G again?

A. Well, we made several calls where no one was available to talk to us and the call was supposed to be returned, it wasn't returned, and we kept calling. I believe Mr. P also spoke.

Q. Did you speak to Mr. P?

A. Yes.

Q. What did you tell Mr. P and when?

A. September, October 1974. Every week in those months, we're talking to the factory about getting something done on this problem. . . . I am telling Mr. G, "I've got to get this straightened out." I am telling Mr. P, "The roof leaks have to be straightened out, I've got to have help up here."

COMMENT: Eventually, the plaintiff contacted the local housing authority, which sent a representative to inspect her home. It didn't take the authority long to condemn her home as a health hazard and, a short time later, replace her roof with one of safer construction. The family never had problems with their roof again, but their work at returning their home to a livable condition was far from over. She still needed to replace her windows. Her large bay window had to be sanded down and refinished. Her plumbing still needed repair, as did her floors, and her moldings had to be replaced.

---

§ 10.19 —Conclusion

In his opening statement, the plaintiffs' counsel described the defendant as "a company that didn't care" about the product that it made, the way it was distributed, how it was sold, or what problems that arose from its defective design.[35]

A Franklin County, Massachusetts, jury found for the plaintiffs on the counts of negligence and breach of warranty.[36] However, the court granted the defendant's motion to dismiss the plaintiff's claim that defendant violated the Consumer Protection Laws of Massachusetts. The court further upheld the defendant's claim of exemption under § 93A on the ground that there was not sufficient evidence that its breach of warranty occurred "primarily and substantially" in the Commonwealth of Massachusetts.[37] On reviewing the record, I felt that the trial judge had erred, and that the plaintiffs had a right to a determination of their § 93A claim by a jury of their peers.

On appeal, I argued that the defendant's breach of implied warranty occurred not only primarily and substantially, but entirely within the Commonwealth. The defendant could not be shielded from a jury determination of liability for violation of the state's consumer protection laws. The evidence established that the sales of defendant's homes included delivery to sites and installation of foundations in Massachusetts. The plaintiffs' units were delivered and installed by dealers of the defendant's homes. The sales of the units were only complete when delivery and installation had been completed.

The Massachusetts Supreme Judicial Court agreed, finding that the subject transaction did occur entirely within the Commonwealth of Massachusetts, and remanded the case to the trial court for determination of the matter.[38]

I also argued that the plaintiffs were entitled to multiple damages under Mass. Gen. Laws Ann. ch. 93A, § 9(3) (West 1979), which permits the trial judge to award up to three, but not less than two, times the amount of the plaintiffs' actual damages if he finds that the use or employment of the unfair or deceptive act or practice was a willful or knowing violation of the statute, or that the refusal to grant relief upon demand was made in bad faith with knowledge or reason to know that

---

[35] *Burnham*, *supra* note 2, opening statement of attorney, Jan Schlictmann, Esq.

[36] Burnham v. Mark IV Homes, No. CA 14131 (Mass. Super. Ct. Oct. 20, 1980), verdict for the plaintiffs.

[37] Regulations of the Massachusetts Attorney General state that "it shall be an unfair and deceptive act or practice to fail to perform or fulfill any promises or obligations arising under a warranty." Regulation VII B, 20 Mass. Regs., Part 5, at 28 (1975), currently found in 940 Code Mass. Regs. § 3.08(2) (1978).

[38] *Burnham*, *supra* note 2.

the act or practice complained of violated the act. The Supreme Judicial Court found that "The [trial] judge would have been warranted in finding that Mark IV had 'reason to know' that certain of the allegations stated a claim of violations of G.L. c.93A, § 2, and that Mark IV's decision not to make a written offer of settlement before trial was made in bad faith."[39] The court remanded the case to the trial court for determination of whether the defendant had acted in bad faith, and to assess damages under Mass. Gen. Laws Ann. ch. 93A.[40]

§ 10.20 Case study: The case of slaughter by textbook[41]

Up until now, I have focused primarily on slaughter by products that injure us at home—products that make our lives so much easier, but simply are not designed with safety in mind. Our schools can likewise be repositories of hazardous products. Until recently, personal injuries occurring in the school setting would conjur up mental images of sports-related accidents or unsafe playgrounds. Little would we suspect that a classroom textbook could become the source of tragedy. But it has become clear, based on a recent case, that the very source of learning can become an instrument of destruction and even death.

Such was the case when a junior high school student, Carolyn C, was conducting an experiment illustrated in her eighth grade science textbook. This girl was severely burned when methyl alcohol exploded as she poured it into a beaker placed near the flame of a Bunsen burner. Although the textbook's authors knew that methyl alcohol was highly flammable and explosive, it was not until nearly the end of the book that any warnings of its hazardous nature were provided to the student.

The afternoon that tragedy struck, the plaintiff's class was conducting experiments listed in their chemistry textbook. As they followed the experiment directions, they noticed that the text directed that "alcohol may be rising" from boiling water.[42] They proceeded to pour the contents of a

---

[39] *Id.* at 1032.

[40] *Id.*

[41] Carter v. Rand McNally & Co., No. 76-1864F (D. Mass. Sept. 1980).

[42] Investigation 34 was entitled *Calibrating a Thermometer*. Materials included an alcohol thermometer, microscope slides, freezer tape, water, beaker, crushed ice, and scissors. A Bunsen burner was needed to heat the water to the boiling point. The student was instructed to place a thermometer into boiling water, then into crushed ice, and write down the temperature registered by the thermometer each time. Immediately following Investigation 34 was Investigation 35, entitled *Water and Ice*. This investigation involved "observing the volume of a sample of water in two phases, solid and liquid." A

jug of methyl alcohol into the heated beaker. Within moments, an explosion ripped through the classroom, and the plaintiff was engulfed in flames. She ran through the hallways, her body in flames, past the school nurse and onto the grass outside. She rolled around in the grass until the fire was extinguished, and the nurse rushed to her with a jacket to wrap her burning body. She asked the nurse, "Am I going to die? I can't believe this is happening to me. Am I going to burn to death?"[43]

The student was rushed to ____________ City Hospital, then to ____________ Burn Institute, where she spent the next seventy-one days undergoing extensive burn treatment. She spent much of this time lying inside a life-support bubble to keep her traumatized body free of bacteria. Although it is difficult to imagine the excruciating pain that she must have suffered, a conversation between this teenaged girl and her mother during this period reflects some of this life-and-death struggle.[44]

> Plaintiff: Boy, I'll tell you that today I thought I was ready for the coffin. I could picture myself in the parlor. . . . Well now what happens to you when you die? Will I ever see you again? I don't want to be reincarnated. I never want to leave the family.
>
> Mother: Someday your prince will come and take you on his white horse into the forest. It might take a long time for the right one to come.
>
> Plaintiff: Will I ever be able to ride a bike or sew my skirt or paint or swim again before the summer is done?
>
> Mother: Of course you will. I don't know when, but we have to be careful at first and eventually you will be able to do all those things.

---

test tube containing ice and a metric ruler were listed as materials required for the experiment. Next was Investigation 36, entitled, *Ice, Salt, Sugar, and Alcohol*. The text described this experiment: "At sea level water boils at 100°C and freezes at 0°C. Body temperatures, room temperature, and the temperature of tap water all fall somewhere between 0°C and 100°C. In this Investigation, you will study temperatures that are below 0°C." Recommended materials for this experiment included: a 250 ml. beaker, alcohol thermometer, spoon or mixing stick, crushed ice, table salt, sugar, and methyl alcohol (or ditto fluid). Students were instructed to reduce the thermometer temperature to 0°C and then to expose it to small amounts of salt, sugar, and alcohol and to measure each element's effect on the temperature measured by the thermometer.

[43] *Carter*, *supra* note 41, testimony of the plaintiff.

[44] *Carter*, *supra* note 41, testimony of the plaintiff's mother.

§ 10.21 —Analysis of case

The use of potentially explosive, flammable chemicals in the school classroom is not a new practice. What makes this girl's case unique is the role played by the textbook itself—using language that was unclear and misleading to students using it, and then failing to warn students and teachers adequately of the dangers associated with the explosive liquid.

Even though students cannot be neatly pigeonholed by grade, age, maturity, or knowledge, and the junior high academic years can encompass a vast spread of learning abilities, the scientific language utilized in the text must be clear and adequate for the understanding and comprehension of the foreseeable user of the text. Where the book is being marketed to noncritical youthful users, a little knowledge can be a very dangerous thing.

§ 10.22 —Testimony regarding foreseeability of user

The girl's textbook was written by a group of high school science teachers who wanted to develop a new, innovative classroom science curriculum. After a brief search, they found a publisher, and within three years had the first edition of their book in print.[45] The book was intended to take materials traditionally taught to eleventh and twelfth graders and teach them to eighth and ninth grade students. One of the book's authors conceded in response to my cross-examination that actual readers may have been even younger, including seventh graders. He admitted that not all of the students reading the textbook would fully understand its meaning. Consider the following excerpt from this witness' testimony.[46]

Q. Is there any statement put out by [the publisher] or you as the authors indicating that the book was written or directed to a mid-ninth grade level?

A. . . .If you are asking if there is any printed material to that effect, I am not aware that there is.

Q. So what level would be the earliest level?

A. We aimed at the ninth grade average level and realized that in many cases it might be used at the eighth grade. I know of one

[45] N.A. Graham, P. Balch, D. Chaney & L. Rohrbaugh, Interaction of Matter and Energy (Rand McNally & Co. 1973).

[46] *Carter*, *supra* note 41, testimony of Mr. C.

case in which it was used at the seventh grade level. It was not our intention to write a seventh grade text.

Q. Was it sold or promoted for seventh or eighth graders also?

A. I don't know of any advertising to that effect. There may well have been some. I know that if you write at the junior high school level, I am sure it was advertised for that.

Q. You found nothing wrong with using it for an eighth grade class, certainly?

A. No. The teacher would select the textbook material that he felt was most appropriate for use in his class.

Q. But the book was aimed at a mid-ninth grade level student?

A. Just an average ninth grade level student, yes.

Q. Did you have an opinion, prior to the time you wrote this book with the other authors, concerning that the ability of students to understand this material since the communication levels of a mid-ninth grade student might differ from that possessed by an average eighth grade student?

A. Yes.

§ 10.23 —Testimony regarding confusion of textbook terms

Even the term "flammable" itself can cause confusion. While the textbook uses the term "flammable," the bottle of methyl alcohol that the plaintiff used in conducting her experiment contained in bold letters the label "INFLAMMABLE." Would this create confusion in the mind of an eighth grade student? A confusion that was foreseeable to the publisher of the text? The publisher admitted in response to my extensive cross-examination that such a confusion might, indeed, be foreseeable.[47]

Q. Does inflammable and flammable mean the same thing to you?

A. Yes.

Q. Does it, to your knowledge, mean the same thing to seventh, eighth, or ninth grade students?

A. I would not know how to answer. To some, yes; to some, no, I suppose.

Q. And with respect to the some that are no, those to whom it

[47] *Carter*, *supra* note 41, testimony of Mr. M.

means a different thing, what does the difference mean with regard to flammable from inflammable?

A. The word inflammable might mean not flammable to some students.

Q. Okay. Is there anything in the textbook that instructs the students about differentiating or not differentiating between flammable and inflammable?

A. Not to my knowledge.

Q. Did it occur to you that the suppliers of methyl alcohol for use in this experiment might use on their containers in which they supplied the alcohol the word "inflammable"?

A. No.

§ 10.24 —Testimony of plaintiff regarding lack of understanding of experiment

The sorry fact was that this teenager did not know or understand the experiment that she was conducting. She knew only that she was to read and mark down the temperatures measured by the thermometer when she placed it into water. Most importantly, she did not know that alcohol was flammable. The plaintiff's lack of understanding is illustrated in the following dialogue between myself and this girl.[48]

Q. Did you understand that the purpose of investigation number 34 was to determine, in calibrating this thermometer, how high it would run when it was immersed in boiling water?

A. I understand all that now, but then I didn't understand that at all.

Q. You didn't understand then the purpose of calibrating a thermometer?

A. I didn't even know what it meant. I just recently found out what it meant.

Q. You mean you didn't know that if you put something in hot water or boiling water, it would grow warm?

A. I knew when you put the thermometer in boiling water, you were supposed to write down the temperature. I didn't know what we were trying to prove because nothing was explained.

---

[48] *Carter*, *supra* note 41, testimony of the plaintiff.

Q. What was not clear to you, if you will tell me, about this experiment?

A. About what we were supposed to prove and the procedures and things like that. They were very vague.

Q. Did you know that alcohol was inflammable?

A. Well, I found out. I didn't know then.

§ 10.25 —Testimony regarding inadequacy of warnings

Although the use of methyl alcohol is recommended throughout the 350-page text, it is not until page 305, after at least five separate references to the highly explosive liquid, that any warnings are given regarding its hazards. My probing cross-examination of one of the book's author's reveals this negligence.[49]

Q. Now going back to . . . page 84, it calls for the use of methyl alcohol, does it not?

A. Yes.

Q. Were any warnings or instructions given there as to the use of methyl alcohol?

A. Instructions were given.

Q. Were any warnings given about its hazards?

A. I believe not.

Q. Going to page 125, investigation 19, where its uses methyl alcohol, are there any warnings about hazards given there?

A. I believe not.

Q. Now going to page 201, methyl alcohol is called for there. Were there any warnings about hazards given there?

A. No.

Q. That, of course, was investigation 36, was it not?

A. Yes.

Q. Now going to investigation 67, at page 305, first of all, does it recommend the use of methyl alcohol in that investigation?

A. Yes.

Q. There is caution called for at page 305, is there not?

---

[49] *Carter*, *supra* note 41, testimony of Mr. C.

A. Yes.

Q. What is that?

A. "Caution: Alcohol is flammable. Do not place a container of alcohol directly over an open flame. Heating the alcohol inside a water bath is relatively safe."

Q. Up to that page, up until we came to this point, is this the first time that a warning or instructions were given in this text, in the teacher's edition, about the use of methyl alcohol?

A. I believe so.

COMMENT: Incidentally, the "water bath" referred to in the caution was the same device called for in the experiment that the plaintiff was conducting when the explosion occurred. The author further testified that the warnings provided in the text were indeed inadequate.[50]

---

* * *

Q. If you are going to somehow instruct a child adequately not to use methyl alcohol with an open flame, in order that the lesson is learned, shouldn't you also tell the child that if he or she did use it with an open flame, what the consequences might be?

A. Yes, it would be desirable for them to know why.

Q. I show you Plaintiff's Exhibit 3 [the bottle of methyl alcohol used by the plaintiff]. It says METHYL ALCOHOL. Down here it says INFLAMMABLE. By the way, as a teacher of children, do you think all children ages twelve and thirteen would know the difference between the words inflammable and flammable?

A. If you are asking me about all children, then certainly the answer would have to be no.

[50] *Id.*

§ 10.26 —Testimony regarding laboratory safety

A variety of protective equipment is available, and recommended by safety experts, to ensure that students remain safe while enjoying the learning experience when hazardous products are used in the classroom. It almost goes without saying that use of protective fume hoods, lab aprons, masks, goggles, gloves, and even safe storage methods should be emphasized as being of paramount importance in any school laboratory text. Yet one of these authors admitted under oath that he was aware when the book was first published that most junior high schools were "probably not" equipped with fume hoods. Lab aprons were not even mentioned in the text. Although the use of masks, goggles, and gloves became recommended practice for school chemistry laboratories after the first edition was published, no such recommendation was included in its later, revised editions. Consider this excerpt from my examination of the text author:[51]

Q. What about the necessity, from the point of view of safe practice, of wearing protective gear, such as flame-retardant aprons, a face mask, etc.? Would that be a safer practice than not using them?

A. Yes. After publication of this book, this became recommended practice. Just prior to the publication of our book, I think the only safety recommendation was lab aprons. Subsequent to the publication of the book, face masks or safety glasses were recommended.

Q. Did you modify your text to include those safety recommendations?

A. No, we did not.

The authors also learned about important storage safety information after the first edition was published—that methyl alcohol should be stored in explosion-proof containers. This witness admitted under oath that he changed his own teaching practices when he learned this new information. Yet, astonishingly, the new information was never incorporated into the revised text. Consider this excerpted testimony:[52]

Q. You are aware, sir, that the proper way to store methyl alcohol, the safest way, is in an explosion-proof container?

---

[51] *Id.*

[52] *Id.*

A. Yes, but I became aware of this subsequent to [publication of the first textbook].

Q. When did you become aware of this?

A. I probably saw recommendations on this in a publication from the National Science Teachers Association on laboratory safety about 1972 or 1974.

Q. And you, of course, since that time, have passed that safety information that you acquired onto the users of your book in the new editions, have you not?

A. No, we have not. The subsequent revisions have not been of such a substantial nature that we added new sections.

Q. You did not make that change in subsequent editions with respect to the storage information of flammable liquids?

A. We provided no information on storage of chemicals.

Q. Did you change your own [teaching] practices when you learned that?

A. Yes.

By this point, the reader might ask why methyl alcohol was even proposed, no less encouraged, for use in a junior high school laboratory. According to this witness, the reason was that the product would be "inexpensive and available." Again, consider the witness' admissions in these excerpts from my cross-examination at trial.[53]

Q. In deciding to use methyl alcohol, obviously you checked on whether the methyl alcohol was absolutely necessary for each experiment, did you not?

A. We gave consideration to whether it was the most reasonable substance to use for that particular experiment—not absolutely necessary, where nothing else would have done, but the best choice of materials.

Q. If something else could have been used that was safer, of course, you would have recommended its use?

A. If something else were available that was reasonable in terms of cost and reasonable in terms of cleanup, yes.

Q. When you came to an experiment that used the materials, such

[53] *Id.*

as the kind we have described here, certainly one of the considerations had to have been the necessity for the experiments when balanced against the risks of using the particular products or materials involved?

A. In the context of that experiment, yes.

Q. Each time in the text you used methyl alcohol or wood alcohol, you had to go through this kind of a balancing or a reasoning process, did you not?

A. I don't recall whether I sat down each time and tried to decide that since methyl alcohol is toxic, should we use it at all? I think we made a decision to use a limited number of chemicals and try to avoid those that had extreme toxicity. We also were concerned at the time because, for many of us, the science budgets were limited, and we were concerned with providing a list of materials that would be as inexpensive and available as possible, and those criteria certainly were applied. We would not use a substance that was especially expensive or especially hazardous unless we had some particularly good reason for using it.

Q. You said you would not use a substance that was extremely toxic, for example?

A. Unless we had a particularly good reason.

Q. Would you consider methyl alcohol or wood alcohol to be extremely toxic?

A. Yes, I would.

Q. How did you justify its usage in this book at all?

A. Because it was the best material to use—given the criteria we had established, it was the best material to use.

Q. Of course, in deciding whether it was the best material to use, you have to take into account all its disadvantages as well as its advantages. Now we are back to the balancing, is that correct?

A. Yes.

Although the authors of this textbook may have been new to the publishing field, it would not have taken them long to discover that other publications in this field did provide their readers with specific emphasis on laboratory safety. One text, in fact, had a section at the beginning of the book entitled *Techniques and Safety Sketches*, with sketches and cartoons to demonstrate safe laboratory practices. Another specifically addressed the student with *Safety Lab Rules*. This witness admitted under cross-examination that their book, in comparison, did not have such emphasis on safety.[54]

Q. Does the book in issue in this case have a safety section at the beginning of it?

A. No, it does not.

Q. So how many books are there presently for seventh and eighth graders that involve general science and general lab work such as yours?

A. I couldn't give you a total number. I am sure there are in excess of twenty.

Q. Have you ever reviewed those texts from the point of view of their safety content?

A. No, I have not.

Q. You were aware that there were other texts in the field for children that had safety sections at the beginning of the books?

A. Published prior to [this text]?

Q. Well, both ways. First prior to [this text]?

A. I am not aware of that.

Q. Did you look for any?

A. Not specifically.

Q. Prior to commencing work on this book, did you check to see if there were any other publishers with safety sections in their chemistry books?

A. No, I don't think we did.

§ 10.27 —Conclusion

In a landmark verdict, the jury found the defendant-publisher negligent in publishing this textbook without adequate warnings of the hazards involved. The plaintiff was awarded $1.1 million for her severe and permanent burn injuries. This was the first time that personal injuries were found to be the result of negligent publishing.[55]

---

[54] *Id.*

[55] *See also* the discussion of this landmark case in Swartz, *You Can't Judge a Book by Its Cover*, TRIAL (Nov. 1981).

This case also illustrated, once again, that generally accepted practices within a profession are not necessarily sufficient to shield a company from liability. The textbook authors were experienced teachers—but they were not editors, safety experts, or experts in how much knowledge could be absorbed and understood at certain levels. Although the authors intended the text for the ninth grade student and focused the material to that level of knowledge and maturity, the marketers promoted the book for junior high school classes.

COMMENT: As attorneys, we must be willing to pioneer new areas of products liability law, because, short of prevention, this kind of prosecution is the only alternative left to encourage adequate preventive safety programs.

Chapter 11

CLOSING THE CASE OF SLAUGHTER BY PRODUCT

KLUWER LITIGATION LIBRARY REFERENCES

JEANS, LITIGATION: Chapter 16, *Summation*.

SMITH & MALANDRO, COURTROOM COMMUNICATION STRATEGIES: CHAPTER 2, *Persuasive Strategies in the Courtroom*; Chapter 3, *Source Credibility in the Courtroom*; Chapter 10, *Summation: A Time for Motivating Jurors.*

§ 11.01 In general

The closing argument in a products liability case is the best opportunity for the plaintiff's lawyer to play the role of advocate for his injured client. All of the evidence has been presented, the technical and legal issues have been resolved, and the lawyer now has the opportunity to reflect on his client's case and put it in perspective for the jury. The mantle of the advocate is put on the lawyer's shoulder, and he has the stage to himself to make believers out of the jury. It is a golden moment in a trial, a time for skillful advocacy. For this reason, this chapter focuses on the closing argument.

The closing argument techniques that are set forth in the excerpts in this chapter illustrate how counsel can use these techniques to communicate his case effectively to members of the jury. Counsel must always be certain to utilize these approaches in the context of the laws, rules, and jurisdictional requirements that apply in each particular case. The themes presented are intended as guidelines. They must be modified to exigencies of every particular set of circumstances and to the law of the jurisdiction involved in each particular case.

§ 11.02 Goals of the closing argument

The successful closing of the plaintiff's case in a products liability matter requires the lawyer to be a vigorous consumer advocate. He should never forget that the jurors are also consumers, and he must help them to see that they, like his client, are also captives of a system that could injure them without warning, without choice, and without any hope of compensation, except through our system of justice. The lawyer must show the jury that the plaintiff did not choose to be slaughtered by a product, but that he was a helpless victim in the face of a defect in design or in the manufacturing, marketing, testing, packaging, or promotion of the particular product that was created behind closed corporate doors.

The final argument is the lawyer's best opportunity to help the jury (or judge, if it is a bench trial) understand his case. If the lawyer has carefully prepared his opening statement and realistically tailored it to the case, the closing argument is the time to show that the promises made in the opening statement have been fulfilled. Even more important, the closing argument is the time to show the jury the essence of the plaintiff's claim—the elemental reason that justice should be done by compensating the plaintiff for the wrong done to him. The closing argument is also the time for helping the jury to make sense out of the frequently confusing evidence that they have heard—and to understand that evidence in a light most favorable to the plaintiff.

§ 11.03 Checklist: Preparing the closing argument

Several factors must be kept in mind when preparing the closing argument. Every good lawyer should develop his own "checklist" of such factors. The following are some of the factors I consider important:

____ (1) Don't use abstract legal terms during final argument. Remember that the jurors did not go to law school, and they are not familiar with the nuances of legal vocabulary that lawyers and judges use every day.

____ (2) Try to illustrate points you make with stories, analogies, and practical points drawn from the everyday lifes of jurors. You want the jurors to stand in the shoes of your client, to *feel* for him, and to do this, you must put your client's problem into a context within which they can relate.

____ (3) In a products liability case, make the final argument a brief for the captive consumer. The defense will do everything it can to pin the problem on some conduct of the plaintiff. Take the offensive in establishing the fact that the consumer is a helpless captive of the defendant's choice to design the product, test it, market it, label it, advertise it, and sell it, in sum, that the plaintiff really had very little, or no choice in the matter.

____ (4) As the case proceeds, continually ask yourself what you would be concerned about if you were on that jury, and then address those concerns in final argument. Throughout the trial, keep a special "final argument" set of notes, i.e., matters that should be addressed in the final argument.

____ (5) If there is a weak point in your case, don't dwell on it in final argument by trying to develop elaborate and constrained explanations, this will only focus the attention of the jury on the weak aspects of your case and make them question everything you say.

____ (6) If you have developed good demonstrative aids, do not hesitate to use them in final argument, but do not get so caught up with the use of aids that you fail to have a "heart to heart" talk with the jury about the essence of your case.

____ (7) If your case is especially complex, reduce it to its essential points, and drive those points home strongly. Repeat your strongest points in different ways, and make sure the jury goes into its deliberations with those points ringing in their heads. The best teachers use recapitulation as a teaching tool. The lawyer should see himself as a teacher who is not just spouting out facts to the jury, but is attempting to make them *understand* those facts.

____ (8) Make the jury *want* to do something for your client. Open every door for the jury, but leave it up to them to walk through. Jurors are typical of the community from which they are drawn—they will have some compassion and some doubt. But most jurors want to do the right thing. In subtle ways, you must let them know that this is their chance to do the right thing, the chance to make a difference.

§ 11.04 Illustration: Painting a "word picture"

In the various sample final arguments that I provide later in this chapter, you will notice how I put the aforementioned concepts to work. You will also notice how I do not spend hours summarizing every bit of evidence. What is needed is not a dry, factual summary, but a hard-hitting statement of the essential facts of the client's claim. The following brief, but dramatic, summary of fact situations from some of my earlier writings illustrate how a "word picture" can be painted for the jury in a minute or two:

> A young father comes home and is asked by his wife to unclog the bathroom sink with the liquid drain cleaner that she has bought for that purpose. The bottle of cleaner falls off the sink and spills all over their two-year-old girl. The cleaner was dangerously and unnecessarily made of more than 30% caustic lye, and the bottle was a dangerously unstable container. The little girl is hideously and irreparably disfigured.[1]
>
> A father of four, rising early to go to the first of his two jobs, goes down into the celler of his home to investigate the apparent failure of the gas-fueled hot water heater. A few seconds after his wife sees him descending the stairs, there is a thunderous explosion, and the father is dead within the hour. Ten cents worth of factory-added rust retardant on a part made of non-rust proof steel would have prevented the buildup of unburnt gas that caused the explosion.[2]

Notice how, in both of these summaries, the essential facts were presented in just a few words, the wrongdoing of the defendant was presented clearly, and the whole picture was painted in the context of an ordinary family doing ordinary things until suddenly, and without warning, disaster struck. This is the kind of scene a jury can relate to and appreciate.

It is possible to let the jury see the human side of the case in just a few words, while letting them also draw a conclusion as to where the blame should be placed:

> A 14-month-old child was playing with tiny wooden play figures . . . when he put one of the figures in his mouth. The figure slipped into his throat, and because of the design, caught there and could not be removed by the child's parents. . . . The anoxia the child suffered between ingestion and extraction left him permanently and severely brain damaged. Had the figure been designed differently . . . so that it was larger . . . the child would have been unable to swallow it in such a manner and would have avoided a tragic disabling injury.[3]

---

[1] Swartz, *Perils at Home*, Case & Com. (Sept.-Oct. 1976).

[2] *Id.*

[3] Swartz, *Toys-R-Dangerous*, Trial 29 (Feb. 1982).

§ 11.05 Dealing with defense tactics

Another goal of an effective closing argument is to help the jury see through the factual and legal smokescreens that often are erected by the defense in a products liability case. Plaintiff's counsel should characterize such tactics for exactly what they are—an attempt to confuse the jury. In the selections from some of my closing arguments, reprinted later in this chapter, the reader will notice how I bluntly call such defense tactics a "red herring" or an "octopus" defense. By use of an analogy of this kind, I illustrate for the jury why they should not be mislead by the defense tactics. Another example is found in a comment I once made in regard to the defense of "misuse" that is often raised by defendants in products liability cases:

> Toys are easily broken, banged, and smashed, and children themselves often delight in disassembling them. . . . The industry's usual retort to any toy-related injury is that it was the result of some "misuse" by the child. To market a toy with all kinds of potential for creative misuse and then cry foul when a child is harmed while departing from the manufacturer's narrowly circumscribed "intended use" is a standard industry ploy.[4]

It is important to communicate to the jury the concept that the injured plaintiff was a "captive consumer." By whatever words the plaintiff's lawyer gets this point across, the jury must be made to grasp the essential fact that the defendant controlled the manufacture, design, testing, packaging, and marketing of the product that caused death or injury. The consumer has no freedom, no choice, no volitional decision in this matter, except to buy or use the product in ignorance of its dangerous and fatal flaws. If the victim is a child, then the concept of the "captive consumer" must be asserted even more vigorously. As I have stated previously:

> Perhaps the most tragic victims are children who have sustained massive burn injuries from the combustion of clothing, bedding or playthings.[5]

§ 11.06 Illustrative closing arguments

The following excerpts from the author's closing arguments illustrate how these themes can effectively be used to convey the plaintiff's case.

---

[4]Swartz, *Inside Santa's Bag of Tricks*, ENVTL. QUALITY 34 (Dec. 1972).

[5]Swartz, *Preventing Burn Injuries*, J. NURSING AD. (Jan.-Feb. 1973).

Commentaries accompanying these illustrative arguments explain the importance of the argument and the manner in which it is presented.

§ 11.07 —Plaintiff's consumer protection case

COMMENT: As I stated in the introduction to this work, the heart of counsel's successful litigation in cases involving slaughter by product is the ability to understand the plaintiff's case essentially as a consumer protection case, and to convey this sense to members of the jury. It is this sense of mission, this sense of justice, that makes jurors want to find for the plaintiff. It takes the right message to convey this sense of mission. Tell jurors of their unique opportunity to send a message to this company as well as to an entire industry to change their practices before additional tragedy strikes. Inspire them to seize the opportunity to send this message that can save consumers' lives and prevent needless injuries. Teach them how they can seize this moment by finding for the plaintiff in this case.

Argument 1

I indicated in my opening remarks that if any of you happen to be a user of propane gas, the place to learn about these hazards is when they sell the product to you, not here in the courtroom. Gas supply companies like this defendant are supposed to educate us so that we can protect ourselves and our families. This is basic products liability law. It is also basic consumer protection law. I think it appeals to the reasonableness of the law.

Argument 2

You now have the opportunity to render a verdict in this case, to speak out and say to this defendant, "Look, if you want to place that product in our stream of commerce and make a profit, then come forward and tell us the whole story about its hazards, no matter how much it might hurt company sales." I ask you to speak out. Be courageous. Return a verdict for the plaintiff and the plaintiff's family in this case. It's too late to prevent this tragedy. It is not too late to sound the alarm to prevent tragedy to others.

Argument 3

Consumer protection, in this context, means bottom line, not lip service. You can say to defendant's executives, "we care."

Rarely in a lifetime do any of us have an opportunity to make a statement, if the facts warrant it, that can change the conduct of an entire industry. This is what the law calls deterrence. You have the opportunity to save lives.

Argument 4

Rarely have six people and, forgive me, alternates, been given an opportunity in a courtroom to affect an industry. You can affect the course of a product by setting a standard as the conscience of the community.

You can tell this corporation, "Listen, if you are going to sell things for teething age children who put things in their mouth all the time, please make them large enough, please give us warnings, and please give us instructions, because sooner or later someone is going to get caught again just like this child and we don't want that on our conscience. . . ." The message that your verdict will send back to this corporation is the only consumer message that will prevent further tragedy.

Argument 5

The message must come out from this courtroom. The law provides a vehicle for that message—simple justice for my client and punitive justice for the defendant. Together you will make a statement because the good Lord has the capacity to protect all of us, even the little sparrow. And if there is a sparrow out there that hasn't fallen yet, I want that family to get the message of what we have learned in this courtroom from the defendants' own mouths.

§ 11.08 —Reviewing the facts

COMMENT: Counsel's description of the facts should focus on the injured plaintiff as the victim of corporate decisions that resulted in a defective product being placed in the stream of commerce and ultimately causing death or injury.

Argument 6

In this tragedy that should not have occurred, the plaintiff's family lost all three sons. They went to bed one night and, as [their mother] testified when she was on the stand, the next morning "half my family was gone." You know the testimony. J____ and her girlfriend got up. The room was filled with smoke. They escaped through a bedroom window. A____ was found by the window in the front bedroom on the floor. The other two boys were on their way to the rear bedroom. These children were afforded no protection. They were wasted because of corporate indifference and callousness.

Argument 7

Ladies and gentlemen of the jury, when I previously had the privilege of addressing you, I told you that on June 20, 1967, ____________ got up in the morning and went to the bathroom to shave. He tried to get some hot water, found there wasn't any, and went down to the basement to check his hot water heater. His wife heard him go through the door or two doors and, about that time, there was an explosion that resulted in his injury and subsequent death.

I told you that in the basement of this home, there were two gas appliances. I indicated that our proof would show that one of the appliances was defective. This resulted in the discharge of raw gas and created an explosive concentration in the plaintiff's basement, a condition that my expert has described as a "booby trap." It is time to disarm these bombs in homes everywhere!

Argument 8

As you have heard from the evidence presented in this case, the defendant placed into the stream of commerce a defective product. This product had a propensity and a certain capacity to render someone quadriplegic or kill someone if it was used in the manner in which they said it should be used and which they foresaw.

When I made my opening remarks, I said to you that this may sound like an easy matter. A kid in a backyard jumps into an aboveground pool with three and a half or four feet of water. Aren't people hit crossing the street every day? You know that I said to wait until we have the whole truth, until we find out how the product was marketed, how it was sold, and how it was promoted. How was it intended by the manufacturer to be used? What was the motivation for selling this product? Was safety subverted for the sake of a few more bucks . . . a few more sales?

§ 11.09 —Criticizing defendant's case: casting doubt on his arguments

---

COMMENT: Counsel should always keep members of the jury suspicious of the defendant's case by casting doubt on the legitimacy of the defendant's arguments. One way to do this is to characterize the defendant's case in descriptive terms that convey this sense of doubt to the jury—not only has this corporation wronged the plaintiff, it is now attempting to pull the wool over the eyes of this jury. I like to use terms such as "red herring defense," "octopus defense," and "phantom defense" to convey this sense of doubt.

"Red Herring" Defense

Argument 9

We are not talking, as the defense would have you believe, about a body of water contained in a cylinder in a training complex like a high school gym, the Y.M.C.A., or a public facility that has a rectangular pool with a deep end and a shallow end. We are talking about what was sold and conceived to be a wading pool or a wading area. I think of a wading pool as two feet deep or two and one-half feet deep. When you are done using it, you pour the water out. We don't place a rope across this pool to designate "diving" and "no-diving" areas like we do with inground rectangular pools. Are they trying to tell us that this cylinder that holds water that we use in our backyard is comparable in any way to a professional facility where we have professional assistance and guidance and professional instructors? What they did was to take a wading pool and, through clever marketing, make it into a "backyard country club."

Argument 10

Defense counsel has raised the questions of how many smoke detectors the plaintiff purchased and where he installed them. These are red herrings in this case. It's beyond dispute that there was a power failure as a result of an overloaded circuit. Remember, there was no electricity. Without battery back-up unit, this so-called lifesaving early detection unit did not perform its function and could not perform its function regardless of how many were purchased or where they were installed.

"Octopus" Defense

Argument 11

You know how an octopus works. It gives off this black, murky stuff that enables it to escape from anyone who might put it in a position of danger. This is the kind of thing you do when you don't have the facts and the law on your side. If you have the facts and the law on your side, you see, you don't comment on things like that. They become very unimportant to you. It is when you have problems with the quality of your defense that you start trying the other attorney and talking about irrelevancies, and you really don't get down to the issues of the case.

For example, you take a picture of a bunch of toys and you line them up like it's a rogues' gallery. The only problem is that you leave off the one toy that did the harm. That's an octopus defense, murkying the water so perhaps the trier of fact won't see the real issue, Plaintiffs' Exhibit 1.

Let's not allow the octopus defense, in any way, to muddy the waters unnecessarily. What they are shamelessly attempting to suggest, ladies and gentlemen, is that the ____________ family has put in a fraudulent claim and has concocted a case against [the defendant].

Let's call it the way it is. There is too much at stake here to get involved with unnecessary niceties.

§ 11.10 —Perception of risk

COMMENT: Defendants often argue in these cases that the plaintiff is to blame for his injuries because the risk was "open and obvious." I have, on a number of occasions, successfully countered this argument by pointing out that the defendant's own executives and experts were not aware of the risks involved, or that the defendant's witnesses provided conflicting testimony regarding product risks. This approach places the defendant in a dilemma. If it didn't know of the risks, how can it argue the risks are "open and obvious" to the plaintiff?

Argument 12

If the big "highfalutin" experts in the courtroom didn't understand that you can become a quadriplegic from diving into three-and-one-half feet of water, how is the average person to know? They look at three-and-one-half feet of water. They figure the water offers resistance and envelops you. It's a trap. You might bump your head and nose. Perhaps a child bumps his head when he is ten, eleven, or twelve years old. Nothing happens. The next year, the child's body weight and height have increased and grown to dangerous levels for diving into three-and-one-half or four feet of water. Now the same dive, safely performed, could lead to tragedy!

§ 11.11 —Criticizing defendant's case: lack of experts

COMMENT: One way for counsel to demonstrate the defendant's continuing lack of concern for the injured plaintiff is to draw the jury's attention to the defendant's failure to provide effective experts to support its case. This reinforces an important component of counsel's consumer protection argument. This defendant does not care about this plaintiff, about this case, or about consumer protection in general.

Argument 13

Here is a company with the resources to hire any expert[s] that they could find on the entire North American continent. Yet, the only people they produce in this courtroom to comment on the quality of the product and the specific hazard we are complaining about are Mr. ____________ and Mr. ____________, both senior company executives.

They provided no doctors for you, no economists, no engineers, no medical library. Where was the independent evaluation that this company could have brought to you? Where were the pediatricians; where were the physicians that could have examined this child? Indeed, where were their economists?

They have demonstrated that they are a cut-rate company. Considering the seriousness of this injury this defendant owed this jury and owed the ____________ family more.

Argument 14

By the way, I didn't hear any economist testify for the defendant. And where are these nameless, faceless executives from ____________? I guess they are not really concerned enough yet. I hope that somehow, either today or tomorrow, their concern will be sharpened a little for the sake of all of us.

Argument 15

Did you notice anything strange about the defendant's expert? I don't mean it in a derogatory sense. They didn't produce anyone to tell us about the defects involved with this pool. You had Dr. A, you had Dr. B, and you had Dr. C. Did you notice that I asked Dr. A and Dr.B, "What about the design of the pool? That is what this case is about. What can you help us with? What can you tell us?" What was the answer from these experts? "Oh, I am not qualified in that. I am not here to give you an opinion on that." The same with Dr. C; he said he is not qualified to tell you about the design of the pool from the point of view of the defect. Therefore, how can an end-user, a captive consumer, be expected to perceive the devastating risks involved?

§ 11.12 —Establishing liability—the defect

COMMENT: Jurors often come to a case with a greatly limited concept of what makes a product defective. Ask a layman about a defect and he will probably talk about a broken leg on a chair. Most jurors never suspect that the concept of defect includes a product's design, manufacture, marketing, promotion, advertising, assembly, certification, inspection, materials, warnings, instructions, and more. Counsel has presented the evidence concerning the defective nature of the product during the course of the trial. The closing argument is the opportunity to make certain that the jurors understand the broad scope of this concept as it applies to your case. You must also understand that they need to find only one defect in order for the plaintiff to recover.

Argument 16

Please remember, the plaintiff has to prove only one defect. You might find one hundred, but only one is sufficient for the plaintiff to recover. I am going to ask you to consider: Was this four-foot-deep, aboveground pool defective inadequate depth for recreational swimming? Was it of sufficient depth for family swimming and diving? That answer is yes or no. How do you answer? I respectfully suggest that based on the admissions by the defendant's own experts, the answer must be that the pool was defective in the manner in which it was sold and promoted, because of this defect or any one of ten other defects about which you have heard testimony.

Argument 17

The fact remains that this defendant can scientifically predict that with every ten thousand of these pools sold, they are going to get one case of quadriplegia or death. Is that a defective product? I submit under the law of ___________ that it is.

§ 11.13 —Defective marketing

COMMENT: One way for jurors to get the sense of justice and the feeling that counsel is providing them with a unique view behind normally closed corporate boardroom doors is to discuss the defendant's marketing tactics with reference to decisions that were made behind those closed doors. Emphasize that those closed door decisions were intended to sell the product in question. This is a prime opportunity to emphasize the defendant's priorities for sales over consumer safety, to ignite the jurors' sense of justice that the injured plaintiff was a victim of the defendant's callous marketing scheme, and to cultivate further the sense in the jurors' minds that they have a consumer protection mission that they can fulfill by finding for the plaintiff in this case.

Argument 18

What came out of this pool manufacturer's corporate boardroom, where the decisions are made that affect you and me, is quite obvious. How are we going to market this cylinder that holds water to make it financially within the reach of everyone? How are we going to put a swimming pool into every backyard in America? The corporate boardroom people started talking about this. They prepared test marketing. "What is going to happen when kids start using it at play, away from the context of school and supervised training," they asked themselves. We are talking about the backyards of America where girls and boys will dive for all different kinds of things and reasons. You heard evidence in this case that kids are going to play in the pools. They dive into the pools. This company decided to market the pools as family fun centers. They advertised them as backyard country clubs. In short, they overpromoted these pools as "full service" swimming pools when, in fact, they were only suitable, if at all, as "wading" pools!

§ 11.14 —Failure to warn/failure to instruct

COMMENT: The defendant's duty to provide adequate warnings and instructions must be stressed in a manner that is easily understood by members of the jury. In this regard, counsel must stress the vital distinction between warnings and instructions in language and concepts that the jurors can relate to and understand. Emphasize how simple it would have been for the defendant to provide the plaintiff with adequate warnings and instructions, and how bereft the culpable product was of even the most elementary information in this regard.

As with other elements of the plaintiff's case, the importance of adequate warnings should be conveyed within a context that stresses the consumer protection aspects of the case. Emphasize how the plaintiff deserved the opportunity to protect his family, which he could have done if he had been provided adequate warnings concerning the product's defects before tragedy struck.

FAILURE TO WARN

Argument 19

Even a perfectly made and designed product may be defective if it is not accompanied by proper warnings and instructions concerning its use. A product supplier must give such warnings and instructions as are required to inform the consumer or the user of the possible risks. Notice I said possible risks, not definite risks; the possible risks that are created by the inherent limitations in such usage. If you find that such warnings or instructions were not given, the defendant is liable for all harm caused thereby.

Argument 20

Why don't they do the right thing and put a warning logo on the bottom of the pool where you can see it when you look in? Tell us the truth;

instruct the purchaser about quadriplegia so that mothers and fathers can decide whether the fun from backyard pools is worth the risk. You cannot make that judgment unless you have the information that we now have in the jury room. Too late for this plaintiff—not too late for those who are still using and shopping for these death traps.

Who have they warned about this death trap to this very day? They send warranty cards out to pool purchasers. Why can't they use this method to warn their customers about the potential for tragedy? If they mean what they say—that one injury to one child is one too many if it can be avoided; that we are interested in accident prevention and don't care about sales—then why didn't they use a stamp to post an adequate warning?

Argument 21

There is a bomb in that house in the form of odorless, colorless, highly volatile liquefied-petroleum gas, and this company has not provided the consumer with one line of written warning or instruction regarding this hazard. My God, when a kid gets a cut finger and you go get a bottle of Mercurochrome, that bottle has a warning of poison risks. Here I am talking about the possibility of losing an entire family from an explosion—and not a word, not one word, about the catastrophic consequences you learned about in this courtroom.

Failure to Instruct

Argument 22

I don't know of another product that is as void of all instructions as the propane gas in this particular case. There is a big cylinder outside the plaintiff's house with no instructions on it. This defendant didn't give these people even a mimeographed sheet to describe a particular hazard that might result from the use of propane gas in basements. We don't want any fancy brochures. We don't need any trimmings. All they have to do is leave with our bill, or put in our mailbox, or leave with the product, a mimeographed sheet of warnings and instructions on how to live with propane, if you must use it in your home. Certainly as their customer, the plaintiff could expect some information. I think it is a reasonable request. I think it is the kind of conduct that can save lives.

WARNINGS VS. INSTRUCTIONS

Argument 23

Remember the difference between warnings and instructions. If I tell you to "Take two Bufferin a day," that is an instruction. If I tell you, "Don't exceed taking two Bufferin a day because you will get an upset stomach," that's a warning. Adequate warnings and instructions tell it to me the way it is so that I am given the opportunity to make my own choice.

§ 11.15 —Failure to test adequately

Argument 24

Opposing counsel is going to talk, I am sure, about the fact that the State of ___________ has a standard governing liquefied-petroleum gas stating that one pound or two pounds of odorant in 10,000 gallons of LP gas creates an odor. But who's ever tested the odorant in the basement of a home? They do their tests in laboratories, under controlled conditions. I'm not interested in what some chemist says with respect to odorants from a laboratory test. I'm talking about a man who is shaving, getting ready for work one morning, who walks down the stairs to the basement of his home, and is struck down by an explosion. That's the guy I want to help. And if they are going to do any testing, they ought to get out in the field and do some meaningful testing in the consumer's home.

§ 11.16 —Failure to respond adequately to alerts of product hazard

Argument 25

It's as if someone got a call saying there were children walking toward a cliff and they are about to fall off, but we are going to give you time to build a fence at the top of the cliff. You have a choice. If you don't build a fence, you can put an ambulance in the valley below. They chose the ambulance, rather than to build a fence. The only thing is, the ambulance didn't do any good in this case—it could only *transport* the worst type of human misery!

§ 11.17 —Defendant violates its own standards

COMMENT: Remind the jurors that the defendant violated its own stated standards of corporate policy in designing, manufacturing, and marketing the culpable product. Draw the jurors' attention to the testimony of the defendant's executives and other evidence demonstrating this breach by the defendant of its own acknowledged standards for proper conduct.

Argument 26

Do you remember when Mr. S was on the witness stand and he said that "even one injury to one child is one too many if it can be avoided"? Is that consistent with the attitude expressed in court here? Is that consistent with the laws of ____________ that the manufacturer or seller of a product is the guarantor of its safety?

Argument 27

Well, let's judge the defendants by their own standard. They violated that standard, right up until the time this tragedy occurred. For example, do you remember Mr. ____________, the man who designed this product, the defendant's chief engineer? This executive was asked in deposition, "Do you stand for the proposition, as a responsible engineer, that even one death or one injury to one person is one too many if it can be avoided?" And he answered, "Absolutely."

Q. And that has been a standard you have had as long as you have been with the company?

A. Yes, that's correct.

Q. And you wouldn't have it any other way?

A. No.

Well, this company violated that standard because they provided the consumer with no information. It's the plaintiffs' position here today that had they done so and had they given the option to the ____________ family, this tragedy wouldn't have occurred.

§ 11.18 —Safer design alternatives

COMMENT: Few facts drive home the defendant's callous indifference to consumer safety as well as the establishment that safety devices, or safer product designs, were available that could have prevented the plaintiff's tragedy, and that the defendant simply chose not to use them. This evidence comes to the essence of the plaintiff's consumer protection case, as it frequently involves the defendant's conscious choice to save a few dollars, or sell more products by placing its priorities on aesthetics, or cutting corners, rather than on safe product design.

Argument 28

Mr. ___________ testified that he could have taken Plaintiffs' Exhibit 1 for identification and redesigned it. You see where that hole is? He could have made it one piece instead of attaching the head with a screw. I don't think you have to be a mechanical genius to understand that one piece construction might have had less of a chance of coming apart. If he made it in one piece, he said as a matter of design that he could have brought the hole all the way through and created an airway.

Dr. ___________testified that if the defendant had designed its product with such an airway, the plaintiff would not be brain damaged today. It would have bought him the time that they needed by creating an airway, which might have avoided the severe brain damage that occurred.

Argument 29

Dr. B's [the Plaintiff's expert's] conclusion was that there were safety caps available and patented that would have prevented the plaintiff's permanent and disfiguring burn injuries. Such a safety cap would have prevented this caustic cleaner from spilling out of its container. This testimony goes unrebutted, in essence—there was no answer—yet the clear inference is that the cap was not used because it would cost a few pennies more.

Argument 30

The evidence is absolutely uncontradicted, from their own sources, that this was an unprotected utility wire. It was uninsulated. It was not fused. Did you hear Mr. ____________ quite honestly say that this girl probably would be alive today, she wouldn't have been hurt, had this electric utility pole had a fuse that costs a couple of dollars and would take one or two men ten minutes to install? For a couple of bucks and ten minutes of their time, this company let this girl die.

§ 11.19 —Evidence from defendant's witnesses

COMMENT: The most striking and effective evidence of the defendant's misconduct often comes from the testimony of the defendant's own witnesses, frequently under the plaintiff-counsel's cross-examination. Remind the jurors of this kind of evidence, as often as possible with testimony that they have just heard in the courtroom. Again, this evidence helps to fuel the jurors' sense of justice and their willingness to find for the plaintiff.

PRODUCT DESIGNER TESTIFIES THAT PLAINTIFF SHOULD BE ADEQUATELY WARNED

Argument 31

The designer of the product was asked a question: "You'd want the ultimate consumer to be impacted with the information about the limitations of this product?" And he said "Yes."

Q. And that's the standard of your corporation, isn't it?

A. Yes.

Defendant's Expert Flip-Flops on Causes of Household Fires

Argument 32

The defendant's expert testified under oath that electrical fires are a prominent cause of household fires. The defendant makes this statement in its product literature. Yet when I asked the defendant's expert on the stand, "Are electrical fires a prominent cause of fire?", he said, "I disagree."

Well, you can't agree and disagree when it suits yourself. You can't just choose one side or the other when it's convenient. You are in a courtroom under oath. The truth has to come out here. The reason for this evasion is clear—protect my company—at all cost!

Defendant's Failure to Supply Information to Plaintiff Because No One Required It is Evidence of Defendant's Callous Disregard for Human Safety

Argument 33

Despite the fact that this company's chief engineer was using a battery backup system for the smoke detector in his own home, nobody told this plaintiff about it. Why not? Because, as the defendant's executive admitted under oath, "No one required it." No one said, "___________ Corporation, ___________ Company, you have got to do it."

They didn't do something because it was not required. What kind of an attitude is that to take where consumers in the United States of America are buying a product that is sold as a lifesaving device?

Misrepresenting the Product

Argument 34

Not only did this defendant not advise the person who bought the product that they had a chance to protect their family adequately by purchasing the safer product, they went one step further. They misrepresented facts. They made statements that were, according to the testimony of the defendant's expert, totally false. This cannot be acceptable—lives depend on the truth being known.

§ 11.20 —Plaintiff's right to recover: the law

Argument 35

The law provides, as His Honor will instruct you, that if someone sells us a product that has hazards attached to it and we are not informed about those hazards, and as a result of this lack of information, we are injured or killed, the plaintiff is entitled to recover. We are entitled to recover, even without fault or negligence, if we prove that the product was not fit for the purposes for which it is sold, because it was unreasonably hazardous, or because we didn't get notice or warning of any hazard or special instructions about how to avoid the hazard.

Argument 36

When a child has sustained an injury under the circumstances that occurred in this case, the law does not require a mother and a father to dedicate their lives totally to the care of that particular individual, to the detriment of a remaining child, without compensation or professional help. That child is entitled to professional help, professional care. That family is entitled to all the professional support that money can buy, if it is reasonable under the circumstances.

§ 11.21 —Damages

COMMENT: Jurors will be confronted with a responsibility that they likely never had before—to place a monetary value on the loss of life or tragic injury. They will often be faced with staggering figures that they may not have dealt with on a practical basis before. Remind them of the duties that they accepted when they took their oath as jurors. Help them by developing analogies to other, more tangible articles, such as a valuable painting, the price of which may be more conceivable to jury members. Explain technical and detailed economics of the plaintiff's costs to make certain that jurors understand the full dimensions of the plaintiff's damages and the reasonable costs of compensation that he is entitled to recover. Convey the full impact of the plaintiff's damages by reminding the jurors of the plaintiff's injuries in a manner that is graphic and clear. Relate those damages back to the jurors' sense of justice. Reiterate how justice demands a full, fair, and reasonable recovery for the plaintiff in this case.

Plaintiff's Economist

Argument 37

The economist said this injured child would need an eighteen thousand dollar car to get around. He did not include the price of a van with an electric lift, which he could have. He calculated this dollar allowance for transportation so that the mother and father would have a car of their own to use and the attendant, whoever takes care of this child, would be able to take him out to the park or do some of the things he would like to do during the course of his day. More expensive methods of transportation were not included in the medical economist's figures.

Injuries to Plaintiff

Argument 38

We can never make this child whole again. There has been uncontradicted testimony that he is brain damaged in the extreme. You could see for yourselves that the child is totally disabled. The doctor from Canada testified that he will never advance further than that level. Dr. K, our child development specialist, testified that he will never advance beyond that level. One doctor testified that, indeed, he might get worse. He is eleven years old now. He is still in the first grade and he is a sub-par first grader at that. He will never be normal again. And yet, he is and will remain a beautiful, loving child.

Out-of-Pocket Expenses

Argument 39

The child has 60.4 years of life remaining, according to testimony that hasn't been contradicted. This figure comes from published tables. This amounts to about $30,000 each year over sixty years. Now, imagine that this defendant lost a piece of machinery that was going to produce "X" number of dollars for them every week. Suppose that a part on the machine broke down and the company was put out of business for a year on that particular production run. You can be sure they would have plenty of economists come in and tell you what their damages were. If their damages came out to $3,000,000, that's what they would expect to recover. They would say that was a full, fair, and reasonable measure of recovery. The plaintiff is entitled to the same justice.

Parents' Loss of Guidance, Care, and Companionship

Argument 40

There is another element of damages here for the parents of ____________ that I think bears commenting on. It's the loss of past, present, and future guidance, care and companionship that ____________ might reasonably have expected from ____________ if the injury had not occurred. As His Honor will instruct you, it will be your duty to put a price on the value of losing a son's companionship. Here you can talk about a father who has been deprived of the companionship and guidance from a growing son.

Pain and Suffering

Argument 41

The law provides for separate elements of damages called conscious pain and suffering. Counsel for the defense pointed out that her death was a few seconds, a few minutes, a few ticks of the clock. Well, what the evidence showed was that she said, "Save me. Save me," while she was burning up alive, and incinerating. Indeed, while she was burning, her left foot, I believe it was her left foot, shredded. The pictures will show you this. That minute of burning alive is a whole lifetime, a miserable and painful end to a beautiful life. The law says, under conscious pain and suffering, that her estate is entitled to recover for this because a wrongdoer shouldn't get away with that kind of conscious pain and suffering if it was negligently inflicted or inflicted with gross negligence. You decide what that whole lifetime is worth. She's burning. She's dying. It's flashing before her. She is searing with pain. I know you will reach a full, fair, and reasonable determination as to that item of damage: conscious pain and suffering.

Past and Future Pain and Suffering

Argument 42

There is an element of damages that I have not talked about. It is called past, present, and future pain and suffering, and a loss of the amenitites of life. This is the item that this jury is going to have to do the most soul-searching on as the trier of fact. You must put a dollar value on what a happy, productive life is worth, free from brain damage, free from paralysis, free from dependency on others. Indeed, free to choose, free to play ball, free to go bowling, free to play with your brother, and free to toss a ball to one's dad and get it back, waiting for the smile on your father's face when he says, "Boy, you are improving. You know, you are really coming along." Those are the little moments that we all remember. That is what pain and suffering means in this case. All of the little amenities of life that are major when you consider the totality of life. This is what God created us for, to lead productive lives free from injury, if possible, and certainly free from hazards that are avoidable or preventable.

Argument 43

This is the system. This is how it has to be done. It's the only way you can compensate people for harm of this kind. So what figure would be reasonable? I suggest you will think hard about that. I might suggest to you that if the economic loss is a ___________ dollars, certainly pain and suffering can't be worth less than that. It has to be worth, I respectfully submit, a sum far greater than that because you are putting a sum on the most precious thing a life has to offer—happiness free of agonizing pain.

I am confident this jury will be able to, as they go through the evidence, reach their own conclusions. Just do not back away from numbers that perhaps I am not used to dealing with in my own life and you are not used to dealing with in your own lives. If that is where the numbers take you, that is what justice demands in this case, a full, fair, and reasonable measure of recovery.

Quality of Life

Argument 44

I want to concentrate on the quality of life itself, and you will forgive me, and forgive the law, for asking you to do justice by focusing on and evaluating matters that you understandably will find it difficult to deal with. The law has no other way of getting the message out except through jurors like yourselves. When you took your oaths as jurors, you made your commitment to put a dollar value on precisely the kinds of things that one might think it would be impossible to put a dollar figure on: not having a family; not getting married; being humiliated and stared at like some kind of freak.

FULL, FAIR, AND REASONABLE RECOVERY, NOT PUNISHMENT

Argument 45

Punishment has no place in this trial, as His Honor will instruct you. The law doesn't permit that, but the law does permit a full, fair, and reasonable measurement of damages.

NO SECOND CHANCE

Argument 46

Remember, the children whose father died in that gas explosion can't come back to you in the future and say, "It wasn't enough, you were wrong, my daddy was worth more, he had more ambition, we had our own house for the first time." We have to give this family everything now that they are entitled to by a fair preponderance of the evidence.

DESCRIBING THE PLAINTIFF'S DAMAGES TO THE JURY

Argument 47

No family that we know would exchange a human life for any amount of money. You could pile up twenty-five million dollars, a hundred million, three hundred million, all the money in the world, and it wouldn't matter. The fact that the plaintiff's damages are in many ways intangible doesn't mean that you can't—this is your task—put a meaningful value on this girl's life and what her loss means to the members of her family.

§ 11.22 —Punitive damages

COMMENT: Punitive damages are a vital part of the plaintiff's consumer protection case. Counsel should stress the need to send a clear punitive message to the defendant, as well as to the industry of which the defendant is a member, that the conduct and practices that resulted in the plaintiff's injuries or death are not acceptable.

Explain that punitive damages have two functions: punishment and deterrence. Compensatory damages are not intended to punish a corporation for its wrongdoing. Punitive damages do that. Punitive damages must also be sufficient to deter corporations and industries from continuing their practices of slaughter by product.

Draw a practical analogy to illustrate the point that the defendant's wanton and reckless conduct resulted in the plaintiff's tragedy. Explain to the jurors that they have the opportunity to teach the defendants a lesson in the language corporations know best—the bottom line. This is the most effective way to prevent such tragedy from occurring again.

Argument 48

It is plaintiffs' position that there is gross negligence that would entitle them to punitive damages. This is where, I submit, the real fight is. Punitive damages are assessed to force a conscience on the corporation that was grossly negligent, or whose gross negligence caused harm to someone else. And please remember, there has to be a relationship between the punishment and the net worth of the perpetrator, otherwise it is not punishment.

A major purpose of punitive damages is deterrence. Teach the defendants a lesson so that they won't place the defective product that can slaughter unsuspecting consumers into our stream of commerce again. Let them hear the message. Say to them, "You are punished and it's going to cost you a percentage of your net income." Then you will see some fast changes—changes that prayerfully will change lives.

Argument 49

Punitive damage means that in addition to the other damages that you will award, you can award a sum that you expect will get the message across to the corporation that what they did under the circumstances was wanton and reckless.

Suppose, by analogy, that you have a circular stadium of 10,000 people. Suppose, furthermore, that I hand you a loaded gun. You close your eyes and pull the trigger. You cripple one person. Is it any defense when that person sues you to say "How can you complain, you statistically had a good chance of survival, ten thousand to one?" In the same way, if this defendant knew it was getting two quadriplegia cases every year, when people dive into four-foot-deep aboveground pools, that comes to equal one for every ten thousand pools sold. Plaintiff's expert called this a scientific certainty. Can this defendant now come to you and complain that the plaintiff had a good chance not to be injured? I don't think so. The evidence was overwhelming that this young man did not know about the risk of quadriplegia, but that the defendants knew or should have known. They had a duty not to make a buck on a product that was so dangerous unless they told us the whole truth. I would consider that to be as wanton and reckless as my being in the middle of the stadium of ten thousand people, swirling around, and firing a gun. I certainly know that I will hurt someone. That is wanton and reckless. They knew with certainty that their product would cripple someone!

§ 11.23 —No discount justice—full compensation

COMMENT: Emphasize to the jurors the plaintiff's right to a full recovery. Appeal to the jurors' sense of right and wrong by explaining to them that anything short of full compensation for the plaintiff's injuries is discount justice, and not full consumer protection. Don't let the defendant walk away from the courtroom thinking it has achieved a victory because the jury provided discount justice. Let members of the jury sense that their job is only done when full justice has been served and the plaintiff has received the full, fair, and reasonable damages required by law.

Argument 50

I believe the real issue in this case comes down to this: "Is this young man going to get a full, fair, and reasonable measure of recovery and full compensatory damages?" Discount justice is no justice at all. If this corporation gets the feeling that a jury in ____________ is going to indulge in discount justice, and thus, the plaintiff perhaps might be short-changed, they will continue to gamble on such unfair results and the cause of consumer protection will thus be subverted.

Argument 51

If [the corporation] leaves this courtroom with partial justice or discount justice, a verdict that reflects less than the value of the case, then they will feel reasonably satisfied that they have done their job, I am sure. But will the triers of fact have done their job under those circumstances? Will the cause of justice have been served truthfully?

Argument 52

Just as you have to have the courage of your convictions in a case like this, you also have to have the courage to write the appropriate numbers down on your slips, no matter what those numbers are, and no matter where they may lead you, and no matter how large the dollar result is—justice demands an accurate and full accounting.

Argument 53

When you have the opportunity to deliberate tomorrow, please don't give discounts. Seventy-five percent justice or twenty-five percent justice is not full justice. No matter where our reasoning takes us, no matter how large a sum we arrive at, the number must be entered since discount justice is really no justice at all.

§ 11.24 —Distinguishing between justice and sympathy

COMMENT: It is vitally important that the jurors understand that the plaintiff is seeking justice, not sympathy. Sympathy has no place in the courtroom, either for the defendant or for the plaintiff. Counsel can fuel the jurors' sense of their mission more effectively by conveying the sense of justice and helping them to distinguish their justice mission from a reaction of sympathy. The plaintiff does not seek sympathy. The defendant does not deserve it.

Argument 54

Sympathy is charity and the plaintiff is not asking for charity. We are asking for justice and there is a difference.

You are not to consider, as His Honor will instruct you, that ____________ is a major corporation, because we should get no particular benefit from that, and that's the truth. We are not here for sympathy. We are here for an accounting, for justice, for a full, fair, and reasonable measure of justice.

You shouldn't have any concern or sympathy for ____________. They have made a profit by marketing these products as safe. People relied on them. This family relied on them. They have made "X" number of dollars by selling these products, and ____________ has been injured as a result of this dangerous marketing practice.

Argument 55

If after you total up all of these damages, it comes out to six or seven or eight million dollars, that's not sympathy. It's an accounting. Corporations are used to that type of accounting, they use it everyday to adjust their balance sheets—justice demands that they settle adequately this accounting as well.

Argument 56

Sympathy has no place in this trial. This mother and these children are not asking for sympathy. But we don't have to try this case in a vacuum, either. I don't think His Honor suggested that we have to try this case with ice water in our veins, that we can't have the consideration and feeling that makes the jury system in this country what it is. Empathy and compassion are needed for the purpose of properly evaluating the effect this injury has had on this precious life . . . justice does not require this decision to be made by machines.

Argument 57

The plaintiffs did not come here today to ask for sympathy. Their pillows are wet with the tears of sympathy. They came here today to ask for justice. Sympathy is not needed—justice is!

INDEX

[References are to sections.]

—A—

[References are to sections.]

Index

[References are to sections.]

[References are to sections.]

[References are to sections.]

—C—

[References are to sections.]

CHEMICALS, INJURIES RELATED TO—Continued

[References are to sections.]

[References are to sections.]

CLOSING ARGUMENTS—Continued

[References are to sections.]

[References are to sections.]

[References are to sections.]

Index

[References are to sections.]

[References are to sections.]

Index

[References are to sections.]

DRAIN CLEANERS, INJURIES RELATED TO

[References are to sections.]

[References are to sections.]

[References are to sections.]

[References are to sections.]

[References are to sections.]

[References are to sections.]

[References are to sections.]

[References are to sections.]

[References are to sections.]

[References are to sections.]

[References are to sections.]

[References are to sections.]

[References are to sections.]

MOBILE HOMES, PRODUCT-RELATED INJURIES

[References are to sections.]

—N—

—O—

—P—

[References are to sections.]

[References are to sections.]

[References are to sections.]

—S—

[References are to sections.]

[References are to sections.]

—T—

[References are to sections.]

TOYS, INJURIES RELATED TO

[References are to sections.]

[References are to sections.]

[References are to sections.]

[References are to sections.]

[References are to sections.]

Slaughter By Product: Winning the Products Liability Case

Edited by Louise M. Cherkis, J.D.

Index by Lucille Boorstein.

Text design and copyediting by Maryellen J. Costa.

Cover and title page design by Patricia J. Collins.

Composition, printing, and binding by Joe Christensen, Inc., Lincoln, Nebraska. Text set in 11 on 13 Times Roman on the Datalogic system and printed on 50 lb. Hammermill Cream Eggshell; four-color signature printed on 70 lb. Productolith Matte; bound in Library Buckram with 90 lb. Scott Vellum White endsheets.

SLAUGHTER BY PRODUCT

WINNING THE PRODUCTS LIABILITY CASE

1993 CUMULATIVE SUPPLEMENT

EDWARD M. SWARTZ
Member of the Massachusetts Bar

The Michie Company
Law Publishers
CHARLOTTESVILLE, VIRGINIA

Place in pocket of bound volume and recycle previous supplement.

ACKNOWLEDGMENTS

I wish to acknowledge and thank the many judges and lawyers who have provided helpful suggestions and ideas. Additionally, I would like to thank Elly D. Swartz for her research and editorial assistance in compiling this supplement. My particular gratitude is extended to Associate Dean Charles P. Kindregan of Suffolk University Law School for his valuable advice.

All members of the Bar are invited to contact me with regard to any recent product cases they may have handled that have either been settled or gone to verdict, which they feel will be of interest and prove helpful to their fellow attorneys.

EDWARD M. SWARTZ, ESQ.
Swartz and Swartz
Boston, Massachusetts
July 1993

NOTE

I would like to inform the reader that effort has been made to use gender-neutral language throughout the book and supplement. Where clarity requires, however, the masculine pronoun has been used as a gender-neutral reference.

ABOUT THE AUTHOR

EDWARD M. SWARTZ is a nationally known and respected trial attorney, consumer advocate and author. Known as a "Lawyer's Lawyer," he has obtained million-dollar verdicts and settlements in courts across America. Through his lectures, books and articles, he has taught innovative trial techniques and imaginative strategies to attorneys and attorneys-to-be. Among his titles utilized by lawyers everywhere are *Slaughter By Product, Hazardous Products Litigation 2d* and *Proof of Product Defect.*

Edward M. Swartz has dedicated over 20 years of his life to the crusade for safety. For each of those years he has issued an annual "10 Worst Toys List" to alert parents and other consumers to the dangers of unsafe toys. To advance the cause of safety, Swartz created and developed an exciting curriculum, *Toys, You, and the Real World,* which teaches children to become critical thinkers and vigilant, safety-conscious consumers.

Mr. Swartz's message has been heard by millions through his appearances on such national shows as "60 Minutes," "Inside Edition," "Good Morning America," "The Larry King Show," "CNN News," "CBS Nightwatch," "The Today Show," and many local television and radio programs.

Mr. Swartz has been honored by his peers, civic and charitable organizations, and a variety of publications. Among his many honors, he was named "Man of Vision" by the Massachusetts Society for the Prevention of Blindness, declared one of America's 100 Best Lawyers by *Town and Country Magazine,* and paid tribute to by *American Lawyer Magazine* as the best civil trial attorney for 1981. Most recently, Swartz was singled out by *Massachusetts Lawyers Weekly* in an editorial praising him "as an example to the public of the unselfishness of lawyers."

Mr. Swartz graduated magna cum laude from Boston University School of Law, where he was Editor-in-Chief of the Law Review. He received an LL.M. graduate degree from the University of Michigan Law School, where he was a W.C. Cook Fellow. He is Past President of the Massachusetts Trial Lawyers, State Coordinator for Trial Lawyers for Public Justice, and former chairman of the Association of Trial Lawyers of America's Continuing

Education Committee. Mr. Swartz is also a member of the Massachusetts Bar and many Bar Associations.

Mr. Swartz is a partner in the Boston firm of Swartz & Swartz.

TABLE OF CONTENTS

Chapter 4
Fabric-Related Burn Injuries — The Torch Cases

IV. Other Flammable Products

VI. Litigation Sources: Bibliography

Chapter 5
Electrical Mayhem

IV. Other Electrical Hazards

VI. Litigation Sources: Bibliography

Chapter 6
Crippled at Leisure: Recreational Product-Related Torts

VI. Litigation Sources: Bibliography

Chapter 7
In the Nursery: Toys That Injure and Maim

V. Preventing Toy-Related Injuries

VI. Litigation Sources: Bibliography

Chapter 8
Medical Products That Do Not Heal

II. Checklists

IIIA. Other Medical Product Hazards [New]

IV. Preventing Medical Device-Related Injuries

Chapter 12
Products Liability Litigation and the Promotion of Public Safety [New]

Chapter 1

RECOGNIZING "WINNABLE" FACT PATTERNS

IV. Theories of Recovery [New]

V. Allegations of Product Defect in Complaint [New]

Page 1:

[Add new Part title as follows:]

I. Overview [New]

Page 8:

[Add new sections following § 1.07.]

§ 1.08 Consumer protection — a fundamental concept for the plaintiff's lawyer in the products case [New]

It is a common myth that consumers of products exercise total freedom of choice in their purchases. In fact, this myth is false. The techno-industrial society in which we live actually constrains true freedom of choice because the consumer has very little information about the product design, the effectiveness of safety design, the testing done on the product, prior reported injuries caused by the product, or other information which can be used to evaluate the dangers involved in using the product.[23]

The lawyer representing the injured consumer should understand the practical value of the concept of the "captive consumer," i.e., the helplessness of the consumer when he or she is buying, renting, or using a product. In a way, we are all captive consumers — we all depend on the manufacturers and sellers of

[23]For an in-depth analysis of this theme *see* Swartz, *Freeing the Captive Consumer: How Do We Get Consumers Off the Hook?*, 22 TRIAL 28 (Apr. 1986); Kindregan & Swartz, *The Assault on the Captive Consumer*, 18 ST. MARY'S L.J. 673 (1987).

the products we use to protect us from the hidden dangers inherent in the product. Technological advances, coupled with the sophisticated methods employed in mass marketing products, place every consumer at the mercy of those who control the testing, design, manufacture, and marketing of the product. The judge, the jury, the lawyers — in a word, everyone who is involved in the litigation process — is such a consumer. It is the role of the plaintiff's lawyer in a product case to bring this simple concept alive during the trial, and to hammer it home during the presentation of your evidence and argument.

COMMENT: The plaintiff's lawyer who approaches his case as a consumer protection case has a great advantage. He can help the factfinder understand the consumer's total dependence on the integrity and skill of the manufacturer and marketer of the product. He must make this a central theme of the plaintiff's case. Was the product tested for safety? Was the consumer warned of the dangers involved in using the product? Are there safety features built into the product? Did the advertiser or marketer oversell the product by ignoring the hidden dangers? The great advantage of this approach is that the members of the jury are themselves consumers of products — and they can identify with the need to protect the purchaser of the product.

Lawyers have not devoted sufficient attention to this aspect of products liability law. We must be more alert to the plight of the captive consumers and the need to protect them from slaughter by product. As a tool of effective litigation, the concept of the captive consumer has everyday application. I have found, for example, that during the presentation of evidence, and especially during argument, the constant restatement of the theme of the captive consumer in some form is an effective device for getting the jury to think of the case as a form of consumer protection; this theme hits home with jurors who are themselves consumers of products.

The basic rationale for this concept was stated in the classic formulation by Justice Traynor (concurring) in *Escola v. Coca Cola*

Bottling Co.,[24] a statement which continues to have validity almost a half century later:

> Consumers no longer approach products warily but accept them on faith, relying on the manufacturer or trademark.... The manufacturer's obligation to the consumer must keep pace with the changing relationship between them.

§ 1.09 Overcoming the "sale" requirement [New]

Product liability lawyers must think creatively about their craft. Black letter case law suggests that strict liability and breach of warranty claims are premised on a sale of the product. Some statutes and much of the reported case law use the word "sale." However, thoughtful lawyers will be aware that the concept of "sale" evolved for two reasons:

(1) to distinguish a strict liability or implied warranty claim in a commercial situation from the transfer of a product by a non-merchant; and
(2) to create more accountability by one who is inserting a defective and dangerous product into the stream of commerce.

If one understands this concept, then the word "sale" will not be read literally. The creative lawyer will put his or her emphasis on the fact that the defendant was putting a dangerous product into the stream of commerce, rather than on the fact that a product was "sold."

COMMENT: Emphasis should be placed on the fact that the defendant released a defective and dangerous product into the stream of commerce, rather than on the technical issue of whether there was a "sale."

A number of reported cases illustrate this proposition. In

[24] 24 Cal. 2d 453, 150 P.2d 436 (1944), Traynor, J., concurring.

Thorpe v. Robert F. Bullock, Inc.,[25] the plaintiff was burned by oil spilled from a defective fryer placed in a restaurant on a free trial basis. Technically, there was no sale; the Georgia court, however, applied strict liability under a statute requiring that the product be "sold," on the theory that strict liability should not be based on the intricacies of sales law, but on the policy of the law regarding the introduction of dangerous products into the marketplace. The same argument can be made with regard to breach of warranty claims under the Uniform Commercial Code.[26]

§ 1.09A Post-sale duty of manufacturer to warn [New]

It is generally recognized that a manufacturer of a product which is unsafe for use must take steps after selling such a product to warn of unreasonable dangers of which he becomes aware after the product has reached the hands of an exposed consumer.[26.1] The duty of giving post-sale warnings has been recognized for at least forty years,[26.2] and most jurisdictions which have addressed the issue have recognized some form of the duty.[26.3]

The courts have generally allowed recovery on a post-sale duty to warn strict liability theory under Section 402A of the Restatement.[26.4]

---

[25] 179 Ga. App. 867, 348 S.E.2d 55 (1986), *aff'd*, 256 Ga. 744, 353 S.E.2d 340 (1987).

[26] *See* Shaffer v. Victoria Station, Inc., 91 Wash. 2d 295, 588 P.2d 233 (1978) (wine glass shattering in restaurant patron's hand gave rise to claim).

[26.1] Allee, *Post-Sale Obligations of Product Manufacturers*, 12 FORDHAM URB. L.J. 625 (1984); Royal, *Post Sale Warnings: A Review and Analysis Seeking Fair Compensation Under Uniform Law*, 33 DRAKE L. REV. 817 (1983).

[26.2] *See, e.g.*, Comstock v. General Motors Corp., 358 Mich. 163, 99 N.W.2d 627 (1959) (automobile manufacturer warned dealers of defect in power brakes, but took no steps to warn consumers who purchased the vehicles).

[26.3] *See, e.g.*, Kozlowski v. John E. Smith's Sons Co., 87 Wis. 2d 882, 275 N.W.2d 915 (1979) (manufacturer of sausage-stuffing machine failed to warn of danger of ammonia fumes after sale, although it incorporated safety bypass valve on machines manufactured after it had sold the machine which killed a user of the machine). Other cases are collected and noted in the articles cited in note 26.1, *supra*.

[26.4] RESTATEMENT (SECOND) OF TORTS, § 402A comment h (1979).

A seller is obligated to warn and instruct as to known dangers. If the product is defective because such warnings or instructions were not given, and the plaintiff was injured because of this, the manufacturer-seller is liable without proof of negligence.[26.5]

There is no logical reason for a manufacturer-seller to escape liability when he fails to warn of dangers of which he became aware after the sale of a dangerously defective product, when he has the ability to send such warnings through the distribution chain in a manner likely to reach persons who are now using the product. An example is found in *Walton v. AVCO Corp.*,[26.6] where a defect in a helicopter engine had caused the crash of the helicopter and the death of a person in the helicopter. The court held that the manufacturer could be held liable for the defect of which it became aware after manufacturing the product and of which the engine repairer was not made aware.

§ 1.09B Choosing a winning theory [New]

Minors are forever climbing utility poles and, as a consequence, receiving serious bodily injury. Many attorneys proceed under the attractive nuisance doctrine. My law firm recently represented the estate of a seventeen-year-old high school student who spent his evening drinking heavily near a utility pole located next to a strip mall. It was later discovered that the boy's blood alcohol content was .16. The minor proceeded to climb the pole in front of three of his friends. As plaintiff minor was about twenty feet off the ground, an electrical arc pinned him to the pole and then sent him hurtling to the ground, his chest on fire. His friends began to put out the fire, but the boy was mortally wounded. We did not proceed on an attractive nuisance theory. Instead, we alleged that the bottom step of the pole was located too close to the ground, even though the pole was in compliance with applicable regulations. One week prior to trial, the case was settled for $950,000.

[26.5] The argument could also be made that the failure to provide the necessary warnings or instructions is itself negligence.

[26.6] 383 Pa. Super. 518, 557 A.2d 372 (1989).

§ 1.09C Avoid blaming the victim [New]

The problem many attorneys face when confronted with machines that cause amputations of the hands and of fingers is the tendency to blame the victim. The injured party should have been more careful or more aware or should not have stuck his hand where it did not belong. We recently had a case where the machine operator stuck his hand in the wrong spot of the same machine for the second time in five years. On this second occasion, the operator's hand was crushed and a finger partially amputated. The defense countered the claim of defective design, alleging that the danger was open and obvious. The jury returned a judgment in the plaintiff's favor in excess of $500,000 with interest.

Page 8:

[Add new Parts II through V to chapter as follows:]

II. Discovery Practice [New]

§ 1.10 Introduction

A product liability case can be won or lost at the discovery stage of litigation. An ineffective use of the valuable opportunities provided by the rules of civil procedure may cause the lawyer to overlook valuable evidence. Discovery can be used to open an opponent's case, to discover his theories, to foresee his trial tactics, and to position him so that he will begin to think seriously about settlement. Discovery provides the lawyer with golden opportunities to learn and exploit his opponent's damaging weaknesses. For the plaintiff, discovery presents an opportunity to penetrate the world of corporate thinking, where sales often have a higher priority than product safety, and where evidence of this attitude is often buried in corporate records and memoranda.

An example will illustrate my point. In a case I handled, two children were placed by their parents in a station wagon while the parents went back into the house to get some things.[27] The

---

[27] Hinckley v. Eastman Kodak Co., No. 69-1338 (D. Mass. 1973).

parents had wrapped the children in a fiber-filled comforter because it was very cold. Suddenly the station wagon was enveloped in smoke. The children were terribly burned by the time their frantic parents pulled them from the vehicle. They will bear the scars of their injuries all their lives. The cause of the fire which ruined the lives of those children could not be established. But the "comforter" melted onto their skin, causing terrible damage. I was determined to discover what caused the comforter to be such a flammable weapon of destruction.

The fiberfill had been manufactured by a nationally known and respected corporation. By examining company officials, I obtained admissions that when fire melts the polyester fiberfill used in the comforter, it adheres to human skin causing the type of horrible burns which were inflicted on my clients. I also obtained damaging admissions that the chemicals used in the fiberfill were so dangerous that workers at the manufacturing plant had been burned and that special protections for the workers had to be instituted. Corporate officials also admitted that a label prominently displayed on the comforter stating that the user could "count on" the product was intentionally designed to promote sales. By patient examination of the voluminous corporate documents I obtained in discovery, I learned that a corporate executive had written "Whom are we trying to kid?" on a memorandum discussing a program to promote the fabric as "registered." Through patient use of discovery I learned that the company had not tested the comforter for flammability, although other products using the fiber had been tested with a result that the fiber tended to melt when exposed to flame. The judgment of $1,415,000, over a decade ago, was the largest rendered in a flammable fabrics case in the United States up to that point. It was a recovery earned in large part by determined and careful use of discovery.

§ 1.11 Discovering the defect

At the outset of discovery, the lawyer should determine to learn as much as possible about the defect in the product which caused the injury. He should not start with any preconception based on law school learning about defective products. Chief Justice Traynor of the Supreme Court of California once pointed out that as to product defect "no definition has been formulated which would resolve all cases."[28]

COMMENT: The lawyer's attitude should be that if a product caused an injury he should presume that it was defective and set out in discovery to learn what the defect was.

In discovery on the issue of product defect, the lawyer should pursue an inquiry about every aspect of the product. He should create a checklist of information to be obtained, including questions such as the following:

How precisely did the product cause the injury?

How was the product designed?

Could the manufacturer and/or marketer of the product foresee danger?

What steps could the defendant have taken to eliminate or reduce the danger?

What testing was done on the product?

What testing should have been done on the product?

Did marketing of the product avoid warnings of danger?

Did advertising of the product induce an unsafe use?

How was the product packaged?

How was the product labeled?

What instructions were given for the use of the product?

---

[28] Traynor, *The Ways and Means of Defective Products and Strict Liability*, 32 TENN. L. REV. 363 (1965).

One definition of a defectively designed product found in Green v. Kautex Machines Co., 159 A.D.2d 945, 552 N.Y.S.2d 794 (1990) is a product which leaves the seller's hands in a condition which is not reasonably contemplated by the ultimate consumer of the product and is an unreasonably dangerous condition for its intended use.

What warnings were given?

Were safety features adequately explained?

These types of questions will get the lawyer thinking about the areas that will have to be explored in discovery to determine what defect caused the injury to the client. In my experience, thinking about such questions before discovery is a major step toward taking advantage of the opportunities presented by discovery to isolate product defect.

§ 1.12 Prediscovery steps

In preparation for discovery, the lawyer should also read as much as possible about the reported cases on the product,[29] consult the major texts,[30] and consult with experts on every aspect of the product.[31]

Certain additional prediscovery steps will also assist the attorney in obtaining maximum benefit from discovery. Obviously, the plaintiff's attorney should take immediate possession of the product which caused the injury, or of a duplicate if the product itself is not available. He should make a record of serial numbers, model numbers, patent numbers, labels, warnings, instructions, directions, warranties, trademarks, lot numbers, and similar information which will be of assistance during discovery. Obvious characteristics of the product should be noted early, such as sharp edges, flammability of parts, use of toxic paint, and so forth. Moreover, your expert should examine the product and note more subtle characteristics which may prove helpful to you during discovery.

---

[29] Modern computerized research methods make such information more easily available. For example, feeding the name of a particular defendant into the computer will sometimes produce other cases involving issues similar to the case you are handling. Feeding words descriptive of the product into the computer will almost certainly produce other reported cases involving that product.

[30] *See, e.g.*, the *Litigation Sources: Bibliography* sections, *infra* Chapters 2-9.

[31] In SWARTZ PROOF OF PRODUCT DEFECT (Lawyers Co-operative Pub. Co. 1985), I examine how a lawyer can make most effective use of his expert consultants.

The original packaging should be obtained, if available. If it is unavailable, try to obtain duplicate packaging. Note the warranties, warnings, and instructions listed on the packaging. Think of the packaging as a potential defect — does it tell the consumer what it ought to tell him? Does the packaging suggest that the consumer make dangerous uses of the product by drawings or suggestions?

Obtain all of the advertisements for the product. These can be useful in preparing for your discovery, although you might want to use discovery to obtain a complete set of advertisements. Ask yourself if the ads promote unsafe use of the product. In one case, in which I obtained a jury verdict in excess of $6,000,000,[32] we learned that the defendant aboveground pool manufacturer was advertising the product by showing people diving into the pools, despite a body count of quadriplegia victims resulting from such diving.

You should also obtain reports from any and all sources available to you before beginning discovery, including fire reports, police reports, coroner's reports, and hospital and medical reports. The same is true of any reports prepared by your experts.

Think through the theories on which you intend to rely. This will help to focus your use of discovery. Among the more common theories you will want to consider are design defect, manufacturing defect, packaging defect, failure to warn, strict liability, breach of implied warranty, breach of express warranty, uncrashworthy vehicle, failure to inspect, failure to keep up with the state of the art, product unreasonably dangerous, violation of code standard, and violation of statute.

§ 1.13 Identifying the defendant

Normally, the plaintiff's attorney will have chosen the target defendants before the complaint is filed. He will generally have identified the manufacturer, suppliers of component parts, vendors, marketers, packagers, testers, lessors, and so on, and named them as defendants before discovery begins. However, the

---

[32] Koenig v. Muskin Corp., No. 701, A-1973 (Pa. Ct. C.P., Erie Cty. 1982).

lawyer should carefully consider how discovery can be used to locate additional potential defendants.

> Through discovery, counsel can learn the names of people involved with the product from original design through manufacture, promotion, distribution and sale. This information is valuable not only in finding potential defendants, but in pinpointing the defect, learning about the intermediate handling of the product before it reached your client, and proving that the defect was created while the product was in the hands of the defendants.[33]

The diethylstilbestrol (DES) cases, involving a drug consumed by the mother or grandmother of the plaintiffs, have caused particular problems for the courts because of the difficulty or even impossibility of identifying the specific manufacturer-defendant who produced the actual item consumed by the ancestors of the plaintiffs. For this reason many courts have allowed suits against all the DES manufacturers, with a proportional imposition of liability based on the market share of each. While an argument can be made for liability based on a statewide share of the market, some courts have also allowed consideration of a national market.[33.1]

§ 1.14 Forms and checklists

Many form books are available, and they frequently provide valuable ideas and language which the products liability litigator can use in discovery.[34] Certainly every lawyer handling a products case should have at least one reliable form book available for use during discovery. However, the lawyer must also particularize his discovery requests and cannot rely blindly on such form

---

[33] E.M. SWARTZ, HAZARDOUS PRODUCTS LITIGATION § 6.1 (Lawyers Co-operative Publishing Co. 1973). See further analysis in E.M. SWARTZ, HAZARDOUS PRODUCTS LITIGATION ch. 6 (Lawyers Co-operative Publishing Co., rev. ed., 1988).

[33.1] *See,* for example, analysis of the New York Court of Appeals in Humowitz v. Eli Lilly & Co., 73 N.Y.2d 487, 539 N.E.2d 1069 (1989).

[34] *See, e.g.,* E.M. SWARTZ & F. SWARTZ, HANDBOOK OF PERSONAL INJURY FORMS (Lawyers Co-operative Publishing Co. 1982).

books. Discovery requests should be pinpointed to the needs and facts of the particular case.

I am a great believer in using checklists during the investigation and discovery of a products liability case. Checklists are somewhat more difficult to obtain than forms, but they are available.[35] The lawyer should begin to develop his own checklist based on a combination of those found in various publications and the lawyer's own experience.

§ 1.15 Using the rules

Since the adoption of Federal Rules of Civil Procedure Rule 26, and its subsequent adoption by the majority of states, the sequence of discovery is no longer a problem.

COMMENT: I do think, however, that plaintiff's counsel ought to serve interrogatories and notice of depositions promptly since the information obtained thereby will greatly assist counsel in answering discovery requests made by the defendant.

Many judges now issue orders limiting the time during which the parties may conduct discovery. It is the practice of some judges, for example, to send out orders in every case limiting the discovery period to six months after issue is joined. Such orders can ordinarily be extended upon a showing of good cause. Other judges, perhaps mindful of the fact that their own schedule will not allow them to reach a case for trial for several years, will allow the parties to conduct discovery up until the time of trial. A third alternative is where the judge imposes no formal discovery deadline, but decides that discovery which has been filed after a case has been assigned for trial has not been filed on a timely

[35] *See, e.g.*, R. CARTWRIGHT & J. PHILLIPS, PRODUCTS LIABILITY ch. 10, *Pretrial Preparation and Procedures;* Kindregan, *Checklist for Handling the Products Liability Claim,* in SWARTZ PROOF OF PRODUCT DEFECT, *supra* note 31.

basis. This approach hardly seems to provide the parties with adequate notice of a cutoff date.

The attorney should consider using every method of discovery available under the rules. The lawyer should utilize depositions, interrogatories, requests to produce documents, requests for admissions, requests to admit the genuineness of documents, requests to inspect, requests to photograph, and so on. Each method of discovery has its own particular advantages, and if carefully used can result in the accumulation of valuable knowledge.

Counsel should also learn to combine the various methods of discovery. For example, documents obtained by a request to produce may not be admissible unless they are identified and authenticated by the defendant. If the documents are obtained shortly before a deposition of the defendant's employees, they can be identified and authenticated at the time of the deposition. This can result in great convenience in trial preparation.

Additionally, if the product which caused the injury is in the possession of the defendant, you will want to demand to inspect it.

Requests for admission of facts are often not used by lawyers. I think this is a mistake. Facts can often be established conclusively by this method of discovery, resulting in an advantage in negotiation or trial of the case. While such requests might be effectively used early on in discovery, they are often extremely helpful late in the discovery process because they can be drafted with pinpoint accuracy based on what the lawyer has learned in the early stages of discovery.

The Federal Rules of Civil Procedure, and most state rules, allow counsel to discover by answers to interrogatories the opinions of his opponent's experts. A party not satisfied with his opponent's answers may move for further discovery by way of expert depositions. In connection with such depositions, written opinions by such experts can sometimes be obtained. Counsel should not go into a trial situation without having been prepared to cross-examine his opponent's experts through discovery. However, some state rules of civil procedure still impose restrictions on discovery of expert's opinions.

§ 1.16 Using sanctions

The products liability defendant will sometimes prove noncooperative, although this is contrary to both the intent and spirit of contemporary discovery practice. Counsel confronted with such a situation should take a hard line and seek the imposition of sanctions. Seeking court orders, costs, and attorney's fees can be a most practical way of compelling cooperation. In addition, many judges will be willing to exclude evidence or impose other heavy sanctions on a party who has failed to meet his discovery obligation. Indeed, I have been successful in obtaining a court order defaulting the defendant for failing to comply with a discovery order.[36]

Answering discovery requests demands great care. The careless answering of interrogatories, for example, can result in a choice of language which can cause problems during negotiation and trial. Therefore, it is wise to have a partner or associate carefully review all answers to discovery requests to insure that they do not create unnecessary problems. In a word, a lawyer should take care not to blindside himself.

III. Library Resources for the Products Liability Lawyer [New]

§ 1.17 Introduction

The following lists in §§ 1.18 to 1.22 contain basic resources that should be available in the library of the lawyer who handles products cases.

§ 1.18 Identifying the manufacturer

The following books list products, give descriptions, and identify the manufacturer or marketer of the product. This is particularly helpful in identifying the manufacturer of products which are no longer marketed but are still being used.

---

[36] Murphy v. Arctic Industries, Inc., CA No. 71-922-S (D. Mass. Jan. 17, 1975), Memorandum and Order, Skinner, I.

See also Note, *Monetary Sanctions Against Attorneys for Discovery Abuse in Federal Court, When Can They Be Appealed?*, 9 CARDOZO L. REV. 1021 (1988).

- *Trade Names Dictionary,* published by Gale Research Co., Book Tower, Detroit, MI 48226. (Over 200,000 products listed)
- *Trade Names Dictionary — The Company Index,* published by Gale Research Co., Book Tower, Detroit, MI 48226. (Over 40,000 manufacturers listed)
- *New Trade Names,* published by Gale Research Co., Book Tower, Detroit, MI 48226. (Subscription service listing new trade names of products)

§ 1.19 Consumer product information

The following contain helpful information about all kinds of products, including safety information, dangerous conditions, product recalls, etc.

- *Consumer Reports,* published by Consumer's Union, Mount Vernon, N.Y. 10553.
- *Consumer Reports Buying Guide,* published by Consumer's Union, Mount Vernon, N.Y. 10553.
- *Consumer Product Safety Commission Fact Sheets,* published by the U.S. Product Safety Commission, Washington, D.C. 20207.
- CPSC News Releases.

§ 1.20 Products liability treatises

- *Hazardous Products Litigation,* rev. ed. by Edward M. Swartz, published by Lawyers Co-operative Publishing Co., Rochester, N.Y. 14694.
- *The Law of Products Liability,* by Marshall Shapo, published by Warren, Gorham & Lamont, Inc., Boston, Mass. 02111.
- *Lawyer's Annotated Products Liability Checklist,* published by Legal-Medical Studies, Inc., Box 8219, Boston, Mass. 02114.
- *The Master Advocates' Handbook,* edited by D. Lake Rumsey, published by the National Institute for Trial Advocacy, 1507 Energy Park Drive, St. Paul, Minn. 55108.

- *Preparing Products Liability Cases,* by T.F. Kiely, published by John Wiley & Sons, 605 Third Avenue, New York, N.Y. 10158
- *Product Liability International,* published by Carswell, P.O. Box 2205, Buffalo, N.Y. 14240.
- *Products Liability,* by R. Cartwright and J. Phillips, published by Kluwer Law Book Publishers, 36 West 44th Street, New York, N.Y. 10036 [3 volumes].
- *Products Liability,* by L. Frumer and M. Friedman, published by Matthew Bender & Co., 11 Penn Plaza, New York, N.Y.
- *Products Liability: The First Twenty-Five Years,* edited by J.R. White, published by the Association of Trial Lawyers of America, 1050 31st St., N.W., Washington, D.C. 20007.
- *Prosser and Keeton on the Law of Torts — Fifth Edition,* published by West Publishing Co., 50 West Kellogg Blvd., St. Paul, Minn. 55164.
- *Swartz Proof of Product Defect,* published by Lawyers Co-operative Publishing Co., Rochester, N.Y. 14694.
- *Handling Soft Tissue Injury Cases,* by Stanley E. Preiser, Monty L. Preiser and Cyril H. Wecht, published by The Michie Co., P.O. Box 7587, Charlottesville, VA, 22906-7587.
- *Products Liability Practice Guide,* edited by John Vargo, published by Matthew Bender Co., 11 Penn Plaza, New York, N.Y. 10001.
- *Handbook of Personal Injury Forms,* by Edward M. Swartz and Fred Swartz, published by Lawyer's Co-operative Publishing Co., Rochester, N.Y. 14694.
- *Handling Federal Tort Claims,* by Lester S. Jayson, published by Matthew Bender Co., 11 Penn Plaza, New York, N.Y. 10001.
- *Personal Injury Review,* edited by Barry Denkensohn and Agnes Fliss, published by Matthew Bender Co., 11 Penn Plaza, New York, N.Y. 10001.
- *Determining Economic Loss in Injury and Death Cases,* by William G. Baker and Michael K. Seck, published by Shepard's/McGraw-Hill, Inc., P.O. Box 1253, Colorado Springs, Colo. 80901-9943.

- *Products Liability — Second Edition,* by M. Stuart Madden, published by West Publishing Co., 50 West Kellogg Blvd., St. Paul, Minn. 55165.

§ 1.21 Service updates

The following services provide regular updates on the developing law of products liability.

- *The ATLA Advocate,* published by the Association of Trial Lawyers of America, P.O. Box 3717, Washington, D.C. 20007.
- *Drugs in Litigation* [annual], published by Michie Co., P.O. Box 7587, Charlottesville, Va. 22906.
- *The Products Liability Law Reporter,* published by the Association of Trial Lawyers of America, 1050 31st St., N.W., Washington, D.C. 20007.
- *Products Liability Reports,* published by the Commerce Clearing House, 4025 W. Peterson Ave., Chicago, Illinois 60604.
- *The Product Safety and Liability Reporter,* published by the Bureau of National Affairs, 1231 25th St., N.W., Washington, D.C. 20037.
- *The Product Safety Letter,* published by Washington Business Info., Inc., 1117 N. 19th St., Arlington, Va. 22209-1798.

§ 1.22 Selected legal sources

Aitken, *The Product Liability Provision of the Civil Liability Reform Act of 1987,* 62 S. Cal. L. Rev. 1449 (1989).

Bieman, *Strict Products Liability: An Overview of State Law,* 10 J. Prod. Liab. 112 (1987).

Buser, *Strict Products Liabilities Litigation in Review,* 70 Ill. B.J. 148 (1981).

Burrows, *Consumer Safety Under Products Liability and Duty to Disclose,* 12 Int'l Rev. Law & Econ. 457 (1992).

Caso, *Unreasonably Dangerous Products From a Child's Perspective,* 20 Rutgers L.J. 433 (1989).

Clark, *Strict Liability for Products Defect,* 1983 J. Bus. L. 130 (1983).

Claybrook, *Going Public About Defective Products,* 25 Trial 34, No. 11 (Nov. 1989).

Comment, *Judicial Response to Constitutional Challenges in a Product Liability Punitive Damage Limitation Statute (McBride v. General Motors,* 737 F. Supp. 1563), W.H. Voltz, M.C. Fayz, 29 Amer. Bus. Law. J. 367 (1991).

Costan, *A Question About Comment K: Have the Courts Expanded Its Scope?,* 23 Trial 62, No. 7 (July 1987).

Cox, *Use of State of the Art Evidence: Confusion, Inconsistency and Absolute Liability,* 10 J. Prod. L. 91 (No. 2, 1987).

Dueffert, *The Role of Regulatory Compliance in Tort Actions,* 26 Harv. L. Rev. 175 (1989).

Durst, *Proving a Defect Without the Product,* 25 Trial 102, No. 1 (Jan. 1989).

Funston, *The Failure to Warn Defect in Strict Products Liability,* 51 Ins. Couns. J. 39 (1984).

Gleckman, *Proposed Requirements for Transnational Corporations to Disclose Information on Product and Process Hazards,* 6 B.U. Int'l L.J. 89 (1988).

Hay, *Conflicts of Law and State Competition in the Product Liability System,* 80 Geo. L.J. 617 (1992).

Humes, *The Application of Strict Liability in Tort to the Retailers of Used Products,* 16 Okla. City U. L. Rev. 373 (1991).

Johnson & Sattler, *Selecting Economic Experts,* 28 Trial Magazine 83 (No. 11, Nov. 1992).

Kindregan & Swartz, *The Assault on the Captive Consumer, Emasculating the Common Law of Torts in the Name of Reform,* 18 St. Mary's L.J. 673 (1987).

Lambert, *Products Liability: Test for Defective Design in Strict Liability,* 30 ATLA L. Rep. 292 (Sept. 1987).

Little, *Eliminating the Fallacies of Comparative Negligence and Proportional Liability,* 41 Ala. L. Rev. 13 (1989).

Nader, *The Assault on Injured Victims' Rights,* 64 Den. U.L. Rev. 625 (1988).

Note, *Protective Orders in Products Liability Litigation: Striking the Proper Balance,* 48 Washington & Lee L. Rev. 1503 (1991).

Oughton, *Liability in Tort for Economic Loss Suffered by the Consumer of Defective Goods,* 1987 J. Bus. L. 370 (No. 9) (1987).

Patterson, *Ten Critical Steps in Handling and Defending Product Liability Cases,* 29 Defense Counsel J. 390 (1992).

Razook, Horrell, & Roblyer, *A Descriptive and Analytical Matrix for Product Liability for Defense,* 30 Amer. Bus. L.J. 69 (1992).

Reske, *Was There a Liability Crisis?*, Jan. 1989 A.B.A. J. 46 (Jan. 1989).

Schwartz, *A Product Safety Agenda for the 1990's,* 45 Wash. & Lee L. Rev. 1355 (1988).

Seidelson, *The Choice of Law Process in Products Liability Actions,* 26 Duq. L. Rev. 559 (1988).

Swartz, *Freeing the Captive Consumer,* 22 Trial 28, No. 4 (Apr. 1986).

Wade, *Multiple Tortfeasor Liability in Products Liability Suits,* 55 Miss. L.J. 683 (1985).

IV. Theories of Recovery [New]

§ 1.23 Checklist: Potential theories of recovery in a products case

___(1) Absolute liability for breach of statutory duty
___(2) Breach of express warranty
___(3) Breach of implied warranty that product is fit for the use for which it is intended
___(4) Breach of implied warranty that product is merchantable
___(5) Defective design of product
___(6) Defective packaging
___(7) Defective testing
___(8) Failure to conform to governmental safety standards
___(9) Failure to conform to industry safety standards
___(10) Failure to inspect for safety hazards
___(11) Failure to meet ordinary and usual consumer expectations as to product safety
___(12) Failure to test for dangers
___(13) Failure to inform consumer product safety commission of substantial product hazard
___(14) Failure to provide understandable instructions on safe use of the product
___(15) Failure to warn of known dangers
___(16) Failure to warn of knowable dangers
___(17) Failure to warn that product is unavoidably unsafe
___(18) Inadequate instructions for safe use
___(19) Inadequate labeling of product
___(20) Inadequate provision of safety features
___(21) Inadequate warning of dangers in use of product

____(22) Misrepresentation of product safety
____(23) Misrepresentation of uses to which product may be safely put
____(24) Negligence in design of product
____(25) Negligence in manufacture of product
____(26) Negligence in promotion of product
____(27) Negligence in testing of product
____(28) Negligent endorsement of defective product
____(29) Negligence in failure to warn
____(30) Negligence in failure to instruct on use of product
____(31) Negligence in failure to improve product to meet contemporary safety standards
____(32) Negligence in handling and transportation of the product
____(33) Negligence in manufacturing of the product
____(34) Negligence in promotion of the product
____(35) Negligence in testing of the product
____(36) Product is imminently dangerous to human health or safety
____(37) Strict liability for physical harm caused to user of unreasonably dangerous and defective product
____(38) Strict liability for ultrahazardous activities
____(39) Violation of federal law intended to protect the consumer under theories of negligence per se or strict liability
____(40) Violation of state consumer protection statute

V. Allegations of Product Defect in Complaint [New]

§ 1.24 Illustrative allegation of negligence

The death of plaintiff's decedent was the direct and proximate result of the carelessness and negligence of the defendant as follows:

(a) Defendant negligently designed, developed, assembled, manufactured, inspected, tested, marketed, advertised, sold and distributed said ________.

(b) Defendant negligently failed to warn or instruct or adequately warn or adequately instruct decedent and other users of said product of its dangerous and defective characteristics, and of the safe and proper method of using said product.

(c) Defendant negligently disposed of said product and placed it in the channels of trade, when it knew or with reasonable care should have known said product to be dangerous and defective in nature, design, and materials and in a dangerous and defective condition, and when, in the exercise of reasonable care, it ought to have foreseen that placing said product in the channels of trade would probably carry said product into contact with persons such as the decedent who were ignorant of its dangerous and defective nature and condition, and defendant negligently failed to use reasonable care to prevent injury to such persons, including the plaintiff.

§ 1.25 Illustrative allegation of breach of warranty

Defendant expressly and impliedly warranted to decedent and to the general public that said product was safe, merchantable and fit for its intended purposes and uses. Defendant breached its warranties to decedent because said product was unsafe, not of merchantable quality and unfit for its intended uses and purposes. Decedent relied on the warranties made by defendant, and decedent was caused to die as the direct and proximate result of the breaches of warranties by defendant. Due notice has been given defendant of its breaches of warranty.

§ 1.26 Illustrative allegation of strict liability

Said defendant placed said defective product in the stream of commerce knowing that it would be used without substantial change, and said product proved to be defective as a result of the failure of the defendant to properly manufacture, develop, design, construct, assemble, test, package, advertise, distribute, sell and supply said product to prevent it from becoming unreasonably dangerous and unsafe for its foreseeable and intended use.

Chapter 2

COMBUSTION CATASTROPHES

III. Case Study: The Case of the Basement Booby Trap

Page 36:

[Add new sections following § 2.09.]

§ 2.09A Hot water heater — the case against the control valve manufacturer [New]

I was retained to represent a man who was badly burned in a flash fire which occurred when he attempted to light the hot water heater in the basement of his home. After investigating the facts, we established that the control valve of the hot water heater was defective because the thermocouple had a tendency to stick in the "open" position. This caused the safety shutoff device to become ineffective — an obvious danger to human life which the manufacturer of the control valve should have anticipated. When the thermocouple stuck in the open position, highly flammable propane gas would leak through the thermocouple and create an explosive atmosphere. My client suffered severe burns. This case was settled for $1,350,000. The party who supplied the propane gas paid $250,000 of the settlement and the manufacturer paid the balance.

§ 2.09B Gas stove — the case against the stove manufacturer [New]

We represented a young child who lost his left eye when he was hit by the container of an aerosol spray product which had exploded on a stovetop. After investigation, we established that the gas stove had an exposed pilot light, a venting hole that ran through the stovetop to the surface. This pilot light was the most probable source of the heat required to explode the aerosol container. It was clear that the product did not need to have a pilot light flame vented directly to the surface, as most contemporary stoves did not incorporate such a feature.

The other possible source of the heat required to explode the container was from the stovetop burners themselves. It was shown that the stove did not incorporate double-action burner knobs, a basic safety feature designed to prevent a person from inadvertently lighting the burners. This case was settled for $637,500 after a jury was impanelled. The stove manufacturer paid the major portion of the settlement.

V. Preventing Combustion-Related Injuries

Page 51:

[Add new section following § 2.17.]

§ 2.17A Insufficiently visible gas flame [New]

In addition to providing sufficient odorization of gas, a manufacturer is also legally obligated to make the flame sufficiently visible so that one using the gas will be warned of the danger. One hazard which can result from an insufficiently visible gas flame is the ignition of the user's clothing.

In one such case, my firm was hired to represent the estate of a deceased telephone lineman who was burned to death. The decedent was engaged in splicing a lead sleeve on a telephone wire with a hand-held torch. To reach the area of the lead sleeve, the decedent was standing in an elevated bucket, which was appended to a truck owned by the telephone company. The torch was fueled by a MAPP gas, which was contained in a 7.5-pound cylinder kept on the truck.

The deceased was working alone and there were no witnesses to the initial happening which triggered his death. A school crossing guard noticed the lineman "dancing" about in the bucket and saw that his clothing was on fire. A large fire erupted in the elevated bucket and the lineman was burned to death.

Suit was brought against the manufacturer, national distributor, and seller of the MAPP gas. I claimed that the flame emitted by the MAPP gas and its accompanying hand-held torch was not reasonably visible, resulting in the hazard of igniting the clothing of a user without sufficient warning of the danger. In discovery, my firm established that the telephone company had utilized the more expensive acetylene gas prior to using MAPP gas, and that the union had complained to the national distributor about the poor visibility characteristics of MAPP gas after the fuel had been put into use. The case was settled for $1,460,000.

VI. Litigation Sources: Bibliography

§ 2.26 Selected laws, regulations, and standards

Page 58:

[Add the following new text under "Statutes."]

(3) Radiation Control Act, 42 U.S.C. § 263b *et seq.* (1982 & Supp. 1987).

(4) Railroad Safety Appliance Act, 45 U.S.C. § 1 *et seq.* (1986).

(5) Toxic Substances Control Act, 15 U.S.C. § 2601 *et seq.* (1982 & Supp. 1987).

§ 2.27 Selected cases

Page 60:

[Add new text as follows:]

Balder v. Haley, 390 N.W.2d 855 (Minn. Ct. App. 1986), **water heater;** explosion.

White v. Robertshaw Controls Co. (D.N.H. 1986), **hot water heater;** propane gas explosion; control valve defective; settlement of $1,350,000.

Nationwide Insurance Co. v. Ducane Industries, 580 A.2d 95 (Conn. Super. 1990), **barbecue grill;** exploding propane gas tank, with resulting fire destroying home.

Andrus v. Gas Co. of New Mexico, 798 P.2d 194 (N.M. 1990), **furnace;** carbon monoxide poisoning; negligently placed door; failure to test.

Cohen v. Steve's Ice Cream Co., 737 F. Supp. 8 (D. Mass. 1990), **flammable liquid;** warning as to flash point; transfer to smaller containers by subsequent purchaser.

Warzynski v. Empire Comfort Systems, 401 S.E.2d 801 (N.C. 1991), **gas heater** exploded, destroying plaintiff's home; seller of heater who was apparent manufacturer holding himself out as such even though heater was manufactured by a Spanish company could be held liable in products liability claim and cannot use a statutory sealed container defense to defeat liability.

§ 2.28 —Illustrative case — fire resulting from defective design, construction, and installation of spray painting facility — opposition to defendant's motion for summary judgment [New]

PLAINTIFFS' MEMORANDUM IN OPPOSITION
TO MOTION OF DEFENDANT
FOR SUMMARY JUDGMENT

________ was burned over 70% of his body on ________, 19____, in connection with a fire in a spray painting facility at ________ Company in ________, Massachusetts. He later died as a result of his injuries. His survivors subsequently brought suit against several entities involved in designing, constructing and installing components of the facility. Also named as a defendant was __________ (__________), an unincorporated association of three insurance companies which inspected the facility on numerous occasions prior to __________'s death.

In the present motion, __________ seeks summary judgment on the basis of M.G.L.A. c. 143, sec. 16A which provides a defense to certain insurers who conduct safety inspections unless those insurers engaged in "active negligence." The statute, in its totality, provides as follows:

> The furnishing of, or failure to furnish, safety inspection or advisory services intended to reduce the likelihood of injury, death or loss shall not subject an insurer, its agent or employee undertaking to perform such services as an incident to insurance, to liability for damages from injury, death or loss occurring as a result of any act or omission in the course of such services. *This provision shall not apply in the event the active negligence of the insurer, its agent or employee created the condition which was the proximate cause of injury, death or loss.*

(emphasis added). Because evidence in the record in this case clearly establishes that a genuine issue of material fact exists with respect to whether __________ was actively negligent in connection with services provided to __________, defendant's motion for summary judgment must be denied.

ARGUMENT: *A genuine issue of material fact exists with respect to whether __________ was actively negligent in connection with its inspections of the __________ facility.*

The __________ "system" of inspecting insured facilities entails practices and procedures unique in the insurance industry. Indeed, evidence in this case establishes that __________ inspections consist of much more than the usual passive, cursory inspections engaged in by some insurers. __________ inspections are designed not only to assist its insurer members in underwriting decisions, but also to result in engineering and system changes within the insured facility. In this case, the inspections conducted by __________ resulted in recommendations which were communicated to and implemented by _________. Implementation of these recommendations helped to create a condition which was the proximate cause of _________'s injury. For this reason, genuine issues of fact exist, precluding the entry of summary judgment on behalf of ____.

A. *The inspection "system"*

_________ is an unincorporated system of three insurers which was formed in 19____ (Deposition of _________ at ____). _________ Insurance Company, which insured _________ against fire losses, is one of the members (Exhibit ____ to Motion of _________ for summary judgment). Under the services agreement creating _________, the purpose of the association is to perform "certain engineering, inspection and adjustment services" for the insurers (Defendant's Exhibit ____ at ____). The type of services performed by _________ in connection with the _________ facility are described in the agreement as "Fire and Other Inspection and Engineering Services" which are defined as follows:

> The term "fire and other inspection and engineering services" shall mean any and all inspection and engineering services relating to property insurance and reinsurance performed by the Association involving insureds or prospective insureds of a Company, including but not limited to (1) *complete loss prevention engineering* in order to preserve property and to prevent losses thereto; (2) the inspection, *evaluation and testing of insured* or prospective insured *property;* (3) the appraisal of insured property; (4) the rendition of appropriate written reports to the Companies in connection with such services.

(Defendant's Exhibit at ____) (emphasis added).
Accordingly, in addition to inspection services, the activities of _________ include "complete loss prevention engineering" and "evaluation and testing of insured . . . property."

_________ is one branch of the _________ "System" which also includes _________ Engineering Corporation (_________) and _________ Research Corporation (_________) (Deposition of _________ at ____). _________ is a _________ corporation which conducts research into fire protection and lends assistance to _________ (*Id.* at ____). _________ publishes recommended practices including practices relating to operation and maintenance of spraying operations, such as the spraying operation at issue in this case (Deposition of _________ at ____, _________ Deposition Exhibit ____).

The _________ System promulgates various documents relating to practices and procedures to be followed during _________ inspections (_________ Deposition Exhibits ____-____). These documents establish that _________ does in fact engage in "complete loss prevention engineering" and "evaluation and testing of insured . . . property" in accordance with the terms of its services agreement. For example, a _________ loss prevention specialist is instructed to make a thorough inspection of the plant and to discuss his findings with the plant manager (_________ Exhibit ____ at ____-____). He is expected to conduct any necessary testing (*Id.* at ____). He is also expected to engage in a final conference with the plant manager in order to "sell" his important recommendations (*Id.* at ____). "Selling" includes "persuading" and "convincing" (*Id.*). The _________ employee is to sell solutions, suggest priorities, explore alternatives and reach agreement on acceptable solutions (_________ Exhibit ____ at ____). The loss prevention specialist "at all times [is] serving as an engineer of the Insured." (*Id.* at ____). The "insured" would be an organization such as _________ (Deposition of _________ at ____).

After completing his inspection, the _________ loss prevention specialist prepares a report (Deposition of_________ at ____). The report is sent to the insurer — _________ Mutual in this case — which insures the facility (*Id.* at ____). The insurer then sends the loss prevention report to the insured — _________ in this case — with the insurer's logo at the top of the report (*Id.* at ____-____; _________ Deposition Exhibit ____). The purpose of sending the report to the insured is to "assist . . . in minimizing loss from fire and associated perils" (_________ Deposition Exhibit ____).

B. *Actions of_________ in the present case*

In the present case, _________ conducted three fire inspections of the _________ facility prior to the incident in which plaintiff was injured — on ____ ____, 19___, ____ ____, 19___, and ____ ____, 19____ (_________ Deposition Exhibits ____,

____ and ____). In addition, __________ conducted two investigations of fire losses on ____ ____, 19____, and ____ ____, 19____ (__________ Deposition Exhibits ____ and ____). __________ also conducted an investigation of the fire itself (__________ Exhibit ____).

In connection with the inspections made prior to the incident, __________ personnel included the following recommendations in reports which were sent to __________:

— Inasmuch as there was no established schedule for cleaning the walls and floors of the spray paint booths, __________ recommended weekly cleaning (__________ Deposition Exhibit ____ at ____, ____). The inspector made this recommendation based on experience at other plants where weekly cleaning was generally adequate (Deposition of __________ at ____). However, the inspector could not recall ever inspecting an electrostatic spray paint facility prior to the __________ inspection (*Id.*). Moreover, in Loss Prevention Data promulgated by the __________ System, *daily* cleaning of booths was recommended (__________ Exhibit ____ at ____; __________ Deposition at ____).

— Inspection was made of blueprints associated with components of the spray painting facility and ventilation was determined to be "adequate" (__________ Deposition Exhibit ____ at ____).

— The inspector noted that __________ engaged in dispensing of lacquer thinner in open drums in the flammable liquids room adjacent to the spray painting area (__________ Deposition Exhibit ____ at ____). A recommendation was made that a pressure resistant wall be erected in order to "improve" the handling of the lacquer thinner (*Id.* at ____).

— The inspector obtained a material safety data sheet for lacquer thinner and determined that its flash point was four degrees Fahrenheit (__________ Deposition Exhibit ____ at ____). Based on the method by which __________ dispensed the lacquer thinner, the inspector concluded that "damage limiting construction" was not necessary (*Id.*).

— On ____ ____, 19____, the inspector investigated a fire which he determined was caused by a spray of lacquer thinner being ignited by a static charge (__________ Deposition Exhibit ____ at ____). He noted that lacquer thinner was piped directly from the flammable liquids room to the spray booths (*Id.* at ____). He made numerous recommendations encouraging the continuance of this practice (*Id.* at ____-____).

— On ____ ____, 19____, the inspector investigated another fire at __________ caused by an electrical short circuit igniting paint overspray deposits (__________ Deposition Exhibit ____ at ____). Again, lacquer thinner was involved (*Id.* at ____). Numerous recommendations were made relating to housekeeping, the electrostatic equipment and over-current protection (*Id.* at ____).

— The inspector determined that the automatic spray booth was being utilized with a paper floor covering (__________ Deposition Exhibit ____ at ____). He made recommendations which encouraged that this practice continue (*Id.* at ____).

— On ____ ____, 19____, less than three months before the fire, the inspector noted that the booth was being cleaned on a weekly basis and deleted his prior recommendation that more frequent housekeeping be done (__________ Deposition Exhibit ____).

— On ____ ____, 19____, an investigation was made of the fire in which __________ had been injured. Numerous recommendations were made relating to the spray paint booth which previously had never been made. Recommendations were made relating to grounding of objects, daily cleanings, setting of the over-current device, supporting of parts to prevent arcing and changing of motors (__________ Deposition Exhibit ____ at ____-____).

C. *A genuine issue of fact exists relating to __________'s "active negligence"*

The above-recited evidence in the record indicates that prior to the __________ incident, __________ made specific recommendations concerning frequency of housekeeping, use of lacquer thinner and related matters. These recommendations were communicated to and discussed among the workers, engineers and executives at __________ and action was taken (Deposition of __________ at ____-____ — ____-____).

__________ would generally try to react to recommendations contained in __________ Reports (*Id.* at ____-____). For example, based on the __________ report of ____, 19____, __________ instituted a scheduled cleaning program (*Id.* at ____-____). When

__________ made recommendations, individuals at __________ would be asked to follow those recommendations (*Id.* at ____-____-____).

A review of the expert testimony expected to be offered by the parties at trial indicates that the matters which were recommended to __________ played a significant role in the cause of the fire. All parties that have disclosed expert testimony are in agreement that the housekeeping of the facility and the use of lacquer thinner were proximate causes of the occurrence. (See Disclosures of Expert Witnesses filed by the parties attached as Exhibits ____, ____, ____ and ____ to the __________ Affidavit filed herewith). Under these circumstances there can be no question whatsoever that a genuine issue of fact exists concerning whether the active negligence of __________ was a contributing cause of the occurrence.

There have been no cases decided in Massachusetts which construe the "active negligence" language contained in M.G.L.A. c. 143, sec. 16A. The one case in which section 16A is discussed, *Swift v. American Mutual Insurance Co.,* 399 Mass. 373, 504 N.E.2d 621 (1987), simply quotes the section and indicates that an insurer is not to be penalized "for collecting data" in the context of a voluntary safety inspection. *Id.,* 504 N.E.2d at 624, note 9. In the instant case, it is obvious that __________, by engaging in complete loss control engineering, testing and evaluation did much more than "collect data." It is equally obvious that a reasonable trier of fact could find that the activities of__________ constituted "active negligence," thus precluding the entry of summary judgment.

While Massachusetts has generally not recognized the concept of active-passive negligence, *see Stewart v. Roy Bros.,* 358 Mass. 446, 265 N.E.2d 357, 365 (1970), the Supreme Judicial Court has indicated that "active negligence" is synonymous with "misfeasance" as opposed to "nonfeasance." *Chelefou v. Springfield Institution for Savings,* 297 Mass. 236, 8 N.E.2d 769 (1937). Misfeasance is the "negligent or improper doing of an act . . . as opposed to nonfeasance, which involves the negligent failure or omission to act." *Narine v. Powers,* 400 Mass. 343, 509 N.E.2d 905 (1987). Where a defendant engages in conduct which contributes to cause a defect or results in an accident, he has engaged in active negligence. *Farrell v. Boston Water Sewer Commission,* 24 Mass.

App. Ct. 583, 511 N.E.2d 357 (1987). Other jurisdictions have defined "active negligence" as follows:

> Active Negligence is defined as the negligent conduct of active operations. It is conduct which may consist of participation with another in an affirmative act of negligence which is the legal cause of injury to a third person. It may also consist of the actual connection with an act or omission of another by knowledge of or acquiescence in such act or omission which is the legal cause of injury to a third person. Passive negligence is the omission or failure to perform a duty of care imposed by law in which there is no participation with another in any affirmative act of negligence which is the proximate cause of injury to a third person.

Jiminez v. Pacific Western Construction Co., 185 Cal. App. 3d 102, 339 Cal. Rptr. 575 (1986). Where a defendant has actual knowledge of a hazardous condition, a finding of active negligence is supported. The issue of active negligence is ordinarily a question of fact for the jury. *Id.*

Under any formulation of the active negligence doctrine, a genuine issue of fact exists in this case whether __________ engaged in active negligence in connection with providing complete loss control engineering services and acting as an engineer for __________. __________ made recommendations which were sold to and implemented by __________. These recommendations related directly to housekeeping, overspray, use of lacquer thinner and associated matters which all parties agree are a proximate cause of the occurrence. __________'s motion for summary judgment must be denied.

Chapter 3

HOUSEHOLD CHEMICAL THREATS

VI. Litigation Sources: Bibliography

§ 3.29 Selected technical sources

Page 112:

[Add new text as follows:]

Baker, *Workship on Neurobehavioral Effects of Solvents,* 6 Neurotoxicology 99 (1985).

Baker & Fine, *Solvent Neurotoxicity: The Current Evidence,* 28 J. Occup. Med. 126 (1986).

Baker, Smith & Landrigan, *The Neurotoxicity of Industrial Solvents: A Review of the Literature,* 8 Am. J. Indus. Med. 207 (1985).

Spencer & Schaumburg, *Organic Solvent Neurotoxicity,* 11 Scand. J. Work Env't & Health 53 (Supp. 1, 1984).

§ 3.32 Selected legal sources

Page 116:

[Add new text as follows:]

Boher, *Fear and Trembling in the 20th Century: Technological Risk, Uncertainty and Emotional Distress,* 1984 Wis. L. Rev. 83.

Kurzman, *Formaldehyde Litigation,* 19 Trial 82, No. 1 (Jan. 1983).

Larson, *Neurotoxic Effects of Solvents,* 22 Trial 87, No. 12 (Dec. 1986).

Madden, *The Duty to Warn in Products Liability,* 89 W. Va. L. Rev. 221 (1987).

Note, *Increased Risk of Disease from Hazardous Waste,* 60 Wash. L. Rev. 635 (1985).

Note, *UREA Formaldehyde Form Insulation,* 11 Amer. J. L. & Med. 81 (1985).

Sargeant, *ATLA ALERT: Lewis Red Devil Lye-Red Devil Drain Cleaner Can Burn, Blind and Disfigure,* 25 Trial 24, No. 11 (Nov. 1989).

Symposium on Toxic Torts, 52 Brooklyn L. Rev. (No. 2, 1986).

§ 3.34 Selected laws, regulations, and standards

Page 117:

[Add the following new text under "Statutes."]

(4) Federal Food, Drug, and Cosmetics Act, 21 U.S.C. § 301 *et seq.* (1972 & Supp. 1987).

(5) Toxic Substances Control Act, 15 U.S.C. § 2601 *et seq.* (1982 & Supp. 1987).

Page 118:

[Add the following new text under "Regulations."]

(4) Environmental Protection Agency, ruling on polychlorinated biphenyls under Toxic Substances Control Act, PCB contamination, 40 CFR Part 761 (OPTS 62051; FRL 3179-1) (April 2, 1987).

(5) Department of Health and Human Services, Public Health Services, toxicology and carcinogenesis studies of commercial grade 2, 4 (80%) and 2, 6 (20%)-toluene diisocyantante (TDI), used in flexible polyurethane foams (furniture, pillows, carpet underlays, wood finishes, shoes, toys, etc.) (Dec. 8, 1986).

(6) Rules and Regulations of the U.S. Product Safety Commission, 16 CFR Part 1500, 52 Fed. Register 47624-03 (Feb. 3, 1988) (revocation of rule requiring label statement "If swallowed, do not induce vomiting" for hazardous substances containing 10% or more by weight of benzene, toluene, xylene or petroleum distillates).

§ 3.35 Selected cases

Page 118:

[Add new text as follows:]

Advance Chemical Co. v. Harter, 478 So. 2d 444 (Fla. Dist. Ct. App. 1985), **Advance 480-cleaning product** containing ammonia; failure to warn of dangerous propensities adequately; custodian suffered lung damage.

Walker v. Maybelline Co., 477 So. 2d 1136 (La. App. 1985), **mascara;** eye infection caused.

Lee v. Crest Chemical Co., 583 F. Supp. 131 (M.D.N.C. 1984), **chemical product;** discussion of alleged misleading instructions and labels.

Cox v. Velsicol Chem. Corp., 704 F. Supp. 85 (E.D. Pa. 1989), **pesticide;** duty to warn, federal pesticide labeling law did not preempt state tort claim.

Mullaney v. Velsicol Chem. Corp., (S.C. Ct. Comm. Pl., 1987), 7 ATLA Prod. Liab. L. Rep. 8 (Feb. 1988), **pesticide;** liability of manufacturer.

Ayers v. Johnson & Johnson Baby Products Co., 59 Wash. App. 287, 797 P.2d 527 (1990), **baby oil;** infant aspirated product, causing brain damage; failure to warn of dangers and need for immediate treatment; $2,500,000 verdict.

Chapter 4

FABRIC-RELATED BURN INJURIES — THE TORCH CASES

IV. Other Flammable Products

§ 4.09 Clothing, generally

Page 149:

[Add new text at end of § 4.09.]

While many burn cases focus on flammable fabrics, the lighting mechanism may itself be defective and the cause of injury. For example, in *Littlejohn v. Bic Corp.*,[21.1] a lighter failed to extinguish completely after being replaced in the victim's pocket, causing clothing to ignite.

[21.1] 5 Prod. Liab. Rep. (CCH) 155 (Dec. 1986).

VI. Litigation Sources: Bibliography

§ 4.30 Selected legal sources

Page 181:

[Add the following new text:]

Lambert, *Flammable Nightgown,* 28 ATLA L. Rep. 390 (Nov. 1985).
Patton, *Flammable Fabrics,* 20 Trial No. 4 (Apr. 1984).

§ 4.32 Selected laws and standards

Page 184:

[Add the following new text under "Statutes":]

(3) Fire Safe Cigarette Act of 1990, Pub. L. No. 101-352, 104 Stat. 405 (Aug. 10, 1990).

§ 4.33 Selected cases

Page 185:

[Add new text as follows:]

Littlejohn v. Bic Corp., 5 Prod. Liab. Rep. (CCH) 155 (Dec. 1986), **clothing ignited;** defective lighting mechanism.

Ellsworth v. Sherne Lingerie, Inc., 303 Md. 581, 495 A.2d 348 (1985), **flannelette nightgown;** severe burns.

Feiner v. Calvin Klein, Ltd., 549 N.Y.S.2d 692 (App. Div. 1990), **flammable cotton blouse;** serious burns to teenager.

Carrizales v. Rheem Mfg. Co., 226 Ill. App. 3d 20, 589 N.E.2d 569, 573 (1991), plaintiff's gasoline-soaked clothing was ignited by the flame of a **gas-fired hot water heater**. The court rejected the defendant's claim that the danger was a matter of common knowledge, holding that the defendant had a duty to warn. In so holding, the court said:

> Judicial notice of the fact that it is the vapors that ignited, that they travel on air and are flammable does not provide a basis for the trial court's summary judgment. The flame is at the base of the water heater, out of sight and enclosed by a metal ring or plate.

Issues as to the remoteness of the flammable liquid from the flame source must be factored into the equation before the danger attendant to such a devise can be considered open and obvious.

The notion that "fuel-energized devices are using the air to sustain themselves" ought to be outside the ambit of judicial notice since this represents an understanding of how such a complex device operates.

Malone v. BIC Corp., 789 F. Supp. 939 (N.D. Ill. 1992), child playing with a **brightly colored lighter** ignited his clothing and suffered second-degree burns on his chest, arms and legs; manufacturer was denied summary judgment when court could not determine, as a matter of law, whether the manufacturer had a duty to incorporate further changes in the design of the lighter in the absence of complete discovery.

Chapter 5

ELECTRICAL MAYHEM

IV. Other Electrical Hazards

Page 211:

[Add new sections following § 5.13.]

§ 5.13A Electric garage door [New]

Over the last decade, more and more people have had electric garage doors installed in their homes or places of business. Such electrical devices present a major hazard to users. In *Lamer v. McKee Industries, Inc.*,[25.1] the court reversed a verdict for the manufacturer of a garage door winding plug because the unit failed to perform as safely as an ordinary consumer had the right to expect. The case involved the ultimate human tragedy, namely the death of a human being caused by a defective product. The nature of this dangerous product was aptly illustrated in the following description by the court:

> On December 9, 1980, Roger . . . was sent with co-worker Mike . . . to repair a garage door . . . . While standing on an I-beam, eighteen and one-half feet above the ground, Roger attempted to make a necessary adjustment by rotating a winding plug with his winding bar. While pushing on the winding bar his hands suddenly flew up; he lost his balance and fell off the I-beam to the floor below. Roger died as a result of this fall. The complaint alleged that this fall occurred because the winding plug fractured at the hold where Roger's winding bar was inserted.
>
> A winding plug is part of the mechanism that raises and lowers overhead garage doors. The mechanism in this case includes upper and lower shaft assemblies which, as they turn, reel in cables that lift the garage door. An electric motor, together with metal springs, supplies the force needed to spin the shaft assemblies.
>
> The tension in each spring can be adjusted by rotating the proper winding plug. This is done by inserting a round steel bar, called a winding bar, into any one of four holes in the winding plug, loosening the set screws that secure the plug to the shaft, and pushing or pulling the bar to rotate the winding plug. If the plug needs to be turned further, a second winding bar can be inserted in the next hole and the rotation continued as necessary. Once the spring tension is correct, the set screws can then be tightened.
>
> The winding plug and winding bar can also be used to completely release spring tension so that the shaft assembly can turn freely. This is done by inserting a winding bar into one of the four holes in the winding plug, loosening the set

---

[25.1] 721 P.2d 611 (Alaska 1986).

screws, and allowing the winding bar to rest against the wall. When this is done, the spring is said to be "barred off."

Each shaft assembly is composed of two halves connected in the center by a coupling. Each half has its own spring and winding plug. To allow the left-hand shaft to turn freely, the left-hand spring must be barred off and the center coupling loosened. Alternatively, the entire shaft can be freed if both springs are barred off.

An electric operator applies power through a chain and sprocket to the right-hand side of the lower shaft assembly. A solenoid brake prevents the operator from turning when not in use. The brake can be manually disengaged by holding down a release cord at the floor level. The locking effect of the electric operator can also be limited to the right-hand side by loosening the center coupling. If this is done, the left-hand shaft can be turned free of the resistance created by the operator and its solenoid brake.

When Roger fell from the I-beam, he was attempting to create just enough slack in the cable so that the left cable drum could be moved along the shaft to its proper place. With the left-hand winding plug secured to the shaft by its set screws, Roger inserted his winding bar into this winding plug and tried to rotate the entire shaft assembly in an attempt to slightly back-wind both springs at once. The electric operator had not been disengaged. Roger was unable to create enough slack in the cable on his first attempt. He changed positions and tried again, but lost his balance and fell when his winding bar suddenly came out of the hole where it was inserted. A later investigation revealed that two of the four holes in the winding plug were broken.[25.2]

§ 5.13B Defective electrical dryer [New]

In *Collins v. Sears, Roebuck & Co.,* 31 Mass. App. Ct. 961, 583 N.E.2d 873, *review denied,* 411 Mass. 1106, 587 N.E.2d 790 (1992), the court held even though an electrical dryer sold to the plaintiffs by the defendant had been moved to another home

---

[25.2] *Id.* at 612-13.

owned by the plaintiffs after several years, where there is no evidence that the electrical system enclosed within the dryer was ever touched, a reasonable inference could be drawn that the dryer was in the same condition as at the time of sale and the plaintiffs could maintain an action based on a theory that the defective dryer started a fire which destroyed the plaintiff's home.

§ 5.14 Smoke detectors

Page 211:

[Add the following new note 25.3 at end of § 5.14.]

[25.3] *See* Butler v. Pittway Corp., 770 F.2d 7 (2d Cir. 1985) (manufacturer of defective smoke detector could be held strictly liable for aggravated fire damage done to home when detectors failed to sound timely alarm).

§ 5.15 —Illustrative case

Page 214:

[Add the following new text at the end of § 5.15.]

On March 31, 1986 the federal First Circuit Court of Appeals announced its landmark decisions in the *Laaperi* case.[38.1] For the first time, a major American court reviewed the duty to warn issue and the evidentiary standards applicable to smoke detectors. The following analysis from the decision of the court illustrates the dangers which can arise from the use of smoke detectors when the distributor fails to warn users of the dangers.

> Defendants contend that the district court erred in denying their motions for directed verdict and judgment n.o.v. First, they claim that they had no duty to warn that the smoke detector might not work in the event of some electrical fires. Second, they maintain that even if they had such a duty, there was insufficient evidence on the record to show that the failure to warn proximately caused plaintiffs damages. We address these arguments in turn.

[38.1] Laaperi v. Sears, Roebuck & Co., 787 F.2d 726 (1st Cir. 1986). *See* 4 LAWYER'S ALERT 6 (July 8, 1985) and 5 LAWYER'S ALERT 8 (May 5, 1986).

A. *Duty to Warn*

We must look, of course, to Massachusetts law. While we have found no cases with similar facts in Massachusetts (or elsewhere), we conclude that on this record a jury would be entitled to find that defendants had a duty to warn. In Massachusetts, a manufacturer[38.2] can be found liable to a user of the product if the user is injured due to the failure of the manufacturer to exercise reasonable care in warning potential users of hazards associated with use of the product. *See, e.g., Mitchell v. Sky Climber, Inc.*, 396 Mass. 629, 487 N.E.2d 1374, 1376 (1986); *Killeen v. Harmon Grain Products,* 11 Mass. App. 20, 413 N.E.2d 767, 770 (1980); W. Prosser & W.P. Keeton, *The Law of Torts* §96, at 685 (5th ed. 1984). The manufacturer can be held liable even if the product does exactly what it is supposed to do, if it does not warn of the potential dangers inherent in the way a product is designed. It is not necessary that the product be negligently designed or manufactured; the failure to warn of hazards associated with foreseeable uses of a product is itself negligence, and if that negligence proximately results in a plaintiff's injuries, the plaintiff may recover. *Schaeffer v. General Motors Corp.*, 372 Mass. 171, 174, 360 N.E.2d 1062, 1065 (1977). *See also Mitchell,* 487 N.E.2d at 1376; *cf. Martinez v. Dixie Carriers, Inc.*, 529 F.2d 457, 465 (5th Cir. 1976) (in a strict liability case, the failure to warn of the hazards associated with a product is itself a product "defect").

The sole purpose of a smoke detector is to alert occupants of a building to the presence of fire. The failure to warn of inherent non-obvious limitations of a smoke

---

[38.2] *The court's footnote 2 reads:* Defendants make no argument that the duty of Sears is any different from that of Pittway, the actual manufacturer. In the present case, Sears advertised the smoke detector as a "Sears Early One Fire Alarm." Pittway Corp. was not mentioned anywhere in these advertisements nor in the twelve-page owner's manual packaged with the detector. Where a seller puts out a product manufactured by another as its own, the seller is subject to the same liability as though it were the manufacturer. RESTATEMENT (SECOND) OF TORTS §400 (1965), *cited with approval in* Jennett v. Colorado Fuel & Iron Corp., 9 Mass. App. 823, 398 N.E.2d 755, 757 (1980); Tibbetts v. Ford Motor Co., 4 Mass. App. 738, 358 N.E.2d 460, 461 (1976).

detector, or of non-obvious circumstances in which a detector will not function, can, we believe, "create an unreasonable risk of harm in that the inhabitants of a structure may be lulled into an unjustified sense of safety and fail to be forewarned of the existence of a fire." *Butler v. Pittway Corp.*, 770 F.2d 7, 11 (2d Cir. 1985). In the present case, the defendants failed to warn purchasers that a short circuit which causes an electrical fire may also render the smoke detector useless in the very situation in which it is expected to provide protection: in the early stages of a fire. We believe that whether such a failure to warn was negligent was a question for the jury.

To be sure, it was the fire, not the smoke detector per se, that actually killed and injured plaintiff's children. But as the Second Circuit recently held, the manufacturer of a smoke detector may be liable when, due to its negligence, the device fails to work:

> Although a defect must be a substantial factor in causing a plaintiff's injuries, it is clear that a "manufacturer's liability for injuries proximately caused by these defects should not be limited to [situations] in which the defect causes the accident, but should extend to situations in which the defect caused injuries over and above that which would have occurred from the accident, but for the defective design."

Butler v. Pittway Corp., 770 F.2d at 9 (citations omitted) (smoke detector manufacturer can be held liable for personal injuries suffered in fire where defective detector failed to sound in timely fashion). *See also Trust Corp. of Montana v. Piper Aircraft Corp.*, 506 F. Supp. 1093, 1094-95 (D. Mont. 1981) (airplane manufacturer can be held liable for lack of shoulder harnesses where harnesses might have prevented some of injuries suffered in crash); *Stahl v. Ford Motor Co.*, 64 Ill. App. 3d 919, 21 Ill. Dec. 667, 381 N.E.2d 1211, 1214-15 (1978) (auto manufacturer held liable for increased damages resulting from failure of seat belt during accident). The "crashworthiness" or "enhanced injury" automobile cases are to the same effect. *See Larsen v. General Motors Corp.*, 391 F.2d 495, 503 (8th Cir. 1968).

It is true that, unlike the above, there was no defect of design or manufacture in this case. But there was evidence from which it could be inferred that the absence of a warning enhanced the harm resulting from the fire. Plaintiff testified that if he had realized that a short circuit that caused an electrical fire might at the same time disable the smoke detector, he would have purchased a back-up battery-powered detector or wired the detector in question into an isolated circuit, thus minimizing the danger that a fire-causing short circuit would render the detector inoperative. We find, therefore, a sufficient connection between the children's deaths and injury and the absence of any warning.

Defendants contend that the district court nevertheless erred in denying their motions because, they claim, the danger that an electrical fire will incapacitate an electric-powered smoke detector is obvious. They point out that anyone purchasing a device powered by house electrical current will necessarily realize that if the current goes off for any reason, the device will not work.

In Massachusetts, as elsewhere, a failure to warn amounts to negligence only where the supplier of the good known to be dangerous for its intended use "has no reason to believe that those for whose use the chattel is supplied will realize its dangerous condition." Restatement (Second) of Torts §388 (1965). *See Fiorentino v. A.E. Staley Manufacturing Co.*, 11 Mass. App. 428, 416 N.E.2d 998, 1004 (1981); *Maldonado v. Thomson National Press Co.*, 16 Mass. App. 911, 449 N.E.2d 1229, 1231, *review denied*, 389 Mass. 1105, 452 N.E.2d 1158 (1983). Where the risks of the product are discernible by casual inspection, such as the danger that a knife can cut, or a stove burn, the consumer is in just as good a position as the manufacturer to gauge the dangers associated with the product, and nothing is gained by shifting to the manufacturer the duty to warn. Thus, a manufacturer is not required to warn that placing one's hand into the blades of a potato chopper will cause injury, *Plante v. Hobart Corp.*, 771 F.2d 617 (1st Cir. 1985), that permitting a three-year-old child to ride on the running board of a moving tractor risks injury to the child, *Kerr v. Koemm,* 557 F. Supp. 283 (S.D.N.Y. 1983), or that firing a BB gun at another at close range can injure or kill, *Sherk v. Daisy-Heddon,* 498 Pa. 594, 450 A.2d 615 (1982). If a manufacturer had to warn consumers against every such obvious danger inherent in a product, "[t]he list of obvious practices warned against would be so long, it would fill a volume." *Plante,* 771 F.2d at 620.

Defendants ask us to declare that the risk that an electrical fire could incapacitate an AC-powered smoke detector is so obvious that the average consumer[38.3] would not benefit from a warning. This is not a trivial argument; in earlier — some might say sounder — days, we might have accepted it. *Compare Jamieson v. Woodward & Lothrop,* 247 F.2d 23 (D.C. Cir. 1957). Our sense of the current state of the tort law in Massachusetts and most other jurisdictions, however, leads us to conclude that, today, the matter before us poses a jury question; that "obviousness" in a situation such as this would be treated by the Massachusetts courts as presenting a question of fact, not of law. To be sure, it would be obvious to anyone that an electrical outage would cause this smoke detector to fail. But the average purchaser might not comprehend the specific danger that a fire-causing electrical problem can simultaneously knock out the circuit into which a smoke detector is wired, causing the detector to fail at the very moment it is needed. Thus, while the failure of a detector to function as the result of an electrical malfunc-

---

[38.3] *The court's footnote 3 reads:* Defendants appear to claim that the obviousness standard should necessarily take into account the knowledge and experience of the individual consumer who is injured. The Massachusetts courts have made clear, however, that warnings are to be construed with the "average user" or "reasonably prudent person" in mind. . . . It is true that where a manufacturer reasonably expects only those with a certain degree of knowledge and expertise to come into contact with a product, the obviousness standard should be considered in light of the reasonable person with that knowledge or expertise. . . . This rule is not relevant to the present case, however, for the smoke detector was marketed through Sears flyers and catalogs to individuals who could not be expected to have any particular expertise in electrical matters. The fact that Laaperi in fact had some such expertise was therefore purely fortuitous, and does not bear on the legal standpoint for obviousness.

tion due, say, to a broken power line or a neighborhood power outage would, we think, be obvious as a matter of law, the failure that occurred here, being associated with the very risk — fire — for which the device was purchased, was not, or so a jury could find.

Our conclusion finds support in a number of Massachusetts cases stating that a court should be extremely reluctant to take from the jury issues regarding the adequacy of warnings. The recent decision of the Massachusetts Supreme Judicial Court in *MacDonald v. Ortho Pharmaceutical Corp.*, 394 Mass. 131, 475 N.E.2d 65, *cert. denied,* — U.S. —, 106 S. Ct. 250, 88 L. Ed. 2d 258 (1985) is instructive:

> The common law duty to warn . . . necessitates a warning "comprehensible to the average user and . . . convey[ing] a fair indication of the nature and extent of the danger to the mind of a reasonably prudent person." Whether a particular warning measures up to this standard is almost always an issue to be resolved by a jury; few questions are "more appropriately left to a common sense lay judgment than that of whether a written warning gets its message across to an average person." A court may, as a matter of law, determine "whether the defendant has conformed to that standard, in any case in which the jury may not reasonably come to a different conclusion," but judicial intrusion into jury decision-making in negligence cases is exceedingly rare.

Id., 475 N.E.2d at 71 (citations omitted). Applying this standard, we think that the issue of obviousness to the average consumer of the danger of a fire-related power outage was one for the jury, not the court, to determine. In the present case, the jury was specifically instructed that if it found this danger to be obvious it should hold for defendants. It failed to do so.

B. *Causation*

While, as just discussed, the danger the detector would fail in these circumstances was not so obvious as to eliminate, as a matter of law, any need to warn, we must also consider whether Laaperi's specialized electrical knowledge constituted a bar to his own recovery. As pointed out [*supra* note 38.3] plaintiff's specialized knowledge is immaterial to whether defendants had a duty to warn, since that duty is defined by the knowledge of the average purchaser. But plaintiff's expertise *is* relevant to whether defendants' failure to warn caused plaintiff's damages. Even though defendants may have been required to provide a warning, plaintiff may not recover if it can be shown that because of his above-average knowledge, he already appreciated the very danger the warning would have described. In such event there would be no connection between the negligent failure to warn and plaintiff's damages.

Defendants here presented considerable evidence suggesting that Laaperi, who was something of an electrical handyman, knew of the danger and still took no precautions. Laaperi, however, offered evidence that he did *not* know of the danger, and that he would have guarded against it had he been warned. The following exchange between Laaperi and his counsel on direct examination, tends to support the jury's determination of liability:

MR. SWARTZ: Sir, did you ever consider when purchasing this smoke detector that an electric outage would render it inoperable?

THE WITNESS [LAAPERI]: I did not.

Q: Did you ever consider or contemplate at any time installing a separate circuit for the smoke detector in and of itself?

A: I did not.

Q Did you ever read the owner's manual?

A: Yes, I did.

Q: If the owner's manual had indicated to you to place this on a separate circuit, would you have done it?

A: Yes, I would have.

Q: Were you ever advised by any literature or any written instructions to purchase a back-up battery system?

A: No.

Q: If you were alerted to that, would have done it?
A: I think I would have, yes.

Self-serving as this testimony was, the jury was free to credit it. In reviewing the denial of a motion for directed verdict or judgment n.o.v., we are obliged to view the evidence in the light most favorable to the verdict winner. *Insurance Company of North America v. Musa,* 785 F.2d 370, 372 (1st Cir. 1986); *Borras v. Sea-Land Service, Inc.*, 586 F.2d 881, 885 (1st Cir. 1978). We are not at liberty to evaluate the credibility of witnesses or the weight of the evidence at trial. *Musa,* 785 F.2d at 372; *Hubbard v. Faros Fisheries, Inc.*, 626 F.2d 196, 199 (1st Cir. 1980). In light of this standard, we cannot say that the district court erred in denying defendants' motions for directed verdict and judgment n.o.v., for the jury could have believed Laaperi's testimony in the colloquy quoted above, among other evidence, and concluded that had he been properly warned, Laaperi would have instituted different fire detection methods in his home to protect his family against the danger that his smoke detector would be rendered useless in the event of a fire-related power outage.

Page 219:

[Add new sections following § 5.17.]

§ 5.17A Washing machine [New]

The decision in *Sears, Roebuck & Co. v. Black,*[47.1] illustrates the potential liability of a vendor who sells an appliance which causes a fire:

The issue is whether there is sufficient evidence to support the jury's finding that defendant "was negligent in failing to have properly designed" the washing machine which it sold to plaintiffs and that such negligence was a proximate cause of the fire which burned plaintiffs' mobile home. The jury also answered in another portion to the charge that the washing machine was not defectively

[47.1] 708 S.W.2d 925 (Tex. Ct. App. 1986).

designed at the time it was manufactured, but there is no point of error urging a conflict in these answers.

Mr. and Mrs. Black bought a Sears Kenmore washer on November 6, 1979. Their mobile home burned on May 10, 1982. They filed suit against Sears, Roebuck and Company, urging several theories of recovery: strict liability under Restatement (Second) Torts § 402A; express and implied warranty; common-law negligence; and the Deceptive Trade Practices-Consumer Protection Act. Following a trial by jury, judgment was rendered in favor of Mr. and Mrs. Black on February 25, 1985, for the sum of $12,000 plus prejudgment interest. Sears, Roebuck and Company appeals. We affirm.

* * *

While appellees' expert was not a specialist in washing machines, he was an electrical engineer with a doctorate degree in electrical engineering who is on the faculty of a major university. The objections to his testimony went to the weight, rather than to the admissibility of his opinion. *See* TEX. R. EVID. 702, 703, and 704. This expert's opinion was that a faulty electrical contact in the washing machine's switch led to overheating which caused the fire to occur. He concluded that there was a faulty design because if the switch housing had been metal instead of plastic, the mobile home fire could have been prevented. The jury was free to accept this testimony, and we are not at liberty to disturb the verdict. The jury was not compelled to believe appellant's expert on all the issues because they agreed with him on some of the issues. Appellant's expert testimony was persuasive, but it was not conclusive. The fact that Whirlpool Corporation manufactured the washing machine does not insulate Sears from liability. Sears had Whirlpool put the Sears' brand name on the machine, and Sears sold the machine as a Sears Kenmore washing machine. As noted by the Restatement (Second) Torts § 400, one who puts out as its own product a chattel manufactured by another is subject to the same liability as though it were the manufacturer. *See, e.g., Maintenance Contractors v. John Deere Co.*, 554 S.W.2d 28 at 32 (Tex. Civ. App. — Houston [14th Dist.] 1977, writ dism'd).[47.2]

§5.17B The anti-kickback clutch that didn't prevent kickback [New]

My firm recently represented a man who was badly injured in an accident involving a chain saw. My client was a mature and careful man. Indeed, he was an attorney. He was standing on a ladder, about fifteen feet in the air, trimming branches from a tree in his yard using a chain saw. While he was using the saw in a careful and prudent manner, the saw kicked back and threw him to the ground. He was severely injured.

The chain saw was manufactured by one company and marketed by a national retail chain of stores. A manual provided with the chain saw represented that the saw contained an "anti-kickback clutch" which prevented the very kind of kickback experienced by the plaintiff. In the course of discovery, we were able to establish that this so-called safety device did not work as represented. Indeed, the safety device was merely a slip clutch designed to prevent motor burnout — it simply did not prevent kickback. This case was settled for $1,460,000.[47.3]

§5.17C Electric stove [New]

In *White Consolidated Industry v. Swiney*,[47.4] homeowners sued the manufacturer and vendor of an electric stove which caused a fire and destroyed their home. There was evidence that the cause of the fire was a connection on the stove which had not been properly constructed or assembled and which caused the deterioration of the insulation on the wire. There was sufficient evidence that an unreasonably dangerous condition existed in the stove when it left the hands of the defendants.

[47.2] *Id.* at 925-28.

[47.3] Hensleigh v. Sears, Roebuck & Co., No. CA 83-1193-MA (D. Mass. 1986).

[47.4] 376 S.E.2d 283 (Va. 1989).

§ 5.17D Toaster oven [New]

A woman in her sixties was killed when her house caught fire due to what we alleged was a defective toaster oven. Plaintiffs contended that the toaster oven was defective because if the oven was mistakenly turned on to broil at the same time the toaster lever was depressed, the safety controls were overridden, causing the toast level thermostat to be inoperative. Plaintiff's reconstruction indicated that is what probably happened to cause the fire. This theory was developed through extensive testing, as there were no witnesses to the fire, and little physical evidence on which to reconstruct the details of how the fire started. The case was settled for six figures.

§ 5.17E Air conditioner [New]

In *Garavalia v. Heat Controller, Inc.*, 570 N.E.2d 1227 (Ill. App. 1991), the court held that it was foreseeable that a defectively designed or manufactured air conditioner would harm an elderly user if it failed. This was premised on the fact that a person using an air conditioner will seal up the house and become entirely dependent on the air conditioner to keep his body in an appropriate heating environment. In this case, an elderly person died of hyperthermia when his air conditioner failed. When the air conditioner fails, the user may be left to swelter in conditions far more stifling and oppressive than if the unit had never been installed and the house had not been sealed up.

VI. Litigation Sources: Bibliography

§ 5.27 Selected legal sources

Page 227:

[Add new text under "Selected legal sources":]

Mongeluzzi, *Electrocution Accidents on the Job,* 25 Trial 68, No. 3 (Mar. 1989).

§5.29 Selected laws, regulations, and standards

Page 229:

[Add the following new text under "*Statutes*":]

(3) Railroad Safety Appliance Act, 45 U.S.C. §1 *et seq.* (1986).
(4) Radiation Control Safety Act, 42 U.S.C. §263b *et seq.* (1982 & Supp. 1987).
(5) Child Protection and Toy Safety Act, 15 U.S.C. §1274 (1987).
(6) Hazardous Substances Act, 15 U.S.C. §1261-1276 (1982 & Supp. 1987).
(7) Occupational Safety and Health Act, 29 U.S.C. §651 *et seq.* (1985 & Supp. 1987).

[Add the following new text under "*Regulations*":]

(3) 56 Fed. Reg. 28050 (No. 118). Implementation of regulations of the United States Consumer Products Safety Commission regulations governing garage door openers, applying to garage door openers manufactured after January 1, 1991 for sale within the United States.

§5.30 Selected cases

Page 232:

[Add new text as follows:]

Interstate Engineering, Inc. v. Burnette, 474 So. 2d 624 (Ala. 1985), death; failure of sensors in **heat detectors.**

Keelon v. K-Mart, 481 So. 2d 896 (Ala. Civ. Ct. App. 1985), fire allegedly caused by **defective box fan;** property damage to home.

Lamer v. McKee Industries, Inc., 721 P.2d 611 (Alaska 1986), wrongful death; **defective garage door winding plug.**

Thorpe v. Robert F. Bullock, Inc., 179 Ga. App. 867, 348 S.E.2d 55 (1986), **automatic deep fryer;** badly burned when boiling oil spilled.

Folson v. Sears, Roebuck & Co., 174 Ga. App. 46, 329 S.E.2d 217 (1985), **microwave oven;** burn injuries to hand.

Trent v. Brasch Mfg. Co., 132 Ill. App. 3d 586, 477 N.E.2d 1312 (1985), injured while checking thermostat; **electric duct heater.**

Laaperi v. Sears, Roebuck & Co., 787 F.2d 726 (1st Cir. 1986), first- and second-degree burns: **electric smoke detector;** failure to warn.

Hensleigh v. Sears, Roebuck & Co., No. CA 83-1193-MA (D. Mass. 1986), "anti-kickback" clutch on **chain saw;** settlement for $1,460,000.

Klein v. General Electric Co., 714 S.W.2d 896 (Mo. Ct. App. 1986), fire originated in **automatic coffeemaker;** damage to home.

Bednarski v. Hideout Homes & Realty, Inc., 711 F. Supp. 823 (M.D. Pa. 1989), **defective electrical outlet** causing house to burn; action against builder allowed.

Beatty v. Roper Corp., 714 S.W.2d 376 (Tex. Ct. App. 1986), **kitchen range;** no liability.

Sears, Roebuck & Co. v. Black, 708 S.W.2d 925 (Tex. Ct. App. 1986), mobile home fire; plastic switch housing; faulty electrical contact in **washing machine switch.**

Home Insurance Co. of Illinois v. National Tea Co., 577 So. 2d 65 (La. App. 1991), shopping mall fire caused by electrical arc in **wiring of an oven;** distributor of oven not liable when purchaser negligently modified wiring to peak load limiter.

Chapter 6

CRIPPLED AT LEISURE: RECREATIONAL PRODUCT-RELATED TORTS

VI. Litigation Sources: Bibliography

§ 6.45 Selected technical sources

Page 287:

[Add new text preceding "Pools."]

ATVs

Abrams, *Taking the ATV Case to Trial,* 26 Trial 42, No. 8 (Aug. 1990).

Page 288:

[Add to text at end of "Pools."]

Duffy, *$10 Million Verdict for Man Hurt in Pool,* 13 Pa. L.J.-Rep. 12, No. 12 (Oct. 29, 1990).

Gilbert, *Promoting Above-Ground Pool Safety,* 18 Trial 81, No. 11 (Nov. 1982).

Page 290:

[Add to text at end of "Football."]

Cohen, *Sports Helmets: More Harm than Protection?*, 25 Trial 74, No. 3 (May 1989).

Torado, *Allocation of Risk Based on the Mechanics of Injury in Sport*, 10 Comm./Ent. L.J. 33 (1987).

Page 290:

[Add to text at end of "Motorcycles."]

Erza, *Motorcycle Design Defects*, 18 Trial 94, No. 11 (Nov. 1982).

§ 6.47 Selected government sources

Page 291:

[Add new text as follows:]

Consumer Products Safety Comm'n, News Release No. 91-64 (1991). Product warning by U.S. Product Safety Commission about dangers of finger amputation with certain kinds of exercise cycles which do not have chain guards.

§ 6.48 Selected legal sources

Page 294:

[Add new text under "Boats and Water Skiing."]

Hogan, *Propeller Guards for Recreational Boats*, 25 Trial 56, No. 3 (Mar. 1989).

Wonacott, *Products Liabilities of Shipbuilders and Repairers*, 62 Tul. L. Rev. 465 (1988).

Page 295:

[Add new text at end of § 6.48:]

All-Terrain Vehicles

Hansen, *The ABCs of ATV Cases*, 23 Trial 66, No. 8 (Aug. 1987).

Buckley & Rooney, *All-Terrain Vehicles*, 24 Trial 56, No. 11 (Nov. 1988).

§6.51 Selected cases

Page 300:

[Add new text as follows:]

First Nat'l Bank of Dwight v. Regent Sports Corp., 803 F.2d 1431 (7th Cir. 1986), **lawn darts;** 2½-year-old plaintiff; permanent brain damage.

Aimone v. Walgreen's Co., 601 F. Supp. 507 (N.D. Ill. 1985), **lawn darts;** foreseeable they would be treated as toys and given to children.

Wessinger v. Vetter Corp., 685 F. Supp. 769 (D. Kan. 1987), defective **motorcycle fairing;** Japanese corporation which designed motorcycle subject to jurisdiction under stream of commerce theory.

Vincent v. Davis-Grabowski, Inc., 638 F. Supp. 1166 (E.D. La. 1986), strict liability, **boating** injury.

Dietrich v. Allstate Ins. Co., 540 So. 2d 358 (La. 1989), action by injured visitor in privately-owned **swimming pool** against owner and pool installer raised issues as to the lighting of the pool area on negligence and strict liability theories.

Makuc v. American Honda Motor Co., 835 F.2d 389 (1st Cir. 1987), **motorbike** injury; breach of warranty and consumer protection laws.

Gittenburg v. Wilcenski, 174 Mich. App. 321, 435 N.W.2d 480 (1989), injury from diving into shallow **pool;** duty to warn of foreseeable risks, *reversed*, 441 Mich. 379, 491 N.W.2d 208 (1992), no duty to warn of danger associated with head-first dive into shallow water.

McCormick v. Custom Pools, Inc., 376 N.W.2d 471 (Minn. Ct. App. 1985), quadriplegic; dive into shallow end of **swimming pool.**

Gentile v. MacGregor Mfg. Co., 201 N.J. Super 612, 493 A.2d 647 (1985), **reconditioned football helmets;** failure to inspect.

Austria v. Bike Athletic Co., 107 Or. App. 57, 810 P.2d 1312 (1991), severe physical and mental head injury suffered by football player wearing **helmet** manufactured, designed and marketed by defendants; when evidence is that hematoma resulted from the kind of trauma that helmets are intended to prevent because improper design which would allow energy of blow to be transmitted to head of user without absorbing sufficient amounts of energy to prevent injury, judgment for plaintiff will be affirmed.

Denkensohn v. Davenport, 144 A.D.2d 58, 536 N.Y.S.2d 587 (1989), genuine issue of material fact existed on issue of whether swimming pool installer had duty to warn as to relative depth of the **swimming pool.**

Castro v. Alden Leeds, Inc., 144 A.D.2d 613, 535 N.Y.S.2d 73 (1988), injuries caused by explosion of canister of **swimming pool chemicals.**

Howard v. Poseidon Pools, Inc., 134 A.D.2d 926, 522 N.Y.S.2d 388, 389-90 (1987) (dissenting opinion of Callahan, J.P., and Denman, J.), whether manufacturer of **aboveground swimming pool** who is aware that hundreds of persons sustained quadriplegic and paraplegic injuries has duty to warn even experienced swimmers of danger is an issue of fact to be determined by the factfinder.

McInnis v. A.M.F., Inc., 765 F.2d 240 (1st Cir. 1985), injured leg; jagged edges and gears on **clutch housing of motorcycle.**

Yamaha Motor Co. v. Thornton, 579 So. 2d 619 (Ala. 1991), eleven-year-old boy killed riding a **motorcycle** marketed for children; sudden acceleration when child confronted by emergency sighting of another child in roadway; defective design inasmuch as natural reaction of operator when confronted with emergency is to rotate the throttle and produce full acceleration; design options such as engine stop switch, thumb throttle or adjustable speed governor were available to manufacturer to prevent emergency-induced acceleration; award of punitive damages upheld.

Muldowney v. Imperial Pools, 509 A.2d 441 (R.I. 1986), death; **diving board.**

Baughn v. Honda Motor Co., 107 Wash. 2d 127, 727 P.2d 655 (1986), **minitrail bike.**

Mulhern v. Outboard Marine Corp., 146 Wis. 2d 604, 432 N.W.2d 130 (1988), defective **throttle device;** liability of manufacturer in absence of direct sale found on theory that manufacturer placed product into the stream of commerce.

O'Connell v. Continental Casualty Co., (Wis. Cir. Ct., 1986), 29 ATLA L. Rep. 333 (Sept. 1986), **swimming pool;** negligent design.

Holloway v. State, 239 N.J. Super. 554, 571 A.2d 1324 (1990), state's third-party claim against pool manufacturer; injury to state prisoner caused by diving injury; defective manufacture and **pool lining.**

Ryan v. KDI Sylvan Pools, Inc., 121 N.J. 276, 579 A.2d 1241 (1990), plaintiff paralyzed after diving into **swimmimg pool** from board; defective design; $500,000 damage award.

King v. National Spa & Pool Institute, Inc., 570 So. 2d 612 (Ala. 1990), **in-ground vinyl-lined backyard pool;** diver suffered broken neck, quadriplegia, and death due to pneumonia secondary to quadriplegia; trade association which published minimum industry standards for residential pools could be held liable if inadequate.

Chapter 7

IN THE NURSERY: TOYS THAT INJURE AND MAIM

V. Preventing Toy-Related Injuries

§ 7.41 Government action needed

Page 360:

[Add the following new text:]

Efforts have been made in recent years to obtain government action for badly needed research on injuries caused to children by dangerous and defective products. The scope of the problem is shown by the fact that the Consumer Product Safety Network has reported that injuries account for half of all deaths of children who are over the age of one; even more startling is that injuries account for two-thirds of all deaths of children over the age of fifteen.[106.1]

Senator Edward Kennedy of Massachusetts has introduced legislation which would fund government research on this problem, but, to date, Congress has not responded with the needed legislation. Senate Bill 2648, introduced into the 99th Congress, would make the Child Injury Protection Act law. It would create a Center for Injury Control within the U.S. Center for Disease Control. This agency would examine the causes, mechanisms, prevention, diagnosis and treatment of injuries, as well as fund other research on the causes of injuries to children. Another proposed piece of legislation, Senate Bill 2689 (99th Congress), would enact the Child Injury Prevention Amendments. This would, in part, establish uniform labeling guidelines for toys — a much-needed federal intervention.

VI. Litigation Sources: Bibliography

§ 7.46 Selected popular sources

Page 366:

[Add new text as follows:]

Gillis and Fise, *The Childwise Catalog: A Consumer Guide to Buying the Safest and Best Products for Your Children* (1986).

Swartz, *Toys That Kill: Make Sure Your Child is Safe* (1986).

§ 7.47 Selected government sources

Page 367:

[Add new text as follows:]

55 Fed. Reg. 42402. Consumer Product Safety Commission announcement of development of rules governing labeling and other requirements for crib toys; interested parties invited to submit comments.

55 Fed. Reg. 42202. Consumer Products Safety Commission proposed rulemaking for infant cushions; existing regula-

---

[106.1] 4 CPSN Newsletter 3, No. 4 (July/Aug. 1986).

tions do not deal with risks of cushions filled with foam plastic beads or granular materials.

§7.48 Selected legal sources

Page 367:

[Add new text as follows:]

Adler, *Toy Safety: No Kidding Around,* 25 Trial 44, No. 11 (Nov. 1989).

Campbell, *The Flammable Fabrics Act and Strict Liability in Tort,* 9 Ind. L. Rev. 395 (1976).

Caso, *Unreasonably Dangerous Products for a Child's Perspective,* 20 Rutgers L.J. 433 (1989).

Gillis & Fise, *The Childwise Catalog: A Consumer Guide to Buying the Safest and Best Products for Your Children — Newborns through Age Five* (1986), Pocket Books, 1230 Avenue of the Americas, New York, N.Y. 10020.

Kindregan, *Review of The Childwise Catalog,* 23 Trial 95, No. 4 (Apr. 1987).

Lambert, *Flammable Nightgown,* 28 ATLA L. Rep. 390 (Nov. 1985).

Legal-Medical Studies, *The Lawyer's Annotated Products Liability Checklist* (1987), Box 8219, Boston, MA 02114.

Palmer, *Express Warranties Arising from Advertising,* 41 J. Air L. 497 (1975).

Patton, *Flammable Fabrics,* 18 Trial No. 4 (Apr. 1984).

Postell, *Trends: Hazardous Toys,* 23 Trial 85, No. 8 (Aug. 1987).

Swartz, *Toys That Kill: Make Sure Your Child is Safe — Avoid the Thousands of Life-Threatening Toys* (1986), Vintage Books-Random House, 201 East 50th St., New York, N.Y. 10022.

Swartz, *Toys-R-Dangerous,* 18 Trial 28, No. 2 (Feb. 1982).

Swartz, *When Products Injure Children,* 25 Trial 50, No. 8 (Aug. 1988).

§7.49 Selected newsletters

Page 368:

[Add new text at end of section.]

Consumer Information

Consumer Sourcebook
Gale Research Co.
Book Tower
Detroit, Mich. 48226

Pets

Pet Dealer Purchasing Guide
Howmark Publ. Corp.
567 Morris Ave.
Elizabeth, N.J. 07208

Toys and Crafts

Toys, Hobbies and Crafts
545 5th Ave.
New York, N.Y. 10017

Toy Safety Reports

Consumer Product Safety Network Newsletter
Consumer Federation of America
1424 16th St. N.W., Suite 604
Washington, D.C. 20036

§ 7.50 Selected laws, regulations, and standards

Page 368:

[Add new text to subsection "Laws Affecting Safety of Toys and Other Children's Products."]

(6) Federal Refrigerator Safety Act, 15 U.S.C. §§ 1211-1214 (1982 & Supp. 1987).

Page 368

[Add the following new subsections before "Regulations":]

U.S. Consumer Product Safety Commission Rule Announcements [New]

(1) 55 Fed. Reg. 42402 (No. 203). The CPSC announced rules regarding potential requirements of labeling for cribtoys. The issue of potential for strangulation of children by cribtoys is of concern.

Toy Recalls or Repair Orders by the U.S. Consumer Products Safety Commission [New]

(1) Music Maker Toys (F.J. Strauss, N.J.). Excessive lead level; potential choking of child hazard. [CPSC News Release No. 90-155].
(2) Toy Bear (Muffy Valentine II; Northern Amer. Bear Co., Ill.). Hazard because of small parts. [CPSC News Release No. 90-154].

Page 369:

[Add new text to subsection "Regulations."]

(7) U.S. Consumer Product Safety Commission, Proposed Rules, 16 CFR, Ch. II; 52 Fed. Reg. 10688-01 (Oct. 10, 1987) (CPSC preliminary determination that there may be an unreasonable risk of injury associated with lawn darts sufficient to warrant regulatory action).
(8) U.S. Consumer Product Safety Commission, administrative adjudicative proceeding and ruling under the Federal Hazardous Substances Act, 15 U.S.C. 1274, for remedial action to protect the public from substantial risks of injury; "Flying Animal Swings"; 52 Fed. Reg. 47624-03.

§7.51 Selected cases

Page 370:

[Add new text as follows:]

Scarano v. Town of Ela, 166 Ill. App. 3d 184, 520 N.E.2d 62 (1988), young boy was injured when he fell off a **sliding**

board. In his lawsuit against the town which maintained the slide, the plaintiff asserted that the handrails were worn, slippery and loose. The court determined that a slide with defective handrails was a greater risk than children would normally appreciate. Compare this decision to the result in *Cozzi v. North Palos Elementary School District No. 117,* 232 Ill. App. 3d 379, 597 N.E.2d 683 (1992), in which the court held that a school district owed no duty to a child who fell from a **jungle gym** because the risk of falling was obvious; the court in *Cozzi* also held that the manufacturer was not liable under a theory of negligence or strict liability since the jungle gym was not unreasonably dangerous when it left the manufacturer's control.

Aimone v. Walgreen's Co., 601 F. Supp. 507 (N.D. Ill. 1985), eight-year-old injured by **lawn dart.**

Cunningham v. Quaker Oats Co., Fisher-Price Div., 639 F. Supp. 234 (W.D.N.Y. 1986), brain-damaged child; injury caused by defectively designed **toy figurine.**

Vincent v. Davis-Grabowski, Inc., 638 F. Supp. 1171 (S.D.N.Y. 1986), presence of foreign toy supplier at New York toy fair and other contacts sufficient basis for **jurisdiction** in products liability action **under long-arm statute.**

Page 372:

[Add new section following § 7.51.]

§ 7.52 The continuing plague of unsafe toys and the failure of the CPSC [New]

The material that follows was extracted from a press conference given by the author on toy safety on December 1, 1986. The toy manufacturers' public relations campaign notwithstanding, we do not have effective, across-the-board toy safety in the United States.

My new book, *Toys That Kill* (Vintage-Random House) reveals that despite the growing public insistence on toy safety and despite the government's authority to take direct action against dangerous toys, toys which could choke, burn, blind, maim, or kill the children for whom they are intended remain on the market today. This is a consequence of industry failure to deal effectively with the problem of hazardous toys and of governmental failure to deal strictly, swiftly, and summarily with the hazardous toys which can be found in abundance in toy and department stores.

Toys That Kill provides safe buying guidelines for toy shoppers as well as names and describes dangerous toys that should be avoided. Some of these toys have already been associated with DOCUMENTED DEATHS, for example:

- *Play Family Figurine* (Fisher-Price)
  Three deaths with another child severely brain-damaged after the small toy became lodged in throat, cutting off the supply of oxygen to the brain. (*Toys That Kill* p. 12)
- *Soft Triplets Crib Gym* (Johnson & Johnson)
  Several deaths from strangulation (*Toys That Kill* p. 68)
- *Crib and Playpen Play Gym* (Fisher-Price)
  Two deaths from strangulation (*Toys That Kill* p. 158)
- *Hold Me Tite Squeeze Toy* (Reliance Products Corp.)
  Two deaths from choking over small end (*Toys That Kill* p. 7)
- *Battlestar Galactica Space Toy* (Mattel, Inc.)
  Two deaths from ingestion of small missiles (*Toys That Kill* p. 76)
- *Big Wheels* (Louis Marx Co.)
  At least three deaths from motorists striking children. The low profile prevents motorists from seeing a child before it is too late. (*Toys That Kill* p. 90)
- *Embo Elephant and Humbugg Bee* (R. Dakin & Company)
  Two deaths from strangulation involving these toys. (*Toys That Kill* p. 2)

Some of these killer toys have been recalled, but many can still be found in toy boxes throughout the United States. With the exception of one or two toys usually involved in high-publicity recalls (brought on by consumer pressure and an unfortunate body count), most parents are not aware of recalls or the deadly propensities of recalled toys. When the government does take action, it is a case of too little too late. These harmful toys remain in circulation due to the government's unwillingness to implement a tough toy recall procedure.

One example is the recent recall of the Johnson & Johnson "Soft Triplets Crib Gym." This toy has been responsible for at least two deaths and was recalled in October, 1986. The hazard associated with this toy was reported to the Consumer Product Safety Commission two years before any deaths had occurred. The agency [was warned] of the lethal nature of this toy fully five times spanning from 1982 to 1985. The agency did not act until there was an actual "body count."

Unfortunately, many American children will be injured or killed this year as a result of harmful playthings still polluting the marketplace and America's toy boxes. I hope *Toys That Kill* and today's release of my nominees for the "Ten Worst Toys" provides the spark to ignite a grass roots national crusade for children's safety. This crusade must begin in our homes, schools, courtrooms, and state legislatures. Parents, grandparents, teachers, and, yes, children, must lead this crusade.

The toy barons and their bureaucratic associates are masters at public relation campaigns which lull us into a false sense of security. *Toys That Kill* refutes the most common assertions of this $15-billion-dollar-a-year toy industry and establishes that:

- *Adults are not to blame for most toy-related injuries — inadequate design and megabuck marketing are the major causes of the appalling body count.*

Toy manufacturers and retailers are masters at shifting blame for injury from themselves to grief-stricken parents who already feel responsible for their child's injury. Part of this "shift the blame" strategy lies in the industry's use of the words "parental supervision" as a substitute for "don't blame us" when tragedy strikes. The industry knows that the vast majority of toys sold will be used without adult supervision, as surrogate "baby-sitters."

- *The government does not tell us the whole story about toy safety.*

Each year [the] Consumer Product Safety Commission (CPSC) sponsors their annual "toy safety campaign" with the toy industry's trade association (TMA). They use our tax dollars to help toy makers get their spurious points across to consumers and to provide free public relations. This is the industry the CPSC is supposed to be regulating. It is a case of the fox guarding the henhouse.

- *Existing toy safety standards do not protect our children.*

The United States lags behind many other countries around the world in establishing stringent, effective, safety standards for toys. The CPSC knows that we could learn a great deal from our nearest neighbor, Canada, on how to develop effective toy safety standards. Yet, they defend inadequate standards which permit the continued marketing of toys and other products that kill our children.

- *We cannot rely on the government or the toy industry to name the names of toys that kill and maim.*

Toys That Kill documents an industry-wide and regulatory agency conspiracy of silence. This conspiracy has permitted the continued sale and use of killer toys. Further, it has resulted in many dangerous toys becoming "silent assassins" since the CPSC and the toy industry have failed to adequately identify and publish the names of toys associated with death or serious injuries.

It is time for the CPSC and the Toy Manufacturers Association to "name names." Where a toy has killed a child the culprit toy should be exposed by "WANTED POSTERS," and distributed through the media and placed wherever parents and children would be most likely to see them.

- *Our toys are not adequately tested for safety before they are placed on the toy market.*

The toy industry is plagued by inadequate or nonexistent premarket testing. No authority exists for impartial, mandatory premarket review of toys. The CPSC does not test prior to the toy reaching the store shelves. If any such testing is done, it is usually paid for by the manufacturers and we are never told about the failures. Testing organizations hired by the industry refuse to reveal the names of toys which their testing has found to be hazardous.

- *Toy makers place inadequate warnings on hazardous toys which do nothing to protect children from harm.*

Most warnings, if they exist, reside on packaging which is tossed away and forgotten moments after opening a toy. [I have] never found a toy which adequately describes and indicates its potential for killing. This is true even when the toy has been the cause of several toy-related deaths.

- *Toy recalls are ineffective in taking hazardous toys off the market.*

Government regulators boast of their successes in recalling hazardous toys and saving children's lives. But the facts speak otherwise. Many life-threatening toys are not recalled until death and destruction rise high enough to force the government and toy makers into belated action. Even then, their actions are often totally inadequate.

The real key to toy safety is safer design, safer production, and more responsive, truthful, safety-conscious labeling and marketing practices by toy manufacturers. Experience indicates that we will get these only when the government vigorously insists that they be provided to the public. The toy industry's standards are inadequate, and prove that self-regulation is very often no regulation at all.

§ 7.53 Dangers of suffocation of infants on adult beds [New]

The Consumer Products Safety Commission has warned that an infant left on an adult or youth bed is in danger of suffocating. *See* Note, *CPSC Warns: Never Leave Infants on Adult Beds,* 26 Trial 16, No. 3 (Mar. 1990). The Commission received over 200 reports of infant deaths from suffocation in such circumstances between 1985 and 1990.

Chapter 8

MEDICAL PRODUCTS THAT DO NOT HEAL

II. Checklists

Page 379:

[Add new section after § 8.04.]

§ 8.04A Checklist: Discovery in a products-drug case [New]

The following list should be helpful to counsel conducting discovery in a products-drug case.

___(1) Pre-discovery investigation:
___(a) Name of drug

____(b) Identity of manufacturer
____(c) Brand name
____(d) Generic designation
____(e) Prescribing physician
____(f) Pharmacist who filled prescription
____(g) Date filled
____(h) Restrictions on refill
____(i) Other restrictions

____(2) Over the counter (non-prescription) drugs:
____(a) FDA Category I (safe and effective)
____(b) FDA Category II (not recognized as safe and effective)
____(c) FDA Category III (safety and/or effectiveness not determined)
____(d) Warnings
____(e) History of client use
____(f) Client's pre-use medical history
____(g) Review of medical literature on drug

____(3) Prescription drug:
____(a) Client's pre-prescription medical history
____(b) Client's post-prescription medical treatment and history
____(c) Pharmaceutical records
____(d) Warnings given with drug
____(e) Instructions given with drug
____(f) Restrictions on use of drug
____(g) Refill history

____(4) Case search to determine if there is prior reported litigation on subject drug:
____(a) Computer search of legal and medical sources
____(b) Check *Drugs in Litigation: Damages Awards Involving Prescription and Non-Prescription Drugs,* published by The Michie Co., P.O. Box 7587, Charlottesville, Va. 22906
____(c) Review data sources in *The Lawyer's Annotated Products Liability Checklist,* published by Legal-Medical Studies, Inc., Box 8219, Boston, Mass. 02114
____(d) Check listing in *Physician's Desk Reference Handbook* (current edition)

___(e) Check *Products Liability Law Reporter,* published by Association of Trial Lawyers of America, 1050 31st St., N.W., Washington, D.C. 20007

___(f) Submit name of drug to The ATLA Exchange, 1050 31st St., Washington, D.C. 20007

___(g) Review applicable statutes and regulations:

___(1) Federal Food, Drug, Cosmetic and Medical Devices Act

___(2) Applicable F.D.A. regulations

___(3) Applicable state statutes

___(5) Determine potential defendants:

___(a) Drug manufacturer

___(b) Manufacturers of component elements

___(c) Physician

___(d) Pharmacist

___(e) Hospital

___(f) Nurse

___(g) Advertiser

___(h) Middleman

___(i) F.D.A.

___(j) Other

___(6) Develop possible theories of recovery (essential not only to pleading but to focusing discovery):

___(a) Generally:

___(1) Negligence

___(2) Breach of express warranty

___(3) Breach of implied warranty of fitness for a particular use

___(4) Breach of implied warranty of merchantability

___(5) Strict liability

___(b) Specifically:

___(1) Defective design

___(2) Manufacturing flaw

___(3) Failure to test

___(4) Concealment of test results from F.D.A.

___(5) Misrepresentation of test results

___(6) Negligence in testing

___(7) Failure to inspect

___(8) Excessive promotion and marketing

___(9) Failure to warn in advertising
___(10) Failure to warn in package inserts
___(11) Failure to warn on label
___(12) Inadequate label
___(13) Inadequate instructions
___(14) Misleading instructions
___(15) Violation of statute
___(16) Violation of regulation
___(17) Violation of express warranty
___(18) Res ipsa

___(7) Discovery focus on the New Drug Application (NDA):
___(a) Copy of application
___(b) Copy of supporting documentation
___(c) Copy of internal memoranda, studies, and other documents developed in relation to the NDA

___(8) Discovery focus on the Investigational New Drug (IND):
___(a) Copy of IND application
___(b) Copy of all records relating to animal testing
___(c) Copy of all protocols relating to proposed human testing
___(d) Copy of all F.D.A. responses
___(e) Copy of all clinical human test reports and results

___(9) Discovery focus on Drug Efficacy Study Implementation (DESI):
___(a) Copy of any documentation relating to classification of older drugs as effective, probably effective, possibly effective, or not effective
___(b) Copy of any documentation relating to GRASE (generally recognized as safe and effective)

___(10) Discovery focus on chemical composition of drug:
___(a) List of chemical components
___(b) Copy of all memoranda relative to chemical research
___(c) Copy of all lab records, research reports, tests
___(d) Copy of all screening tests

___(e) Identities of all persons involved in chemical research and testing

___(11) Discovery focus on drug testing:

___(a) Identities of all persons involved in testing process

___(b) Initial animal effectiveness testing records

___(c) Dosage level testing

___(d) Additional animal testing during human testing

___(e) Copy of Notice of Claimed Investigational Exemption for a New Drug

___(f) Copy of all protocols

___(g) Identities of members of monitoring committee for human testing of drug

___(h) IND human testing records, documents, results

___(i) Records relating to Phase I Human Testing (dosages, means of absorption into body, safety)

___(j) Records relating to Phase II Human Testing (effectiveness)

___(k) Records relating to Phase III Human Testing (safety and effectiveness of drug used in dosages in which it is intended to be marketed)

___(12) Discovery focus on package insert and labeling:

___(a) Copy of all memoranda relating to package inserts and labeling

___(b) Copy of reports, applications, etc., to F.D.A. regarding package inserts and labeling

___(c) Copy of all inserts, packaging, and labeling ever used on drug since first marketed

___(13) Discovery focus on post-NDA records:

___(a) Copy of records relating to production methods

___(b) Copy of records relating to safety

___(c) Copy of records relating to effectiveness

___(d) Copy of any complaints, comments, or other communications received from physicians as to the drug

___(e) Reports of any alleged injuries caused by drug

___(f) Reports of any contamination

___(g) Reports of adverse reactions

___(h) Reports by company representatives (detailmen, salespersons, etc., of problems, concerns, etc., about the drug)

___(i) All reports filed with F.D.A. after NDA, including three-month, six-month and annual reports

___(j) All Supplemental New Drug Applications prepared and filed, with supporting documentation

___(14) Discovery focus on advertising and promotion of drug:

___(a) Copy of all medical journal and other print advertising for drug

___(b) Copy of all video advertising for drug

___(c) Copy of all literature on drug prepared for and distributed to health professionals, hospitals, clinics, etc.

___(d) Copy of all information, brochures, samples, promotional materials, etc., distributed by detailmen and salespersons

___(e) Copy of all remedial letters or other communications mailed to health professionals regarding this drug

___(15) Discovery of opponent's expert witness:

___(a) Identity

___(b) Qualifications

___(c) Reports prepared

___(d) Admissions or reservations

Page 390:

[Add new Part IIIA to chapter as follows:]

IIIA. Other Medical Product Hazards [New]

§ 8.12A Marketing dangerous drugs

In *Rose Garabedian v. Johnson & Johnson and McNeilab, Inc.,*[14.1] I was retained by the plaintiffs to bring suit on behalf of their deceased mother against the defendants for the negligent

[14.1] CA No. 84-90 5-WD (D. Mass. 1986).

marketing and the inadequate warnings which accompanied the drug Zomax. She was given a prescription for Zomax by her doctor in May of 1981 for mild pain.

Upon taking the Zomax, the patient suffered an anaphylactic reaction. She developed a rash and swelling all over her body, suffered wheezing and was unable to talk. Her immediate family at first thought she was suffering the effects of a stomach flu or something of that nature, as her health prior to this was excellent. The family waited two days before admitting their mother to the hospital, where she died within seventy-two hours of her admission.

Plaintiffs brought suit against the drug manufacturer alleging that the company was negligent in the testing and marketing of Zomax. In particular, it was shown that the defendant only tested 700 people on a multiple-dose basis; i.e., 700 clinical patients were given Zomax for one week or more. As Zomax was a drug prescribed for mild to moderate pain, it was going to be prescribed for one week or more. The defendant then marketed the drug stating in the Physicians' Desk Reference that 3,600 patients were tested.

Plaintiff also alleged that Zomax was similar to another NSAID (nonsteroidal, anti-inflammatory drug), Tolectin. Tolectin is significant in that it causes a higher rate of anaphylactic reactions than any other NSAID drug. The defendant never alerted physicians to the structural and chemical similarities between Zomax and Tolectin, even though it represented to the FDA that Zomax was "an analogue" of Tolectin in its New Drug Application.

The defendant was further negligent in its reporting of adverse drug reactions to the FDA. The defendant systematically minimized adverse reactions reports to the FDA.

The case was settled for an amount which by court order is to remain undisclosed.

IV. Preventing Medical Device-Related Injuries

§8.17 Incorporating safety-related technological advances in medical products

Page 392:

[Add new text as follows:]

Products used in close proximity to patients should encompass the best safety features available. The decision in *Honey v. Barnes Hospital*[15.1] illustrates the danger when persons providing such products fail to account for safety factors. The court affirmed a judgment against a hospital, contractor and manufacturer who failed to provide safety features for windows in a psychiatric hospital, causing the death of a young patient. As to the indifference of the window manufacturer to patient safety, the court commented:

> [The] window manufacturer knew these windows were to be used in psychiatric patient rooms. Window manufacturer also knew the windows would be installed on the fifteenth floor. Safety was an obvious concern with these windows. A simple inspection by window manufacturer would have disclosed these windows fit too tightly in their frames. With this defect, psychiatric room windows which were supposed to lock securely when closed might only appear locked when closed, a dangerous situation on the fifteenth floor. We find sufficient evidence of aggravating circumstances on the part of window manufacturer.[15.2]

Page 392:

[Add new section after § 8.04:]

§ 8.17A Reporting unsafe medical devices [New]

With the enactment of Public Law 101-629, the Safe Medical Devices Act of 1990, which amends the United States Food, Drug and Cosmetic Act, hospitals and other health care facilities are required to report deaths and serious injuries if there is a probability that a medical device caused or contributed to the harm. The report must go both to the manufacturer of the product and to the U.S. Food and Drug Administration.

Manufacturers and distributors of such products must report any corrections to the product after a report of injury or death. The Secretary of Health and Human Services may order the

---

15.1 708 S.W.2d 686 (Mo. Ct. App. 1986).

15.2 *Id.* at 704.

recall of any medical device if there is a reasonable probability that the device causes serious adverse health consequences or death.

V. Litigation Sources: Bibliography

§ 8.23 Selected legal sources

Page 393:

[Add new text as follows:]

Allan, Blackmore & Toseland, A Choloroform Inhalation Fatality — An Unusual Asphyxiation, 28 Med. Sci. & L. 120 (No. 2, 1988).

Brushwood, *Drug Induced Birth Defects: Difficult Decisions and Shared Responsibility,* 91 W. Va. L. Rev. 51 (No. 1, 1988-89).

Burroughs, et al., *Products Liability Actions in Medical Negligence,* 4 J. Legal Med. 201 (1983).

Bushwood, *Drug Induced Birth Defects,* 91 W. Va. L. Rev. 51 (1988-89).

Christensen & Parker, *Don't Overlook Products in Medical Cases,* 25 Trial 78, No. 11 (Nov. 1989).

Ciresi & Walburn, *Preemption in Pharmaceutical Cases,* 24 Trial 75, No. 3 (Mar. 1988).

Comment, *A Primer on Medical Device Regulation,* 20 FDA Consumer (No. 4) 24 (1986).

Comment, *Product Liability — Duty to Warn — MacDonald v. Ortho Pharmaceutical Corp.,* 11 Am. J. Law & Med. 136 (1985).

Hensley, *Polio Vaccine Warnings,* 11 J. Prod. Liab. 39 (1988).

Hinman, *The National Vaccine Program and the National Vaccine Injury Compensation Program,* 44 Food Drug Cosm. L.J. 663 (No. 6, 1989).

Howlett, *Compensation for Drug Induced Fetal Deformities in Common Law and Civil Law Systems,* 2 Touro J. Transnat'l L. 243 (1991).

Hutton, Hanna, Tierno & Pickett, *Tampons and Toxic Shock Syndrome,* 24 Trial 54, No. 2 (Feb. 1988).

Jenner, *Identifying HIV-Infected Blood Donors,* 25 Trial 47, No. 6 (June 1989).

Mandell & Boisclair, *Working with Biomedical Engineers to Prove Causation,* 27 Trial 44, No. 11 (Nov. 1991).

McDonald, *Product Liability — Utah Extends Comment K Protection from Strict Products Liability to all Prescription Drugs,* 26 Suffolk U. L. Rev. 321 (1992).

McMamara, *Performance Claims for Skin Care Cosmetics,* 41 Food Drug Cosm. L.J. 151 (1976).

Note, *Liability for Transfusion-Transmitted Disease,* 14 Wm. Mitchell L. Rev. 141 (1988).

Note, *Long-Term Pill Use May be Linked to Cervical Cancer,* 12 International Fam. Planning Perspectives 141 (No. 4, Dec. 1986).

Note, *A Question of Competence: Judicial Role in the Regulation of Pharmaceuticals,* 103 Harv. L. Rev. 773 (1990).

Note, *A Contractual Solution to the Contraceptive Crisis,* 8 Yale L. & Pol'y Rev. 146 (1990).

Pegalis & Wachsman, *Bacterial Infections and Negligence,* 24 Trial 35, No. 5 (May 1988).

Peters & Hutton, *Reye's Syndrome: The Link Between Aspirin and Reye's,* 23 Trial 36, No. 11 (Nov. 1987).

Raffath, *Does the Pharmacist Have a Duty to Warn Patients of a Prescription Medication's Potential Risks or Dangers?,* 1 Journal of Pharmacy & Law 61 (1991-92).

Roach, et al., *Medical Records and the Law,* Aspen Systems Corp., Rockville, MD, 317 pp. (1985).

Rodriguez, *Cosmetic or Drug? The Minotaur's Labyrinth Revisited,* 44 Food Drug Cosm. L.J. 63 (1989).

Rosen, *Litigation Involving Manufacturer's Liability for Defective Medical Products,* 2 Am. J. Law & Med. 245 (1977).

Sage, *Drug Product Liability and Health Care Delivery Systems,* 40 Stan. L. Rev. 989 (1988).

Sigelman, *Halcion: Waking Up to the Dangers of a Sleeping Pill,* 25 Trial 38, No. 11 (Nov. 1989).

Spitz, *From Res Ipsa to Diethylstilbestrol,* 65 Ind. L.J. 591 (1990).

Swartz, *Products Liability: Manufacturer's Responsibility For Defective or Negligently Designed Medical and Surgical Instruments,* 18 DePaul U.L. Rev. 348 (1969).

Wivell & O'Fallon, *Drug Overpromotion: When is a Warning Not a Warning?,* 28 Trial Magazine 20 (No. 11, Nov. 1992).

§8.25 Selected laws, regulations, and standards

Page 399:

[Add the following new text under "*Federal Laws.*"]

(2) National Swine Flu Immunization Program Act, 42 U.S.C. §247b (1976).

(3) National Childhood Vaccine Injury Compensation Act, Pub. L. No. 99-660, Title III (1986).

(4) Safe Medical Devices Act of 1990, Pub. L. No. 101-629, amending the U.S. Food, Drug and Cosmetic Act as to the regulation of medical devices. Summary of act and dates for implementation of act's provisions found at 56 Fed. Reg. 14111.

§8.26 Selected cases

Page 400:

[Add new text as follows:]

Morris v. Parke, Davis & Co., 667 F. Supp. 1332 (C.D. Cal., 1987), injury caused by **DPT vaccine;** claim of defect not preempted by federal law; defective design actionable under market share theory.

Brown v. Superior Court & Abbott Labs., 245 Cal. Rptr. 412, 751 P.2d 470 (1988), **diethylstilbestrol,** injuries to child in utero; failure to warn; joint and several liability but not on market share theory.

Zichichi v. Middlesex Mem. Hospital, 204 Conn. 399, 528 A.2d 805 (1987), serum hepatitis caused by defective **blood transfusion;** effect of "blood shield" statute.

O'Gilvie v. International Playtex, Inc., 821 F.2d 1438 (10th Cir. 1987), **tampon;** toxic shock syndrome causing wrongful death.

Rose Garabedian v. Johnson & Johnson and McNeilab, Inc., No. 84-90 5-WD (D. Mass. 1986), anaphylactic reaction to drug **Zomax;** settlement amount undisclosed.

Cornelison v. Tambrands, Inc., 710 F. Supp. 706 (D. Minn. 1989), **tampon;** held that state law claims based on failure to warn were preempted by the Medical Device Amendments.

Honey v. Barnes Hosp., 708 S.W.2d 686 (Mo. Ct. App. 1986), **defective window** in psychiatric hospital.

Falk v. Puritan Pride, Inc., 5 Prod. Liab. Rep. (CCH) (N.J. Super. Ct. 1986), inadequately tested **Vitamin B-6;** fiber sensory neuropathy.

Otis v. Bausch & Lomb, Inc., 532 N.Y.S.2d 933 (App. Div. 1988), **contact lenses** causing corneal ulcer; defendant's motion for summary judgment should be denied.

Coursen v. A.H. Robins Co., 764 F.2d 1329 (9th Cir. [Or.] 1985), defectively designed **IUD contraceptive;** uterus infection.

Keeler v. Richards Mfg. Co., 817 F.2d 1197 (5th Cir. [Tex.] 1987), defectively manufactured **hip screw;** broke in patient.

Suber v. Ohio Medical Products, Inc., (Tex. 1987), 6 ATLA Prod. Liab. Rep. 59 (May 1987), defectively designed **anesthesia gas machine;** brain damage caused.

Sabel v. Mead Johnson & Co., 737 F. Supp. 135 (D. Mass. 1990), **antidepressant** causing priapism; failure to warn of danger of impotence after recommendation of F.D.A.

Shields v. Eli Lilly & Co., 895 F.2d 1463 (D.C. Cir. 1990), cancer allegedly caused by mother's consumption of **DES;** injury in utero; factual issue of causality.

Pollard v. Ashby, 793 S.W.2d 394 (Mo. App. 1990), strict liability; sexual dysfunction, headaches, incontinence and pain caused by **chymopapain;** post-injury remedial measures by drug manufacturer admissible; failure to warn; $700,000 verdict.

Khan v. Shiley, Inc., 266 Cal. Rptr. 106 (Cal. App. 1990), concealment of dangers of **artificial heart valve** malfunctioning; fraud on consumer.

Witthauer v. Burkart Roentgen, Inc., 467 N.W.2d 439 (N.D. 1991), second- and third-degree burns suffered by infant being operated on under **surgical lamp;** distributor of lamp held liable for failing to warn of the danger of using the surgical lamp without its heat-protection filter.

Adams v. G.D. Searle & Co., 576 So. 2d 728 (Fla. 1991), user of **intrauterine device** became pregnant and suffered premature rupture of membranes and uterine infection which resulted in stillbirth of child; parents' claim of fraud against manufacturer of intrauterine device allowed if based on fraud claim that defendant misrepresented and omitted material facts on which patient and physician relied in making decision to use product.

Reaves v. Ortho Pharmaceutical Corp., 765 F. Supp. 1287 (E.D. Mich. 1991), woman developed arterial thromboembolism after thirteen-year use of **oral contraceptive;** failure to warn; court held that duty to warn under Michigan law extended only to the medical community under the learned intermediary doctrine and therefore there is no duty to warn the ultimate consumer of a prescribed medicine.

West v. Searle & Co., 305 Ark. 33, 806 S.W.2d 608 (1991), user of **oral contraceptive** suffered hepatic adenoma which caused liver tumor to rupture and create life-threatening situation; while Arkansas learned intermediary rule applies to prescribed oral contraceptive issue of whether adequate and timely warning was given to medical community is question of fact.

Hufft v. Hurowitz, 4 Cal. App. 4th 8, 4 Cal. Rptr. 2d 377 (1992), plaintiff who underwent surgical implantation of **penile prosthesis** to alleviate a penile erection dysfunction thereafter experienced almost constant penile erection, causing him pain and emotional distress; subsequent corrective surgery failed to correct problem; in products claim against manufacturer of device, court held claim on negligence and breach of warranty would lie; an issue of material fact existed as to whether manufacturer of inflatable penile prosthesis knew or should have known that there was a risk the product would cause patient to have a spontaneous and continuing penile erection as to impose a duty to warn.

Chapter 9

INDUSTRIAL ACCIDENTS: DEATH AT THE WORKPLACE

I. Introduction

Page 407:

[Add new section following § 9.01.]

§ 9.01A Overcoming the worker's compensation exclusivity bar [New]

Often the greatest hurdle to a lawyer representing an injured worker is the worker's compensation exclusivity bar, which makes the worker's compensation remedy the exclusive form of relief against the employer for a man or woman injured on the job.

Where the product which injures the worker is defective because of its use, modification, or other conduct attributable to the employer, the injured employee may find himself, at times, limited to the relatively small compensation obtainable under the worker's compensation system. If, of course, the defect is caused by the manufacturer of the product, an action in tort could lie against that manufacturer.

Four major exceptions to the exclusivity bar of the worker's compensation laws which seem to be evolving in the United States promise to open the door to potential remedies for injured workers:

(1) An employer should be held liable for intentional torts. Thus, an employer should not be able to escape liability for intentionally abusing a worker.

(2) Where the employer knows that a threat of harm is substantially likely to occur and he still requires the employee to act, the employee should have a remedy in tort and not face the exclusivity bar. This has important ramifications for products liability law, since it covers the situation where an employer requires a worker to work on a machine which he knows or should know is dangerous.[2.1]

(3) Where the employee is injured by a product which the employer is manufacturing for the general public, under what is sometimes called the dual capacity doctrine, the employer is deemed both an employer and the manufacturer of the dangerous and defective product which has caused injury.[2.2]

(4) An injured worker may have a claim against the parent corporation of his employer. Given the large number of mergers and corporate takeovers in recent years, this promises to be a significant exception.[2.3]

[2.1] *See* Jones v. VIP Dev. Corp., 15 Ohio St. 3d 90, 472 N.E.2d 1046 (1984), noted and discussed at 28 ATLA L. Rep. 6-8 (Feb. 1985).

[2.2] *See, e.g.,* Douglas v. E. & J. Gallo Winery, 69 Cal. App. 3d 103, 137 Cal. Rptr. 797 (1977); Note, *The Employer-Manufacturer and the Dilemma of Dual Capacity,* 34 HASTINGS L.J. 461 (1982).

[2.3] *See, e.g.,* Boggs v. Blue Diamond Coal Co., 590 F.2d 65 (6th Cir.), *cert. denied,* 444 U.S. 836 (1979); *see also* Gaines v. Excell Industries, Inc., 667 F. Supp. 569 (M.D. Tenn. 1987); Lambert, *Employee Safety: Outflanking Exclusivity*

IV. Other Workplace Hazards

Page 437:

[Add new sections following § 9.14.]

§ 9.14A Sandblasting machines [New]

In one case, a worker sustained severe injuries when his left foot and leg were caught and crushed under a silent, slow-moving sandblasting machine at a naval shipyard on October 27, 1980. This twenty-ton capacity, vehicle-like machine moved in and out of a sandblasting booth on railroad truck runners. It was pulled in and out on a steel cable set under the floor and powered by a low gear, three-horsepower electric motor installed behind the booth. The machine, which ran silently on its tracks, without a horn or beepers to alert the worker, was designed with an unguarded space between the bottom of the machine and the floor. This space was big enough to trap a worker's foot, but too small to allow a worker to extricate himself once trapped.

The worker was injured as he was walking in the loading area of the vehicle, when the machine caught his foot and drew him under. A fellow worker responded to his cry for help and turned the machine off.

§ 9.14B Inadequate safety devices [New]

A common problem with regard to industrial accidents arises when the safety devices placed on the machine used by the worker are inadequate to prevent foreseeable injuries. This problem is illustrated by a case which I recently settled.

My client was operating a jig machine, used to dye cloth, when his left arm became entangled with some cloth which was wrapped around moving rolls. The moving rolls propelled my client's hand into the hot dye below the rolls, resulting in the loss of three of his fingers.

I contended that the jig machine presented foreseeable hazards to users due to nip points on the rolls of cloth. In

---

Bar of Worker's Compensation Act, 31 ATLA L. Rep. 9, No. 1 (Feb. 1988) (in his article, Prof. Thomas Lambert provides an excellent review of this exception).

addition, although my client's employer had installed a self-designed emergency stop cord which was run into a limit switch, that limit switch, which was made of a zinc alloy, had become corroded by the humid atmosphere of the dye room. Consequently, it failed to prevent the occurrence of the injury, even though my client had pulled the emergency cord.

COMMENT: A manufacturer of industrial machinery, as well as a manufacturer of safety devices for such machinery, should foresee the danger to which a worker using that machinery is exposed. If they fail to take reasonable steps to prevent foreseeable injury, they can be held legally liable. The danger that safety devices may be made inoperative by the environment in which the machine is used is a major factor in determining such liability.

In this case, I successfully contended that the limit switch should have been made of a noncorrosive material, such as stainless steel, since it was foreseeable that the limit switch would be exposed to a humid atmosphere which would cause corrosion. Both the manufacturer of the machine and the manufacturer of the switch contributed to the final settlement of $260,000 in favor of my client.

§ 9.14C Hydraulic grease gun [New]

I was retained to represent a man who sustained an injury to his right (minor) hand while operating a hydraulic grease gun. The gun inadvertently discharged in the client's hand while he was operating it. After investigating the facts, we established that the hydraulic control valve was defective because it could be easily and inadvertently activated. There was no guard for the control lever, nor was there a safety latch, which would require two distinct motions to activate the gun. During discovery, the manufacturer's engineer admitted that both safety devices were readily available at the time of manufacture. The client sustained a penetrating wound to his hand which required several surgical procedures to remove grease from the wound site. This case was settled for $67,500.00.

VI. Litigation Sources: Bibliography

§ 9.24 Selected legal sources

Page 443:

[Add new text as follows:]

Birnbaum & Wrubel, *Worker's Compensation and the Employer's Immunity Shield,* 316 PLI/LIT 425 (1986).

Broder, *Elevator Accident Cases,* 24 Trial 73, No. 5 (May 1988).

Comment, *The Asbestos Claim,* 24 Duq. L. Rev. 833 (1986).

Comment, *Asbestosis: Who Will Pay the Plaintiff?,* 57 Tul. L. Rev. 1491 (1983).

Gale, *Recovery for Cancerphobia,* 15 Cumb. L. Rev. 723 (1985).

Gallagher, *Exploding the Myths: How to Prevent Industrial Accidents,* 24 Trial 53, No. 4 (Apr. 1988).

Gavin, *Railroad Welders, Lung Disease, and the Federal Employers' Liability Act,* 29 Trial Magazine 50 (No. 2, Feb. 1993).

Gloss, *Helping Asbestos Victims,* 23 Trial 28, No. 10 (Oct. 1987).

Hedrich and Ream, *Deadman Switches and Defective Design,* 32 For the Defense 2, No. 2 (1990).

Kanner, *Trying the Toxic Tort Case,* 23 Trial 32, No. 10 (Oct. 1987).

Leflar, *Compensation for Work-Related Illness in Arkansas,* 41 Ark. L. Rev. 63 (1988).

Locks, *Asbestos-Related Disease Litigation,* 28 Vill. L. Rev. 1184 (1983).

Mongeluzzi, *Electrocution Accidents on the Job,* 25 Trial 68, No. 3 (Mar. 1989).

Mullaney, *Torts in the Workplace,* 25 Trial 40, No. 6 (June 1989).

Sitzman, *A Look at the Federal Employers' Liability Act in the Eighth Circuit,* 21 Creighton L. Rev. 1073 (1988).

Tompkins, *Admissibility of Reports: OSHA, Regs., Standards and Publications,* 57 Def. Couns. J. 446, No. 4 (1990).

§ 9.26 Selected laws, regulations, and standards

Page 445:

[Add the following new text under "Statutes."]

(3) Railroad Safety Appliance Act, 45 U.S.C. § 1 *et seq.* (1986).

(4) Federal Employers Liability Act, 45 U.S.C. § 51 *et seq.* (1986).

(5) Radiation Control Act, 42 U.S.C. § 263b *et seq.* (1982 & Supp. 1987).

(6) Price-Anderson Act (Nuclear injuries), 42 U.S.C. § 2210 (1987).

(7) Toxic Substances Control Act, 15 U.S.C. § 2601 *et seq.* (1982 & Supp. 1987).

(8) Tandem Truck Safety Act of 1984, 49 U.S.C. § 2301 *et seq.* (Supp. 1987).

(9) Comprehensive Environment Response, Compensation and Liability Act, 42 U.S.C. § 6901-6975 (Supp. 1988), as amended by the Superfund Amendments of 1986, P.L. 99-499.

(10) Emergency Planning and Community Right to Know Act, 42 U.S.C. § 11001-11050 (Supp. 1988).

§ 9.27 Selected cases

Page 446:

[Add new text as follows:]

Borden, Inc. v. Cyphers, 486 N.E.2d 635 (Ind. Ct. App. 1985), meat cutter exposed to fumes emitted from **polyvinyl chloride (pvc)** meat wrapping film during employment; chronic obstructive lung disease (meat wrapper's asthma).

Ingram v. Caterpillar Machinery Corp., 535 So. 2d 723 (La. 1988), injury from jumping from **forklift** which was overturning; duty to warn of dangers from foreseeable normal use.

Bell v. Jet Wheel Blast, 462 So. 2d 166 (La. 1985), defective **shot blast machine**.

Richard v. American Mfg. Co., 21 Mass. App. Ct. 967, 489 N.E.2d 214 (1986), crushed hand; design defect in **bag bundling press.**

Tasca v. GTE Products Corp., 175 Mich. App. 617, 438 N.W.2d 625 (1988), injured worker and wife sued cobalt suppliers and designers and manufacturers of **grinding machines for cobalt;** claims for breach of warranty and loss of consortium should not have been dismissed.

Keenan v. Hydra-Mac, Inc., 422 N.W.2d 741 (Minn. App. 1988), **skid-steer loader;** absolute liability for employer's violation of Child Labor Standards.

Germann v. F.L. Smithe Machine Co., 381 N.W.2d 503 (Minn. Ct. App. 1986), **hydraulic press;** failure to warn or instruct as to its safe use.

Gogal v. Johns-Manville Sales Corp., 595 F. Supp. 971 (D.N.J. 1985), exposure to **asbestos** on job; asbestos sold to plaintiff's employer by defendant; asbestosis.

Butler v. PPG Industries, Inc., 201 N.J. Super. 558, 493 A.2d 619 (1985), **caustic soda flakes** exploded during employment; failure to warn; judgment for plaintiff.

Goldman v. Packaging Industries, Inc., 144 A.D.2d 533, 534 N.Y.S.2d 388 (1988), plaintiff injured while changing a die on a **thermoforming machine;** seller of machine could be held liable to injured worker on theory that it negligently failed to warn of defects in machinery.

McGavin v. Herrich & Cowell Co., 118 A.D.2d 982, 500 N.Y.S.2d 85 (1986), employee's right hand came in contact with saw blade of a **rung sawing and chucking machine;** modification to machine.

Lopez v. Precision Papers, Inc., 107 A.D.2d 667, 484 N.Y.S.2d 585 (1985), **forklift** violated O.S.H.A. standards.

O'Neal v. Sherck Equipment Co., 751 S.W.2d 559 (Tex. App. 1988), worker injured by malfunctioning **backhoe;** allegation that defect was caused by lessor's negligence did not preclude claim based on strict liability theory.

Jackson v. Deft, Inc., 223 Cal. App. 3d 1305, 273 Cal. Rptr. 214 (1990), painter suffering harm to respiratory system as result of exposure to **paint** manufactured by defendant and used by the plaintiff while working as civilian employee of Navy; genuine issue of whether defendant gave sufficient unambiguous and conspicuous warning of dangers of overexposure to its paint; as to the military contractor, defense issue existed as to whether the warning label required by the Navy could have been supplemented by additional warnings.

Koske v. Townsend Engineering Co., 551 N.E.2d 437 (Ind. 1990), injury to hand caught in **meat skinner/slasher machine;** material issue existed as to whether manufacturer of machine had knowledge of danger that employee using machine would not be able to extricate herself from machine; open and obvious danger doctrine does not itself preclude recovery from a defendant who acts in willful or wanton manner.

Hansen v. Abrasive Engineering & Manufacturing, Inc., 112 Or. App. 586, 831 P.2d 693 (1992), plaintiff who was cleaning a **sanding machine** had his glove pulled into a kip point by the sanding belt, sanding off all of the plaintiff's left hand except the thumb and a portion of the palm; plaintiff's theory was that his injuries were caused by failure of the defendant to design, build and install machine safety features consistent with state and federal safety standards, as well as standards promulgated by the American National Standards Institute (ANSI).

Boyer v. Eljer Manufacturing, Inc., 830 S.W.2d 535 (Mo. App. 1992), shank flew off a **saw** manufactured by the defendant's predecessor corporation, causing blindness in one of plaintiff's eyes; plaintiff was not wearing safety goggles at the the time of injury; court erred in giving a contributory fault instruction when there was no evidence that plaintiff knew that safety glasses might have prevented or reduced the danger.

Klein v. Sears, Roebuck & Co., 92 Md. App. 477, 608 A.2d 1276 (1992), court held that plaintiff's complaint stated claim; plaintiff purchased a **10″ radial arm saw** and had four fingers of his hand amputated by the saw blade; plaintiff was ready to show that the same vendor sells a 12″ radial arm saw with a lower blade guard, and that it would have been feasible to design and equip his 10″ radial arm saw with a similar lower blade guard.

Gean v. Cling Surface Co., 971 F.2d 642 (11th Cir. 1992), case involving a plaintiff whose arm had to be amputated after getting caught in a conveyor belt; court held that the manufacturer had a duty to warn that **smooth-lagged pulleys** caused belt slippage when used in a wet environment and the manufacturer's failure to warn was the proximate cause of the plaintiff's injury.

Campbell v. Robert Bosch Power Tool Corp., 795 F. Supp. 1093 (M.D. Ala. 1992), action against the manufacturer of a **grinder disk** which shattered and caused injury to the unprotected eye of the user; held that assumption of the risk of having small particles of wood or metal striking the eye was insufficient to prove that the user assumed the risk of injury from a shattering grinding disk.

Bursch v. Beardsley & Piper, a Division of Pettibone Corp., 971 F.2d 108 (8th Cir. 1992), plaintiff's right forearm and hand became trapped between two pneumatically-driven parts on a **core-making machine**; plaintiff's forearm and hand were severely burned because the core-box halves had been heated to approximately 500 degrees fahrenheit; coworker's failure to activate the correct valve when the worker's hand and forearm became caught in the machine was deemed a foreseeable mistake and not a superseding cause.

Chapter 10

OPENING NEW DOORS: LANDMARK LITIGATION

Page 497:

[Add new sections after § 10.27.]

§ 10.28 Other landmark products cases [New]

Downing v. Overhead Door Corp., 707 P.2d 1027 (Colo. Ct. App. 1985). Evidence of post-sale, pre-accident warning supported inference that warning of defective door was inadequate.

Wheeler v. The Andrew Jergens Co., 696 S.W.2d 326 (Ky. Ct. App. 1985). The shampoo manufactured by the defendant caused the plaintiff to lose 80% of her hair. The failure of the defendant to make its product tamper-proof could be the basis of recovery.

Prejean v. Great Atlantic and Pacific Tea Co., 457 So. 2d 60 (La. 1984). Defective roast caused cook to become nauseous and vomit blood. There was no need for the plaintiff to have eaten the meat in order to recover.

Kelley v. R.G. Industries, Inc., 304 Md. 124, 497 A.2d 1143 (1985). The Maryland court held that the manufacturer of a "Saturday night special" handgun could be held liable to the victim of a crime who was shot by a gun manufactured by the defendant. Such a gun has no social utility, cannot be used for sport, and is primarily used for illegal activities.

The defendant violated a duty to the public when he put such a product on the market.

Yakubowicz v. Paramount Pictures Corp., 404 Mass. 624, 536 N.E.2d 1067 (1989). Plaintiff's son murdered by person who had just attended a motion picture showing violent scenes. Producer and exhibitor of commercial film owed a duty of reasonable care to the public in producing, exhibiting and advertising of films, but because of protection of First Amendment no liability will be imposed if film does not inherently incite viewers to tortious action.

Kotler v. American Tobacco Co., 685 F. Supp. 15 (D. Mass. 1988). Cigarette smoker's estate may have claim against manufacturer of tobacco products for defective design and breach of implied warranty of merchantability on theories of inadequate testing and content of toxic and carcinogenic ingredients.

Gianitsis v. American Brands, Inc., 685 F. Supp. 853 (D.N.H. 1988). In action against manufacturer of tobacco product, the Federal Cigarette Labeling and Advertising Act preempted smoker's failure to warn action arising after date of the Act, but it did not preempt claim for failure to warn arising prior to the effective date of the Act.

Dewey v. R.J. Reynolds Tobacco Co., 121 N.J. 69, 577 A.2d 1239 (1990). Failure to warn that tobacco products are unsafe; damages recoverable.

Carlisle v. Phillip Morris, Inc., 805 S.W.2d 498 (Tex. App. 1991). The Federal Cigarette Labeling and Advertising Act did not preempt state common-law claims for injury caused by the smoking of cigarettes.

Coursen v. A.H. Robins Co., 764 F.2d 1329 (9th Cir. 1985). The defendant manufacturer of an I.U.D. contraceptive marketed the product knowing of its damages to users. The defendant placed in evidence the sexual histories of the plaintiffs. This is a good example of gross corporate irresponsibility.

Birmingham v. Fodor's Travel Publications, Inc., 73 Haw. 359, 833 P.2d 70 (1992). The plaintiff went to Hawaii on his honeymoon after consulting a travel book published by the defendant which mentioned a particular beach in Hawaii. The plaintiff was injured while using the beach, and brought suit against the publisher on a theory that the publisher knew or should have known that the wave and water conditions along Kehaha Beach were dangerous to swimmers and failed to warn the plaintiff of these dangerous conditions. The court denied relief, holding that there is no case in which a publisher has been liable in negligence for personal injury in reliance upon information contained in a publication, except in cases where the publisher authored or guaranteed the information. See also *Winter v. G. P. Putnam's Sons,* 938 F.2d 1033 (9th Cir. 1991) (publisher not subject to strict liability or negligence for ideas contained in book).

Motter v. Everest & Jennings, Inc., 883 F.2d 1223 (3rd Cir. 1989) (en banc). Person injured when caster of shower chair fell off leg of chair has claim for injuries caused by defectively designed caster-affixing system, including damages for pain and suffering, embarrassment and loss of the pleasures of life (including disrupted sleep, effect on sexual relations with husband, interference with vacations, depression, etc.).

Malek v. Miller Brewing Co., 749 S.W.2d 521, 524-26 (Tex. App. 1988) (Evans, C.J., dissenting). Person injured by drunk driver may have products claim against manufacturer of beer, based on its alleged failure to give its consumers information about safe levels of beer consumption.

Ayers v. Johnson & Johnson Products Co., 59 Wash. App. 287, 797 P.2d 527 (1990). Infant suffering brain damages; failure of manufacturer of baby oil to warn of danger of aspirating product; $2,500,000 verdict.

Burke v. Safeway Stores, Inc., 554 So. 2d 184 (La. App. 1989). Exploding soft drink bottle; laceration of hand; plaintiff unable to work as legal secretary or cosmetologist.

McGuire v. Joseph Seagram & Sons, Inc., 790 S.W.2d 842 (Tex. App. 1990). Whiskey is chattel under Restatement of Torts § 402B; failure to warn of genetic or psychological predisposition to alcoholism; claims for conspiracy to suppress information about dangers of alcoholism.

East Penn Mfg. Co. v. Pineda, 578 A.2d 1113 (D.C. App. 1990). Exploding battery; partial blinding of plaintiff; failure to warn of dangers in charging battery.

Perry v. Red Wing Shoe Co., 597 So.2d 821 (Fla. App. 1992). Purchaser bought a pair of work boots in order to protect his toes while working with heavy equipment. The boots purchased contained a steel toe and had a tag attached which lead the purchaser to believe that the steel toe would cause the boots to withstand the pressure of heavy falling objects. While at work, a weight fell on the purchaser's foot, crushing his small toes, and resulting in their amputation. The plaintiff's expert testified that the boots manufactured by the defendant were inadequate because the small toes were susceptible to injury. The expert also testified that technology was available whereby the manufacturer could have produced a shoe which would have protected the small toes. The court held that there was sufficient evidence of negligence by the defendant manufacturer to allow the case to go to a jury.

Cippollone v. Liggette Group, Inc., 112 S. Ct. 2608 (1992). In an action against a tobacco manufacturer, the Supreme Court of the United States held that the Federal Cigarette Labeling and Advertising Act and the Federal Public Health Cigarette Smoking Act of 1969 did not preempt all state product liability claims. The court held that federal preemption applied only if Congress expressly stated an intent to preempt a state law or if the state law actually conflicted with federal law.

Sedgwick v. Kawasaki Cycleworks, Inc., 71 Ohio App.3d 117, 593 N.E.2d 69 (1991). While attempting to avoid a car, the plaintiff's hands became trapped between the handlebars and wind fairing of a motorcycle, causing him to lose control. Plaintiff suffered blunt abdominal trauma, multiple rib fractures, ankle fractures, back fracture, knee fracture and pelvic fracture; plaintiff was awarded $738,000 in damages.

§ 10.29 Checklist: Chemical contamination cases [New]

In *Sterling v. Velsicol Chemical Corp.,*[56] a landmark case, the court examined the growing problem of chemical contamination

---

[56] 647 F. Supp. 303 (W.D. Tenn. 1986).

of local aquifers through careless disposal of hazardous waste, and concluded that the defendant chemical company could be held liable on theories of strict or absolute liability, negligence, trespass, and nuisance.[57]

The following factors, relied on by the *Sterling* Court, outline theories which plaintiff's counsel may find useful in plotting future claims of hazardous waste pollution, and provide a helpful checklist of possible legal theories and factual allegations for pleading such a case.

___(A) Strict or Absolute Liability:

___(1) A high degree of risk of some harm to the person, land, or chattels of others;

___(2) The likelihood that the resulting harm would be great (such as the increased risk of many diseases, including cancer, and the destruction of plaintiffs' quality of life);

___(3) The inability to eliminate the risk by the exercise of reasonable care;

___(4) The extent to which the activity at the dump site was not a matter of common usage and, as a means of disposal, violated the state of the art;

___(5) The inappropriateness of the location of the dump site; and

___(6) The extent to which the value to the community (none) was outweighed by the dangerous attributes (great).

___(B) Negligence:

___(1) There was a duty, a standard of conduct, imposed by law on the defendant, to protect others from unreasonable harm arising from the dumping of the chemicals.

___(2) The defendant breached that duty by its failure to do the following:

___(a) Investigate the geological makeup or strata under the dump site prior to its purchase or operation;

---

[57] *Id.* at 316-17.

____(b) Investigate the hydrological, or water-bearing, zones under the dump site prior to its purchase or operation;

____(c) Hire knowledgeable persons to investigate the geological and hydrogeological area under the dump site prior to its purchase or operation;

____(d) Install proper monitoring procedures in and around the dump site prior to commencing dumping operations at the dump site;

____(e) Investigate the geological and hydrogeological situation at the dump site after being warned by a report that chemicals were escaping from their burial trenches and contaminating the local water table aquifer;

____(f) Hire professional geologists or hydrogeologists at the time of the report to properly analyze the data generated therein, as any reasonable person would do;

____(g) Heed the warning in the report by continuing to dump, and even expanding the size of the dump;

____(h) Heed warnings about the expansion of the dump site;

____(i) Select locate, operate, and maintain the dump site under the prevailing state of the art for such operation during the entire length of time the dump site was open;

____(j) Obey an administrative order, by continuing to dump hazardous materials, an activity which was illegal and amounted to negligence per se;

____(k) Take steps to halt the leakage that was already occurring from the dump site;

____(l) Properly monitor the dump site from its opening until its closing;

____(m) Monitor the dump site at all times from its closing until the forced monitoring imposed by the state;

____(n) Operate the dump site according to the state-of-the-art methods to protect the plaintiffs, by failing to cover wastes daily, thereby allowing an increase in the infiltration rate;

____(o) Properly close the dump site, pursuant to the state of the art;

____(p) Timely register the dump site as a hazardous waste disposal site as required by the state;

____(q) Timely, completely, and correctly respond to the requests of governmental agencies as to what was put into the dump site;

____(r) Warn the plaintiffs to watch their water for the presence of any chemical odors or tastes;

____(s) Transport the chemicals from the plant site in a safe and proper manner to insure the safety of the plaintiffs and their property;

____(t) Contain the chemicals within the boundaries of their own property, by allowing them to escape and pollute the drinkable ground water used by plaintiffs; and

____(u) Contain the chemicals within the boundaries of their own property, by allowing the fumes from said chemicals to escape into the air which drifted onto the property and into the houses of the plaintiffs.

§ 10.30 Bibliography on developing landmark law affecting product litigation [New]

Airbags

Bryant, *Airbag Litigation,* 25 Trial 30, No. 2 (Feb. 1989).

McGowan, *Airbag Claims: Is there Federal Preemption?,* 24 Trial 31, No. 2 (Feb. 1988).

Miller, *Deflating the Airbag Preemption Controversy,* 37 Emory L.J. 897 (1988).
Note, *Preemption of Airbag Litigation,* 76 Va. L. Rev. 577 (1990).

Alcohol

Comment, *A Case for Alcohol Beverage Warning Labels,* 53 Mo. L. Rev. 555 (1988).

Computers

Weber, *Bad Bytes: The Application of Strict Products Liability to Computer Software,* 66 St. John's L. Rev. 469 (1992).

Franchisor Liability

Phillips, *Liability of Franchisors for the Torts of Their Montana Franchisees,* 49 Mont. L. Rev. 123 (1988).

Motor Vehicle

Cohen, *The Tide has Turned: Federal Preemption Cannot Defeat Motor Vehicle Design Claims,* 29 Trial Magazine 75 (No. 1, Jan. 1993).
Wegis, *Honda ATV Litigation in Retrospect,* 28 Trial Magazine 36 (No. 11, Nov. 1992).

Seat Belts

Slavik, *Defective Seat Belts,* 24 Trial 34, No. 2 (Feb. 1988).
Swartz, Swartz & Cantor, *Seat-Belt Injury Litigation,* 24 Trial Magazine 46, No. 11 (Nov. 1988).
Wilton & Campbell, 11 J. of Products Liability 1 (1988).

Smoke Detectors

Swartz, Swartz & Cantor, *Smoke-Detector Litigation: A Way to Save Lives,* 22 Trial Magazine 30, No. 11 (Nov. 1986).

Tobacco

Ausness, *Cigarette Company Liability,* 39 Syracuse L. Rev. 897 (1988).

Daynard & Morin, *The Cipollone Documents: Following the Paper Trail to Tobacco Industry Liability,* 24 Trial 40, No. 11 (Nov. 1988).

Daynard & Sweda, *Redressing Injuries from Secondhand Smoke,* 28 Trial 50, No. 3 (March 1992).

Dusinki, *Products Liability-Preemption and Retroactivity, Federal Cigarette Labeling and Advertising Act,* 22 Seton Hall L. Rev. 193 (1991).

Gerrard & Leech, *Cigarette Smokers — More Sinned Against Than Sinning,* 140 New L.J. 1141 (August 1990).

Gordon & Granoff, *A Plaintiff's Guide to Reaching Tobacco Manufacturers: How to Get the Cigarette Industry Off Its Butt,* 22 Seton Hall L. Rev. 851 (1992).

Johnson, *Regulation, Remedy and Exported Tobacco Products,* 25 Suffolk U. L. Rev. 1 (1991).

McGuire & Daynard, *When Cigarettes Start Fires: Industry Liability,* 28 Trial Magazine 44 (No. 11, Nov. 1992).

Note, *Tobacco Litigation,* 16 Brooklyn J. Int'l L. 275 (1990).

Novello, *Health Hazards of Cigarette Use,* 28 Trial 46, No. 3 (March 1992).

Schmidt, *Preemption of Failure to Warn and Misrepresentation Claims Under the Cigarette Act,* 60 U. Cin. L. Rev. 251 (1991).

§ 10.31 Selected government sources [New]

CPSC News Release No. 91-60 (1991). Warning by U.S. Consumer Product Safety Commission about danger of certain auger-type log splitters which have allegedly caused death and injury to users.

CPSC News Release No. 91-62 (1991). Manufacturer's voluntary repair program, in conjunction with the U.S. Consumer Products Safety Commission, as to certain models of audio system speakers which tend to overheat and burn.

Chapter 11

CLOSING THE CASE OF SLAUGHTER BY PRODUCT

§ 11.01 In general

Page 500:

[Add the following note to end of § 11.01.]

* *See generally* KLIEMAN, HOW TO USE COURTROOM DRAMA TO WIN CASES (Prentice-Hall, Inc. 1987).

§ 11.06 Illustrative closing arguments

§ 11.21 —Damages

Page 552:

[Add the following new text at end of Comment.]

In proposing a final argument on damage issues, counsel should be certain to explain the nature of each damage claim and the impact the injury had on the plaintiffs. For example, in a consortium claim the attorney should carefully explain the impact of the injury on the spouse of the injured victim. For example, in *Burns v. Pepsi-Cola Metropolitan Bottling Co.*,[6] the plaintiff-husband ingested glass con-

---

[6] 353 Pa. Super. 571, 510 A.2d 810 (1986).

tained in a soft-drink bottle and sustained serious injuries. These injuries, however, also harmed his marriage because they created mood swings, idiosyncratic eating habits, and a refusal to have sexual relations with his wife. Thus, the plaintiff's wife equally became a victim of the defective soft-drink product, and the court properly awarded damages of $15,000 to his wife.

§ 11.22 —Punitive damages

Page 527:

[Add new text following Argument 49:]

Further readings on punitive damages:

Gibbins, *Post-*Haslip *Cases Approve State Punitive Damage Laws,* 28 Trial Magazine 54 (No. 11, Nov. 1992).

Volt & Fayz, *Judicial Response to Constitutional Challenges in A Products Liability Punitive Damage Limitation Statute,* 29 Amer. Bus. L.J. 367 (1991).

Chapter 12

PRODUCTS LIABILITY LITIGATION AND THE PROMOTION OF PUBLIC SAFETY [NEW]

§ 12.01 Serving the client and the public at the same time

It is a common perception that personal injury attorneys who represent clients in claims against manufacturers and sellers of dangerous and defective products benefit only their clients when they succeed in recovering money damages. From my own experience, I can testify that this is not so. While my focus — when I take a case — is on the best interests of my client, in representing my client, I also serve the best interests of society. This is especially true in regard to the promotion of public safety, which is an inevitable result of products litigation. Since many of my cases involve products which have injured or killed children or adults in the home and in the workplace, proving the danger of those products in those cases has resulted, as a spin-off, in a safer environment for all consumers.

Much neglected in the current debate over tort reform is the fact that society benefits from the vigorous litigation of product-related injury claims by the creation of incentives to improve product safety. In reviewing the current tort system, the recent report of the United States Attorney General's commission on the "Crisis in Insurance Availability" ignores this aspect of products liability law. It is important that this fact not be ignored, because tort litigation has provided a major prod to manufacturers and vendors of products to improve their product design, production process, advertising, instructions, warnings, and other features of product availability and marketing.

In my three decades of practice, I have tried to become a responsible public voice for consumer product safety, along with other attorneys. I know that the litigation of my clients' claims against careless manufacturers of dangerous and deadly products has also had a substantial impact on product safety.

Foremost among the areas of product safety where my law practice has had a substantial impact is in the area of children's toys. My books on this subject have played a major role in educating legislatures, consumer groups, parents, and the general public about the terrible consequences of marketing toys that injure and kill our children. I cannot stress enough that these books and legislative efforts grew directly out of my litigation experiences in representing injured children.

COMMENT: The cases I mention in this chapter have been discussed in detail elsewhere in this book. I mention them now from a new perpective — i.e., the public safety side-effects of products litigation. I am sure that other good trial lawyers can cite similar examples from their own practices. As a profession, we should give more attention to this important public service of the plaintiff's bar in products cases.

---

§ 12.02 Educating the public through litigation

Education of the public about the dangers of certain toys designed for young children is a noteworthy effect of the representation of private clients in products cases. For example, in *Cunningham v. Quaker Oats Co., Fisher-Price Div.*,[1] I established that a toy figurine which had widespread public acceptance could easily become lodged in the throat of a young child. I also showed that the manufacturer had previous warnings of the danger, and that the design had not been changed, even though children had died or suffered brain damage. Because of this litigation, parents, professionals, and the general public became better educated about the need to promote product safety for very young children.

COMMENT: This often overlooked "educational" function of products liability claims is a major benefit of our tort system.

In many other instances, the effective use of litigation and consumer education has directly resulted in improvement of the safety of the toys used by our children. The following are a few examples from my own experience:

(1) Doll bottles designed with removable caps posed serious ingestion problems; today, doll bottles are designed in one piece.

(2) Flammable play tunnels which easily ignited were recalled by the FDA after I identified them as a hazardous product.

(3) Baby rattles with exposed metal points were demonstrated to be lethal, resulting both in adverse publicity and reduced marketing of the product.

(4) Toy xylophones assembled with sharp nails and spikes which could seriously injure children have been redesigned to reduce exposure.

(5) Little people figurines were designed small enough to fit in a child's mouth, yet, large enough to get lodged in a child's throat, presenting a serous choking hazard. Today,

---

[1] 107 F.R.D. 66 (W.D.N.Y. 1985) (No. 1973-343).

the little people figurines have been redesigned as larger figures, eliminating the prior suffocation risk.

(6) Crib gym was recalled due to strangulation hazard.

(7) Electric ovens and irons ran on 110-volt household current, without adequate warnings of shock and burn hazards. Today, adequate warnings are required and toys that generate heat can be marketed only to children ages eight and older.

(8) Tops contained removable bases that exposed a spike-like protrusion. These bases have been redesigned to be securely fastened.

(9) Doll bottles were previously designed with removable caps that posed an ingestion hazard. These bottles no longer have the removable caps.

(10) Dolls were sold with ribbons in their hair, bells on their booties and pacifiers in their mouths. The ribbons were attached with sharp pins, the bells and pacifiers were removable and, as such, posed ingestion hazards. Dolls today are generally designed without pins in their hair and bells on their booties. Additionally, dolls contain warnings on the ingestion hazard associated with the pacifiers.

§ 12.03 Getting the government to act as result of litigation

Children are particularly vulnerable to burn injuries caused by unduly flammable clothing, sleepwear, and accessories. In one case involving a flammable children's fiber-filled comforter, *Hinckley v. Eastman Kodak Co.,*[2] I succeeded in calling the attention of the public to the serious problem of the melting tendencies of certain materials, which tendencies had the effect of seriously compounding burn injuries to children. Furthermore, children's sleepwear cases have motivated governments to more seriously regulate the distribution of flammable products by legislation, such as the Flammable Fabrics Act and various regulations, although much more remains to be done.

---

[2] No. 69-1338-J (D. Mass. 1973).

§ 12.04 Improving the safety of a product because of litigation

A dramatic and illustrative example of the impact which products liability law can have on child safety is provided by a case involving a textbook intended for use by high school students. In *Carter v. Rand McNally & Co.*,[3] we established that a young woman had been seriously burned because the author and publisher of the book had failed to warn about the dangers of doing a chemistry experiment discussed in the book, and had used confusing and misleading directions on how to perform the experiment. Not only were the defendants required to pay damages to the injured student, but later publications of this type were more clearly written and warnings were provided, thus contributing directly to the safety of other children performing similar experiments.

COMMENT: Children are frequently exposed to hazards in their own homes. Many of these hazards are preventable with slight product modifications, but until the manufacturer has been forced to pay damages and has risked exposure to public attention because of a lawsuit, many producers remain unmotivated to make such modifications.

Another example of public exposure of hidden risks through products litigation is found in a case which was brought by my firm against the manufacturer of a vacuum cleaner. In *Larue v. National Union Electric Co.*,[4] I represented a young boy who had his penis amputated by a fan in a vacuum cleaner. I showed that the injury could have been prevented by insertion of a safety screen in the vaccum cleaner, and, indeed, such screens are now more often found in these devices. In this case, we established the important legal principle that a manufacturer of home-use products has a duty to consider the environment in which his product will be used and to anticipate safety problems, including

[3] No. 76-1864F (D. Mass. 1980).

[4] 571 F.2d 51 (1st Cir. 1978).

the fact that, in a home environment, children with healthy curiosities will be exposed to certain dangers. It is clear that a case such as this will improve the safety environment, since manufacturers will now be required to consider the human factors in designing safety features for their products.

§ 12.05 Bringing previously unknown dangers to light through litigation

Children are often exposed to the risk of fire or explosion during their sleeping hours. The growing use of fire detector devices helps to reduce the potential for injury from these dangers, but if the smoke detector is itself improperly designed, the risk to sleeping children and other household members becomes that much greater. In a landmark case, my firm established the great danger of electrically operated smoke detectors which do not have battery backup sources of power. In *Laaperi v. Sears, Roebuck and Co.*,[5] children died in a fire because the smoke detector installed in their home was made inoperative when the electrical system failed and no battery power backup had been built into the system. Manufacturers of electrically operated smoke detectors are now more commonly using battery backup systems, and this case has increased public awareness of the problem.

§ 12.06 Forcing improvements in product advertising by litigation

As the use of aboveground swimming pools has become more common in recent years, the dangers faced by children using these pools has substantially increased. In one case, *Koenig v. Muskin Corp.*,[6] I established that a young man had become a quadriplegic due to the fact that the manufacturer of an aboveground pool had actually promoted unsafe use of the pool and had ignored safety features, in order to better promote the pool as a kind of backyard pleasure place. This was only one aspect of this significant case, but an important one. Instead of warning consumers about the dangers of diving into this type of pool, manufacturers were actually promoting their products by

[5] 787 F.2d 726 (1st Cir. 1986).

[6] No. 701, A-1973 (Pa. Ct. C.P. 1982).

illustrations of people diving into the pools from positions well above the water. In recent years, such advertisements have largely disappeared, an indication of the direct impact that tort litigation can have on product advertising that is harmful to safety.

§ 12.07 Using the expertise of the trial bar to promote product safety

Many more examples of the impact of products litigation on public safety could be given. Such examples would include the better design and packaging of household chemicals, such as drain cleaners, improvements in the chemical composition and warning labels on detergents and cleaning products, and the better design of safety factors on household appliances, such as hairdryers. These common household products often pose risks, especially to unsuspecting children, and many of the improvements which have been made in these products are due directly to the work of trial lawyers who, like my firm, have established in court the nature of the risks and dangers posed by the products to which consumers are all too often exposed.

COMMENT: Lawyers have played a major role in revealing safety problems through the representation of clients in products liability cases. As lawyers, we have a duty to use the knowledge and expertise that we have developed in handling these cases to create a greater public awareness of the scope of the problem of product safety. The tort system is under attack today. We have a duty to make the public understand that the tort system does not benefit only lawyers and clients — it also benefits every consumer in this nation, i.e., it benefits everyone.

---

§ 12.08 Reporting defective products

For many years, a major defect in legislation designed to protect the public from defective products was the fact that manufacturers were not required to report incidence of successful claims against them in products liability suits. In 1990, the

Consumer Product Safety Act was finally amended to correct this situation.

Under the Consumer Product Safety Improvement Act of 1990 [P.L. 101-608], amending the Consumer Product Safety Act, manufacturers are now required to report certain specific information to the Consumer Product Safety Commission about lawsuits brought against them in products liability cases.

The manufacturer must report when there have been three civil actions seeking damages for death or grievous bodily harm which have been found to have been caused by their product by a judgment or settlement. The claims must have been brought within a time frame of two years.

In a set of regulations published at 56 Fed. Reg. 5984, the United States Consumer Product Safety Commission announced the procedures to be followed by manufacturers of products for the reporting of claims based on product injuries.

Some critics have found The Consumer Product Safety Improvement Act of 1990 [P.L. 101-608], to be less than adequate in terms of protecting the public. See the criticism of the act in Adler, *New CPSC Act: A Disappointment,* 27 Trial 19, No. 11 (Nov. 1991). *See also* Zick, *Reporting Substantial Product Safety Hazards Under the Consumer Product Safety Act: The Product Liability Interface,* 80 Geo. L.J. 387 (1991); Lemov & Woolf, *Underreporting Defects Is Risky,* National Law J. (Dec. 14, 1992).

INDEX

[References are to sections.]

—B—

—C—

[References are to sections.]

[References are to sections.]

—D—

—E—

[References are to sections.]

[References are to sections.]

[References are to sections.]

—L—

—M—

—N—

[References are to sections.]

[References are to sections.]

—S—

—T—

[References are to sections.]